Introduction to
Microsoft® ASP.NET

THOMSON
™
COURSE TECHNOLOGY

Australia • Canada • Mexico • Singapore • Spain • United Kingdom • United States

Introduction to
Microsoft® ASP.NET

Kathleen Kalata

THOMSON

COURSE TECHNOLOGY

Australia • Canada • Mexico • Singapore • Spain • United Kingdom • United States

THOMSON
------------*------------ TM
COURSE TECHNOLOGY

Introduction to Microsoft® ASP.NET
is published by Course Technology

Managing Editor:
Jennifer Locke

Product Manager:
Tricia Boyle

Acquisitions Editor:
Bill Larkin

Production Editor:
Kristen Guevara

Development Editor:
Lynne Raughley

Associate Product Manager:
Janet Aras

Editorial Assistant:
Christy Urban

Composition House:
GEX Publishing Services

Text Designer:
GEX Publishing Services

Cover Designer:
Joseph Lee, Black Fish Design

Associate Marketing Manager:
Angela Laughlin

Manufacturing Coordinator:
Laura Burns

BRIEF
Contents

TABLE OF

Contents

CHAPTER SIX
Managing Data Sources   245

CHAPTER SEVEN
Building Data-driven ASP.NET Applications   291

Preface

Introduction to Microsoft ASP.NET will familiarize you with ways to create dynamic Web applications using server-side programming technologies. A well-rounded Internet programmer needs to be able to integrate server technologies to produce Web applications that not only interact with visitors, but also integrate other computer applications.

Web sites today need to validate form data, as well as provide ways of interacting with visitors. In the past, you might have used JavaScript to create client-side scripts. You may have worried about which browser application and browser version would support your Web site. Today, with the wide range of Internet-enabled devices, Internet applications must support devices such as mobile phones and hand-held devices that do not support JavaScript. Your challenge is to create applications that can be used in a variety of settings and on a variety of devices. With Visual Studio .NET you can create ASP.NET Web applications that are portable. These applications can be displayed on a simple hand-held device, or in the latest browser.

In the early days of the World Wide Web, a company might have created a Web presence consisting of a few Web pages that contained general information about the company. Today, companies are building Web applications to manage and deliver information to their customers and business partners. They are using databases to store, retrieve, and display data on the Web. Although the need for business-to-business applications was recognized early, Internet programmers did not have the tools or skills to develop these types of Web sites. Large companies could afford to build custom applications, while small to medium size businesses lacked the resources to develop Internet business applications Visual Studio .NET and ASP.NET are Microsoft's solution to building e-business applications with a new type of Internet application known as a Web Service. Web Services are built on Internet standards and allows companies to share data and build applications that communicate over the Internet. Microsoft provides tools within Visual Studio .NET and ASP.NET to build Web Services.

In this book, you will learn how to use ASP.NET to process form data from the client, and to send out e-mail from a Web page. You will also learn how ASP.NET can be used to interact with other computer applications on the server. You will learn how to use ASP.NET to read and write information to a file on the server, and how ASP.NET can also be used to build Web applications that interact with a database. Finally, you will learn how to develop Web Services and mobile Web applications.

THE INTENDED AUDIENCE

Introduction to Microsoft ASP.NET is intended for the individual who wants to create dynamic Web applications. You should be familiar with the Windows operating system and know how to use Internet Explorer to view Web pages. A basic understanding of the Internet and HTML is recommended. No prior knowledge of programming is required.

This book provides background chapters on beginning programming concepts, including object-oriented programming and Visual Basic .NET, as well as the .NET Framework and the ASP.NET model. No prior knowledge of server programming is required. In later chapters, the book describes how to create Web pages that interact with a Microsoft Access database and a SQL Server database. These chapters explain relational database concepts, and use the Access database environment to upsize your database to SQL Server. No prior knowledge of database programming is required.

THE APPROACH

To facilitate the learning process, this book presents content and theory integrated with sample exercises. Each chapter includes references to additional Internet resources, and a summary and review questions that highlight and reinforce major concepts that were presented. The Hands-on Projects are guided activities that let you practice and reinforce the techniques presented in the chapter. They also enhance your learning experience by providing additional ways to apply your knowledge in new situations. At the end of each chapter, there are several Case Projects that allow you to use the skills that you have learned in the chapter to solve real world problems.

The examples provided in each chapter were developed to provide you with the opportunity to practice the skills discussed within the chapter. They are not dependent upon successful completion of the previous chapter. Therefore, you can always move ahead to another chapter, while still reviewing content presented in a previous chapter.

The approach and sequence of topics was chosen based upon experience teaching ASP.NET in the classroom. Beginning ASP.NET developers need to have a strong grasp of the basic concepts. They need to see a variety of techniques that are used in real-world applications. In this book, a layering approach is integrated within the chapters. Instead of jumping in to Web databases, this book begins with form processing and validation. Then, it moves to binding data using controls and data structures such as ArrayLists and HashTables. In later chapters students take another step to bind to data objects such as the DataReader and DataSet. Then, they extract this knowledge to build a data component in Visual Basic .NET. Finally, they expose their Web database application as a Web Service. By using this layered approach, students build upon the knowledge that they learned in previous chapters. This helps them review the information, and focus on learning the new concepts and skills.

Too much variety in a complex course tends to be difficult for students because they cannot focus on the learning objectives, and instead spend more time on assessment of the case study. Therefore, the majority of this book uses a sample fictional store called Tara Store as the focus of the hands-on activities. This is not a running case study. Rather, it provides a conceptual framework for students, so that they can focus on learning the material, instead of learning about a new company in each chapter.

OVERVIEW OF THIS BOOK

The examples, hands-on exercises, projects, and cases in this book will help you achieve the following objectives:

- Describe the architecture of the .NET Framework and the ASP.NET object model
- Create basic Web pages using ASP.NET
- Use Server controls to create dynamic Web applications
- Validate form data using server-side Validation controls
- Locate Internet resources that include information ASP.NET and Visual Studio .NET
- Create XML documents and transform them into XHTML using XSLT style sheets
- Become familiar with object-oriented programming and Visual Basic .NET programming techniques
- Become familiar with relational database concepts and learn how to create queries using SQL
- Create and manage databases using Microsoft Access and SQL Server
- Create dynamic Web applications that interact with a database using server-side programming
- Create reusable server components to retrieve data from SQL Server using stored procedures and Visual Basic .NET
- Configure your Web applications to optimize Web performance and minimize security risks
- Become familiar with methods to debug and troubleshoot your Web application.
- Create Web Services that allow your Web application interact with other server based applications
- Use server-side programming to process forms, send e-mail from a Web page, and read and write to files on the server
- Create Web applications that can be displayed on mobile devices

In **Chapter 1**, you will learn about the ASP.NET object model. You will also learn about the new HTML and ASP.NET Server controls, and about how Visual Basic .NET programs are integrated with ASP.NET pages. You will locate Internet resources that provide additional information on ASP.NET, and you will learn about the architecture of the .NET Framework. In **Chapter 2**, you will use the Visual Studio .NET tools to create a Web application. You will learn to create User controls to store reusable content and code. You will create ASP.NET pages using HTML Server controls. You will build cascading style sheets using the Style Builder tool. You will learn how to customize the toolbox. In **Chapter 3**, you will create ASP.NET pages with ASP.NET Server controls. You will create, validate, and process forms. You will use ASP.NET controls to bind to data lists such as ArrayLists and HashTables. In **Chapter 4**, you will learn how to enhance your Web application using Rich controls. You will create XML data files, XSLT style sheets, and transform them into an XHTML page using the XML control. You will create an XML file to store your Web site banner ads, and use an AdRotator control to manage your banner ads. You will use the File Upload control to upload files to the Web Server without requiring a file transfer program (ftp). **Chapter 5** explains how to program using Visual Basic .NET. You will learn basic object-oriented-programming concepts such as how to create classes, functions, and procedures. You will learn how to create code to handle server events and store data. You will use decision control structures to alter the execution order of a program and looping control structures to repeat blocks of code.

There are three chapters that focus specifically on Web databases. **Chapter 6** provides database basics. In this chapter, you will learn about the ADO.NET Framework. You will learn how to create database connections, create SQL Server databases, and build SQL scripts and stored procedures. You will use Access to upsize your database to SQL Server. You will also learn to use the database tools within Visual Studio .NET to create your table structures, insert data, and build SQL queries. **Chapter 7** shows you how to create data-driven Web pages. This chapter explains how to bind a Data object to various Data controls which are located within the Web page. You will also learn to work with a variety of new Data controls such as a DataGrid and Repeater. **Chapter 8** describes how to build more complex Web database applications. You will learn how to use different Data objects such as the DataReader and DataSet to retrieve data. You will learn to customize the DataGrid control to sort and filter data. You will use SQL commands to insert, modify, and delete data. You will also build reusable Visual Basic .NET components using Visual Studio .NET to store your database logic.

In **Chapter 9**, you will learn how to maintain state between the client and the server using the Global Application File, application variables, session variables, and cookies. You will learn to read and write cookies using the Response object. You will learn how to maintain state without cookies. You will also learn about the methods used to build secure Web sites. In **Chapter 10**, you will learn how to handle errors within your applications. You will learn to interpret error messages, and create custom error messages. You will learn how to use structured exception handling to help you capture and identify your errors. In **Chapter 11**, you will learn to create Web Services. You will describe the standards and protocols used to create Web Services. You will locate and consume third party Web Services from a Web page. In **Chapter 12**, you will learn to integrate your Web application with the file system. You will learn how to manage files and directories on the server and to store and retrieve data from a file on the server. You will learn how to send e-mail from a Web page. Finally, you will create Web pages that can be viewed on mobile devices using Mobile Server controls.

FEATURES

- **Chapter Objectives:** Each chapter in this book begins with a list of the important concepts to be mastered within the chapter. This list provides you with a quick reference to the contents of the chapter as well as a useful study aid.

- **Step-By-Step Methodology:** As new concepts are presented in each chapter, tutorials are used to provide step-by-step instructions that allow you to actively apply the concepts you are learning. Many of the Hands-on Projects at the end of the chapter also provide step-by-step instruction. Students often need additional cases to apply the concepts learned in the chapter. These hands-on activities provide a great way to reinforce the material.

- **Modular Approach:** Each chapter contains exercises, Hands-on Projects, and Case Projects that are self-contained. Many of the chapters can be taught in a different scope and sequence.

- **Figures and Tables:** Figures help you visualize Web-architecture components and relationships, and other basic concepts. Tables list examples of code components and their variations in a visual and readable format.

- **Tips:** Chapters contain Tips designed to provide you with practical advice and proven strategies related to the concept that being discussed. Tips also provide suggestions for resolving problems you might encounter while proceeding through the chapters.

- **Chapter Summaries:** Each chapter's text is followed by a summary of chapter concepts. These summaries provide a helpful way to recap and revisit the ideas covered in each chapter.

- **Review Questions:** End-of-chapter assessment begins with a set of approximately twenty Review Questions that reinforce the main ideas introduced in each chapter. These questions ensure that you have mastered the concepts and understand the information you have learned.

Hands-on Projects: Along with conceptual explanations and step-by-step tutorials, each chapter provides Hands-on Projects related to each major topic aimed at providing you with practical experience. Some of the Hands-on Projects provide detailed instructions, while others provide less detailed instructions that require you to apply the materials presented in the current chapter with less guidance. As a result, the Hands-on Projects provide you with practice implementing Web programming in real-world situations.

Case Projects: Approximately four cases are presented at the end of each chapter. These cases are designed to help you apply what you have learned in each chapter to real-world situations. They give you the opportunity to independently synthesize and evaluate information, examine potential solutions, and make recommendations, much as you would in an actual business situation.

TEACHING TOOLS

The following supplemental materials are available when this book is used in a classroom setting. All of the teaching tools available with this book are provided to the instructor on a single CD-ROM.

Electronic Instructor's Manual. The Instructor's Manual that accompanies this textbook includes:

- Sample course syllabi. Although ASP.NET is a complex topic, this book can be used in a variety of settings such as an eight-week class or an online course.

- Additional instructional material to assist in class preparation, including suggestions for lecture topics. It is critical for the instructor to be able to help the students understand how to use the help resources and how to identify problems. The Instructor's Manual will help you identify areas that are more difficult to teach, and provide you with ideas of how to present the material in an easier fashion. There is also additional information on how to install and configure the Windows operating systems, Web Servers, and Visual Studio .NET.

- Solutions to all end-of-chapter materials, including the Review Questions, and, when applicable, Hands-on Projects and Case Projects.

- Suggestions for Web sites with more information on the relevant topics.

ExamView®. This textbook is accompanied by ExamView, a powerful testing software package that allows instructors to create and administer printed, computer (LAN-based), and Internet exams. ExamView includes hundreds of questions that correspond to the topics covered in this text, enabling students to generate detailed study guides that include page references for further review. The computer-based and Internet testing components allow students to take exams at their computers, and also save the instructor time by grading each exam automatically

PowerPoint presentations. This book comes with Microsoft PowerPoint slides for each chapter. These are included as a teaching aid for classroom presentation, to make available to students on the network for chapter review, or to be printed for classroom distribution. Instructors can add their own slides for additional topics they introduce to the class.

Solution Files. Solutions to steps within a chapter and end-of chapter exercises are provided on the Teaching Tools CD-ROM and may also be found on the Course Technology Web site at *www.course.com*. The solutions are password protected.

Distance Learning. Course Technology is proud to present online courses in WebCT and Blackboard, as well as MyCourse 2.0, Course Technology's own course enhancement tool, to provide the most complete and dynamic learning experience possible. When you add online content to one of your courses, you're adding a lot: self tests, lecture notes, a gradebook, and, most of all, a gateway to the twenty-first century's most important information resource. Instructors are encouraged to make the most of your course, both online and offline. For more information on how to bring distance learning to your course, contact your local Course Technology sales representative.

ACKNOWLEDGMENTS

No book is written on an island. So, I'd like to thank Lynne Raughley, Developmental Editor, who did a great job managing the project and keeping me on track. I'd like to thank Jennifer Muroff, for all your support and pearls of wisdom. I would also like to thank Tricia Boyle, who had the great task of keeping us on schedule with a product that was always in beta! Thanks to Bill Larkin, and the entire production team for making this book happen. Thank you to the QA team: John Bosco, Nicole Ashton, Serge Palladino and Alex White. They had the huge task of testing the projects during several beta cycles and on several operating systems. Their effort has greatly improved the quality of this book. Thanks to the reviewers who provided invaluable comments and suggestions during the development of this book: Warren Boe, University of Iowa; Terry Felke, William Rainey Harper College; Marylu Gowen, Bishop Kenny High School; Anne Nelson, High Point University; Bonnie Ryan-Gauthier, New Brunswick Community College; and Michael Walters, Laramie County Community College.

The Tara Store case (*www.TaraStore.com*) is modeled after Joy of Ireland, which is a real brick and mortar store located in Chicago, Illinois. Their Web site at *www.Joy-Of-Ireland.com* is well known for their customer service, quality products, and vast product line. I'd like to thank the owner Mike Joy for allowing me to use the photographs of his store and products in the Tara Store Hands-on Projects and case studies. Slainte!

Thanks to my students who continually inspire me to continue learning. Thanks to Kitty Tabers at Oakton Community College (*www210.oakton.edu*), who allows me be innovative in the classroom and continue to support my work in the World Wide Web. Thanks to my student Tatyana Kiseleva (*www.kiseta.net*) who helped me test the Case Projects and develop the support materials. Thank you to my three daughters, Molly, Erin, and Christy, and to my brother Jim Shea. Thank you to my dear friends Cindy, Daniel, Carolyn, and Elizabeth Niersbach for supporting me during this time. Thank you to John and Mary Ann Kalata who were supportive. Many chapters of this book were written at their dining room table!

I'd like to dedicate this book to my wonderful husband, John Kalata. You are my inspiration. You are where I find my strength, courage, energy, and commitment. As I said, no book can be written on an island. But if I had to pick someone to be on that island with, it would be you. The process of researching to completion of this book was almost two years. Without you I would not have been able to write this book, or develop and teach new courses in cutting-edge Web technologies to my students. Thank you.

Read This Before You Begin

TO THE USER

You can use your own computer to complete the exercises, Hands-on Projects, and Case Projects in this book. To use your own computer, you will need the following:

- **Microsoft Windows 2000 Professional or Windows XP Professional.** Your computer must be configured so that you can connect to the Internet. You must have TCP/IP software loaded on your computer. You can learn more about these operating systems at *www.microsoft.com/windows.*

- **Internet Information Server (IIS).** The IIS Web Server is packaged with the Windows 2000 Professional and Windows XP Professional disks. However, Windows 2000 Professional does not install IIS by default. You can install it via Add/Remove Programs in the Control Panel. The Web server must have the FrontPage 2000 server extensions installed and configured. IIS can be used to host multiple Web sites on the same physical server. On Windows 2000 Server, you can run Internet Information Server 5.0 (IIS), which is included in Windows 2000 Professional CD-ROM. IIS 5.0 is installed on Windows 2000 Server by default. For Windows 2000, the IIS executable is located at C:\winnt\system32\Inetsrv. In IIS 5.0, the tool for managing the Web server is called Internet Information Server snap-in. You can verify that IIS is installed by opening the IIS snap-in. To open the IIS snap-in click Start, point to Settings, then click Control Panel. Double-click the Administrative Tools folder, and then double-click Computer Management. Under the Server Applications and Services node, expand IIS. Once the Web server has been installed, the complete documentation for IIS 5.0 for Windows 2000 Server is available at *http://localhost/.* You can also view additional information at *www.microsoft.com/windows2000/technologies/web/default.asp.*

- **Microsoft Visual Studio .NET Professional, Visual Studio .NET Developer, or Visual Studio .NET Enterprise Architect.** You can select the default installation. However, all of the documentation is not installed by default. It is recommended that you load the documentation locally so that you do not need the CD each time you view a Help file. You should read the ReadMe file that comes with the installation disks. The entire installation requires at least three gigabytes of free disk space on your hard drive. It is important that you install Visual Studio .NET correctly; otherwise, some of the features of ASP.NET may not be available. Your instructor has detailed information in the Instructor's Manual on installing Visual Studio .NET in Windows 2000 Professional and Windows XP Professional systems. You can learn more about the features of Visual Studio .NET at *http://msdn.microsoft.com/vstudio.*

- **Microsoft Access XP.** You'll need Access XP to create the database tables and queries, and upsize your database to SQL Server. If you have Access 2000, you can still use the database, but you may not be able to upsize your database to the server without installing the Access upgrade. You can download the upgrade at *http://office.microsoft.com/downloads/2000/Accsql.aspx.* You will learn how to upsize an Access database in Chapter 6. You can learn more about the features in Access at *www.microsoft.com/office/access.*

- **Microsoft SQL Server Data Engine (MSDE).** MSDE is needed to create the database tables, queries, and stored procedure in SQL Server. You will learn how to install the MSDE and the database samples in Chapter 6. Alternately, you can use the full version of SQL Server. You can learn more about the features of SQL Server at *www.microsoft.com/sql/default.asp.* You should learn how to install and configure the MSDE database server before you start Chapter 6. Instructions on installing and configuring the MSDE database server are located in the Chapter 6 data files directory. The directions are also found in the Instructor's Manual.

- **Student Data Files.** To complete the steps and projects in the chapters, you will need data files that have been created specifically for this book. You may obtain these files from your instructor. You may also download them from the Course Technology Web site at *www.course.com.* Enter the ISBN number in the Search text box on the home page, and then click the hyperlink labeled Introduction to ASP.NET. You will need a place to store your data files. The data files are named after the chapter, for example Chapter01Data, Chapter02Data, etc.

- **Web folder on a Web Server.** In each chapter, you will create a single project named after the chapter, for example, Chapter1, Chapter2, and Chapter3. You will be creating many files as you proceed through the tutorials, Hands-on Projects, and Case Projects within this single project. This way you will be able to manage all of your files for the chapter within a single location.

- **Microsoft Mobile Internet Toolkit.** The toolkit is used to develop Mobile Forms that are Web pages displayed on mobile devices. You can download this for free from Microsoft at *http://msdn.microsoft.com/msdn-files/027/001/817/Search.asp.* You will learn how to install the Toolkit in Chapter 12.

- **The QuickStart Web Site and .NET Framework Samples.** These samples are used to help you learn how to build Web Forms. You will learn how to install these samples in the book. If you would like to preview these samples, you can view them online at *http://samples.gotdotnet.com/quickstart/.*

TO THE INSTRUCTOR

To complete all the exercises and chapters in this book, your users must work with a set of user files, called a Data Disk, and download software from Web sites. The data files are included on the Instructor's Resource CD. They may also be obtained electronically through the Course Technology Web site at *www.course.com*. Follow the instructions in the Help file to copy the user files to your server or standalone computer. You can view the Help file using a text editor, such as WordPad or Notepad.

After the files are copied, you can make Data Disks for the users yourself, or tell your students where to find the files so they can make their own Data Disks. Make sure the files are set up correctly by having students follow the instructions in the "To the User" section of Read This Before you Begin.

COURSE TECHNOLOGY DATA FILES

You are granted a license to copy the data files to any computer or computer network used by individuals who have purchased this book.

VISIT OUR WORLD WIDE WEB SITES

The author's home page can be viewed at *www.oakton.net*. Additional materials for your course may be available at the Course Technology Web site. Go to *www.course.com*. Periodically search this site for more information and materials to accompany this text. You can also view the Tara Store Web site at *www.TaraStore.com*.

1

INTRODUCTION TO **ASP.NET**

> **In this chapter, you will:**
> - Learn about the differences between static and dynamic Web pages
> - Identify the controls used in ASP.NET pages
> - Describe how server-side processing occurs with ASP.NET pages
> - Learn about the ASP.NET object programming model
> - Identify Internet resources about ASP.NET and Visual Studio .NET
> - Import a namespace
> - Describe the common language runtime
> - View an assembly

Businesses use the Internet to promote their companies, or to allow customers to purchase their products online. The cost of developing and maintaining a custom e-commerce solution, such as an online store, can vary from a few thousand to millions of dollars per year. Research predicts that the majority of Internet activities in the future will be business-to-business transactions, which are often referred to as e-business. Microsoft has redesigned ASP.NET and Microsoft Visual Studio .NET to support developers who need to build both e-commerce solutions and e-business applications.

ASP.NET is a language-independent technology that is used to develop Web applications. ASP.NET enables Web developers to create a new type of business application for the Web called Web Services. In this book you will learn how to use Visual Studio .NET to generate ASP.NET applications and Web Services. In this chapter, you will learn how ASP.NET processing allows you to create dynamic Web applications.

STATIC AND DYNAMIC WEB APPLICATIONS

In the first years of the World Wide Web, the Hypertext Markup Language (HTML) was the primary tool for developing Web pages. HTML generates static content that can be viewed via a browser over the Internet. Browser software interprets HTML tags and formats the output. Every time a **static** Web page is loaded in a browser, the browser displays the same content. As the Internet expanded from governments and universities to businesses and individuals, Web applications needed to become more dynamic. A **dynamic** Web application enables the user to interact with the Web application in ways that change the appearance or the content of the Web page. Examples of dynamic Web applications include shopping carts, membership databases, online catalogues, and personalized Web sites.

You cannot create dynamic Web applications using HTML alone. You can use many other different technologies along with HTML, including client- and server-side scripting, and server-side programming. A major limitation of client-side scripting is browser dependency, since client-side scripts are executed via the browsers' scripting engines, and not all browsers support all scripting languages. Another major limitation of client-side scripting is security. The client can easily view the scripts within the Web page. Server-side programs allow you to create dynamic Web applications that can process a form or manage a database. With server-based applications, you can create a secure Web site because the programs are run on the Web server. The Web server sends static HTML to the client's browser. Because the processing of the script occurs on the server, you can hide code from the client. There are several types of server-side programming technologies, such as Perl CGI programming and Java programming.

Microsoft's implementation of Web server programming technology is referred to as Active Server Pages (ASP). ASP makes it easier for Web developers to create dynamic Web applications. An **Active Server Page (ASP)** is a Web page that contains server-side scripting. The two common scripting languages are VBScript and JavaScript. Both the server script and HTML coexist within the same file. When the client requests an ASP page, the Web server passes the request to the ASP application. The ASP application detects if there are any global scripts that need to be processed in the Global Application File (global.asa). Then, the ASP application inserts the code from any server-side include pages. Server-side include files are text files that end with the file extension inc or .asp. Server-side include pages contain code and content that is used in several pages. Frequently Web sites use server-side include files to store database connections, frequently used scripts, headers, menus, and footers. The server-side scripts are executed by the Web Server scripting engine. When the server script finishes processing code, it sends the HTML and any client-side scripts to the browser. Figure 1-1 shows how ASP Web pages are processed on the Web server.

Processing ASP

Figure 1-1   Processing ASP pages

The most recent version of ASP is called ASP.NET, and the two main types of Web resources created with ASP.NET applications are WebForms and Web Services. **WebForms** allow you to quickly develop and process forms on Web pages, and develop cross-browser Web applications. WebForms are Web pages identified with the file extension **.aspx**. Any page ending in **.aspx** is directed to the ASP.NET engine, which is located in a file named **XSPISAPI.DLL**. An example of an ASP.NET application is a shopping cart. WebForms can be used to target any browser or device without requiring you to write a separate application for each.

Web Services are ASP.NET Web pages that contain publicly exposed code so that other applications can interact with them. Web Services are identified with the file extension **.asmx**. A company could, for example, expose the product-ordering functionality of its Web site, in order to allow other Web sites to connect to this function. For each sale that originated from other Web sites, the company could pay a referral fee. You will learn how to create Web Services later in this book.

Both types of ASP.NET applications support several new features, including support for a variety of programming languages, enhanced performance, improved session management, enhanced scalability, improved error handling, tracing capability, debugging capability, simpler deployment, and support for multiple platforms.

WEBFORMS

WebForms are ASP.NET pages within an ASP.NET application. In previous versions of ASP, HTML is intermixed with ASP code within the same script. The ASP.NET WebForm is separated into two logical areas, the HTML template and a collection of code behind the WebForm.

The **HTML template** usually contains the design layout, content, and controls. (*Note*: Most HTML books refer to controls as tags or elements. Within ASP.NET these are known as HTML controls.) The HTML template creates the user interface, or **presentation layer**. These controls tell the browser how to format the Web page. Although there are many controls available in ASP.NET, WebForms can also use any of the traditional HTML controls. The HTML template is created by using a combination of HTML controls, HTML Server controls, Mobile controls, and ASP.NET controls.

Server Controls

HTML Server controls are similar to HTML controls, except that they are processed by the server. In a traditional HTML page the developer creates a text box by writing `<input type="text">`. Using HTML Server controls, you only need to write `runat = "server"` to transform the HTML control into an HTML Server control. In this case, you would write `<input type="text" runat="server"/>`. When the runat property is set to server, the control is processed by the server. By transforming HTML controls to HTML Server controls, you can create server-side programs that interact with the control before it is rendered as a plain HTML control and sent to the browser. Below is a sample of an HTML Server control.

```
<input type="radio" runat="server" value="Yes"/> Yes
```

Notice in the sample above that the HTML Server control ends with `/>`. In previous versions of HTML, HTML elements such as the line break only required the opening tag. However, the most recent version of HTML, known as XHTML, requires that all HTML elements be compliant with XML standards. XML is another type of markup language that can be used to build applications. One of the rules of XML is that all controls must have a closing tag, or end with `/>`. So, all controls that do not have a closing tag are closed in the initial tag with `/>`. The XML, HTML, and XHTML standards are maintained by the World Wide Web Consortium. For more information on XHTML visit the World Wide Web Consortium at *www.w3c.org*.

 A common error is forgetting to specify the runat attribute for the Server control. When you refer to the control in your code behind the page, the compiler displays an error message with the message ID BC30451, and text that specifies that the control was not declared.

There are a variety of new controls, including ASP.NET Form controls, Data Validation controls, User controls, and Mobile controls. ASP controls are usually identified with the prefix asp: followed by the name of the control. ASP.NET Form controls are similar to HTML Server controls. For example, the control for an ASP.NET button is written: `<asp:Button id="ShowBtn" runat="server" Text="Show the message." />`. Notice that the forward slash is also used with ASP.NET Form controls to indicate that there is no closing tag. ASP.NET Form controls also have different properties than their HTML Server control counterparts. ASP.NET Form controls allow you to create controls that render HTML output and that provide more flexibility when you are creating your programs. ASP.NET Form controls can interact with client-side events such as the user clicking a button. When the event occurs, ASP.NET can trigger a script to run on the server. ASP.NET Form controls will create the HTML code. HTML Server controls and ASP.NET Server controls use different properties to generate output. In the following sample code, the HTML Server Label control named Message1 contains an InnerHTML property that is used to assign the value to an HTML tag. But, the ASP Server Label control named Message2 uses the Text property to assign the value to the HTML tag.

```
Message1.InnerHTML = "Product 1"
Message2.Text = "Product 2"
```

 It is very important that you look at the browser source code of each ASP.NET page that you create in order to understand what the Web server is sending to the browser. ASP.NET code is never sent to the browser. Only HTML tags, along with client-side scripts, are sent to the browser. Many errors are related to the syntax of the HTML code that is sent to the browser, such as a missing closing tag, or a missing quotation mark. By viewing the source code in the browser, you can more quickly locate the HTML syntax errors. Sometimes it's also useful to paste the code into an editor such as FrontPage XP, which can help you locate and identify HTML errors quickly.

Data Validation controls are a series of controls that validate form data without extensive JavaScript programming; they are supported in both Internet Explorer and Netscape Navigator. Data Validation controls also have some unique properties and methods.

User controls are external files that can be included within other WebForms. User controls allow you to reuse code across multiple files. For example, you can create a User control that displays the top ten music selections this week. You can use this control on the home page, and on the product category pages. User controls are often used to create self-contained code, headers, menus, and footers. User controls replace the functionality of ASP server-side include pages. They are identified with the file extension .asmx. When the User control is inserted into the Web page, the control can be assigned a custom prefix instead of ASP.

Mobile controls are a series of controls that provide form functionality within wireless and mobile devices. The rendering of the user interface occurs automatically, depending upon which device is used.

Literal controls are page content that is not assigned to a specific HTML control. For example, any text sent to the browser is a Literal control. Literal controls can be used to send a combination of HTML tags and text to the browser.

The Web developer uses these new controls to build their Web pages. Figure 1-2 shows some of the Server controls in the Visual Studio .NET Toolbox. You will learn how to use each of these types of controls in this book.

Figure 1-2   Server controls within Visual Studio .NET

The Code Behind the Page

The WebForm contains the HTML controls, client-side scripts, and Server controls. In previous versions of ASP the server scripts were written within the Web page. With WebForms, the server programs are written in a separate file known as the code behind the page. The **code behind the page** contains programming routines that are directly related to the various Server controls on the WebForm. Only Server controls can interact with the code behind the page. The code behind the page may be written in any ASP.NET-compatible language, including Visual Basic .NET, C#, Perl, and Java. The code behind the page has the same filename as the WebForm. However, the file extension varies with the programming language used. The filename for the code behind the page has the extension **.vb** if the code is written in Visual Basic .NET. (In this book, you will use Visual Basic .NET to create the code behind the page.) If the page is written in C#, the file has the extension **.cs**.

The location of the code behind the page is determined by a property that is set on the first line in the page, using the @Page directive. The **@Page** directive allows you to set the default properties for the entire page. There are many properties that can be set using the @Page directive, as you will learn later in this book. In the following sample code, the default Language property is set to vb to indicate that the code behind the page is written in Visual Basic .NET. The **CodeBehind** property indicates that the code behind the page is located in a file named WebForm1.vb. The **Inherits** property indicates that the code behind the page inherits the page class named TaraStore.WebForm1. This class contains the compiled code for the entire page.

```
<%@ Page Language="vb" Codebehind="WebForm1.vb" ¬
Inherits="TaraStore.WebForm1"%>
```

 The code above should be displayed on one line as indicated by the symbol ¬. This symbol is used throughout this book, to identify lines of code that are longer than one line of printed text.

The compiled code behind the page is the class definition for the page. A **class** is a named logical grouping of code. The **class definition** contains the functions, methods, and properties that belong to that class. In Visual Studio .NET, the process of compiling a class is called **building**. When you build the application, you compile the code into an executable file.

When you use Visual Studio .NET to create your application, Visual Studio .NET compiles the code behind the page into an executable file and places the file in the `bin` directory. As you can see in Figure 1–3, the code behind the page is compiled into a class and cached on the Web server. When there is a change in the page class file, the page class is recompiled, and cached again.

There are several reasons for separating the server code and the page. For example, assume that you place an HTML Server control button on a page. When the user clicks the button, an event signals the server that the event occurred. An event handler named OnServerClick is called. The code for the OnServerClick event handler is located in the code behind the page. The OnServerClick event handler could display a message in the Web page. By separating the programming logic and the presentation layer, the application becomes easier to maintain. When the message changes, you need only change it within the logic code behind the page. You don't need to modify the page itself.

 In this book, you will use Visual Studio .NET to create all of your ASP.NET applications. However, some programmers prefer to create their ASP.NET templates and the code behind the page in a single file and not use Visual Studio .NET. In this situation, there is only one ASP.NET file, and the entire page is compiled at runtime. If you do not use Visual Studio .NET to manage your projects, and instead create the ASP.NET template and the code behind the page in a text editor, then you must compile your components using a command-line compiler. You must also set the Web server permissions of your `bin` directory to execute, and the ASP.NET directories to read and script.

Figure 1-3   Compiling the ASP.NET page and the code behind the page into the Page class

Postback

When a user fills out a form and clicks the Submit button, the data is sent to the Web server for processing. If the user enters an invalid value, the form is redisplayed to the client. It is helpful to redisplay the values that the user entered. Maintaining this information across browser requests is known as **maintaining state**. The server code must retrieve the values from the initial page and merge them with the code for the subsequent page.

Server controls allow you to send data to the browser without writing the data-gathering and data-rendering code. By default, the Server control automatically supports the posting of data back into the form, a process known as **postback**. When the user enters the data into a text box on a form, the server collects the value and rerenders the text box with the data. A hidden form field named **_ViewState** is a very long string that contains information required to maintain the form data across multiple page requests. The Web server decodes this encoded string. Therefore, the value of _ViewState changes each time the form is reposted back to the server. Then, the values that are stored with the page remain with the page, even if it is redirected to a different Web server. In an enterprise network, it is common to have a group of Web servers called a WebFarm. In a WebFarm, when one server stops, the clients are redirected to another server. By storing the information on the client and not on the server, you enable the information to travel with the client across page requests and across servers. In Figure 1-4, the _ViewState hidden field demonstrates how postback maintains state. You will learn more about how state management works later in this book.

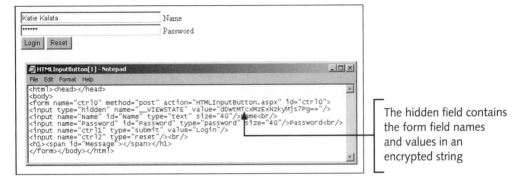

Figure 1-4　Postback data using the _ViewState hidden field

The Web page does not have to support the postback feature. You can turn the property on or off by setting the EnableViewState property to true or false within the @Page directive. You can also turn the EnableViewState property on or off by setting the property for any individual Server control, or for the entire application by setting the property in the application configuration files. In the following sample code, the Postback property is turned off for the entire page for all Server controls.

```
<%@ Page EnableViewState="false" %>
```

Page Class Events

All Web pages created with ASP.NET are objects based upon the Page class in the .NET environment. The **Page class** consists of a variety of methods, functions, and properties that can be accessed within the code behind the page. The first time a page is requested by a client, a series of page events occurs. As shown in Figure 1-5, the first page event is the **Page_Init** event, which initializes the page control hierarchy.

After the page control hierarchy is initialized, the Page_Load event loads any Server controls. You can access the Page_Load event handler within code behind the page. When the Page_Load event occurs, all controls on the page are loaded into memory. You can place code that you want to execute when the page opens in the Page_Load event handler. The Page_Load event occurs every time the page is executed.

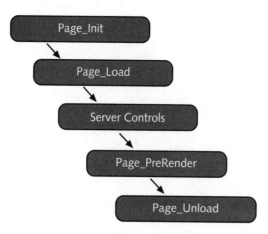

Figure 1-5   Page class event cycle

In the following sample code, a message is displayed when the Page_Load event occurs. In Visual Basic .NET, the event handler is known as a **procedure**. When you create a procedure, you must identify the beginning of the procedure with the keyword Sub, and the ending with the keywords End Sub. You also need to indicate if any values, known as **parameters,** are passed to the procedures. (*Note:* You will learn how to create procedures and pass parameters in the following chapter.)

```
Sub Page_Load(sender As Object, e As EventArgs)
    Message.InnerHtml = "Welcome!"
End Sub
```

Within the Page class you can define specific **server control events**, which occur when the page is posted back to the server. Control events can be **action events**, such as the click event for a Server Button control, or **change events**, such as when the value of a server Text control changes. For example, if a user clicks a Server Button control, then you can execute code in the OnServerClick event handler. Server control events are only executed when the event related to the Server control occurs. In the following sample code, the page contains an HTML Server Button control named MyBtn and a span tag named Message.

```
<button id="MyBtn" runat="server" ¬
OnServerClick="MyBtn_Click"> Click me!</button>
<h1><span id="Message" runat="server"/></h1>
```

When the page first opens, no message would be displayed. However, when the user clicks the button, an OnServerClick event handler is called. The event handler calls a procedure named MyBtn_Click. In the code behind the page, the OnServerClick event handler can send a message back to the browser. Figure 1-6 shows the results of the server code. Notice that the message in the span tag has changed. Also notice how the client page contains client-side code written in JavaScript. The client-side JavaScript is created by the server to trigger the event that returns a server click event, which is processed on the server. That is how the server knows that the click event has occurred in the browser. (*Note*: If there is a client- and server-side OnClick event handler, the server-side OnClick event handler takes precedence.)

```
Sub MyBtn_Click(sender As Object, E as EventArgs)
    Message.InnerHtml = "You clicked me!"
End Sub
```

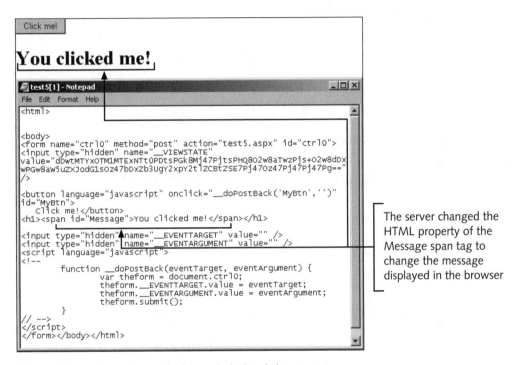

The server changed the HTML property of the Message span tag to change the message displayed in the browser

Figure 1-6 Interacting with the code behind the page

You will most likely add your server code to the Page_Load event handler, event procedures, and functions. However, there are additional page events such as the Page_CommittTransaction and Page_AbortTransaction. These events are used in combination to define a sequential series of events that together are called a **transaction**. In a transaction, all events must occur; otherwise all events are rolled back to their original state.

The **Page_PreRender** event occurs immediately before the control hierarchy is rendered and sent to the browser. Although the page contains Server controls, the client only sees the rendered Client controls, such as HTML and client script. Not all controls need to be rendered to the client. For example, you may not want to render a control to the browser until the user completes the login form correctly.

If you want to view the order in which the Server controls are rendered to the Web page, turn on the Trace feature. The **Trace** feature allows you to view the page controls, the order in which they are loaded, and the time it takes to load the control. To turn on the Trace feature, on the first line of code set the Trace property for the page to true, as shown in the sample code below.

```
<% @Page trace = "true" %>.
```

When the trace feature has been turned on, the page is displayed along with the Page class Tree. Figure 1-7 shows the Page class Control Tree. Notice how the type of control is listed, along with the time it takes to load each control. The ID is a property that is assigned to the Server control in the Web page. If no ID is provided for the Server control, a generic ID value is assigned. The Control Tree uses indentation to illustrate how the objects are organized within the page class hierarchy.

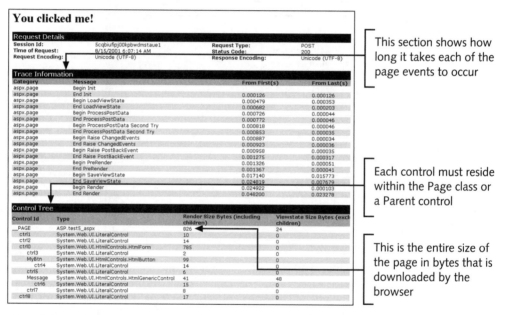

This section shows how long it takes each of the page events to occur

Each control must reside within the Page class or a Parent control

This is the entire size of the page in bytes that is downloaded by the browser

Figure 1-7   The Page class Control Tree

When the page unloads, the Page_Unload event occurs, and the page is removed from the server's memory. You can use the Page_Unload event handler to close database connections, close files, and release any programming variables or objects. In the sample code below, a message is displayed on the Web page when the page is unloaded.

```
Sub Page_UnLoad(sender As Object, e As EventArgs)
    Message.InnerHtml = "Goodbye!"
End Sub
```

It is a common programming practice to release programming variables or objects after they have been used. However, in the .NET framework, the server collects any unused memory assigned to objects that are no longer referenced in your program. It reconfigures the memory storage to free the memory. Although you do not have to release your variables and objects, it is still a recommended programming practice.

Built-in ASP.NET Objects

ASP.NET pages have access to objects that are built into the Web server, along with their properties and methods. You can access built-in ASP.NET objects in the code behind the page. The following is a list of some of these built-in objects.

- *HTTPRequest*—Used to access information that is passed from the client's browser to the Web server. For example, the Request object retrieves information that a user filled in a form. The names and values are stored within a collection that can be accessed from the code behind the page. The HTTPRequest object is mapped directly to the Request property of the Page object. Although you can access this data in other ways, it is much easier to access the Request object directly using the Page object.

- *HTTPResponse*—Used to send information from the Web server to the client's browser. For example, the Response object redirects the user to another Web page. The HTTPResponse object is mapped directly to the Response property of the Page object. Although you can access this data in other ways, it is much easier to access the Response object directly using the Page object.

- *Session*—Used to share information between a single client and the Web server. The Session object stores data during the course of a session. For example, the name of the visitor can be shared as a session variable. When the user closes the browser, the session ends, and the session variable no longer exists. The session can also end when the default session timeout is reached.

- *Application*—Allows developers to treat a sequence of Web pages as a single application, which means that information, such as the name of the application or the total number of visitors on the Web site, can be shared among all the users of an ASP application. The capacity to treat a collection of pages as a single application greatly broadens the possibilities for application development.

The Page.Request Property

The Page object contains a Request and Response property. When a browser sends a request for a Web page to the Web server, the Web server receives the request and some additional information in the TCP/IP header. The **TCP/IP header** is a portion of the data packet that includes information that determines how and where to send the file. The TCP/IP header includes the date and time, the type of request (get or post), the page requested, and the HTTP version. Additional information includes the default language, the referring page, the IP address of the client, the cookies associated with that domain, and the user agent. The **user agent** can be used to identify the client software. If the client has a certificate, the values from the certificate are sent with the request. This information can be retrieved from the TCP/IP header as server variables or with the Request property. The Request property allows you to retrieve any information sent by the browser, including the names and values of form fields and the server variables. Because the Request property belongs to the Page class, you can refer to the Request property using `Page.Request.PropertyName` or `Request.PropertyName`.

In the sample code below, three server variables are written to the browser. Server variables are variables that are passed in the TCP/IP header. This example displays the physical path to the file, using Request.PhysicalPath. The page also displays the IP address of the client, and the domain name of the previous page that contained the link to the current page. Notice that the ASP.NET Response property is used to write out the content to the browser. In the next section you will learn more about the Response property.

```
Response.write(Request.PhysicalPath)
Response.write(Request.UserHostAddress)
Response.Write(Request.UrlReferrer.Host)
```

The Request property can also provide you access to additional properties. For example, the user agent provides a string that can be used to detect the browser version. However, the string must be parsed to locate the browser application name and version. With the Browser property, you can directly access the browser application's name and version without the user agent. The following sample code uses the Browser property to display the client browser's version, then writes out the short name of the browser application, the version number, and the platform.

```
Response.Write(Request.Browser.Browser)
Response.Write(Request.Browser.Version)
Response.Write(Request.Browser.Platform)
```

The Request property provides access to the form field names and values. If there is a form on the page, the form field name and value pairs are sent to the Web server. If the form method is GET, then the form is sent appended to the URL requested as a single string called the **QueryString**. If the form method is POST, it is sent as part of the HTTP request body. The Request property contains a Form collection and QueryString collection that allow you to collect form information from both methods. In the sample code below, a QueryString containing the values of two form fields, name and topic, is attached to the URL. The QueryString is separated from the URL by a question mark.

```
http://www.tarastore.com/index.asp?name=katie&topic=asp
```

The sample code below creates a text box named password and a button named MyBtn.

```
<span id="Message" runat="server">
Please enter your password</span>
<input id="PWD" type="password"
size="8" runat="server"><br/>
```

```
<input id="MyBtn" type="submit" value="Login"
OnServerClick="MyBtn_Click" runat="server"/>
```

This page uses the Request property to retrieve information from the form field and displays the value.

```
Response.write(Request.Form("PWD"))
```

A simpler method for retrieving the value from a form field is to directly access the value properties of the form field. The property name that you use to access the value is different for each type of Server control. However, this method only works with Server controls. If you use a simple HTML control, you must request the form or QueryString collection to retrieve the form field values. For the exercises in this book, you will work primarily with Server controls and can, therefore, use the Value property to directly access the value of a particular form field.

To retrieve the value of the form field you can create an event handler that processes the form. For example, the event handler could be the OnClick event handler for the Submit button. When the user clicks the Submit button, the OnClick event handler is called. Then, in the code behind the page, you retrieve the value of the text box in the event handler. If the value is correct, then the page displays a welcome message. (*Note*: To detect if the value matches a string, such as Course, you need to put the string in quotation marks. You can use an If-Then-Else statement to structure your code. The Then keyword must be on the same line as the If keyword. The code following the keyword Then is executed only if the password matches. The code following the keyword Else is executed if the password does not match.) Otherwise, if the password does not match, the page displays a message instructing the user to try again.

```
Sub MyBtn_Click(As Object, e As EventArgs)
   If (PWD.Value = "Course") Then
      Message.InnerHtml = "Welcome!"
   Else
      Message.InnerHtml = "Try again!"
   End If
End Sub
```

Figure 1-8   Using Page.Request to retrieve form values and server variables

You can obtain information about the members of the Request property by going to the Visual Studio .NET documentation at *ms help://MS.VSCC/ MS.MSDNVS/cpref/html/frlrfsystemwebhttprequestmemberstopic.htm*.

The Page.Response Property

The Response object is used to send information to the browser. Some of this information identifies the server and server properties. For example, the IP address of the server, and the name and version number of the Web server software are sent to the client. The Cookies collection is used to send cookies to the browser. A status code is sent to indicate whether the browser request was successful or encountered an error.

The Response object has several methods, such as Write and WriteFile. The **write method** allows you to send a string to the browser. You can send text, HTML and client script to the browser using the write method. You can use a variable or expression to store the string. Then, you can write out the contents of the variable with the write method. The **WriteFile method** allows you to send the entire contents of a text file to the Web page. In the sample below, the write method is used to write out a string and a variable that contains a string. The WriteFile method is used to write the entire contents of a file named copyright.txt to the Web page.

```
Response.Write("Copyright by TaraStore<br/>")
Dim strMessage as String = "Copyright by TaraStore<br/>"
Response.File(strMessage)
Response.WriteFile("c:\copyright.txt")
```

The Response object allows you to redirect the browser to another page. The Response object also allows you to hold the contents of the page in an area of memory called the **buffer** until you send the page. The methods and properties of the Response object allow you to control the caching of content from the ASP page. **Caching** is the process by which a page is generated and stored on the server. This copy of the page is known as a cached page. If you enable caching on the Web server, the next time the user requests the page, the cached copy is sent. All data sent to the browser is sent using the Response object either via the HTTPResponse object or via the Page.Response property. The following sample code shows how to redirect the visitor to another page. Because this redirection occurs on the server, the visitor never knows that they have been redirected to a new page.

```
Response.Redirect("http://www.course.com/")
```

LOCATING YOUR ASP.NET APPLICATION

You can only view ASP.NET Web pages on a Web server that supports ASP.NET. A local Web server allows you to preview ASP applications on the desktop without connecting to the Internet. In this book, you use the Microsoft Internet Information Server (IIS), which comes with Windows 2000 Professional, Windows 2000 Server, and Windows XP. When you install the Web server software, it creates a default directory for the root Web site at

`C:\Inetpub\wwwroot`. The root Web site is mapped as **localhost**. Therefore, you can reach the Web site with a browser by typing in *http://localhost/*. If you enter this URL in the browser, the IIS help and documentation windows appear. (*Note*: You can stop this by renaming the default.aspx page in the wwwroot folder default_old.aspx.)

When you create your ASP.NET Web applications in Visual Studio .NET, the program places a folder in the root directory, named after your application. (*Note*: Don't put blank spaces in the names of the projects you create. The name is used in the URL for the application. Some browsers do not recognize blank spaces in URLs.) When you have finished creating your applications, you can deploy them to a production Web server on the Internet. To **deploy** a Web application, you copy all of the Web application files to a live Web server on the Internet. You will learn how to deploy your application in a later chapter.

If you do not have your own Web server, you can use a third-party Web server. There are several hosting service providers that are currently supporting ASP.NET applications. Brinkster (*www.brinkster.com*), EraServer (*www.eraserver.com*), and Media3 (*www.media3.com*) all support ASP.NET applications. If you choose to setup an account with an ISP, you may have to write your ASP.NET pages with the ASP.NET code and the code behind the page all within the same file. Some providers may not allow you access to a bin directory either. Some providers require you to use their file transfer software, while others require you to use your own File Transfer Protocol (FTP) software to upload your Web pages to the Web site. WS_FTP by Ipswitch (*www.ipswitch.com*) is a commonly used file transfer program (FTP). You can also locate other FTP programs through Tucows (*www.tucows.com*). Currently, if you use Media3, you can use the deployment features within Visual Studio .NET to deploy your application directly to the Media3 Web server.

WEB SERVICES

Web Services allow you to expose part or all of your programs over the Internet. For example, if your business partner is Course Technology and you want to query that company's product catalog from your Web site, you could post a link with the query that sends the user to Course Technology's Search Page. A newer and controversial method is to scrape the site. **Scraping** a Web site is the process of using a program to view a Web site and capture the source code. The programmer has to create an application that parses the HTML from the data, as well as a program that integrates the new data into the Web site.

A better solution is for Course Technology to provide a Web Service to their catalog application. Then you can use the Catalog Web Service within your own Web applications. Course Technology could limit access to the Catalog Web Service; it could expose the entire program as a Web Service, or only certain parts of the catalog application. Once the catalog application is public, you can use Visual Studio .NET tools such as Server Explorer to view the Web Services available from Course Technology. Currently, there is a public registry known as UDDI that contains registered public Web Services. You can learn more about UDDI at *www.microsoft.com/uddi.* You can also locate more Web Services at *www.xmethods.com.*

In Visual Studio .NET the Web Services source file is contained in a file that has the extension .asmx. When a Web Service is created in Visual Studio .NET, a discovery file containing information on how to interact with the Web Service, and how to format and send data to the Web Service, is created. Because Web Services are built using open standards, Web Services are supported across applications and platforms. For example, a Web Service could be accessed from a Windows application, a Web application, or a mobile application. The client accessing the Web Service might be on a Windows system, UNIX system, or mobile device.

Web Services are used to create business-to-business applications. For example, in Figure 1-9 the Tara Store has a Web Service that exposes the product-ordering functions within its inventory application to its business partners and distributors. Then, visitors can view the product catalog, determine which products are in stock, and order products directly from Tara Store, or from one of their partners and distributors. You will learn more about Web Services in a later chapter.

Figure 1-9 The Tara Store Web Service

THE .NET FRAMEWORK

ASP.NET is used to develop dynamic Web applications within the .NET Framework. In ASP.NET, the Page class is a class in the .NET Framework. This means that the page code must conform to the .NET Framework standards. Therefore, it is important to understand the basics of the Page Class hierarchy and the .NET Framework. The .NET Framework consists of a common language runtime (CLR) and a hierarchical set of Base Class Libraries (BCL). As shown in Figure 1-10, the **.NET Framework** is the architectural model for creating programs that interface with the operating system and the base class libraries.

Figure 1-10   The .NET Framework

The Base Class Libraries

The **base class libraries** are commonly used code that provides general functions that can be accessed from any application. The base class libraries are organized into logical groupings of code called **namespaces**. These compiled .NET programs and base class libraries are called **assemblies**.

Microsoft has created a large group of these code libraries known as the .NET base class libraries. These libraries contain fundamental code structures and methods that allow you to communicate with the operating system software and other applications. The actual library of code is located in one or more dynamic link library files. For example, the code for accessing a database object is stored in the database class library, located in the file called System.Data.dll. By storing commonly used code in libraries, the code can be reused across applications.

Namespace

A namespace is a hierarchical way to identify resources in .NET. The System object is at the top of the namespace hierarchy, and all objects inherit from it. Because all objects inherit the System object, you can refer to any object within the System namespace as System.Object.ObjectName. All ASP.NET applications must inherit the System.Web namespace. WebForms is a base class in the .NET Framework that is used to create WebForm applications. So, all WebForms must also inherit the System.Web.UI namespace. All ASP.NET WebForm pages also inherit the System.Web.UI.Page namespace. The System Base Class known as System.Web.UI.Page.dll. is required to create the Page Class. The ability to store information in the _ViewState hidden field is controlled by the StateBag namespace. The StateBag namespace is known as System.Web.UI.StateBag. Web Services is the .NET base class library that is used to create Web Service applications. So, all Web Services must also inherit the System.Web.WebService namespace.

When you use Server controls, you must see that they inherit the appropriate Server control namespace. (*Note*: As you learn the different controls and classes, you should read the documentation for the corresponding namespace from the help files. You can read the documentation that describes the .NET namespaces at *ms-help://MS.NETFrameworkSDK/cpguidenf/html/cponthenetframeworkclasslibrary.htm*.) Figure 1-11 shows that the HTML Server controls that you learned about belong to the System.Web.UI.Control.HTMLControl namespace. In the next chapter you will learn to add these HTML Server controls to your WebForm.

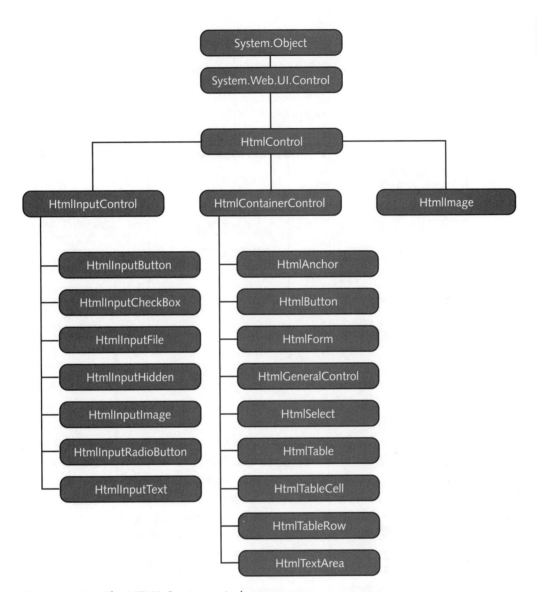

Figure 1-11   The HTML Server controls namespace

Figure 1-12 shows that the ASP.NET Server controls that you already learned about belong to the System.Web.UI.Control.WebControl namespace. As you can see, there are many other ASP.NET Server controls. Later in this book you will learn to add these ASP.NET Server controls to your WebForm.

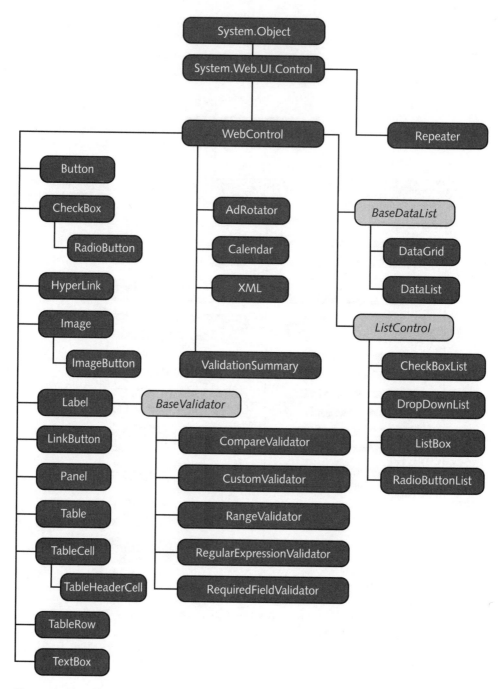

Figure 1-12   The ASP.NET Server controls namespace

Visual Studio .NET adds references to your projects' commonly used namespaces by default. (*Note:* You must ensure that any code library you use in your application inherits the appropriate namespace. You can import a namespace more than once without causing any errors or diminished performance.) You can import the namespaces into your page by using the @Import directive. The following is the syntax for importing a .NET namespace.

<%@ Imports NamespaceName %>

Below is a sample of how you would import the ASP.NET Page class.

```
<%@ Imports System.Web.UI.Page %>
```

It is possible to extend the .NET Framework and create your own set of code in a user-defined namespace. You can import a .NET namespace, or a user-defined namespace. You must import each namespace individually. When you compile your application, the .dll file contains a namespace with all of your compiled code. The namespace is named after your application. (*Note:* You can create additional namespaces within your application.) The following is the syntax used to import a user-defined namespace in the code behind the page.

<@ Import NamespaceName = "MyNamespaceName" %>

Common Language Runtime

Visual Studio .NET and the **Common Language Runtime** are language independent. Out of the box, Visual Studio .NET supports Visual Basic, scripting languages such as JavaScript and VBScript, Java, and C# (pronounced C Sharp). Over 100 third-party code providers of languages such as PERL, COBOL, Fortran, and Eiffel will also support .NET. This open language model allows companies to leverage their existing skills, because they don't need to retrain their programmers to use a new language in order to improve application performance. Language independence is achieved via the use of the common language runtime (CLR). The CLR supports new features such as a Common Type System (CTS), garbage collection (GC), and an intermediate language (IL).

Each .NET language provides a compiler that supports the CLR. Therefore, each language must support the CTS. The **Common Type System (CTS)** requires that all applications built within .NET, including ASP.NET applications, support the same basic data types. Examples of data types are strings and integers. These common data types are derived from the System namespace. Each of these languages store data in different formats on the computer, and use different syntax. **Syntax** is the rules that are applied when the code is written so that the compiler can correctly transform the program code into compiled code. Each of the languages continues to maintain its own syntax.

When the program code is compiled, the code is transformed into an intermediate language called the **Microsoft Intermediate Language** (MSIL or IL). At that time, an integer in Visual Basic .NET or an int in C# is converted to the same .NET data type, which is Int32. No matter what language is used to create the program, the IL that is created is the same. (*Note*: This also means that you can create applications using multiple languages at the same time.)

The **assembly** is the compiled .NET program. The assembly contains the intermediate language along with additional information called **metadata**. Metadata contains information about the assembly. Web Services uses this metadata to describe the contents of the IL in a discovery file so that developers can find out how to create an application that can communicate with the Web Service.

When the application is requested, the Loader program (also called Verifier) loads the program into a compiler called **JIT** (also called **JITter** or **Just in Time compiler**). The compiler converts the IL code to **managed code**, and then executes the code.

You can use the IL Disassembler (ildasm.exe) to view the IL within an assembly. There is a tutorial on using the IL Disassembler at *ms-help://MS.NETFrameworkSDK/cptutorials/ html/il_dasm_tutorial.htm*.

In the following exercise you will create a simple class in Visual Basic .NET, compile the class into an assembly, then view the class using the IL Disassembler. The Visual Basic file will be saved as hello.vb and compiled using the Visual Basic command-line compiler named **vbc**. You can then run the program from the executable file.

1. Make a directory named **Chapter1** in the C:\Inetpub\wwwroot directory. Click **Start**, and then click **Run**. In the Run dialog box, type **cmd /c md c:\Inetpub\wwwroot\Chapter1** in the Open text box and click **OK**.

2. Open a new document in Notepad and type in the code below.

```
' hello.vb - displays hello world
' Created 06/01/2002
Imports System
Public Module Hello
   Sub Main( )
```

In this code, the Imports System statement imports the System namespace into the application. You use the single apostrophe to identify inline comments. You create a public module named hello. Modules declared with the Public keyword have public access. You call the Main method as a sub procedure. (*Note*: Sub procedures are public by default, so the keyword Public is not required.)

3. Type in the code below to create the string. The .NET Framework requires that you declare the data type for all variables. In the next line of code, you will create a variable that contains a string, so you have to declare the variable as a string data type. Notice the Dim keyword is used to declare the variable. The variable can be declared and then assigned a value in the same statement.

```
Dim s1 As String = "1 - Hello World"
Console.WriteLine(s1)
```

4. Add the closing End statements, which are used to end the code blocks. Additional comments are added at the end of the file.

```
    End Sub
End Module
' Run this at the command line
' vbc hello.vb
```

5. Save the file as **hello.vb** in your c:\Inetpub\wwwroot\Chapter1 directory. Make sure to save the file using quotation marks.

6. Exit Notepad.

7. Click **Start**, point to **Programs**, point to **Microsoft Visual Studio .NET**, click **Visual Studio .NET Tools,** and then select **Visual Studio .NET Command Prompt**. (*Note:* You cannot go to the run command and get to the Visual Studio .NET Command Prompt. The path to the SDK tools is not installed into the default command prompt.)

8. Change to your c:\Inetpub\wwwroot\Chapter1 using the **cd c:\Inetpub\wwwroot\Chapter1** command.

9. Type **vbc hello.vb** and press **Enter**. This compiles your program into an executable file named hello.exe in the same folder.

10. Type **hello** at the command prompt and press **Enter**. The program runs and displays the Hello World string.

11. View the compiled assembly using the IL Disassembler. At the command prompt, type **ILDASM hello.exe**. The ILDASM window opens. (*Note:* The name of your assembly is hello, which is the name of your executable. You can compare where the class appears in your program and in the assembly.)

12. Close the ILDASM window by clicking **File**, then clicking **Exit**.

13. Close the command window by clicking the **Close** button.

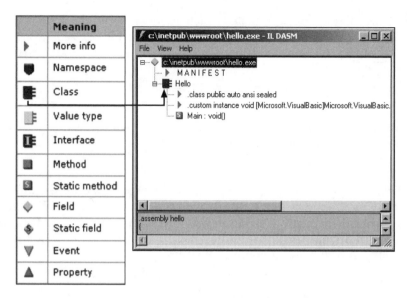

	Meaning
▶	More info
▆	Namespace
▐█	Class
▐	Value type
▐▌	Interface
■	Method
⬛	Static method
◆	Field
◈	Static field
▽	Event
▲	Property

Figure 1-13   Using the ILDASM to view the assembly and classes

Garbage Collection

Programs that don't release references to objects cause memory leaks. **Memory leaks** occur when memory is no longer being used by the application, but cannot be reassigned to another object. In .NET, the common language runtime uses the garbage collector to manage memory. **Garbage collection (GC)** is the process of allocating and managing the reserved memory known as the managed heap. The **managed heap** is a reserved address space in memory that can be subdivided into and allocated in smaller pieces. All .NET objects are allocated memory at the top of the heap when the object is created. The garbage collector is an object that runs periodically within a background thread. Starting from the root, it removes the objects from the heap that are no longer referenced by the application and moves objects to lower areas in the heap. This process is known as **compaction**. Because of the garbage collection process, .NET applications have less problems with memory leaks and circular references than current Windows applications. (*Note*: Although you can also explicitly call the garbage collector using the Finalize method of the object that you are removing, it is not recommended.)

OTHER RESOURCES

There are numerous Web sites that provide help, documentation, support, sample code, and sample applications. One sample ASP.NET application is an online catalogue and shopping cart application for the fictitious company I Buy Spy. I Buy Spy was created to help developers learn about using WebForms, accessing a database from the Web, and creating a simple Web Service. I Buy Spy sells spy products. The online catalogue allows you to view and place orders for one or more products. Products placed within the shopping cart are temporary, and are deleted when the customer leaves the Web site, unless they have registered and logged in. In order to place an order, the customers must register with the site and provide their contact and shipping information. If they have logged into the site, the shopping cart information is recorded directly within the database. Then, if a customer exits the browser, they can retrieve the shopping cart by simply logging into the Web site. The Web site also allows for other companies to place orders, and check the status of an order using a Web Service. The Web Service allows these business partners to integrate their Web site with I Buy Spy. The I Buy Spy Store can be found at *www.IBuySpy.com/store*. You can download the files to recreate the store at *http://www.IBuySpy.com*.

Another sample ASP.NET application that contains several Web Services is Margie's Travel, written by Clarity Consulting. This Web site was created to help developers learn to integrate multiple Web Services. Margie's Travel is a fictitious travel company that uses their ASP.NET application to provide their members with a single Web site, which can handle all of their travel needs. This ASP.NET application focuses on integrating multiple Web Services provided by other, third-party organizations in the travel industry. You can download files to recreate the ASP.NET application at *www.margiestravel.com*.

The following is a list of some useful Web sites that cover Visual Studio .NET, Visual Basic .NET, ASP.NET, ASP, Web Services, and the .NET Framework.

- *msdn.microsoft.com/net/aspnet*

- *msdn.microsoft.com/net*

- *msdn.microsoft.com/vstudio*

- *www.microsoft.net*

- *www.asp.net*

- *www.gotdotnet.com*

- *www.microsoft.com/trainingandservices*

- *uddi.microsoft.com/default.aspx*

- *xmethods.com*

- *www.microsoft.com/tools/vb.htm*

- *www.asp101.com*

- *www.ibuyspy.com*

- *www.scottgu.com*

- *www.brinkster.com*

- *www.margiestravel.com*

- *www.fmstocks.com*

Some of the applications created by Microsoft and third-party developers are located in the QuickStart Web site that is installed with the Visual Studio .NET Framework SDK. If you install the .NET SDK that comes with Visual Studio .NET, you also have access to additional local Web sites to help you become familiar with .NET. The local Web site known as **QuickStart** provides tutorials and walkthroughs. All of the tutorials and sample code can be accessed from *http://localhost/quickstart/*. You can access these samples via a browser at *http://localhost/quickstart*. If you do not have access to the local version of the QuickStart Web site, you can view it remotely at *www.gotdotnet.com/*. These sites contain many samples of WebForms.

CHAPTER SUMMARY

- ❐ Active Server Pages are Web pages containing scripting programs that are interpreted by the scripting engines on the Web server. ASP page filenames end in .asp. The default language for ASP pages is VBScript. The main ASP objects are Request, Response, Server, Session, Application, and ASPError. ASP pages are supported in the .NET framework if the ASP.DLL engine is installed on the Web server.

- ❐ ASP.NET pages can contain programs written in a variety of programming languages. The default language for ASP.NET pages is Visual Basic .NET. ASP.NET pages end in a variety of file extensions. WebForms end in .aspx. Web Services end in .asmx. User-defined controls end in .ascx. ASP.NET pages and WebForms are synonymous.

- ❐ ASP.NET contains all of the ASP objects plus some additional objects, properties, methods, and events. The entire ASP.NET Web page is a class called the Page class. Therefore all items on an ASP.NET page and the page itself are objects.

- ❐ The .NET framework is the architectural framework in which ASP.NET applications are created. ASP.NET applications interface with the .NET framework, instead of interfacing directly with the operating system. .NET applications are compiled to an intermediate language (IL) that contains metadata. These compiled programs are called assemblies. Namespaces is a hierarchical way to organize objects. All objects are derived from the System.Objects.dll class. .NET applications import the namespaces so that they can refer to the .NET base class objects without using their fully qualified names.

- ❐ .NET requires strict data typing. You must identify the type of data stored in the variable. At compile time, all languages must support the same common .NET data types. Option explicit requires you to declare your variable before you can use it.

- ❐ The Page class hierarchy loads all the controls into the Web page. The Page class renders the HTML and Server code to the browser. The Page class contains the HTML and the code behind the page, which is located in a separate file.

❑ Web Services allow you to publicly expose code to other businesses and applications.

❑ When you create a WebForm in Visual Studio .NET, you do not have to compile the code behind the form manually. Visual Studio .NET places the Page class file into the BIN directory. The BIN directory must have execute permissions.

❑ You do not need to have Visual Studio .NET installed to create or run ASP.NET pages. However, you do need a Web server to post your pages, and a platform that supports the .NET framework. There are a variety of help resources within Visual Studio .NET and on the Internet.

REVIEW QUESTIONS

1. Which is the file extension for an ASP.NET page?

    a. .asp

    b. .html

    c. .aspx

    d. .apx

2. Which of the following is not an ASP.NET object?

    a. Session

    b. Application

    c. Client

    d. Response

3. What web server can be used to view ASP.NET Web pages on windows 2000?

    a. O'Reilly Web Server

    b. Apache

    c. Internet Information Server

    d. Personal Web Server

4. Which of the following sends output to the browser?

    a. Response.File

    b. Document.Write

    c. Document.Writeln

    d. Response.Write

5. Which concept provides a universal type format for types in the .NET framework?

    a. Universal type system

    b. garbage collector

    c. Page class

    d. Common Type System

6. What is the name of the feature that ensures that the data types such as integers and strings are consistent within each language within the .NET framework?

   a. common language runtime

   b. Common Type System

   c. garbage collection

   d. Web Service

7. What object is used to create other objects in ASP.NET?

   a. system.variant

   b. system.variable

   c. system.object

   d. system.new

8. What is as the name for the hierarchical treelike structure used to identify the base class resources within the .NET framework?

   a. namespace

   b. common language runtime

   c. Command-line compiler

   d. portable executable

9. What tool is used to view the managed IL code?

   a. Command-line compiler

   b. IL Disassembler

   c. Just in Time compiler

   d. Command-line Interpreter

10. Which technique allows you to automatically send data back to Form controls on a web page?

    a. Postback

    b. Data Validation controls

    c. Response.write

    d. Flush

11. Which tool is used to create e-business applications that can be exposed over the Internet?

    a. WebForms

    b. WinForms

    c. WebServices

    d. ASPServices

1

12. Where is the web site that contains the local support documentation files for ASP.NET?

   a. www.asp.net

   b. http://quickstart

   c. http://localhost/quickstart

   d. http://localhost/help

13. What type of application is a shopping cart?

   a. static

   b. dynamic

   c. local

   d. none of the above

14. What technique is used to retrieve data from other Web sites?

   a. scraping

   b. garbage collecting

   c. redirecting

   d. integrating

15. Where is the Visual Basic code usually located?

   a. with the HTML Server controls

   b. with the ASP.NET Server controls

   c. with the HTML body tag

   d. with the code behind the page

16. What property transforms an HTML control to an HTML Server control?

   a. runat= "server"

   b. id= "mybtn"

   c. value= "onserverclick"

   d. onclick= "onerverclick"

17. Which of ASP.NET controls do not require the prefix ASP?

   a. Data Validation controls

   b. User controls

   c. Mobile controls

   d. Literal controls

18. What property of the @page directive is used to set the location of the code behind the page?

    a. inherits

    b. language

    c. codebehind

    d. href

19. Which phase of the page class event cycle is responsible for initializing the controls?

    a. Page_Init

    b. Page_Load

    c. Page_Prerender

    d. Page_Unload

20. What is the correct way to import the WebForm page namespace in Visual Basic .NET?

    a. Imports System.Web.Ui.Page

    b. Using system.Web.Ui.Page

    c. Import MyNamespaceName= System.Web.Ui.Page

    d. Imports Web.Ui.Page

HANDS-ON PROJECTS

Project 1-1

In this project you create a simple Visual Basic program in Notepad and view the IL with the IL Disassembler.

1. Open a new document in Notepad.

2. Type in comments to identify the file, the purpose of the program, and date the file was created, as follows. (*Note*: It is also common to include the name of the programmer in the comment section in your code.)

```
' Ch1Proj1.vb
' Displays hello world
' Created 06/01/2002
```

3. Type in the code that imports the System namespace. The Imports System statement imports the System namespace into the application. A public module named hello is created. Modules declared with the Public keyword have public access. The Main method is called as a sub procedure.

```
Imports System
```

4. Type in the code to create a public module named **hello**. Modules declared with the Public keyword have public access.

```
Public Module Hello
```

5. Type in the code that creates the Main method. It is the first procedure called when the application is started.

```
Sub Main()
```

6. Create the string. Use the keyword *Dim* to declare the variable. The variables can be declared on one line when they are both of the same data type. The variable can be declared and then assigned a value in the same statement.

```
Dim s1, s2 As String
s1 = "Hello"
s2 = " World"
```

7. Add the code to write out the contents of the variables to the window using the Write and WriteLine methods. (*Note*: Because the window is the command window, you must use the Console object to access the command window.)

```
Console.Write(s1)
Console.WriteLine(s2)
```

8. Write the closing End statements to end the code blocks.

```
End Sub
End Module
```

9. Add comments to the end of the file. Comments at the end of the file often include information about how the file was processed. This comment indicates that the code is compiled using the vbc command-line compiler.

```
' Run this at the command line
' vbc Ch1Proj1.vb
```

10. Save the file as **Ch1Proj1.vb** in your c:\Inetpub\wwwroot\Chapter1 directory. Make sure to save the file using quotation marks.

11. Exit Notepad.

12. Click **Start**, point to **Programs**, point to **Microsoft Visual Studio .NET**, point to **Visual Studio .NET Tools**, then click **Visual Studio .NET Command Prompt**.

13. Change to **c:\Inetpub\wwwroot** using the cd c:\Inetpub\wwwroot\Chapter1 command.

14. Type **vbc Ch1Proj1.vb** and press **Enter**. This compiles your program into an executable file named Ch1Proj1.exe in the same folder.

15. Type **Ch1Proj1** at the command prompt and press **Enter**. The program runs and displays the Hello World string.

16. View the compiled assembly using the IL Disassembler. At the command prompt type **ILDASM Ch1Proj1.exe**. The ILDASM window opens.

17. Click **File** on the menu bar, then click **Dump Tree View**.

18. In the Filename text box type **Ch1Proj1.txt**. You should save the file within quotation marks in order to save the information as a text file. Save the file in the directory c:\Inetpub\wwwroot\Chapter1.

19. Close the ILDASM window by clicking **File** on the menu bar, then click **Exit**.

20. Close the command window by clicking the **Close** button.

21. Open the Ch1Proj1.txt file, which is located in c:\Inetpub\wwwroot\Chapter1, in Notepad. Click **File** on the menu bar, then click **Print**. Then, exit Notepad.

Project 1-2

In this project you create a simple Visual Basic program in Notepad and view the IL with the IL Disassembler.

1. Open a new document in Notepad.

2. Type in comments to identify the file, the purpose of the program, and date the file was created.

```
' Ch1Proj2.vb
' Displays hello world
' Created 06/01/2002
```

3. Add the code to import the System namespace into the application, create a public module named hello, and create the Main method. Modules declared with the Public keyword have public access. The Main method is called as a sub procedure. It is the first procedure called when the application is started.

```
Imports System
Public Module Hello
   Sub Main()
```

4. Create the string using the keyword *Dim* to declare three variables. The variable can be declared in the same statement. Then, assign values to each variable. Use the Visual Basic .NET concatenation operator (&) to display both s1 and s2 in the s3 variable.

```
Dim s1, s2, s3 As String
s1 = "Hello"
s2 = " World"
s3 = s1 & s2
```

5. Add the code to write out the s3 variable to the console window.

```
Console.WriteLine(s3)
```

6. The closing End statements are used to end the code blocks. Additional comments are added at the end of the file.

```
   End Sub
End Module
' Run this at the command line
' vbc Ch1Proj2.vb
```

7. Save the file as **Ch1Proj2.vb** in your c:\Inetpub\wwwroot\Chapter1 directory. Make sure to save the file using quotation marks.

8. Exit Notepad.

9. Click **Start**, point to **Programs**, point to **Microsoft Visual Studio .NET** point to **Visual Studio .NET Tools**, then click **Visual Studio .NET Command Prompt**.

10. Change to your c:\Inetpub\wwwroot\Chapter1 directory using the cd **c:\Inetpub\wwwroot\Chapter1** command.

11. Type **vbc Ch1Proj2.vb** then press **Enter**. This compiles your program into an executable file named Ch1Proj2.vb in the same folder.

12. Type **Ch1Proj2** at the command prompt and press **Enter**. The program runs and display the hello world string.

13. At the command prompt type **ILDASM Ch1Proj2.exe**. The ILDASM window opens, and displays the compiled assembly.

14. Click **File** on the menu bar, then click **Dump Tree View**.

15. In the Filename text box type **Ch1Proj2.txt** and save the file to c:\Inetpub\ wwwroot\Chapter1. This allows you to save the information as a text file.

16. Close the ILDASM window by clicking **File** on the menu bar, then clicking **Exit**.

17. Close the command window by clicking the **Close** button.

18. Open the file in c:\Inetpub\wwwroot\Chapter1\Ch1Proj2.txt. Click **File** on the menu bar, then click **Print**. Click **File** on the menu bar, then click **Exit**.

Project 1-3

In this project you will install the samples from the Framework SDK. These samples, are not installed by default.

1. Go to the SDK Tutorials and Samples page, which is located at C:\Program Files\Microsoft.NET\FrameworkSDK\Samples\StartSamples.htm. To get to this page Click **Start,** point to **Programs**, point to **Microsoft .NET Framework SDK**, then click **Samples and QuickStart Tutorials**.

2. Click the link **Install the .NET Framework Samples Database**.

3. In the File Download box, click the **Open** button to run this program from its current location.

4. Click the **Set up the Quickstarts** link to configure the samples for your computer.

5. Click the **Open** button to run the program from its current location. This configures the QuickStart virtual directory and creates the sample SQL Server database files and some registry keys.

6. When the samples are installed, you see a window that says Congratulations. Click the **Launch** button. (Note: If you get any other message, view and save the log file. It will indicate where the installation was halted.)

7. You will know when the samples are installed correctly by visiting this page in a browser: *http://localhost/quickstart/*. If the page exists, then it's installed correctly.

8. Exit Internet Explorer.

Project 1-4

In this project, you view the samples that come with the Framework SDK. (*Note*: You must complete Hands-on Project 1-3 before completing this project or you can visit an online version of the QuickStart samples at *http://samples.gotdotnet.com/quickstart/Default.aspx*)

1. Start **Internet Explorer**.

2. Go to the SDK Tutorials and Samples page at *http://localhost/quickstart/*.

3. Click the link **Start the ASP.NET QuickStart Tutorial**.

4. Click the **list arrow** in the upper-right corner of the page labeled I want my samples in, then click **VB.NET**, if it is not already selected. All samples are given in Visual Basic .NET by default. (*Note*: You can change this for individual samples by clicking on the language box below the sample code.)

5. Click the **Language Support** hyperlink in the left menu. Read the sample code for the following statements. (*Note*: You will learn more about how to implement these Visual Basic .NET statements later in this book.)

   ❏ Declare a variable

   ❏ Comment my code

   ❏ Declare a simple property

   ❏ Declare and use a method

   ❏ Statically initialize a variable

   ❏ Write an if statement

   ❏ Write a case statement

   ❏ Write a for loop

   ❏ Write a while loop

   ❏ Concatenate a string

   ❏ Declare an event

   ❏ Declare an event handler

   ❏ Add an event handler

   ❏ Declare a class or interface

   ❏ Write a standard module

6. Print the page for your reference.

7. Click the **Back** button on the browser.

8. Click the **Introducing Web Forms** link in the menu.

9. Read the sections listed below.

   ❐ What is ASP.NET Web Forms?

   ❐ Writing Your First Web Forms Page

   ❐ Code-Behind Web Forms

   ❐ Introduction to ASP.NET Server Controls

10. Click the **Run Sample** link under the Introduction to ASP.NET Server Controls topic.

11. Click **View** on the browser's menu bar, then click **Source**. The client's view is displayed in Notepad. (*Note:* The square brackets [ ] indicate that you are opening a temporary file that contains the client's view of the code, not the actual server-side source code for the page.)

12. Click **View**, click **Source**, then print this page and close Notepad.

13. Compare the two printouts. Write a one-page paper describing how the ASP.NET form works and posts back data into the form fields. Provide specific details based on the examples you printed out. Save the paper as a Web page named **Ch1Proj4.aspx** in your c:\InetPub\wwwroot\Chapter1 directory.

14. Exit your browser

Project 1-5

In this project you view more Framework SDK samples. Make sure you have installed the Framework SDK samples before doing this exercise, or you can visit an online version of the QuickStart samples at *http://samples.gotdotnet.com/quickstart/Default.aspx*.

1. Start **Internet Explorer**.

2. Go to the SDK Tutorials and Samples page at *http://localhost/quickstart/*.

3. Click the link **Start the ASP.NET QuickStart Tutorial**.

4. Click the link **A Personalized Portal** on the lower-left corner to open a new window displaying the Portal Application. Click the **Run sample** hyperlink.

5. Click the link **Create New Account**.

6. Click **View** on the menu bar, then click **Source**. The source code is displayed in Notepad.

7. Click **File** on the menu bar, then click **Print** to print the source code. Locate where the _ViewState hidden field is located. Underline the value of the _ViewState field. Close the Notepad window.

8. Fill out the entire form without entering a User ID.

9. Click the **Create Account** button. A red asterisk (*) appears after each field that is required. Your data for the other fields is posted back to the page.

10. Click **View** on the menu bar, then click **Source**. The source code is displayed in Notepad.

11. Click **File** on the menu bar, then click **Print** to print the source code. Find where the _ViewState hidden field is located. Underline the value of the _ViewState field. Close the Notepad window.

12. Write a one-page paper that compares the two values of the _ViewState field, and that explains why they are different or not different in each version of the page. Save the paper as a Web page named **Ch1Proj5.aspx** in your c:\InetPub\wwwroot\Chapter1 directory.

13. Exit your browser.

Project 1-6

In this project you view more Framework SDK samples. Make sure you have installed the Framework SDK samples before doing this exercise.

1. Start **Internet Explorer**

2. Go to the SDK Tutorials and Samples page at *http://localhost/quickstart/*.

3. Click the link **Start the ASP.NET QuickStart Tutorial**.

4. Click the link **Web Forms Controls Reference** in the left-hand corner. This contains links to documentation for HTML Server controls and Web Server controls. Pick three server controls to read about.

5. Click on each link for the control you selected, then read about the control.

6. For each control you selected, view the sample. Print the client's view of the source code by clicking **View** on the menu bar, then clicking **Source**. In the new window that opens, click **File** on the menu bar, then click **Print**.

7. For each control you selected, view and print the server source code.

8. Write a one-page paper describing the differences between the server source code and the client's view of the source code. Save the paper as a Web page named **Ch1Proj6.aspx** in your c:\InetPub\wwwroot\Chapter1 directory.

9. Exit your browser.

Project 1-7

In this project you view more Framework SDK samples. Make sure you have installed the Framework SDK samples before doing this exercise.

1. Start **Internet Explorer**.

2. Go to the SDK Tutorials and Samples page at *http://localhost/quickstart/*.

3. Click the link **Start the ASP.NET QuickStart Tutorial**.

4. Click the link **Web Forms Controls Reference** in the left-hand corner. This contains links to documentation for HTML Server controls and Web Server controls. Pick one HTML Server control and the corresponding ASP.NET Server control.

5. Click each link for the control you selected, then read about the control.

6. For each control you selected, view the sample. Print the client's view of the source code by clicking **View** on the menu bar, then clicking **Source**. In the new window that opens, click **File** on the menu bar, then click **Print**.

7. For each control you selected, view and print the server source code.

8. Write a one page paper describing the differences between the server source code and the client's view of the source code. Compare the differences between the HTML server control and the ASP.NET server control. Save the paper as a web page named **Ch1Proj7.aspx** in your c:\InetPub\wwwroot\Chapter1 directory.

9. Exit the browser.

CASE PROJECTS

Microsoft Support Sites for .NET Programming

Your project manager would like to know what new events are occurring that relate to the .NET technologies. Visit at least one of the following Microsoft Web sites mentioned in the chapter that frequently discusses the .NET technologies.

❐ *www.microsoft.net*

❐ *msdn.microsoft.com*

❐ *www.asp.net*

Read the documentation that appears on the Web site. After you have read the documentation, pick a topic that relates to ASP.NET or Visual Studio .NET. Create a one-page report that summarizes your findings. The one-page report should contain the answers to the following information:

❐ What topic did you read about?

❐ Provide a 5–6 paragraph summary of the topic.

❐ At which URL did you find your information?

❐ Provide one sample of code you found during your research.

Sample Business ASP.NET Web Sites — I Buy Spy

Visit the IBuySpy Web site listed in the first section of the chapter at *www.ibuyspy.com/store*. After you have read the documentation, create your report in a Web page format. The one-page report should contain the answers to the following questions:

❑ Who built the store?

❑ How many files were required to create the store?

❑ What programming languages were used to create the Web site?

❑ What was required to build and run the store?

ASP.NET and Visual Studio .NET Web Resources

Your project manager wants to know where she can learn more about ASP.NET, because your company cannot send her for off-site training. You know that there are many Web sites that discuss ASP.NET and Visual Studio .NET. Visit five of the links listed in this chapter. Within each site, visit at least five web pages. Using Notepad, create an ASP page named `Ch1_Case3.aspx`. Add links to at least five sites, and the five pages you visited. Add a short paragraph about why the site is valuable to ASP Web programmers, and summarize the contents of each page. Use your knowledge of HTML and ASP to format the page. Add graphics, fonts, and color to enhance the page. You may add additional links to other resources if you think that might be useful to your project manager. Print out the Web page and the source code.

2

INTRODUCTION TO VISUAL STUDIO .NET

In this chapter, you will:

♦ Familiarize yourself with the Visual Studio .NET user interface
♦ Create Web pages using the Visual Studio .NET HTML editor
♦ Use Visual Studio .NET to create reusable User controls
♦ Create Cascading Style Sheets with the Style Builder
♦ Customize the Toolbox
♦ Locate help resources within Visual Studio .NET

One of the challenges companies face is adapting to the ever-changing software industry. Software applications are usually created with a single programming language. But to take advantage of newer techniques software developers often must learn programming languages as they are created. Learning to program in a new language is as difficult as learning to speak a new language, and there are hundreds of different programming languages and versions. Visual Studio .NET allows programmers to learn one interface for many languages. More importantly, you can use Visual Studio .NET to build programs using a combination of languages.

In this chapter you will learn how to use Visual Studio .NET to generate ASP.NET Web applications. You will learn how to manage project files and create basic Web pages. You will create cascading style sheets with the Style Builder to format your Web pages. You will also create User controls that can be reused across multiple ASP.NET pages.

VISUAL STUDIO .NET USER INTERFACE

Where once applications were hand-coded by developers, today rapid application development (RAD) tools allow them to build higher-quality applications more quickly. RAD tools allow developers to create prototypes, develop reusable software components, and facilitate communication and file management. Visual Studio .NET is a RAD geared to the creation of Web applications and Web services

Visual Studio .NET provides a new user interface called the **Integrated Development Environment (IDE)**, which is shown in Figure 2-1. All of Microsoft's major programming languages such as C++, C#, J#, JScript, Visual Basic, Transact-SQL, and Visual FoxPro share this single IDE. For example, the IDE provides a better interface between Visual Studio .NET and Visual Basic .NET. For a Visual Basic developer, the most important benefit of the .NET Framework is direct and easy access to the underlying .NET platform, using a consistent programming model. As a Visual Basic 6.0 developer, you have access to the same features and capabilities of the .NET Framework as you do with other platform languages. The IDE is consistent across languages and applications. You can manage your Windows applications, Web applications, and Web services all within the same development environment using a **Solution Explorer** to manage all of the files and resources

Main window
Toolbox
Solution Explorer window
Toolbars
Web page in Design view
Server Explorer window
Properties window
Design view
HTML view

Figure 2-1   Visual Studio .NET IDE layout

Visual Studio .NET was formerly known as Visual Studio 7. Some of the features within the Visual Studio .NET user interface were previously available in Visual InterDev, an application used to create Web applications. However, Visual InterDev is no longer a standalone product. Most of the functionality of Visual InterDev is now integrated within the Visual Studio .NET IDE.

2

There are many other windows, controls, and toolbars within the Visual Studio .NET user interface. The **main window** is used to view your project files. When you open multiple documents in the main window at the same time, a **document tab** appears in the main window of the IDE to allow you to easily switch between documents. If you open a large number of documents, you can use the next and previous buttons to navigate through the other tabs. (*Note*: These buttons appear to the right of the document tabs.)

When you create a project, Visual Studio .NET includes the appropriate references to the base class libraries in the Solution Explorer window. Visual Studio .NET also imports the namespaces required when you use the templates to create your files. And, when you build Windows Applications, Web Applications, or Web Services, Visual Studio .NET creates all of the other ancillary files and folders, including the bin directory.

As you learned in the previous chapter, the code behind the ASP.NET page is compiled by Visual Studio .NET. When you call the Build command, Visual Studio .NET compiles the ASP.NET code into a file with the extension .dll and places this file within the bin directory of the project. Visual Studio .NET assigns the bin directory execute permissions so that the code can be executed at runtime. Therefore, you can build and deploy your application from within Visual Studio .NET.

 Some developers have chosen to create ASP.NET applications with other editors such as Notepad. If you do not use Visual Studio .NET to create, build, and deploy your application, you have to manually compile your application with a command-line compiler. You also need to use other various XCOPY methods, such as FTP, to deploy your application.

Each Visual Studio .NET project template contains several default files. Figure 2-2 shows the default Web application files in the Solution Explorer window. The Web application contains WebForms, global configuration files, and different built-in references to the .NET base classes such as System.Web. In the Solution Explorer window, you can click the Show All button to view all of the files in the Web project. A Windows application contains different types of files such as a Visual Basic Windows Form and references to .NET base classes such as Windows.Forms.

Visual Studio .NET provides many more features to help developers be more productive. For example, Visual Studio .NET supports Add Item, Application, and Solution Wizards that you can use to quickly create .NET applications. You can access these wizards via the menu or by right-clicking on the project or solution in the Project Explorer window. The Documentation Viewer is now part of the IDE, and not a separate application as it was in Visual Studio 6.

Figure 2-2   The Solution Explorer window

The **Server Explorer** provides access to public components on your network servers. The Server Explorer also provides you with wizards to create Data Connections to databases. Data Connections are required when you want your application to access data from a database. The Server Explorer provides access to the server event logs, performance counters, and services without requiring you to have physical access to the server. You can record macros that perform activities, such as adding a form to the Web page, that can be shared with other developers. You can manage your macros in the **Macros Explorer**. The **Task window** allows you to manage a to do list. You can mark code so that you can locate it quickly. You can use a common debugging tool to debug an entire application at once, and do so across physical servers. You can control the source code within Visual Studio .NET by checking out files. These are only a few of the basic features that Visual Studio .NET supports.

Creating a Web Application

A Web application consists of many projects. When you create a Web application, you need to create a solution to maintain the projects. A **solution** contains several solution files, which are used to maintain information about each of the projects within the application. Each **project** maintains its own set of **project files**. The types of files within each project vary with the type of project. For example, in a Web project, you find Web related files such as WebForms.

By default Visual Studio .NET creates the project files and places them in a folder named after the project. By default the project folder is located in the Visual Studio projects folder within My Documents. The Web files are published to the default Web directory in a folder named after the project. The default Web directory is located at c:\Inetpub\wwwroot. (*Note:* Your system administrators may change the default location of the Visual Studio projects folder and the default location of the Web server.) You can preview your Web page on a Web server such as Internet Information Server.

When you create the Web application, you need to specify name of the Web server and the name of the project. The project name is also the name of the folder on the server which stores the project Web pages. When you create a Web application, the Name text box in the New Project window is dimmed. You must enter the name of the project in the Location text box. Therefore, you must have access to a Web server when you create Web applications with Visual Studio .NET. However, you can change the folder that stores your solution files by clicking the Browse button in the New Project dialogue box. Many of the Web pages are not viewable until the Web pages are stored on a Web server.

The name of the local Web server is usually the name of your computer. If your machine name is Course, then your Web address would be *http://Course/Chapter2*. You can also use the IP address of the computer. In addition, you can use the keyword **localhost** or the loopback address 127.0.0.1 to refer to the local Web site. The localhost keyword and loopback IP address is a reserved IP address that only works while you are logged in at the local computer. In this case the Web address would be *http://localhost/Chapter2* or *http://127.0.0.1/Chapter2*. If you want to create your Web application on a remote Web server, you must type in a valid URL to the Web server, and you must be connected to the Internet while you are creating and editing the Web application.

In the exercise below, you will create a Web application. You will create a new solution named Chapter2, and a project named Chapter2. You will use this solution and project for the rest of the examples in the chapter.

1. Start **Visual Studio .NET**. (On most computers, you click **Start**, point to **Programs**, point to **Microsoft Visual Studio .NET**, then click **Microsoft Visual Studio .NET**.)

2. Click **File** on the menu bar, point to **New**, then click **Project** to open the New Project window. (*Note:* The New Project window displays the various types of project templates available.)

3. The Visual Basic Projects project type is selected by default. Click the **ASP.NET Web Application** icon in the Templates pane.

4. Enter the name of the Web server and the name of the project in the Location text box. Type **http://localhost/Chapter2** in the Location text box to name the project Chapter2. The new project is created on your default Web server. The Web address of the project is *http://localhost/Chapter2*.

5. Click **OK** to create the solution, project, and default files. Look at the files that were created in the Solution Explorer window. A WebForm named WebForm1.aspx is created in the project file by default. This WebForm is opened by default in the main window.

6. Click the **plus sign** next to the References folder to expand the references. You can see the references that are included with the project. These are references to the .NET base classes within the .NET framework.

7. Click the **minus sign** next to the References folder to hide the references.

When you start Visual Studio .NET, a **Start Page** provides access to your recently created applications, and Help Resources opens. Once you have created an application, you can click the application name on the Start Page to reopen the solution and related project files.

While you are working with the project, you have access to the .NET Framework. The .NET Framework is the foundation on which you build and run applications. For example, you can access the .NET data class, which provides you with objects to connect your Web application to a database. Visual Studio .NET also provides you with graphical tools that represent these data objects. Having such a foundation makes it easier to build applications, using a consistent, simplified programming model.

NAVIGATING THE WINDOWS

Visual Studio .NET has a variety of productivity tools that you can access from the various windows. Each window has four common properties that determine where the window is positioned on the desktop. You set these properties by right-clicking on the window. The first window property is the **Dockable** property. Windows that are Dockable can be moved to other locations on the desktop. The Dockable feature is checked by default. Docked windows can also be placed on top of one another. When one window is docked on top of another window, the user interface creates several tabs that you can use to move back and forth between each window. Any time windows are docked on top of each other you can click a named tab to place the corresponding window on the top layer. A second common feature of windows is the Hide property. Setting the **Hide** property hides, or closes, the window. You can reopen a hidden window via the View menu. The third window property is the **Floating** property. The Floating property allows you select the window and drag and drop it to any location on the desktop. It is different from the docked property in that the floating window does not have to be placed on top of another window. The **Auto Hide** property is a new feature that allows you to store the window on the desktop as a tab. The tab is labeled with the name of the window. When you click the tab, its associated window slides open. To turn this feature off, and make the windows stick to the desktop, click the pushpin icon on the window's menu bar. By default, the Server Explorer and the Toolbox windows are set to Auto Hide. When there are multiple windows that are set to Auto Hide, some of the names of the windows may not appear on the tab. Only the icon that represents the window appears on the tab. This feature allows you to have quick access to many windows at the same time. When Visual Studio .NET first opens, the Solution Explorer window and the Properties window are both open. They split half of the window on the right side of the monitor. You can expand either window by placing the pointer over the top of the Properties window. When the cursor changes to a double-headed arrow, click and drag the cursor up or down. When you move the cursor up, the Properties window is enlarged. When you move the cursor down, the Solution Explorer window is enlarged. You can also resize the other windows in the same way.

The Solution Explorer Window

You use the **Solution Explorer** window to manage your files and projects. For example, the Solution Explorer offers a means to manage and publish a solution without requiring that you use a file transfer program such as FTP. In the following exercise, you will add files to the Chapter2 project using the Solution Explorer window. You will also learn how to work with the sliding windows.

1. Right-click **Chapter2** in the Solution Explorer window to display the shortcut menu. (*Note:* The shortcut menus that are displayed when you right-click an object are also called pop-up menus. Just as in other Microsoft applications, any task listed in the pop-up menus can also be accessed via the standard menus or a keyboard shortcut.) Point to **Add**, then click **New Folder**.

2. Type **images** to name the folder, then press **Enter**. You will store the application images in this folder.

3. Right-click the **images** folder, point to **Add**, then click **Add Existing Item**.

4. Navigate to your **Chapter02Data** directory. (*Note:* The Chapter02Data directory contains the data files required for this chapter. If you do not have the data files for this chapter, you can download them from the Course Technology Web site at *www.course.com.*) In the Files of type drop-down list box, change the selection from Common VB Code Files to **Image Files**.

5. Select the files **header.jpg**, **menu.gif**, **bullet.gif**, and **CustomerSupport.jpg**. Click the **Open** button. This imports the images into the images directory of your Chapter2 project.

6. Right-click **Chapter2** in the Solution Explorer window, point to **Add**, and then click **Add New Item**. The Add New Item Chapter2 window displays typical Web Project and Windows Project files.

7. In the Categories pane click **Web Project Items** if necessary, and in the Templates pane click **WebForm**. (*Note:* Although you can use the pop-up menu to add a WebForm, use the templates for this step.) See Figure 2-3.

8. In the Name text box, type **home.aspx** and then click **Open**. (*Note:* The default file extension for WebForms is aspx.) The WebForm is added to the project and opens in the main code window.

9. Click **File** on the menu bar, then click **Save All**.

10. Click the **Close** button to close the page.

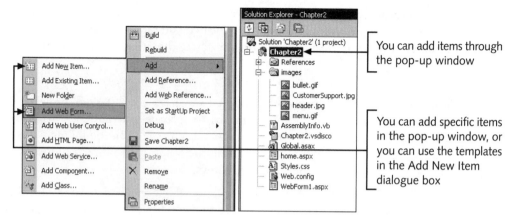

Figure 2-3   Adding items to the project

The Toolbox

The Visual Studio .NET **Toolbox** contains a set of commonly used controls, including HTML controls and WebForm controls, which are organized using tabs. The HTML tab provides access to the HTML controls. The WebForms tab contains the ASP.NET Server controls. The Toolbox is a window and can be hidden. The Toolbox slides out when you drag the pointer over the Toolbox tab.

The Properties Window

You use the **Properties window** to set properties for objects, controls, and classes. The object can be a Windows Form, a WebForm, an image, a form field, or even a label on the page. Figure 2-4 shows what the Properties window looks like. When you click an object, such as the document window, the properties for that object are displayed in the Properties window.

HTML Controls

Hypertext Markup Language (HTML) is a markup language that consists of a predefined group of tags that identify and format content on a Web page. The World Wide Web Consortium (*www.w3c.org*) maintains HTML standards. The current HTML standards allow you to enter HTML tags in uppercase, lowercase, or a mixture of uppercase and lowercase. The case in the beginning tag does not have to match the case in the closing tag. Most HTML tags contain a beginning and an ending tag. However, some tags, such as the horizontal rule, do not require a closing tag. The HTML standards allow HTML tags to contain minimized attributes. **Minimized attributes** can be specified by a keyword, instead of the name of the attribute and the keyword. For example, you specify the property of the check box by using the minimized attribute "checked". No value has to be provided with the checked attribute.

All of the properties of a control can be set in the Properties window

You can enter a value for the property, use the drop-down list to select a value, or use one of the build tools to select a value for the property

A description of the individual properties is available at the bottom of the Properties window

Figure 2-4 The Properties window

The newest version of HTML is known as Extensible Hypertext Markup Language (XHTML). **XHTML** is an updated version of HTML that applies the syntax from Extensible Markup Language (XML). XML represents a new standard. It was created to provide a universal format for structured documents and data. XHTML is a version of HTML that is compliant with XML standards. HTML was updated to XHTML because Web content is being ported to a variety of browsers and devices, such as cell phones and PDAs. XML requires that all tags consist of a beginning and closing tag. Tags that do not use a closing tag can be closed using a forward slash at the end of the beginning tag. Minimized attributes must be written using a name and a value. When you create Web applications using Visual Studio .NET, the HTML controls create HTML that is XHTML compliant. For example, instead of `<hr noshade>` the HTML editor writes `<hr noshade="noshade"/>`.

You can learn more about HTML, XML, and XHTML by visiting the W3C Web site at www.w3c.org.

In Visual Studio .NET, you can create pages with HTML using the HTML editor. The HTML editor is also known as the **HTML Designer**. There are several views within the HTML Designer. The view can be identified by the tabs at the bottom of the Web page. The Design view allows you to add HTML controls to the page via the Toolbox. The HTML view allows you to view and edit the HTML code. When you create a page, the page opens in Design view by default. You can click the HTML tab to change to the HTML view.

When you are editing the page in HTML view, you must choose how you want to position the HTML controls on the Web page. There are two types of page layout settings. The **MS_POSITIONING** property maintains the page layout settings. In HTML view the body tag has a property **MS_POSITIONING** set to GridLayout by default. **GridLayout** allows the page to use absolute positioning to place objects. **FlowLayout** positions elements on the page in top down format. Controls are displayed in the page in the order in which they appear in the HTML view. You can use a grid to assist you when you are placing controls on the page. When the showGrid property is set to True, the grid is displayed in Design view. The grid is not shown when the Web page is viewed in the browser. The showGrid property is set to True by default.

You should also determine which browsers your Web site will support. You can target any level of browser by configuring the targetSchema property for the page. The **targetSchema** property is Internet Explorer 5.0 by default.

There are several document properties that correspond to the attributes of the HTML body tag. The alink, vlink, link, text, bgColor, and background properties are all configurable via the Properties window. The alink, vlink, and link properties allow you to configure the color of the active hyperlinks, visited hyperlinks, and default hyperlinks, respectively. The Text property allows you to configure the color of the default text. The bgColor allows you to configure the color of the page background. The Background property allows you to configure the URL of a graphic as the page background. If you insert a background image, the image will tile across and down the page by default. bgProperties is a property that allows you to set the background image to a fixed position. So, if the user scrolls down the page, the background image will not scroll. It will remain in place while the content of the page changes. The rightMargin, leftMargin, topMargin, and bottomMargin properties allow you to set the margin properties for the page. Not all browsers support the setting of Web page margins.

The HTML Designer supports a new feature called IntelliSense. **IntelliSense** detects what you have typed, and tries to predict what you will type next. IntelliSense detects built-in keywords and properties, as well as third-party controls installed with your application. Drag-and-drop controls and IntelliSense are available for all languages within .NET. You can jump to the listings that begin with "b" by pressing the B key. Because you can select the keyword from a predefined list, IntelliSense helps prevent syntax errors in your HTML code.

The Web page can be created using the menu commands or Toolbox controls, or edited directly in HTML view. In the following exercise you will use all three techniques to create a basic Web page. In the first steps, you will use the HTML view to add code to the page. You will learn how to use the IntelliSense feature. You will verify the page properties using the Properties window. You will also modify the code in HTML view using the Properties window.

1. Right-click **Chapter2** in the Solution Explorer window, point to **Add**, then click **Add HTML Page**.

2. In the Name text box type **feedback.htm**, then click **Open**.

3. The Properties window shows the DOCUMENT properties by default. Verify the DOCUMENT properties in the Properties window. Verify that the value of the pageLayout property is GridLayout. Verify that the targetSchema property is Internet Explorer 5.0. Verify that the showGrid property is set to True.

4. In the Title property field, type **Tara Store**. The Title property corresponds to the HTML title tag.

5. In the Keywords property field type **Irish Gifts, Ireland, Tara Store**.

6. Drag the **header.jpg** image from the Solution Explorer window to the page and:

   a. Position the image in the upper-left corner of the page.

   b. In the Properties window of the header.jpg image, type **Tara Store** in the alt field.

7. Click the **HTML** tab to change to HTML mode. Notice that the keywords were placed inside a meta tag, and the title was added using a title tag.

8. Insert a blank line below the image tag, then type **<**. The IntelliSense feature detects that you have started to enter a beginning tag. The list of tags is presented in a drop-down list.

9. Click the **br** tag to select it, as shown in Figure 2-5, and then press **Enter**.

10. Close the tag by typing **>**. Add three more **
** tags.

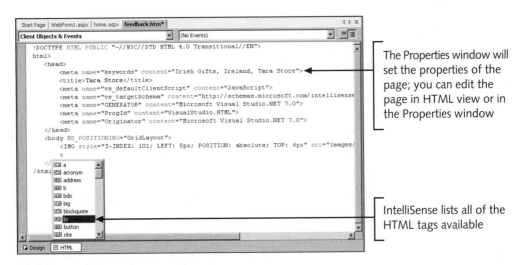

Figure 2-5   Selecting an HTML tag

11. Add a horizontal rule tag, **<hr>**.

12. Click inside the <hr> tag. The Properties window displays the property page for the hr tag. Change the noshade property to **True** using the drop-down list box in the property page. Notice that the keyword noshade is added to the HTML tag.

13. Click **File** on the menu bar, then click **Save All**.

In the following steps you will add a table to the page you just created, using the Table menu. You will use the Properties window to set the properties of individual HTML controls. You will also use the HTML controls to add a form.

1. Click the **Design** tab to switch to Design view.

2. Click **Table** on the menu bar, point to **Insert**, then click **Table**. Change the number of rows to **6** and columns to **1**. Click **OK**.

You can configure the table properties and the cell properties when you create the table; you can also configure the properties using the Properties window after you create the table

Figure 2-6 The Insert Table dialog box

3. Change the properties of the table using the Properties window.

   a. Change the border from 1 to **0**.

   b. Change the style property to **Z-INDEX: 106; LEFT: 244px; POSITION: absolute; TOP: 132px**. (*Note*: Depending on your screen resolution, you may have to resize the Properties window to edit the style property. Place the cursor over the edge of the window and drag the edge to the left until you can see the entire style property value text box.)

4. Click in the first table cell, then type **Tara Store Feedback Form**.

   a. Select the entire phrase **Tara Store Feedback Form**.

2

    b. In the Formatting toolbar, change the format from Normal to **Heading2** in the Style drop-down list box

    c. In the Formatting toolbar, change the font to **Verdana** and the size to **4**.

5. Place the pointer over the **Toolbox** tab to slide out the Toolbox. Click the **pushpin** icon to make the Toolbox remain open.

6. In the Toolbox, click the **HTML** tab, if necessary, to show the HTML controls.

7. Drag the **HTML Label** control to the page and position the control inside the second table cell. The icon for the Label control is the letter A.

    a. Click inside the new Label control, then delete the text Label.

    b. Type **Complete the form**. Press **Shift+Enter** to insert a single line break.

    c. Then, type **and click on the submit button**.

    d. Drag the handles on the Label control to make the text fit the table cell.

    e. In the Properties window, in the Class property field, type **TSHeading**.

8. Drag a **Text Field** control to the page and position it inside the third table cell.

    a. In the Properties window, change the value property to **Enter your e-mail address**.

    b. Set both the (ID) property and the Name property of the text box to **Email**.

    c. Set the Size property of the text box to **30**.

    d. Set the Class property to **txtBox**.

In the following steps you will use the HTML controls to add a form. You will use the Properties window and the HTML view to set the properties of individual HTML controls.

1. Drag a **Text Area** control from the HTML tab and drop it in the fourth cell.

    a. In the Properties window, set the Cols property to **25** and the Rows property to **5**.

    b. Set the Name property of the Text Area control to **comments**.

    c. Set the (ID) property of the Text Area control to **comments**.

    d. Set the Class property to **txtBox**.

2. Right-click the **Text Area** control, then click **View HTML Source**. The HTML view is displayed in the code window.

    a. Locate the <IMG> tag. The image tag has the alt property specified as "Tara Store".

    b. Place the cursor between the <TEXTAREA> tags. (*Note:* You can also change modes by clicking on the HTML tab.)

    c. Type **Enter your comments** in between the <TEXTAREA> tags, after cols = "25".

3. Click the **Design** tab to return back to Design mode.

4. Drag a **Submit** button from the HTML tab to the page and position the button inside the fifth cell.

   a. In the Properties window change the Value property of the Submit button to **Send**.

   b. Change the Name and (ID) properties of the Submit button to **btnSubmit**.

   c. Change the Class property to **TSButton**.

5. Click **File** on the menu bar, then click **Save All**.

In the following steps you will use the menu to insert a hyperlink. Then, you will use the Hyperlink dialog box to set the properties to the hyperlink.

1. In the last table cell, type **E-mail us at info@tarastore.com**. Press **Enter**, then type **Visit us at www.tarastore.com**.

2. Select the text **info@tarastore.com**.

3. Click **Insert** on the menu bar, then click **Hyperlink**.

4. In the Hyperlink dialog box, change the type in the drop-down list box from http:// to **mailto**, if necessary.

5. If necessary, type the e-mail address **info@tarastore.com** in the URL text box. Click **OK**. Because the hyperlink is an e-mail address, Visual Studio .NET automatically formats the address as a hyperlink. The text in Design view is blue and underlined to indicate the text is a hyperlink.

   a. Click the e-mail hyperlink.

   b. In the Properties window verify that the href property is mailto:info@TaraStore.Com.

   c. Set the class property to **TSLinks**.

6. Click the text **www.tarastore.com**.

   a. Verify the href property is set to http://www.tarastore.com.

   b. Set the class property to **TSLinks**.

7. Highlight all the text in the fifth cell, then click the Bullets icon on the Formatting toolbar. This creates an unordered list.

8. Click **File** on the menu bar, then click **Save All**.

You can preview your page within Visual Studio .NET or in a Web browser by typing in the URL of your project, the path, and the name of the Web page. Visual Studio .NET also allows you to start the application by clicking the Start button on the Standard toolbar. The Start button is a blue arrowhead located to the left of the debug drop-down list. This method always opens the starting page, which is not necessarily the page you want to preview. You can change the start page by right-clicking on the desired page in the Solution Explorer window and selecting Set Start Page. If you use the Start button, Visual Studio .NET indicates that your application is running. As a result, you must close the browser window before Visual Studio .NET allows you to make further changes to your Web application.

In the following steps you will preview your Web page using a browser and from the browser within Visual Studio .NET. You will also set the page as the start page of the project and view the page.

1. Start your **Internet Explorer** browser.

2. Enter **localhost/Chapter2/feedback.htm** in the location box to view the page.

3. Close the browser window.

4. In Visual Studio .NET, verify that you are in Design view.

5. Right-click on the Web page, then click **View in Browser**. Your results should look like the page shown in Figure 2-7. The name of the window is Browse – Tara Store.

Figure 2-7   An HTML page created with Visual Studio .NET

6. Click the **Close** button to close the Browse window.

7. Right-click **feedback.htm** in Solution Explorer window. Click **Set As Start Page**.

8. On the Standard toolbar, click the **Start** button (a blue triangle). The browser opens with the page loaded. The Output window also opens.

9. Close the browser.

10. Close the Output window within Visual Studio .NET, then close the feedback.htm page.

USER CONTROLS

To make it easier to maintain Web pages, you could use server-side include files for code and images that are repeated across many Web pages in a Web site. For example, if you create a Web page that contains an image tag, you can reference that file from other pages within your site. Then, if the filename changes, you need only modify the original server-side include file. Server-side include files can contain HTML and server-side code. Both Windows and UNIX systems support server-side include files.

 It is important to plan your Web application before you start to develop the code. After planning the desired outcome of your Web site, you can try to identify areas where code can be reused. Then, you can create User controls to replace this code.

In Visual Studio .NET, server-side include files are also called User controls. User controls are a form of ASP.NET pages. Therefore, User controls can contain HTML, client-side scripts, and ASP.NET server code. (*Note*: User controls were formerly known as Pagelets.) Similarly to include files, **User controls** allow you to separate content that can be reused in other pages.

User controls are compiled by Visual Studio .NET and must be registered with each ASP.NET page. You cannot include the <html>, <head>, or <body> elements in the user control. The User control file extension must have the file extension **.ascx**. The first line of User control must identify the file as a User control with the keyword Control. All User controls are identified with this keyword. Because the User control can contain code, it also contains a reference to the code behind the page. You can place the server code within the code behind the page, or you can include the code within the HTML view.

The following sample code creates a user control that displays a list of months and could be saved in a file named months.ascx.

```
<%@ Control %>
<select id=months>
<option>January</option>
<option>February</option>
<option>March</option>
<option>April</option>
<option>May</option>
<option>June</option>
<option>July</option>
<option>August</option>
<option>September</option>
<option>October</option>
<option>November</option>
<option>December</option>
</select>
```

2

Because ASP.NET pages place a form tag within the ASP.NET page, you should not include an additional <form> control in the Web page. If the <form> element is used in the User control and the User control is nested within a <form> element, your code will not work.

Within each ASP.NET page that contains the User control, you must register the user control. To register the control, the first line of the page must contain the **@Register** directive. The @Register directive allows you to include the file as a custom control. The **TagPrefix** property is used to identify the User control's namespace, like the ASP prefix used with ASP controls. The following sample code shows how you would register the user control from the previous sample.

```
<%@ Register TagPrefix="Months" TagName= ¬
"ListMonths" src="months.ascx" %>
```

You can also add the code to register and insert the User control by dragging the User control from the Solution Explorer window to the Web page in the Design view. This adds the Register code and the user control tags to the new Web page. You can still edit this code manually in HTML view.

Once the TagPrefix has been registered, you can add an ASP.NET tag with the TagPrefix. You can use the new tag anywhere in the Web page. You can reuse any User control many times within the same page. However, you must provide a unique ID name for each user control. Below is a sample of how you would add a User control to the Web page by inserting the new ASP.NET tag.

```
<UC:Months id = "Month1" runat = "server"/>
```

User controls can contain HTML code or ASP.NET code. The User control may be as simple as a heading image, or as complicated as a list of records returned from a database. Because the page is compiled, you can include code within the User control, or in the code behind the page for the User control. The User control can be reused in other Web pages within the same application, and across projects.

User controls are setup to use the flow layout mode as the default. You can change the layout to grid layout so that you can use absolute positioning of controls. To do this, you open the HTML tab on the Toolbox and add a Grid Layout Panel control. Then, you can position the elements within the Panel. This places the items within a DIV tag in the resulting Web page.

The following exercise illustrates how to create and register a User control. The User control contains an image and some basic ASP.NET code. In the Web page, you will register the User control and add the new tag to the Web page.

1. Right-click **Chapter2** in the Solution Explorer window, point to **Add**, then click **Add Web User Control**.

2. In the Name text box type **header.ascx**. Click the **Open** button.

3. Click the **HTML** tab. Notice that the first line includes the keyword Control. The first line also identifies the default language, "vb" for Visual Basic .NET, and other properties, which will be covered in the next chapter.

4. Click the **Design** tab to return to the Design view.

5. Drag the file **header.jpg** from the images folder in the Solution Explorer window to the page and position the image in the upper-left corner. (*Note:* You may need to place the cursor at the end of the header image and press **Enter** to position the label below the image.)

6. Drag a **Label** control from the Toolbox to the Web page and position it beneath the header image.

7. Click the **HTML** tab. Under the image tag, enter the following code. (*Note:* You must type this code all on a single line. The Visual Studio .NET editor will place this code on the line below the @ Page directive.)

```
<% Response.write("<h1 align='center'> ¬
Welcome to Tara Store</h1>") %>
```

8. Click the **Design** tab to return to Design view.

9. Right-click on the page, then click **View Code**. The code behind the page located in header.ascx.vb opens.

10. Locate the Page_Load event procedure. As you learned in the first chapter, the Page_Load event procedure is run when the page is loaded in memory on the Web server.

11. Below the comment, enter the following code, which sets the Text property of the Label control named Label1 to the current date. The Now class provides you with access to the date and time. The Date class returns the Date object for the current date. The date is formatted as mm/dd/yy by using the ToShortDateString method. (*Note:* The comment is colored green.)

```
Label1.Text = Now.Date.ToShortDateString
```

12. Click **File** on the menu bar, and then click **Save All**.

13. Close the header.ascx.vb page and the header.ascx page.

In the following steps, you will open the home page you created earlier, register the User control, and add the new tag to the Web page. When you register your User control, it is useful to use the name of the application or project as the TagPrefix. If you use the same name as the TagPrefix, it will be easier for you to recognize and maintain your User controls. The user control must be compiled before you can view the page. The Build command instructs Visual Studio .NET to compile your application.

1. Double-click **home.aspx** in the Solution Explorer window to open the Web page.

2. Right-click on the Web page, then click **View HTML Source**.

3. Insert a blank line above the @Page directive.

4. On the blank line, type the following code to register the User control.

```
<%@ Register TagPrefix = "Chapter2" ¬
TagName = "MyHeading" src= "header.ascx" %>
```

5. Scroll down the page to the opening body tag. The next tag is the form tag. Below the opening form tag, insert a blank line. Then, on the blank line, type the following code, which inserts the User control. (*Note*: Notice that an ID is used to identify the control. The naming convention for the User controls is to use the tag name and add a number.)

```
<Chapter2:MyHeading id = "MyHeading1" runat = "server"/>
```

6. Click the **Design** tab to return to Design view. The User control appears as a graphical control in the page. This helps you plan where to insert your user controls in the Web page.

7. Click **Build** on the menu bar, then click **Build Solution**.

8. Right-click on the page, then click **View in Browser**. Your results should look like the page in Fig 2-8.

Figure 2-8   Inserting User controls in an ASP.NET page

9. Close the **Browse** window.

CREATING CASCADING STYLE SHEETS

Most Web applications use cascading style sheets to store information about how to present the Web site. **Cascading style sheets (CSS)** can be used to separate page content from presentation. The World Wide Web Consortium (*www.w3c.org*) is responsible for developing and maintaining the CSS standards. There are several versions of the CSS standards. A browser must support HTML 4.0 to support CSS. Older browsers simply ignore the CSS. Cascading style sheets can be used with Web pages created using HTML, XML, and ASP.NET. Web sites that use Cascading style sheets are easier to maintain. For example, when you need to make a change to the font color of the H1 tag, you can simply change the Color property within the style sheet. The change is reflected immediately across the entire Web site. Because style sheets can be used to help manage the presentation of the Web site, it is important to plan and create your style sheets before you start developing your application.

Visual Studio .NET supports the ability to create and maintain cascading style sheets. You can create your cascading style sheet manually or use a Style Builder graphical user interface to create your style sheet. The Style Builder allows you to quickly build and preview complicated style sheets.

CSS Overview

A **style rule** is the information that is applied to a single HTML tag. There are three style formats that are used to create style rules. The syntax for the style rules varies depending upon where the style sheet rule is located. The inline style rules add the style information within the HTML tag. The inline style rule would only be applied to the single tag. In an embedded style sheet, the style rules are located in the heading section of the Web page. A single pair of style tags, <style></style>, is used to identify the embedded style rules. Embedded style rules can apply to all tags within the same page. For example, a paragraph tag that is formatted in the embedded style sheet is reflected in all the paragraph tags within the Web page. External style sheets are used to apply style rules across multiple Web pages. Each Web page must include a reference to the external style sheet using a <LINK> tag. When a paragraph tag is formatted in an external style sheet rule, all of the paragraphs within the Web pages will apply the new style rule.

Inline Style Sheets

Inline style sheets format a single HTML tag. Inline style sheet rules are also called internal style sheet rules. When referring to an HTML tag within a style sheet, the tag is referred to as an **element**. The style information is stored with the HTML tag using the keyword style. In the style rule, you separate the name of the property and the value that is assigned to that property with a colon. You can format multiple style rules by separating each name and value pair with a semicolon. Below is the syntax for using an inline style rule. (*Note*: Not all tags contain content.)

```
<tagname "style=property1:value;property2:value2">
    Content goes here
</tagname>
```

In the sample below, HTML used the Color property of the <FONT> tag to format the color of the text.

```
<FONT COLOR="green">
    <H1>Welcome to Tara Store!</H1>
</FONT>
```

2

Using cascading style sheets, you can format a heading using an inline style rule. The Color property is formatted using the color style rule. There is no need to include the <FONT> tag.

```
<H1 style="color:green;size:12">Welcome to Tara Store!
</H1>
```

Embedded Style Sheets

Embedded style sheets are style rules that are placed in the heading section of the HTML page. Because embedded style sheet rules are placed in the heading section, they can be applied to more than one tag within the HTML page. Below is the syntax for inserting an embedded style sheet. All style sheet rules are contained within this pair of style tags. In this example, the ElementName represents any valid XML or HTML control. Examples of HTML controls are <H1>, <P>, and <DIV>. The entire listing of property names and values are enclosed within a single pair of curly braces. The PropertyName represents any property that is valid for that control. For example, you can format the font color with the Color property. The value represents any value that is valid for that property. You can learn about the valid controls, property names, and values on the W3C cascading style sheet Web site at *www.w3c.org/Style/CSS.*

```
ElementName {
    PropertyName: value;
    PropertyName: value;
}
```

 Although some programmers prefer to write the CSS rules on a single line, it is a good idea to enter only one style rule on a single line. Then, you can easily detect if there is a colon or semicolon missing from the style rule. You can also easily detect if there is a missing curly brace.

Embedded styles are useful when you need to create custom style rules that apply to all elements within the same page. Below is a sample of an embedded style sheet. All of the <H1> tags on the page format the text as 12 point, green.

```
<HTML><HEAD><TITLE>Sample Embedded Style
Sheet</TITLE>
<STYLE>
H1{
     color:green;
     size:12"
}
</STYLE>
</HEAD>
<BODY>
<H1>Welcome to Tara Store!</H1>
</BODY></HTML>
```

External Style Sheets

The third type of cascading style sheets is the external style sheet, which is also known as a linked style sheet. The **external style sheet** contains style rules that can be used by many files at the same time. The link tag (<LINK>) is used to attach a style sheet to the Web page. Because the style sheet is external to the Web page, the style rules can be reused. The benefit of using an external style sheet is that if you need to make a change to a style rule, you only have to make the change in one location. All of the Web pages that use that style sheet would instantly display the new style rule. Because this is an efficient way to manage style rules, external style sheets are commonly used in business Web sites. External style sheets provide the greatest flexibility.

Below is a sample of the code that would be inserted in the external style sheet. The style sheet format for external style sheet rules is the same as the format for embedded style sheet rules. However, you do not need to include the style (<STYLE>) tags within the external style sheet. The name of the file of the external style sheet ends with .css. In the example below, the name of the style sheet is MyStyle.css.

```
H1{
     color:green;
     size:12;
}
```

The <LINK> tag is an HTML tag that is used to identify the location of the external style sheet. The **rel** property indicates that the linked document contains a style sheet. In an external style sheet, the style tags are omitted because the rel property indicates that the linked file is a style sheet. The **Type** property is used to indicate the MIME type of the linked file. The MIME type is used to indicate which types of programs can open the files. The MIME type indicates that the file is a text file, and contains cascading style information. The **href** property is used to indicate the location of the external style sheet. The URL can be the absolute URL, such as http://www.domain.com/path/StyleSheetName.CSS, or a relative URL such as /includes/StyleSheetName.CSS. The URL should be placed within quotation marks. Below is the syntax for adding the external style sheet to the Web page using the <LINK> tag.

<link rel=stylesheet type="text/css" href="URL">

The sample code below uses the </LINK> tag to insert the external style sheet into the Web page. (*Note:* The code for the <LINK> tag is entered on one line.)

```
<HTML><HEAD><TITLE>Sample Embedded Style Sheet</TITLE>
<LINK REL="stylesheet" TYPE="text/css" HREF="MyStyle.css">
</HEAD>
<BODY>
<H1>Welcome to Tara Store!</H1>
</BODY></HTML>
```

Comments within Cascading Style Sheets

You can add inline comments in the style sheet by adding two forward slashes (//) before the comment. You can add a multiline comment by adding the symbol /* before the comment, and */ after the comment. You can add comments to external style sheets or embedded style sheets. The following sample code uses comments to document the external cascading style sheet. A multiline comment is used to document the style sheet. An inline comment is used to indicate the purpose of the style information.

```
/* Styles.CSS
Created By: Katie Kalata
Date Created: 9/5/2002
This style sheet is used to format the main menu
*/
H1 {color:green}      // Green
corporate logo
H2 {color:red}        // Red
heading
H3 {color:blue}       // Blue menu
```

Cascading Style Sheets Rules

These three types of cascading style sheets can contain conflicting styles rules. These conflicts are resolved through a series of **cascading rules**. In most cases, inline style sheet rules take precedence over embedded style rules, and embedded style rules take precedence over external style rules. In other words, if the external style sheet indicates that the heading tag is to be formatted in blue, and the embedded style sheet indicates that the heading tag is to be formatted in green, and the inline style rule indicates that the heading tag is to be formatted in red, then the heading tag is formatted in red.

Classes

Style sheets are often used to create a class. A **class** can be used to format a group of different tags or a subgroup of a specific tag. For example, you can use a class named MyHeader to format the heading1 tags. The following sample code changes the color of all heading 1 tags in the document to green. The class named BlueHead is used to change the color of the BlueHead element to blue.

```
H1 {color:green}
.SelCat {color:red}
.BlueHead {color:blue}
```

Then, in the Web page, you could format any element with the class. In the sample code below, the first message would appear in green. The SelCat class is used only with one item to indicate that the category was selected by formatting the text as red. The <H2>

and <H3> headings are formatted with the BlueHead class. Both of these headings would appear in blue.

```
<h1>Welcome to Tara Store!</h1>
<h2 class="BlueHead">Product Listing:</h2>
   <ul>
   <li>Gifts</li>
   <li class="SelCat">Jewelry</li>
   <li >China & Crystal</li>
   <li>Food</li>
   <li>Clothing</li>
   <li>Books, Music, & Videos</li>
   </ul>
<h3 class="BlueHead">About Tara Store</h3>
   <ul>
   <li>What's New</li>
   <li>Current Sales</li>
   <li>Location</li>
   <li>Contact Us</li>
   <li>Members Only</li>
   </ul>
```

There are several books that cover cascading style sheets, including *Designing Web Pages with Cascading Style Sheets* by J. Sklar (Course Technology, © 2001) which can be located at www.course.com/webwarrior.

In some cases a Web designer may develop the external style sheet. The Web designer is a computer graphic arts specialist who has Web page layout and design skills. He or she can assist you with selecting the appropriate colors, fonts, and images for your Web site.

Using the CSS Editor

Although you can create style sheets in a text editor, it is useful to use a CSS editor to create your style sheets. A **CSS editor** uses a graphical user interface to represent the Web page elements and properties. Although many programs, such as Visual Studio .NET, integrate a Web page editor and a CSS editor into their development environment, CSS editors are available independently of Web page editors. However, having the CSS editor integrated with the development environment makes it easier for you to design and create cascading style sheets. For example, as you make changes to your cascading style sheets, you can see the resulting effects within Visual Studio .NET. CSS editors help ensure that you use only valid tags, properties, and values. Most CSS errors are caused by incorrect syntax.

Visual Studio .NET comes with a complete CSS editor called the **Style Builder**. You can use the dialog boxes to build your style rules, or you can enter them manually by typing in the style rules. You can create the style sheets, view the CSS code, and preview the output within the Style Builder. Visual Studio .NET also helps you build style rules with the Add Style Rule dialog box and IntelliSense. When you create an ASP.NET application, a default style sheet named styles.css is created.

Visual Studio .NET includes the IntelliSense feature within the CSS editor, which is useful when you choose to enter your style rules manually. For example, when you type font-family: the IntelliSense feature displays a list of font faces to choose from. You can use the arrow keys to navigate through the list, or type the first few letters to go directly to the entry in the list. When you have selected the font you want to use, press Enter to make the selection. After you add the semicolon, the IntelliSense feature provides a list of other PropertyNames to choose from. You can quickly build style sheets using the IntelliSense features.

The Style Builder recognizes any style properties you enter manually. All of the properties are organized using the tabs located on the left of the Style Builder. The Style Builder lets you select the property names and values for fonts, background, text, position, layout, edges, lists, and other properties. You can navigate across these style properties by using the menu located on the left side of the Style Builder window.

The Style Builder includes a **Color Picker** feature, which can be used to help you select a color. The Color Picker is useful because you can select your colors from a predefined palette based on your design and business objectives. Some Web sites prefer to use only the Web colors. The Web colors are 216 colors that are supported by the majority of computers and browsers. Therefore, if you select a color from the Web Colors palette, you can be confident that the end users see the same color on their monitor. There are four tabs in the Color Picker, which identify how the colors are commonly used. The **Web Palette** tab provides 216 basic Web colors. Clicking a color selects the color, and displays the hexadecimal equivalent at the bottom of the table. The **Named Colors** tab provides the 16 Windows colors and the 122 other named colors. Although some browsers only support the name feature for the 16 Windows colors, it is useful to refer to the colors by name because the colors are commonly used in daily life. The **System Colors** tab allows you to select a color that matches the colors used to create system graphical user interfaces such as windows, menus scroll bars, and buttons. This is usually a more useful feature for intranets and Windows applications where you can be certain of the users' color schemes. The **Custom Color** tab allows you to use three slider controls to select the red, green, and blue (RGB) values for the color. In addition to displaying the hexadecimal equivalent of the RGB value, a preview of the color is displayed. The Custom Color palette allows you to select any one of millions of possible colors. However, some computers and browsers may not display all of these colors properly. It is useful to test your Web application to ensure that the colors applied in your Web site are acceptable on different browsers and platforms.

Creating a Cascading Style Sheet

When you create an ASP.NET Web application in Visual Studio .NET, a default cascading style sheet is created. The default style sheet is named Styles.css. The default style sheet already contains many commonly used style rules. You can edit these style rules or remove them in the code view, or in the Style Builder. In the following example, you will modify the default style sheet using the Add Style Rule dialog box, IntelliSense, and the Style Builder.

1. Double-click the **Styles.css** file in the Solution Explorer window.

2. The style sheet opens. Locate the BODY tag in the style sheet.

   a. Locate the style rule for the default FONT-FAMILY.

   b. Insert the font type **Arial,** before the Verdana font name, as shown in Figure 2-9. This formats all of the fonts in the page with the Arial typeface. (*Note*: Make sure to include the comma between Arial and Verdana.)

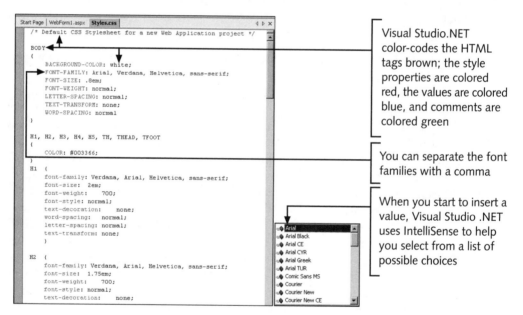

Figure 2-9   Cascading style sheet

   c. To change the background color of the page, right-click the word **BODY,** and then click **Build Style**. Notice that the first value in the Font Family property is Arial.

   d. Click the **Background** tab in the Style Builder dialog box.

   e. Click the drop-down **list arrow** in the Color property. Notice that the 16 Windows named colors are listed. Do not select a color.

f. Click the **Build** button next to the color list to open the Color Picker dialog box.

g. Click the **Web Palette** tab, as shown in Figure 2-10. Do not select a color. Click **Cancel** twice. (*Note*: The preview box in the Style Builder dialog box displays the color selected with sample text.)

Figure 2-10   Changing style properties in the Style Builder

 The Background property is often used to add a color or image to the background of an object. In browsers, the background applies to the entire line, not just the text. By specifying margins, you can specify where the background color is implemented.

3. To insert another style rule, right-click on the CSS page above the BODY tag, then click **Add Style Rule**. HTML elements, Class Names, and Element IDs are provided in three drop-down lists.

4. In the Element drop-down list box select **TABLE** as shown in Figure 2-11. Click the **>** button to place the element in the Style rule hierarchy, then click **OK**.

5. Use the process described in Steps 3 and 4 to insert the **HR** and **TD** tags. The style rules are added to the bottom of the style sheet. Click **OK**.

6. Right-click within the curly braces of the H2 tag, then click **Build Style**. The Style Builder dialog box opens. Click the Color drop-down **list arrow**. Select **Green** from the 16 Windows named colors list, then click **OK** to close the dialog box.

7. Right-click the **HR** style rule at the bottom of the page, then click **Build Style**. In the Color drop-down list box select **Green**. Click the **OK** button.

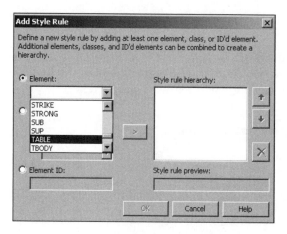

Figure 2-11 The Add Style Rule dialog box

8. Right-click in the **UL LI** style rule, then click **Build Style**.

   a. Click the **Lists** tab and then click the **Custom bullet** check box to select it.

   b. Click the **Build** button next to the Image text box. In the Projects pane select the **images** folder. In the Contents of Images pane select **bullet.gif**. (*Note:* You can browse the directory tree on your computer to insert images, or select images from within the project files.) Click the **OK** button. Click the **OK** button in the Style Builder.

9. Right-click the **Table** element, then click **Build Style**.

   a. Click the **Edges** tab.

   b. Change the border by changing the style setting in the drop-down list box to **Solid Line**.

   c. Change the table Color property to **Green**. Click the **OK** button.

10. Right-click on the **TD** element, then click **Build Style**.

    a. Click the **Text** tab.

    b. Change the Horizontal property to **Centered**. Click the **OK** button.

11. Add a class by right-clicking on the style sheet, then clicking **Add Style Rule**.

    a. Click the **Class name** radio button to select it. In the text box type **TSHeading**. Click the **>** button and the **OK** button.

    b. Right-click in the **TSHeading** class style rule, then click **Build Style**.

    c. In the Font tab, set the Small caps property to **Small caps**.

    d. Check the Specific radio button and enter **12** and **pt** for the size of the text font. Click **OK**. The units drop-down list box automatically selects pt.

2

12. Add a class by right-clicking on the style sheet and then clicking **Add Style Rule**.

   a. Click the **Class name** radio button to select it. In the text box, type **TSLinks**. Click the > button and the **OK** button.

   b. Right-click in the **TSLinks** class style rule, then click **Build Style**.

   c. In the Font tab, change the color to **Green**.

   d. Check the **Specific** radio button and enter **10** and **pt** for the size of the text font. Click **OK**.

13. Add a class by right-clicking on the style sheet and then clicking **Add Style Rule**. Click the **Class name** radio button to select it. In the text box, type **txtBox**. Click the > button and the **OK** button.

14. Right-click in the **txtBox** class style rule, then select **Build Style**.

   a. In the Font Color drop-down list box, select **Green**.

   b. In the Bold section, the Absolute radio button is selected. Click **Bold** from the drop-down list.

   c. Check the **Specific** radio button and, in the Size text box, enter **10** and **pt**.

   d. In the Font Family text box, use the Build button to select **Verdana**, press the > button, then click **OK**.

   e. On the Edges tab, change the style to **Solid Line** and the color to **Green**. Click **OK**.

15. Add a class by right-clicking on the style sheet and then clicking **Add Style Rule**. Click the **Class Name** radio button to select it. In the text box, type **TSButton**. Click the > button and the **OK** button.

16. Right-click in the **TSButton** class style rule, then select **Build Style**.

   a. On the Font tab, set the Family to **Verdana**.

   b. Set the Small caps property to **Small caps**.

   c. In the Font Color drop-down list box, select **White**.

   d. Check the **Specific** radio button and, in the Size text box, enter **10** and **pt**.

   e. In the Bold section, the Absolute radio button is selected. Click **Bold** from the drop-down list.

   f. On the Background tab, change the Color to **Green**.

   g. On the Edges tab, change the Style to **Ridge** and the Color to **Yellow**. Click **OK**.

17. Click **File** on the menu bar, then click **Save All**.

In the following steps, you will apply the style sheet to the feedback.htm page you created earlier. You can simply drag the cascading style sheet from the Solution Explorer window to the Web page. Visual Studio .NET will insert and configure the <LINK> tag for you. (*Note:* You can also enter the link information manually in HTML view.)

1. Preview the style sheet by right clicking in the style sheet and then clicking **View in Browser**. The CSS Editor Preview Page opens with a preview of what the style sheet looks like when applied to a sample Web page.

2. Close the CSS Editor Preview Page.

3. Open the **feedback.htm** page if it is not already open.

4. Click the **Design** tab to view the Web page in Design view.

5. Drag the **Styles.css** file from the Solution Explorer window to the feedback.htm page. This adds the link tag into the HTML code.

6. Click **File** on the menu bar, then click **Save All**.

7. Right-click on the page, then click **View in Browser**. Your page should look like the one on the left-hand side in Figure 2-12.

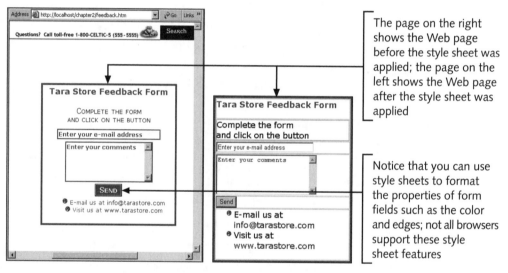

Figure 2-12   Linking a style sheet to a Web page

8. Close the feedback.htm page and the style sheet.

Customizing the Toolbox

The Clipboard Ring is a Toolbox tool that stores the list of items that have previously been copied to the Clipboard. The **Clipboard** is the area in memory that Windows uses to copy information that can be used in another part of a document, or even in another program. The Clipboard is also found in Windows Office applications. If you do not create a custom control for a piece of code, and you happen to have recently copied it

2

somewhere, the code might appear in the Clipboard Ring. However, if you create code that you plan to reuse, it is best to customize the Toolbox and add the code to the General tab. You can add additional tabs to the Toolbox to help organize your frequently used code. You can add third-party customized controls, including code fragments, to any of the tabs in the Toolbox.

In the following exercise you will create a new tab and add a code fragment to this new tab.

1. Right-click in the Toolbox area below existing tabs, then click **Add Tab**. Type **My Tools**, then press **Enter**.

2. Open the **feedback.htm** page.

3. Click the **My Tools** tab which is at the very bottom of the Toolbox area.

4. Click and drag the **header.jpg** image to the My Tools tab. The code is represented as MarkUp Fragment on the toolbar.

5. Right-click the **MarkUp Fragment**, then click **Rename Item**. Type **HeaderImage**, then press **Enter**.

6. Right-click **Chapter2** in the Solution Explorer window, point to **Add**, then click **Add Web Form**.

7. In the Name text box, type **Contact.aspx**, then click the **Open** button.

8. Click the **My Tools** tab. Drag the new custom **HeaderImage** code from the My Tool tab to the top-left corner of the Contact page. This places the control on the Web page. The image appears in the Web page.

9. Click **File** on the menu bar, then click **Save All**.

10. Close the Contact page.

Using Visual Studio .NET Help Resources

In the exercise below, you learn how to locate Help resources within Visual Studio .NET. **Dynamic Help** provides help for the currently selected item. The **Search Help** provides a text box to enter a search phrase. **Index Help** provides a dictionary index that you can search for a term alphabetically. **Contents Help** allows you navigate the help documentation using a table of contents. All Help methods provide results in a ranked list. You can double-click on the items in the list to view the documentation from within the user interface. You do not have to leave the Visual Studio .NET application to locate Help or documentation. You can view the actual URL of the Help files in the URL drop-down list box on the Web toolbar.

1. With the file feedback.htm open in Visual Studio .NET, right-click the page, then click **View HTML Source**. Highlight the word **HTML**. Click **Help** on the menu bar, then click **Dynamic Help**. In the Dynamic Help window

click the **HTML View, HTML Designer** hyperlink to open a Web page within the main window that contains information about the HTML editor.

2. Read the documentation on the Object Selector and Event Selector. By default the HTML Designer shows you the HTML and any scripts. They are both drop-down list boxes that appear at the top of the HTML page. The **Object Selector** is a list of all scriptable objects in the current document. The **Event Selector** is a list of all events sent to the selected object for which you can write handlers. Close the Dynamic Help window.

3. Click **Help** on the menu bar, then click **Search**. In the Look for text box, type **Style Builder**. In the Filtered by drop-down list box, click **Internet Development**. Click the **Search** button. The Search Results window opens with your results.

4. In the Search Results window, double-click **Introduction to Cascading Style Sheets**. The documentation appears in a new window. Read the documentation for creating cascading style sheets. When you are finished, close the page.

5. Click Help on the menu bar, then click **Index**. The **Filtered by** text box should still say Internet Development. In the **Look for** text box, type **STYLE tag**. The list changes as you type the characters. Click the STYLE tag selection. In the Index Results window, the selection Introduction to Cascading Style Sheets is displayed. Click this selection to open the same help window you saw in the previous step. Close the page.

6. Click **Help** on the menu bar, then click **Contents**. Click the **plus sign** to expand the selections as follows. Expand **Visual Studio .NET**. Expand **Developing with Visual Studio .NET**. Expand **Working with Code, HTML, and Resource Files**. Expand **Editing Code, HTML, and Text**, then expand **HTML**. Expand **Working with CSS Styles**. Click **Introduction to Cascading Style Sheets**, as shown in Figure 2-13. (*Note*: Although this method requires more clicks to locate what you're looking forward, you might stumble upon other useful information as you browse through the documentation. You can search the MSDN & the Visual Studio .NET SDK documentation and Help files all from within the same user interface.)

2

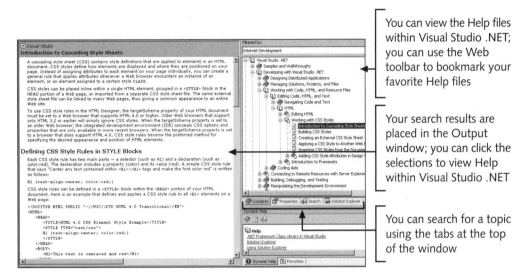

You can view the Help files within Visual Studio .NET; you can use the Web toolbar to bookmark your favorite Help files

Your search results are placed in the Output window; you can click the selections to view Help within Visual Studio .NET

You can search for a topic using the tabs at the top of the window

Figure 2-13   Help search results

CHAPTER SUMMARY

❑ Visual Studio .NET provides many options for configuring the Visual Studio .NET desktop. Auto-hiding allows you to shelve windows until they are needed. Floating windows allow you to drag windows anywhere on the desktop.

❑ The Solutions window allows you to manage all of your project files from one location.

❑ The Properties window allows you to set properties for objects.

❑ The Toolbox contains a set of commonly used controls, which are organized into tabs. You can customize the Toolbox to include your own custom controls.

❑ The HTML editor can be used to create HTML pages. You can write the HTML code directly in the HTML view, or use the Design view and drag-and-drop controls from the HTML tab in the Toolbox. HTML tags can be formatted using the Formatting toolbar, the menus, or the Properties window.

❑ You can create your own custom controls called User controls. User controls can contain HTML code and programming code. User controls must be registered within an ASP.NET page before they can be used. Once a tag has been registered as a User control, you can use the tag throughout the Web page. User controls are compiled, and can be reused across multiple pages within the same application.

❑ There are three types of cascading style sheets. The inline style sheet rules apply only to a single element. The embedded style sheet rules can be applied to multiple elements within the same page. A linked style sheet contains rules that can be applied to multiple pages. Cascading style sheets can be created manually or with the Style Builder.

❏ Additional features such as IntelliSense and Dynamic Help provide additional features to help programmers learn how to use Visual Studio .NET.

REVIEW QUESTIONS

1. If you want the window to be hidden, but want the ability to click on the name of the window on the desktop and show the window, which selection should you choose?

    a. Hide

    b. Auto Hide

    c. Floating

    d. Sliding

2. What is the file extension for a WebForm?

    a. .asp

    b. .aspx

    c. .asx

    d. .asxp

3. Which property allows you to position elements on a page using absolute positioning?

    a. pageLayout

    b. pageView

    c. positionTab

    d. positionProperty

4. What character(s) is/are used to comment out code in a style sheet?

    a. /* */

    b. *

    c. //

    d. #

5. You have just created a page named Spooks.htm. If your project name is ghosts, and you created your project using the default settings, where can you view your page in a browser?

    a. *http://www.ghost.com/spooks.htm*

    b. *http://localhost/ghost.htm*

    c. *http://255.255.255.0/ghost.htm*

    d. *http://localhost/ghost/spooks.htm*

2

6. Which tab in the Toolbox is most commonly used to insert custom code fragments?

   a. HTML

   b. General

   c. WebForm

   d. WinForm

7. Which property is used to set the target browser for the Web page?

   a. targetPage

   b. targetSchema

   c. targetBrowser

   d. none of the above

8. Which toolbar provides access to text format tools?

   a. Design toolbar

   b. Image editor

   c. Format toolbar

   d. Paint toolbar

9. The Start window has been closed. What menu allows you to reopen the Start window?

   a. File

   b. Window

   c. Help

   d. Edit

10. What feature supplies context-sensitive help?

    a. Index

    b. Start Page

    c. Dynamic Help

    d. Contents

11. Which type of style sheet takes precedence over all other style rules?

    a. inline

    b. external

    c. linked

    d. embedded

12. What tag is used to attach an external style sheet to a Web page?

    a. Link

    b. MIME

    c. Rel

    d. Href

13. What is the character that separates the name and values within a style rule?

    a. :

    b. *

    c. { }

    d. ,

14. Which style element can be applied to more than one element?

    a. Class

    b. ID

    c. H2

    d. none of the above

15. What is the file extension of a cascading style sheet?

    a. .css

    b. .ccs

    c. .html

    d. .ascx

16. Which keyword is used to define a User control?

    a. control

    b. pagelets

    c. fragments

    d. register

17. Which tag(s) can not be included within a User control?

    a. HTML

    b. head

    c. body

    d. all of the above

HANDS-ON PROJECTS

Project 2-1

In this project you will use the Visual Basic .NET to create a feedback form.

    1. Start **Visual Studio .NET** and open your **Chapter2 solution** if necessary.

    2. Create a new HTML page named **Ch2Proj1.htm**.

    3. Add a title to the page using the title tag that says **Feedback Form**.

4. Add the header.jpg, menu.gif, and Customer Support.jpg images to the Web page.

5. Add a heading that says **Feedback Form** using the Label control on the HTML tab of the Toolbox. Format the text as Heading2. Drag the handles of the control to show the text on one line.

6. Add HTML Text controls to collect the user's name and e-mail address Add labels for each of the Text controls.

7. Add a Label control that says **How did you hear about our Web site?** Add a drop-down list box containing five choices such as "Magazine, Radio, E-mail, Friend, Television". Right-click on the drop-down list box to display the Select Property Pages dialog box. Enter the options. The options should be the same value as the text displayed, as shown in Figure 2-14. You must click the Insert button after each Text and Value pair you enter. Leave the **Allow multiple selections** check box unchecked. Change the Size property to **1**. Click **OK**.

Figure 2-14   Using the Select Properties Pages to enter the options list

8. Add a Label control that says **What products are you interested in?** Add three check boxes and corresponding Label controls that say **Jewelry**, **Clothing**, and **China**. (*Note:* You may add additional check boxes and radio buttons to enhance the form.)

9. Add a Submit button that says **Send Your Comments**.

10. You can make it look presentable and professional by adding color, changing the text fonts, and adding graphics.

11. Go to the **File** menu and select **Save All** to save all of your solution files.

12. Click **Build** on the menu bar, then click **Build Solution**.

13. View your page in a browser. Go to *http://localhost/chapter2/Ch2Proj1.htm*. From the browser, print the page and the source code view. Your page should look like the one in Figure 2-15.

Figure 2-15   Building a feedback form with the HTML Editor

14. Close the page.

Project 2-2

In this project you will create an external Cascading Style Sheet using the Style Builder.

1. Start **Visual Studio .NET** and open your **Chapter 2 solution** if necessary.

2. Create a new style sheet named **Ch2Proj2.css**.

3. Add the following elements to the style sheet: TABLE, UL, H1, H2, and HR.

4. Modify the BODY, TABLE, UL, H1, H2, and HR elements using the Style Builder. Choose at least three properties to modify with each element.

5. Create a class named **Ch2Proj2**. Format the class with the Style Builder. Choose at least three properties to modify.

6. Go to the File menu and select **Save All** to save all of your solution files.

7. Preview the style sheet using the **CSS Editor Preview Page**. Print the page and the style sheet.

Project 2-3

In this project you will create a custom user control. You will register the User control in an ASP.NET page, and use the control in the Web page.

1. Start **Visual Studio .NET** and open your **Chapter2 solution** if necessary.

2. Create a new web User control named **Ch2Proj3.ascx**.

3. Go to the HTML tab in the Toolbox and drag the **Grid Layout Panel** to the page.

4. Place the **header.jpg**, **menu.gif**, and **CustomerSupport.jpg** image files inside the panel on the user control page.

5. Add a label that says **Welcome to Tara Store Customer Support** and format the label with the Heading3 tag.

6. Create an ASP.NET Web page named **Ch2Proj3.aspx**. Make sure to select **Add WebForm** when you create the page. The page opens in Design view.

7. Drag the **Ch2Proj3.ascx** file from the Solution Explorer window place it on the Ch2Proj3.aspx Web page.

8. Click the **HTML** tag to view the code that registered and inserted the User control.

9. Make the page look presentable and professional by adding content and color, changing the text fonts, and adding graphics.

10. Click the **Save All** button on the Toolbar to save all of your solution files.

11. View your page in a browser. Go to *http://localhost/chapter2/Ch2Proj3.aspx*. From the browser, print the page and the source code view. Your Web page should appear like the one in Figure 2-16.

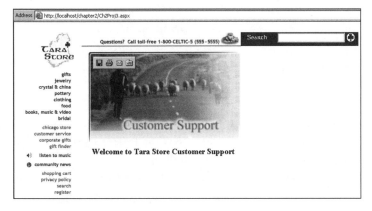

Figure 2-16   Inserting a User control

Project 2-4

In this project you will create a custom User control that contains a menu.

1. Start **Visual Studio .NET** and open your **Chapter2 solution** if necessary.

2. Create a new web User control named **Ch2Proj4Header.ascx**.

3. Add the **header.jpg** file to the User control.

4. Create a new web User control named **Ch2Proj4Menu.ascx**.

5. Add the **menu.gif** image to the User control.

6. Create an ASP.NET Web page named **Ch2Proj4.aspx**. Make sure to select **Add WebForm** when you create the page.

7. Create a table using the Table menu that contains two rows and two columns. Change the Border property to 0.

8. To merge the first two cells, click inside the first cell in the first row. Change the colspan property in the Properties window to **2**. Click inside the second cell in the first row. Right-click in the cell, point to **Delete**, then click **Cells**.

9. Drag the **Ch2Proj4Header.ascx** user control from the Solution Explorer window to the first cell in the first row. The User control graphic is placed in the cell.

10. Drag the **Ch2Proj4Menu.ascx** User control from the Solution Explorer window to the first cell of the second row. The User control graphic is placed in the cell.

11. Click the **HTML** tab to view the code that registered and inserted the User control into the Web page.

12. Make the page look presentable and professional by adding content and color, changing the text fonts, and adding graphics.

13. Click the **Save All** button to save all of your solution files.

14. Click **Build** on the menu bar, then click **Build Solution**.

15. View your page in a browser. Go to *http://localhost/chapter2/Ch2Proj4.aspx*. From the browser, print the page and the source code view.

Project 2-5

In this project you will locate additional help topics within Visual Studio .NET. You will use the Help Windows within Visual Studio .NET to learn more about ASP.NET. You will create a Web page that summarizes your findings.

1. Start **Visual Studio .NET** and open your **Chapter2 solution** if necessary.

2. Open the **Search** Help window. Make sure to select Internet Development as the filter from the drop-down list.

2

3. Select a topic and enter the topic in the text box. Topics you can select from:

   - Introduction to ASP.NET
   - Introduction to WebForms
   - Creating an ASP.NET Applications
   - Web Server Controls
   - Other ASP.NET related topics

4. Create a page named **Ch2Proj5.aspx**. Summarize your findings in this page. Format the page using the HTML editor.

5. Visit the Microsoft Design Gallery Live (Formerly known as Clipart Gallery Live) at *http://dgl.microsoft.com/*. Select three graphics. Right-click each graphic and select **Save Picture As**. Save the graphics to your Chapter02Data directory. Import the three graphics from your Chapter02Data directory to your images folder in your Chapter2 project. Add the three graphics to your Web page.

6. Make the page look presentable and professional by adding content and color, changing the text fonts, and adding graphics

7. Click the **Save All** button to save all of your solution files.

8. View your page in a browser. Go to *http://localhost/chapter2/Ch2Proj5.aspx*. From the browser, print the page and the source code view. (*Note:* Your Web page will vary depending upon which topic you selected, which content you added, and which graphics you added.)

CASE PROJECTS

Creating Web Pages with Visual Studio .NET

You are hired as the Web developer for a new Web site called MyStore. You are responsible for creating the home page for the Web site. Use Visual Studio .NET to create a home page for your Web site. Add at least three graphics, three hyperlinks, a bulleted list, and a table. Use the Properties window to modify the appearance of the controls and the Web page. Format the page using additional graphics, content, fonts, and color to enhance the appearance of the page. You may change the name of the store. Save the home page as Ch2Case1.htm. View your Web page in your browser. Print your Web page and the source code from the browser.

Creating Style Sheets with Visual Studio .NET

You are hired as the Web developer for a new Web site called MyStore. Your store manager has requested that you make several product category pages. Choose at least five product categories such as shirts, accessories, china, jewelry, or books. Create a Web page for each product category named Ch2Case2Cat1.aspx, Ch2Case2Cat2.aspx, Ch2Case2Cat3.aspx,

Ch2Case2Cat4.aspx, and Ch2Case2Cat5.aspx. On each Web page, include a menu that lists all product categories. Each category listed contains a hyperlink to the specific category page.

Create a style sheet that formats the category menu. There should be two classes defined in the style sheet. The first class, named Unselected, is used for the categories that are not selected. The Selected class is used to format the current hyperlink. The current hyperlink is the hyperlink that would take you to the current page. The Selected class changes the format of the link to a different color and font size using a style sheet rule. For example, each of the categories may be formatted blue with a font size of 10 pt. When the user is on the books page, the books hyperlink is red, with a font-size of 12 pt. Add a link from the external style sheet to each of the Web pages using the link tag. Format each page using additional graphics, content, fonts, and color to enhance the appearance of the page. You may change the name of the store. View your Web pages in your browser. Print each Web page and the source code from the browser.

Creating User Controls with Visual Studio .NET

Your store manager has requested that you make several product category pages. However, you don't have the budget to create custom pages and to maintain individual pages. Create a Web page for each product category. The product category pages should be named Ch2Case3Cat1.aspx, Ch2Case3Cat2.aspx , Ch2Case3Cat3.aspx , Ch2Case3Cat4.aspx, and Ch2Case3Cat5.aspx. Create three User controls, named Ch2Case3Header.ascx, Ch2Case3Menu.ascx and Ch2Case3Footer.ascx. In the Ch2Case3Header.ascx control, add a banner graphic. Create a menu in the Ch2Case3Menu.ascx user control that lists at least five product categories. Each category listing should contain a hyperlink to the category home page. In the Ch2Case3Footer.ascx control, add the store address, and a hyperlink to the store home page. Within each page, register the three controls, and insert them into the page. Format each page using additional graphics, content, fonts, and color to enhance the appearance of the page. You may change the name of the store. View each Web page in your browser. Print each Web page and the source code from the browser.

Customizing the Visual Studio .NET Desktop

You need to customize your desktop within Visual Studio .NET so that you will be able to more efficiently locate resources that you will commonly use. Create an HTML page named Ch2Case4.htm. Create a form on the page with at least five form fields. Set a default value for the name and id properties for each field. You can select which additional properties you would like to modify. For example, the default property for a text box name might be txtName. Customize the toolbar. Add a new tab with your name. Create an HTML fragment on the General tab in the toolbox that contains one of the form fields from the WebForm. Rename the HTML fragment according to the name of the form field. With the custom tab displayed, capture a screen shot of your desktop by using the Print Screen key. Open WordPad. Paste the screen shot into WordPad. Press Ctrl+V to paste the screen shot, or go to the Edit menu in WordPad and select Paste. Print the screen shot and the Ch2Case4.htm page.

Locate Help Using the Built-in Resources

As project manager you need to customize Visual Studio .NET for all the programmers. Your Web pages will be used by the other programmers to learn how to customize Visual Studio .NET. You also have to provide training for your programmers so that they know how they can customize the development environment. To do this, you need more information about customizing the user interface. Use Dynamic Help, Contents, Index, Search, and the Start Page to locate information on three of the following topics listed below.

❑ Customizing the Toolbox

❑ Setting Properties using the Properties Window

❑ Customizing the Toolbox

❑ Docking Windows

❑ Modifying the Start Page

❑ Customizing the User Interface

❑ The Clipboard Ring

Create three Web pages, named Ch2Case5Topic1.aspx, Ch2Case5Topic2.aspx, and Ch2Case5Topic3.aspx. Provide a summary of the information you learned about the topics you researched. In your Web page, provide step-by-step instructions how to customize the development environment. Modify the presentation of the pages using the toolbars, Toolbox, and properties window. View each Web page in your browser. Print each Web page and the source code from the browser.

Creating a Form with Visual Studio .NET

You are responsible for developing a survey for your Web site. Develop a survey that uses multiple choice questions, true and false questions, short answer and open-ended questions. Use Visual Studio .NET to create the form in an ASP.NET page named Ch2Case6.aspx. The form should consist of questions that use text boxes, radio buttons, check boxes, drop-down lists, and command buttons. Add hyperlinks and images to the Web page. Modify the presentation of the page using the toolbars, Toolbox, and properties window. View the Web page in your browser. Print the Web page and the source code from the browser.

3

USING SERVER CONTROLS

In this chapter, you will:

♦ Create Web pages using HTML Server controls and ASP.NET controls

♦ Examine the difference between HTML Server controls and ASP.NET controls

♦ Create and process a form using HTML Server controls

♦ Create and process a form using a ASP.NET Server controls

♦ Populate form field controls dynamically using ArrayLists and HashTables

♦ Populate a list control dynamically using ArrayLists and HashTable

♦ Validate a form using Validation controls.

One of the responsibilities of a Web developer is to create and process WebForms. In the past, WebForms were created using HTML, and processed and validated using client-side JavaScript. However, forms processed using client-side JavaScript are not secure because they can be easily altered before the form is submitted by the user. Also, client-side JavaScript is browser dependent. Today, most WebForms are validated on the Web server, which is both more secure and browser independent.

In this chapter, you will learn to use HTML Server controls and ASP.NET controls to create, process, and validate WebForms. You will create form fields that can be changed dynamically by using data structures such as ArrayLists and HashTables.

USING HTML SERVER CONTROLS

As you learned in Chapter 1, the two types of server controls are HTML Server controls and ASP.NET Server controls. HTML Server controls are HTML controls that are converted to Server controls by setting the runat attribute to "server". HTML Server controls generate the HTML controls that are sent to the browser. In Visual Studio .NET, all of the Web page HTML Server controls and ASP.NET controls are objects on the Web server. **Object-oriented programming** allows you to use objects, which can be accessed by other programs, including Web pages. An **object** is a set of related methods and properties that are compartmentalized. **Properties** are used to set the value of a variable defined within an object. You change the values of the properties of the Web Server objects by using the Properties window in Visual Studio .NET.

All HTML Server controls inherit from the same HTMLControl class, which is known as `System.Web.UI.HTMLControl`. So, all HTML Server controls inherit the same properties and methods from the HTMLControl class. For example, all HTML Server controls inherit a property called ID. The ID property is used to identify the control within server programs. The ID property is also used to generate the ID for the HTML control on the client. All HTML Server controls also inherit a property called Visible. All HTML Server controls are visible by default because the Visible property is True by default. The **Visible property** is a Boolean value that indicates whether a Server control is rendered as an HTML control on the page. Another commonly used property is the Style property. The Style property retrieves a collection of all cascading style sheet (CSS) rules applied to a specified HTML Server control. The Style property can be configured by using a cascading style sheet, or by using the Style Builder. You can access the Style Builder for a specific control by using the pop-up menu or the Properties window. The ToString method returns the value of the object in the form of a string. If, for example, a text box contains a value, you can use the ToString method to write out that value in a browser. Although each HTML Server control inherits these properties, each type of HTML Server control has additional properties specific to that control.

The properties and methods common to all HTML Server controls can be found in the Visual Studio .NET online documentation for the HTMLControl class.

All that's required to turn any HTML element into a Server control is the addition of the extra attribute runat="server". This attribute enables the server to recognize the control as a Server control. One of the most cumbersome tasks when creating interactive Web sites and applications is managing the values passed to the server from HTML Form controls, and maintaining the values in these controls between page requests. So one of the core aims of ASP.NET is to simplify this programming task. This involves no extra effort on the part of the programmer, and works on all browsers that support basic HTML and above. You can access the properties of Server controls by using server programs. In plain HTML, it is difficult for the server to retain the values and properties of the HTML control across page requests. With HTML Server controls, the state of the control can be maintained using ASP.NET.

The four main groups of HTML Server controls are the HTMLImage, HTMLContainer, HTMLGeneric, and HTMLInput controls. The **HTMLImage control** is used to represent simple images and returns an image tag. The **HTMLContainer control** group represents tags that can contain other elements and that must have a closing tag. HTMLContainer controls create HTML controls such as the italic, bold, and div tags. The **HTMLGeneric control** is used for other HTML elements not listed in the HTMLControls such as the DIV and SPAN tags. The **HTMLInput control** group retrieves information from the user. For example, the HTMLInputText generates a text box in a form. Table 3-1 lists the HTML controls and the HTMLControl class that it inherits.

Table 3-1 HTMLControls Generate Client HTML Controls

Control Name	Inherits from this Class	HTML Generated
HtmlAnchor	HTMLContainerControl	`<a href="page.aspx" runat="server">`
HtmlButton	HTMLContainerControl	`<button runat="server">`
HtmlSelect	HTMLContainerControl	`<select runat="server">`
HtmlTextArea	HTMLContainerControl	`<textarea runat="server">`
HtmlInputButton	HTMLInputControl	`<input type="button" runat="server">`
HtmlInputCheckBox	HTMLInputControl	`<input type="check" runat="server">`
HtmlInputRadioButton	HTMLInputControl	`<input type="radio" runat="server">`
HtmlInputText	HTMLInputControl	`<input type="text" runat="server">` and `<input type="password" runat="server">`
HtmlInputHidden	HTMLInputControl	`<input type="hidden" runat="server">`
HtmlInputImage	HTMLInputControl	`<input type="image" runat="server">`
HtmlInputFile	HTMLInputControl	`<input type="file" runat="server">`
HtmlForm	HTMLContainerControl	`<form runat="server">`
HtmlImage	HTMLImage	`<img src="page.jpg" runat="server">`
HtmlTable	HTMLContainerControl	`<table runat="server">`
HtmlTableRow	HTMLContainerControl	`<tr runat="server">`
HtmlTableCell	HTMLContainerControl	`<td runat="server">`
HtmlGenericControl	HTMLContainerControl	Any other unmapped tag, such as `<span runat="server">`, `<div runat="server">`, etc.

HTML Control Server Event Handlers

Web developers have used client-side scripting to interact with the user. JavaScript, cascading style sheets are used in combination to create Dynamic HTML (DHTML). DHTML allows you to interact with the user when he or she completes a form, or click a hyperlink. There are various levels of browser support for JavaScript. There are many different types of platforms that are now Web enabled. With Server controls, you do not have to write the client-side script. Rather, you write the code to configure the properties and events of the Server controls. By using a server-side control, you generate output that is supported by the client. If the client's browser supports JavaScript and DHTML, the output is generated using JavaScript and DHTML. Events such as the form validation could be performed on the client. If not, then the output is HTML, and events such as form field validation are performed on the server.

When the control in the browser detects an event, such as a mouse click, the browser can respond to the event by using an event handler, which executes code statements when the event occurs. HTML Server control events include OnServerChange and OnServerClick. The **OnServerChange event** occurs when an HTML Server control value has changed. The HTML Server controls that support the OnServerChange event are HTMLInputCheckBox, HTMLInputRadio, HTMLInputHidden, HTMLInputText, HTMLTextArea, and HTMLSelect. The **OnServerClick event** occurs when the visitor clicks an HTML Server control. The HTML controls that support the OnServerClick event include HTMLInputImage, HTMLAnchor, HTMLButton, and HTMLForm.

Visual Studio .NET Help provides information about all of the HTML Server controls. This information can be accessed within Visual Studio .NET or via a browser. For example, the HTMLImage control Help information is located at *ms-help://MS.VSCC/MS.MSDNVS/cpref/html/frlrfsystemwebuihtmlcontrols htmlimageclasstopic.htm*. There is a tutorial on server-side events in the Help documentation located at *ms-help://MS.VSCC/MS.MSDNVS/csref/html/ vcwlkEventsTutorial.htm*. The Help files contain the members, properties, and events for each HTML Server control. At the end of the chapter is a listing of the documentation on the HTML Server controls and ASP.NET controls within Visual Studio .NET.

Client- and server-side event handlers can sometimes conflict with each other. For example, if you create a hyperlink tag using an HTML Server control, the output created is a simple anchor tag. If there is a client-script such as mouseover, and the user points at the hyperlink, the mouseover event occurs. If the user clicks the hyperlink, the server click event handler is executed. However, if the anchor tag contains both a server-side click event handler and a client-side event handler, an autogenerated client-side script intercepts the click event and directs the handler to the server-side click event handler. The client-side click event handler is ignored.

The HTML Server controls generate the HTML control, as well as JavaScript to capture the events on the client, including the onchange and onclick events. In the sample code below, the input text box captures the onchange event and calls the JavaScript function _doPostBack. A **function** is a named grouping of one or more programming statements. This JavaScript function only occurs once in the page, no matter how many controls are used. This function is used to pass information to the server. The Web page contains two hidden fields, named _EVENTTARGET and _EVENTARGUMENT, that are used to determine which control called the function and what parameters were passed with the control. Then, the client-side script calls the submit method to submit the form to the server. Note that, although these events are called HTML Server control events, they do require the client to capture the initial event and call the function. They are called HTML Server control events because the event is processed, or handled, by the server event handler, and not by the client event handler.

```
<input name="WebAddress" type="text" id="WebAddress"
    onchange="__doPostBack('WebAddress','')"
    language="javascript" />
<input type="submit" name="GoBtn" value="Go" id="GoBtn" />
<input type="hidden" name="__EVENTTARGET" value="" />
<input type="hidden" name="__EVENTARGUMENT" value="" />
<script language="javascript">
<!--
function __doPostBack(eventTarget, eventArgument) {
    var theform = document.ctrl0;
    theform.__EVENTTARGET.value = eventTarget;
    theform.__EVENTARGUMENT.value = eventArgument;
    theform.submit();
}
// -->
</script>
```

In the following exercise, you will create an ASP.NET page that uses HTML Server controls to dynamically change the contents of the page. You will add Image controls and HTML Server Button and Label controls to the Web page. Because the Layout property is already set to Grid Layout, you will be able to position your controls absolutely, by dragging and dropping the controls onto the Web page. The HTML Server Button control creates the HTML code equivalent to the input tag with the Type property set to button. The Label control creates a DIV tag within the Web page. You will use Visual Basic .NET code to change the properties of the Label controls.

1. Start **Visual Studio .NET**.

2. Click **File** on the menu bar, point to **New**, then click **Project** to open the New Project window.

3. In the Project Types pane, click **Visual Basic Projects**. In the Templates pane, click the **ASP.NET Web Application** icon. Change the text in the

location text box to **http://localhost/Chapter3**. Click **OK** to create the solution, project, and default files.

4. To add a folder, right-click the project name, point to **Add**, then click **New Folder**. Type **images** as the folder name, and then press **Enter**.

5. Right-click the images folder, point to **Add**, and then click **Add Existing Item**. Browse to locate the Chapter03Data folder. (*Note*: In the Files of type drop-down list box, you must change the selection from Common VB files to **Image Files**.)

6. Select all from the files in the Chapter03Data\images folder. (*Note*: In some versions of Windows, you can also use the Ctrl+A key combination to select all of the files.) Click the **Open** button to import the images into the images directory of the Chapter3 project. (*Note*: You can collapse the list of files in your Solution Explorer window by clicking the minus sign in front of the images folder.)

7. Right-click the project, point to **Add**, then click **Add WebForm**. Type **HTMLButton.aspx** to name the WebForm, and then click the **Open** button.

8. To add the header graphic, drag the **header.jpg** graphic in the images folder and drop the image at the top of the page. Click the **Style** property in the Properties window. Click the **Style Builder** button, which is a button with three dots. The Style Builder window opens. Click the **Position** tab. Make sure that the Top and Left properties are both set to **0**. Click **OK**.

9. To add the menu graphic, drag and drop the **menu.jpg** graphic from the images folder and to the left side of the page. Click the **Style** property in the Properties window. Click the **Style Builder** button. Click the **Position** tab. Make sure that the Top and Left properties are set to **85** and **17** respectively. Click **OK**.

10. To add the main graphic, drag and drop the **waterfordgifts.jpg** graphic from the images folder to the left side of the page. Click the **Style** property in the Properties window. Click the **Style Builder** button. Click the **Position** tab. Make sure that the Top and Left properties are set to **38** and **134** respectively. (*Note*: The Z-Index order value may vary. You do not need to change this number.) Click **OK**.

11. Click the **HTML** tab in the Toolbox. Drag and drop the **Label** from the Toolbox to the page. Right-click the control, and then select **Run As Server Control**. In the Properties window, change the Label (ID) property to **lblTitle**. Click the **Style** property and the **Style Builder** button. Change the Font Family to **'Trebuchet MS'** and the Font Size to **15 pt**. Go to the position tab and change the position to top: **243**, left: **139**, height: **26**, and width: **365**. Click **OK**. Click inside the Label control and delete the word **Label**.

3

12. Drag and drop the **Button** control from the HTML tab to the page. Right-click the control, and then select **Run As Server Control**. In the Properties window, change the (ID) property to **btnMale** and the value to **Male**. Open the **Style Builder** and change the position to top: **274**, left: **138**, height: **27**, and width: **89**. Click **OK**.

13. From the Toolbox, drag and drop the **Button** control from the HTML tab to the page. Right-click the control, and then click **Run As Server Control**. In the Properties window, change the Label (ID) property to **btnFemale** and the value to **Female**. Open the **Style Builder** and change the position to top: **310**, left: **138**, height: **27**, and width: **89**. Click **OK**.

14. Drag and drop the **Label** control from the HTML tab to the page. Right-click the control, and then click **Run As Server Control**. In the Properties window, change the (ID) property to **lblGiftIdeasWomen**. Click the **Style** property and the **Style Builder** button. Change the Font Family to **'Trebuchet MS'** and the Font Size to **12 pt**. Change the position to top: **275**, left: **235**, height: **210**, and width: **250**. Click **OK**.

15. Click inside the label you just created. Delete the default text within the Label control. Add the following text in the control, placing each item on a separate line: **Make-Up Brush**, **Tyrone Bell**, **Butterfly**, **Balmoral Vase**, **Abbey Clock**, **Heart Shaped Ring Holder**, **Wellsley Picture**. Then, select all of the items and click the **Bullets** icon on the Formatting toolbar to change the list into a bulleted list.

16. Drag and drop the **Label** control from the HTML tab to the page. Right-click the control and click **Run As Server Control**. In the Properties window, change the (ID) property to **lblGiftIdeasMen**. Click the **Style** property and the **Style Builder** button. Change the Font Family to **'Trebuchet MS'** and the Font Size to **12 pt**. Change the position to top: **275**, left: **500**, height: **210**, and width: **250**. Click **OK**.

17. Click inside the label you just created and delete the default text. Add the following text in the control, placing each item on a separate line: **Golf Ball**, **Golf Club**, **Male Golfer**, **Letter Opener**, **Business Card Holder**, **Shamrock Paperweight**. Then, select all of the items and click the **Bullets** icon on the Formatting toolbar to change the list into a bulleted list. Click outside of the Label control.

18. To move the label that you just created onto another label, you need to change the Position properties. Click the label, then click the **Style** property and the **Style Builder** button. Change the left position to **235**. Click the **OK** button. (*Note*: Do not reposition the label by dragging and dropping the label on top of another label. You may inadvertently place the label within the other label.)

19. Click the **Save All** button.

You have created the WebForm and added the HTML controls. In the following steps, you will add the code that will hide the two Label controls when the page loads. Then, you will add code to create two buttons. When you click one button, one of the labels will be visible. When you click the second button, the second label will be visible.

1. Double-click somewhere on the page, other than on a control. The file containing the code behind the page, called HTMLButton.aspx.vb, opens. Add the code below within the Page_Load event handler. This code changes the Visible property for the two Label controls to false. When the page loads, these controls will not be seen by the visitor.

```
lblGiftIdeasMen.Visible = False
lblGiftIdeasWomen.Visible = False
```

2. Click the **HTMLButton.aspx** page tab to return to the Design page. Double-click the **Male** button to return to the code behind the page. This action also inserts a server click event handler for the Male button. Add the code below to this new event handler. This code changes the message within the title label and shows the lblMale Label control, which contains the list of recommended products for male customers. (*Note*: Do note break the string across two lines. All strings must be typed on a single line.)

```
lblTitle.InnerHtml = ¬
"<b>We have lots of gift ideas for men.</b>"
lblGiftIdeasWomen.Visible = False
lblGiftIdeasMen.Visible = True
```

3. Click the **HTMLButton.aspx** page tab to return to the Design page. Double-click the **Female** button to return you to the code behind the page. This action also inserts a server click event handler for the Female button. Add the code listed below to this new event handler. This code changes the message within the title label and shows the lblFemale Label control, which contains the list of recommended products for female customers.

```
lblTitle.InnerHtml = ¬
"<b>We have lots of gift ideas for women.</b>"
lblGiftIdeasWomen.Visible = True
lblGiftIdeasMen.Visible = False
```

4. Click the **Save All** button. Click **Build** on the menu bar, then click **Build Solution**.

5. Click the **HTMLButton.aspx** page tab to return to the Design page. Right-click the page, and then click **View in Browser**. Click the **Male** and **Female** buttons to see the contents of the labels change. Figure 3-1 shows how the page looks after you click to the Male button.

6. Close the Browser page, the HTMLButton page, and the code behind the page (HTMLButton.aspx.vb).

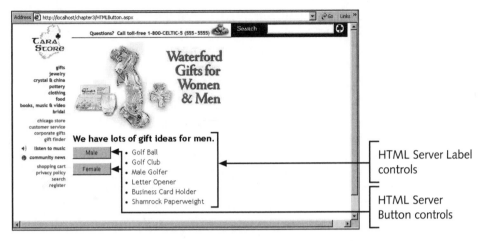

Figure 3-1   HTML Server Button and Label controls on a WebForm

HTML Server Button Controls

There are many kinds of HTML controls that can be added to a Web page. Some controls, such as text boxes and check boxes, are used to obtain information from the user. Some controls, such as buttons, are used to provide a means for the visitor to interact with the Web page. When the user clicks a button, you can capture the button click event and create a response. The response may be to change the properties of the button, such as hiding the button, or to change the message on the button. You can also change the properties of another control.

The properties of individual controls can be changed via the Properties window. You can also change the properties of individual controls by adding code to the code behind the page. You can change the property when the page loads, or when an event occurs, such as a button click. In order to access the HTML controls, you must set the runat attribute to server. Then, the code behind the page will be aware of the HTML control. You can set the property in the HTML view or by selecting Run As Server Control in the controls pop-up menu.

You can add new pages to a Web site. You can also import an existing Web page into a project. Visual Studio .NET will create the code behind the page that is associated with the Web page. Visual Studio .NET refers to the code behind the page as a class file. The page is an object that is derived from the class code within the code behind the page. Therefore, after you import a Web page, you will have to build your solution before you can view the Web page in the browser.

The properties are not always the same for HTML Server controls and ASP.NET Server controls. You can change the values of the Label controls by using the Properties window. Two properties often used to assign the value of an HTML Server Label control are **InnerHTML** and **InnerText**. However, in ASP.NET controls, the property that changes the value of the Server Label controls is **text**.)

In the following exercise, you will insert several buttons that change the properties of a control when the button is clicked. The Image button creates the HTML code that uses the button tag. The button tag is not supported in all browsers. You will also use the Input Button control to create an image input button. In the following exercise you will create an ASP.NET page that uses HTML Server controls to create and process a registration form.

1. Right-click **Chapter3** in the Solution Explorer window, point to **Add**, and then click **Add Existing Item**. Click the **Browse** button and navigate to the Chapter03Data folder. Select **All Files** in the Files of type drop-down list box. Select **HTMLImageButton.aspx**, and then click **Open**. The following pop-up message appears: "There is no class file in the project associated with the Web Form 'HTMLImageButton.aspx'. Create a new class file now?" Click **Yes**.

2. Double-click the **HTMLImageButton.aspx** file to open it.

3. Drag and drop the **Button** control from the HTML tab to the left of the lblGiftIdeasMen label.

4. Right-click on the control, and then select **Run As Server Control**. In the Properties window, change the Label (ID) and Name properties to **btnMale**.

5. Note that the property sheet does not allow you to change the type of the button, and that there is no Image Button control on the HTML tab in the Toolbox. Click the **HTML** tab to view the HTML code. Change the code for the control from type = "button" to **type= "image"**. Click the **Design** tab to return to Design view. Additional properties appear in the Properties window for the Image Button control. Change the src property to **images/Male.gif**.

6. Click the **Style Builder** in the Properties window, and change the position to top: **280**, left: **150**. Click the **OK** button.

7. Drag and drop the **Button** control from the HTML tab to below the Male Image Input button. Right-click the control, and then click **Run As Server Control**. In the Properties window, change the (ID) and Name properties to **btnFemale**.

8. Click the **HTML** tab to view the HTML code. Change the code for the control from type = "button" to **type= "image"**. Click the **Design** tab to return to Design view. Additional properties appear in the Properties window for the Image Button control. Change the src property to **images/Female.gif**.

9. Click the **Style Builder** in the Properties window, and change the position to top: **315**, left: **150**. Click **OK**.

10. Drag and drop the **Image** control from the HTML tab to below the Menu.gif image. Right-click the control and click **Run As Server Control**.

3

In the Properties window, change the (ID) and Name properties to **imgLogo**. Change the src property to **images/logo.gif**.

11. Click the **Style Builder** in the Properties window, and change the position to top: **390**, left: **40**. Click **OK**.

12. Double-click the **Male** button to open the code behind the page. In the click event handler type the following code to change the title label contents and show the label with the gift ideas for men.

```
lblTitle.InnerHtml = ¬
"<b>We have lots of gift ideas for men.</b>"
lblGiftIdeasWomen.Visible = False
lblGiftIdeasMen.Visible = True
```

13. Click the **HTMLImageButton.aspx** tab to return to the Web page. Double-click the **Female** button. In the click event handler type the following code to change the title label contents and show the label with the gift ideas for women.

```
lblTitle.InnerHtml = ¬
"<b>We have lots of gift ideas for woman.</b>"
lblGiftIdeasWomen.Visible = True
lblGiftIdeasMen.Visible = False
```

14. Click the **Save All** button. Go to the **Build** menu and click **Build Solution**. Right-click the page, and then click **View in Browser**. Click the **Male** and **Female** buttons. Close each of the pages you created.

You can add HTML Form controls within a WebForm. The Form controls can be added from the HTML tab or the WebForms tab. However, the Form controls from the HTML tab are generic HTML controls. WebForm controls have additional properties that are not available with HTML controls. You can create server code that will interact with HTML control events—for example, when the user clicks on a button. You must configure the form field to be a Server control in order for you to create server code that will interact with the HTML Form control. You can modify the properties of the form fields. In the activity below you can hide the Help button if the help text field is visible. You can also get the values of form fields, and perform calculations, or evaluate their contents. For example, the code can detect if the username and password match a predefined string. The strings are always case sensitive, which means that you must type the values as they are shown. If the user is not authenticated, a message instructing him or her to click on the Help button is displayed in the label, and the Help button is made visible.

When you have code that is very long, you can use an underscore to split the code across multiple lines. It is important not to break the contents of a string across multiple lines unless each string is contained within its own pair of quotation marks, and the string is concantenated. Concantenation is the process of putting together two or more expressions. The ampersand (&) is used to separate the concatenated expressions.

In the following exercise you add HTML Form controls to a Web page. You will add input and password text boxes, and Submit, Reset, and Help buttons. When the Help button is displayed, a label appears with a helpful message, as shown in Figure 3-2. When the user is authenticated, the title label displays a message to the user.

Figure 3-2   HTML Form controls

1. Right-click **Chapter3** in the Solution Explorer window, point to **Add**, and then click **Add Existing Item**. Navigate to the Chapter03Data folder. Select the file **HTMLInputButton.aspx**, and then click **Open**. The following pop-up message appears: "There is no class file in the project associated with the Web Form 'HTMLInputButton.aspx'. Create a new class file now?" Click **Yes**.

2. Double-click the file **HTMLInputButton.aspx** to open it.

3. Drag and drop the **Text Field** control from the HTML tab in the Toolbox to the left of the Username label. Right-click the control, and then click **Run As Server Control**. In the Properties window, change the (ID) and Name properties to **txtUsername**. Click the **Style** property and the **Style Builder** button. In the Position tab, change the position to top: **280**, left: **145**. Click **OK**.

4. Drag and drop the **Text Field** control from the HTML tab to the left of the Password label. Right-click the control, and then click **Run As Server Control**. In the Properties window, change the Label (ID) and Name properties to **txtPassword**. Click the **Style** property and the **Style Builder** button. In the Position tab, change the position to top: **310**, left: **145**. Click the **OK** button.

5. Drag and drop the **Submit Button** control from the HTML tab to below the Password control. Right-click the control, and then select **Run As Server Control**. In the Properties window, change the Label (ID) and Name properties to **btnSubmit**. Change the Value property to **Sign In**. Click the

Style property and the Style Builder button. In the Position tab, change the position to top: 345, left: 150. Click the OK button.

6. Drag and drop the Reset Button control from the HTML tab to below the Password control. Right-click the control, and then click Run As Server Control. In the Properties window, change the (ID) and Name properties to btnReset. Click the Style property and the Style Builder button. In the Position tab, change the position to top: 345, left: 230. Click OK.

7. Drag and drop the Button control from the HTML tab to below the Password control. Right-click the control, and then select Run As Server Control. In the Properties window, change the (ID) and Name properties to btnHelp. Change the Value property to Help. Click the Style property and the Style Builder button. In the Position tab, change the position to top: 345, left: 450. Click OK.

8. Right-click on the page, and then select View Code. In the Page_Load event handler, type the code below where the comment stipulates. This code assigns the default message using the InnerHTML property, and hides the Help button and the Help label.

```
lblTitle.InnerHtml = ¬
"Please log into our Customer Support Area."
lblHelp.Visible = False
btnHelp.Visible = "Help"
```

9. Click the HTMLInputButton.aspx page to return to the Design view. Double-click the Sign In Submit button. In the Sign In Server Click event handler, type the code below. This code hides the Help button if it's visible. If the user is not authenticated, a message instructing him or her to click on the Help button is displayed in the label, and the Help button is made visible.

```
lblHelp.Visible = False
If ((txtUsername.Value = "Course") And _
(txtPassword.Value = "Technology")) Then
    lblTitle.InnerHtml = "You are authenticated!"
Else
    lblTitle.InnerHtml = _
    "Please click on the Help button for help!"
    txtUsername.Value = ""
    txtPassword.Value = ""
    btnHelp.Visible = True
End If
```

10. Click the HTMLInputButton.aspx tab to return to the page. Double-click the Reset button. Do not enter any code in this click event handler.

11. Click the **HTMLInputButton.aspx** tab to return to the page. Double-click the **Help** button. Enter the following code, which displays the Help label.

```
lblTitle.InnerHtml = ¬
"Please log into our Customer Support Area."
lblHelp.Visible = True
btnHelp.Visible = False
```

12. Click the **HTMLInputButton.aspx** tab to return to the Web page. Click the **Save All** icon. Go to the **Build** menu and select **Build Solution**. Right-click the page, and then select **View in Browser**. Close each of the pages you created.

Hyperlinks and Form Fields

Hyperlinks allow you to create links to other pages or to internal targets within the same page. Check boxes, radio buttons, and drop-down lists are form fields that allow you to select from lists of options. The difference between check boxes and radio buttons is that you can only select one option from a group of radio buttons. Therefore, the radio button group must all be identified with a single name. (*Note:* You will learn how to process check boxes with ASP.NET controls later in this chapter.)

Creating a Web Page with Radio Button Controls

1. Right-click **Chapter3** in the Solution Explorer window, point to **Add**, and then click **Add Existing Item**. Navigate to the Chapter03Data folder. Select the file **HTMLRadioButton.aspx**, and then click **Open**. The following pop-up message appears: "There is no class file in the project associated with the Web Form 'HTMLRadioButton.aspx'. Create a new class file now?" Click **Yes**.

2. Double-click the file **HTMLRadioButton.aspx** to open it.

3. Drag and drop the **Radio Button** control from the HTML tab to below the existing radio buttons. Right-click the control, and then select **Run As Server Control**. In the Properties window, change the Label (ID) to **rdBridal** and the Name property to **category**. The Checked property should be **False**. Click the **Style** property and the **Style Builder** button. In the Position tab change the position to top: **383**, left: **310**. Click **OK**.

4. Double-click the **Search** button. Type the following code, which determines which radio button is checked.

```
If (rdBridal.Checked = True) Then
    lblTitle.InnerHtml = "Celebrate Your Wedding!"
    imgTop.Src = "images/28.jpg"
ElseIf (rdBooks.Checked = True) Then
    lblTitle.InnerHtml = ¬
"Your Favorite Irish Book Selections!"
    imgTop.Src = "images/27.jpg"
```

```
ElseIf (rdClothing.Checked = True) Then
    lblTitle.InnerHtml = "Traditional Irish Clothing!"
    imgTop.Src = "images/26.jpg"
ElseIf (rdFood.Checked = True) Then
    lblTitle.InnerHtml = ¬
"Traditional Irish Food Products!"
    imgTop.Src = "images/25.jpg"
ElseIf (rdPottery.Checked = True) Then
    lblTitle.InnerHtml = ¬
"New Pottery from Belinda Bradshaw!"
    imgTop.Src = "images/24.jpg"
ElseIf (rdCrystal.Checked = True) Then
    lblTitle.InnerHtml = ¬
"Quality Crystal & Traditional China!"
    imgTop.Src = "images/23.jpg"
ElseIf (rdJewelry.Checked = True) Then
    lblTitle.InnerHtml = ¬
"Quality Jewelry at Affordable Prices!"
    imgTop.Src = "images/22.jpg"
ElseIf (rdGifts.Checked = True) Then
    lblTitle.InnerHtml = ¬
"Let us help you find the best gift!"
    imgTop.Src = "images/21.jpg"
End If
```

5. Click the **HTMLRadioButton.aspx** tab to return to the Web page. Click the **Save All** icon. Go to the Build menu and select **Build Solution**. Right-click the page and select **View in Browser**. The page should look like the one shown in Figure 3-3. Close each of the pages you created.

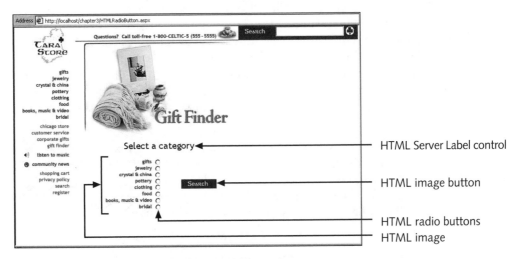

Figure 3-3   HTML Radio Button controls

Creating a Page with a Drop-down List Control

In the following exercise, you will create a drop-down list box using the HTML Server controls. You will also populate the control using HTML code, and dynamically add items to the list using server-side programming.

HTML Drop-down List controls are created with the HTML Select tag. Option tags are used to create each individual item in the list. A value can be associated with each item in the list. The value of the item does not have to match the displayed text of the item. For example, sometimes your username is displayed, but not your ID number. The ID number is used as the value, and would be passed to the server when the form was submitted. You can obtain information about the option selected by using the SelectedIndex property of the drop-down list box. When nothing has been selected the SelectedIndex property returns the value -1.

With Server Drop-down List controls, you can add items dynamically to the Drop-down List control, or add them through the Properties window. The add method allows you to add items to the list dynamically when the page loads, or when an event occurs. Each Drop-down and List control contains an Items collection with properties and methods. The add method adds an item to the Items collection. You might use the ServerChange event to detect a change in the drop-down list. If the user chooses the first option on the list, which is checked by default, there is no change, and the page is redisplayed. Otherwise, the new list is displayed along with a graphic, and the old list is removed. The contents of the drop-down list are cleared before new items are added, because the user may repeat the exercise and select the other option. In some cases this results in the items being appended to the list instead of replacing the items in the list. It's useful to clear the items from the list anytime you are beginning a list.

In this example, you will use the isPostBack Page property to determine if the user has visited the page before. This is the Boolean value that is set to true when the user has visited the page. The_doPostBack function is created by ASP.NET to handle events that must be returned to the Web server. For example, if the user clicks a button, the server click event is handled on the server. But, you need to pass the object that called the event and any parameters to the server. The isPostBack property will be able to recognize the visitor based upon the _ViewState and the information obtained from the _doPostBack function.

1. Right-click **Chapter3** in the Solution Explorer window, point to **Add**, then click **Add Existing Item**. Navigate to the Chapter03Data folder. Select **HTMLSelect.aspx**, and then click **Open**. The following pop-up message appears: "There is no class file in the project associated with the Web Form 'HTMLSelect.aspx'. Create a new class file now?" Click **Yes**.

2. Double-click the file **HTMLSelect.aspx** to open it.

3. Drag and drop the **Dropdown** control from the HTML tab to the left of the picture frame. Right-click the control, and then click **Run As Server**

3

Control. In the Properties window, change the (ID) and Name to **CatList**. Click the **Style** property and the **Style Builder** button. In the Position tab change the position to top: **320**, left: **150**. Click **OK**.

4. Click the **HTML** tab and find the default pair of Option tags (<OPTION selected></OPTION>) associated with the CatList control. Enter **Select a Main Category** as the text displayed for the option. Click the **Design** tab to return to Design view. (Note: The Drop-down List control is displayed on top of the picture from image. When you view the page in a browser, the picture frame image is not displayed while the Drop-down List control is displayed.)

5. Drag and drop the **Dropdown** control from the HTML tab to the left of the Submit button. Right-click on the control, and then click **Run As Server Control**. In the Properties window, change the (ID) and Name to **ProductList**. Click the **Style** property and the **Style Builder** button. In the Position tab change the position to top: **320**, left: **350**. Click **OK**.

6. Double-click the page. In the Page_Load event handler type the code below, which displays the drop-down list. Notice that the add method allows you to add items to the list dynamically. Each Drop-down and List control contains an Items collection with properties and methods. The add method adds an item to the Items collection.

```
If (Not IsPostBack) Then
    lblTitle.InnerHtml() = ¬
"Select the gender of the gift recipient."
    imgProduct.Visible = False
    ProductList.Visible = False
    CatList.Items.Add("Gifts for Men")
    CatList.Items.Add("Gifts for Women")
End If
```

7. After the Page_Load event handler, type the code below, which determines which selection the user makes from the CatList drop-down list box, and displays the new drop-down list box.

```
Sub CatList_ServerChange(ByVal sender As System.Object, ¬
    ByVal e As System.EventArgs) ¬
Handles CatList.ServerChange
    CatList.Visible = False
    btnSubmit.Visible = False
    ProductList.Visible = True
    imgProduct.Visible = True
    ProductList.Items.Clear()
    If CatList.Value = "Gifts for Men" Then
        lblTitle.InnerHtml() = _
        "We have lots of gift ideas for men."
        ProductList.Items.Clear()
        ProductList.Items.Add("Golf Ball")
        ProductList.Items.Add("Golf Club")
```

```
        ProductList.Items.Add("Male Golfer")
        ProductList.Items.Add("Letter Opener")
        ProductList.Items.Add("Business Card Holder")
        ProductList.Items.Add("Shamrock")
        ProductList.Items.Add("Paperweight")
    Else
        lblTitle.InnerHtml() = _
        "We have lots of gift ideas for women."
        ProductList.Items.Clear()
        ProductList.Items.Add("Makeup Brush")
        ProductList.Items.Add("Tyrone Bell")
        ProductList.Items.Add("Butterfly")
        ProductList.Items.Add("Balmoral Vase")
        ProductList.Items.Add("Abbey Clock")
        ProductList.Items.Add("Heart-shaped Ring Holder")
        ProductList.Items.Add("Wellsley Picture Frame")
    End If
End Sub
```

8. Click the **HTMLSelect.aspx** tab to return to the Web page. Click the **Save All** icon. Click **Build** on the menu bar, then click **Build Solution**. Right-click the page, and then select **View in Browser**. The drop-down list should look like the one in Figure 3-4. Close each of the pages you created.

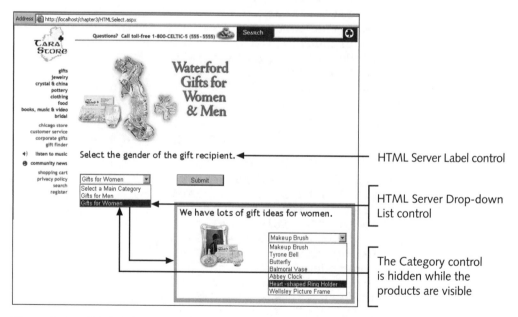

Figure 3-4   HTML Select controls

3

Creating a Page with a Hyperlink Control

In this final HTML Server control exercise, you will add several hyperlinks to a Web page. The hyperlinks can act as anchor tags and redirect the visitor to a new page, using the URL property. You can use a relative or absolute URL. You can set the URL property of the hyperlink dynamically when the page loads, or in one of your functions or procedures. You can also capture the click from the hyperlink and initiate the click event handler for the hyperlink.

1. Right-click **Chapter3** in the Solution Explorer window, point to **Add**, and then click **Add Existing Item**. Navigate to the Chapter03Data folder. Select the files **GiftsForWomen.aspx**, **GiftsForMen.aspx**, and **HTMLAnchor.aspx**, and then click **Open**. An alert box appears for each of these three files. Click **Yes** to create a new class file for each.

2. Double-click the file **HTMLAnchor.aspx** to open it. Note that there is no Hyperlink control in the HTML Toolbox. You need to insert the link for each piece of text.

3. Click in the **Male** label and select the word **Male**. Click **Insert** on the menu bar, and then click **Hyperlink**. Type the URL **http://www.tarastore.com** in the text box. (*Note*: http:// has already been entered for you.) Click **OK**. Right-click the control, and then select **Run As Server Control**. Click the **Male Hyperlink** control, then in the Properties window, change the (ID) and Name property to **AMale**.

4. Click in the **Female** label and select the word **Female**. Click **Insert** on the menu bar, and then click **Hyperlink**. Type the URL **http://www.tarastore.com** in the text box. Click **OK**. Right-click the control, and then click **Run As Server Control**. Click the **Female Hyperlink** control, then in the Properties window, change the Label ID and name to **AFemale**.

5. Click in the **Tara Store Home Page** label and select the words **Tara Store Home Page**. Click **Insert** on the menu bar, and then click **Hyperlink**. Type the URL **http://www.tarastore.com** in the text box. Click **OK**. Right-click the control, and then click **Run As Server Control**. In the Properties window, change the Label (ID) and Name to **AHome**.

6. Double-click on the page. In the Page_Load event handler, type the code below, which changes the href properties of the hyperlinks and hides the label that displays the sale items.

```
AMale.HRef = "GiftsForMen.aspx"
AFemale.HRef = "GiftsForWomen.aspx"
AHome.HRef = "http://www.tarastore.com"
```

 If IntelliSense displays the URL in blue and underlined, along with a message indicating that href is not a member of the control group, ignore it. Href is a valid property of the anchor tag.

7. Click the **HTMLAnchor.aspx** tab to return to the Web page. Click the **Save All** icon. Click **Build** on the menu bar, and then click **Build Solution**. Right-click the page, and then select **View in Browser**. The page should appear as shown in Figure 3-5. Close each of the pages you created.

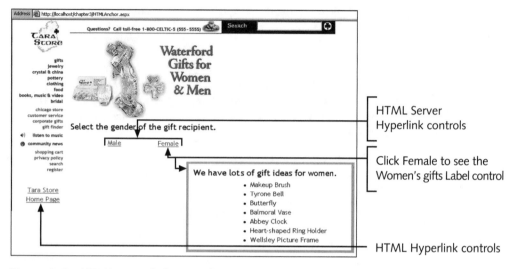

Figure 3-5   HTML Hyperlink controls

USING ASP.NET WEBFORM CONTROLS

The ASP.NET controls are located on the WebForms tab in the Toolbox. The ASP.NET WebForms inherit from the **Web control class** which is found in the `System.Web.UI.WebControls` namespace. ASP.NET controls are similar to HTML Server controls, but they support additional properties, methods, and events. ASP.NET controls generate the necessary HTML and DHTML, which is supported by the client. ASP.NET controls can be grouped into WebForm controls, Rich controls, Data controls, Validation controls, and Mobile controls. In this section you will learn about WebForm controls.

Dynamically assigning properties and calling methods to WebForm controls is different from calling HTML Server control properties. For example, to change the text displayed in an HTML Server Label control, you set the InnerHTML property. To change the text value for the ASP.NET label, you set the Text property. If you assign a property to the Label control you can simply assign the value using a string. However, if you assign the value dynamically, using programming code, you must be careful how you assign the value to the property. For example, the Color properties must be assigned using a different syntax. Color is an object that inherits its properties from the System.Drawing.Color namespace. So, to retrieve a color, you have to directly or indirectly inherit from the Color namespace.

You can assign the value by the known color name, a 32-bit value, a hexadecimal value, or property of an object. In the following sample code, the BorderColor property is assigned Green. Green is one of the known colors that you can refer to by name.

```
MyControl.BorderColor = System.Drawing.Color.Green
```

You can select the property using the known color name, such as Green, or from a value from another object. The following sample code shows how to assign the color value from the text box or form.

```
MyControl.BackColor = Color.FromName(txtBackColor.Value)
```

Some of the properties of ASP.NET controls require a numeric value. You cannot simply assign the numeric value dynamically; ASP.NET requires that you use a new object, known as a unit. The unit class represents numeric values for the properties of other objects. You need to use the keyword New to create the Unit object, and then pass the numeric value to the class. In the following example, you can assign the BorderWidth property using the Unit object.

```
MyBtn.BorderWidth = New Unit(4)
```

Drop-down Lists and Image Controls

In the following WebForm Server control exercise, you will add a drop-down list to a Web page, and dynamically add the options to the list when the page first loads. You will also add the code to retrieve the value of the item the user clicked.

In this exercise, you will change the property of an Image control. The WebForm Image control class produces an <img> tag to display an image on the Web page. This control only displays an image. If you need to capture mouse clicks on the image, you use the ImageButton control. The ImageURL property provides the path to the image by creating the **SRC property** for the IMG tag. The AlternateText property provides the text that is displayed when the image is not available, or when the user places the pointer over the image. The **AlternateText property** generates the ALT property in the HTML tag. The **ImageAlign property** provides the Image Alignment property.

1. Right-click the project, point to Add, and then click **Add Existing Item**. **Browse** Navigate to the Chapter03Data folder. Select **ASPSelect.aspx** within the Chapter03Data folder. The following pop-up message appears: "There is no class file in the project associated with the Web Form 'ASPSelect.aspx'. Create a new class file now?" Click **Yes**.

2. Double-click the file **ASPSelect.aspx** to open it.

3. Drag and drop the **DropDownList** control from the WebForms tab in the Toolbox to the left of the Select a Category button. Change the (ID) property to **dlCategory**. Change the Height property to **25** and Width property to **155**.

4. Double-click on the page. In the Page_Load event handler, enter the code below to add the items to the drop-down list box. The code checks whether the user has visited the page before by using the IsPostback property. In this example, you only add the items to the control the first time the control is created.

```
If (Not IsPostBack) Then
    dlCategory.Items.Add("Gifts")
    dlCategory.Items.Add("Jewelry")
    dlCategory.Items.Add("China and Crystal")
    dlCategory.Items.Add("Pottery")
    dlCategory.Items.Add("Clothing")
    dlCategory.Items.Add("Food")
    dlCategory.Items.Add("Books, Music, and Video")
    dlCategory.Items.Add("Bridal")
End If
```

5. Click the file **ASPSelect.aspx** tab to return to the Web page. Double-click the **Submit** button (labeled Select a Category) to display the click event handler. Add the code below to determine which value the user selected from the drop-down list, and change the Source property for the Image control.

```
Select Case dlCategory.SelectedIndex
    Case 0
        lblTitle.Text = _
        "Let us help you find the best gift!"
        imgTop.ImageUrl = "images/21.jpg"
    Case 1
        lblTitle.Text = _
        "Quality Jewely at Affordable Prices!"
        imgTop.ImageUrl = "images/22.jpg"
    Case 2
        lblTitle.Text = _
        "Quality Crystal & Traditional China!"
        imgTop.ImageUrl = "images/23.jpg"
    Case 3
        lblTitle.Text = _
        "New Pottery from Belinda Bradshaw!"
        imgTop.ImageUrl = "images/24.jpg"
    Case 4
        lblTitle.Text = _
        "Traditional Irish Clothing!"
        imgTop.ImageUrl = "images/26.jpg"
    Case 5
        lblTitle.Text = _
        "Traditional Irish Food Products!"
        imgTop.ImageUrl = "images/25.jpg"
    Case 6
        lblTitle.Text = _
        "Our Favorite Irish Book Selections!"
        imgTop.ImageUrl = "images/27.jpg"
```

```
Case 7
    lblTitle.Text = _
    "Celebrate Your Wedding!"
    imgTop.ImageUrl = "images/28.jpg"
Case Else
    lblTitle.Text = _
    "Select a Product Category"
    imgTop.ImageUrl = "images/WaterfordGifts.jpg"
End Select
```

6. Click the **ASPSelect.aspx** tab to return to the Web page. Click the **Save All** icon. Click **Build** on the menu bar, then click **Build Solution**. Right-click the page, and then click **View in Browser**. The page should appear as shown in Figure 3-6. Close each of the pages you created.

Figure 3-6   Drop-down lists using ASP.NET Server controls

Panel, Placeholder, and Literal Controls

There are many similarities between HTML Server and ASP.NET controls. However, there are new ASP.NET controls that are not available as HTML Server controls. This section discusses some of these new controls, specifically the Panel, Placeholder, and Literal controls.

The **Panel control** can contain other controls and creates a DIV tag to enclose the contents. You can set properties such as wrapping, absolute positioning, font type, and scroll bars. For example, if you want to add some text to a panel, simply add a Label control within the panel tags or enter the text directly into the panel. The Label control creates contents within a Panel control using the SPAN tag. You use the Text property to display text in a Label control. You can also use a **Literal control** to write content directly to the page. Literal controls are often used to add client-side HTML and text to the page.

1. Right-click **Chapter3** in the Solution Explorer window, point to **Add**, and then click **Add Existing Item**. Navigate to the Chapter03Data folder. Select the file **ASPpanel.aspx**, and then click **Open**. The following pop-up message appears: "There is no class file in the project associated with the Web Form 'ASPpanel.aspx'. Create a new class file now?" Click **Yes**.

2. Double-click the file **ASPpanel.aspx** to open it.

3. Drag and drop the **Panel** control from the WebForms tab in the Toolbox to below the Community News graphic. Change the (ID) property to **PanelAboutNews**. Change the Height property to **180** and Width property to **235**. Change the ForeColor to **Teal**. You can click the drop-down list arrow and select the color. It is the fifth color in the sixth column in the Custom tab. Click on the **plus sign** next to the Font property to expand the Font properties. Change the Name to **Trebuchet MS**. Change the Size property to **X-Small**.

4. Click inside the panel, delete the word **Panel**, and type the following paragraphs: **"Please sign up for our Tara Store eBulletin for future updates. Editorial contributors wanted. Do you have a passion for Irish culture? A flair for writing? Tara Store is currently seeking individuals with experience in journalism and/or editing to contribute to our Community News section."** Add a blank line by pressing **Enter**, and then add this sentence: **"Please contact co-owner Katie Kalata for additional information at info@TaraStore.com."**

5. Click the **Save All** icon. Click **Build** on the menu bar, then click **Build Solution**. Right-click on the page, and then click **View in Browser**. Your page should appear as shown in Figure 3-7. Close each of the pages you created.

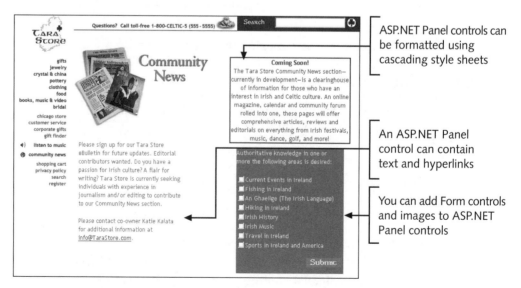

Figure 3-7   ASP.NET Panel control

The Placeholder control inherits from the control class. The **Placeholder control** is used as a container to store dynamically added Server controls. The Placeholder control does not produce any visible output without the use of other controls. To add, insert, or remove a control from the Placeholder control, you can use the controls class of the control namespace. To do this, you must know how to use the constructor to create a control dynamically. For example, say you create and initialize a new instance of the button class. This won't display anything. You have to add it to the Controls Property collection of the Placeholder class. Then, it will display the control in its place, and format the Button properties.

In the example below, you will dynamically create a HyperLink control. The HyperLink control is used to create an anchor tag that can link to another page or a target by using the ImageURL property. The displayed text is configured using the Text property. The Text property also becomes the ToolTip by default. The **ToolTip** is a new property that is used to display a message when the user places the pointer over the object. Notice that the image hyperlink does not have to be any specific size, color, or font. You can change the Target property of the hyperlink. The **target** is the window or frame used to load the Web page linked to when the HyperLink control is clicked. The default value for the target is String.Empty. You can change the target to any named window, or one of the reserved window names. The named window must begin with a letter in the range of a through z and is case sensitive. The reserved windows are as follows:

- *_New*—renders the content in a new window
- *_blank*—renders the content in a new window without frames
- *_parent*—renders the content in the immediate frameset parent
- *_self*—renders the content in the frame with focus
- *_top*—renders the content in the full window without frames

In the example below you will dynamically create a HyperLink control using the Placeholder control.

1. Right-click **Chapter3** in the Solution Explorer window, point to **Add**, and then click **Add Existing Item**. Navigate to the Chapter03Data folder. Select **ASPPlaceholder.aspx**, and then click **Open**. The following pop-up message appears: "There is no class file in the project associated with the Web Form 'ASPPlaceholder.aspx'. Create a new class file now?" Click **Yes**.

2. Double-click the file **ASPPlaceholder.aspx** to open it.

3. Drag and drop the **Placeholder** control from the WebForms tab in the Toolbox directly onto the empty Label control. Change the (ID) property to **placeholder**.

4. Double-click the page to open the code behind the page. Add the following code to the Page_Load procedure to dynamically create a label and place the label within the placeholder.

```
' Create a label to contain text
Dim MyLabel As New Label()
placeholder.Controls.Add(MyLabel)
MyLabel.Text = "Please select one or more topics"
MyLabel.ForeColor = ¬
System.Drawing.Color.FromName("#004040")
MyLabel.Font.Name = "Trebuchet MS"
MyLabel.Font.Size = MyLabel.Font.Size.Smaller
MyLabel.ID = "lblMessage"
```

5. Below the code above, add the following code to dynamically create a Literal control and place the controls within the Placeholder control. The Literal control writes out line breaks using the <br /> tag.

```
' Create HTML controls using the Literal Control class
Dim MyLiteralBR As New Literal()
placeholder.Controls.Add(MyLiteralBR)
MyLiteralBR.Text = "<br /><br />"
```

6. Below the code above, add the following code to dynamically create a HyperLink control. Assign the properties of the HyperLink control and place the control within the placeholder.

```
' Create a hyperlink
Dim MyLink As New HyperLink()
placeholder.Controls.Add(MyLink)
MyLink.Text = ¬
"Click here to go to <br /> the Tara Store home page"
MyLink.ForeColor = ¬
System.Drawing.Color.FromName("#004040")
MyLink.Font.Name = "Trebuchet MS"
MyLink.Font.Size = MyLabel.Font.Size.Smaller
MyLink.ID = "HLHome"
MyLink.NavigateUrl = "http://www.tarastore.com"
MyLink.Target = "_new"
```

7. Below the code above, add the following code to dynamically create a Literal control and place the controls within the Placeholder control. The Literal control writes out line breaks using the <br/ > tag, and place the controls within the placeholder. Notice that because there is already one Literal control, you must declare the control with a different name because each control must be uniquely identified by its ID property.

```
' Create HTML controls using the Literal Control class
Dim MyLiteralBR2 As New Literal()
placeholder.Controls.Add(MyLiteralBR2)
MyLiteralBR2.Text = "<br /><br />"
```

8. Add the following code to dynamically create an Image Hyperlink control. Assign the properties of the Image Hyperlink control and place the control within the placeholder.

```
' Create an image hyperlink
Dim MyImageLink As New HyperLink()
placeholder.Controls.Add(MyImageLink)
MyImageLink.Text = ¬
"Click here to go to the Tara Store home page"
MyImageLink.ForeColor = ¬
System.Drawing.Color.FromName("#004040")
MyImageLink.Font.Name = "Trebuchet MS"
MyImageLink.Font.Size = MyLabel.Font.Size.Smaller
MyImageLink.ImageUrl = "images/logo.gif"
MyImageLink.ID = "HLHome"
MyImageLink.NavigateUrl = "http://www.tarastore.com"
MyImageLink.Target = "_new"
```

9. Click the **ASPPlaceholder.aspx** tab to return to the Web page. Click the **Save All** icon. Click **Build** on the menu bar, then click **Build Solution**. Right-click the page, and then click **View in Browser**. Your page should appear as shown in Figure 3-8. (*Note:* The check boxes do not work yet. You will learn to work with check boxes in the next activity.) Close each of the pages you created.

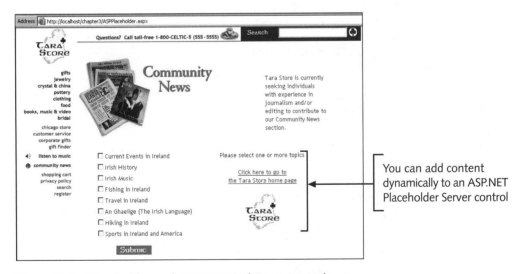

Figure 3-8   Placeholder and ASP.NET WebForm controls

Working with Checkboxes

You previously learned how to process a form using HTML Server control radio buttons. In this exercise, you will learn how to work with check boxes using ASP.NET

CheckBox control. The control has some additional properties to help you format the check boxes and retrieve the values.

1. Right-click **Chapter3** in the Solution Explorer window, point to **Add**, and then click **Add Existing Item**. Navigate to the Chapter03Data folder. Select **ASPCheckbox.aspx**, and then click **Open**. The following pop-up message appears: "There is no class file in the project associated with the Web Form 'ASPCheckbox.aspx'. Create a new class file now?" Click **Yes**.

2. Double-click the file **ASPCheckbox.aspx** to open it.

3. Drag and drop the **CheckBox** control from the WebForms tab in the Toolbox to directly beneath the Hiking in Ireland CheckBox control. Change the (ID) property to **CB8**. Change the Text property to **Sports in Ireland**. Change the ForeColor to **#004040**. You can enter the value in the drop-down list box. Click the **plus sign** next to the Font property to expand the Font properties. Change the name to **Trebuchet MS**. Change the Size to **X-Small**.

4. Double-click the **Submit** button to go to the click event in the code behind the page. Add the following code to the click event procedure to determine which check boxes were clicked, and write the results to the string.

```
Dim MyMessage As String
MyMessage = "<b>You selected:</b><br /><br />"
If CB1.Checked Then
    MyMessage += CB1.Text & "<br />"
End If
If CB2.Checked Then
    MyMessage += CB2.Text & "<br />"
End If
If CB3.Checked Then
    MyMessage += CB3.Text & "<br />"
End If
If CB4.Checked Then
    MyMessage += CB4.Text & "<br />"
End If
If CB5.Checked Then
    MyMessage += CB5.Text & "<br />"
End If
If CB6.Checked Then
    MyMessage += CB6.Text & "<br />"
End If
If CB7.Checked Then
    MyMessage += CB7.Text & "<br />"
End If
If CB8.Checked Then
    MyMessage += CB8.Text & "<br />"
End If
MyMessage += "<br /><b>Thank you.</b>"
lblTopics.Text = MyMessage.ToString()
```

5. Click the **ASPCheckbox.aspx** tab to return to the Web page. Click the **Save All** icon. Click **Build** on the menu bar, then click **Build Solution**. Right-click the page, and then click **View in Browser**. Close each of the pages you created.

USING VALIDATION CONTROLS

There are five built-in ASP.NET Validation controls. All five controls can be added to your ASP.NET page using the WebForms tab on the Toolbox. The five validation controls are:

- *RequiredFieldValidator*—Makes sure a form field is not left blank

- *RangeValidator*—Makes sure a field's value falls within a given range

- *CompareValidator*—Compares field's value with other values or other fields' values

- *RegularExpressionValidator*—Evaluates data against a regular expression

- *CustomValidator*—Evaluates data against custom criteria

The Validation controls inherit from the BaseValidator class, which inherits from the label class. Therefore, Validation controls can display custom error messages using labels. They all support common properties and methods such as ForeColor. The **ForeColor property** sets the color of the error message. The default ForeColor property is red. Validation controls that perform comparisons also inherit from the BaseCompareValidator base class, and therefore inherit additional properties.

One of the common properties of all Validation controls is display. When the Display property is set to dynamic, space for the validation message is dynamically added to the page if validation fails. The Validation control is inserted into the page and assigned to a hidden field. The error message takes up space in the page, which can offset your HTML elements. If the display is set to static then space for the validation message is allocated in the page layout. If the validation does not fail, then no message is sent to the browser. However, the space for the message is still reserved on the page. If the display is set to none, then the validation message is never displayed in the browser.

Each of the controls inherits the validate method which performs validation on the associated Input control and updates the IsValid property. The IsValid property indicates whether the control that is being validated is valid. The sample below shows how you can check if the entire page is valid at the same time by calling the `Page.Validate` method and then using the `Page.IsValid` property.

```
Page.Validate()
If Page.IsValid Then
    Message.Text = "Result: Valid!"
Else
```

```
        Message.Text = "Result: Not valid!"
    End If
End Sub
```

The **RequiredFieldValidator control** is used to determine if any value is entered or selected. The **ControlToValidate property** specifies the Input control to validate. This control can be combined with other controls, for further validation. For example, this control can detect whether you typed in a number for your credit card, but would not apply any rules to see if the number is valid.

The **RangeValidator control** checks whether the value of an Input control is within a specified range of values. In addition to the ControlToValidate property, you must assign the **MinimumValue** and **MaximumValue properties** to specify the minimum and maximum values of the valid range. Then, the value entered in the field is compared against these two values. The values may be any valid data type. The Type property is used to specify the data type of the values to compare. The values to compare are converted to this data type before the validation operation is performed. The following list shows the different data types that can be compared.

- *String*—A string data type

- *Integer*—An integer data type

- *Double*—A double data type

- *Date*—A date data type

- *Currency*—A currency data type

The **CompareValidator control** inherits from the BaseCompareValidator class. This Validation control compares the value entered by the user into an Input control, such as a text box, with the value entered into another Input control, or with a constant value. You must specify the Input control to validate by setting the ControlToValidate property. If you want to compare a specific Input control with another Input control, set the **ControlToCompare property** to specify the comparison control. If you want to compare the Input control with a constant value, you can specify the constant value with the **ValueToCompare property**. You must use the Operator property to specify the type of comparison to perform between the Input control and the CompareToControl or ValueToControl.

The **RegularExpressionValidator control** inherits from BaseCompareValidator class. This control checks whether the value of an Input control matches a pattern defined by a regular expression. A regular expression can be used to check for predictable sequences of characters, such as those in Social Security numbers, e-mail addresses, telephone numbers, and postal codes.

3

 Make sure the clientTarget property is set to downlevel. Also, it's important to note that the validation will succeed if the Input control is empty. Therefore, you should use the RequiredFieldValidator in conjunction with this control.

You can set the validation to occur on the client, if the client supports JScript, or on the server. If the validation occurs on the client, then JScript regular expression syntax is used. If the validation occurs on the server, then, the `System.Text.RegularExpressions.Regex` syntax is used. Since the JScript regular expression syntax is a subset of `System.Text.RegularExpressions.Regex` syntax, it is recommended that you use the JScript regular expression syntax in order to obtain the same results on both the client and the server.

You must provide the ValidationExpression property to compare the Input control to the regular expression. There are several basic regular expressions already built in to Visual Studio .NET. A global RegExp object is used for creating pattern-matching expressions called regular expressions. The regular expression pattern is stored in the Pattern property of the RegExp object. You can construct a regular expression by putting the various components of the expression pattern between a pair of delimiters. In JScript, the delimiters are a pair of forward slash (/) characters. The components of a regular expression can be individual characters, sets of characters, ranges of characters, choices between characters, or any combination. Below is a listing of some common regular expressions that are included with Visual Studio .NET.

- *Social Security Number*—/\d{2}-\d{5}/
- *Internet E-Mail Address*—\w+([-+.]\w+)*@\w+([-.]\w+)*\.\w+([-.]\w+)*
- *Internet URL*—http://([\w-]+\.)+[\w-]+(/[\w- ./?%&=]*)?
- *US Phone*—((\(\d{3}\) ?)|(\d{3}-))?\d{3}-\d{4}
- *US Zip Code*—\d{5}(-\d{4})?
- *Phone Number*—\d{3}-\d{2}-\d{4}

The **ValidationSummary control** is used to summarize the error messages from all validators on a Web page, in one location. Like other Validation controls, the ValidationSummary class inherits properties and methods from the WebControl class. The ValidationSummary control has additional properties such as the DisplayMode, ShowSummary, ShowMessageBox, and HeaderText. This ValidationSummary can display the summary as a list, a bulleted list, or a single paragraph by setting the **DisplayMode property** to BulletList, List, or SingleParagraph. The **ShowSummary property** shows the entire list of error messages from invalid controls. You can display an additional message in an alert box by setting **ShowMessageBox property**. The **HeaderText property** allows you to display a heading message. The other validation properties, such as the ForeColor property, still apply to the ValidationSummary control. You can format the validation summary list and the error messages.

If none of these Validation controls is applicable to your form field, you can create your own validation functions on the client or server using the **CustomValidator control**. When you use Visual Studio .NET to validate your forms, you don't have to write the client-side scripts. The benefit of using the Validation controls is that the single control works for multiple browsers. Even if you select client-side validation, the data is still validated on the server.

Validate Form Data

The following exercise demonstrates how to add required field and regular expression Validation controls to a Web page.

1. Right-click **Chapter3** in the Solution Explorer window, point to **Add**, and then select **Add Existing Item**. Navigate to the Chapter03Data folder. Select **ASPValidateForm.aspx**, and then click **Open**. The following message appears: "There is no class file in the project associated with the Web Form 'ASPValidateForm.aspx'. Create a new class file now?" Click **Yes**.

2. Double-click the file **ASPValidateForm.aspx** to open it.

3. Drag and drop the **RequiredFieldValidator** control from the WebForms tab in the Toolbox to the left of the lblFirstName label. Change the (ID) property to **ValRFirstName**. Change the ControlToValidate property to **txtFirstName**. Verify that the Display property is **static** and that the ForeColor property is **Red**. Change the ErrorMessage to *****.

4. Drag and drop the **RegularExpressionValidator** control from the WebForms tab in the Toolbox to below the E-mail Address label. Change the (ID) property to **ValREPhone**. Change the ControlToValidate property to **txtPhone**. Change the Font Name property to **Trebuchet MS** and the Size property to **X-Small**. Verify that the Display is **static** and the ForeColor property is **Red**. Change the ErrorMessage to **Please submit the phone number as (999) 999-9999**. Click the **ValidationExpression Build** icon in the Properties window, and from the Regular Expression Editor select **U.S. Phone Number**, and then click **OK**. Change the Height property to **34px** and the Width property to **166px**.

5. Click the **Save All** button. Click **Build** on the menu bar, then click **Build Solution**. Right-click the page, and then click **View in Browser**. Your page should appear as shown in Figure 3-9. Close each of the pages you created.

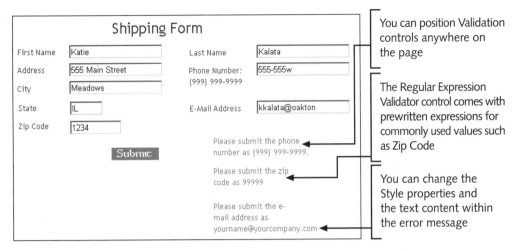

Figure 3-9   Using a Validation control to validate form field data

The following exercise demonstrates how to add a Validation Summary control to a Web page. The individual error messages are not displayed, because the individual Validation controls have the Display property set to none. The ShowMessageBox property is set to true, which displays an alert box with the error messages in the newer browsers.

1. Right-click **Chapter3** in the Solution Explorer window, point to **Add**, and then click **Add Existing Item**. Navigate to your Chapter03Data folder. Select **ASPValidationSummary.aspx**, and then click **Open**. The following pop-up message appears: "There is no class file in the project associated with the Web Form 'ASPValidationSummary.aspx'. Create a new class file now?" Click **Yes**.

2. Double-click the file **ASPValidationSummary.aspx** to open it.

3. Drag and drop the **ValidationSummary** control from the WebForms tab in the Toolbox to below the Submit button. Change the (ID) property to **ValSummary**. Change the DisplayMode property to **List** and verify that ShowSummary is **True**. Change the ShowMessageBox to **True** and the HeaderText property to **"You have one or more errors that must be corrected. Please resubmit the form."** Change the Height to **41px** and Width to **346px**. Change the Font Name property to **Trebuchet MS** and the Size to **X-Small**.

4. Click the **Save All** button. Click **Build** on the menu bar, then click **Build Solution**. Right-click the page, and then click **View in Browser**. Your page should appear as shown in Figure 3-10. Close each of the pages you created.

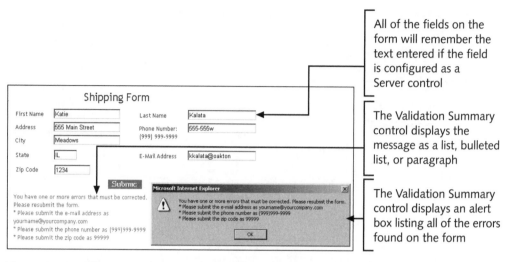

Figure 3-10   The ASP.NET Summary Validation control

BINDING TO SIMPLE DATA

Visual Studio .NET makes it easy to bind Form controls to data sources. In a later chapter, you will learn how to bind controls to databases such as Access, SQL Server, and Oracle. In this section, you will learn how to bind data from ArrayLists and HashTables.

Binding RadioButtonLists to ArrayLists

In the example below, you will bind the data from an ArrayList to an ASP.NET RadioButtonList control. **RadioButtonList controls** allow you to group a series of one or more radio buttons. You can easily bind the RadioButtonList to several types of data sources such as ArrayLists, HashTables, and databases. By grouping them together in a single control, you can set the properties for the entire group. For example, you can set the **RepeatDirection property** so that the group is displayed horizontally or vertically. You can specify the **RepeatLayout property**, which will group the list using a table or using paragraph tags.

The System.Array class is the base class of all array types. The **ArrayList** is a type of array whose size dynamically increases as required. The ArrayList is declared using the keyword dim, the name of the array, and the keyword new. The Capacity property is the number of items the list can hold. As items are added to an ArrayList, the capacity is automatically increased as required through reallocation. You must pass the number of items in the array as a parameter when the array is first created. The ArrayList is **zero-based**, which means that the counting of items in the ArrayList starts at 0 and not 1. If the **Capacity property** is explicitly set to zero, the CLR sets the Capacity property to a default capacity of 16. The **Count property** determines the number of items that are actually in the ArrayList. You can add items to the ArrayList by using the add method of the Items collection, which is the collection that belongs to the ArrayList object for storing the items.

In the example below, you will create a simple ArrayList that will populate a RadioButtonList control, as shown in Figure 3-11. After creating the RadioButtonList control and the ArrayList object, you must assign the ArrayList object to the RadioButtonList control by using the DataSource property. Then, you need to bind the data to the control by using the DataBind method of the RadioButtonList control. You can also bind all the controls on a Web page by using the DataBind property of the Page object.

1. Right-click **Chapter3** in the Solution Explorer window, point to **Add**, and then click **Add Existing Item**. Navigate to the Chapter03Data folder. Select **ASPDBRadioButtonList.aspx** within the Chapter03Data folder and click **Open**. The following pop-up message appears: "There is no class file in the project associated with the Web Form 'ASPDBRadioButtonList.aspx'. Create a new class file now?" Click **Yes**.

2. Double-click the file **ASPDBRadioButtonList.aspx** to open it.

3. Drag and drop the **RadioButtonList** control from the WebForms tab in the Toolbox to the inside of the empty Panel control. Change the (ID) property to **RBL**. Verify that the AutoPostback property is **False**. Change the Font Name property to **Trebuchet MS**, the Size to **X-Small**, and the ForeColor to **#004040**. Verify that the RepeatDirection is set to **Vertical** and the RepeatLayout property is set to **Table**.

4. Double-click the page to open the code behind the page. Add the following code to the Page_Load procedure to check if the page is being loaded for the first time using the IsPostBack property. Then set the RadioButtonList properties. Declare the array that contains the category. Add each category to the array. Then, assign the array to the DataSource property and bind the data to the RadioButtonList by using the DataBind method.

```
If Not Page.IsPostBack Then
    RBL.RepeatLayout = RepeatLayout.Table
    RBL.RepeatDirection = RepeatDirection.Vertical
    Dim AR1 As New ArrayList(9)
    AR1.Add("Current Events in Ireland")
    AR1.Add("Fishing in Ireland")
    AR1.Add("An Ghaeilge (The Irish Language)")
    AR1.Add("Hiking in Ireland")
    AR1.Add("Irish History")
    AR1.Add("Irish Music")
    AR1.Add("Irish Step and Set Dancing")
    AR1.Add("Travel in Ireland")
    AR1.Add("Sports in Ireland")
    RBL.DataSource = AR1
    RBL.DataBind()
End If
```

5. Click the **ASPDBRadioButtonList.aspx** tab to return to the Web page.

6. Double-click the **Submit** button to view the submit click procedure in the code behind the page. Add the code below, which determines which element is selected with the SelectedItem object. The SelectedItem object contains a value and Text property. Assign the Text property to a variable, which is used to change the Text property of the Label control.

```
Dim strResult As String
strResult = "<b>You selected: </b><br /><br />"
If RBL.SelectedIndex > -1 Then
    strResult += RBL.SelectedItem.Text
End If
lblTopics.Text = strResult
```

7. Click the **ASPDBRadioButtonList.aspx** tab to return to the Web page. Click the **Save All** button. Click **Build** on the menu bar, then click **Build Solution**. Right-click on the page, and then click **View in Browser**. Your page should appear as shown in Figure 3-11. Close each of the pages you created.

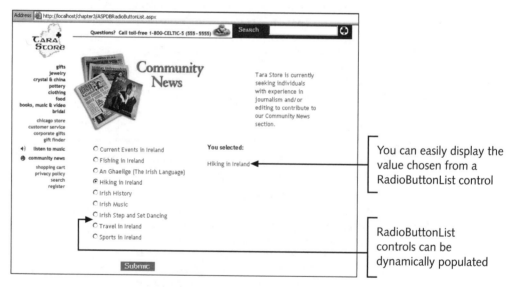

Figure 3-11   The ASP.NET RadioButtonList control

Binding CheckBoxLists to HashTables

In the following example you will bind the data from a HashTable to an ASP.NET CheckBoxList control. **CheckBoxList controls** allow you to group a series of one or more CheckBox controls. You can easily bind the CheckBoxList to almost several types of data sources such as ArrayLists, HashTables, and databases. By grouping them together in a single control, you can set the properties for the entire group. For example, you can set the **RepeatDirection property** so that the group is displayed horizontally or vertically. You can specify the **RepeatLayout property**, which will group the list using a table or using paragraph tags.

In the steps below, you create a simple HashTable that populates a CheckBoxList control. You can create a HashTable by declaring the object using the keyword dim, the name of the HashTable, and the keyword new. You do not need to identify the number of items in the HashTable. You can add items to the HashTable by using the add method of the HashTable object to store the items. The items are added using a key and value pair. You can use the key in your programming to retrieve the value for a particular item. Because you have a key and value pair, you must specify the key and value using the **DataTextField** and **DataValueField properties**. The DataValueField is used to create the value for the control, and the DataTextField is used to create the text displayed for the control.

1. Right-click **Chapter3** in the Solution Explorer window, point to **Add**, and then select **Add Existing Item**. Navigate to the Chapter03Data folder. Select **ASPDBCheckboxList.aspx**, and then click **Open**. A pop-up message will appear stating that "There is no class file in the project associated with the Web Form 'ASPDBCheckboxList.aspx'. Create a new class file now?" Click **Yes**.

2. Double-click the file **ASPDBCheckboxList.aspx** to open it.

3. Drag and drop the **CheckboxList** control from the WebForms tab to the inside of the empty Panel control. Change the (ID) property to **CBL**. Verify that the AutoPostback property is **False**. Change the Font Name property to **Trebuchet MS**, the Size to **X-Small**, and the ForeColor to **#004040**. Verify that the RepeatDirection is set to **Vertical** and the RepeatLayout property is set to **Table**.

4. Double-click the page to open the code behind the page. Add the following code to the Page_Load procedure to check if the page is being loaded for the first time using the IsPostBack property. Then set the CheckboxList properties. Declare the HashTable, which contains the category key and value. Add each pair of key and values to the HashTable and specify the DataTextField and DataValueField properties. Then, assign the HashTable to the DataSource property and bind the data to the CheckboxList by using the DataBind method.

```
If Not Page.IsPostBack Then
    Dim HS1 As New HashTable(9)
    HS1.Add("Current Events in Ireland", ¬
"Current Events in Ireland")
    HS1.Add("Fishing in Ireland", "Fishing in Ireland")
    HS1.Add("An Ghaeilge (The Irish Language)",
"An Ghaeilge (The Irish Language)")
    HS1.Add("Hiking in Ireland", "Hiking in Ireland")
```

```
      HS1.Add("Irish History", "Irish History")
      HS1.Add("Irish Music", "Irish Music")
      HS1.Add("Irish Step and Set Dancing", ¬ "Irish Step
and Set Dancing")
      HS1.Add("Travel in Ireland", "Travel in Ireland")
      HS1.Add("Sports in Ireland", "Sports in Ireland")
      CBL.DataSource = HS1
      CBL.DataTextField = "Value"
      CBL.DataValueField = "Key"
      CBL.DataBind()
  End If
```

5. Click the **ASPDBCheckboxList.aspx** tab to return to the Web page.

6. Double-click the **Submit** button to view the submit click procedure in the code behind the page. Add the code below, which determines which items are selected by using the Selected property. The Selected property indicates if the item was selected. However, because you can have multiple items selected, you must loop through each control in the list and read the Selected property for each control. Then, you can assign the Text property of that control to a variable, which will be used to change the Text property of the Label control.

```
' This determines if any item was ¬
selected CBL.SelectedIndex > -1
' This will get the number of items ¬
in the list CBL.Items.Count
Dim strResult As String
If CBL.SelectedIndex > -1 Then
    strResult = ¬
"You selected the following categories:<br /><br />"
    Dim i As Integer
    For i = 0 To CBL.Items.Count - 1
        If CBL.Items(i).Selected Then
        strResult += CBL.Items(i).Text + "<br />"
    End If
  Next
Else
  strResult = "You did not select a category."
End If
lblTopics.Text = strResult
```

7. Click the **ASPDBCheckboxList.aspx** tab to return to the Web page. Click the **Save All** button. Click **Build** on the menu bar, then click **Build Solution**. Right-click the page, and then click **View in Browser**. Your page should appear as shown in Figure 3-12. Close each of the pages you created.

8. Exit Visual Studio .NET by clicking **File** on the menu bar, and then clicking **Exit**.

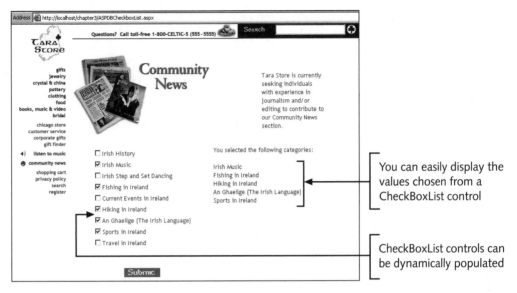

You can easily display the values chosen from a CheckBoxList control

CheckBoxList controls can be dynamically populated

Figure 3-12   The ASP.NET CheckBoxList control

CHAPTER SUMMARY

❑ Visual Studio .NET allows you to create Web pages using HTML controls, HTML Server controls and ASP.NET controls. In order to use HTML Server controls or ASP.NET controls, you must save your page as an ASP.NET page. You can only use HTML controls when creating a basic HTML page.

❑ HTML Server controls are HTML controls where the runat attribute has been set to server. Because the server is aware of the control, you can create server code to manipulate the control's properties and values. ASP.NET controls are Server controls by default. The server will generate the output required by the browser to view and interact with the ASP.NET control.

❑ Both HTML Server controls and ASP.NET controls are used to build forms. Forms are used to collect information from the user, and to increase interactivity with the user. Both HTML Server controls and ASP.NET controls support text boxes, radio buttons, and check boxes. However, ASP.NET controls include collections of radio buttons and check boxes called RadioButtonLists and CheckBoxLists.

❑ There are many other types of controls such as HyperLink, Panel, and Placeholder controls. You can modify the contents and properties of these controls by using the Properties window, or dynamically through the code behind the page.

❑ Validation controls are a form of ASP.NET controls that allow you to assign validation rules to other controls. You can build custom validation rules to validate your form fields, or use one of the prepackaged form field Validation controls.

❏ Server controls can be modified programmatically. Some controls, such as simple lists and drop down lists, can be populated programmatically using arrays ArrayLists and HashTables.

REVIEW QUESTIONS

1. A(n) _____ is a set of related procedures and properties that are compartmentalized.
   a. object
   b. control
   c. method
   d. function

2. Which class is inherited by the HTMLControl class?
   a. System.Web.UI.HTMLControl
   b. System.Web.HTMLControl
   c. System.UI.WebControl
   d. System.HTML.UI.Control

3. Which property is used to uniquely identify the Server controls?
   a. ID
   b. Name
   c. GUID
   d. Style

4. What are the possible values of the Visible property?
   a. True
   b. False
   c. Visible
   d. a and b

5. Which HTMLControl is used to create hyperlink?
   a. HTMLAnchor
   b. HTMLTarget
   c. HTMLHyperlink
   d. HTMLImageLink

6. Which events does the HTMLControls object intercept?
   a. ServerChange
   b. ServerClick

    c. MouseClick

    d. a and b

7. What is the name of the function that is created by the server event handlers?

    a. _PostBack

    b. _doPostBack

    c. _EVENTTARGET

    d. _EVENTARGUMENT

8. What property is used to change the text displayed by an HTML Label control?

    a. Text

    b. InnerHTML

    c. DisplayMode

    d. OuterText

9. What must you do to change an HTML control into an HTML Server control?

    a. Add runat = "server" in the control tag

    b. Right-click the control and select Run As Server Control

    c. Type "server" in the runat property in the Properties window

    d. a and b

10. What does the Build Solution command do?

    a. opens the debugger

    b. compiles the code behind the page

    c. executes the code

    d. opens the page in a browser

11. What is the name of the event handler that activates when the page is visited?

    a. IsPostback

    b. IsValid

    c. Page_Load

    d. Page_OnLoad

12. What property is used to retrieve the value of a TextBox control?

    a. Value

    b. Text

    c. ID

    d. InnerText

3

13. What method is used to remove all the items in a Drop-down List control?

a. Remove

b. Delete

c. Clear

d. none of the above

14. Which Server controls inherit from the System.Web.UI.WebControls namespace?

a. WebForm controls

b. Rich controls

c. Validation controls

d. all of the above

15. Which method(s) are used to assign a color to a control?

a. MyControl.BackColor = Color.FromName(txtBackColor.Value)

b. MyControl.BorderColor = System.Drawing.Color.Green

c. MyControl.BorderColor = Green

d. a and b

16. Which type of control is often used to dynamically write content directly to the page?

a. Label control

b. Panel control

c. Placeholder control

d. Literal control

17. What type of ASP.NET controls is used as a container to store dynamically added Server controls to the Web page?

a. Label control

b. Panel control

c. Placeholder control

d. Literal control

18. Which is not a valid value for the Target property of a hyperlink?

a. New

b. _blank

c. parent

d. href

19. Which control is used to turn off the display of a Validation control error message?

    a. dynamic

    b. none

    c. static

    d. off

20. Which Validation control is the best choice to ensure that the zip code values are all numeric?

    a. RequiredFieldValidator

    b. RangeValidator

    c. CompareValidator

    d. RegularExpressionValidator

HANDS-ON PROJECTS

Project 3-1

In this project you create a Web page that uses HTML Server controls to change the Source property of an image. This page will change the image when you click on the buttons.

1. Start **Visual Studio .NET** and open your **Chapter3** solution.

2. Start the browser. Open the page named **CaseProducts.htm** in your browser.

3. In Visual Studio .NET create a WebForm named **Ch3Proj1.aspx**. Add HTML Server controls that replicate the same features as the caseProducts.htm page without using client-side JavaScript. Use the example you created in the chapter and the sample code below to help you change the Source property of the image in the code behind the page. (*Hint:* You will need to intercept each button ServerClick event and then assign a new image name as the source of the switcher graphic control.)

```
Private Sub Button1_ServerClick(ByVal ¬
sender As System.Object, ¬
ByVal As System.EventArgs) Handles ¬
Button1.ServerClick
     switcher.Src = "images/yellowNotepad1.gif"
End Sub
```

4. Save the file. Build the solution. Open the page in your browser. Print the Web page and the ASP.NET source code and code behind the page within Visual Studio .NET.

Project 3-2

In this project you create a Web page that uses HTML Server controls to open new windows using server-side hyperlinks. To enable you to manipulate the window dimensions and toolbars, you will use a client-side script.

1. Start **Visual Studio .NET** and open your **Chapter3** solution.

2. Open the browser. Open the page named **Caseterm.htm** in your browser.

3. In Visual Studio .NET create a WebForm named **Ch3Proj2.aspx**. Add HTML or ASP.NET server controls that replicate the same features as the Caseterm.htm page without using client-side JavaScript. Use the example you created in the chapter to help you change the hyperlink to open the page in a new window. You can use link buttons for the hyperlinks. In the code behind the page, you can create a function that will write out the client-side script.

```
Function newWin(ByVal varWindow As String)
Dim WinCode As String
WinCode = "<script>" & _
"window.open(" & varWindow & ",'newWin'," & _
"'height = 465, width = 450, status = no, toolbar = no, ¬
    menubar = no, location = no'); " & _
"</script>"
Response.write(WinCode)
```

4. Then, you can call the client-script and pass the URL to the function as shown below. You will have to call the function and pass the new URL for each button click event.

```
Private Sub LinkButton1_Click(ByVal ¬
sender As System.Object, ¬
ByVal e As System.EventArgs) Handles ¬
LinkButton1.Click
    newWin("'documentobjectmodel.htm'")
End Sub
```

5. Save the file. Build the solution. Open the page in your browser. Print the Web page, the ASP.NET source code, and code behind the page within Visual Studio .NET.

Project 3-3

In this project you create a Web page that uses server events to change the Source property of an image.

1. Start **Visual Studio .NET** and open your **Chapter3** solution.

2. In your browser open the page named **zoo.htm**, which is located in your Chapter03Data folder. The page contains questions and images. When the visitor clicks the image, a new image appears, showing the answer to the question.

3. In Visual Studio .NET create a WebForm named **Ch3Proj3.aspx**. Create an ASP.NET page using HTML or ASP.NET Server controls that replicates the same features as the zoo.htm page without using client-side JavaScript. (*Hint:* You can use the ImageButton to create the Image controls.) You can change the code so that the user must click on the image to change the image and view the answer as shown below.

```
Private Sub ImageButton1_Click(ByVal ¬
sender As System.Object, ¬
ByVal e As System.EventArgs) ¬
Handles ImageButton1.Click
    ImageButton1.ImageUrl = "images/farm.gif"
End Sub
```

4. Save the file. Build the solution. Open the page in your browser. Print the Web page, the ASP.NET source code, and code behind the page within Visual Studio .NET.

Project 3-4

In this project you create a Web page that uses Server controls to change the page properties dynamically when the form is submitted.

1. Start **Visual Studio .NET** and open your **Chapter3** solution.

2. In your browser open the page named **MemberPrefs.htm**, which is located in your Chapter03Data folder. This page retrieves user information, then that information is used to redisplay the page according to the member's preferences.

3. In Visual Studio .NET create a WebForm named **Ch3Proj4.aspx**. Add HTML or ASP.NET Server controls that replicate the same features as the MemberPrefs.htm page without using client-side JavaScript. (*Hint:* You should assign default values to the fields.)

4. You should refer to the example code provided in the chapter to change the color of a property dynamically. The code below is a sample of what you will need to do to the <body> tag to change the property of the page text color and the background color.

```
<body text="<% = txtFgColor.text %>"
    bgColor="<% = txtBgColor.text %>"
    MS_POSITIONING="GridLayout">
```

5. Then, you can display the Welcome message, change the Source property of the logo image, and change the background color of the table as shown below.

```
Private Sub Button1_Click(ByVal ¬
sender As System.Object, ¬
ByVal e As System.EventArgs) ¬
Handles Button1.Click msg.Text = "Welcome " & txtUser.Text
    logoImage.Src = ¬
    animal.SelectedItem.Value.ToString Table1.BgColor = ¬
    txtTableColor.Text
End Sub
```

6. Save the file. Build the solution. Open the page in your browser. Print the Web page, the ASP.NET source code, and code behind the page within Visual Studio .NET.

Project 3-5

In this project you create a Web page that retrieves user login information, authenticates the user, then redirects the user to the appropriate member or administration home page.

1. Start **Visual Studio .NET** and open your **Chapter3** solution. Import the **Admin.htm** page from the Chapter03Data folder into your solution.

2. In your browser open the page named **AdminLogin.htm**, which is located in your Chapter03Data folder. The page retrieves the user login information, then uses that information to redirect the user to his or her home page. You can create the additional member and administrative home pages in Visual Studio .NET.

3. In Visual Studio .NET create a WebForm named **Ch3Proj5.aspx**. Add HTML or ASP.NET Server controls that replicate the same features as the AdminLogin.htm page without using client side JavaScript.

4. Retrieve the values of the form fields when the user clicks on the button as shown below.

```
Private Sub Submit1_ServerClick ¬
(ByVal sender As System.Object, ByVal e As ¬
System.EventArgs) ¬
Handles Submit1_.ServerClick
    Dim strUserName, strPassword
    strUserName = txtUsername.Value
    strPassword = txtPassword.Value
```

5. Use the code below to determine if the username is the manager. Then, determine if the password field matches "pwd". If yes, then redirect the user to the Admin.htm page. If the password does not match, redirect them to the login page.

```
Select Case StrUserName
Case "manager"
    If (strPassword = "pwd") Then
        Response.Redirect("admin.htm")
    Else
        Response.Redirect("Ch3Proj5.aspx")
    End If
```

6. You will need to repeat the Case-Select and If-Then-Else control structures for each user that you allow in the site. You should include at least one administrator, named admin, with a password named pass, to log in to the Web page.

7. Save the file. Build the solution. Open the page in your browser. Print the Web page, the ASP.NET source code, and code behind the page within Visual Studio .NET.

Project 3-6

In this exercise you create an ASP.NET page that displays data in a list.

1. Start **Visual Studio .NET** and open your **Chapter3** solution.

3

2. In your browser open the page named **RedRiverBoats.htm,** which is located in your Chapter03Data folder. The page displays employee information dynamically.

3. In Visual Studio .NET create a WebForm named **Ch3Proj6.aspx**. Add an ASP.NET RadioButtonList control that is populated with the employee data without using client-side JavaScript. You should refer to the sample code provided in the chapter to add items to the list dynamically when the page loads. (*Hint:* You can use an ArrayList to populate the list, then bind the ArrayList to the RadioButtonList.)

4. Save the file. Open the page in your browser. Print the Web page, the ASP.NET source code and code, behind the page within Visual Studio .NET.

Project 3-7

In this exercise, you will create an ASP.NET page that processes and validates form data.

1. Start **Visual Studio .NET** and open your **Chapter3** solution.

2. In your browser open the page named **ApplebeeBooks.htm**, which is located in your Chapter03Data folder. This page processes and validates form data.

3. In Visual Studio .NET create a WebForm named **Ch3Proj7.aspx**. Add at least four ASP.NET Validation controls that validate the form fields. If the form is valid, display a message in the browser. (*Hint:* The code below is a sample of how you can detect if the entire page is valid by using the IsValid property.)

```
Private Sub Submit1_ServerClick(ByVal ¬
sender As System.Object, ¬
ByVal e As System.EventArgs) ¬
Handles Submit1.ServerClick
    If Page.IsValid = True Then
        Label1.Text = ¬
"Thank you for completing the form."
    End If
End Sub
```

4. Save the file. Build the solution. Open the page in your browser. Print the Web page, the ASP.NET source code and code, behind the page within Visual Studio .NET.

CASE PROJECTS

World Culture Foundation — Using HTML Server Controls

The World Culture Foundation has hired your company to create a Web site to promote cultural awareness and diversity. The project manager has asked you to create a sample Web site using Visual Studio .NET. Select a culture that you are interested in. Visit Web sites that discuss your topic. If you don't have any information about your topic, you can visit Life Beyond Yahoo! at www.lifebeyondyahoo.com to locate subject links to many culture-related Web sites. Create a Web site containing at least two Web pages that present the information you researched. Use the HTML Server controls to create the Web pages. At least one of the pages must contain a form. Save the Web pages as Ch3Case1_1.aspx and Ch3Case1_2.aspx. Print out your Web pages and the source code for the ASP.NET page and the code behind the page.

Tara Store Product List Page — Passing Form Field Data to a Web Page

The project manager has asked you to create a sample Web site that displays Tara Store's products. Create a form that displays five product images, along with their product name, price, and product number, as shown in Figure 3-13. Add a Submit button that is labeled "Add to My Cart" below each of the products. Display the quantity ordered as a single text box. You can add additional form fields and ASP.NET controls as needed.

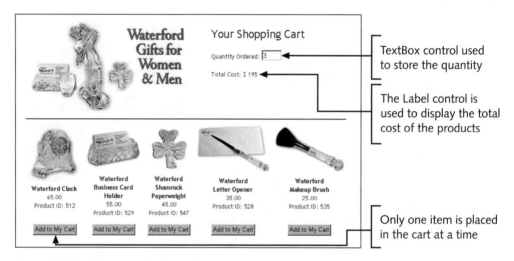

Figure 3-13   Form controls

When the visitor clicks the Submit button, calculate the price by using the quantity times the cost of the item. Display the total cost to the user. Save the Web pages as Ch3Case2.aspx. Print out your Web page and the source code for the ASP.NET page and the code behind the page. (*Hint*: On each button click, you will calculate the total cost and change the Text property of a Label control to the total cost as shown below.)

```
Private Sub Button1_Click(ByVal ¬
sender As System.Object, ¬
ByVal e As System.EventArgs) ¬
Handles Button1.Click
    Dim Cost As Integer
    Cost = quantity.Text * l512.Text
    lblOrder.Text = "Total Cost: $ " & Cost.ToString
End Sub
```

Tara Store Product Shipping Form — Form Field Validation

Your project manager has asked you to create the shipping form for the Tara Store Shopping Cart. Create a form for the visitor's name, address, phone, and e-mail address. Use the ASP.NET Validation controls to validate the form. Modify the error messages to indicate the error to the visitor. Once the page is validated, display a thank you message to the visitor. (*Hint:*You can use the IsValid property to detect if all of the Validation controls have been used successfully.) Save the Web pages as Ch3Case3.aspx. Print out your Web pages and the source code for the ASP.NET page and the code behind the page.

Tara Store Product Main Category list — Displaying the Main Categories Using Dynamic Lists

Your project manager has asked you to create the main category list for the Tara Store Online Catalogue. Create a Web page that displays the category list as a radio button list control, as shown in Figure 3-14. When the visitor clicks a Submit button, its associated category page should open. Save the Web page as Ch3Case4.aspx. You can use an ImageButton for the Submit button. You will need to create each of the associated category pages. (*Hint:*You can add the items directly using the Collections property, or use an ArrayList and programmatically add the items when the page loads.) Place a menu on each category page, so the user can jump to any of the category pages from any Web page. Print out your Web page and the source code for the ASP.NET page and the code behind the page.

Figure 3-14   RadioButtonList controls

Tara Store Product List — Displaying the Product List using Dynamic Lists

Your project manager has asked you to create the product list page for the Tara Store Online Catalogue. Create a Web page that displays the product list as a CheckBoxList control. Display a default graphic when the page loads. When the visitor clicks the Submit button, the related product image should be displayed in place of the default graphic. (*Hint*: You can use the strResult variable to store the path to the image. The CheckBoxList control values should be the name of the graphic image, and the text should be the name of the product. You must obtain the value of the item selected. If two products are selected, no product image will appear. So, you should change the selected property of the checked box to false, so that the box will become unchecked. The user will have to reselect the next product. Save the Web page as Ch3Case5.aspx. Print out your Web page and the source code for the ASP.NET page and the code behind the page.

4

USING ASP.NET RICH CONTROLS

In this chapter, you will:

♦ Learn how ASP.NET Rich controls can enhance your Web applications

♦ Identify the format and structure of an XML document

♦ Create an XSLT stylesheet

♦ Use the XML controls to read and display an XML data file

♦ Create a rotating banner advertisement on the Web page using the AdRotator control

♦ Create an interactive calendar using the Calendar control

♦ Create ASP.NET pages that allow you to upload a file to the Web server

Today businesses need to be able to enhance the appearance of the Web pages, as well as to manage the data within the Web site. In this chapter, you will learn about the Rich controls that will enhance your Web pages, not only in appearance, but also by providing the user with more information and interactivity. XML is the glue that allows applications to share information. By using XML files and data sources, you can share data across networks and firewalls to any application that supports the XML standards. Companies can use XML-based data to create data-driven Web applications that are not database dependant. Once the data has been provided to your Web site, you will want to format the data so that the output will appeal to your visitors. You will learn to edit the XML data file by using the XML editor built into Visual Studio .NET. You will learn to use the ASP.NET XML control to read and format XML data. You will use the ASP.NET Rich controls to create XML-based rotating banner ads and display an interactive calendar. You will also learn to upload files using the HTMLInputFile control. Although the HTMLInputFile control is not classified as a Rich control, it provides the same function as a Rich control, which is to enhance the interactivity within a Web site.

ASP.NET Rich Controls

As you learned in Chapter 1, you use ASP.NET Rich controls to enhance your Web applications. There are several Rich controls that are installed with Visual Studio .NET. The File Upload control allows you to upload a file to the Web server. The XML control allows you to read and display XML document data in a Web page. The Adrotator control allows you to display rotating banner advertisements based upon the data stored in an XML data file. The Calendar control allows you to insert a customized calendar into the Web page. Rich controls are Web controls and inherit the Web control class from the `System.Web.UI.WebControl` namespace. Third-party software companies also provide Rich controls.

The XML Control

Extensible Markup Language (XML), like HTML, is a markup language that provides access to structured content. But, unlike HTML, XML is not limited to a set of tags or to being displayed in a browser. XML allows you to define your own elements. XML documents can be shared across applications, file systems, and operating systems.

The XML standards are maintained by the World Wide Web Consortium (*www.w3c.org*). The XML standards allow you to add content, referred to as data, to an XML document. However, an XML document can also include information that describes the data, which is known as the data structure or schema. The XML standards contain the **XML Document Object Model (DOM)**, which is a standard language-neutral interface for manipulating XML documents from a script or program. With a DOM, a program or script can access and update the content, structure, and style of an XML document.

There are many technologies that work with XML documents. You can add a hyperlink to an XML document using the **Xlink** standard. You can point to parts of an XML document using the **XPointer** and **XFragments** standards. The XML document can be formatted using a style sheet known as **XSLT stylesheets**. **XSL Transformations (XSLT)** is a language for transforming XML documents. XSLT stylesheets use XSLT to interact with an XML document. XSLT stylesheets can format individual elements or groups of elements within the XML document.

You can view the XML document using an XML parser. An **XML parser** is an application that can read and interpret both the data and processing instructions in an XML document. You can view XML files using the **MSXML Parser (version 2.0)** built into Internet Explorer 5.5 browser or any later version of Internet Explorer. Just open the page in the browser to view the XML document. The latest version of the MSXML Parser is available from Microsoft for free at *http://msdn.microsoft.com/xml*. You can locate information about the versions of the MSXML Parser in the MSDN library. In a browser, go to *http://msdn.microsoft.com./default.aspx?scid=kb;EN-US;q269238*.

XML documents can be used by other types of applications, such as Window Forms. These applications access the data in the XML document using the XML Document Object Model (DOM) and the Simple API for XML (SAX).

You can insert an XSLT style sheet directly into the XML document and view the formatted output using an XML parser. However, if you do this, the stylesheet is hard-coded into the XML document. If you want to switch to a new XSLT stylesheet, you would have to manually change the code in the XML document. With the XML control, you can create a Web page that formats the XML document using an external XSLT stylesheet.

The benefit of using the XML control is that you can programmatically change the XML document source or the XSLT stylesheet without directly altering the XML document. To use the XML control, you use an XML document, an XSLT stylesheet, and an ASP.NET Web page.

This chapter will provide introductory information about XML, XSLT, and the XML control. You can learn more about the standards for creating a well-formed XML document at *www.w3c.org/XML*.

Figure 4-1 XML technologies

Although you can integrate your ASP.NET applications with XML documents and XSLT stylesheets, you do not need to use ASP.NET to build XML applications. However, Visual Studio .NET contains many tools that will help you create and modify your XML documents, and integrate them within your existing ASP.NET applications. The benefit of using XML technologies is that the technology is platform independent and language neutral. You can share your XML document with an application that was created with Java on a UNIX platform. Web Services, which is built on XML technologies, helps call applications remotely across the Internet and share data. You will learn more about how to use XML documents to integrate your databases and Web Services in later chapters.

XML Editing Tools

To create XML documents, you can use a variety of tools, including a simple text editor such as Notepad. Visual Studio .NET provides HTML/XML editor that you can use to create and edit HTML or XML files. Another editor, named Microsoft XML Notepad, provides a graphical view of the XML hierarchical document object model. (*Note*: The Microsoft XML Notepad executable file is called xmlpad.exe, and you can download it from Microsoft at *http://msdn.microsoft.com/xml/notepad/intro.asp*.)

Because all XML documents self-describe their contents, it is not necessary to use the application that created the XML document in order to modify it. XML documents are generally saved with the file extension .xml. Some applications, including Visual Studio .NET, Access XP, and SQL Server 2000, allow you to save a set of data from a database as an XML document. These XML documents are saved with the file extension .XSD. Visual Studio .NET comes with many XML templates and tools to help you create XSLT and other XML documents.

XML Introduction

The XML standards contain rules regarding how to create and format XML documents. The most important rule is that the XML document must be well formed. A **well-formed document** follows XML standards and can therefore be read by any XML parser. All XML documents must comply with these rules. In a well-formed document, there can be only one root element, within which all other elements are nested. You cannot mix nesting elements. For example, in HTML, you can write `<b>Welcome to <i>Tara Store</b></i>`. In the new, XML-compliant version of HTML, known as **XHTML**, this statement is illegal. You must rewrite the statement as `<b>Welcome to <i>Tara Store</i></b>`. In a well-formed document, you must enclose the values of properties within double quotation marks. XML is case sensitive. The case for the opening and closing tags of an element must match. (*Note*: It is recommended that you use lowercase letters when naming elements.) So, in a well-formed document the tag `<b>` does not correspond to the closing tag `</B>`. In a well-formed document, all tags must be closed.

You should read through the XML standards on the W3C Web site. Some of the tags, such as the <br> tag have been changed. If you have an empty element, such as the line break tag <br>, that does not usually have a closing tag, you can add a forward slash (/) before the closing bracket to close the tag. The resulting tag would then be <br />. To support older browsers which implement previous versions of HTML, you need to add a space after the br characters. By leaving a space the browser will read <br and recognize that this tag is a line break tag. When the browser sees a space and a slash it interprets the code as an unrecognized attribute. The browser ignores the slash while still using the <BR> tag correctly. However, if you do not leave a space before the slash, some browsers will not recognize <br/> as a valid tag, and ignore it. For more information, you can read the XHTML standards located at *www.w3.org/TR/xhtml1/#guidelines*.

 It is useful to validate your XML code to ensure that it is well-formed. Microsoft has a free validation tool located at *http://msdn.Microsoft.com/downloads/ samples/Internet/xml/xml_validator/sample.asp*.

The Prologue

When you create an XML document, you must first select which version of XML standards you will be working with. The first section, known as the **prologue**, contains global information such as the XML version, formatting information, and schema definitions.

XML Version

The first line in an XML document specifies the version of XML, using the **Version property**, as shown below. The question mark indicates that this tag, XML, is a processing instruction and therefore does not contain data. The version property identifies the XML standards version to be used to read the document. You can also indicate the Character-encoding property used such as UTF-8 or UTF-16. The Character-encoding property is optional and describes any coding algorithms that are used within the page. (*Note*: The W3C is currently working on the second version of XML.)

```
<?xml version="1.0" encoding="utf-8" ?>
```

Formatting XML Documents

The prologue of the XML document can contain a reference to an external cascading style sheet (CSS) or an XSL file. CSS files are often used to format HTML documents or XML documents. Unlike HTML, elements contained within XML documents do not contain any formatting instructions. You must include the formatting instructions within the processing instructions inside the XML document, or use an external file such as a CSS or XSL stylesheet. The sample code below shows how to add a reference to a CSS stylesheet in an XML document. This code would appear in the prologue below the XML version.

```
<?xml:stylesheet type="text/css" href="taragifts.css">
```

You can also use XSL stylesheets to process and format XML documents. XSL is Extensible Style Language. XSLT is a form of XSL that transforms the XML data by using processing rules in the XSLT stylesheet. There are two types of XSL stylesheets. XSLT is responsible for transforming an XML document. The XSLT stylesheet can analyze the XML document, process instructions, and produce output such as HTML. The other type of XSL stylesheet, called XSL-FO, contains formatting objects, and is used to format the XML document. In this chapter, you will work with XSLT stylesheets.

The XML Body

The XML document complies with the XML DOM standards. (*Note:* You can locate the DOM specifications at *www.w3c.org/TR/REC-DOM-Level-1/*.) The two parts of the XML DOM are the DOM Core and DOM HTML. The DOM Core is used to represent XML documents, and also serves as the basis for DOM HTML. The DOM HTML is used to represent XML/HTML documents. (*Note:* you can read more about the DOM HTML at *www.w3c.org/TR/REC-DOM-Level-1/level-one-html.html*.) The XML DOM was influenced by the document object models that were used by browsers. The document object model within a browser is used to enable JavaScript to interact with objects and events within the browser. This application of JavaScript to manipulate the document object model in the browser is called Dynamic HTML (DHTML). However, the objects, properties, and methods within the XML DOM are very different from the DHTML document object models.

The XML DOM states that XML documents must have a logical structure. The body of the XML file contains the elements, attributes, and data in the XML document. In an XML document, you must define a root container element to carry all the elements and data in the file. All tags must be nested within the **root node**. The root node in an XML document is also known as the root tag.

A **container element** is an element in which other elements can nest. The root node is a container element because all elements must be nested within the root element in an XML document. In an HTML page, the HTML tag is the root element. The HTML element is a container element because it contains child elements such as <head></head> and <body></body>. In this case, the element is also the **parent element** for the head and body tags. The head and body tags are referred to as the **child elements**.

In the sample code below productlist is the root node. The root node can contain many other elements. In this sample, the productlist node contains two product nodes.

```
<productlist>
 <product>
 </product>
 <product>
 </product>
</productlist>
```

You can create elements that are containers for other elements. In an HTML page, the <title> tag is nested within the <head> tag. The <head> tag is a container element, and the parent element for the <title> tag. In the sample below, the productlist element is the root element. The product element contains data about a single product. There are multiple product elements contained within the productlist root element. The product element is a container element because it contains the code, name, price, category, image, and rating elements. Notice that each element has a beginning and closing tag.

```
<productlist>
 <product>
  <code>387-463-55-00</code>
  <name>Waterford Crystal Shamrock Paperweight</name>
  <price>99.00</price>
  <category>Waterford</category>
  <image>547.gif</image>
  <rating>4</rating>
 </product>
 <product>
  <code>978-979-53-00</code>
  <name>Waterford Crystal Business Card Holder</name>
  <price>59.00</price>
  <category>Waterford</category>
  <image>529.gif</image>
  <rating>3</rating>
 </product>
</productlist>
```

Modifying an XML Document

In the previous chapter, when you edited an ASP.NET page, you were able to edit the page manually in HTML view, or you could have used the visual editor in Design view. You clicked the HTML and Design tabs to switch back and forth between the two views. When you edit an XML document in Visual Studio .NET, you can edit the data manually in XML view, or in Data view. Data view is the visual tool that you use to enter or modify data in an XML file. Data view allows you to enter the data using a table structure. You can use the XML and Data tabs to switch between the XML view and Data view.

In the products.xml document the root node is named productlist, as shown in the sample code below. The productlist node contains one or more product elements. Each product element contains six child elements.

```
<?xml version="1.0" ?>
<productlist>
    <product>
        <code></code>
        <name></name>
        <price></price>
```

```
            <category></category>
            <image></image>
            <rating></rating>
        </product>
<productlist>
```

 XML view supports IntelliSense and color coding to help you create your XML code. If you type the < character, the list of elements is displayed. You can use the arrow keys to move up and down the list of elements. You can use the Enter key to select the element. If you press the spacebar, a list of attributes associated with the element will be available to you in a list. When you insert an element using IntelliSense, the closing tag will also be inserted for you.

In the following exercise, you will modify the products.xml file. You will use the **XML Designer** in Visual Studio .NET to add a product to the XML document. The XML Designer allows you to edit the document in XML view or Data view. You will add the product using the XML view. Then, you will modify some data in the XML file using the Data view. You will display the XML document structure using the Document Outline window. The **Document Outline window** opens and displays the structure of the XML document. Later in this chapter you will use the XML control to display the XML data.

1. Start **Visual Studio .NET**. (In most computers, you can go to the **Start** menu, select **Programs**, **Microsoft Visual Studio .NET**, then **Microsoft Visual Studio .NET**.)

2. Click **File** on the menu bar, point to **New**, then click **Project** to open the New Project window.

3. Under Project types, click **Visual Basic Projects**, and under Templates, click **ASP.NET Web Application**. The location of your project should be http://localhost/WebApplication1. Change WebApplication1 to **Chapter4** in the Location text box, then click **OK** to create the solution, project, and default files.

4. To add a folder, right-click **Chapter4** in the Solution Explorer window, point to **Add**, then click **New Folder**. Type **images**, then press **Enter**.

5. Right-click the **images** folder, point to **Add**, then click **Add Existing Item**. Browse to locate your data files for this chapter. (*Note*: In the Files of type drop-down list, change the selection from VB Code Files files to **Image Files**.)

6. Select all of the images from the images directory within the Chapter04Data folder. (*Note*: You can use the Ctrl+A key combination to select all of the files.) Click the **Open** button to import the images into the images directory of the Chapter4 project. (*Note*: You can collapse the list of files in the Solution Explorer window by clicking the minus sign in front of the images folder.)

7. Right-click **Chapter4** in the Solution Explorer window, point to **Add**, then click **Add Existing Item**. Browse to locate your data files for this chapter in the Chapter04Data folder. Select the file **products.xml**. (*Note*: In the Files of type drop-down list, change the selection from VB Code Files files to **All Files**.) Click the **Open** button to import the page into your project. (*Note*: No pop-up message appears in this case because there are no class files associated with XML or XSLT files.)

8. Double-click the file **products.xml** in the Solution Explorer window. Your document opens in XML view. Scroll down the page and look at the structure of the XML document. Verify that the first line contains the version of the XML document, that the productlist element is the root node, and that there are eight product nodes.

9. Below the opening productlist node, type the following code to create another product record. Your page should look like the XML document in Figure 4-2.

```
<product>
  <code>387-463-55-00</code>
  <name>Waterford Crystal Shamrock Paperweight</name>
  <price>120.00</price>
  <category>Gifts</category>
  <image>547.gif</image>
  <rating>2</rating>
</product>
```

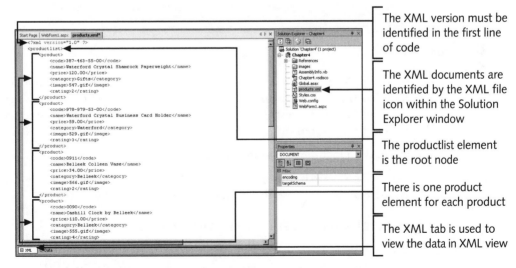

The XML version must be identified in the first line of code

The XML documents are identified by the XML file icon within the Solution Explorer window

The productlist element is the root node

There is one product element for each product

The XML tab is used to view the data in XML view

Figure 4-2   An XML document in XML view

10. Click the **Data** tab to open the file in Data view using the XML editor. Place the cursor over the divider line between the code and name cells in the header row. When you move the cursor over the divider lines between the columns, the cursor changes from a single arrow to a double-headed arrow. Click and drag the divider to the right until you can see all of the codes.

11. Place the cursor over the divider line between the name and price cells in the header row. Click and drag the divider to the right until you can see all of the product names.

12. Change the price of the Waterford Crystal Shamrock Paperweight to **99.00**. Change the rating from 2 to **4**. Change the category from Gifts to **Waterford**, as shown in Figure 4-3.

Data view displays the data in a table

The heading row name is assigned based on the name of the element

The name of the table is based on the name of the first-level elements

The Data tab is used to display the XML file in Data view

Figure 4-3   An XML document in Data view

13. Click the **XML** tab. Right-click on the XML document, and then click **Synchronize Document Outline**. Note that in the Document Outline window the productlist element is the root node, and that the product elements are all nested under the productlist element.

14. Close the Document Outline window.

15. Click the **Save All** button. Click **Build** on the menu bar, and then click **Build Solution**. Close the Output window. Close the page.

Using Special Characters in an XML Document

In early versions of HTML, special characters had to be entered using their markup code. For example, the blank space was represented by . In XML, certain characters are not supported within the tags because they are used to separate XML elements. You must replace these characters with the equivalent element markup codes. Listed below are several common XML characters and their markup codes.

Table 4-1 XML character entity references

Character	XML Character Markup Code
'	&apos;
"	&quote;
&	&amp;
<	&lt;
>	&gt;

4

You can find additional information on commonly used characters at *ms-help://MS.VSCC/MS.MSDNVS/DHTML/workshop/author/dhtm/lreference/charsets/charset1.htm*. This is the ISO Latin-1 character set that represents the first 256 values of the Unicode character set. In HTML, you can use the decimal code or named entity to represent the character. You can find additional information on escape characters at *ms-help://MS.VSCC/MS.MSDNVS/cpgenref/html/xsdrefcharacterclassescapes.htm*. You will find links to single-character escapes such as the ampersand and other types of escape characters.

XSLT Stylesheets

The XSTL stylesheet is an XML document that contains information about how to format a different XML document. The XSLT stylesheet can contain HTML, style rules, and XSTL commands. The XSTL stylesheet must be formatted according to the XML standards, and therefore the first line identifies the version of XML. A root node is used to indicate that the document is an XSTL stylesheet. The sample below shows the basic code required to create an XSLT stylesheet. The usual file extension for a cascading style sheet is .css. However, the file extension for the XSLT stylesheet is .xsl. The name for the root node for the XSLT stylesheet is xsl:stylesheet. The xmlns:xsl attribute indicates the schema to be supported for the stylesheet. The schema or rules is the XSL Transform standards which are maintained by the W3C. These standards describe how XSLT stylesheets are used to format XML documents. Like other XML documents, you can include comments within the stylesheet using the <! - - and - - > tags. You must close the root element at the bottom of the XSLT stylesheet.

```
<xsl:stylesheet version="1.0"
  xmlns:xsl="http://www.w3.org/1999/XSL/Transform">
<!- - Put your formatting code here - - >
</xsl:stylesheet>
```

Within the comment tag, do not use any blank spaces between the exclamation point and the hyphen, between the two hyphens, or between the hyphen and the closing bracket.

Formatting the Main Template

XSLT stylesheets use templates to group together formatting rules. You can create a generic template, or you can create custom templates that can be used to format specific elements. You can format all the elements at the same time by using the generic template, or you can specify how you want to format each element within the document with the custom template. The following sample code formats several of the elements within the XML document. In this example, the products element is the root node. Notice that the images element is missing from the XSLT document. You do not have to use all of the elements that are contained within the XML document. You can specify which fields to retrieve and which fields to display. In this first segment of code, the default template is defined. This is the main template, as indicated by the match attribute with a forward slash, and is used to format the XML document. You must match the root node of the existing XML document. This is used by the XSLT processor to read the document and to know where to start formatting the document.

Notice that the main template, **xsl:template**, is also used to send basic HTML output to the browser. You can nest basic HTML tags within the templates. The first template, shown below, will start applying the template, using the root node in the XML document. (*Note:* You do not have to use the entire XML document when formatting the page.) In the HTML code, an embedded style sheet is used to format the heading. You can mix stylesheets across traditional Web pages, and XSL Stylesheets. You can still use embedded and external style sheets. The **xsl:for-each** statement is a processing instruction that is applied to the node provided in the selected attribute. In this example, for each product node, the product name element, a colon, and the product category element would be written, followed by a line break tag.

```
<xsl:template match="/">
  <html><head><title>Tara Store Product List</title>
  <style type="text/css">
  H1 {color:#003366; font-size:16pt;}
  </style>
  </head>
  <body>
    <H1>Products and their categories.</H1>
    <xsl:for-each select="//product">
          <xsl:apply-templates select="name" />:
          <xsl:apply-templates select="category" /> <br />
    </xsl:for-each>
  </body></html>
</xsl:template>
```

In the sample below, processing is applied to the product elements. Different formatting can then be applied to each child element within the product element. Classes are defined within the embedded style sheet and applied to the product elements. For example, the `<xsl:apply-templates select="name"/>` code means that there is a template in the page that is outside of the main template, that contains the formatting instruction for the name element. In the example above, there was no template created for the elements. The XML templates can use the stylesheets defined here to format the XML output to a browser. Although the output is the value of the element, no formatting is applied yet. You will need to create the element template and the formatting within the element template. The sample below only shows the main template, which corresponds to the root node of the XML document.

4

```
<xsl:template match="/">
  <html><head><title>Tara Store Product List</title>
  <style type="text/css">
  .heading {font-family: trebuchet ms;
      color:#003366; font-size:16pt;}
  .product {font-family: Verdana;
      color:#003366; font-size:10pt;}
  </style>
  </head>
  <body>
  <div class="heading">
   <br /><img src="logo.gif" align="left" hspace="10" />
   <p>Tara Store <br /> Product List</p>
   <br /><br />
  </div>
  <hr size="1" width="550" align="left" color="#003366"/>
  <xsl:for-each select="//product">
        <xsl:apply-templates select="name" />
        <xsl:apply-templates select="category" />
        <xsl:apply-templates select="code" />
        <xsl:apply-templates select="price" />
        <xsl:apply-templates select="rating" />
  </xsl:for-each>
  <hr size="1" width="550" align="left" color="#003366"/>
  </body></html>
</xsl:template>
```

Formatting the Elements Using Element Templates

After using the main template, you can define individual templates for individual elements. In the following sample code, a template is defined for each element. The match attribute indicates the name of the element to apply the template. When the name element template is called, a string is displayed, along with the value of the contents within the name element. The xsl:value-of attribute indicates that the value of the element is retrieved and displayed. So, to display the contents of any node, just use `<xsl:value-of select="." />`. The period means that everything within the node is selected.

```
<xsl:template match="product">
  <b><xsl:value-of select="." /> </b>
</xsl:template>
```

If you want a template to apply to all the other elements, you can use an asterisk as the value for the Match property.

```
<xsl:template match="*">
  <div class="product"><xsl:value-of select="."/></div>
</xsl:template>
```

The DIV tag uses the class defined in the embedded style sheet to determine how to format the output. In addition, the bold tag is applied locally to format the output. You can use a mixture of inline, embedded, and linked styles to format the output. You can add other HTML tags such as the line break tag to format the output for a Web page.

```
<xsl:template match="name">
  <div class="product">
    <b>Product Name: <xsl:value-of select="." /> </b><br />
  </div>
</xsl:template>
```

Element templates are applied to the category, code, price, and rating elements. Each of the elements defined in the for-each code in the main template references the style template shown below. This technique allows you to create very custom XSLT stylesheets.

```
<xsl:template match="name">
  <div class="product">
    <b>Product Name: <xsl:value-of select="." /> </b><br />
  </div>
</xsl:template>
<xsl:template match="category">
  Category: <xsl:value-of select="." /><br />
</xsl:template>
<xsl:template match="code">
  Product Code: (<xsl:value-of select="." />)<br />
</xsl:template>
<xsl:template match="price">
  Price: <b>$ <xsl:value-of select="." /></b> <br />
</xsl:template>
<xsl:template match="rating">
  Rating: <xsl:value-of select="." /> stars<p />
</xsl:template>
```

Creating an XSLT Stylesheet

In the exercise below, you will create a simple XSLT stylesheet named listproducts.xsl that will be used to display the data in the products.xml file. The XSLT stylesheet merely displays the data in a list. The style information is located in the ASP.NET page and in the stylesheet.

1. In Visual Studio .NET, open the **Chapter4** project if it is not already open.

2. Right-click **Chapter4** in the Solution Explorer window, point to **Add**, and then click **Add New Item**. Under Templates click **Style Sheet**, type **listproducts.xsl** in the name text box, and then click **Open**.

3. Notice that the body { } style element has been inserted, but you cannot use the style builder. Delete **body { }**.

4. On the first line, indicate the XSL stylesheet standard version, as follows:

```
<xsl:stylesheet ¬
xmlns:xsl="http://www.w3.org/1999/XSL/Transform" ¬
version="1.0">
```

5. In between the xsl:stylesheet tags, add the code to create the main template, as shown below. (*Note:* You must include a closing stylesheet tag, </xsl: stylesheet>, at the bottom of the page. All of the code must be nested within the stylesheet tags. It's a good idea to add it when you create the opening tag.) The main template will retrieve the name, category, code, price, and rating elements.

```
<xsl:template match="/">
</xsl:template>
```

6. In between the main template tags, add the for-each processing instruction as shown below. The **product** is the name of the node that you want to retrieve. The for-each statement should look like this:

```
<xsl:for-each select="//product">
    <xsl:apply-templates select="name" />
    <xsl:apply-templates select="category" />
    <xsl:apply-templates select="code" />
    <xsl:apply-templates select="price" />
    <xsl:apply-templates select="rating" />
</xsl:for-each>
```

7. Enter the code to display and format the data from the name element in the XML file. Add a horizontal ruler, which will divide each product listing.

```
<xsl:template match="name">
    <hr size="1" width="400" align="left" ¬
  color="#003366" />
    <b>Product Name: <xsl:value-of select="."/></b><br />
</xsl:template>
```

8. Enter the code to display and format the data from the other four elements in the XML file.

```
<xsl:template match="category">
  Category: <xsl:value-of select="."/><br />
</xsl:template>
<xsl:template match="code">
  Product Code: (<xsl:value-of select="."/>)<br />
</xsl:template>
<xsl:template match="price">
  Price <b>$ <xsl:value-of select="."/></b><br />
```

```
      </xsl:template>
      <xsl:template match="rating">
        Rating: <xsl:value-of select="."/> stars<p/>
      </xsl:template>
```

9. Click the **Save All** button. Click **Build** on the menu bar, then click **Build Solution**. Your page should look like the one in Figure 4-4.

Figure 4-4   XSLT stylesheet

Using the XML Control

Creating the XML control in a Web page involves three steps. First, you must determine how to locate the source document. There are three attributes that can be configured to locate the XML data. The **Document property** indicates that the XML data is located in an object called **XMLDocument**. The **DocumentContent property** indicates that the XML data is a string containing the entire text of the XML document. The **DocumentSource** allows you to identify a physical or virtual path to the XML document.

In the XML control, you also have to specify where the style information is located. The **Transform attribute** allows you to use an object called **XSLTransform**, which contains the XSL or XSLT stylesheet. This stylesheet is then used to transform the document before displaying it. You can also use the **TransformArgumentList**, which contains a reference to an object called **XsltArgumentList** that contains the arguments to be passed to the stylesheet. Finally, you can use the **TransformSource** attribute to identify the physical or virtual path to the XSL or XSLT stylesheet.

Recall that because this is an ASP.NET Rich control, the control is identified with the prefix ASP and a semicolon. In the XML control, you must set the runat property to server to indicate that the control is a Server control. Below is an example of how you insert an XML control in a Web page. You can close the tag with /> or </asp:Xml>. You do not need to type this code in the Web page because Visual Studio .NET provides a graphical tool in the Toolbox to insert the XML control.

```
<asp:Xml runat="server" id="Xml1" ¬
TransformSource="listproducts.xsl" ¬
DocumentSource="products.xml" />
```

In the exercise below, you will create a Web page that displays an XML document named products.xml using an XSLT stylesheet. The XML control allows you to read, process, and display XML data using an XSLT stylesheet. This process is known as transformation. You will use the DocumentSource and TransformSource properties of the XML control to identify the physical path to the XML document and the XSTL stylesheets.

1. In Visual Studio .NET, open the **Chapter4** project if it is not already open.

2. Right-click **Chapter4** in the Solution Explorer window, point to **Add**, and then click **Add WebForm**. In the name text box enter **listproducts.aspx**, and then click **Open**.

3. Drag the **header.jpg** from the images folder in the Solution Explorer window to the top of the page. Drag the **menu.gif** from the images folder in the Solution Explorer window to the left of the page below the header.jpg image. Drag the **giftfinder.jpg** image from the images folder in the Solution Explorer window below the header.jpg image and just to the right of the menu.gif file.

4. In the Toolbox, drag the **Panel** control from the WebForms tab to the page. Position the panel below the giftfinder.jpg file. Drag the handle on the lower-right corner of the panel to enlarge the panel to fill the window. Delete the word **Panel** in the Panel control.

5. In the Toolbox, drag the **XML** control from the WebForms tab onto the Panel control. The XML control is labeled Xml.

6. In the Properties window change the DocumentSource property to **products.xml**. Change the TransformSource property to **listproducts.xsl**. (*Note:* You can type in the names of the files, or you can use the Build button to open the dialog box and browse to locate the file.)

7. Click the **Save All** button. Click **Build** on the menu bar, then click **Build Solution**.

8. Right-click on the page, and then click **View in Browser**. Close all of the pages you have created.

The XML control appears as a visual element on the Web page; it is not processed until you view the page in a browser

The TransformSource and DocumentSource properties are configured in the Properties window

Figure 4-5   XML control

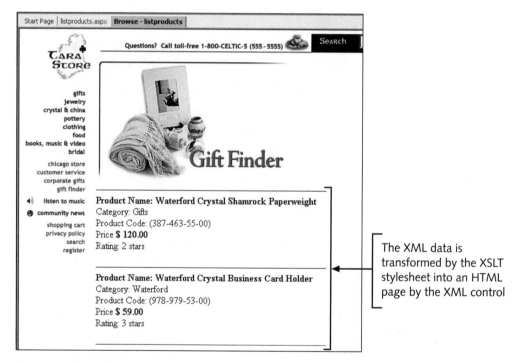

The XML data is transformed by the XSLT stylesheet into an HTML page by the XML control

Figure 4-6   Displaying the XML control in an ASP.NET Web page

Modifying XSLT Stylesheets

There are many ways to format XSLT stylesheets. You can insert HTML, embedded style sheets, and XSLT commands. This means that all of the HTML tags are available for use within an XSLT stylesheet. As shown in the sample code below, you can insert images, tables, and hyperlinks within an XSTL stylesheet. You can specify the attributes for any of the HTML properties in the template by using the **xsl:attribute** command. You can insert the value using the data retrieved from an XML file.

```
<xsl:template match="image">
  <a>
    <xsl:attribute name="href">
      <xsl:value-of select="." />
    </xsl:attribute>
      Click here to go to the Web site.
  </a>
</xsl:template>
```

Inserting a Table with XSLT Stylesheets

The following sample code shows how you can change the above code to format the contents as a table. Instead of using line breaks, the cell tag is used to separate individual elements. The heading of the table is separated outside of the for-each loop so that the heading only appears once. The closing table tag is also located outside of the for-each loop.

```
<xsl:template match="/">
<table border="0" cellspacing="10">
   <tr><th>Image</th><th>Name</th><th>Category</th>
     <th>Code</th><th>Price</th></tr>
   <xsl:for-each select="//product">
     <tr><td><xsl:apply-templates select="image"/></td>
     <td><xsl:apply-templates select="name"/></td>
     <td><xsl:apply-templates select="category"/></td>
     <td><xsl:apply-templates select="code"/></td>
     <td><xsl:apply-templates select="price"/></td></tr>
   </xsl:for-each>
   </table>
</xsl:template>
<xsl:template match="*">
     <div class="product">
         <xsl:value-of select="."/>
     </div>
</xsl:template>
```

Inserting an Image with an XSLT Stylesheet

To output an image to a Web page, you simply modify the image element template. In the previous version the name was simply displayed. In the sample code below, the image is displayed using an <img> tag. Recall that the template is processed by the XML parser built into the browser. The browser uses the img tag to create an <img> tag, but you must retrieve the properties for the image tag, such as the Source property. In this example, you define the src property of the image tag. The value is assigned from the contents of the image element in the product node in the XML document. The Align attribute is used to define the Align property for the image tag. In this sample, the value was hard-coded as left-aligned. (*Note:* The align value can also come from the XML document, if the data is available there.)

```
<xsl:template match="image">
  <img>
    <xsl:attribute name="src">
      <xsl:value-of select="." />
    </xsl:attribute>
    <xsl:attribute name="align">left</xsl:attribute>
  </img>
</xsl:template>
```

One of the common things people want to do is to create a link to another document using the XML date. When you want to combine the values, it is simpler to create the hyperlink within the main template. The sample code below creates a hyperlink to a URL, and passes the name of the image in a querystring. The **xsl:text** instruction is used to write out the value of the text. You can use this instruction to write out literal text, as well as special control characters, which are listed in Table 4-1. The disable-output-escaping attribute is used to generate characters without escaping, such as the single < character. (*Note:* You need to be careful not to split the xsl:text instruction across multiple lines because the XML parser will process the carriage return and blank spaces. In this example, the text is wrapped to illustrate how the code is spliced across XSLT instructions.) You create an anchor tag that creates a basic hyperlink such as `<a href = "ProcessingPage.aspx?ImageUrl=15.jpg">Belleek Frames & Clocks</a>`. Then, in the processing page, you can retrieve the image name. You can use this technique to create and process more complex querystrings based on values in the XML document.

```
<xsl:template match="/">
  <xsl:for-each select="//Category">
    <xsl:text disable-output-escaping="yes">
        &lt;a href="ProcessingPage.aspx
    </xsl:text>
    <xsl:text disable-output-escaping="yes">
        ?ImageUrl=
    </xsl:text>
    <xsl:value-of select="ImageUrl" />
    <xsl:text disable-output-escaping="yes">
        "gt;
    </xsl:text>
    <xsl:value-of select="CategoryName" />
    <xsl:text disable-output-escaping="yes">
        &lt;/a&gt;
    </xsl:text>
    <br />
  </xsl:for-each>
</xsl:template>
```

You can alter this code slightly to create simple links to the images. In the sample below, a simple hyperlink is used to display the image when the hyperlink is clicked. The link is created using the anchor tag, and the href property is set to the ImageUrl value from the XML document.

```
<xsl:template match="/">
  <xsl:for-each select="//Category">
     <xsl:apply-templates select="ImageUrl" />
     <xsl:apply-templates select="CategoryName" />
  </xsl:for-each>
</xsl:template>
<xsl:template match="ImageUrl">
     <a>
          <xsl:attribute name="href">images/
              <xsl:for-each select=".">
          </xsl:attribute>
          Click here to see the image.
     </a>
</xsl:template>
<xsl:template match="CategoryName">
     <b><xsl:for-each select="."></b>
</xsl:template>
```

Processing XML Data with an XSLT Stylesheet

In addition to retrieving the data and formatting the output, the XSLT stylesheet can analyze the contents of the element and performs actions. This sample code looks at the contents of the XML document and displays the product name and rating. If the product rating is equal to or greater than 4, then it displays a clover image and the message "Excellent". The text is formatted using a class called over, which is defined in the embedded stylesheet. If the product rating is 3, then only the message "This is within current projections" is displayed. No special formatting is applied to the message. If the product rating is equal to or less than 2, then a message is displayed that says "WARNING: this is below our target." This message is formatted using the over class, which is defined in the embedded style sheet. Below is the stylesheet code that must be added to define the over and under classes.

```
.over {font-family:Verdana; font-size:11pt;
    color:green; font-weight:bold}
.under {font-family:Verdana; font-size:10pt;
    color:red; font-weight:bold}
```

In the XSLT stylesheet, you can use the xsl:for-each statement to select which elements to retrieve. Again, this does not mean that you must display them, only that they are retrieved. You can use the template listed in the select attribute to format the output, which may contain the value of the element.

```
<xsl:for-each select="//product">
    <xsl:apply-templates select="name"/>
    <xsl:apply-templates select="rating"/>
</xsl:for-each>
```

In the name templates, the name is displayed and formatted with the product class defined in the embedded style sheet and the inline bold tag.

```
<xsl:template match="name">
  <div class="product">
    <b><xsl:value-of select="." /></b>
  </div>
</xsl:template>
```

In the rating templates, the rating is displayed with some additional text. Then, **xsl:choose** is used to allow you to analyze the value of the rating. The **xsl:when** statement is used if the condition listed in the test attribute is met. Notice that the greater than sign is written as >. As you saw earlier, this is necessary because otherwise the XML parser may interpret the sign as part of an XML tag. If the first condition is met, then the formatting within the statement occurs. Otherwise, the parser moves to the next condition. The **xsl:otherwise** statement is used to format any data that may not apply to the other choices listed. (*Note:* Don't forget to always include the closing HTML tags.)

```
<xsl:template match="rating">
  <blockquote>Average Customer Rating:
    <b><xsl:value-of select="."/></b> stars.
    <xsl:choose>
      <xsl:when test=". &gt; 3">
        <span class="over">
          <img src="clover.gif" align="bottom" ¬
              hspace="5"/>
          Excellent!
        </span>
      </xsl:when>
      <xsl:when test=". &lt; 3">
        <span class="under">
          WARNING: this is below our target.
        </span><br />
      </xsl:when>
      <xsl:otherwise>
        This is within current projections.
        <br />
      </xsl:otherwise>
    </xsl:choose>
  </blockquote>
  <hr size="1" width="550" align="left" ¬
      color="#003366"/>
</xsl:template>
```

You can locate more information on the XSL attributes within the Visual Studio .NET Help files at *ms-help://MS.VSCC/MS.MSDNvS/xmlsdk30/htm/ xmrefxslvalueofelement.htm.*

There are many other processing instructions that can be used with XSLT stylesheets. You can sort the data by using the **xsl:sort** command. You can create and use variables and parameters with XSLT instructions. You can use the test instruction to determine if a condition has been met—for example, to determine the length of the element. The following sample code tests to see if the length of the element named ProductImage is greater than zero. You can use the period (.) to represent the element data or the element name. You can also use the > to represent the greater than symbol. The **xsl:if** statement is similar to the xsl:if-else-end if control statement, but does not run unless the conditional statement resolves to true.

```
<xsl:template match="ProductImage">
<xsl:if test="string-length(ProductImage)>0">
  <img><xsl:attribute name="src">
       <xsl:value-of select="." />
   </xsl:attribute></img>
</xsl:if>
</xsl:template>
```

XML Schemas

One of the benefits of XML is that it allows you to define your own markup language. You can create a document that contains a set of rules, and share them with other programmers. You have to be careful when you are using XML documents to follow the same set of rules. For example, one XML document may use the <p> tag to mean a paragraph, and another XML document may use <p> to represent a person. To eliminate confusion when working with multiple XML documents, XML documents can identify a namespace associated with the document. This set of rules, or namespace, is called a **schema**. Schemas are used to define the structure, content, and semantics of XML documents.

The schema can be written in a Document Type Definition (DTD) document or an XML schema document. **Document Type Definition (DTD)** is an older method used to identify the rules used to structure a document. Different types of documents implement different DTDs. Below is the DTD that is used with Web pages that comply with the strict HTML 4.0 standards. This statement must be the first line in the Web page, before the beginning <html> tag. You can read more about how to use the DTD within a Web page at *www.w3.org/TR/html401/sgml/dtd.html.*

```
<!DOCTYPE HTML PUBLIC "-//W3C//DTD HTML 4.01//EN" ¬
    "http://www.w3.org/TR/html4/strict.dtd">
```

The ¬ character is not part of the code. It is used where a single line of code is split over multiple lines to fit it on the book page.

The W3C is upgrading DTD to a newer format called **XML schemas**. XML schemas will eventually replace DTD. An XML schema is like a DTD document in that they both are ways to structure elements. Both data and schema are transportable through HTTP and can be used on any platform that understands XML.

The two models of XML schemas are available from the W3C and Microsoft. The Microsoft XML schema is extensible because you can add elements to a document without invalidating the document. This is not possible within the W3C XML schemas. You can learn more about XML schemas at *http://msdn.microsoft.com/xml/reference/schema*, and *www.w3c.org/XML/Schema*.

When you create your XML document, you can point to the schema to identify the rules that the document will follow. To do this, you place a reference to a DTD or (an) XML schema in the prologue of the XML document. Then, the XML parser uses that schema to validate the structure of the XML document. When you create an ASP.NET page with Visual Studio .NET, the property used to identify the schema is called **TargetSchema**. Parsers use the schema to determine the rules to validate the XML data.

When you edited the product.xml file, you used the XML Designer. You inserted the new element using the XML view and modified the element using the Data view. Any XML document can be created or edited in XML view. However, only XML documents that end in .xml can be edited in Data view. The XML Designer supports another view, called the Schema view. The Schema view is used to edit schema documents. The Schema view can display the schema using a DataSet view or an XML View. The DataSet view displays the schema using tables, while the XML view displays the schema using XML code. Visual Studio .NET can create a schema for you based on an existing XML document within the XML Designer. The schema document file extension is .xsd. The XML Designer will create the schema document and name it after the XML document, except that it will change the file extension to .xsd. The xmlns attribute is added to the inventory element to identify the XML schema document associated with the XML document as shown in the sample code below.

```
<elementname xmlns="http://tempuri.org/schemaname.xsd">
```

In the following exercise, you will create a schema, using Visual Studio .NET, based on an existing XML document named inventory.xml. You will then modify the schema. The inventory document contains information about the products, the number of items currently in inventory, the reorder level, and the number of items on order. When the number of items in stock reaches the number of items in the reorder level, the manager must place an order for the product. The current values in the inventory document are all strings. In the schema, you will change the types from strings to integers.

1. In Visual Studio .NET, open the **Chapter4** project if it is not already open.

2. Right-click **Chapter4** in the Solution Explorer window, point to **Add**, then click **Add Existing Item**. Browse to locate your data files for this chapter in the Chapter04Data folder. Select the file **inventory.xml**. (*Note*: In the Files of type drop-down list, change the selection from VB Code Files files to **All Files**.) Click the **Open** button to import the page into your project.

3. Double-click the file **inventory.xml** in the Solution Explorer window. Your document opens in XML view.

4. Click the **Data** tab to open the file in Data view using the XML editor.

5. Right-click on the page, and then click **Create Schema**. A new document named inventory.xsd appears in the Solution Explorer window.

6. Click the **XML** tab to return to XML view. Notice that the inventory node has been changed. The attribute `xmlns="http://tempuri.org/incentory.xsd"` has been added to the inventory element. This identifies the XML schema document associated with the inventory.xml document.

7. Double-click the **inventory.xsd** document to open the document in the XML Designer. Notice that the values in the first column are all E, which identifies the entry as an element. The second column contains the name of the element. The third column contains the description of the type. In the inventory.xsd file all of the element types are defined as string.

8. Click the word **string** for the instock element. Click the arrow that appears in the string cell. A list of data types appears. Scroll down the list and click **integer**, as shown in Figure 4-7.

9. Click the **Save All** button.

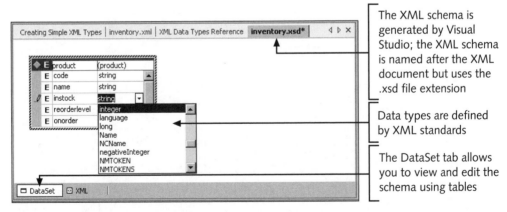

Figure 4-7   The DataSet view of the inventory XML schema

10. Go back to the inventory.xml page by clicking the **inventory.xml** tab.

11. Change the instock value for the Waterford Crystal Business Card Holder from 5 to **5abc**.

12. Click the **Data** tab. Notice that the value displayed in the Data view for the instock value is listed as (null). Because a schema is used with the XML document, the values must conform to the rules in the schema document.

13. Click the **XML** tab and change the value to **-5**. Click the **Data** tab. Notice that the value is displayed in the Data view. Because you do not use negative numbers for inventory, you can change the data type in the schema to only accept positive integers.

14. Click the **XML** tab and change the value back to **5**.

15. Go back to the XML schema by clicking the **inventory.xsd** tab. Change the instock data type from integer to **positiveInteger**. Click the **Save All** button.

16. Go back to the inventory.xml page by clicking the **inventory.xml** tab.

17. Click the **XML** tab and change the in stock value to **-5**. Click the **Data** tab. Notice that the value displayed is (null).

18. Click the **XML** tab and change the value to **5**. Click the **Save All** button.

19. Go back to the XML schema by clicking the **inventory.xsd** tab. Change the type for the reorderlevel and onorder elements to **positiveInteger**.

20. Click the **XML** tab. The XML schema is displayed using XML code. Notice that the elements are identified using the name attribute and the data type using the type attribute. The type for the code and name elements is string, and the type for the other elements is positiveInteger. The XML schema should look like the XML schema in Figure 4-8. (*Note:* The layout of the xs:schema element appears was modified so that you can view the entire file.)

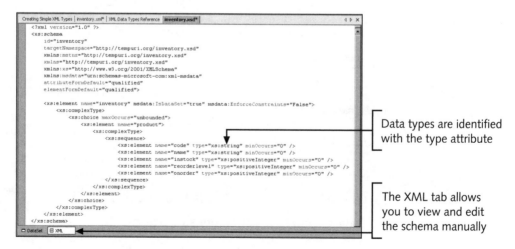

Figure 4-8   The XML view of the inventory XML schema

21. Click the **Save All** button. Click **Build** on the menu bar, then click **Build Solution**.

 Visual Studio .NET contains a vast amount of documentation on XML. If you are using the Contents window from the Help menu to locate Help documents, you can click on the MSDN Library, select Web Development, then XML and Web Services, XML (General), SDK Documentation, and then XML (Extensible Markup Language). From there you can browse the developer's guide, reference, tutorials, and samples. You can also locate XML documentation online at *http://msdn.microsoft.com/xml*.

4

THE ADROTATOR CONTROL

The **AdRotator control** allows you to display a banner ad on a Web page. When you refresh the page, the banner ad is changed to another image. The AdRotator control class is contained within the `System.Web.UI.WebControl.AdRotator` namespace. The two parts to the AdRotator are the AdScheduler File and the Web page. The **AdScheduler File** is an XML document that stores the ad information. This file is also known as the rotation file because it includes the information about the rotating ads. You will see each ad for the proportion of time that you indicate in the AdScheduler File. The Web page is an ASP.NET page that contains a WebForm, which displays the ads.

The banner ad is a hyperlinked image. So, you need to obtain your graphics and import them into your Web application. You can create your own image using a graphics software package, such as PhotoShop or Paint Shop Pro, or use an existing graphic. You don't have to use the dimensions in a traditional banner ad. You can use any type of rectangular graphic.

 You can locate graphics from Life Beyond Yahoo! at *www.lifebeyondyahoo.com/graphics.asp*. You can create banner ads that display text messages using various free Web tools such as Banner Generator at *www.coder.com*.

The information used to create the banner ad is stored in an external file called the AdScheduler File. The AdScheduler File is an example of an XML document. The AdScheduler File contains information that creates the HTML image tag, which inserts the image in the Web page. The file also contains information that creates the hyperlink using an anchor tag. When you click the banner ad, you are redirected to the URL defined within the hyperlink. The image source and the URL for the hyperlink are defined within the AdScheduler File. Each time the page is displayed, the AdRotator class retrieves a different image and hyperlink from the AdScheduler File.

The XML document can be edited with a basic text editor such as Notepad, or an XML editor. Visual Studio .NET contains an editor that can create and edit XML documents such as the AdScheduler File. Because the AdScheduler File is an XML document, the filename has the file extension .xml.

The first line of the AdScheduler File indicates the version of the XML document. Below is the syntax for defining the XML version that is used in the XML document. It follows the same format as all XML documents.

```
<?xml version="1.0" encoding="utf-8" ?>
```

The rest of the file is contained within a root node named advertisements. In an XML document, all tags must be nested within the root node. The root tag in an XML document is also known as the **root node**. Contained within the advertisement tag are one or more repeating groups of tags named ad. The **ad tag** is an element that contains the individual properties for the ad.

Each ad contains several properties that are used to create the image and hyperlink tags within the Web page. The ImageURL identifies the absolute or relative location of the image. Only images in the JPG, GIF, or PNG formats are currently supported on most Web browsers. The ImageURL is used to create the SRC property in the image tag. The NavigateURL identifies the URL to which the browser will be directed when the user clicks on the image. The NavigateURL is used to create the href property in the hyperlink. AlternateText identifies the text that is displayed when the user places the mouse icon over the image. AlternateText is used to create the ALT property of the image tag. If the user's browser does not support images, the text is displayed instead of the image.

Remember that the NavigateURL corresponds to the href property in the hyperlink created by the anchor (<a>) control. You may want to redirect the user to a Web site outside of your Web site, or to another page within your Web site. You can also pass additional information with the hyperlink in a hard-coded querystring. For example, you could use the value getproduct.aspx?id=529.jpg. The querystring is separated by the URL with a question mark. When the user clicks on the image, the hyperlink takes them to the getproduct.aspx page and passes the querystring to the next page. The next page can retrieve the name and value pairs in the querystring using the Page.Request.Querystring collection.

There are two properties that do not have a corresponding HTML function. The **impressions property** is used to indicate the frequency with which the banner ad is displayed. The Ad Scheduler File may contain data for thousands of banner ads. You can indicate how often you would like each banner ad to be displayed. Then, when the banner ad is created, the AdRotator class selects a banner ad from the XML file based upon the impressions property. The Impressions property identifies the relative frequency with which the ad should be displayed. So, if there are four banner ads defined in the file, and the first banner ad Impressions property is 20, and the other banner ads Impressions properties are 35 and 45, then the first banner ad would appear in the Web page 20 times out of 100 page views. This property is important because you can specify to a customer the number of times that their banner ads are displayed within the Web page. You can also refer to your log files to determine the exact number of times that the ad was displayed.

The AdRotator control can be configured to only display images from a group of banner ads. The Keyword property is used to indicate one or more words that categorize the banner ad. The AdRotator class uses the keyword to group the banner ads. For example, a newspaper Web site may contain one area that is for adults and another area for children. The adult Web site can display all of the banner ads. However, not all of the banner ads may be appropriate for children. Therefore, the newspaper can configure the AdRotator control using the KeywordFilter property. In the children's area on the Web site, the banner AdRotator would screen the banner ads in the XML file for those where the Keyword property matched the KeywordFilter property. Children would only be able to see age-appropriate content. Thus, one AdScheduler File can be used to create the banner ads in multiple pages. If you want a banner ad to belong to multiple categories, you can create an additional entry with the other keywords. Below is a sample of the code used to display two banner ads.

```
<Advertisements>
  <Ad>
    <ImageUrl>banner1.gif</ImageUrl>
    <NavigateUrl>http://www.course.com/ </NavigateUrl>
    <AlternateText>Course Technology</AlternateText>
    <Impressions>60</Impressions>
    <Keyword>Books</Keyword>
  </Ad>
  <Ad>
    <ImageUrl>banner2.gif</ImageUrl>
    <NavigateUrl>http://www.microsoft.com/ </NavigateUrl>
    <AlternateText>Microsoft</AlternateText>
    <Impressions>40</Impressions>
    <Keyword>Software</Keyword>
  </Ad>
</Advertisements>
```

Creating the AdvertisementFile File

In the example below, you will import an AdvertisementFile file. Then, you will use the XML editor to add a new banner ad.

1. In Visual Studio .NET, open the **Chapter4** project if it is not already open.

2. Right-click **Chapter4** in the Solution Explorer window. Point to Add, then click **Add Existing Item**. Browse to your Chapter04Data directory and select the **ads.xml** file, then click **Open**. This step imports the AdvertisementFile file.

3. Double-click the **ads.xml** file in the Solution Explorer window. Notice that you can edit the XML code manually. Under the opening Advertisements tag, add the following code to create a new banner ad element. (*Note*: Remember that the ¬ symbol means that the line of code should be written on one continuous line. Do not type the ¬ character in the code.) The document should appear as shown in Figure 4-9.

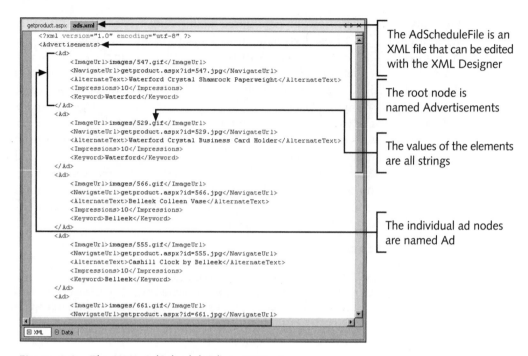

Figure 4-9   The XML AdScheduleFile in XML view

```
<Ad>
  <ImageUrl>images/547.gif</ImageUrl>
  <NavigateUrl>getproduct.aspx?id=547.jpg  ¬
  </NavigateUrl>
  <AlternateText>Waterford Crystal Shamrock
      Paperweight</AlternateText>
  <Impressions>10</Impressions>
  <Keyword>Waterford</Keyword>
</Ad>
```

4. Click the **Data** tab to edit the XML file in Data view.

5. Place the cursor over the divider line between the ImageURL and NavigateURL cells in the header row. Click and drag the divider to the right until you can see all of the names of the graphic images.

6. Place the cursor over the divider line between the NavigateURL and AlternateText cells in the header row. Click and drag the divider to the right until you can see all of the URLs.

7. Place the cursor over the divider line between the AlternateText and Impressions cells in the header row. Click and drag the divider to the right until you can see all of the alternate text.

8. Click the column heading **ImageURL** cell to sort the rows based on the ImageURL.

9. In the last row, enter the data for a new record as shown in Figure 4-10. (*Note:* When you first click in the last row, all of the values will be null.) The ImageUrl value is **images/803.gif**. The NavigateUrl value is **getproduct.aspx?id=803.jpg**. The AlternateText value is **Traditional Music of Ireland**. The Impressions value is **10**. The Keyword value is **Music**.

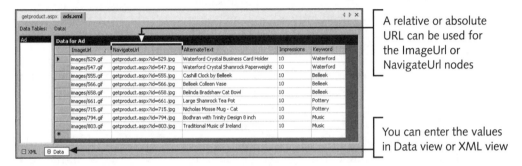

A relative or absolute URL can be used for the ImageUrl or NavigateUrl nodes

You can enter the values in Data view or XML view

Figure 4-10   XML AdScheduleFile in Data view

10. Click the **Save All** button. Click **Build** on the menu bar, then click **Build Solution**. Close the ads.xml file and the Output window.

Inserting the AdRotator Control

When you insert the banner ad in the Web page, you must insert the banner ad control, which is called **AdRotator**. Recall that because this is an ASP.NET Rich control, the control is identified with the prefix ASP and a semicolon. In the AdRotator control, you must set the runat property to server to indicate that the control is a Server control. Also, you must configure the **AdvertisementFile** property to point to the location of the AdScheduler File. Below is an example of how you insert an AdRotator control in a Web page. You can close the tag with /> or </asp:AdRotator>. You do not need to type this code in the Web page because Visual Studio .NET provides a graphical tool in the Toolbox to insert the AdRotator control.

```
<asp:AdRotator runat="server" id="AdRotator1" ¬
AdvertisementFile="ads.xml" ¬
KeywordFilter="Waterford" />
```

The ID property should be explicitly assigned to each Server control. If you do not assign an ID, the code behind the page still recognizes the object, and the Web server assigns an ID to the control. If you do not assign an ID to the control, you cannot create programs to interact with the control.

There are several additional properties that can be set in the AdRotator control. The Height and Width properties define the height and width of the image that will be displayed. If you want to display images that have different Height and Width properties, then you should not set the Height and Width property of the AdRotator control. However, if you use the AdRotator control from the Toolbox within Visual Studio .NET, the default Height and Width are 468px and 60px.

You can also use the Style property within Visual Studio .NET to configure the styles for the AdRotator control. Recall that the AdRotator control inherits the properties from the Web control class. Therefore, you can configure many of the basic Web control Style properties that you learned in the previous chapter, such as BorderColor, BorderWidth, BorderStyle, Visible, TabIndex, and Absolute Positioning.

By default, when you click a hyperlink, the browser opens the new URL in the current window. You can force the browser to open the new URL in a different window or frame by using the **Target property**. The Target property is set to _top by default. When the target is set to _top, the URL is displayed in the current, unframed window. If the target is set to _blank, the URL is displayed in a new unframed window. If the hyperlink is within a frame, you can set the target to display the URL in the current frame, or, in the parent frameset. The _self value displays the URL in the current frame, and the _parent value displays the URL in the parent frameset. The Target property also can place the URL in the Search window by changing the value to _search.

The **KeywordFilter property** retrieves only those banner ads from the XML document whose keyword matches exactly. Because the Keyword property can contain one or more words, the keyword value should be contained within quotation marks. The ToolTip property is used to provide more information about the banner ad. The ToolTip property stores a message as a string. The browsers display the message in the ToolTip when the user mouses over the banner image.

There are several help resources within Visual Studio .NET that document the AdRotator control and the AdRotator class. Documentation about the AdRotator class can be found at *ms-help://MS.VSCC/MS.MSDNVS/cpref/html/frlrfSystemWebUIWebControlsLabelClassTopic.htm*. Documentation about the members of the class can be found at *ms-help://MS.VSCC/MS.MSDNVS/cpref/html/frlrfsystemwebuiwebcontrolslabelmemberstopic.htm*.

In Visual Studio .NET you can insert the AdRotator control directly in the HTML code, or drag and drop the control from the WebForms tab in the Toolbox. In the following exercise you create a banner advertisement in a Web page using the AdRotator control from the Toolbox.

1. In Visual Studio .NET, open the **Chapter4** project if it is not already open.

2. Right-click **Chapter4** in the Solution Explorer window, point to **Add**, then click **Add Web Form**. Enter **displayBanner.aspx** in the name text box, and then click **Open**.

3. Double-click on the **displayBanner.aspx** page in the Solution Explorer window to open the page if it does not open automatically.

4. Drag the **header.jpg** file from the images folder in the Solution Explorer window to the top of the page. Drag the **menu.gif** file from the images folder in the Solution Explorer window to the left of the page, below the header.jpg image. Drag the **waterfordgifts.jpg** image from the images folder in the Solution Explorer window to below the header.jpg image and just to the right of the menu.gif file.

5. From the Toolbox, drag a **Label** control to the Web page. Change the Text property of the label to **Click on the image to view the item**.

6. In the Toolbox, click the **WebForms** tab if necessary, then drag the **AdRotator Button** control to the page, placing it below the Label control. In the Properties window, verify that the Target property is set to **_top**. Change the KeywordFilter property to **Waterford**. Change the AdvertisementFile property to **ads.xml**.

7. To add the file getproduct.aspx to your solution, right-click **Chapter4** in the Solution Explorer window, point to **Add**, then click **Add Existing Item**. Navigate to your Chapter04Data folder, select the file **getproduct.aspx**, and click **Open**. The following message appears: "There is no class file in the project associated with the Web Form 'getproduct.aspx'. Create a new class file now?" Click **Yes**.

8. Double-click the **getproduct.aspx** page to open the code behind the page. In the Page_Load handler type the code below. This code retrieves the value from the URL and displays the image.

```
Dim imagename As String
imagename = Page.Request.QueryString("ID")
Image1.ImageUrl = "images/" & imagename
```

9. Click the **Save All** button. Click **Build** on the menu bar, then click **Build Solution**.

10. Click the **displayBanner.aspx** tab to return to Design view.

11. Right-click on the page, and then click **View in Browser**. Click **View** on the menu bar, and then click **Refresh** to reload the page. Note which image is displayed.

12. Repeat the previous step 10 times, noting each time which image is displayed. Figure 4-11 shows how the banner advertisement appears in the Web page.

13. Click the image. The getproduct.aspx page should open, displaying a larger picture of the product.

14. Close all of the pages.

> You should always have some way for users to observe that their file has been uploaded. You can add code to the page to display links to the files, display a custom message with the filename, or redirect the browser to the newly created file.

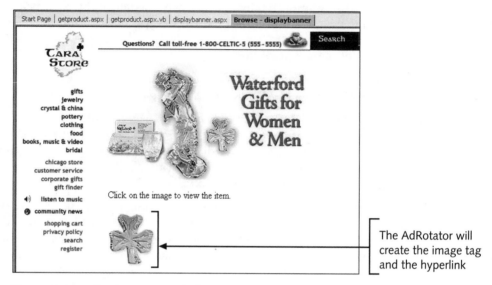

Figure 4-11   Creating a rotating banner advertisement in a Web page

The AdRotator will create the image tag and the hyperlink

THE CALENDAR CONTROL

You can use the **Calendar control** to insert and configure an interactive calendar within the Web page. The Calendar control is created by the calendar class. The calendar class is located in the `System.Web.UI.WebControls.Calendar` namespace. The calendar displays a single calendar month. By default, the current month is displayed. You can configure the appearance of the calendar by setting the properties of the Calendar control. You can create programs that interact with the calendar using methods and event handlers. Each date is displayed as a hyperlink. You can retrieve the current date or a data that the user selects by clicking on the hyperlink. (*Note:* The Date data type is equivalent to the .NET framework's DateTime data type.)

In Visual Studio .NET, you can insert the Calendar control directly in the HTML code, or drag and drop the control from the WebForms tab in the Toolbox. Below is the code to insert the Calendar control. Because the control is an ASP.NET Rich control, the name of the control includes the prefix ASP: followed by calendar. The runat property must be assigned to server, and you should assign a value to the ID property. You can close the tag with /> or </asp:Calendar>. You do not need to type this code in the Web page because Visual Studio .NET provides a graphical tool in the Toolbox to insert the Calendar control.

```
<asp:calendar id="MyCal" runat="server" />
```

The Calendar control supports several properties that you can configure when you insert the control. You can also change these properties dynamically in the code behind the page. There are several styles that can be configured to change the appearance of the calendar. Most of the Style properties can modify the background color; text color; font face, size, and style; alignment; width and height; wrapping; and border style. You can also assign a CSS class to the property, which can be used to configure the styles from an external style sheet. The various Calendar control Style properties that can be configured are listed below.

4

- *DayHeaderStyle*—sets the style for the days of the week
- *DayStyle*—sets the style for the individual dates
- *NextPrevStyle*—sets the style for the navigation controls in the heading
- *OtherMonthDayStyle*—sets the style for dates that are not in the current month
- *SelectedDateStyle*—sets the style for the dates that are selected
- *SelectorStyle*—sets the style for the month date selection column
- *TitleStyle*—sets the style for the title in the heading
- *TodayDateStyle*—sets the style for the current date
- *WeekendDayStyle*—sets the style for weekend dates

There are several properties that allow you to modify the Calendar control's appearance. The ShowDayHeader property is used to show or hide the days of the week heading row. The ShowGridLines property is used to show or hide the gridlines that divide the days of the month. The ShowNextPrev property is used to show or hide the navigation controls. The Navigation controls are used to navigate to the next or previous month. The ShowTitle property is used to show or hide the title in the heading.

There are several methods exposed by the Calendar control. The SelectionChanged event occurs when the user clicks a new date. This event changes the selected date to a new selected date. The SelectedDate property is the new selected date. The Calendar control visually indicates to the user which date is selected.

There are several events that can be intercepted by the code behind the page. You can write event handlers to intercept the event and execute your own custom code. The VisibleMonthChanged event occurs when the user clicks on the next or previous month hyperlinks. If you create an event handler for the VisibleMonthChanged event, you also pass the MonthChangedEventHandler object as a parameter to the event handler. The MonthChanged event handler object contains several properties. For example, when you click on the next or previous month, a new month appears in the calendar. The NewDate property is the current date in the new month. The property is the selected date in the previously selected month.

There are several Help documents within Visual Studio .NET that document the Calendar control and the calendar class. Documentation about the calendar class can be found at *ms-help://MS.VSCC/MS.MSDNVS/cpref/html/frlrfSystemWebUIWebControlsLabelClass Topic.htm.* Documentation of the members of the class can be found at *ms-help://MS.VSCC/ MS.MSDNVS/cpref/html/ frlrfsystemwebuiwebcontrolslabelmemberstopic.htm.*

The calendar output on the client may support new features such as altering the month name without page reloading. You can configure the target client browser using the **ClientTarget property**.

Creating a Program to Interact with the Calendar Control

You can build code within the code behind that page to interact with Calendar controls. You can assign a default selected date using the SelectedDate property. When the user clicks a date, you can create an event handler to capture the selected date. Then, you can retrieve the value that was clicked using the SelectedDate property. You can use the **ToShortDateString property** of the SelectedDate to display the selected date using the short date format. (*Note:* The short date format is mm/dd/yyyy). As shown in the sample code below, you can refer to each date selected by its position within the SelectedDates object such as `MyCalendar.SelectedDates()`.

```
Label1.Text = _
Calendar1.SelectedDate.ToShortDateString()
```

In the following exercise, you will create a calendar in a Web page using the Calendar control located in the WebForms tab in the Toolbox. You will also set the properties of the Calendar control. The calendar you create is shown in Figure 4-12.

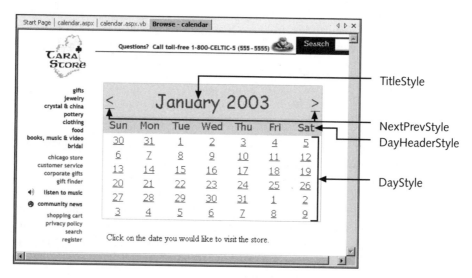

Figure 4-12   Creating a calendar in a Web page

1. Open the **Chapter4** project in Visual Studio .NET, if it is not already open.

2. Right-click **Chapter4** in the Solution Explorer window, point to **Add**, then click **Add Web Form**. Enter **calendar.aspx** in the name text box, and then click **Open.**

3. Drag the **header.jpg** file from the images folder in the Solution Explorer window to the top of the page. Drag the **menu.gif** file from the images folder in the Solution Explorer window to the left of the page, below the header.jpg image.

4. Click the **WebForms** tab in the Toolbox if necessary, then drag the **Calendar** control to the page, placing it below the heading graphics.

5. In the Properties window, change the Height property to **240px** and the Width property to **400px**.

6. In the Properties window, click the **plus sign** in front of DayHeaderStyle to expand the properties. Change the BackColor property to **#E0E0E0**. This turns the background color a light shade of gray. Click the **ForeColor** property drop-down list arrow, click the **Web** tab, then click **Firebrick** to change the ForeColor property to **Firebrick**. Click the **plus sign** next to the Font property to expand the Font properties. Change the Name property to **Verdana**. Change the Size property to **Medium**.

7. Click the **plus sign** in front of DayStyle, then click the **ForeColor** property drop-down list arrow. Click the **Web** tab, then click **Maroon**, which changes the ForeColor property to Maroon. Change the HorizontalAlign property to **Center**. Click the **plus sign** in front of the Font property to expand the Font properties. Change the Name property to **Verdana**. Change the Size property to **Small**.

8. Click the **plus sign** in front of the NextPrevStyle properties, then click the **plus sign** in front of Font. Change the Font Name property to **Trebuchet MS**. Click the **ForeColor** property drop-down list arrow, click the **Web** tab, then click **Firebrick** to change the ForeColor property to FireBrick.

9. Click the **plus sign** in front of the TitleStyle properties, then click the **plus sign** in front of Font. Change the Font Name property to **Comic Sans MS** and the Font Size property to **X-Large**. Change the BackColor property to **#FFE0C0**. Change the ForeColor to **Firebrick**.

10. From the Toolbox, drag a **Label** control to the Web page below the header.jpg. Change the Text property of the label to **Click on the date you would like to visit the store.**

11. Click the **Save All** button.

In the exercise below, you will add the code behind the page to the calendar.aspx page. You will create an event handler to detect when the user clicks a new date, and display a message in the Web page indicating the value of the new date. You will use an If-Then control structure to determine if the date selected is the current date. If the date selected is the current date, you will display a different message in the Label control.

1. Right-click the page, and then click **View Code**. This opens the code behind the page.

2. Type the following code below the Page_Load procedure. This code executes when the user clicks a new date. The code changes the Text property of a Label control named Label1. The message displayed includes a string message. (*Note:* The ¬ character indicates that a single line of code has been split across lines to fit on the page. Type this code on one line. The underscore (_) represents the line continuation character. You should always type the underscore in your code as it is shown in the sample code.)

```
Private Sub Calendar1_SelectionChanged(ByVal ¬
sender As System.Object, ByVal e As System.EventArgs) ¬
Handles Calendar1.SelectionChanged
   Label1.Text = "You selected: " _
   & ChrW(60) & "br" & ChrW(62) _
   & ChrW(60) & "br" & ChrW(62)
```

 The ChrW(60) and ChrW(62) functions insert the opening and closing brackets (< >) using Visual Basic .NET. You can add these characters directly by using a Literal control and defining the value of the Literal control as <br>.

3. Below the code above add an If-Then control structure to determine if the selected date is equal to today's date. You need to use the ToShortDateString property for both Date objects when comparing the dates.

```
If Calendar1.SelectedDate.ToShortDateString()= ¬
     Date.Now.ToShortDateString() Then
     Label1.Text &= _
     "Today all Waterford products are 30% off."
Else
     Label1.Text &= _
     "All products are 10% off during this month."
End If
End Sub
```

4. Click the **Save All** button. Click **Build** on the menu bar, then click **Build Solution**.

5. Click the calendar.aspx tab, then click the **Design** tab to return to the Design view. Right-click the page, and then click **View in Browser**. Click the link for next Monday.

6. Click the link for today. The message should appear as shown in Figure 4-13.

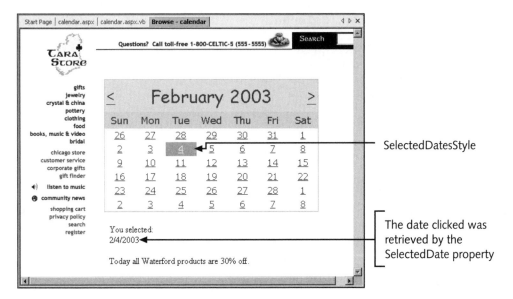

SelectedDatesStyle

The date clicked was retrieved by the SelectedDate property

Figure 4-13   Creating an interactive calendar in a Web page

7. Close all of the pages.

When the visitor clicks multiple dates, you can retrieve the values selected with the SelectedDates object. You will use a **For–Next loop** to iterate through each date that was selected. The **Count property** provides the number of dates that were selected. You can refer to each date selected by its position within the SelectedDates object such as `MyCalendar.SelectedDates(i)`. The position within the object is often called the **index position**. The first index position in all arrays and collections in Visual Basic .NET is 0. The value of the last index position in the SelectedDates object is equal to the value of Count property minus 1. You can use a **loop counter** to keep track of how many times the looping structure repeats.

For example, you can loop through the list of dates that were selected by the user by looping through the SelectedDates collection. The loop counter is declared as an integer outside of the loop. The counter is initialized at a beginning value such as 0. Because the loop counter started with the number 0, the loop should repeat until the counter reaches the value of Count property minus 1. If there are three dates selected, the Count property equals 3. Because the first element in the array is at index position 0, the loop counter begins at 0. The loop displays the first date. During the second loop, the loop counter is 1, and the second date is displayed. During the third loop, the loop counter is 2, and the third date is displayed. During each loop, the loop counter is also used to retrieve the ToShortDateString property of the SelectedDate. The loop ends when the loop counter reaches the value of the Count property minus one. You need to include the minus one so that the loop will continue to run the code for the last iteration.

```
Private Sub Calendar1_SelectionChanged(ByVal sender ¬
As System.Object, ByVal e As System.EventArgs) ¬
Handles Calendar1.SelectionChanged
  Label1.Text = "You selected:" _
  & ChrW(60) & "br" & ChrW(62)
  Dim i As Integer
  For i = 0 To Calendar1.SelectedDates.Count - 1
      Label1.Text &= _
      Calendar1.SelectedDates(i).ToShortDateString() _
      & ChrW(60) & "br" & ChrW(62)
  Next i
End Sub
```

 You can compare the value of an object to determine if the object contains a value. A null reference is assigned when an object has no value assigned. In Visual Basic, the keyword is Nothing. In some database languages, the word null represents the null reference. In .NET, the null is represented by the System.DBNull namespace.

USING THE FILE UPLOAD CONTROL

The **File Upload control** allows you to upload a file to a Web server. There are many uses for a File Upload control. For example, in an online store, the store manager is often required to complete an online form when adding a product to the store database. You can use a File Upload control to allow the manager to upload a graphic image of the product. Community and volunteer organizations often have several people who submit materials such as monthly newsletters and event flyers to be placed on the Web site. By using a File Upload control, the members can upload the documents to the Web site without having to learn how to use a Web editing tool or a file transfer program (*Note*: File transfer programs are also known as an FTP programs because they use the File Transfer Protocol). Business Web sites will also find many uses for the file upload component. Businesses often share documents with other businesses. These documents can be delivered through e-mail as attachments. However, some types of files such as graphics are very large. If the document is delivered to a large number of employees or a mailing list, the mail server could have difficulty storing the files and could crash. Because of this, businesses have limited the size of the files that can be sent through e-mail attachments to their company mailing lists. In order to make these documents accessible, you can use the File Upload control to upload the file to the Web server. Then, you can create a Web page that will provide employees with the ability to view or to download the document.

Although the File Upload control is not listed as a Rich control, it is included here, because it does significantly enhance a Web application. In the previous version of ASP, Rich controls did not exist. Rich controls were external components that were installed on the Web server to enable you to enhance your Web applications. In early versions of HTML and ASP, no File Upload control was available. In recent versions of HTML, the

File Field control allows you to browse your network and locate a file. The File Field control consists of a browse button that allows you to search your network and locate the file, and a textbox that stores the URL of the file. This control allows you to select and store the URL of the file. However, it does not allow you to upload the file to the Web server.

To actually upload the file, you have to use an external COM component to handle the file upload. You could use third-party file upload components such as SA-FileUp by Software Artisans (www.softwareartisans.com), or Posting Acceptor from Microsoft. Both of the components must be installed on the Web server. The file upload capability is completely built into ASP.NET, and is available to all ASP.NET applications. The upload services are built into the ASP.NET runtime. Once you start building your ASP.NET applications, you won't need a third-party file upload component anymore. You can now use the File Upload control to upload files such as Web pages, PDF documents created with Adobe Acrobat, word-processing documents, spreadsheets, and databases.

The key to building an upload feature into your Web site is the InputFile HTML server control. The File Upload control is an HTML Server control. The File Upload control class inherits from the `System.Web.UI.HTMLInputControl` namespace. Therefore, you cannot only browse your file system and select a file, you can also upload the file to the Web server.

You do not need to set a folder to allow anonymous users' create and write rights. Again, the ASP.NET runtime is able to save the file to any folder on the server you designate without requiring that you grant create and write rights to the user. This means they can safely add file-upload services to their Web site without weakening security on the Web server.

Creating the File Upload Page

When you create the page that uploads the file, you must include the File Upload control within a form. The form tag must contain an attribute named enctype that is set to multipart/form-data. This property indicates that there is a file attached to the URL request. The following sample code shows the File Upload control named uploadFilePath and the Form control. The form field named txtFileName is used to retrieve a different filename for the file. There is also a button named btnUpload. The OnServerClick server event handler detects when the user clicks the button. Then, the server handler specifies the file parameters and uploads the file. This code appears in the HTML view of the ASP.NET Web page.

```
<form enctype="multipart/form-data" runat="server">
    <INPUT id="uploadFilePath" type="file"
    size="40" name="txtFileName" runat="server">
    <input id="FileName" type="text" runat="server">
    <br /><br />
    <input type=button id="btnUpload"
    value="Upload a File" runat="server"
    OnServerClick="btnUpload_Click">
</form>
```

In addition to the type attribute, the file field accepts the Accept attribute. The Accept attribute allows you to specify the MIME formats that can be uploaded. To upload only JPEG images, you would set the Accept attribute to image/jpg. If you want to upload any image, you can set the attribute to image/*. The asterisk represents any image type. You can enter multiple MIME formats if they are delimited with a comma. You can set the MaxLength property in the file field to limit the length of the filename that can be entered in the text box. The Size attribute allows you to set the width of the file field text box as shown in the sample code below. In your HTML code, you don't see the properties listed in the Properties window. You can set the properties in the code behind the page in a procedure such as the Page_Load event procedure just as you can set the properties of other HTML and ASP.NET Server controls.

```
<INPUT id="uploadFilePath" type="file" MaxLength="50"
    size="40" name="txtFileName" runat="server"
Accept = "images/*, text/css, text/htm">
```

In the btnUpload_Click event handler, you can include the code to set the File Upload properties, then upload the file. In the code sample below, the path is hardcoded in the event handler. The name of the file is retrieved from a form field named txtFileName. This code appears in the code behind the ASP.NET Web page. The file is uploaded using the HTTPPostedFile class. To save the file, you must call the PostedFile.SaveAs command and pass the path to the file on the client's computer. The PostedFile allows you to upload the file, manipulate the file, and retrieve information about the file.

```
Private Sub btnUpload_ServerClick(ByVal ¬
sender As System.Object, ByVal e As System.EventArgs) ¬
Handles btnUpload.ServerClick
    strFilePath = "c:\upload\images\" & txtFileName.Value
    uploadFilePath.PostedFile.SaveAs(strFilePath)
End Sub
```

Once you have selected the file, the PostedFile object handles the file. You can obtain the size of the file using the ContentLength property. You can use this information to determine if the user has not selected a file to upload as shown in the sample below. You can also detect the MIME type of the file using the ContentType property. You can retrieve the path, filename, and file extension using the FileName property. The InputStream property of the PostedFile is used to create a Stream object which will be used to place a binary image file within a database.

```
Dim UploadedFile as HttpPostedFile = _
UploadedFile.PostedFile
If UploadedFile.ContentLength = nothing then
    "No file was selected. Pick a file to upload."
Else
    "The file has been uploaded."
End if
```

The Server contains a MapPath method to map the path to a file. This code is written as Server.Mappath(filename). Once you get the filename, you can retrieve the file extension using the GetExtension method of the Path object. The Path object is derived from the **System.IO** namespace. The FileName property retrieves the complete filename on the client's computer. The following sample code shows how to retrieve the path and filename from the uploaded file and the Path object.

```
Dim UploadedFile as HttpPostedFile = _
UploadedFile.PostedFile
Dim FilePath As String = UploadedFile.FilePath
Dim FileName As String  Path.GetFileName(FilePath)
Dim FileExtension As String = Path.GetExtension(FileName)
Dim ContentType As String = UploadedFile.ContentType
```

Tip

You must determine where you want to store your images. If you store them in the server's file system, it's more difficult to manage the files. If you store the images within the database, the images are stored in a central location, and are therefore easier to maintain. However, when you store images in a database, they are stored as BLOB objects (Binary Large Objects). Not all databases support BLOBs. When you store binary files in a database, the physical size of the database may become very large, requiring more hard drive space and memory on the database server.

Creating the File Upload Page

You may want to enable only authenticated users to upload a file. In the following exercise, you will create a login form. After the user is authenticated, you will show the file upload control. Then, you will allow the user to upload the file to the Web server. Figure 4-14 shows the screen when the user logs in and after when the user selects a file to upload.

Figure 4-14   Uploading a file to the Web server from a Web page

1. In Visual Studio .NET, open the **Chapter4** project if necessary.

2. Right-click **Chapter4** in the Solution Explorer window, point to **Add**, then click **Add Existing Item**. Browse to your Chapter04Data directory and double-click the file **uploadfile.aspx**. The following pop-up message appears: "There is no class file in the project associated with the Web Form 'uploadfile.aspx'. Create a new class file now?" Click **Yes**. Double-click the file in the Solution Explorer window to open it. (*Note:* This page contains many overlapping Form controls. Do not move these controls. When the user first accesses the page, only the Authentication controls are displayed. After the user is authenticated, the Upload controls are displayed. When the file has been uploaded, the upload message is displayed.)

3. Click the **HTML** tab in the Toolbox to open it, if necessary. Then drag the **File Field** control, which is the File Upload control, from the HTML tab to the page. Position the control below the hyperlink. Right-click the control, and then click **Run As Server Control**. In the Properties window, change both the Label (ID) and Name properties to **uploadFilePath**. Change the size property to **50**.

4. In the Properties window, click the button with three periods next to the Style property to open the Style Builder, which you can use to change the control's properties. Click the **Position** tab. Change the Z-Index property to **107**, POSITION to **Absolutely position**, the Left property to **145px**, the Width property to **376px**, the Top property to **280px**, and the Height property to **23px**. Click the **OK** button.

5. Double-click the page to open the code behind the page. Delete the entire **Page_Load** event handler.

6. Click **File** on the menu bar, point to **Open**, then click **File**. Browse to your Chapter04Data folder, click the **uploadfile.txt** file to select it, and then click **Open**.

7. Select all the text in the file by clicking **Edit** on the menu bar and selecting **Select All**. Click **Edit** on the menu bar again, then click **Copy**. Open the **uploadfile.aspx.vb** page by clicking the **Document** tab in the main window. Place the insertion point on the line where you deleted the Page_Load event handler. Click **Edit** on the menu bar, then click **Paste**.

8. Below the comment that says 'Enter the code below to upload the file', type the following code. This code declares the path variable, retrieves the path from the path of the current file, and uploads the file that was received from the form. (*Note:* The ¬ character indicates that a single line of code has been split across lines to fit on the page. Type this code on one line. Do not split strings across multiple lines without concatenating the string. It is important to split the strings correctly or your code may not work properly. If you can avoid it, try not to split your code across multiple lines.)

```
Dim strFilePath As String
strFilePath = ¬
System.IO.Path.GetDirectoryName ¬
(Server.MapPath ("uploadfile.aspx"))
uploadFilePath.PostedFile.SaveAs((strFilePath & "\" & ¬
txtFileName.Value))
```

9. Click the **Save All** button. Click **Build** on the menu bar, then click **Build Solution**.

10. Click the **uploadfile.aspx** file tab in the main window. Click the **Design** tab to change to the Design view, if necessary. Right-click on the page and click **View in Browser**. (*Note:* You can also view the page in your browser at *http://localhost/chapter4/uploadfile.aspx*.) In the username text box type **Course**. In the password text box type **Technology**. Click the **Sign In** button.

11. Click the **Browse** button to locate a file in your Chapter04Data\images folder named uploadimage.gif. Enter **uploadimage.gif** in the File Name text box. Click the **Open** button. The filename and path appear in the text box. Click the **Upload the Image** button.

12. A message is displayed, indicating the image was uploaded. Click the button labeled **Upload Another Image** if you want to upload another image. (*Note:* In a real situation, you would also include a button to return to the login screen. Although this example is used to upload images, you can also use this code to upload files. You can practice uploading a file with this sample using a file named uploadtest.txt located in your Chapter04Data folder.)

13. Close any open pages.

CHAPTER SUMMARY

❑ Rich controls enhance the user interface and increase interactivity within Web pages. Examples of Rich controls are the XML control, the AdRotator control, and the Calendar control. Third-party providers are likely to create additional Rich controls, which can be added to your application.

❑ XML standards are maintained by the World Wide Web Consortium. XHTML is a version of HTML that is XML compliant. An XML parser is an application that can read the file and process the instructions in the file. A Web browser such as Internet Explorer 5.5 or above can read XML files. XML files can be formatted with cascading style sheets or XSLT stylesheets. XML files must be well formed. They must follow the rules defined by the W3C. The XML schema is a set of rules. Schemas are used to define document format and structure. Industries can create their own schemas and define their own sets of tags. The XML control allows you to read, process, and display XML data using an XSLT stylesheet. This process is known as transformation.

- The banner AdRotator control allows you to display rotating banner ads. The banner contains a hyperlink, alternate text, and an image. If you do not specify the height and width, you can display images of varying sizes. The AdScheduler File is an XML file that is used to store the ad information. The AdScheduler File can be edited with a text editor, such as Notepad, or an XML editor. The root node is named advertisements. The Impressions property determines the ad's relative display frequency. The Keywords property is used to group banner ads. You can apply a filter and only show some of the banner ads using the KeywordFilter property.

- The Calendar control displays an interactive calendar. There are many properties that you can use to format the calendar. The SelectionChanged event allows you to detect when the user clicks on a new date. The SelectedDate property indicates the value of the currently selected date. You can retrieve the value of the date that users click, or execute code when they click a particular date.

- The File Upload control is an HTML Server control that allows you to upload files to a Web server. The Form Encrypt property must be set to multipart/form-data. The upload file field type must be set to file. On the server, you must retrieve the filename. You can change the filename or path on the server in the code behind the page. The SaveAs method saves the file to the Web server.

Review Questions

1. Which of the following is not a Rich control, but still enhances the Web application?

   a. FileUpload control

   b. AdRotator control

   c. Calendar control

   d. XML control

2. Which class is inherited by the FileUpload class?

   a. System.Web.UI.HTMLControl

   b. System.Web.HTMLControl

   c. System.UI.WebControl

   d. System.Web.UI.HTMLInputControl

3. Which property is used to identify a file that is attached to the form?

   a. multipart/form-data

   b. type=form-data

   c. attachedFile

   d. type=form/file

4. What is the value of the Type property for the upload file field?

    a. Upload

    b. File

    c. Text

    d. Attached

5. What method is used to upload the file to the server?

    a. Upload

    b. FileUpload

    c. Save

    d. SaveAs

6. Where is the banner ad information stored?

    a. in memory

    b. in the AdScheduler File

    c. in the AdRotator File

    d. in the Windows Registry

7. Who is responsible for the maintenance of the XML standards?

    a. Microsoft

    b. Sun Microsystems

    c. IBM

    d. W3C

8. In the AdScheduler File, what is the name of the root node?

    a. Ad

    b. AdSchedule

    c. AdRotator

    d. Products

9. What is the name of the tag used to insert the Calendar control?

    a. calendar

    b. asp:calendar

    c. xml:calendar

    d. asp/calendar

10. Which property is used to create the hyperlink in the banner AdRotator control?

    a. ImageURL

    b. NavigateURL

    c. NavigateHREF

    d. HREF

11. Assume that you have four banner ads, and all four banner ad impression properties are set to 20. You visit your page 100 times. How many times would you expect to see each banner?

    a. 4

    b. 10

    c. 20

    d. 25

12. What property is used to search for a subset of the banner ads in the AdScheduler File?

    a. keyword

    b. KeywordFilter

    c. advertisement

    d. impressions

13. What property of the Calendar control is used to capture the date that the user clicked on?

    a. VisibleMonthChanged

    b. SelectedDate

    c. DayChanged

    d. SelectionChanged

14. Which word describes the position of an item in a collection?

    a. index position

    b. counter

    c. loop index

    d. counter

15. Which of the following rules is not part of the XML standards?

    a. Element names must not be more than 32 characters long.

    b. All container elements must be closed.

    c. The opening and closing element tags must have the same case.

    d. A child container element can be nested within a parent container element.

16. Which prefix is used to indicate that the XML document should use a cascading style sheet?

    a. xml:css

    b. xml:stylesheet

    c. asp:stylesheet

    d. type = css

17. What character code is not part of the XML markup code by default?

   a. '

   b. "

   c. &

   d. @

18. Which of the following is used to add a comment to an XML document?

   a. <! - - comment - - >

   b. /* comment /*

   c. ' comment

   d. # comment

19. Which XML processing instruction retrieves the contents of any element within the node?

   a. `<xsl:value-of select="." />`

   b. `<xsl:apply-templates select="*" />`

   c. `<xsl:template match="/*">`

   d. `<xsl:apply-templates select="." />`

20. Which property is used to identify the XSL stylesheet in an XML control?

   a. DocumentContent

   b. TransformSource

   c. HREF

   d. XML:CSS

HANDS-ON PROJECTS

Project 4-1

In this project, you create an XML data file using Visual Studio .NET.

1. Open your **Chapter4** solution in Visual Studio .NET, if it is not already open.

2. Right-click **Chapter4** in the Solution Explorer window, point to **Add**, then click **Add New Item**. Click the **XML File** icon, type **Ch4Proj1.xml** in the name text box, and then click **Open**. The prologue with the version and encoding attributes has already been entered for you.

3. On the second line, create a root node named **ProductCategories**.

4. Create a child node named **Category** for each of the eight product categories.

5. Create elements named **ImageURL**, **CategoryID**, and **CategoryName** for each product category.

6. Add the data to each of the category nodes using the table below. (*Hint:* You will have to replace each of the ampersands (&) with the character code **&**.)

ImageURL	CategoryID	CategoryName
21.jpg	1	Irish & Celtic Gifts
22.jpg	2	Jewelry
23.jpg	3	Crystal & China
24.jpg	4	Pottery & Handblown Glass
25.jpg	5	Foods from Ireland & England
26.jpg	6	Irish Clothing
27.jpg	7	Books, Music & Video
28.jpg	8	Bridal Department

7. Save the file. Open the page in your browser using the following URL: *http://localhost/chapter4/Ch4Proj1.xml*.

8. Print the page from the browser.

9. In Visual Studio .NET, create a schema based on the XML document. (*Hint:* You can right-click on the XML document in XML view or Data view and select **Create Schema**.)

10. Print the schema. You can then open the Ch4Proj1.xsd document and print the schema within XML view.

11. Click the **Save All** button. Click **Build** on the menu bar, then click **Build Solution**. Close all files.

Project 4-2

In this project, you create an XSLT stylesheet to format an XML file. The XML file named Ch4Proj2.xml contains a listing of product categories.

1. Open your **Chapter4** solution in Visual Studio .NET, if it is not already open.

2. Right-click **Chapter4** in the Solution Explorer window, point to **Add**, then click **Add Existing Item**. Browse to locate your data files for this chapter in the Chapter04Data folder. Double-click the file **Ch4Proj2.xml**.

3. Right-click **Chapter4** in the Solution Explorer window, point to **Add**, then click **Add New Item**. Click the stylesheet icon, type **Ch4Proj2.xsl** in the Name text box, then click **Open**.

4. Delete the Body style rule. The Body style rule that you will delete is **body { }**.

5. On the second line, add the main template using the code below. Add the horizontal line, which inserts a line in between each row of data.

```
<xsl:stylesheet xmlns:xsl= ¬
"http://www.w3.org/1999/XSL/Transform" ¬
version="1.0">
<xsl:template match="/">
  <xsl:for-each select="//Category">
    <xsl:apply-templates select="ImageUrl" />
    <xsl:apply-templates select="CategoryName" />
    <xsl:apply-templates select="CategoryID" />
    <hr size="1" width="550" align="left" ¬
color="#003366" />
  </xsl:for-each>
</xsl:template>
```

6. Add the code to display the image and create a hyperlink to the image. Set the Border property to 0.

```
<xsl:template match="ImageUrl">
  <a>
    <xsl:attribute name="href">
      images/<xsl:value-of select="." />
    </xsl:attribute>
    <img>
      <xsl:attribute name="src">
        images/<xsl:value-of select="." />
      </xsl:attribute>
      <xsl:attribute name="border">0
      </xsl:attribute>
    </img>
  </a>
</xsl:template>
```

7. Add the code to display and format the CategoryID and CategoryName.

```
<xsl:template match="CategoryName">
  <div class="cat">Category Name:
      <b><xsl:value-of select="." /></b>
  </div><br />
</xsl:template>
<xsl:template match="CategoryID">
    <div class="cat">Category ID:
    (<xsl:value-of select="." />)
    </div><br />
</xsl:template>
</xsl:stylesheet>
```

8. Save the file. Print the page within Visual Studio .NET. Close all of the pages.

Project 4-3

In this project, you create an ASP.NET page that displays the data in the Ch4Proj3.xml file using the XML control. The XML file named Ch4Proj3.xml contains a listing of product categories. The XSLT stylesheet named Ch4Proj3.xsl contains the style rules to format and display the XML document.

1. Open your **Chapter4** solution in Visual Studio .NET, if it is not already open.

2. Right-click **Chapter4** in the Solution Explorer window, point to **Add**, then click **Add Existing Item**. Browse to locate your data files for this chapter in the Chapter04Data folder. Select the files **Ch4Proj3.xml**, **Ch4Proj3.aspx**, and **Ch4Proj3.xsl**. You can hold the Ctrl key down and select all three items. Click **Open** to import the files into the project. The following message appears: "There is no class file in the project associated with the Web Form 'Ch4Proj3.aspx'. Create a new class file now?" Click **Yes**.

3. Double-click on the **Ch4Proj3.aspx** in the Solution Explorer window to open the page, then double-click on the page to open the code behind the page. In the Page_Load handler, type the code below. This code retrieves the value from the URL and displays the image.

```
Dim ImageUrl As String
  If Request.QueryString.Count > 0 Then
  ImageUrl = Page.Request.QueryString("ImageUrl").ToString
  If ImageUrl.Length > 0 Then
    Image1.ImageUrl = "images/" & ImageUrl
  Else
    Image1.ImageUrl = "images/giftfinder.jpg"
  End If
End If
```

(*Note*: The editor places the End If statement when you create an If-Then statement. There should only be one End If statement for each If-Then statement.)

4. Click the **Ch4Proj3.aspx** tab to return to Design view. Drag an ASP.NET **XML** control from the Toolbox and place the control inside the Panel control. Set the DocumentSource property to **Ch4Proj3.xml**. Set the TransformSource property to **Ch4Proj3.xsl**.

5. Click the **Save All** button. Click **Build** on the menu bar, then click **Build Solution**.

6. Right-click on the page, and then click **View in Browser**. The page should appear as shown in Figure 4-15.

7. Print the Web page, the ASP.NET source code, and the code behind the page. Close all of the pages.

Figure 4-15   Using XLST to transform an XML document into a Web page

Project 4-4

In this project, you create a Web page that displays a rotating banner ad using the AdRotator control.

1. Open your **Chapter4** solution in Visual Studio .NET, if it is not already open.

2. Create the AdScheduler file named **Ch4Proj4.xml** using the data below. (*Note*: If you imported the entire folder of images in the chapter, then you do not have to import them again. However, if you did not import these images, then you need to import them into your images directory in your project.)

ImageURL	NavigateURL	AlternateText	Keyword	Impressions
images/15.jpg	images/15.jpg	Frames & Clocks	Belleek	10
images/16.jpg	images/16.jpg	Decorated Plates	Belleek	15
images/17.jpg	images/17.jpg	Vases	Belleek	20
images/18.jpg	images/18.jpg	Claddagh Theme	Belleek	25
images/19.jpg	images/19.jpg	Tabletop Pieces	Belleek	30
images/20.jpg	images/20.jpg	Gifts for Women	Belleek	35

3. Right-click **Chapter4** in the Solution Explorer window. Point to **Add**, then click **Add Existing Item**. Browse to your Chapter04Data directory and select the **Ch4Proj4.aspx** file, then click **Open** to import the file into the project. The following message appears: "There is no class file in the project associated with the Web Form 'Ch4Proj4.aspx'. Create a new class file now?" Click **Yes**.

4. Double-click the **Ch4Proj4.aspx** file in the Solution Explorer window.

5. Drag and drop the **AdRotator** control from the WebForms tab in the Toolbox to the Web page, placing it below the header.jpg image.

6. Change the Advertisement property in the Properties window to **Ch4Proj4.xml**.

7. Delete the Height and Width properties in the Properties window.

8. Click the **Save All** button. Click **Build** on the menu bar, then click **Build Solution**.

9. Right-click on the page, and then click **View in Browser**. Click **View** on the menu bar, then click **Refresh** to reload the page.

10. Repeat the previous step 10 times, noting which image is displayed each time.

11. Print the ASP.NET source code within Visual Studio .NET. In the Browser view of the Web page, print the Web page and the source code. Close all of the pages.

Project 4-5

In this project, you create a Web page that uses File Upload Server controls to upload a file. You should always have some way for end users to view that their file has been uploaded. After the file is uploaded, you are redirected to the newly created file.

1. Start **Visual Studio .NET** and open your **Chapter4** solution.

2. In Visual Studio .NET create a WebForm named **Ch4Proj5.aspx**.

3. Click the **HTML** tab to edit the HTML code.

4. Add the code below to the form tag.

```
enctype="multipart/form-data"
```

5. Click the **Design** tab to return to Design view.

6. Drag the file **header.jpg** from the images folder in the Solution Explorer window to the top of the page. Drag the **menu.gif** file from the images folder in the Solution Explorer window to the left of the page below the header.jpg image. Drag the **uploadheader.jpg** image from the images folder in the Solution Explorer window to below the header.jpg image and just to the right of the menu.gif file.

7. Add the File Upload Server control to the Web page. The File Upload control is located on the HTML tab and is named File Field. Right-click the control, and then click **Run as Server Control**.

8. Drag and drop a **TextBox** control from the WebForms tab in the Toolbox to the Web page, placing it below the File Upload control.

9. Drag and drop a **Label** control from the WebForms tab in the Toolbox to the Web page, placing it next to the TextBox control.

10. Drag and drop an **ImageButton** from the WebForms tab in the Toolbox to the Web page, placing it below the text box. Change the ImageUrl property to **images/upload.gif**.

11. Double-click the **Upload** button. Add the code below, which allows you to upload the file in the ImageButton1_Click procedure.

```
Dim Path As String
Path = System.IO.Path.GetDirectoryName ¬
    (Server.MapPath("Ch4Proj5.aspx"))
File1.PostedFile.SaveAs((Path & "\" ¬
    & txtFileName.Text))
Response.Redirect(Path & "\" & txtFileName.Text)
```

12. Click the **Save All** button. Click **Build** on the menu bar, then click **Build Solution**.

13. Switch to Design view. Right-click on the page, and then click **View in Browser**.

14. Print the source code of this page from the browser.

15. Click the **Browse** button. From your data directory select the file **uploadtest.txt**. In the text box, enter **uploadtest.txt**. Click the **Upload** Button.

16. The file should be uploaded to the directory where your Web application is installed. You view the page in a browser at *http://localhost/chapter4/test.txt*.

17. Print the ASP.NET source code and the code behind the page within Visual Studio .NET. Close all of the pages.

Project 4-6

In this project, you create a Web page that uses server events to display a Calendar control.

1. Open your **Chapter4** solution in Visual Studio .NET, if it is not already open.

2. Create an ASP.NET page named **Ch4Proj6.aspx**.

3. Drag the file **header.jpg** from the images folder in the Solution Explorer window to the top of the page. Drag the **menu.gif** file from the images folder in the Solution Explorer window to the left of the page, below the header.jpg image.

4. Drag and drop the **Calendar** control from the WebForms tab in the Toolbox to the Web page. Place the calendar below the header.jpg image.

5. In the Properties window, change the Height property to **240px** and the Width property to **400px**.

6. Click the **plus sign** in front of the DayHeaderStyle to expand the properties. Change the BackColor property to **#C0C0FF**. Change the ForeColor property to **MidnightBlue**. Change the Font property to **Trebuchet MS**. Change the Size property to **Medium**.

7. Click the **plus sign** in front of the DayStyle properties. Change the ForeColor property to **MidnightBlue**. Change the HorizontalAlign property to **Center**. Change the Font Name property to **Verdana** and the Size property to **Small**.

8. Click the **plus sign** in front of the NextPrevStyle properties. Change the Font Name property to **Trebuchet MS**. Change the ForeColor property to **MidnightBlue**.

9. Click the **plus sign** in front of the TitleStyle properties. Change the Font Name property to **Trebuchet MS** and the Font Size property to **X-Large**. Change the BackColor property to **#C0C0FF**. Change the ForeColor to **MidnightBlue**.

10. Add a Label control from the WebForms tab to the Web page and position the control below the Calendar control. Change the Text property from Label to **Select your birthday.**

11. Right-click on the page, and then click **View Code** to open the code behind the page.

12. Type the following code below the Page_Load procedure. This code executes when the user clicks a new date. The code displays a message and the selected date.

```
Private Sub Calendar1_SelectionChanged(ByVal sender As
System.Object, ByVal e As System.EventArgs) Handles
Calendar1.SelectionChanged
    Dim Msg As String
    Msg = Calendar1.SelectedDate.ToShortDateString()
    Label1.Text= "You selected: " & Msg
End Sub
```

13. Add an If-Then control structure to determine if the selected date is equal to today's date. You need to use the ToShortDateString property for both date objects when comparing the dates. If the user's birthday is today, display a Happy Birthday message.

```
If Calendar1.SelectedDate.ToShortDateString = ¬
    Date.Now.ToShortDateString() Then
    Label1.Text &= _
    "<br /><br /><b>Happy Birthday!</b>"
Else
End If
```

14. Click the **Save All** button. Click **Build** on the menu bar, then click **Build Solution**.

15. Click the **Design** tab to return to the Design view. Right-click on the page, and then click **View in Browser**. Click the link for next Monday. Click the link for today. Note what messages are displayed on each date.

16. Print the Web page and the source code from the browser. Print the ASP.NET source code and code behind the page within Visual Studio .NET. Close all of the pages.

CASE PROJECTS

Tara Store — Data Storage with XML

Your store provides products from a distributor named Shea's Superstore, in Ireland. Shea's would like you to provide an XML file of your Belleek product inventory. In Visual Studio .NET, you will use the table below to create an XML file named Ch4Case1.xml in your Chapter4 solution. The root node should be ProductNode. The elements should be named ProductID, SubCatID, ModelName, ProductImage, UnitCost, and Thumbnail. Create a schema for your XML file. When you are finished, go to your browser and view the XML file at *http://localhost/chapter4/Ch4Case1.xml*. Print out the view from the browser. View the schema in the browser at *http://localhost/chapter4/ch4Case1.xsd*. Print the schema from the browser.

4

ProductID	SubCatID	ModelName	Product Image	Unit Cost	Thumbnail
550	16	Marriage Blessing Plate	550.jpg	75.00	550.gif
551	16	Claddagh Plate	551.jpg	45.00	551.gif
552	16	Irish Blessing Plate	552.jpg	75.00	552.gif
554	15	Shamrock Picture Frame	554.jpg	70.00	554.gif
555	15	Cashill Clock	555.jpg	110.00	555.gif
557	15	Killarney Clock	557.jpg	70.00	557.gif
559	15	Child's Picture Frame - Boy	559.jpg	50.00	559.gif
561	17	Glendalough Vase	561.jpg	45.00	561.gif
564	17	Tall Daisy Vase	564.jpg	65.00	564.gif
568	19	Shamrock Creamer	568.jpg	50.00	568.gif
570	19	Cup	570.jpg	48.00	570.gif
571	19	Saucer	571.jpg	35.00	571.gif
573	18	Claddagh Bud Vase	573.jpg	30.00	573.gif
556	15	Oval Shamrock Picture Frame	556.jpg	50.00	556.gif
560	15	Child's Picture Frame - Girl	560.jpg	50.00	560.gif
563	17	Claddagh Bud Vase	563.jpg	30.00	563.gif
565	17	Galway Vase	565.jpg	25.00	565.gif
566	17	Colleen Vase	566.jpg	34.00	566.gif
567	19	Shamrock Sugar	567.jpg	50.00	567.gif
572	19	Dinner Plate	572.jpg	80.00	572.gif
574	18	Claddagh Plate	574.jpg	45.00	574.gif
575	18	Claddagh Makeup Bell	575.jpg	25.00	575.gif
576	18	Heart-Shaped Trinket Box	576.jpg	30.00	576.gif
578	18	Heart-Shaped Claddagh Dish	578.jpg	40.00	578.gif
579	20	Kylemore trinket Box	579.jpg	35.00	579.gif
580	20	Shamrock Ring Holder	580.jpg	35.00	580.gif
581	20	Kylemore Bowl	581.jpg	100.00	581.gif
582	20	Claddagh Makeup Bell	582.jpg	25.00	582.gif
583	20	Daisy Candle Holder	583.jpg	45.00	583.gif
584	20	Child's Cup for a Girl	584.jpg	25.00	584.gif
585	20	Child's Cup for Boy	585.jpg	25.00	585.gif
553	16	Mother's Blessing Plate	553.gif	65.00	553.gif
569	19	Shamrock Teapot	569.jpg	250.00	569.gif

Tara Store — Data Transformation with the XML Control

Shea's Superstore has asked you to create a Web page to view the data. Use an XSLT stylesheet to transform the data in the Ch4Case2.xml document into a Web page. First, create an XSLT stylesheet to read and format the data. You should use the Thumbnail data to create an image that is displayed in the Web page. You should format the price of the products with a dollar sign. You should format the data using a table. Save this stylesheet as Ch4case2.xsl in your Chapter4 solution.

Create a Web page named Ch4Case2.aspx. Add the XML control to the Web page. Change the DocumentSource property to Ch4Case2.xml. Change the TransformSource property to Ch4Case2.xsl. Your page should appear as shown in Figure 4-16. Add your company logo, graphics, color, and content to enhance the appearance of the page. Print out your Web page and the source code. Print out the XSLT stylesheet.

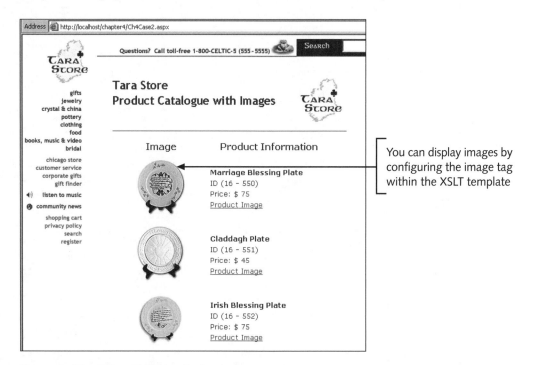

Figure 4-16   Using XLST to display images

Tara Store — Data Transformation with the XML Control

Your manager would like you to create a report that will display graphic images for the product ratings. Your manager created an XML file named Ch4Case3.xml and an XSLT stylesheet named Ch4Case3.xsl to display and format the report. He also created a third file, named Ch4Case3.aspx, that contains the page layout. You will need to add these files to the Chapter4 solution. The report applies a different format style based upon the number of stars awarded to the product. Your boss would like to add the product data from the XML document. Use the XML control to add the data to the Web page. You will need to set the XML control properties to point to the XML document and XSLT stylesheet. Modify the XSLT stylesheet and the ASP.NET page to enhance the appearance of the page. Add your company logo, graphics, color, and content to enhance the appearance of the page. Printout the Web page and the ASP.NET source code. Print out the XSLT style sheet and the XML document.

4

Figure 4-17   Using XLST to process data

Tara Store — Filtering Data with XSLT

Your boss only wants to display the Belleek products for Shea's department store. Use an XSLT stylesheet to transform the data in the Ch4Case4.xml document into a Web page. First, create an XSLT stylesheet to read and format the data. Only display Belleek products, where the subcategory ID is 20. You may format the stylesheet using tables and display the product images. Save this stylesheet as Ch4case4.xsl in your Chapter4 solution.

Create a Web page named Ch4Case4.aspx. Add the XML control to the Web page. Change the DocumentSource property to Ch4Case4.xml. Change the TransformSource property to Ch4Case4.xsl. Add your company logo, graphics, color, and content to enhance the appearance of the page. Print out your Web page and the source code. Print out the XSLT stylesheet.

Tara Store — Creating a Rotating Banner Ad

The marketing manager at Tara Store has sold contracts to several other Irish Web sites to allow them to display their banner on the Tara Store Web site. Create a page named Ch4Case5.xml that contains the ads, using data from the table below.

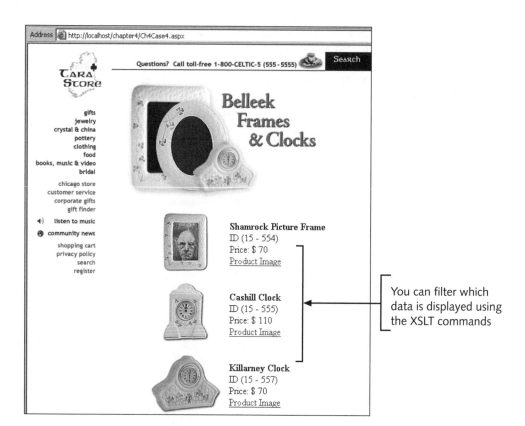

Figure 4-18   Using XLST to filter data

ImageURL	NavigateURL	AlternateText	Keyword	Impressions
Images/4a.jpg	http://www.joyofireland.com	Joy of Ireland	Store	10
Images/4b.jpg	http://www.rootsweb.com/~irish	The Irish Genealogical Society-International	Culture	15
Images/4c.jpg	http://www.aoh.com	Ancient Order of Hibernians	Culture	20
Images/4d.jpg	http://www.ireland.com	The Irish Times	News	25
Images/4e.jpg	http://home.iol.ie	Ireland On-Line	News	30
Images/4f.jpg	http://www.irelandseye.com	Ireland's Eye	Culture	35
Images/4g.jpg	http://www.irishamhc.com	Irish American Heritage Center	Culture	25

Create a page named Ch4Case5.aspx. Add an AdRotator control to the page. Filter the ads to only show culture-related links. Enhance the page with text, color, and graphics. View the page and print out the Web pages and the ASP.NET source code.

Tara Store — Creating an Interactive Calendar Control

The store manager needs a method to display a calendar to his employees in order to schedule employee vacation time. Create a Web page with the Calendar control, named Ch4Case6.aspx. Create two buttons labeled Start Date and End Date. When the user clicks on a date, then clicks the Start Date button, display a message confirming the start date of the vacation. When the user clicks on a date, then clicks the End Date button, display a message confirming the end date of the vacation. Display the start and ending dates to the user using Label controls. Save the Web pages as Ch4Case6.aspx. Add your company logo, graphics, color, and content to enhance the appearance of the page. Print out your Web page, the source code for the ASP.NET page, and the code behind the page.

4

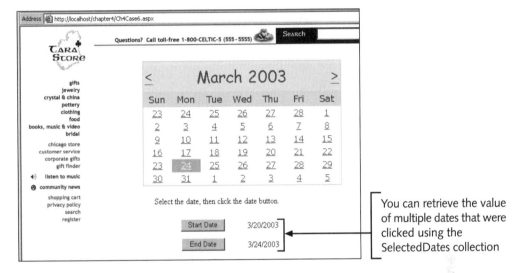

Figure 4-19   The Calendar control

Tara Store — Creating an Administration File Upload Tool

You have been asked to create an administration tool for the shopping cart on the Tara Store Web site. Open the Chapter4 solution in Visual Studio .NET. Create a login form that authenticates the user. Save the page as Ch4Case7Login.aspx. If the user is validated, allow the user to the upload the file. If the user is not authenticated, redisplay the form. Add the File Upload control to the page. Allow the user to enter a new filename in a text box. (*Note:* The user must enter a valid file name and extension.) Create a new folder in your project, named Ch4Case7, in your c:\InetPub\ wwwroot\Chapter4 directory. Allow only the store manager to upload only image files to the Ch4Case7 directory. (*Note:* Using the Accept property feature may only work in some browsers.) His username is StoreMan and his password is GalwayBay. Enhance the page with text, color, and graphics. Provide a link to the Ch4Case7 folder so that users can browse the folder and view their uploaded image. Print your Web pages and the source code for each ASP.NET page and the code behind the page.

5

USING VISUAL BASIC .NET WITHIN AN ASP.NET PAGE

In this chapter, you will:

♦ Define object-oriented programming

♦ Use Visual Basic .NET to manipulate the code behind the page

♦ Create classes using Visual Basic .NET

♦ Use variables to store data

♦ Learn how data types are stored in the .NET Framework

♦ Use collections to store groups of data elements

♦ Create and use procedures in Visual Basic .NET

♦ Learn how to use Visual C# .NET instead of Visual Basic .NET to create ASP.NET pages

---

Today, companies want programs that can be easily maintained and integrated with other applications. Companies need to build reusable programs with different data sources. To accomplish this, programmers use object-oriented programming techniques to encapsulate the business logic. Then, they create applications that can access the business logic, regardless of how the program was written. ASP.NET code can be written using a variety of programming languages. In this chapter, you will learn how to use object-oriented programming techniques and Visual Basic .NET within an ASP.NET page.

The entire ASP.NET application is compiled into one or more logical groupings known as namespaces. Within the namespace, you can build reusable code from classes. Within the .NET Framework, the Base Class Library provides access to many built-in classes. You can also create your own class, which in turn enables you to create objects. These objects can be used in your program to store reusable code. You can store data in a variety of data structures—variables, constants, collections, and databases—and retrieve it at a later time. In this chapter, you will learn to create classes, store data using several data structures, and access the data using functions and methods.

OBJECT-ORIENTED PROGRAMMING

In the very early days of BASIC (the precursor to Visual Basic), each line of code was given a number, and the statements were executed sequentially in a single file. Commands such as GOTO allowed you to divert the code to another line in the program. Later, decision control structures were used to control the execution order of the program. **Decision control structures** use conditional expressions to determine which block of code to execute. The code is a group of one or more programming statements. If a condition is met, then a block of code is executed, otherwise, an alternate block of code is executed. Visual Basic allows you to create decision control structures, as well as functions and procedures, which are used to control the order that the programming statements were executed. This type of programming is often referred to as procedural programming and the programming statements are known as **procedural code**.

Today an ASP.NET application organizes code into several physical files called **modules**. When the application is written in Visual Basic .NET, each module ends in the file extension .vb. Modules consist of one or more classes. Within each module are programming statements. Some of these programming statements are grouped as event handlers and procedures. These programming statements are stored in a class definition. An **object** is a set of related code that is compartmentalized. In **object-oriented programming**, you create objects based upon a class, and then you can access the procedures and properties of the object across multiple Web pages.

The creation of an object consists of two separate tasks. The first task is to create the object definition, called the **class**. The class is not an object that you can access directly; it is the code that contains the procedures and properties of the object. Once you create the class, you can create objects based upon the class definition. In other words, the class is the template for the new object. When you create an object, you are really creating an instance of the class. **Instantiation** is the process of declaring and initializing an object from a class. You can create many objects from the same object definition. This process in analogous to making cookies. If you have a recipe to make cookies, you know what the ingredients are, and you know how to combine the ingredients to make the cookies. But a recipe is not a cookie. First you make the cookie dough, then you bake it, and only then have you made cookies. The class is like the cookie recipe, since it contains the directions to create a cookie. Instantiation is like the process of mixing and baking the dough.

The ability to create many cookies based on a single recipe is useful, because then all of the cookies have the same properties (for example, they all taste the same). Each object you create from the class inherits the properties and procedures from the class definition. However, there may be times when you want to make oatmeal cookies instead of chocolate chip cookies. If the cookie recipe contains general information about making cookies, you can reuse the recipe to make an oatmeal cookie by changing some of the ingredients and measurements. Similarly, you can create multiple objects from the same class, and also assign different values to each object's properties.

Below is a sample of how to create a class named TaraStoreClass. The line `Public Class TaraStoreClass` means that the class is available to other applications, and that the name of the class is TaraStoreClass. The line `End Class` identifies the end of the code within the class definition. This class contains one variable named StoreName. Later in this chapter, you will learn to create a class, instantiate an object, and reuse the code stored within the object.

```
Public Class TaraStoreClass
    Private StoreName As String = "Tara Store"
End Class
```

In the class definition, you can restrict which applications have access to the class. Only procedures and properties that are declared **Public** can interact with other objects outside of the base class. Procedures and properties that are declared as **Private** can only be called within the base class. Protected procedures and properties can be called from within the base class, and within subclasses. **Subclasses** are used to create a class that inherits from a base class. Procedures and properties that are declared as **Friend** can be called from anywhere within the same application.

After you have created the class definition, you can instantiate an object based on the class definition. You must use the keyword dim to declare a variable in which to store the object, and the keyword new to identify that this is an object based on a class definition. The class in the sample code below is named TaraStoreClass. The object is stored in the variable named Ch5Class. The class is contained within the Chapter5 namespace. Therefore, the class is referred to as `Chapter5.TaraStoreClass`.

```
Dim Ch5Class As New Chapter5.TaraStoreClass()
```

Both procedures and event handlers can also contain one or more programming statements. Some of these statements are action statements, for example changing the value of a text box. Some of the statements are decision control structures, which allow you to organize the order in which the code is executed. As you learned previously, when an action occurs, such as the button being clicked, the click event triggers the OnClick event handler. The event handler executes code when the event occurs. Procedures are executed only when they are called by another procedure or event handler.

There are two types of procedures: **subprocedures** and **functions**. Both contain one or more programming statements, and both are a named grouping of one or more programming statements. You can pass values, called parameters, to subprocedures and functions in the class. These values are called **parameters**. Parameters can be passed to the method in a comma delimited list within a pair of parentheses. The parentheses are required even if no parameters are passed. Built-in functions include mathematical functions, date and time, string, and formatting functions, among others. However, functions can return a value to the program that called the function. When the function ends, a value can be returned to the main program by using the return keyword. Below is an example of a function named GetStoreName that returns the name of the store. The keyword return is used to identify a value that is returned to the code that called the function. You will learn more about functions later in this chapter.

```
Public Function GetStoreName() As String
    Return "Tara Store"
End Function
```

Properties are used to set the value of a variable defined within an object. You can call any of the object's methods and properties that are defined in the class. You can also assign values to properties that are declared in the class after the object is created, and you can assign values to the properties when you create the object from the class. Then, when you create the object, you use the class to create a new instance of the object, which contains different values for the properties. The sample code below shows how a property is defined within a class. You will learn more about defining properties later in this chapter.

```
Public ReadOnly Property StoreName() As String
    Get
        Return StoreName
    End Get
End Property
```

Properties are identified by the name of the object, followed by a period, followed by the name of the property. Some properties are assigned to the object by default within the object definition. Then, all new objects inherit the same properties as the original object definition. However, if an object does not assign a value to a property, and a new object is created without assigning a value to the property, the property is assigned the default value "undefined." (*Note*: In the next section, you will learn to use property methods to expose private variables that are defined within the class.)

```
lblContact.Text = Ch5Class.StoreName.ToString()
```

Object-oriented programming languages support concepts such as inheritance, encapsulation, abstraction, and polymorphism. **Inheritance** allows you to derive the interface and behaviors from another class. The keyword **inherits** allows you to inherit from another .NET class. With the Common Language Runtime, all objects are inherited from the System namespace, and these objects are referred to as types. Each object inherits properties and procedures from the System namespace, including Equals, GetHashCode, GetType, and ToString. Therefore, because all objects are inherited from the System namespace, some of the properties such as ToString apply to most objects. For example, all of the form fields are objects within the System.UI.Web class, and so they all can use the ToString function to display their values as a string. The ToString function is inherited from the System class. It is also possible to override the interface and behaviors that were inherited from another class.

The ability to assign different values to each object's properties is called encapsulation. **Encapsulation** means that the inner workings of the object, such as the procedures and properties, are maintained within the object. Encapsulation enables you to create objects

5

or programs that are self-contained. You can create multiple objects based on the same class, as long as the names are unique. For example, your inventory application needs to interact with the shopping cart application to provide the number of items in stock. Both applications contain objects that interact with each other. If the Purchasing Department changes the database server application that stores the inventory data, the inventory application needs to be changed to reflect the new database software. However, the shopping cart application does not have to be altered because the interface between the two applications remains consistent. The business logic within the inventory application is isolated from the business logic within the shopping cart application. Therefore, encapsulation makes it easier to upgrade applications that interact with other applications.

Abstraction is the ability to create a concept using code. For example, a customer is a person who makes purchases from a company. A customer object is the programming code that represents the customer. The customer object may contain information about the customer, such as the shipping address and purchases. The objects interact with each other via a public **interface** that is defined in the class. You can use the functions, properties, events, and attributes to interact with the interface.

Polymorphism is the ability to create code that can be applied to objects that are derived from different classes. If you have an application that contains a student object and a faculty object, you can write an application that retrieves the name property from both objects. Polymorphism allows you to apply programs across different classes.

INTRODUCTION TO VISUAL BASIC .NET

It's important to have an understanding of where Visual Basic .NET fits within ASP.NET and Visual Studio .NET. Visual Basic .NET code can be created using simple text editors such as Notepad. This code must be compiled manually using the command-line compiler that is provided with the .NET Framework. The code is compiled into the MSIL, Microsoft Intermediate Language. In Chapter 1, you used the compiler to create a simple Visual Basic .NET program. When you create an ASP.NET application using Notepad instead of Visual Studio .NET, you may include your Visual Basic .NET code within the Web page. Typically the code is inserted at the top of the Web page. Logically, this code represents the code behind the Web page that you created in the previous chapter. You lose the developer tools, such as the debugging tools, that are part of Visual Studio .NET.

A typical Visual Basic .NET application contains a graphical user interface called a **form** through which the program interacts with the user. The form is an object that is inherited from the `System.Windows.Forms` namespace. The Visual Studio .NET Toolbox contains a tab called WinForms that contains controls that are typically added to a Windows Form. The form contains code behind the graphical interface, which is used to interact with any of the objects contained on the form. When you build the application, Visual Studio .NET compiles the code and stores the .dll file that contains the namespace in the projects bin directory. The bin directory has execute permission, which allows the code to be executed at runtime.

In this book, you use Visual Studio .NET to create the code behind the ASP.NET page, and not behind the Windows Form. Because you are working on a Web page and not a Windows Form, you do not have the same type of controls available. However, you do have the same access to the Visual Basic .NET programming language. You can create classes using an external file, or create the class in the code behind the page. If you want to use a class that is located in a different file, you need to import the class into the Web page, and then create a new object using the class. Then, all of the properties and procedures of the class will be available to the new object.

In the .NET framework, the ASP.NET page is a class within the application that inherits from the class that is inherited from the ASP.NET page class. The ASP.NET page inherits the code behind the page. By default, when you create an ASP.NET Web page in Visual Studio .NET, a class that represents that page is created. The name of the class is the same as the name of the Web page. On the first line of the Web page, Visual Studio .NET inserts the keyword inherits and identifies the name of the class that is created in the code behind the Web page.

Within your ASP.NET page, you have access to the same System namespace as Windows Forms. Therefore, your application can inherit the same value and reference types as Visual Basic .NET. You can also define your own classes, and the properties and procedures within those classes. When the build method is called, the code behind the page is compiled into the same .dll file that contains the namespace for the application.

Most of the documentation on ASP.NET contains code samples created in Notepad. In these examples, the Visual Basic .NET code is contained within the ASP.NET page. However, it is better to use Visual Studio .NET to create your Visual Basic .NET code in the code behind the page. The code is split between two files, which makes your code easier to maintain. Not only do you have the benefits of Visual Studio .NET development and debugging tools, but you also have the ability to work in a multiuser environment, and all of the project files can be managed within Visual Studio .NET. The Visual Studio .NET Enterprise Edition comes with an additional application called Visual Safe Source, which provides additional resources to help teams of developers who want to work on the same project files, but don't want the problems of having multiple versions of documents and developers deleting other developers' work.

Creating a Class

In the following exercise, you will create a new project and define a class. Because you have only created the class definition, and have not created an instance of the object yet, you cannot refer to the object by its name within the class definition. Therefore, the keyword Me can be used in place of the object name within the class definition. (*Note*: In C# the keyword Me is replaced with the keyword This.) Procedures are identified by the name of the object followed by a period, followed by the name of the procedure. After you define the class and create the object, you will modify the value of the variables defined within the object.

1. Start **Visual Studio .NET**.

2. Click **File** on the menu bar, point to **New**, then click **Project**. This opens the New Project window.

3. Under Project Types, click **Visual Basic Projects**, and under Templates click **ASP.NET Web Application**. Type **Chapter5** in the Location text box in place of WebApplication1. Click **OK** to create the solution, project, and default files.

4. Right-click **Chapter5** in the Solution Explorer window, point to **Add**, then click **New Folder**. Type **images** for the folder name, then press **Enter**.

5. Right-click the **images** folder, point to **Add**, then click **Add Existing Item**. Browse to locate your data files for this chapter. (*Note*: In the Files of type drop-down list, you need to change the selection from VB Code Files to **Image Files**.)

6. Select all of the files in the images directory of the Chapter05data\images directory. (*Note*: You can use the Ctrl+A key combination to select all of the files.) Click the **Open** button to import the images into your project within the images directory.

7. Right-click **Chapter5** in the Solution Explorer window, point to **Add**, then click **Add New Item**. In the dialog box, under Templates, click the **Class** icon. In the Name text box replace the default name by typing **TaraStoreClass.vb**, then click **Open**. The page opens in Code view. The class declaration is already inserted for you.

8. Within the TaraStoreClass definition, add the following code. This code creates two variables that can be called from your Web pages. The keyword dim is not used here, because then each variable would be made private to the class by default. The keyword public is required to ensure that the class in the Web page can retrieve the variables. The StoreName and StoreEmail variables are instance variables that are private to the TaraStoreClass class. They are not available outside of the TaraStoreClass class.

```
Public StoreName As String = "Tara Store"
Public StoreEmail As String = "info@TaraStore.com"
```

9. Click Edit on the menu bar, point to **Outlining**, then click **Start Automatic Outlining**. This allows you to visually see the code using a graphical outline. (*Note*: If this option is already running, it is not displayed on the Outlining menu.)

10. Click **Tools** on the menu bar, then click **Options**. The Options window opens. Click the folder labeled **Text Editor**, click the folder labeled **Basic**,

then, click the **Line numbers** check box to select it. Click the **OK** button to close the window, as shown below in Figure 5-1.

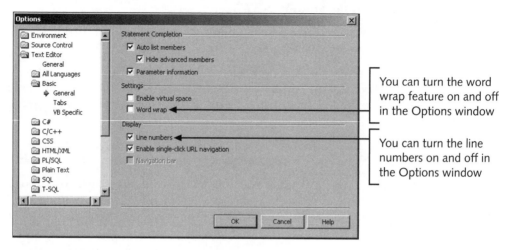

You can turn the word wrap feature on and off in the Options window

You can turn the line numbers on and off in the Options window

Figure 5-1 Configuring the Code view options

11. Click the **Save All** button. The code to create the class should look like the code in Figure 5-2.

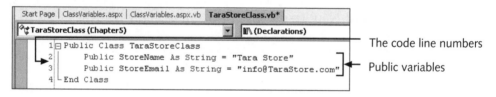

The code line numbers

Public variables

Figure 5-2 Creating a class in an external VB file

12. Right-click **Chapter5** in the Solution Explorer window, point to **Add**, then click **Add Existing Item**. Navigate to your Chapter05data directory, and double-click the file **ClassVariables.aspx**. You will have to change the File of type list box to **All Files**. The following pop-up message appears: "There is no class file in the project associated with the Web Form 'ClassVariables.aspx'. Create a new class file now?" Click **Yes**. Double-click the file in the Solution Explorer window to open it.

13. Double-click on the page to open the code behind the page. In the Page_Load procedure add the following code to create a new object named **Ch5Class** based on the TaraStoreClass. Because the variable contains an object, you must use the keyword new to instantiate the object from a class. As you type each period, notice that the IntelliSense list box appears. Your Chapter5 namespace contains a class named TaraStoreClass. As you type the

name of the assembly, Chapter5 and the period, a list of objects defined is displayed in a drop-down list box. You can use the arrow keys or the pointer to make your selection, as shown in Figure 5-3.

```
Dim Ch5Class As New Chapter5.TaraStoreClass()
```

Figure 5-3   Instantiating an object in a Web page

14. On the next line, add the code to retrieve the values from the new class. By default, this new object inherits the properties and methods of the TaraStoreClass. You can assign the properties to the Text property of the Label control that is located on the WebForm. The ToString method is used to retrieve the value of the two variables from the string objects. The values are inherited when the object was created from the initial class. The code should appear as shown in Figure 5-4.

```
lblContact.Text = Ch5Class.StoreName.ToString() _
& "<br />" & Ch5Class.StoreEmail.ToString()
```

Figure 5-4   Retrieving the values of variables defined within an object

15. Click the **Save All** button. Click **Build** on the menu bar, then click **Build Solution**.

16. Click the **ClassVariables.aspx** tab in the main window. Click the **Design** tab to change to the Design view if necessary. Right-click on the page and click **View in Browser**. (*Note:* You can also view the page in your browser at *http://localhost/chapter5/ClassVariables.aspx*.) The page should appear as shown in Figure 5-5.

Figure 5-5   Viewing the ClassVariables page

You can use the IL Disassembler (ILDASM) tool to view the namespace and locate any of the classes created within your Windows or Web application. The ILDASM is the graphical tool used to visually look at the objects within the application. In the following steps you will view the Chapter5 assembly using the ILDASM.

1. Go to the Visual Studio .NET command prompt. In most computers, to access this command click **Start** menu, point to **Programs**, point to **Microsoft Visual Studio .NET**, point to **Visual Studio .NET Tools**, then click **Visual Studio .NET Command Prompt**.

2. At the command prompt enter **cd Inetpub\wwwroot\Chapter5\bin**. By default your assembly is compiled and placed within this directory.

3. At the command prompt enter **ILDASM Chapter5.dll** to open the ILDASM window. (*Note:* The name of your assembly and the namespace is Chapter5, which is also the name of your .dll file.)

4. Click the **plus sign** next to the Chapter5 icon to expand the Chapter5 namespace.

5. Click the **plus sign** next to the TaraStoreClass icon to expand the class information. Double-click **StoreEmail:public string**. This opens a window that tells you that the StoreEmail is a field within the TaraStoreClass type, and is a public variable of type string. Notice in Figure 5-6 that the ClassVariables.aspx and WebForm1.aspx are also shown as classes because all Web pages are now classes within the application namespace.

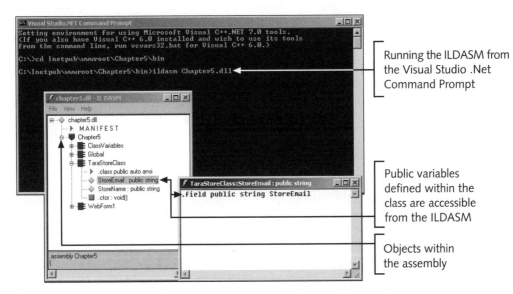

Running the ILDASM from the Visual Studio .Net Command Prompt

Public variables defined within the class are accessible from the ILDASM

Objects within the assembly

Figure 5-6 Viewing the new object properties in the ILDASM Tool

6. Close all of the ILDASM windows and the Command Prompt window by clicking the **Close** button in each window.

7. Close any open pages.

Variables

In the previous example you created a variable and retrieved the value. In this section, you will learn more about how to use variables within your application. **Variables** are used to store data that can be retrieved at a later time. For example, a variable might be used to store a value that is to be used during a calculation. If you need to calculate several values, compare values, or perform multiple operations on a value, then it is worthwhile to use variables to store them, in lieu of using the values themselves. The program can then refer to the variable instead of the value. In the previous exercise, you created a class that contained two variables. You declared each variable as a string, and assigned it a value. Because the variable is defined within a class definition, you are able to retrieve the values from within the Web page by creating an object based upon that class definition.

A **variable declaration** consists of two parts: a **variable name** and a **data type**. While it is obvious that the name refers to the variable name, it is less obvious that the name also refers to a section of memory on the computer. The exact location of the variable in the computer's memory is unimportant because you can refer to the location by using the name of the variable.

The data type identifies what kind of data the variable can store. For example, a variable might be an **integer** used in a calculation, or it might be a **string** of characters that is used to store the name of the company.

 Although Visual Basic .NET and Visual C# .NET support different data types, when the application is compiled, the managed code converts the data types to the same data type across all languages.

Variable Declaration

Some programming languages, including Visual Basic .NET, require that you declare variables before using them in scripts or programs. When you declare a variable, the computer reserves the memory required to store the variable. **Declaring** a variable is the process of reserving the memory space for the variable before it is used in the program. Variables that are declared in the class are referred to as **members**, **member variables**, or **instance variables**.

The variable is defined within a class, event handler, or procedure. Where the variable is defined will determine where the variable can be used within the application. You use the keywords private, public, friend, and protected to specify the scope of the variable. Private variables are only available to code within the local class and are defined with the keyword public. Global or public variables are used outside the class. Friend variables are used only within the current application or project. Protected variables can only be called from within the base class, and from within subclasses.

In Visual Basic .NET, you declare a variable using the keyword dim and the name of the variable. Variables declared exist as long as the procedure or function in which they are declared exists.

```
dim intQuantity as Integer
dim intPrice as Integer
dim strName as String
dim strEmail as String
```

If you have multiple variables to declare, you can declare each one on a separate line, or use a single line. To declare several variables on a single line, use the declaration keyword once, followed by the list of variables separated by a comma. The following examples illustrate how to declare multiple variables in Visual Basic .NET.

```
dim intQuantity, intPrice as Integer
dim strName, strEmail as String
dim decPrice, decCost as Decimal
```

You can force a program written in Visual Basic .NET to declare all variables before the variables can be used. Declaring variables before they are used makes it easier to debug your code. For example, it helps you catch spelling and syntax errors. If you type in the wrong name for a variable, the program will not run until you declare the variable with the correct name. The option explicit mode is used to require the page to declare all variables before they can be used. Use the phrase `<%@Page Option Explicit = true %>` in the first line within the HTML code view to force all variables to be declared before they can be used. This statement must be placed at the top of the Web page before any other HTML or scripts. You can also place this code in the Web.config configuration file. Then, all pages inherit this property. Although by default you are required to declare all variables before they can be used, you can turn off this feature using `<% option explicit = false %>` at the top of the Web page.

Naming Variables

When naming variables, your options are almost infinite, but there are certain naming rules in Visual Basic .NET that you must adhere to. Violations of these conventions result in errors in your programs.

- You cannot use any of the Visual Basic .NET commands or keywords as your variable name.

- Variable names must begin with a letter.

- You cannot use a period or space within a variable name.

- Avoid using any special characters in a variable name except for the underscore.

Variables are more useful if you name them with a standardized naming convention. This makes them easier to identify, and also makes spelling and syntax errors less likely. One important convention is case sensitivity. Visual Basic .NET commands and variables are not case sensitive. Therefore, Visual Basic .NET interprets intPrice and INTPRICE and intPrice the same way. However, it is useful to be consistent in the naming of variables because other programming languages, such as C#, would interpret those variable names as two separate variables. Variables often consist of two or more combined words. The first letter of each word is often capitalized, for example, as in the variable names LastName and IntPrice.

It is also useful to provide your variables with a descriptive name, one that has some meaning or association with the contents or purpose of the variable. Using the data type prefix and a descriptive variable name makes your code much more readable. The naming convention does not affect how the memory space is reserved for the variable. For example, the variable that holds the price of a product can be named IntPrice to indicate that the variable contains an integer that describes the price of a product. This technique, known as Hungarian notation, uses the first three characters to identify the datatype. Table 5-1 contains a list of common prefixes used in Visual Basic .NET.

5

Table 5-1   Common prefixes used in Visual Basic .NET

Data Type	Prefix	Sample Variable Name
Boolean	Bln	BlnMember
Byte	Byt	BytZero
Char	Chr	ChrLetter
Date	Dat	DatBirthdate
Double	Dbl	DblWeight
Decimal	Dec	DecProductPrice
Integer	Int	IntNumberProducts
Long	Lng	LngSalary
Single	Sng	SngAverage
Short	Sho	ShoYears
String	Str	StrLastName

Assigning Values to Variables

You can store values in variables using the assignment operator. The **assignment operator** is the equal sign (=). To assign a value to a variable, enter the name of the variable on the left side of the assignment operator, and enter the new value on the right side of the assignment operator. You can assign the value to the variable when you declare the variable, or after the variable has been created. The sample code below shows you how to declare multiple variables at the same time, and how to assign a value to a variable when the variable is declared.

```
Dim LastName, FirstName as String
Dim StoreName As String = "TaraStore"
```

Note that the equal sign is an assignment operator, and not an arithmetic operator.

Constants

You can use a **constant** instead of a variable when you want to assign a value to a variable that does not change. For example, you can use constants for tax rates, shipping fees, and values used in mathematical equations. The keyword const is used to declare a constant. The naming rules for variables also apply to constants. However, the names of constants are usually all uppercase. In addition, when you declare a constant, you need to assign the value to the constant.

```
Const TAXRATE As Integer = 8
```

Concatenation

In Visual Basic .NET, strings can be manipulated using several techniques. **Concatenation** is the process of joining together one or more strings. The string can be a literal string, the result returned from an expression, or a variable that contains a string data type. You can also use built-in methods to determine the length of the string, locate characters within the string, and truncate the spaces at the beginning or end of the string. In the sample code below, the variable is used to store the result of an expression. The expression is built using the values from the properties, and a line break tag. The ampersand is used to concatenate the expression to one single string. (*Note*: Because the code is long, the underscore character is used to continue the code to the next line.) Then, the variable is assigned to the Text property of the Label control.

```
Dim lblControlContent = Ch5Class.StoreName.ToString() _
& "<br />" & Ch5Class.StoreEmail.ToString()
lblContact.Text = lblControlContent
```

Data Types

There are several data types built into the .NET framework. All of the variables are declared as a data type, or type. The two categories of types are reference types and value types. Examples of **reference types** are strings, classes, arrays, collections, and objects. Value types are also referred to as **primitive types** or **structures**. Examples of **value types** are Boolean, Integer, Decimal, Char, and DateTime. These datatypes are also referred to as **subtypes**, and are as follows:

- String
- Char
- Byte
- Short
- Long
- Integer
- Date
- Boolean
- Decimal

Value types and reference types are stored in different locations in memory. Value types store their data in an area called the **stack** because they contain numeric data that can be stored using a fixed number of bytes. Searching for variables that contain value types is more efficient if they are stored in the stack than in the managed heap. Reference types are stored in the managed heap because the amount of memory required to store them may vary. The **managed heap** contains memory addresses that are used to store variables that are reference types. The garbage collector from the Common Language Runtime allocates and manages the managed heap. All newly created objects are allocated at the top of the managed heap. Periodically, the garbage collector removes objects that are no longer referenced from the heap.

String

The string is used to store text, which can consist of numbers, characters, and date information. Number values not used in mathematical expressions are more efficiently stored as strings. Social Security numbers, zip codes, and phone numbers are typically stored as strings. However, strings are stored as basic text, and must be explicitly converted to a numerical data type before a string value can be used in an arithmetic expression. When you assign a string a value, the value must be within quotation marks. All strings are stored as Unicode. Unicode allows you to have more letters than the 26 letters of the American alphabet. Strings are variable in length. Therefore, you don't have to specify the number of characters in the string when you create the string object.

There are several methods built into the string object.

- The **Ltrim, Rtrim**, and **Trim methods** remove the blank spaces from the preceding, ending, and both ends of the string, respectively.

- The **Asc method** provides the string's ANSI (American National Standards Institute) character equivalent.

- The **Chr method** provides the ASCII (American Standard Code for Information Interchange) character equivalent. Chr is a useful method when you want to create control characters such as carriage returns.

- The **Replace method** replaces one string with another.

- The **Split method** returns a string that has been split, using a delimiter to identify where to split the string.

- The **Concat method** allows you to join strings together without using the concatenation operator.

- The **Compare method** allows you to compare two strings. If they are equal, the method returns 0. If the value on the left side is less than the value on the right side, then a negative integer is returned; otherwise a positive integer is returned.

- The **LCase** and **UCase methods** convert the case to lowercase and uppercase, respectively.

The sample code below retrieves the value from a text box and stores the value in a variable as all lowercase.

```
Dim Password As String
Password = LCase(txtPassword.Value)
lblPassword.Text = Password
```

The **Format method** allows you to format numeric output. The Format method allows you to format the string using currency, percent, and other format properties. The sample code below illustrates how to format the number as currency, decimal, number, hexadecimal and percentage. The Number property is used to format the number using commas.

```
System.Console.WriteLine({"0:c"}, 1441.33)
System.Console.WriteLine({"0:D"}, 1441.33)
System.Console.WriteLine({"0:N"}, 1441.33)
System.Console.WriteLine({"0:x"}, 255)
System.Console.WriteLine({"0:00%"}, 255.25)
```

Char

Char data type allows you to store a single text value as a number. The char datatype stores a number between 0 and 65, 535. The char data type can be used to create new character sets for other types of languages that use Unicode standards.

Numeric

The numeric data types include Byte, Short, Long, and Integer. Real number data types are represented by the types Single, Double, and Decimal.

- A **byte** stores an integer between 0 and 255. A byte data type is stored in a single byte on the computer. (*Note*: A byte is composed of 8 bits. Each bit is represented by 0 or 1.)

- A **Short data type** is a 16-bit number. Therefore, a short data type can only store values from −32,768 to 32,767.

- The **Integer data type** is a 32-bit whole number and is the preferred data type for representing a 32-bit number on a 32-bit operating system.

- The **Long data type** is a 64-bit number and is the preferred data type for representing a 64-bit number on a 64-bit operating system.

- The **Single data type** represents a single-precision floating point number.

- The **Double data type** supports larger numbers than the single data type.

- The **Decimal data type** can store numbers up to 28 decimal places and is often used to store currency data. Variables that store monetary values have a subtype called decimal. (*Note*: In previous versions of Visual Basic .NET this data type was known as **currency**. You can use formatting methods to change the appearance of the decimal data type to currency.)

When you convert a long number to an integer, you may lose some data. Visual Studio .NET sets the option strict on by default so that any conversion that would result in data loss is halted. Only widening conversions are allowed, because there is no data loss. If you place `<% option strict %>` in the Visual Basic .NET code, you enable your code to implicitly convert Long data types to integers.

You can learn more about the System namespace data types at *ms-help://MS.VSCC/MS.MSDNVS/cpref/html/frlrfsystem.htm*.

DateTime

The **DateTime data type** is used to store dates. The date and time values are stored in the formats mm/dd/yyyy and hh:mm:ss. The date value is enclosed within a pair of pound signs. Visual Basic .NET can store any date between 01/01/0001 and 12/31/9999. Use the DateTime class to declare a date object. You can retrieve or assign a value to the date using the pound sign before and after the date, as shown in the sample code below.

```
Dim MyBirthday As DateTime
MyBirthday = #3/22/2002#
```

You can learn more about the System namespace data types at ms-help://MS.VSCC/MS.MSDNVS/cpref/html/frlrfsystemdatetimeclassmember-stopic.htm. You can also find information about retrieving the current date at *ms-help://MS.VSCC/MS.MSDNVS/cpref/html/frlrfsystemdatetimeclass-nowtopic.htm*.

Boolean

A **Boolean data type** only has two possible values. The Boolean data type is used to store either a True value or False value. (*Note*: George Boole developed the branch of mathematics related to outcomes of true or false.) Typically, in binary math, one represents true and zero represents false. However, when a Boolean value is used within a mathematical expression, the value of the Boolean variable is converted to a number. When these values are converted to an integer, the True value is converted to −1, and the False value is converted to 0. (*Note*: In the previous version of Visual Basic, the True value was converted to 1.)

Using a Property to Retrieve and Set the Value of a Variable

To use an instance variable outside of a class from a different class, you need to use the property function, or to declare the variable public. A property is not the same thing as a variable. A **property** is a method that is used to get and set values. These values may be stored within a variable within the class. You can use the property method to make the instance variable available to code outside of the class. In the code below, the Store method is used to retrieve the value of the internal instance variable named StoreName. By having the property store the value of the variable, the internal variable is not exposed outside of the class. Property methods are used to keep private the variables internal to your code.

```
Public Class TaraStoreClass
  Private StoreName As String = "Tara Store"
  Private StoreEmail As String = "info@TaraStore.com"
  Public ReadOnly Property StoreName() As String
    Get
       Return StoreName
    End Get
  End Property
End Class
```

You should not declare the property public or friend, because that directly exposes the variable outside of the class. Rather, you can use the property to retrieve the variable within the class. Then, only the property is exposed outside of the class.

You can set the value of the variable directly, or by using the property method. The following sample passes the NewValue string to the SetName method. Then, the value assigns a new value to the NewStoreName variable. The GetName method retrieves the value of the variable named NewStoreName. No value is passed to the GetName method. Therefore, you can simply return the value as a string data type using the return keyword. You must identify the data type of the variable that is returned to your main code.

```
Public Class TaraStoreClass
  Public Sub SetName(ByVal NewValue As String)
    NewStoreName = NewValue
  End Sub
  Public Sub GetName() As String
     Return NewStoreName
  End Sub
End Class
```

The above technique offers direct access to your variables. You can use the property method to retrieve and set the value of the variables. In the following sample the value of the variable is set using the property. Although it may appear that you are still using the get and set keywords, the values are set and retrieved indirectly.

```
Public Class TaraStoreClass
  Private StoreName As String = "Tara Store"
  Public Property NewStoreName() As String
    Get
       Return StoreName
    End Get
    Set(ByVal NewValue As String)
       NewStoreName = NewValue
    End Set
  End Property
End Class
```

You can set the GetName property to read-only by using the keyword ReadOnly. This prevents you from writing to the property. You can also set the SetName property to write-only with the keyword WriteOnly. This allows the value to be changed, but not retrieved from the property. The ReadOnly and WriteOnly keywords are placed before the Property keyword.

Collections

Data can be stored in structures called collections. A **collection** is an object that can store other elements. A collection is like an egg carton. The collection and the egg carton are both containers. You can refer to the carton as a whole, or to an individual egg in that carton. In the same way, you can refer to the collection as a whole, or to each element within the collection.

These elements can be any valid data type such as a string, integer, an object, or even another collection. Sometimes collections are used to group items you intend to treat in a similar manner. For example, a list of employee names, a list of states, a list of tax rates would all be used for similar purposes, and so could easily be stored within a collection. This data could also be stored in other types of structures such as a database. However, some data such as the names of the states would require significant processing for every time the Web application had to retrieve the list, because it would need to return to the database to get the values. By storing some types of data in a collection, you would not need to use a database.

The `System.Collections` namespace provides access to classes that manage data. The `System.Collections` namespace defines five types of collections. These five collections are the ArrayList, HashTable, SortedList, Queue, and the Stack. All collections can store objects such as integers, strings, dates, other objects, and other collections.

There are differences between the collections. The Queue and Stack collections need to rotate through the collection sequentially in order to locate an element. Because each collection is created within the `System.Collections` namespace, they share several properties and methods. The ArrayList, HashTable, and SortedList collections can provide access to any element without having to rotate through the other elements. In the previous chapter you learned to use the ArrayList to store related data. Arrays, ArrayLists, SortedLists, and HashTables are all collections used to store data. You can use the collection to refer to the group of items, or to refer to an individual item within the collection. Each item in the collection is also referred to as an **element**.

ArrayList

An **ArrayList** is a series of related data items. The ArrayList object is inherited from the `System.Array` class. Arrays are objects that are also reference values, which means that they are stored in the memory heap. The ArrayList stores each item in sequential order, and each item is indexed with a number. Therefore, you do not have to worry about defining the size of the ArrayList when you create the array, add items, or remove items.

These items are grouped together using a group variable name. Each item in the ArrayList is identified using an index number that indicates its position within the ArrayList. All of the items within the ArrayList must be of the same data type. When you declare the ArrayList, you specify the name of the ArrayList, but you do not need to specify the size of the ArrayList. You must specify that the collection is an ArrayList. The ArrayLists are zero-based, which means the first item in the ArrayList is at position 0. So, an ArrayList size of three means that the ArrayList has four items.

Assigning values to elements in an ArrayList is called **populating the ArrayList**. You can populate the ArrayList when you declare it, or you can obtain values from the user with which to populate the ArrayList. To populate the ArrayList, specify the index number, and then specify the value for each element. You populate an element by using Add method. As with all variables, the value of each element within the ArrayList is undefined until you assign it a value. The following sample code illustrates how to create an ArrayList named StateAbbrev. The ArrayList is populated with three elements.

```
Dim StateAbbrev As New ArrayList
StateAbbrev.Add = "IL"
StateAbbrev.Add = "MI"
StateAbbrev.Add = "IN"
```

 The erase command can be used to clear the values of all of the elements in the array. The IsArray function returns a Boolean value that indicates whether a variable is an ArrayList. If the variable is an ArrayList, the function returns True, otherwise it returns False.

After the ArrayList is populated, the program can retrieve the value of any element in the array. To retrieve the value of an ArrayList element in the ArrayList, you use the ArrayList name and the index number of the element. You can then use this value in an expression, display it in a Web page, or assign it to a variable. When the array element is used in an expression or assigned to a variable, it must appear on the right side of the assignment operator (=). To write out the first element of an ArrayList to the Web page using Visual Basic .NET, you can write `Response.write(StateAbbrev(0))`. In the example above, you added elements using the Add method. You can create an ArrayList and rotate through the list using the For-Next loop. The following is a list of methods that apply to the ArrayList collection.

- The **Add** and **Remove methods** add or delete a single element.

- The **Insert** and **RemoveAt methods** add and remove elements at a specific location within the ArrayList. You can insert or remove an element at a specific index position within the ArrayList by specifying the elements index position number.

- The **AddRange** and **RemoveRange methods** allow you to add or remove a group of elements. When you remove a range, you must specify the index number of the first element you want to delete, and then the number of elements you want to delete.

- The **IndexOf property** returns an integer which represents the index position of the element in the list. A value of -1 means that the element was not found in the list.

- The **Count property** identifies the number of items in the array, which will be the largest index number plus 1.

- The **Clear method** allows you to remove all of the elements within the ArrayList.

In the following sample code, an ArrayList is inserted into the first position, and then removed.

```
StateAbbrev.Insert(0, "OK")
StateAbbrev.Remove("OK")
```

ArrayList elements can be directly manipulated, or the values of the ArrayList elements can be assigned to variables and the variables can be manipulated. In the following sample code, the index position of the OK element is retrieved and all of the values are written to a TextBox control.

```
Dim iPos as Integer
iPos = StateAbbrev.IndexOf("OK")
Dim MyCount As Integer
MyCount = StateAbbrev.Count
For I = 1 to MyCount -1
    MyStates.Text = StateAbbrev(I) & "<br />"
Next
```

HashTables

In a previous chapter you used a hashtable to populate a CheckBoxList control in a Web page. The HashTable collection is different from an ArrayList—it creates the index of elements using an alphanumeric key. In other words, each item is referenced by an alphanumeric key, like an encyclopedia. The order in which the elements are stored is based upon a built-in set of rules known as the hashing algorithm. The keys are a collection of alphanumeric values, and the values are a collection of elements. When you call the add method, the key is the first parameter and is passed using quotation marks. The second parameter is the value. The value parameter is separated from the key parameter with a comma.

You can also create a HashTable within a class by declaring the object using the keyword Dim, the name of the HashTable, and the keyword New. You do not need to identify the number of items in the HashTable. You can add items to the HashTable using the add method of the HashTable object to store the items. The items are added using the key and value pair. You can use the key in your programming to retrieve the value for a particular item. Because you have a key and value pair, you must specify the key and value. The **DataValueField** is used to create the value for the control, and the **DataTextField** is used to create the text displayed for the control. You can add and remove items using the **add** and **remove methods**. The following sample code would create a HashTable within a class.

```
Public Shared Sub Main()
   ' Create & initialize a new Hashtable.
   Dim HS1 As New HashTable()
   HS1.Add("1", "Current Events in Ireland")
   HS1.Add("2", "Fishing in Ireland")
   HS1.Add("3", "An Ghaeilge (The Irish Language)")
   HS1.Add("4", "Hiking in Ireland")
   HS1.Add("5", "Irish History")
   HS1.Add("6", "Irish Music")
   HS1.Add("7", "Irish Step and Set Dancing")
   HS1.Add("8", "Travel in Ireland")
   HS1.Add("9", "Sports in Ireland")
End Sub
```

The **clear method** of the HashTable class lets you delete all of the elements in the HashTable. The **ContainsKey** and **ContainsValue methods** can help you determine if a key or value exists. This method is often used before adding or removing an item. For example, you might only want unique values in the HashTable. You could use the ContainsKey to verify that the element does not already exist before calling the add method. If the key or value exists, the method returns True.

The SortedList

The SortedList class collection also uses a key, but the collection is indexed by both the key and the item. Because the sorting of the list is based on the key, the index position of the element changes frequently. Therefore, you cannot insert the element based on its index position. You can iterate through the list with a For-Next loop. The add method allows you to add an element to the SortedList. You can remove the element using the **Remove or RemoveAt method**. The **GetKeyList method** is used to provide the collection of keys within the list.

The Queue

The Queue class can only be used to provide sequential access to the elements. This is similar to a roller coaster ride. Typically, the people in the first car are let out first. This sequential ordering system is known as first in, first out (FIFO). There are two parts to the list: the tail, called the enqueue, and the head, called the dequeue. When you add an element to the list, they are added using the enqueue and dequeue methods. You can iterate through the list with a For-Next loop. Below are some methods used to add and remove items from the queue.

- **Enqueue** is used to retrieve an element from the tail of the class.

- **Dequeue** returns each element from the head of the queue. You can remove elements from the head of the queue.

- **Clear** removes all elements.

- **Peek** looks at the head withoutaltering the elements. Peek returns the element at the head of the queue without removing the element from the queue. If you try to look at an empty queue with the peek method, the InvalidOperationException is thrown.

- **Contains** is a method that can be used to determine if an element is a member of the queue. If the element exists within the queue, the method returns True.

The Stack

The Stack class provides sequential access but stores them in last in, first out (LIFO) order. The stack is similar to the line in a theatre, church, or crowded elevator. The first one to enter the room is the last one to leave the room. Below are some methods used to add and remove items from the stack.

- Add an element in the stack using **push method**.

- Remove an element from the stack using the **pop method**.

- Peek to look at the top of the stack without removing the element from the stack.

Procedures

There are two types of procedures in Visual Basic .NET. Using functions in Visual Basic .NET, you can create a block of code, assign a name to it, and call it from another location. You can also create another kind of code block, called a method. A **subprocedure** is similar to a function in that it is a block of code that can be called from other locations. This allows you to create blocks of code that can be reused within your Web application rather than writing the same code over and over again. (*Note*: subprocedures are also called subroutines or methods.)

Subprocedures

Like a function, a subprocedure can accept zero or more arguments. Variables declared within the subprocedure are local and are only available to the subprocedure. When you create the subprocedure, you declare it public or private. The keyword Public is used to explicitly declare the subprocedure public. Public subprocedures are available to all other methods in all the applications, while private subprocedures are only available to other subprocedures in the context in which they are declared.

The main differences between functions and subprocedures are that subprocedures do not return values, and cannot be used in an expression value. Subprocedures are declared using the keyword sub. You can use the `exit sub` statement to exit the subprocedure.

Subprocedures are often used to respond to an event such as a button click. The syntax for a subprocedure is shown below. The keyword Sub indicates that the subprocedure is being created. The name of the subprocedure and the parameters are identified in the sub statement. The subprocedure can issue action and control statements. The end of the subprocedure is identified with the keywords `end sub`. It is important to note that the order in which procedures are declared does not affect the order of their execution. Subprocedures always execute in the order in which they are called, not the order in which they are created. You can call multiple subprocedures in the same function.

```
Sub SubprocedureName (parameters)

    Action and Control Statements

End Sub
```

Subprocedures can be used more than once and anywhere within your application, including within other subprocedures, functions, or control structures. Once your method has been declared, it is executed by specifying the name of the subprocedure. The keyword Call can be used to call a function or subprocedure and is optional. If you use the Call keyword, then the parameters passed to the subprocedure must be enclosed in parentheses. Multiple arguments are passed in a comma-delimited list. Below is the syntax for calling a method in Visual Basic .NET.

```
[call] SubprocedureName (arguments)
```

Functions cannot define other functions, but they can call other functions and subprocedures. You can call multiple subprocedures in the same function. This allows for a program to be segmented. Segments can be reused in other scripts, which can help you produce more efficient code. The subprocedures are executed in the order they are called. Each step can be called separately from the program. One benefit of using multiple methods is that if one of the steps changes, then only that step needs to be modified. By using multiple subprocedures instead of combining them into one, each subprocedure can be reused without having to rewrite entire sections of code. If multiple variables are to be used across functions and procedures, they need to be global to the application and defined before the functions and procedures that reference them.

You previously learned that subprocedures do not return values. However, there are ways to access values from a subprocedure. The subprocedures can assign their value to the value property of one of the WebForm controls. This way, the values can be made available to multiple subprocedures.

Event Procedure

As you previously learned, when you call event handlers from within the ASP.NET controls, the event handler is identified with the prefix "on" and the event name. Events such as click are intercepted by event handlers such as onServerClick. You can intercept the event using an **event handler**. An event handler is also known as an event procedure. When you open the code behind the page the Page_Load event procedure is created by default. An **event procedure** is a procedure that is attached to an object. An event procedure is not executed until an event triggers the event procedure. The Page_Load event procedure is triggered when the page is loaded into the browser. An event procedure does not return a value. When an object recognizes an event, it immediately calls the event procedure. The event procedure provides a connection between the object and the code.

Event procedures' names are based upon the name of the object and the event name. An underscore (_) is used to separate the object name and the event name. For example, if you create a button named btnExit that calls an event procedure when it is clicked, you name the event procedure btnExit_onServerClick. You must assign the name of the object in the page code before you define an event procedure. If you change the name of an object after defining an event procedure for that object, you must change the name of the procedure to match the new name of the object. Note that the event procedure is not called, but rather is triggered when the event occurs for that specific object. The object calls the event procedure when it detects that the event has occurred. Below is the syntax for creating event procedures.

```
Sub objectName_eventHandler(sender as Object, e as EventArgs)

        action and control statements

End Sub
```

Functions

A **function** is a block of code that is grouped into a named unit. Functions are also procedures and are implemented with the keyword Function. Visual Basic .NET supports built-in and user-defined functions. Built-in functions are inherited from a class within the .NET Framework. There are hundreds of built-in functions available within the .NET Framework. For example, you can locate more information on string functions at *ms-help://MS.VSCC/MS.MSDNVS/vbcn7/html/vaconManipulatingStrings.htm*.

You use the keyword function to identify the start of a function. The function is identified by a unique name. You can declare a function as public, private, protected, or friend. The public, private, friend, and protected status is identified before the Function keyword, as shown below.

```
Public Function GetStoreName() As Integer
'This function returns an integer
    Return 23422
End Function
```

Passing an Argument to a Function

A pair of parentheses follows the name of the function. Within the parentheses you include zero or more arguments, also known as parameters, which are passed to the function when it is called. If no arguments are passed, you use an empty pair of parentheses.

If multiple arguments are used, you use a comma to separate each argument. You can call the function several times, passing different arguments each time. The result of the function is different each time, because the argument that was passed was different each time.

Returning a Value from a Function

The block of code can contain any number of action statements or control statements. A function can return a value—one value only—to the script that called it, but it does not necessarily return a value. The keyword Return is used to identify the value that is returned to the function call. Usually the code assigns the value returned by the function to a variable. If no return value is explicitly identified by the function, the return value is the last value in memory.

Exiting a Function

In Visual Basic .NET the keywords exit function are used to exit a function. Exit Function is a jumping control; jumping controls allow you to temporarily halt the execution of a code block, and move to another section of code. Unlike the End Function statement that appears at the end of a function, the Exit Function statement can appear as an action statement in the middle of the function code, as shown below.

```
Public Function GetStoreName() As String
    Dim UserName as String
    UserName = txtUserName.text.ToString
    If UserName = "Admin" then
        Return "Welcome Administrator!"
        Exit Function
    Else
        Return "Welcome!"
        Exit Function
    End If
End Function
```

Creating a Function

You can create a function within the class of the Web page, or within the Visual Basic .NET file. In the following sample, the function GetStoreName returns a string to the code that called the function. The function is public, so it can be accessed from outside of the class. (*Note*: If you want to make the methods and functions public, you can also put them into a Visual Basic .NET module. The module is not contained within any one class, so it is available to all classes.)

```
Public Class TaraStoreClass
    Public Function GetStoreName() As String
        Return "Tara Store"
    End Function
End Class
```

You can call the function from within the code behind the page, or from within another section of code within the class. The following sample instantiates a new object and calls the GetStoreName function from the new object.

```
GetTheFunction(New TaraStoreClass.GetStoreName)
```

Using Visual Basic .NET in a Web Page

In the following exercise, you will use Visual Studio .NET to create an ASP.NET page, and you will insert your business logic in the code behind the page using Visual Basic .NET.

1. Right-click **Chapter5** in the Solution Explorer window, point to **Add**, then click **Add Existing Item**. Navigate to your Chapter 5 data directory, select the file **SampleUsingVB.aspx**, then click **Open**. The following pop-up message appears: "There is no class file in the project associated with the Web Form 'SampleUsingVB.aspx'. Create a new class file now?" Click **Yes**. Double-click the file in the Solution Explorer window to open it.

2. Double-click on the page to open the code behind the page. Add the following code in the Page_Load event handler to declare three string variables and to assign the default message in the topics and title Label controls. You can see the complete code as it appears in Visual Studio .NET in Figure 5-7.

```
Dim strClass, strStoreName, strStoreImage As String
lblTopics.Text = "Please select the Tara Store" & _
    " you would like to visit:"
lblTitle.Text = "Welcome to Tara Store"
```

3. Type the code below to create an If-Then statement that determines if the user has visited the page before. If this is the first time, then set the properties of the RadioButtonList control and declare an array that contains two values. Bind these two values to the RadioButtonList control using the DataBind method.

```
If Not Page.IsPostBack Then
   RBL.RepeatLayout = RepeatLayout.Table
   RBL.RepeatDirection = RepeatDirection.Vertical
   Dim AR1 As New ArrayList(2)
   AR1.Add("Tara Store in Chicago.")
   AR1.Add("Tara Store in New York.")
   RBL.DataSource = AR1
   RBL.DataBind()
```

 Visual Studio .NET inserts the End statements when you insert a beginning statement such as If-Then or Select-Case. If you enter the End statement twice you will generate an error.

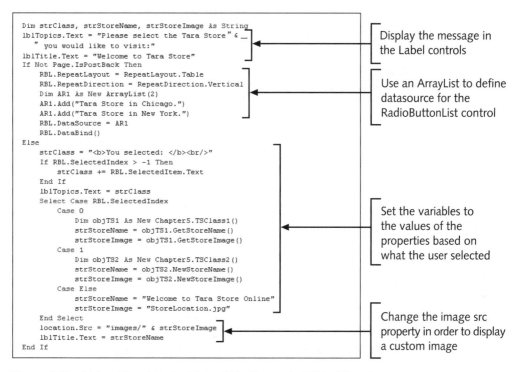

```
Dim strClass, strStoreName, strStoreImage As String
lblTopics.Text = "Please select the Tara Store" & _
   " you would like to visit:"
lblTitle.Text = "Welcome to Tara Store"
If Not Page.IsPostBack Then
    RBL.RepeatLayout = RepeatLayout.Table
    RBL.RepeatDirection = RepeatDirection.Vertical
    Dim AR1 As New ArrayList(2)
    AR1.Add("Tara Store in Chicago.")
    AR1.Add("Tara Store in New York.")
    RBL.DataSource = AR1
    RBL.DataBind()
Else
    strClass = "<b>You selected: </b><br/>"
    If RBL.SelectedIndex > -1 Then
        strClass += RBL.SelectedItem.Text
    End If
    lblTopics.Text = strClass
    Select Case RBL.SelectedIndex
        Case 0
            Dim objTS1 As New Chapter5.TSClass1()
            strStoreName = objTS1.GetStoreName()
            strStoreImage = objTS1.GetStoreImage()
        Case 1
            Dim objTS2 As New Chapter5.TSClass2()
            strStoreName = objTS2.NewStoreName()
            strStoreImage = objTS2.NewStoreImage()
        Case Else
            strStoreName = "Welcome to Tara Store Online"
            strStoreImage = "StoreLocation.jpg"
    End Select
    location.Src = "images/" & strStoreImage
    lblTitle.Text = strStoreName
End If
```

Display the message in the Label controls

Use an ArrayList to define datasource for the RadioButtonList control

Set the variables to the values of the properties based on what the user selected

Change the image src property in order to display a custom image

Figure 5-7   Using Visual Basic .Net within the code behind the page

4. Type the code below. If the user has visited the page before, then IsPostback is True. In this case, assign a value to the strClass variable, which is a concatenated string. The string contains a bolded heading statement and the value of the Text property of the Radio Button control that the user selects.

```
Else
  strClass = "<b>You selected: </b><br />"
  If RBL.SelectedIndex > -1 Then
    strClass += RBL.SelectedItem.Text
  End If
lblTopics.Text = strClass
```

5. Type the following code to create a select case statement to determine which Radio Button control is selected using the SelectedIndex property. If the first item is selected, then create a new object named **objTS1** based upon the TSClass1. The TSClass1 contains two values which can be accessed using the functions GetStoreName and GetStoreImage. Both functions return strings that can be assigned to the strStoreName and strStoreImage variables. The GetStoreName returns a message that identifies the store name as the Tara

Store – Chicago. The GetStoreImage returns a message that identifies the store image as ChicagoStore.jpg.

```
Select Case RBL.SelectedIndex
Case 0
   Dim objTS1 As New TSClass1()
   strStoreName = objTS1.GetStoreName()
   strStoreImage = objTS1.GetStoreImage()
```

6. Add the code that runs if the second item is selected, then create a new object named **objTS2** based upon the TSClass2. The TSClass2 contains two values, which can be accessed using the properties NewStoreName and NewStoreImage. Both Property methods return a string that can be assigned to the strStoreName and strStoreImage variables. The NewStoreName returns a message that identifies the store name as the Tara Store – New York. The NewStoreImage returns a message that identifies the store image as NewYorkStore.jpg. These values are not stored in the properties, but within the private variables within the Property method. Therefore, you are accessing the values of these variables indirectly.

```
Case 1
   Dim objTS2 As New TSClass2()
   strStoreName = objTS2.NewStoreName()
   strStoreImage = objTS2.NewStoreImage()
```

7. Create a select case statement that runs if neither item is selected. Assign strings to the strStoreName and strStoreImage variables that contain the name of the store and the filename of the image to be displayed in the Web page. (*Note*: Don't forget to end the Select-Case statement with the keywords end select.)

```
Case Else
   strStoreName = "Welcome to Tara Store Online"
   strStoreImage = "StoreLocation.jpg"
End Select
```

8. Now you use the variables that have been retrieved from the classes to set the properties of the Web page controls. Type the code below. The strStoreImage variable is concatenated with the path to the images directory and assigned to the Source property of the Image control named location. The strStoreName variable is assigned to the Text property of a Label control named lblTitle. (*Note*: Make sure to not delete the End Sub and End Class keywords at the bottom of the code.)

```
location.Src = "images/" & strStoreImage
lblTitle.Text = strStoreName
End If
```

9. Create a new class named **TSClass1**. Add the code to create a function named **GetStoreName** that returns a string that contains the name of the

store in Chicago. Add another function named **GetStoreImage** that returns a string with the filename of the Chicago Store image. (*Note*: Don't forget to add the code to end the class.) You can refer to Figure 5-8 to see how the code appears within Visual Studio .NET.

```
Public Class TSClass1
  Public Function GetStoreName() As String
    Return "Tara Store - Chicago"
  End Function
  Public Function GetStoreImage() As String
    Return "ChicagoStore.jpg"
  End Function
End Class
```

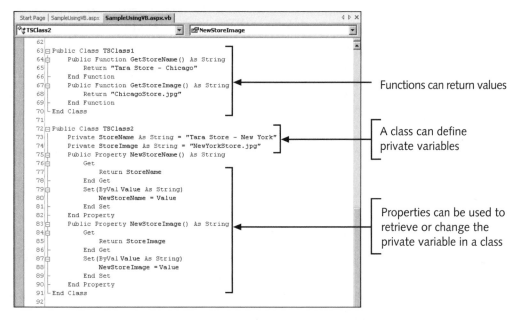

Figure 5-8   Creating functions and properties within Visual Studio .Net

10. Create a new class named **TSClass2**. Add the code to create two private instance variables, named **StoreName** and **StoreImage**. Declare both as string and assign the values of the store name and image to the variables.

```
Public Class TSClass2
    Private StoreName As String = "Tara Store - New York"
    Private StoreImage As String = "NewYorkStore.jpg"
```

11. Create a property called **NewStoreName**. Return the value of the private StoreName variable to the NewStoreName property when it is called. Create the code to allow the class to set the property of the variable as shown below.

IntelliSense sets up the basic code structure after you enter the Public Property. Be careful not to repeat this code.

```
Public Property NewStoreName() As String
    Get
        Return StoreName
    End Get
    Set(ByVal Value As String)
        NewStoreName = Value
    End Set
End Property
```

12. Create a property named **NewStoreImage**. Return the value of the private StoreImage variable to the NewStoreImage property when it is called. Create the code below to allow a class to set the property of the variable as shown below. (*Note*: Don't forget to add the code to end the class.)

```
Public Property NewStoreImage() As String
    Get
        Return StoreImage
    End Get
    Set(ByVal Value As String)
        NewStoreImage = Value
    End Set
End Property
End Class
```

13. Click the **Save All** button. Click **Build** on the menu bar, then click **Build Solution**.

14. Click the **SampleUsingVB.aspx** tab in the main window. Click the **Design** tab to change to the Design view if necessary. Right-click on the page, and then click **View in Browser**. When you click the radio buttons, the messages in both Label controls change, and the image changes as shown in Figure 5-9. (*Note*: You can also view the page in your browser at *http://localhost/ chapter5/SampleUsingVB.aspx*.)

15. Close any open pages.

The value selected will change the image source property and the message in the Label control

5

Figure 5-9   Using Visual Basic .NET to display variables within a Web page

INTRODUCTION TO C#

C# is a new language created by Microsoft to allow non-Visual Basic .NET programmers to take advantage of the powerful features of Visual Studio .NET. The syntax of C# is similar to JavaScript and C++. However, it is important to remember that when the program is compiled by the C# compiler, the code is compiled into the same managed Intermediate Language code that is also generated by the Visual Basic .NET compiler.

As you learned in Chapter 1, all of the .NET Framework, the .NET base classes, and the Visual Studio development environment are available across programming languages. So, you can include programs written with C# within your ASP.NET application. In addition, you have access to the same Windows Form tools and ASP.NET WebForm tools. Therefore, the user interface to your application is not language dependent. You can create your WebForm the same way for all .NET programming languages. In this book, you use Visual Basic .NET primarily because most beginning programming courses use Visual Basic. However, once you learn one programming language, the programming concepts are similar with other languages. It is useful to be aware of the differences between programming languages. In addition, some of the samples you may find on the Internet are written in C#. If you are familiar with some of the structure of the C# application, you can convert the C# code into Visual Basic .NET.

When you open the QuickStart Web site at *http://localhost/quickstart/*, you can specify the samples to be displayed by default using C# by changing the drop-down list box located in the upper-right corner from VB to C#.

One of the first things that you will notice in a C# program is that each statement ends with a semicolon. The semicolon is called the line termination character because it indicates the end of the statement. Therefore, you can write statements that extend across multiple lines without using an underscore, because the program knows that the end of the statement occurs where the semicolon is located. C# uses the plus sign as the concatenation operator instead of the ampersand that is used in Visual Basic .NET. The following sample code shows how to concatenate strings in C#.

```
var s1 : String;
var s2 : String = "Welcome to ";
s2 += "Tara Store";
s1 = s2 + " !!!";
```

To improve performance, you can use the StringBuilder class. The StringBuilder class is available to both Visual Basic .NET and C#. The following sample code shows how to concatenate strings in C# using the StringBuilder class. The Append method is used to concatenate two or more strings.

```
var s1:StringBuilder = new StringBuilder();
s1.Append("Welcome to ");
s1.Append("Tara Store");
s1.Append(" !!!");
```

One difference between the two programs is that C# is case sensitive. You must be careful about the names of variables, properties, namespaces, functions, and other programming keywords. In C# you often use lowercase for the names of programming elements within the C# language.

When you assign a value to a variable in C#, you do not have to use the keyword dim or var to declare it. When you declare a string variable, you must indicate in both languages that the variable is a string data type. In Visual Basic .NET, you use the keywords As String after the variable name. In C# you specify the data type first, String, then you specify the variable name; don't forget that the data types are different and are transformed to the Common Language Runtime data types at compile time. When you create an object data type in Visual Basic .NET you declare the object using the keyword dim and the object name. Then, you assign the name using the keyword **As** to **New Object()**, where Object is the name of the class that is used to create the new object. In C#, you do not use the dim or as keywords. You specify the data type of the object first, then the name of the object. You use the assignment operator **new Object()**, where the keyword new is lowercase. If you declare the variable public in Visual Basic .NET, you capitalize the first letter in public. If you declare the variable public in C#, you use all lowercase letters for the keyword public. The sample code below shows how to declare a variable and assign it a value in C#.

```
String StoreName = "Tara Store";
int counter = 1;
```

Comments in C# are similar to comments in JavaScript. A single line comment is preceded by two forward slashes. A multiline comment begins with a forward slash and an asterisk. After the comment, an asterisk and forward slash mark the end of the comment. The following sample code illustrates how to create a comment in C#.

```
// This is a single line comment
/*
This is a multiline comment
Always document your code
*/
```

5

When you create an array using C# instead of using parenthesis around the index position, use square brackets. Anytime you work with one or more statements, you enclose the code in curly braces. This nesting of code within curly braces is the same in JavaScript and C#. Certain types of control structures use the curly braces to indicate which blocks of code should be executed. In a Visual Basic .NET If-Then statement, the keyword then is used to identify the first block of code. Because there are no curly braces, there is also an End If statement to indicate when the function ends. In C#, the If-Then statement does not require the then or end If keywords because the curly braces indicate which blocks of code are executed when the statement is True or False.

CHAPTER SUMMARY

- Object-oriented programming languages support concepts such as abstraction, encapsulation, polymorphism, and inheritance. The process of creating an object from a class is called instantiation.

- The keyword inherits identifies the name of the class that is created in the code behind the Web page. The keyword imports is used to identify the namespaces used within the code behind the page.

- The IL Disassembler (ILDASM) can be used to view the assembly, namespaces, classes, functions, methods, and properties within your compiled .dll file. The compiled .dll file is located in the bin directory. You can create multiple classes within a single class file. The compiler places all the classes into a single namespace by default.

- Variables are used to store data. You must assign a data type to a variable when the variable is created. You can also assign a value to the variable when the variable is created. All data types are the same across languages after the application is compiled into managed code. Data types in Visual Basic .NET include string, Boolean, Date, Char, Byte, Short, Integer, Long, Decimal.

- Instance variables are variables defined within a class. Option explicit is used to force all variables to be declared before they can be used. You cannot start a variable with a number. You can start the name of a variable with an underscore or letter.

❑ Value types are stored in the stack and consist of primitive types such as Boolean, Integer, Decimal, Char, and Datetime. Reference types are stored on the managed heap and consist of strings, classes, arrays, collections, and objects. The garbage collector manages the memory addresses within the managed heap.

❑ Properties are used to set the value of a variable defined within an object. Public means that the properties and methods can interact with other objects outside of the base class. Private variables can only be called within the base class. Protected variables can be called from within the base class, and within subclasses. Friend variables can be called from anywhere within the same application or project.

❑ A property is a method that is used to get and set values. You can directly manipulate variables within a class, or you can use a property to indirectly read and change the variable.

❑ Constants are used to store values in variables that do not change within the application. The keyword const is used to declare the constant. The value must be specified when the constant is declared.

❑ The concatenation operator in Visual Basic .NET is the ampersand. In C# the concatenation operator is the plus sign. In Visual Basic .NET there is no line termination character. If you write code that expands over multiple lines you must use the line continuation character, which is the underscore. In C# the line termination character, which is the semicolon, is used to identify the end of a statement.

❑ ArrayLists, HashTables, SortedLists, Queues, and Stacks are examples of System.NET Collections. When you create a collection, you must declare the name of the collection first. Each item in the collection is referred to by its index position, which is in parenthesis. In C# the index position is contained within square brackets. The Add method can be used with the HashTable or ArrayList to add items to the collection. Remove is used to remove items from the HashTable or ArrayList.

❑ Procedures are used to organize the order in which the code is executed. The Event handlers are used to execute code when an event occurs. The two types of procedures are functions and subprocedures. Functions are used to return values. Subprocedures do not return a value to the code that called it. Functions use the keyword return to return the value to the code that called the function. The values that are passed to the subprocedure or function are called parameters. Multiple parameters are separated by commas when they are passed to the procedure.

❑ C# is a new programming language that can be used to create ASP.NET applications. Although the syntax of C# code is different from that of Visual Basic .NET, they share the same development tools, .NET base classes, and .NET Framework.

REVIEW QUESTIONS

1. Which of the following is not a value type?

   a. Boolean

   b. Integer

   c. Char

   d. ArrayList

2. Where is the reference type stored in memory?

   a. in the garbage heap

   b. in the memory heap

   c. in the memory stack

   d. in the managed heap

3. Which object-oriented feature enables you to create code that can be applied to objects that are derived from different classes?

   a. abstraction

   b. encapsulation

   c. polymorphism

   d. inheritance

4. Which object-oriented feature is the ability to create a concept using code?

   a. instantiation

   b. encapsulation

   c. polymorphism

   d. inheritance

5. What is the process for creating an object from a class?

   a. instantiation

   b. polymorphism

   c. inheritance

   d. abstraction

6. Which property makes an element available anywhere within the application or project?

   a. public

   b. private

   c. friend

   d. dim

5

7. Which property makes an element available anywhere to any class?
   a. public
   b. private
   c. friend
   d. protected

8. Which keyword is used to identify the name of the class created in the code behind the Web page?
   a. instantiate
   b. inherits
   c. imports
   d. integer

9. Which term when used in code requires you to declare all variables before they are used?
   a. instantiation
   b. instance
   c. option explicit
   d. option strict

10. Which is the only variable name that is allowed in Visual Basic .NET?
    a. My_ImageName
    b. Public
    c. Image Name
    d. $NewImage

11. What is the concatenation operator in Visual Basic .NET?
    a. $ (dollar sign)
    b. ' (single quotation mark)
    c. '' (quotation marks)
    d. + (plus sign)

12. What is the line termination character in C#?
    a. _ (underscore)
    b. & (ampersand)
    c. ; (semicolon)
    d. + (plus sign)

13. Which collection is used to create multiple related dimensions of data?

    a. HashTable

    b. Variables

    c. Properties

    d. Array

14. Which of the following returns a value?

    a. subprocedure

    b. procedure

    c. event Procedure

    d. function

15. What is a subprocedure also known as?

    a. a function

    b. a subroutine

    c. an event procedure

    d. an event handler

16. What is used to separate multiple arguments passed to a function?

    a. ; (semicolon)

    b. : (colon)

    c. / (forward slash)

    d. , (comma)

17. Which keyword is used to stop a program from writing to a private variable within a property?

    a. read only

    b. WriteOnly

    c. ReadOnly

    d. Write Only

18. Which are possible values for a Boolean variable?

    a. 0 or 1

    b. T or F

    c. True or False

    d. On or Off

5

19. Which format method outputs the value 1441.33 with a dollar sign preceding the value?

   a. `System.Console.WriteLine({"0:c"}, 1441.33)`

   b. `System.Console.WriteLine({"0:N"}, 1441.33)`

   c. `System.Console.WriteLine({"0:D"}, 1441.33)`

   d. `System.Console.WriteLine({"0:x"}, 1441.33)`

20. What numeric data type is a 32-bit number?

   a. Byte

   b. Short

   c. Long

   d. Integer

21. Which data type stores values between –32,768 and 32,767?

   a. Byte

   b. Short

   c. Long

   d. Integer

22. Which keyword is used to declare a constant variable?

   a. Var

   b. Dim

   c. Con

   d. Const

HANDS-ON PROJECTS

Project 5-1

In this project, you will create an ASP.NET page that creates a class using Visual Basic .NET.

1. Start **Visual Studio .NET** and open your **Chapter5** solution, if it is not already open.

2. In Visual Studio .NET create a class named **Ch5Proj1** that is stored in a file named **Ch5Proj1.vb**.

3. Create a public instance variable named **StoreAddress** that is a String data type. Assign the value **555 Michigan Avenue, Chicago, IL 60016** to the variable.

4. Click the **Save All** button to save the class file.

5. Right-click **Ch5Proj1** in the Solution Explorer window, point to **Add**, then click **Add Existing Item**. Browse to the Chapter05data directory, select **Ch5Proj1.aspx**, and then click **Open**. The following pop-up message appears: "There is no class file in the project associated with the WebForm 'Ch5Proj1.aspx'. Create a new class file now?" Click **Yes**. Open the newly imported page. The Layout property is already set to Grid Layout. You will be able to absolutely position your controls on the page.

6. Double-click the page to open the code behind the page. In the Page_Load procedure add the following code to create a new object named **Ch5Proj1Class**, based on the Ch5Proj1 class. Because the variable contains an object, the keyword new must be used to instantiate the object from a class. As you type each period, notice that the IntelliSense list box appears. Your Chapter5 namespace contains a class named Ch5Proj1.

```
Dim Ch5Proj1Class As New Chapter5.Ch5Proj1()
```

7. Type the following code to retrieve the values from the new class and assign the variable from the class to the Text property of the lblContact Label control in the Web page. (*Note:* You need to use the ToString method to retrieve the value from the string stored in the variable.)

```
lblContact.Text = Ch5Proj1Class.StoreAddress.ToString()
```

8. Click the **Save All** button. Click **Build** on the menu bar, then click **Build Solution**. Return to the Design view of the file Ch5Proj1.aspx.

9. Right-click on the page, and then click **View in Browser**. (*Note:* You can go to a browser and try to view the page at *http://localhost/chapter5/Ch5Proj1.aspx*.)

10. Print the Web page, the ASP.NET source code, and the code behind the page within Visual Studio .NET. Close all your pages.

Project 5-2

In this project, you view the compiled assembly and class you created in the previous exercise using the ILDASM tool. You must complete Project 5-1 before you can complete this project.

1. Start **Visual Studio .NET** and open your **Chapter5** solution if necessary.

2. Go to the Visual Studio .NET command prompt. In most computers, to access this command prompt, click **Start**, point to **Programs**, point to **Microsoft Visual Studio .NET**, point to **Visual Studio .NET Tools**, then click **Visual Studio .NET Command Prompt**.

3. At the command prompt, enter **cd Inetpub\wwwroot\Chapter5\bin**. By default, your assembly is compiled and placed within this directory.

4. Open the .dll file using the ILDASM. At the command prompt, type **ILDASM Chapter5.dll**. The ILDASM window opens. (*Note:* The name of your assembly and the namespace is Chapter5, which is also the name of your .dll file.)

5. Click the **plus sign** next to the Chapter5 icon to expand the Chapter5 name-space. The namespace is the blue shield icon.

6. Click the **plus sign** next to the Ch5Proj1 icon to expand the class information. The class icon has the blue rectangle with three outputs.

7. Double-click the **StoreAddress**: **public string** icon to open a window that tells you that the StoreAddress is a field within the Ch5Proj1 type, and is a public variable of type string.

8. Click **File** on the menu bar, and then click **Dump TreeView**. In the Save As dialog box type the filename "**Ch5Proj2.txt**". Make sure to save the file in your C:\Inetpub\wwwroot\Chapter5\ directory. Then, click the **Save** button.

9. Start **Notepad**, click **File** on the menu bar, then click **Open**. Browse to locate your C:\Inetpub\wwwroot\Chapter5\ directory. Select the file **Ch5Proj2.txt**, and then click **Open**. A text view of the assembly will be displayed in the file.

10. Scroll down the page and locate the StoreAddress variable in the Ch5Proj1 class, as shown in Figure 5-10.

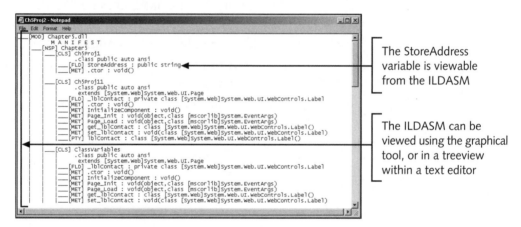

Figure 5-10   The ILDASM

11. Print the file, and then exit Notepad.

12. Close the ILDASM windows and the Command Prompt window by clicking the **Close** button in each window.

13. Close any open pages.

Project 5-3

In this project, you create a Web page that uses a property to retrieve the values of private variables defined in a class.

1. Start **Visual Studio .NET** and open your **Chapter5** solution if necessary.

2. Right-click **Chapter5** in the Solution Explorer window, point to **Add**, then click **Add Existing Item**. Browse to locate your Chapter05data directory, select the file **Ch5Proj3.aspx**, click **Open**, then click **Yes** to create a new class file. Open the page.

3. Double-click on the page to open the code behind the page. In the Page_Load procedure add the following code to create a new object named **objCh5Proj3Class**, based on the Ch5Proj3Class class. Because the variable contains an object, the keyword New must be used to instantiate the object from a class.

```
Dim strClass As String
Dim objCh5Proj3Class As New Chapter5.Ch5Proj3Class()
```

4. Type the following code to retrieve the property named NewStoreAddress from the object you just created. Assign the value to the strClass varible. Assign the variable contents to the Text property of the topics Label control. (*Note*: Don't delete the End Sub and End Class keywords that were put in by Visual Studio .NET.)

```
strClass = objCh5Proj3Class.NewStoreAddress()
lblTopics.Text = strClass
```

5. Type the following code to create a public class named **Ch5Proj3Class**.

```
Public Class Ch5Proj3Class
```

6. Type the following code to assign the street address provided to the private variable named **StoreAddress**. The variable should be a String data type.

```
Private StoreAddress As String = _
    "555 Michigan Avenue, Chicago, IL 60016"
```

7. Type the following code to create a read-only property named **NewStoreAddress** which contains a string. Return the private StoreAddress variable when the NewStoreAddress property is called. (*Note*: Don't delete the End Class keywords that Visual Studio .NET adds to the page.)

```
Public ReadOnly Property NewStoreAddress() As String
    Get
        Return StoreAddress
    End Get
End Property
End Class
```

8. Click the **Save All** button. Click **Build** on the menu bar, and then click **Build Solution**. Return to the Ch5Proj3.aspx page.

9. Click the **Design** tab to return to the Design view if necessary. Right-click the page, and then click **View in Browser**. The store's name and address are displayed under the graphic.

10. Print the Web page, the ASP.NET source code, and code behind the page within Visual Studio .NET. Close any open pages.

Project 5-4

In this project, you create a class and create a custom message based on the user input from the ASP.NET page.

1. Start **Visual Studio .NET** and open your **Chapter5** solution if necessary.

2. Right-click **Chapter5** in the Solution Explorer window, point to **Add**, then click **Add Existing Item**. Browse to locate your Chapter05data directory, select the file **Ch5Proj4.aspx**, click **Open**, and then click **Yes** to create a new class file. Open the page. The Layout property is already set to Grid Layout. You will be able to position your controls absolutely on the page.

3. Double-click on the page to open the code behind the page. In the Page_Load procedure, use the IsPostBack property to determine if the user has been to the page before. If the user has not been to the page before, display the default message and image. Add the following code to assign the Source property for the location image and Text property of the Title control.

```
If Not Page.IsPostBack Then
    location.Src = "images/" & "StoreLocation.jpg"
    lblTitle.Text = "Welcome to Tara Store"
```

4. Type the following code, which determines if the user has visited the page before, and declares a variable named strEntered to store the value the user types in the text box named txtLocation. Assign the value entered to the strEntered variable. Use this variable to change the Text property of the title Label control named lblTitle.

```
Else
    Dim strEntered As String
    strEntered = txtLocation.Text
    lblTitle.Text = strEntered
```

5. Add the following code to create a new object named **objCh5Proj4Class** based on the Ch5Proj4Class class. Because the variable contains an object, the keyword new must be used to instantiate the object from a class.

```
Dim objCh5Proj4Class As New Chapter5.Ch5Proj4Class()
```

6. Add the following code to call a function named **ChangeImage** within the class. Pass the strEntered variable as a parameter to the function. The variable contains the information that the user typed in the text box. The function uses this information to change a property which stores the image name.

```
objCh5Proj4Class.ChangeImage(strEntered)
```

7. Type the following code to declare a string variable named **strNewImage** to store the name of the new image. Use the NewStoreImage property to retrieve a new image name and assign it to the variable you just created. Then, display the message and the image name in the topics Label control. Change the source property of the location image object to the images directory and to the new image filename that is stored in the strNewImage variable.

```
      Dim strNewImage As String
      strNewImage = objCh5Proj4Class.NewStoreImage()
      lblTopics.Text = "The image above is: " & strNewImage
      location.Src = "images/" & strNewImage
   End If
```

8. Create a new file named **Ch5Proj4Class.vb**, which contains a public class named **Ch5Proj4Class**. Verify that the class definition is entered correctly by Visual Studio .NET.

```
   Public Class Ch5Proj4Class
   End Class
```

9. Within the class definition, type the following code to assign the street address provided to the private variable named StoreImage. The variable should be a String data type. Assign StoreLocation.jpg as the default value in the StoreImage variable.

```
   Private StoreImage As String = "StoreLocation.jpg"
```

10. Type the following code to create a property named **NewStoreImage**, which contains a string. Return the private StoreImage variable when the NewStoreImage property is called.

```
   Public Property NewStoreImage() As String
     Get
        Return StoreImage
     End Get
```

11. Type the following code, which uses the set keyword to assign a new value to the StoreImage private variable.

```
     Set(ByVal Value As String)
        StoreImage = Value
     End Set
   End Property
```

12. Type the following code, to create a function named **ChangeImage**. The function receives a string value when it is called. Use the Select-Case control structure to determine which city the user entered in the text box. Provide a default selection for users who did not enter the correct text. This function assigns a new value to the private variable in the property method. (*Note*: Don't delete the End Class keywords that Visual Studio .NET adds to the page.)

```
   Public Sub ChangeImage(ByVal StoreLocation As String)
        Select Case StoreLocation
           Case "Chicago Store"
               StoreImage = "ChicagoStore.jpg"
           Case "New York Store"
               StoreImage = "NewYorkStore.jpg"
           Case Else
               StoreImage = "StoreLocation.jpg"
        End Select
   End Sub
```

13. Click the **Save All** button. Click **Build** on the menu bar, and then click **Build Solution**. Return to the Ch5Proj4.aspx page.

14. Click the **Design** tab to return to Design view if necessary. Right-click on the page, and then click **View in Browser**.

The value selected will change the image source property and the message in the Label control

Figure 5-11 Using properties to change variables with Visual Basic .NET

15. Print the Web page, the ASP.NET source code, and code behind the page within Visual Studio .NET.

CASE PROJECTS

Tara Store — Using a Class to Store Global Variables

You have been assigned to create a class to store variables that will be reused throughout your Web site. Your manager would like you to create a class named Ch5Case1Class.vb, which will contain the properties for the Web site. The properties should be public so that they can be directly changed via the Web page. You must create a Web page to retrieve and display these values. Create a Web page named Ch5Case1.aspx that displays these properties. You need to create properties to store the name of the store (Tara Store), the address (555 Michigan Ave, Chicago IL 60016), e-mail address (info@tarastore.com), phone number (800-555-5555), store description (We provide a variety of Irish cultural products including china, crystal, pottery, food, clothing, books, music, jewelry, bridal, and gifts.), number of visitors per year (3,245,120), and tax rate (8%). Add graphics, color, content, and text to enhance the appearance of your Web page. Print out the Web page and the source code of the Web page and the code behind the page, and the Ch5Case1.vb page.

Tara Store — Using Properties to Store Global Variables

You have been assigned to create a method to store variables that will be reused throughout your Web site. Your manager would like you to create a class named Ch5Case2Class.vb, which will contain the properties for the Web site. The properties should be private so that they cannot be directly changed via the Web page. You must create a Web page to retrieve and display these values. Create a Web page named Ch5Case2.aspx that displays these properties. You need to create properties to store the name of the store (Tara Store), the address (555 Michigan Ave, Chicago IL 60016), e-mail address (info@tarastore.com), phone number (800-555-5555), store description (We provide a variety of Irish cultural products including china, crystal, pottery, food, clothing, books, music, jewelry, bridal, and gifts.), number of visitors per year (3,245,120), and tax rate (8%). Add graphics, color, content, and text to enhance the appearance of your Web page. Print out the Web page and the source code of the Web page, the code behind the page, and the Ch5Case2Class.vb page.

Tara Store — Object-oriented Programming with Visual Basic .NET

The current Web site was created using ASP. Before you upgrade the site to ASP.NET, your manager would like you to explain what changes in programming would need to be performed during the upgrade process. Specifically, you are to focus on the changes within Visual Basic .NET. Visit the QuickStart Web site at *http://localhost/quickstart* and click the How Do I? hyperlink. In the left menu, click the hyperlink Languages. The Language Support documentation page opens in the browser. Read the documentation provided. List at least five techniques that are used within Visual Basic .NET. Provide an example of each. Create a Web page named Ch5Case3.aspx to display your research. Add graphics, color, content, and text to enhance the appearance of your Web page. Print out the Web page and the source code of the Web page.

Tara Store — Object-oriented Programming with C#

Your manager would like you to explain what changes in programming would need to be performed if the company used C# or Visual Basic .NET. Visit the QuickStart Web site at http://localhost/quickstart/aspplus/ and click the How Do I? hyperlink. In the top menu, click the hyperlink How Do I...?. (*Note:* The same documentation can be found online at the GotDotNet Web site at *http://samples.gotdotnet.com/quickstart/howto/*.) The Common Tasks documentation page opens in the browser. Read the documentation provided in the Languages section. List at least five techniques that are used in Visual Basic .NET and C#. Provide an example of each technique in both languages. Create a Web page named Ch5Case3.aspx to display your research. Add graphics, color, content, and text to enhance the appearance of your Web page. Print out the Web page and the source code of the Web page.

Tara Store — Researching Web Programming Careers

Your coworker suggests that you learn Visual Basic .NET because the company plans to use Visual Studio .NET to create their Web applications. Your coworker doesn't know if other companies are planning to use Visual Basic .NET. Visit at least three of the Web sites listed below to locate information on Web Programming careers.

- ❑ Chicago ComputerJobs.Com - *www.chicago.computerjobs.com*
- ❑ CNET Online Career Center - *www.cnet.com/techjobs/0-7067.html?tag=boxhl1*
- ❑ Dice.com - *www.dice.com*
- ❑ Information Technology Talent Association (ITTA) - *www.it-ta.com*
- ❑ IT Headhunter.com - *www.itheadhunter.com*
- ❑ Techies.com - *www.techies.com*
- ❑ Monster - *www.monster.com*

After reading the information, create a Web page named Ch5Case5.aspx that discusses your findings. Discuss what positions are available, what programming skills and languages are required, what educational requirements are required. Provide information about three specific jobs. Add graphics, color, content, and text to enhance the appearance of your Web page. Print out the Web page and the source code of the Web page.

6

MANAGING DATA SOURCES

In this chapter, you will:

♦ Learn about the ADO.NET model

♦ Build a database connection

♦ Create a SQL Server database using Visual Studio .NET

♦ Manage a database using the Visual Studio .NET database tools

♦ Create SQL scripts using Visual Studio .NET

♦ Create SQL stored procedures using Visual Studio .NET

In order to develop flexible and effective data-driven Web applications, you must use multiple tools to access data from a wide variety of sources. Internet applications integrate Web pages, style sheets, multimedia, Web servers, e-mail servers, e-commerce servers, certificate servers, and authentication servers in addition to databases and database servers. As the number of available Web development tools increases, the task becomes ever more complex. Visual Studio .NET integrates many of these Web development tools into one development environment. In this chapter, you will learn how to create, manage, and access Web data using the tools available in Visual Studio .NET.

OVERVIEW OF THE ADO.NET FRAMEWORK

In the past, database management systems were proprietary; stored data could only be accessed via the program that was used to create the database. Programs could not share data unless you built an interface to the database application. Today, business needs demand database management systems that are more flexible. This flexibility has been achieved by means of the **Universal Data Access Model (UDA)**, which provides a method whereby data can be shared across different applications and platforms. The UDA is implemented by means of standards called Open Database Connectivity (ODBC) and Object Linking and Embedding (OLE-DB), as well as XML and the ActiveX Data Object Model (ADO.NET). The ODBC drivers and OLE-DB providers provide the low-level interface to the database. The ActiveX Data Object Model (ADO) provides objects that allow you to interface with the database. With the .NET Framework, a new version of ADO called ADO.NET is installed. XML is a standard that allows you to describe and store data within text files. ADO.NET allows you to retrieve data from a variety of sources, including XML data. By using these technologies together, you can exchange data across products and platforms.

To learn more about how the UDA is implemented, refer to the Microsoft UDA Web site at *www.microsoft.com/data/default.htm*.

There are many ways to connect your Web application to a database using this UDA Model. First you must build your database tables and determine what information you want to retrieve from them. Then, you decide what technology you will use to connect to your database, and how the connection information will be stored on the server. The connection information identifies the location of the database (the data source) and the connection method (an ODBC driver, OLE-DB provider, or an OLE-DB.NET data provider), along with any other connection settings such as username or password. Once all these elements are in place, you can create a Web page that connects to the database using technologies such as ADO.NET. You can use the built-in objects within ADO.NET to connect to the database, execute commands, and return data from the database. From there, you can interact with the data, display the data, perform calculations on the data, or upload changes to the database.

There are many acronyms used in programming. ASP, ADO, ODBC, OLE-DB, XML, .NET, IIS, PWS, and VB are all commonly used programming acronyms. The large number of acronyms can make programming seem more complicated than it really is. It is very useful to create a listing of these acronyms and their definitions as you read about them. Then, as you learn more about these acronyms, you will be able to differentiate them.

ADO.NET Model

The ADO.NET model separates the process of connecting to the data source from the manipulation of the data. For example, suppose your company uses a non–Microsoft database server. They then create a Web application using Visual Studio .NET that can access their products database and display their products on the Web. The Web application makes the connection using the .NET providers for OLE-DB data sources. The Web pages use the ADO.NET data objects to retrieve the data from the products table, and display the data using a DataGrid control. The following year, the company decides that they are going to support all future Web applications with SQL Server, a database server from Microsoft. After the database has been converted to the new database server, the only changes you must make are those to the connection methods. You do not have to modify the Web application itself, because the data connection is separate from the application layer.

ODBC, OLE-DB, and OLE-DB .NET

In the United Nations, many members need to communicate with members from other countries. They use translators to translate their language into another language. A member who speaks American English would use a translator who could speak French. The French Prime Minister would receive the message in French, and respond with a return message in French. The translator would translate the message from French to American English. This kind of simultaneous translation, when applied to databases, allows you to interact with a database using its own proprietary interface. You can use a standard such as Open Database Connectivity (ODBC) or Object Linking and Embedding Database (OLE-DB) to translate commands between your application and the database.

In 1992, the standard known as **Open Database Connectivity (ODBC)** was created to provide a common interface to relational database systems. ODBC drivers are used to provide access to an ODBC-compliant database. Using ODBC drivers, an application can access a database without an application- or database-specific interface. You do not need to know how the database application stores the data in order to access the data. The ODBC drivers provide the low-level interface to the database applications. ODBC drivers are available for most Database Management Systems (DBMSs), including Access, SQL Server, and Oracle. Therefore, if you want to create an application that accesses an Access database, you would use the ADO objects to create a connection to the database via the ODBC driver.

E-mail programs, such as Exchange Server, store data in a different format than relational database applications. The UDA Model provides a method for accessing relational database stores, as well as these nonrelational data stores, which is called **Object Linking and Embedding Database (OLE-DB)**. Using OLE-DB allows your application to access a database without an application- or database-specific interface. In other words, you do not need to know how the database application stores the data in order to access it. OLE-DB providers are available for most common data stores, including Access, SQL

Server, and Exchange Server. Microsoft provides an OLE-DB provider that will inter-face with the ODBC driver in order to support legacy database applications. For exam-ple, if your database application does not have an OLE-DB provider, but does have the ODBC driver, you can use the OLE-DB provider for ODBC to access the database.

 Microsoft provides an excellent presentation on the development of OLE-DB at *www.microsoft.com/data/oledb/olap/presentations/muda/sld01.htm*.

The ODBC drivers and OLE-DB providers provide the low-level interface to the data-base, which enables you to write code that can transfer data between applications. The method for sending requests to and receiving responses from ODBC and OLE-DB is provided by Microsoft Data Access Components (MDAC) version 2.6 or higher, which incorporates not only the OLE-DB provider and ODBC drivers, but also the compo-nents that interface to ODBC and OLE-DB. This collection of components is known as ADO (ActiveX Data Objects). If your application accesses Access data using ADO objects, and you upgrade your data to a SQL Server database, you will only have to make a few changes to your application. The ADO interface to the data will remain largely the same.

MDAC contains ODBC drivers for text files, Access, FoxPro, Paradox, dBase, Excel, SQL Server, and Oracle. MDAC also provides additional files, including the ODBC Driver Manager. The ODBC Driver Manager is located in C:\Windows\system\odbc32.dll. You can access the ODBC Driver Manager via the Control Panel. The ODBC Driver Manager is used to create Data Source Names. Data Source Names (DSN) contain the connection information required to connect to an ODBC or OLE-DB data source. In Windows 2000 Professional, the ODBC Driver Manager is accessed via the Administrative Tools folder, which is located in the Control Panel.

The ADO model, ODBC drivers, and OLE-DB providers reside on the server, not the client. The Web application interacts with objects built within the ADO Model, as shown in Figure 6-1. Then ADO objects interface with the database via the ODBC and OLE-DB. Your Web application interfaces with the ADO objects.

Figure 6-1   ODBC drivers, and OLE-DB and .NET data providers

Visual Studio .NET includes a new set of data providers, known as **Managed Providers** or .NET providers. There are two versions of the .NET managed providers available by default. The SQL Server .NET data provider is used to connect to a SQL Server database. The OLE-DB .NET data provider is used to connect to any other data source that can be accessed via the OLE-DB interface. The ASP.NET application interacts with ADO.NET objects built into the ADO.NET model. Then, ADO.NET uses the interface of the .NET managed provider to access the database, as shown in Figure 6-2.

Figure 6-2   .NET managed data providers

There are some important differences between the SQL Server .NET data provider and the OLDE-DB .NET data provider. The SQL Server .NET data provider uses a native communication method to communicate with SQL Server. The SQL Server .NET data provider does not have to convert the COM data types from the OLE-DB providers to the .NET data types in the SQL Server .NET data providers. Therefore, there is about a 70% performance improvement when you use the SQL Server .NET data provider.

ADO.NET Object Model

When you use the ADO.NET data provider, you can access the data source using ADO.NET objects. When you use the SQL Server .NET data provider, these objects are known as the SqlConnection, SqlCommand, SqlDataReader, and SqlDataAdapter. When you use the OLE-DB data provider, these objects are known as the OleDbConnection, OleDbCommand, OleDbDataReader, and OleDbDataAdapter. There is also a DataSet object that is used to retrieve data from the database. Within the Web page, the ASP.NET data controls are bound to the DataReaders or DataSets.

The **Connection object** provides the connection to the database. Within the data connection, you must specify the location of the database, the access permissions, and any additional required parameters using a **connection string**. The connection string format is different for each .NET data provider because each provider has its own name. The provider is identified with the keyword **Provider**. The name of the server is identified as the **Data Source**. The User ID and Password identify the authentication data required to connect to the database. The following sample code shows how to create a connection string to an OLE-DB data source.

```
Dim CS
CS = "Provider=msdaora; Data Source=TheOracleDBName;
        User ID=MyUserID; PASSWORD=MyPassword;
```

In SQL Server, the name of the database is identified as the **Initial Catalog**. Below is a sample of an OLE-DB connection string to a SQL Server database. (*Note*: The default user ID in SQL Server is sa and the password is blank.) The name of the SQL Server OLE-DB provider is Provider=SQLOLEDB.1. You do not include the name of the SQL Server .NET data provider because it is selected by default. This string should be placed on one line.

```
Dim CS
CS = "Data Source=WindamereServer;
        User ID=sa; PASSWORD=;
        Initial Catalog=MyDatabase;"
```

The Connection object provides access to the **Transaction object**, which allows you to group data commands together as a logical **transaction**. If any command within the transaction fails, the entire transaction fails, and all data is returned to the original values. Transactions are often used with credit card processing. The BeginTransaction method of the Connection object begins a transaction and returns a Transaction object, which is used to commit or abort transactions.

The ADO.NET **Command object** is used to identify a SQL command or a stored procedure. SQL is the **structured query language** that is used to identify what records to add, delete, or modify within the database. **Stored procedures** are SQL commands that are stored within the database. The Command object also exposes a **Parameters collection** that can be used to apply parameters, which are passed to stored procedures. The connection used by the Command object is defined in the **Connection property**. The command is defined in the **CommandText property**. The CommandType is used to indicate the type of command being executed. The **CommandType property** is Text by default, which indicates that the command is a SQL text string. The CommandType property can also be **TableDirect**, which specifies the name of a table to return. The CommandType property can also be **StoredProcedure**, which specifies the name of a stored procedure. The **execute method** of the Command object executes the command and passes the results to the DataReader object. The **ExecuteNonQuery method** does not return rows because it's used to insert, modify, and delete data. Therefore, the method returns an integer representing the number of rows affected by the command.

The **DataReader object** is used to deliver a stream of data from the database. It is included in the ADO.NET model in order to provide a high-performance method of accessing read-only data. The DataReader object is another object in the ADO.NET model, as shown in Figure 6-3. The DataReader provides a read-only, forward-only stream of data from the database. Therefore, you cannot make changes to the database using the DataReader. The DataReader requires continual access to the database, while the DataAdapter uses a disconnected dataset to access the data. You can access the DataReader using the Command object.

Figure 6-3   ADO.NET core objects

When you call the **ExecuteReader method** of the Command object, the DataReader opens a connection to the database and then retrieves rows of data as they are located in the database. The **read method** of the DataReader returns a single row and caches each row in memory only once, then moves the current record pointer to the next record or row. You must remain connected until you have finished reading the stream of data. When you are finished, you need to close the connection using the **CommandBehavior property** of the Command object. If you set the CommandBehavior to **CloseConnection**, the connection closes automatically when the close method of the DataReader object is called. You must call the close method to close the Reader object and release the references to the rowset. (*Note*: Some features of ASP.NET Data controls won't work with the DataReader. For example, automatic paging with the DataGrid control won't work with DataReader. Instead, you will have to use a DataView object, which is available through the DataSet object.)

The **DataAdapter object** is primarily used to access a DataSet object, as shown in Figure 6-4. The DataAdapter object provides four commands that you can use to access the DataSet object. **SelectCommand** is used to retrieve data. When you use SelectCommand, the data must be inserted into the DataSet object. The **fill method** of the DataAdapter inserts the data returned from the SelectCommand into the DataSet object. The DataSet object is effectively a private copy of the database, and does not necessarily reflect the current state of the database. If you want to see the latest changes made by other users, you can refresh the DataSet object by calling the appropriate fill method of the DataAdapter object. **InsertCommand** is used to add a new record. **UpdateCommand** is used to modify the data within an existing record. **DeleteCommand** is used to permanently remove a record from the database. (*Note*: If no records are returned, then the command returns a count of records affected.) These four commands are used to access the DataSet object. The **DataSet object** is a disconnected collection of one or more tables that are stored in memory on the server. Because the DataSet object is disconnected, there must be methods used to maintain the original set of data, and the changes. When the code has completed making changes to the DataSet object, there must be a method to upload the changes to the database. The DataAdapter contains the methods required to maintain the list of changes made to the DataSet object. The DataAdapter connects to the database and reconciles changes made to the data in the DataSet object with the data source when the **update method** is called.

6

Figure 6-4   Using ADO.NET objects to access a DataSet object

One useful feature of Visual Studio .NET is that when you use the DataAdapter, the DataAdapter commands are automatically generated via the **CommandBuilder object**. So, the DataAdapter provides the bridge between the DataSet object and the data source. The DataSet object is a passive container for the data. The DataSet object is accessed through the `System.Data` namespace. To actually fetch data from the database and (optionally) write data to the database, you use the DataAdapter object.

The DataSet object consists of the DataTableCollection and the DataRelationCollection. As shown in Figure 6-5, the **DataTableCollection** is a collection of one or more **DataTable objects**. Each DataTable object consists of a DataRowCollection, DataColumnCollection, and ConstraintCollection. The DataRowCollection and DataColumnCollection store information about the rows and columns of data. (*Note*: The column is also referred to as the field.)

The **ConstraintCollection** includes information about the primary and foreign keys, and constraint rules. A **primary key** is used to ensure that no duplicate records appear in this column. Therefore, if one customer has the customer number, no other customer can have that number. The **Constraint rules** are used to ensure that the field contains the correct datatype and values. The UniqueConstraint and ForeignKeyConstraint are used to create the relationships. The **DataRelationCollection** contains the data required to maintain relationships between the DataTables. Relational data can be exposed via ADO.NET because relationships can be made between DataTables. The tables are joined using the primary and foreign keys that are defined in the DataTable object. The **ExtendedProperties property** of the DataSet object allows you to specify information that can be stored with the DataSet object and later retrieved. The ExtendedProperties can be used to store the date the DataSet object was generated, the SQL statement, or any other data.

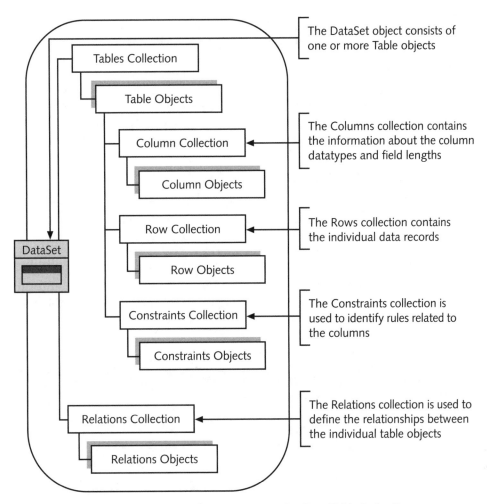

6

Figure 6-5   Using the DataSet object to access the DataTableCollection

A **DataView** object contains the data from the DataSet object for a single DataTable or subset of records from a table. The DataTable object has a DefaultView property that returns all the records in the DataTable. However, you can select a subset of records from a table. You can add columns to the DataColumnCollection as well as filter and sort the data in a DataView object. The **RowFilter property** of the DataView object allows you to filter a subset of the DataView object. The **Sort property** of the DataView object also allows you to sort the data based upon a specific criterion in one or more of the columns.

If you have XML data, you can use it in the Web application by converting the XML data to a DataSet object. The XML data contains the data as well as the definitions (or schema) of the data. The DataSet object can also store the data as XML in memory, and store the schema as an XSD document. XSL is the XML Schema Definition language used to define the schema of a DataSet object. Visual Studio .NET generates your XML data and the XSD document for you when you create a DataSet object and fill it with data.

In Visual Studio .NET you can generate a DataSet object and the XSD documents from your data source whether it's a database or an XML document. However, if you don't have access to Visual Studio .NET, both SQL Server 2000 and Access XP are able to generate XML data. You can export a table or query from Access XP into XML. Thus, a component can transmit a data set to another component using XML. The receiving component receives the data set as a DataSet object within the .NET framework. In the same way, the DataSet object can generate the XML and XSD documents, which can be used by applications that do not support DataSet objects.

Data Related Namespaces

The ADO.NET data objects are stored within the database class. You can access these objects via the data namespaces. These namespaces must be imported into your Web application. (*Note*: These namespaces are the same for both Web and Windows applications.) You can manage these namespaces within the config.web global application file. The SQL Server .NET data provider has its own namespace, called SqlClient. The OLE-DB .NET data providers use the OleDb namespace. (*Note*: The OLE-DB .NET data provider only works with OLE-DB versions 2.6 or higher.) The table below lists the common data-related namespaces.

Table 6-1   Data related namespaces

ADO.NET Object	Namespace
Data objects (contains DataSet, DataTable, and DataRelation objects)	`System.Data`
SQL Server OLE-DB .NET data provider (includes the Connection, Command, DataReader, and DataAdapter objects)	`System.Data.SqlClient`
OLE-DB .NET data provider (includes the Connection, Command, DataReader, and DataAdapter objects)	`System.Data.OleDb`

BUILDING DATABASE CONNECTIONS

Visual Studio .NET provides a graphical user interface that you can use to create a connection to a database. The Server Explorer window provides you access to your local and network databases and data connections. The two nodes within the Server Explorer window are Data Connections and Servers. The Servers node provides you with access to the services running on the computer, such as a database server. The Data Connections node provides you with access to the data connection to a database, and to the graphical tool used to create a database. Once a data connection is made, the information is stored in the data connection properties. The properties of the data connection include the ConnectString, Database, Driver, Server, State, Type, and User. The **ConnectString property** contains all of the values of the data connection properties in a single string. It also may contain additional properties required to connect to the database such as the username and password. The **Database property** is the name of the database, and the **Server property** is the name of the server. The **Type property** is the name of the database application such as Microsoft Access Database or SQL Server 2000 Database. The **Driver** is the name of the ODBC driver, OLE-DB provider, or .NET managed data provider that is used to communicate with the database. The **State property** indicates if the database is currently connected. You can create data connections to remote databases. If the remote computer crashes, then the data connection will no longer work. The State property indicates if the connection to the database is still valid. The **User property** identifies the name of the user account that created the database. The creator of the database is known as the database owner, or dbo.

When you installed Visual Studio .NET, by default a version of SQL Server called the **Microsoft SQL Server Desktop Engine (MSDE)** may have been installed. The name of the SQL Server is *MachineName*\NetSDK, where *MachineName* is the name of your local computer. This server can also be referred to as (local)\NetSDK or localhost. (There can be several versions of the SQL Server installed on the same computer. Your system administrator may have changed the default settings.

The MSDE server uses Windows authentication by default. The ASP.NET Windows account must have permission to access each database you create. You can find instructions on assigning database permissions in the ReadMe.doc file, which is located in the Chapter06Data directory.

The following exercise shows you how to install the samples that come with the .NET Framework and the data server. (If you have already installed the samples and QuickStart tutorials, then you can skip this exercise.)

1. Start **Internet Explorer**.

2. Go to the SDK Tutorials and Samples page by typing in the address text box **C:\Program Files\MicrosoftVisualStudio.NET\FrameworkSDK\ Samples\StartSamples.htm**. (*Note:* You can also get to this page by using the shortcuts in the Start menu. Click **Start**, point to **Programs**, point to **Microsoft .NET Framework SDK**, then click **Samples and QuickStart Tutorials**.)

3. Click the link **Install the .NET Framework Samples Database**.

4. In the File Download box, select **Run this program from its current location**, and then click the **OK** button. When the security warning opens, click the **Yes** button. This will install the sample database server.

5. When the installation is finished, click the hyperlink **Complete the installation**.

6. In the File Download box, select **Run this program from its current location**, and then click **OK**. When the security warning opens, click the **Yes** button. This will install the virtual directories and database files and some registry keys.

7. When the samples are installed, a window that says Congratulations! opens. Click the **Launch** button. (*Note*: If you get any other message, then you should click the **View log** hyperlink to view and save the log file.)

8. In the browser, go to **http://localhost/quickstart** to view the documentation. If the page loads, then the samples and the data environment were installed correctly. (*Note*: The documentation for the .NET framework SDK can be found by clicking **Start**, **Programs**, **Microsoft .NET Framework SDK**, **Tools**.)

9. Exit the browser.

It is important to have enough random access memory (RAM) on the computer to use Visual Studio .NET and the database server. Database processing requires a significant amount of memory. If you do not meet the minimum requirements for the installation of Visual Studio .NET, you should not attempt to create or maintain your databases using the Visual Studio .NET MSDE. You may, however, be able to use Visual Studio .NET in conjunction with a database server located on a different computer.

You can find detailed information about the SQL Server installation process and the .NET Framework SDK samples in C:\Program Files\Microsoft Visual Studio .NET\FrameworkSDK\Samples\Setup\html\ConfigDetails.htm. If you are working with Internet Information Server version 6.0, you should refer to this page for information on how to configure your application so that it will be authenticated by the SQL Server database.

Once the samples are installed, the server appears in the Visual Studio .NET Server Explorer window. The sample databases that are installed include GrocerToGo, Northwind, Portal, and pubs. GrocerToGo and Portal were created primarily to display the capabilities of data-driven ASP.NET applications. In the exercise below, you create a new Web application named Chapter6, view the list of databases installed on your server, and list the columns within the Products table in the GrocerToGo database.

1. Start **Visual Studio .NET**.

2. Click **File** on the menu bar, point to **New**, then click **Project**. This opens the New Project window.

3. Under Project Types, click the **Visual Basic Projects** folder icon, then under Templates, click the **ASP.NET Web Application** icon. Type **Chapter6** in the Location text box in place of WebApplication1. Click **OK** to create the solution, project, and default files.

4. Click the **Server Explorer** tab to slide the window out. (*Note*: If the tab is not visible, click **View** on the menu bar, then click **Server Explorer**. If the window is open, but you cannot see it, click the **Server** tab next to the Toolbox tab near the bottom left of the window.) Then, click the **pushpin** on the title bar of the Server Explorer window to make the window remain open.

5. Click the **plus sign** next to the Servers icon to expand the list of your local and network servers. (*Note*: This may already have been expanded on your system.) Click the **plus sign** next to the name of your computer (the MachineName). Click the **plus sign** next to the SQL Servers icon. Click the **plus sign** next to the database that is named *MachineName*\NETSDK, where MachineName is the name of your computer.

6. Click the **plus sign** next to the GrocerToGo icon. Click the **plus sign** next to the Tables icon. Click the **plus sign** next to the Products table icon to display the list of fields in the Products table.

7. Click the **ProductID** field. The list of properties of the ProductID field is displayed in the Properties window. The properties include the DataType and Length, as shown in Figure 6-6.

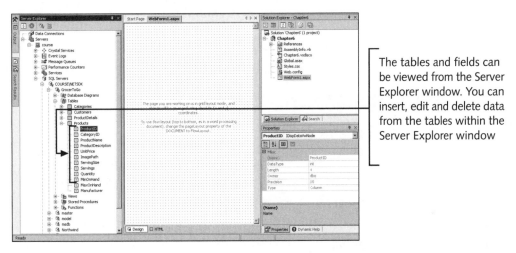

The tables and fields can be viewed from the Server Explorer window. You can insert, edit and delete data from the tables within the Server Explorer window

Figure 6-6   Displaying fields within tables in the Server Explorer window

8. Click the **minus sign** next to the Servers icon to collapse the list of your local and network servers.

In the exercise below, you will make a connection to the GrocerToGo database. (*Note*: This does not create a Connection object, just the connection to the database. You will create the Connection objects in the next chapter.) The exercises in this chapter can be applied to both Web and Windows applications created with Visual Studio .NET.

1. In the Server Explorer window, right-click the **Data Connections** icon, which is located at the top of the window, and then click **Add Connection**. The Data Link Properties dialog box opens.

2. In the Server Name text box enter your database server name, which is **(local)\NETSDK**. (*Note*: You can also use the name for the local server, which is known as localhost or *MachineName*\NetSDK.)

3. Select the authentication mode for the SQL Server. There are radio buttons, which indicate the two possible methods to authenticate your connection with the SQL Server database.

   a. If you use the default installation, you can select the first radio button, which indicates that the connection should use integrated Windows NT security. With this option, you do not have to enter a username or password.

   b. If you have installed your own version of SQL Server, then you should select the second radio button. If you installed SQL Server, you can enter the default username and password. The default username is sa with no password. Then, in the **User name** text box type **sa** and check the **Blank password** check box. If you did not install the sa user, you must type the name of the user account that was configured during the installation of the SQL Server software. (*Note*: If you did not install the software, you should contact your system administrator to obtain the permission settings to connect to the SQL server.)

4. In the drop-down list box, select **GrocerToGo**, as shown in Figure 6-7. (*Note*: You will only see the databases that you have permission to access.)

Figure 6-7   Creating a database connection to the GrocerToGo database

5. Click the **Test Connection** button. An alert box should appear that says Test connection succeeded. Click the **OK** button to close the alert box. (*Note*: If the connection does not occur, an alternate message is displayed, showing the type of error. If an error occurs, you should verify that the database and the settings are correct, and then create a new connection to the database.)

6. Click **OK**. The connection is named *MACHINENAME\NETSDK. GrocerToGo.dbo* and is placed in the list under Data Connections in the Server Explorer window. You can use this connection later, to create the Connection object. (*Note*: Remember that this is not a Connection object, just a reference to the database connection in the project. If you click the connection, the connection properties are displayed in the Properties window. The properties are dimmed because the values were set with the Visual Studio .NET program and are not meant to be edited manually.)

7. Click the **plus sign** next to the *MACHINENAME\NETSDK. GrocerToGo.dbo* icon. Click the **plus sign** next to the Tables icon. Click the **plus sign** next to the Products table icon to display the list of fields in the Products table. These are the same fields that you displayed earlier using the Servers node.

8. Click the **minus sign** next to the *MACHINENAME\NETSDK. GrocerToGo.dbo* icon to collapse the view.

You can use the Data Link Properties box with nonlocal data sources. You have to provide the URL to the SQL Server database in the server name text box.

VISUAL STUDIO .NET BUILT-IN DATABASE TOOLS

There are a variety of Visual Studio .NET tools that allow you to create and manipulate a database. Once you have created your database in the Server Explorer, you will want to add tables and stored procedures. You can add a table using the Table Designer. There is also a Query and View Editor for creating database queries. (*Note*: In some databases, such as Access, you must use queries to create stored procedures, and pass the parameter to the query.) The Visual Studio .NET SQL Editor is used to create and edit SQL scripts and stored procedures.

Creating a SQL Server Database in Visual Studio .NET

Visual Studio .NET provides a graphical user interface that you can use to create a connection to a database. When you create the database, you need to know which type of authentication is required for access to the SQL Server. You can use the authentication built within Windows NT, or SQL Server authentication.

You must have permission to create the database. Within SQL Server, a user ID is used to identify users and control which users can access the Database objects. Each user has roles that identify if they are able to create or modify a Data object. You can read more about the permissions and authentication modes at *ms-help://ms/vscc/MS.MSDNVS/ vsintro7/html/dvrefCreateDatabaseDialogueBox.htm*. You can read more about managing SQL Server security at *ms-help://ms/vscc/MS.MSDNVS/adminsql/ad_security_05bt.htm*.

In the following exercise, you will create a basic database named Chapter6.

1. In the Server Explorer window, right-click **Data Connections**, and then click **Create New SQL Server Database**.

2. In the Create Database dialog box, enter the name of your SQL server in the Server text box, which is **(local)\NetSDK**. (*Note:* You can also enter *Machine*\NETSDK, where *Machine* is the name of your computer.)

3. In the New Database Name text box type **Chapter6**, as shown in Figure 6-8. The Use Windows NT Integrated Security option is selected by default. (*Note:* If you use SQL Server Authentication, click the **Use SQL Server Authentication** radio button to select it, and enter the login name and password.)

Figure 6-8   Creating a database

 If you use the default SQL Server installation, the Login Name is sa and the password is blank. If you have a SQL Server username that you want to use instead of the sa account, you can enter that in the Login Name text box, and the corresponding password in the Password text box.

4. Click **OK** to create the Chapter6 database. The connection to the *MACHINENAME*\NETSDK.Chapter6.dbo database appears under the Data Connections in the Server Explorer window. The Chapter6 database also appears under *Machine*\NETSDK within the SQL Servers. (*Note:* You may need to right-click **Data Connections** in the Server Explorer, then click **Refresh** to view the view data connection.)

 While using Visual Studio .NET, if your database connection does not work, you should close Visual Studio .NET, then reopen Visual Studio .NET and your solution. If you still cannot create a database, you should consult the security documentation or your system administrator to verify your SQL Server authentication settings.

The Table Designer

The Table Designer allows you to create the schema for the table and enter the data. In Table Design view, you can create new columns, and modify the properties of the columns. In Table Data view, you can create a new row, modify an existing row, or delete a row. In Table Design view, the top half of the Table Designer allows you to create the structure of the columns within the table. You define the name of the column, and the data type. Each column is defined within a row in the Table Designer. Each row contains a row selector bow, a Column Name, Data Type, Length, and Allow Nulls. The currently selected row can be identified by the triangle in the row selector box. The **row selector** is the gray square located next to the column name. The row selector can also be used to select the current row. The lower half of the Table Designer allows you to modify the properties of the column. The properties within the second half of the Table Designer vary with the data type selected. Most of the data types provide a description property and a default value for the column length property.

You must specify a name for the column and a data type. Do not use any blank spaces or special characters in a column name other than an underscore. It is best to keep the column name short, but descriptive. For example, the column name LastName describes a field that might contain customer last names. However, if the column name is LN, it's not clear what information is stored in the column. You must select a data type from a drop-down list. You must also provide the length of the columns in bytes, and whether or not the column requires a value. If a column does not contain a value for a particular record, a null value is returned.

You must specify a data type for each column when you create the column. The ADO.NET managed providers convert the data types to Managed .NET data types when you retrieve your data using ADO.NET. There are many data types defined within SQL Server. For example, the int data type is used to identify an integer. You can learn more about SQL Server data types at *ms-help://ms/vscc/MS.MSDNVS/cpref/html/ frlrfSystemDataSqTypes.htm*.

The possible data types for SQL Server 2000 are as follows:

- bigint
- binary
- bit
- char
- datetime
- decimal
- float

- image
- int
- money
- nchar
- ntext
- numeric
- nvarchar

- real
- smalldatetime
- smallint
- smallmoney
- sql_variant
- text
- timestamp

- tinyint
- uniqueidentifier
- varbinary
- varchar

You can set the default column properties such as column length using the Visual Studio .NET Options window. You can access the Options window by clicking Tools on the menu bar, then clicking Options. The SQL Server column options are shown below in Figure 6-9.

The Options settings allow you to change the settings for the editors, as well as any of the developer tools within Visual Studio .NET

Figure 6-9   The SQL Server column options

There are many properties that can be set in the Properties pane. The properties that you can set will depend upon the data type you selected. For example, you can specify if a column with an int datatype is an **identity column** with the **Identity property**. The identity column is used to provide a unique value for each row. This value can be used to locate a specific row of data. To change a column to an identity column, change the Identity property from No to Yes. Then, you can set the Identity Seed and Identity Increment properties. The **Identity Seed property** shows the initial value of the column, which is used to create the value for the first row. The **identity increment** is the value that is used to increment the seed when a new row is added. For example, you can increment the identify column by one, so that the value of the identity column increases by one for each new record.

The **primary key** is used to identify the column as a unique column. Each value for each row must be unique within this column. All rows must have a value for this column. No record will be allowed that contains a null value for this column. The primary key is configured for a specific column by using the row selector, the Table toolbar, or the Diagram menu.

In the following exercise, you will create a table named Products and create the columns using the Table Designer.

1. In Server Explorer, click the **plus sign** next to the Data Connection for the *MACHINENAME*\NETSDK.Chapter6.dbo database. Right-click the **Tables** icon, and then click **New Table** to open the Table Designer.

2. In the first row, type **ProductID** as the column name. Select **int** as the data type from the drop-down list. The length should be **4**. Click the **Allow Nulls** check box to deselect it, since all products are required to have a ProductID. In the properties at the bottom half of the window, change the Identity from No to **Yes** using the drop-down list arrow. Identity Seed should be set to **1**, and identity increment should be set to **1**. This creates a new value for each new record entered in the database.

3. Right-click the **ProductID** row selector, and then click **Set Primary Key**. A yellow key appears at the side of the column name to indicate that this column is the Primary Key column.

4. Add the other columns as shown in the table below and in Figure 6-10. You can leave the default properties for each column.

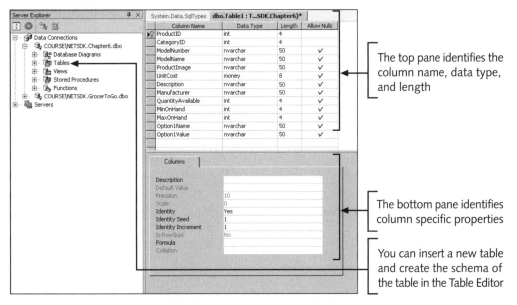

The top pane identifies the column name, data type, and length

The bottom pane identifies column specific properties

You can insert a new table and create the schema of the table in the Table Editor

Figure 6-10   Creating a database table using the Table Editor

Table 6-2   The Products table for the Chapter6 database

Column Name	DataType	Length	Allow Nulls
ProductID	Int	4	No
CategoryID	Int	4	No
ModelNumber	Nvarchar	50	Yes
ModelName	Nvarchar	50	Yes
ProductImage	Nvarchar	50	Yes
UnitCost	Money	8	Yes
Description	Nvarchar	200	Yes
Manufacturer	Nvarchar	50	Yes
QuantityAvailable	Int	4	Yes
MinOnHand	Int	4	Yes
MaxOnHand	Int	4	Yes
Option1Name	Nvarchar	50	Yes
Option1Value	Nvarchar	50	Yes

5. Click the **Save All** icon. The Choose Name dialog box opens. Enter **Products** as the table name, and then click **OK**. Close the Table Designer window.

6. Right-click the *MACHINENAME*\NETSDK.Chapter6.dbo data connection icon, and then click **Refresh**. The Products table should appear under the Tables icon.

7. Click the **plus sign** next to the *MACHINENAME*\NETSDK.Chapter6.dbo database to expand the database objects.

8. Click on the **plus sign** next to the Tables icon to expand the tables list. Click the **plus sign** to expand the Products table and view the columns that you created in Step 4.

In the following exercise you will add data for four records into the table.

1. Right-click the **Products** table name, and then click **Retrieve Data from Table**. The table opens in Data view. You can enter data for each record in Data view. The cursor is placed in the ProductID column. Because SQL Server assigns this value, press the **Tab** key to move to the next column. Enter **1** for CategoryID.

2. Add the values for the other fields using the table below. Leave the other fields empty and press **Enter**. Notice that the option1 and value1 columns are replaced with the keyword null in the first record.

3. Enter the other three records. The data for all of the records is shown in Table 6-3 below. The ProductID field has been assigned a value of 1, 2, 3, and 4 respectively as shown in Figure 6-11.

Table 6-3   The Products table for the Chapter 6 database

Column Name	Row 1 Data	Row 2 Data	Row 3 Data	Row 4 Data
ProductID	1 (to be filled in by the database)	2 (to be filled in by the database)	3 (to be filled in by the database)	4 (to be filled in by the database)
CategoryID	1	1	1	1
ModelNumber	756-224-00-09	387-463-55-00	978-979-53-00	978-979-53-79
ModelName	Letter Opener	Shamrock Paperweight	Business Card Holder	Cat Bowl
ProductImage	528.jpg	537.jpg	529.jpg	658.jpg
UnitCost	69	99	59	22
Description	Letter Opener by Waterford.	Shamrock Paperweight by Waterford	Business Card Holder by Waterford	Cat Bowl by Belinda Bradshaw
Manufacturer	Waterford	Waterford	Waterford	Bradshaw
QuantityAvailable	10	5	50	25

Table 6-3   The Products table for the Chapter 6 database (continued)

Column Name	Row 1 Data	Row 2 Data	Row 3 Data	Row 4 Data
MinOnHand	5	10	25	10
MaxOnHand	20	30	100	75
Option1Name		Size		Color
Option1Value		S, L		Yellow, Blue

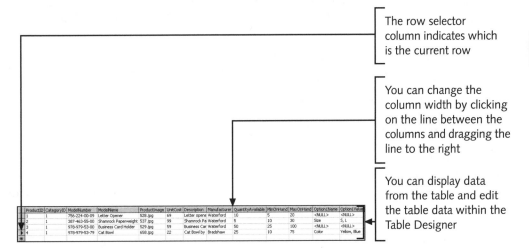

The row selector column indicates which is the current row

You can change the column width by clicking on the line between the columns and dragging the line to the right

You can display data from the table and edit the table data within the Table Designer

Figure 6-11   Table values

Tip If you do not enter a value, the column will display <NULL>. If you make a mistake, you can delete the value you entered and configure the column to display <NULL>. When you press Ctrl key and 0 while inside the column, the contents of the column will be replaced with the <NULL> value.

4. Click the **Save All** icon and close the window.

5. Create a second table by right-clicking **Tables** and clicking **New Table**. The table has two columns. The name of the first column is **CategoryID**. Enter the CategoryID is an integer (**int**) with a length of **4** bytes. Click the **Allow Nulls** check box to deselect it. A CategoryID is required for all categories. In the properties at the bottom half of the window, change the Identity from No to **Yes** using the drop-down list arrow. The Identity Seed should be set to **1**, and the identity increment should be set to **1**. This creates a new value for each new record entered in the database.

6. Right-click the **CategoryID** column name in the row selector, and then click **Set Primary Key**. A yellow key appears at the side of the column name to indicate that this column is the Primary Key column.

7. The name of the second column is **CategoryName**. Enter **nvarchar**, as the datatype and the length as **50** bytes. The CategoryName column is allowed to have null values, so leave the Allow Nulls check box checked.

8. Click the **Save All** icon. The Choose Name dialog box opens. Enter **Categories** for the table name, and then click **OK**.

9. Open the table and add two records. Right-click on the **Categories** table in the Server Explorer window and select **Retrieve Data from Table**. In the first row, press the **Tab** key to move to the CategoryName column. The database server adds the CategoryID for you. Type **Waterford** as the CategoryName.

10. Press the **Tab** key twice to get the CategoryName for the second row. Enter **Pottery** for the Second Row, and then press **Enter**.

11. Click the **Save All** icon. Close the window.

Creating a View with the Query and View Editor

The Query and View Editor allows you to create a query in the database. There are four windows called **panes** displayed within the editor. The top pane is the Table pane. In the **Table pane**, you can add tables and select which columns to include in the query. The query is displayed visually with icons next to the columns. For example, if you sort the table based on a column, a sort icon is placed next to the column name in the Table pane. This provides a quick method for viewing the query. The second pane is the Grid pane. You use the **Grid pane** to select columns and criteria, just as you do when using Microsoft Access. The **column name** and **table** indicate where to retrieve the values for the column. The **Output property** indicates if the column should be visible in the results when the query is executed. (*Note*: The Output property is like the "show" check box in Access.) The **sort order** is used to specify one or more columns for sorting the results. You can number the sort order to specify which column should be sorted first. (*Note*: The sort order with the lowest number is sorted first.) You can specify the sort order as ascending or descending by using the **Sort Type property**. The **Alias property** is used to display an alternate name in the results. Because the field names do not contain spaces or special characters, it is sometimes useful to provide a more readable alias name for the end user. You use the **Criteria property** to create a conditional statement that must be met before the record can be retrieved. The **Or property** indicates an alternate condition that could be met for the record to be retrieved.

The third pane is the SQL pane. The **SQL pane** generates the SQL for you based upon the Table pane and Grid pane. However, you can edit the SQL directly within the SQL pane. The Grid pane and Table pane are updated automatically when you make a change to the SQL pane. The last pane is the Output pane. In the **Output pane**, the output from the Query is displayed. Therefore, you can test your queries from within Visual Studio .NET before you place them in your Web pages.

In the following example, you will use the Query and View Editor to create a view that will display the products from the Waterford manufacturer.

1. In Server Explorer, under the *MACHINENAME*\NETSDK.Chapter6.dbo data connection, right-click **Views**, then click **New View**. The Query and View Editor opens along with the Add Table dialog box. You need to select which tables you would like to add to the query. Select the **Products** table, click the **Add** button, and then click the **Close** button. The Products table is added to the Table pane.

2. In the Table pane, click the **check box** next to the following column names to select them: **ProductID**, **CategoryID**, **ModelName**, and **Manufacturer**. This places the column names into the query in the Grid pane and the SQL pane.

3. In the Grid pane go to the Sort Type property for the ModelName column, and select **Ascending** from the drop-down list. The sort order is entered as **1**, which indicates that this is the first column to be sorted.

4. In the Manufacturer column enter **= Waterford** in the Criteria property.

5. Right-click the Table pane, and then click **Run**. (*Note*: You can also click the **Run Query** icon in the SQL toolbar. The **Run Query** is the red exclamation point icon.) The three Waterford products are displayed, with the Business Card Holder displayed first, as shown in Figure 6-12.

Figure 6-12   The Query and View Editor

6. Click the **Save All** icon to save the view. In the Save New View dialog box, enter **DisplayWaterford** as the name of the view, and then click **OK**.

7. Close the Query and View Editor.

8. To rerun the query, click the **plus sign** next to the Views icon under Data Connections to display the list of views.

9. Right-click the **Display Waterford** view, and then click **Retrieve Data from View**. The query runs and display the results, but does not display the Query and View Editor.

10. Close the window.

Creating a Relationship with the Data Diagram

The **Database Designer** allows you to define relationships between tables using columns. In the Database Designer, each table contains a **title bar**, which displays the name of the table. If the table has an owner, the owner's name is shown in parenthesis in the title bar after the table name. By default the tables are displayed showing the table names in the title bar and the column names. This view of the table is called the **Column Names view**. You can change the view of the tables using the Table view property. When you right-click on a table, you can change the view from Column Names by selecting **Table View** and then selecting the view name. The **Standard view** displays the column names and the schema for the columns. The **Keys view** displays the names of the tables in the title bar and the names of the primary key columns. The **Name view** displays only the names of the tables in the title bar. The **Custom view** allows you to add any of the properties to the view.

A line is drawn from a field from one table to another to indicate which fields are used to define the relationship between the tables. The endpoints of the line indicate whether the relationship is one-to-one or one-to-many. If a relationship has a key at one endpoint and a figure eight at the other, it is a one-to-many relationship. However, if the relationship has a key at each endpoint, then it is a one-to-one relationship.

It's important to note that these diagrams are useful before building the database and entering the data. Once the data has been entered, if you try to create a relationship that is not valid, the Database Designer will not let you create the relationship. For example, if you entered the records for the Products table but not the Categories table, then you cannot create a relationship between the two tables based on the CategoryID. (*Note:* This enforcement of referential integrity also applies to Microsoft Access and other relational databases.) In the following example, you will use the Database Designer to create a relationship between the Categories table and the Products table. The CategoryID is used to create a one-to-many relationship.

1. In Server Explorer, under the *MACHINENAME*\NETSDK.Chapter6.dbo data connection, right-click **Database Diagrams**, then click **New Diagram**. The Data Diagram Editor opens along with the Add Table dialog box. Select both the **Categories** table and the **Products** table by holding down the **Shift** key while you make the selections. Click the **Add** button and then the **Close** button. The tables are added to the Database Designer.

2. Click the **row selector** next to the CategoryID column in the Categories table and drag the row to the row selector next to the CategoryID column in the Products table. The Create Relationship window opens. Select the

CategoryID in the drop-down list for both the Categories and Products table. (*Note:* These may have been entered by default when you dragged the CategoryID.)

3. Click **OK**. The line now indicates a one-to-many relationship between the two tables. There is only one CategoryID value in the Categories table. There can be many products that have the same CategoryID value. In the example shown below in Figure 6-13, the relationship is a one-to-many relationship.

Figure 6-13   Database diagram

4. Click the **Save All** icon to save the view. In the Save New Database Diagram dialog box, type **Category_Products** as the name of the view, and then click **OK**. A warning message may appear indicating that the tables will be saved to the database. Click **Yes**.

5. Close the window.

BUILDING SQL SCRIPTS AND STORED PROCEDURES

Stored procedures can be used to create a SQL command that is stored within the database. Because the command is stored with the database server, it has already been parsed and compiled by the server. Therefore, the stored procedure is more efficient than a SQL statement. Prior to Visual Studio .NET, you had to create the stored procedure from within a SQL Server tool such as Query Analyzer or Enterprise Manager. Today, you can create your stored procedure from within Visual Studio .NET.

You can use a stored procedure to run a SQL query. You can also create a stored procedure that uses input and output parameters. An **input parameter** is a value that is passed to the stored procedure when it is called. This value must match the data type and length that is specified within the stored procedure. The name of the parameter within the stored procedure always begins with the @ symbol. Any of the values within the SQL statement can be replaced with the input parameters. Usually, the input parameter is compared to a value. Then, the subset of matching records is retrieved, modified, or deleted. The other type of parameter is the output parameter. **Output parameters** can send values back to the object that called the stored procedure. (*Note*: Text, ntext, and image parameters can be used as output parameters. However, in SQL Server 2000 the output parameter cannot have the data type as Text.) You can also have a value that is passed to and returned from the stored procedure. This value is known as an **InputOutput parameter**. In addition, you can have a return value passed back to the stored procedure call. The return value is indicated with the keyword **Return** and is known as a **ReturnValue parameter**. It is often used for queries that don't return columns, such as an INSERT query. You can specify information such as the number of records affected in the return value. You can specify a default value for the parameter in the stored procedure. Therefore, if the user does not enter a parameter, the default is used. The default value must be a constant or it can be null. You can return values of integer, money, and varchar but not text. (*Note*: Wildcard characters, such as the asterisk, are permitted with the default value. Information about the user of parameters can be found in the Visual Studio .NET help files at *ms-help://MS.VSCC/MS.MSDNVS/tsqlref/ ts_create_4hk5.htm*.)

Visual Studio .NET provides a **SQL Editor** to create and edit SQL scripts and stored procedures. Although the SQL Editor does not have IntelliSense prompting, it does color-code SQL keywords, which helps minimize syntax and spelling errors. Comments in the SQL skeleton script are indicated with /* and */ characters. The comments are displayed in green text to differentiate the comments from SQL commands. The SQL Editor also inserts a skeletal stored procedure when you create a new stored procedure. You can change the editor's default behaviors such as tab size, word wrapping and line numbers by selecting Options on the Tools menu.

Creating Stored Procedures with the SQL Editor

In the following exercises, you will create stored procedures using the SQL Editor. The first procedure will retrieve all of the records from the table where the QuantityAvailable column is less than the MinOnHand. This creates a listing of products that must be reordered because there are not enough units available. The stored procedure will return the number of rows affected, and the @RETURN_VALUE. The @RETURN_VALUE is the value of the output parameter. If there is no value, then the value 0 is returned. The results are displayed as text in the Output window, which can be saved as a text file.

1. In the Server Explorer window, under the *MACHINENAME*\NETSDK. Chapter6.dbo data connection, right-click **Stored Procedures**, and then click **New Stored Procedure**. The stored procedure document opens with the default text for creating the stored procedure.

2. Replace the text dbo.StoredProcedure1 with **dbo.sp_ReorderProducts**.

3. Under the As keyword insert a new line and type the following code which retrieves all of the columns from the database where the QuantityAvailable column is less than the MinOnHold column. The asterisk is a wildcard character,

which indicates that all columns are selected. Because this is SQL and not Visual Basic .NET, you do not have to add the underscore to continue onto the second line. A blue line will appear around the code, which indicates that the code can be edited manually or in the graphical user interface within the SQL Editor.

```
SELECT * FROM Products
WHERE QuantityAvailable < MinOnHand
```

```
dbo.sp_Reorde...SDK.Chapter6)*                          ◁ ▷ ✕
    CREATE PROCEDURE dbo.sp_ReorderProducts
    /*
        (
            @parameter1 datatype = default value,     ──── Comments are written in green
            @parameter2 datatype OUTPUT
        )
    */
    AS                                                 ┐ The blue line indicates that
    SELECT * FROM Products                             │ the code can be built using
    WHERE QuantityAvailable < MinOnHand                │ the Query and View Editor
        /* SET NOCOUNT ON */                           ┘
        RETURN
```

Figure 6-14   The SQL Editor

4. Click the **Save All** icon. The stored procedure is saved. The first line SQL command changes from CREATE PROCEDURE to ALTER PROCEDURE. This means that the procedure has been created. At this point, you can only change the procedure using the ALTER PROCEDURE command.

5. Click the **plus sign** next to Stored Procedures in the Server Explorer window. Right-click the **sp_ReorderProducts** stored procedure, and then click **Run Stored Procedure**. The results are displayed in the **Output window**. There should be one row returned, which contains ProductID 2. The results will return the number of rows affected which is 2, and the @RETURN_VALUE which is 0. (*Note:* You can save the output as text by clicking the **File** menu and selecting **Save Output As**.)

 You can read more about SQL Server parameter queries at *ms-help://ms/vscc/ MS.MSDNVS/vdbt7/html/dvconparameterqueries.htm*. You can read more about input and output parameters and the return value at *ms-help://ms/vscc/ MS.MSDNVS/cpguide/html/cpconinputoutputparametersreturnvalues.htm*. It is also important to know that the purpose of these exercises is to demonstrate specific content. You should read about the application of coding techniques and programming practices at *ms-help://ms/vscc/MS.MSDNVS/ dnvsgen/html/cfr.htm#cfr_bestprac*. Some of these suggestions apply directly to Web and data-driven applications.

Now you will create a stored procedure that returns the products that match an input parameter value. Then you will create another stored procedure to display the product information for a single product, based upon the product name supplied by the end user.

1. In the Server Explorer window, under the *MACHINENAME\ NETSDK.Chapter6.dbo* data connection, right-click **Stored Procedures**, and then click **New Stored Procedure**. The stored procedure document opens with the default text for creating the stored procedure.

2. Replace the text dbo.StoredProcedure1 with **dbo.sp_DisplayProduct**.

3. Insert a blank line after the CREATE PROCEDURE line. Type the code below to define a parameter named @param_ModelName. The column name that will be mapped to the parameter is **ModelName**. The data type for the parameter and column is **nvarchar**, with a length of **50** bytes.

```
@param_ModelName nvarchar(50)
```

4. Under the as keyword create a new line and type the following code, which retrieves a subset of the columns from the database. You must supply the name of the product when the stored procedure is called. The stored procedure is also shown in Figure 6-15.

```
SELECT ProductID, ModelName,
UnitCost, ModelNumber, ProductImage
FROM Products
WHERE ModelName = @param_ModelName
```

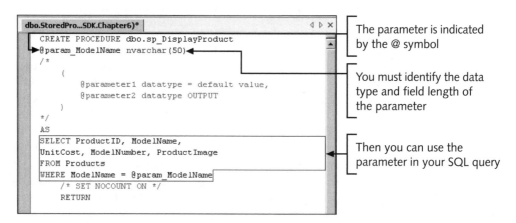

Figure 6-15   Creating stored procedures using the SQL Editor

5. Click the **Save All** icon. The stored procedure is saved. The first line of the SQL command changes from CREATE PROCEDURE to ALTER PROCEDURE. This means that the procedure has been created. At this point, you can only alter the procedure, using the ALTER PROCEDURE command.

6. Right-click the **sp_DisplayProduct** stored procedure, and then select **Run Stored Procedure**. The Run stored procedure window appears. (*Note:* You can have multiple input parameters listed here.) In the Value column for the @param_ModelName, enter **Letter Opener**, and then click the **OK** button, as shown in Figure 6-16. Only one column matches the criteria. The columns listed for the first record are displayed.

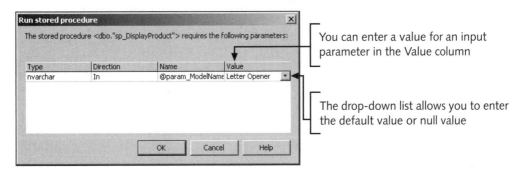

Figure 6-16   Running the stored procedure

7. Close the output window and the stored procedure.

In the following exercise, you use the SQL Editor to create a stored procedure that will insert a new record in the Categories table and return the value of the identity column.

1. In the Server Explorer window, under the *MACHINENAME\\ NETSDK*.Chapter6.dbo data connection, right-click **Stored Procedures**, and then click **New Stored Procedure**. The stored procedure document opens with the default text for creating the stored procedure.

2. Replace the text dbo.StoredProcedure1 with **dbo.sp_InsertCat**.

3. Insert a blank line after the CREATE PROCEDURE line. Type the code below, which defines an input parameter named @param_CatName. The column name that will be mapped to the parameter is CategoryName. The data type for the parameter and column is nvarchar, with a length of **50** bytes. All parameters are considered input parameters by default, so you don't have to indicate that the parameter is an input parameter.

```
@param_CatName nvarchar(50)
```

4. Under the as keyword insert a new line and type the following code, which inserts the new row using the value passed from the parameter as the value for the CategoryName column. You can pass a list of column names separated by commas. You must pass the values for each of the columns in a comma-separated list if there is more than one column. The values that are passed must be in the same order as the column names.

```
INSERT INTO Categories (CategoryName)
VALUES (@param_CatName)
```

5. After the return keyword type the following code which retrieves the identity column, as shown in Figure 6-17.

```
RETURN @@Identity
```

Figure 6-17   Creating a stored procedure to insert a row

6. Click the **Save All** icon and close the window. The stored procedure is saved
in the SQL Server database.

7. Right-click the **sp_InsertCat** stored procedure, and then click **Run Stored
Procedure**. The Run stored procedure window opens. In the Value column
for the @param_CatName, type **Jewelry**, and then click the **OK** button, as
shown in Figure 6-18.

Figure 6-18   Passing an input parameter

8. Right-click the **Categories** icon under the Tables list, and then click
Retrieve Data from Table. The Jewelry entry should be listed in a new
record in the third row, as shown in Figure 6-19.

9. Close the all of the windows.

CategoryID	CategoryName
1	Waterford
2	Pottery
3	Jewelry

When you run the stored procedure, a text view of the results is displayed. You can also view the table directly to see that the new record has been added

Figure 6-19   Viewing the new record

In the following exercise, you will create a stored procedure that searches a field in the database for a matching value. You will search a text string under the ModelName field, then display the results.

1. In the Server Explorer, under the Chapter6 data connection, right-click **Stored Procedures**, and then click **New Stored Procedure**. The stored procedure document opens with the default text for creating the stored procedure.

2. Replace the text dbo.StoredProcedure1 with **dbo.sp_SearchProducts**.

3. Insert a blank line after the CREATE PROCEDURE line. Enter the code below, which defines an input parameter named @param_SearchProducts. The column name that will be mapped to the parameter is ModelName. The data type for the parameter and column is nvarchar with a length of 50 bytes.

```
@param_SearchProducts nvarchar(50)
```

4. Under the as keyword, insert a new line and type the following code, which retrieves a subset of the columns from the database.

```
SELECT ProductID, ModelName,
ModelNumber, UnitCost, ProductImage,
Manufacturer
FROM Products
```

5. Type the following code, which uses the Where clause to search for a condition that contains the string that was passed with the parameter. It uses the wildcard character and the like keyword to locate any text that contains the string passed, as shown in Figure 6-20.

```
WHERE
ModelNumber LIKE '%' + @param_SearchProducts + '%'
OR
ModelName LIKE '%' + @param_SearchProducts + '%'
OR
Description LIKE '%' + @param_SearchProducts + '%'
OR
Manufacturer LIKE '%' + @param_SearchProducts + '%'
```

6. Click the **Save All** icon and close the window.

6

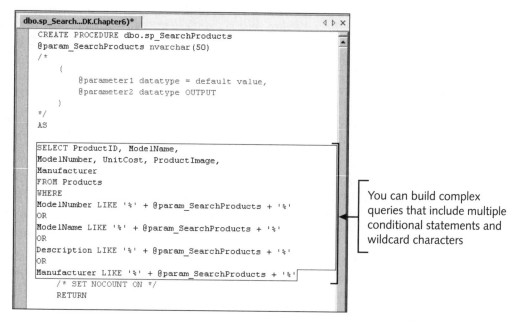

```
dbo.sp_Search...DK.Chapter6)*                                        ◁ ▷ ×
    CREATE PROCEDURE dbo.sp_SearchProducts
    @param_SearchProducts nvarchar(50)
    /*
        (
            @parameter1 datatype = default value,
            @parameter2 datatype OUTPUT
        )
    */
    AS

    SELECT ProductID, ModelName,
    ModelNumber, UnitCost, ProductImage,
    Manufacturer
    FROM Products
    WHERE
    ModelNumber LIKE '%' + @param_SearchProducts + '%'
    OR
    ModelName LIKE '%' + @param_SearchProducts + '%'
    OR
    Description LIKE '%' + @param_SearchProducts + '%'
    OR
    Manufacturer LIKE '%' + @param_SearchProducts + '%'
        /* SET NOCOUNT ON */
        RETURN
```

You can build complex queries that include multiple conditional statements and wildcard characters

Figure 6-20   Using wildcards

7. Right-click the **sp_ SearchProducts** stored procedure, and then click **Run Stored Procedure**. The Run stored procedure window opens. In the Value column for the @param_ModelName, type **Letter** and then click the **OK** button. Only one column matches the criteria. The columns listed for the first record are displayed.

8. Run the stored procedure again with a different value entered for the input parameter. Right-click the **sp_ SearchProducts** stored procedure and click **Run Stored Procedure**. The Run stored procedure window opens. In the Value column for the @param_ModelName, type **Waterford** and then click the **OK** button. Now all three columns match the criteria.

9. Close the windows.

Modifying Stored Procedures with the SQL Query Builder

The SQL Query Builder has the same user interface as the Query and View Editor that you used earlier. However, the code to create the query is stored in the stored procedure. Within the stored procedure, you can edit the blocks of code that are enclosed within a blue line, via the SQL Query Builder. Simply right-click the block and select Design SQL Block. In the following exercise, you will modify a stored procedure using the SQL Query Builder.

1. In the Server Explorer window, under the Chapter6 data connection, right-click the **sp_ReorderProducts** stored procedure, and then click **Edit Stored Procedure**. The stored procedure script you created earlier opens.

2. Right-click the blue-outlined block of code, and then click **Design SQL Block**. This opens the block of code within the SQL Query Builder.

3. In the SQL pane change the QuantityAvailable criteria under < MinOnHand to **<=10**.

4. Click the **Save All** icon.

5. (*Note*: If the stored procedure and the Query Toolbar are open, you can also click the **Run Query** button. The Run Query button looks like a red exclamation point.) There should be two records displayed in the Results pane.

6. Close the window. When you are asked to save your changes, click **Yes**.

6

INTERNET RESOURCES

This chapter provides an introduction to the database tools contained within Visual Studio .NET. You can learn more about SQL from a variety of Internet resources. These Internet resources contain information about SQL, databases, and data-driven Web applications. While Microsoft supports ADO.NET technology, other vendors may not support it. For example, Java provides an alternate solution that involves using JDBC, the Java Database Connection. Because these technologies change frequently, the latest information about ADO.NET is located on the Internet through the Microsoft MSDN Library at *www.msdn.microsoft.com/library/*. You should try to review these Web sites frequently to keep current with the latest database technologies.

- Microsoft UDA—*www.microsoft.com/data/default.htm*

- MSDN Library—*www.msdn.microsoft.com/library*

- SQL at Microsoft—*www.microsoft.com/sql*

- Yahoo! SQL Link—*dir.yahoo.com/Computers_and_Internet/ Programming_Languages/SQL*

- SQL & Websites—*www.sqlWeb.com*

- ANSI—*www.ansi.org*

- JCC SQL Standards links—*www.jcc.com/SQLPages/jccs_sql.htm*

- Oracle—*www.oracle.com*

- Sybase—*www.sybase.com*

- Informix—*www.informix.com*

- SQL FAQ Berkley—*epoch.cs.berkeley.edu:8000/sequoia/dba/montage/FAQ/ SQL_TOC.html*

- Tutorials from MuppetLabs—*www.muppetlabs.com/library/tech/tutorials*

- Programming Tutorials on the Web—*www.eng.uc.edu/~jtilley/tutorial.html*

- Access on the Web—Princeton—*www.princeton.edu/~hannahk/WebPubl.htm*

- MySQL—*www.tcx.se*

- SQL from Cramsession—*www.cramsession.com*

- Database Jump Site—*www.pcslink.com/~ej/dbwebWeb.html*

- SQL Interpreter and Tutorial—*www.sqlcourse.com*

- Learn SQL Jim Hoffman—new—*www.willcam.com/sql*

- SQL.Com—*www.sql.com*

- Ask the SQL Pro—*www.devx.com/gethelp*

- SQL Tutorial—*www.geocities.com/SiliconValley/Vista/2207/sql1.html*

- More SQL Sites—*www.sql-zone.com/sites.asp*

- Links to Developer Support—*www.borland.com/devsupport/sqllinks*

CHAPTER SUMMARY

- In the ADO.NET model, you connect to data sources using managed providers. The .NET managed data provider for SQL Server is located in the System.Data.SqlClient namespace. The .NET managed data providers for OLE-DB are located in the System.Data.OleDb namespace.

- ADO.NET object model consists of four objects: Connection, Command, DataAdapter, and DataReader. The DataAdapter serves as a bridge between the DataSet object. The DataReader object is a high-performance object that provides a stream of data. The data is read-only and forward-only.

- The DataSet object is a disconnected set of data that is stored in memory. Therefore, the DataSet is not the most current version of the data. The DataAdapter maintains the changes in the DataSet, and pushes the changes to the server. The DataSet consists of DataTableCollection and DataRelationConnection. The DataTable can consist of many DataViews. A DataView is a subset of data from a single DataTable. A DataSet can be persisted as an XML document. You can import XML data into a DataSet object, or store the DataSet as an XML document.

- You can use the Visual Database Tools within Visual Studio .NET to create and maintain your databases. The Table Editor allows you to create tables and enter data. The Query and View Editor allows you to create queries called views. The SQL Editor allows you to create stored procedures. Stored procedures are SQL commands that are stored with the SQL Server, and compiled. Therefore, stored procedures run faster than SQL commands that are stored in a Web page. The SQL Query Builder allows you to use the visual tools to build your stored procedures.

❒ Database and Web technologies change frequently. There are a variety of Web sites that you can consult for up-to-date information about ADO.NET, SQL Server, SQL, queries, and stored procedures.

REVIEW QUESTIONS

1. Which of the following is not a data type in SQL Server 2000?

   a. int

   b. nvarchar

   c. char

   d. array

2. What is required to connect a database to an ADO.NET Web application?

   a. an ODBC provider

   b. a Managed Provider

   c. a UDA database

   d. an OLE-DB driver

3. Which object is used to connect the Web application to the database?

   a. connection

   b. command

   c. parameter

   d. transaction

4. What is the keyword used to identify the server within a connection string?

   a. provider

   b. data source

   c. server

   d. initial catalog

5. What is the name of property that is used to identify the values that are passed to the Command object?

   a. Connection

   b. ActiveConnection

   c. Parameter

   d. CommandText

6. Which is not a valid option for the CommandType property?

a. Text

b. SQL

c. TableDirect

d. StoredProcedure

7. Which object provides a read-only, forward-only stream of data from the database?

a. DataReader

b. Connection

c. Recordset

d. Command

8. Which property is used to close the connection using the Command object?

a. CommandClose

b. Close

c. CommandBehavior

d. ConnectionClose

9. Which is not one of the ADO.NET objects?

a. Connection

b. Recordset

c. DataReader

d. DataAdapter

10. Which method is used to populate a DataSet object from a DataAdapter object?

a. SelectCommand

b. Select

c. Fill

d. InsertCommand

11. What is used to ensure that no duplicates can appear in a column?

a. a foreign key

b. a primary key

c. a constraint

d. a relationship

12. What property allows you to to specify information that can be stored with the DataSet object and later retrieved?

a. DataView

b. DataSet

c. CommandBuilder

d. ExtendedProperties

13. Which property allows you to retrieve a subset of the DataView?

a. RowFilter

b. Sort

c. Filter

d. GetRows

14. What is the file extension for the DataSet generated from the database?

a. .xml

b. .xsl

c. .xslt

d. .xsd

15. What is the name of the namespace for the OLE-DB .NET managed provider?

a. System.Data.SqlClient

b. System.Data

c. System.Data.OleDb

d. System.Data.ODBC

16. What is the tool used to create a new table in Visual Studio .NET?

a. Table Designer

b. Database Designer

c. SQL Builder

d. Query and View Editor

17. Which pane in the SQL Editor shows the criteria as visual icons?

a. Table pane

b. Grid pane

c. SQL pane

d. Results pane

18. What is the value of a column within a row that has no value assigned?

a. 0

b. an empty string " "

c. false

d. null

6

19. If the relationship in the database diagram has a key at each endpoint, then what type of relationship is it?

    a. one-to-one

    b. many-to-one

    c. one-to-one

    d. many-to-many

20. What symbol is used to identify the parameter in a stored procedure?

    a. @

    b. $

    c. #

    d. *

HANDS-ON PROJECTS

Project 6-1

In this project, you will create a connection to the Pubs database. The Pubs database is one of the sample databases installed when you installed the MSDE samples.

1. Start **Visual Studio .NET** and open your **Chapter6** solution.

2. Right-click the **Data Connections** in the Server Explorer window, and click **Add Connection**.

3. Type **(local)\NetSDK** in the server name text box.

4. Click the radio button labeled **Use Windows NT Integrated security** to select it. (*Note*: If your server uses SQL Server authentication, in the User name text box type **sa**. Leave the password text box blank. Click the **Blank password** check box to select it.)

5. In the "Select the database on the server" drop-down list box, select **pubs**.

6. Click the **Test Connection** button. Click **OK** in the alert message. Click the **OK** button in the dialog box.

7. Look at the database contents within the Data Connections tool and answer the following questions:

    ❑ What are the names of the tables in the Pubs database?

    ❑ How many records are in the authors table?

    ❑ What is the primary key column for the authors table?

    ❑ Which data types are used in the authors table?

    ❑ Which columns are required to have a value?

    ❑ Which field(s) must contain unique values within the column?

8. Look at the **titleview** view and answer the following questions:

❑ What are the three tables that are joined together in the query?

❑ What is the relationship between the titleauthor table and the titles table?

❑ What field is used to establish a relationship between the authors table and the titleauthor table?

❑ How many records are displayed in the titleview?

9. Look at the **byroyalty** stored procedure and answer the following questions:

❑ What is the name of the table being used?

❑ What is the name of the parameter?

❑ What symbol is used to identify the parameter?

❑ What is the data type of the parameter?

❑ Is the parameter an input or output parameter?

❑ Why does the stored procedure say ALTER PROCEDURE instead of CREATE PROCEDURE?

10. Create a Web page named **Ch6Proj1.aspx** that displays your answers. Save the page in your Chapter6 solution. Print the Web page.

Project 6-2

In this project, you will create a connection to the Northwind database. The Northwind database is one of the sample databases that was installed when you installed the MSDE samples.

1. Start **Visual Studio .NET** and open your **Chapter6** solution if necessary.

2. Right-click the **Data Connections** in Server Explorer, and then click **Add Connection**.

3. Type **(local)\NetSDK** in the server name text box.

4. Click the radio button labeled **Use Windows NT Integrated security** to select it. (*Note*: If your server uses SQL Server authentication, in the User name text box type **sa**. Leave the password text box blank. Click the **Blank password** check box to select it.)

5. In the "Select the database on the server" drop-down list box, click **Northwind**.

6. Click the **Test Connection** button. Click **OK** in the alert message. Click **OK** to close the dialog box box.

7. Look at the database contents within the Data Connections tool and answer the following questions:

❑ What are the names of the tables in the Northwind database?

❑ How many records are in the customers table? (*Hint*: You can count them manually or create a stored procedure which will return to you the number of records.)

❑ What is the primary key column for the customers table?

□ Which data types are used in the customers table?

□ Which columns are required to have a value?

□ Which field(s) must contain unique values within the column?

8. Look at the **Products by Category** view.

□ What are the two tables that are joined together in the query?

□ What is the relationship between the tables?

□ What field is used to establish a relationship between the tables? How many records are displayed in the view?

9. Look at the **Ten Most Expensive Products** stored procedure.

□ What is the name of the table being used?

□ What is the purpose of the ROWCOUNT property?

□ What are the keywords used to sort the data?

10. Look at the **CustOrderHist** stored procedure.

□ What is the name of the table being used?

□ What is the name of the parameter?

□ What symbol is used to identify the parameter?

□ What is the data type of the parameter? Is the parameter an input or output parameter?

□ Why does the stored procedure say ALTER PROCEDURE instead of CREATE PROCEDURE?

11. Create a Web page named **Ch6Proj2.aspx** that displays your answers. Save the page in your Chapter6 solution. Print the Web page.

Project 6-3

In this project, you will create a customer database using Visual Studio .NET.

1. Start **Visual Studio .NET** and open your **Chapter6** solution if necessary.

2. In Visual Studio .NET, create a database named **Ch6Proj3**.

3. Use the table below to determine the column names, datatypes, lengths, and properties.

Column Name	DataType	Length	Allow Nulls
CustomerID	int	4	No
CustomerName	nvarchar	50	Yes
EmailAddress	nvarchar	50	Yes
Password	nvarchar	50	Yes
MembershipLevel	int	4	Yes

4. In the properties at the bottom half of the window, change the Identity for the CustomerID column from No to **Yes** using the drop-down list arrow. The Identity Seed should be set to **1**, and the Identity Increment should be set to **1**. This creates a new value for each new record entered in the database.

5. Right-click the **CustomerID** column name and select **Set Primary Key**. A yellow key appears at the side of the column name to indicate that this column is the primary key column.

6. Click the **Save All** button to save the table as **Customers**.

7. Enter the following data listed in the table below. Let the MSDE assign the values for the CustomerID column.

Column Name	Row1	Row2	Row3	Row4
CustomerID				
CustomerName	June Mayzer	Ralph Waldon	Joseph Reno	Kevin Marx
EmailAddress	JM@ tarastore.com	RW@ tarastore.com	JR@ tarastore.com	KM@ tarastore.com
Password	Franklin	Bears	Crypto	Loyola
MembershipLevel	2	1	2	3

8. Print the table and the schema. (*Note:* You can print the screen by pressing the **PrntScrn** key. You can also copy the screen shot by pressing the **Shift** key and the **PrntScrn** key at the same time. Then, you can paste this into a word processor.)

Project 6-4

In this project, you will create an orders database table using Visual Studio .NET.

1. Start **Visual Studio .NET** and open your **Chapter6** solution if necessary.

2. In Visual Studio .NET, create a database named **Ch6Proj4**.

3. Use the table below to determine the column names, datatypes, lengths, and properties.

Column Name	DataType	Length	Allow Nulls
OrderID	int	4	No
CustomerID	int	4	No
ProductName	nvarchar	50	Yes
ProductDescription	nvarchar	50	Yes
ShippingMethod	int	4	Yes

4. In the properties at the bottom half of the window, change the Identity for the OrderID column from No to **Yes** using the drop-down list arrow. The Identity Seed should be set to **1**, and the identity increment should be set to **1**. This creates a new value for each new record entered in the database.

5. Right-click the **OrderID** column name and select **Set Primary Key**. A yellow key appears at the side of the column name to indicate that this column is the primary key column.

6. Click on the **Save All** button to save the table as **Orders**.

7. Enter the following data listed in the table below. Let the MSDE assign the values for the OrderID column.

Column Name	Row1	Row2	Row3	Row4
OrderID				
CustomerID	1	1	3	4
ProductName	Letter Opener	Business Card Holder	Cat Bowl	Shamrock Paperweight
ProductDescription	Letter Opener by Waterford.	Business Card Holder by Waterford	Cat Bowl by Belinda Bradshaw	Shamrock Paperweight by Waterford
ShippingMethod	1	2	3	1

8. Print the table and the schema. (*Note:* You can print the screen by pressing the **PrntScrn** key. You can also copy the screen shot by pressing the **Shift** key and the **PrntScrn** key at the same time. Then, you can paste this into a word processor.)

Project 6-5

In this project, you will create a stored procedure in the GrocerToGo database using Visual Studio .NET.

1. Start **Visual Studio .NET** and open your **Chapter6** solution if necessary.

2. Create a new stored procedure named **sp_DisplayProducts** in the GrocerToGo database.

3. The stored procedure should display the ProductID, CategoryID, ProductName, and Manufacturer columns from the Products table as shown below. All records should be displayed.

```
SELECT ProductID, CategoryID,
ProductName, Manufacturer
FROM Products
```

4. Run the stored procedure. Print the results displayed in the Output window. Save the results as **Ch6Proj5.txt** in the C:\Inetpub\wwwroot\Chapter6 directory.

Project 6-6

In this project, you will create a stored procedure in the GrocerToGo database using Visual Studio .NET.

1. Start **Visual Studio .NET** and open your **Chapter6** solution if necessary.

2. Create a stored procedure named **sp_ProductDetails**.

3. The stored procedure should display all of the columns. It should display only the records that match the ProductID that is provided when the stored procedure is called.

4. Add an input parameter named **@param_ProductID** that has a datatype of **int**. (*Note:* You do not specify the size of this input variable.)

5. Add the **SQL SELECT** statement to retrieve the values from the database. Select all products from the Products table where the ProductID equals the input parameter named **@param_ProductID**.

6. Run the stored procedure. Use the ProductID **3002** when you are asked for an input parameter.

7. Save the stored procedure. Print the results displayed in the Output window. Save the results as **Ch6Proj6.txt** in the C:\Inetpub\wwwroot\Chapter6 directory.

CASE PROJECTS

Tara Store — The ADO.NET Data Model

Your customer has requested that your company support the .NET framework. Their application requires access to a SQL Server database. Research the use of ADO.NET in enterprise applications. Use the Help menu in Visual Studio .NET, the *www.asp.net* Web site, the *www.msdn.microsoft.com/library* Web site, the QuickStart Web site (localhost/quickstart), and the *www.GotDotNet.com* Web site to locate more information. Write up a chart that compares the ADO.NET object model to the ADO object model. Save the page as Ch6Case1.aspx. Save the page in your Chapter6 solution. Print the Web page.

Tara Store — Creating a Database using Visual Studio .NET

Your boss has asked you to create a demonstration shopping cart application. Your first step is to set up a sample database. Create a database named Ch6Case2 using your local SQL server. Create a Product table and a Categories table. Each table must have a primary key. Create the database diagram. Establish a relationship between the tables using the primary keys. Save the diagram as Categories. Enter sample data into the tables. Print the database diagram, the table schema, and the data for the two tables.

Tara Store — Creating Stored Procedures with Visual Studio .NET

Your boss has heard that it's more efficient to use a stored procedure than a SQL query. He would like you to test out several queries using stored procedures. Using the Northwind database, create a new stored procedure named sp_USCustomers. Retrieve the records for all customers in the USA. Sort the results based on the Region and CompanyName columns. Run the stored procedure and print out the results. Save the results as Ch6Case3.txt in your c:\Inetpub\wwwroot\Chapter6 directory.

I Buy Spy — Creating a Database for a Shopping Cart with Visual Studio .NET

You are developing a sample Web database shopping cart to teach new Web developers how to create tables in Visual Studio .NET. Recreate the I Buy Spy online store located at *www.IBuySpy.com*. Visit the I Buy Spy store online. Read the documentation. Reconstruct the database and the tables in the shopping cart. Name the database Ch6Case4. Create a data diagram using the Database Designer. Name the data diagram Ch6Case4Diagram as shown below in Figure 6-21. Print each of the table schemas and the data.

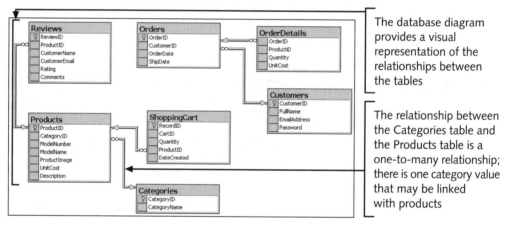

The database diagram provides a visual representation of the relationships between the tables

The relationship between the Categories table and the Products table is a one-to-many relationship; there is one category value that may be linked with products

Figure 6-21   Database diagram

7

BUILDING DATA-DRIVEN ASP.NET APPLICATIONS

In this chapter, you will:

♦ Learn about the various methods used to bind data to ASP.NET controls

♦ Bind an array to various Data controls

♦ Bind a hash table to a DataGrid and Repeater control

♦ Populate a DropDownList control from an array

♦ Populate a DataGrid control from a hash table

♦ Modify the appearance of a DataGrid control using templates

♦ Modify the appearance of a Repeater control using templates

♦ Modify the appearance of a DataList control using templates

One of the challenges that Web developers face is the variety of data sources and the variety of ways in which data can be displayed in Web applications. For example, a data source can be a simple hash table, an array, or a database. Data can be displayed as a simple list, a drop-down list, or a table. A Web developer must be able to use various techniques to build data-driven Web applications. Using ASP.NET, you can separate the data source from the presentation of the data. In the previous chapter, you learned how to connect to and manage a database. In this chapter, you will learn how to work with various controls to display data in your Web applications.

DATA BINDING TECHNIQUES

Data can be in the form of a single item, such as the name of an image, or it can be in the form of multiple items, for example a list or an array containing the names of many images. Data can be bound to a control. The two types of data binding are single-value binding and repeat-value binding. When a single piece of data or a single expression is bound to a control, it is called **single-value binding**. Single-value binding is sometimes used to store single values such as constants and read-only properties. **Repeat-value binding** allows you to bind your control to multiple items. Examples of repeat-value binding include databases, hash tables, and ArrayLists. This chapter illustrates how to bind controls to databases, hash tables, and ArrayLists.

Data binding can occur with a variety of data sources, such as mail servers. There are many advantages to binding data to controls. If the data changes, the data control automatically reflects the change. Data binding allows you to get records asynchronously—the ability to retrieve records is not tied to the page loading process. As a result the whole page is more responsive and loads more quickly. Data binding results in fewer trips to the server, since you normally won't need to interact with the server once the requested data has been downloaded. Any interaction with the database requires a round trip to the server to refresh the page, which ensures total browser compatibility. However, you can improve performance when interacting with database by caching the pages on the server. You will learn more about caching databases in the next chapter.

Single-expression Binding

Single-value binding is used to bind a single value or expression to a control. To bind a single expression to an ASP.NET control, you use the pound sign (#) before the expression's name. The expression is enclosed within inline server tags (<% %>). No other code can be placed inside the tags, as shown in the code below. The ImageURL variable stores the location of the image. Later in the page, the image location can be retrieved and used to display the image.

```
<% dim ImageURL As String = "logo.gif" %>
<img name="Logo" src="<%# ImageURL %>" alt="Logo" />
```

In the previous example, you retrieved the value from a variable. The data that is being bound can also be in the form of a property, procedure, or expression. You can use the bound expression to display the value in a Web page, to store a value, or to use the value in another expression.

The data is not bound until the DataBind method is called from the page, or from the control. The DataBind method for the page is called using Page.DataBind(). The Page.DataBind procedure is often called within the Page_Load event handler so that the data is bound before the page is displayed. You can also bind the expression to a single control by calling the DataBind method of an individual control, such as Logo.DataBind().

In the following exercise, you will create a Web page that contains a read-only property and a function. You will bind all the page Data controls using Page.DataBind, then display the bound Data controls in the Web page. The Label and Text Box controls are bound to the value from the ImageURL property. The Image Button control is bound to the value returned by the GetImageURL function. When the page is rendered, the controls are bound to the values, and displayed in the Web page.

1. Start **Visual Studio .NET**.

2. Click **File** on the menu bar, point to **New**, then click **Project**. This opens the New Project window.

3. Click the **Visual Basic Projects** folder icon, then click the **ASP.NET Web Application** icon under Templates. Type **Chapter7** in the Location text box in place of WebApplication1. Click **OK** to create the solution, project, and default files.

4. In the Solution Explorer window, right-click **Chapter7**, point to **Add**, then click **New Folder**. Type **images** to name the folder, and then press **Enter**.

5. Right-click the **images** folder, point to **Add**, and then click **Add Existing Item**. Change the Files of type drop-down list from VB Code Files to **All Files**. Browse to locate the images folder within the Chapter07Data folder. Select all of the images in the images folder. (*Note:* You can drag the mouse to select all of the images, or use the Shift key to select each image, or use the Ctrl + A key combination to select all of the images.) Click the **Open** button to import the images into the images directory of the Chapter7 project.

6. Right-click **Chapter7** in the Solution Explorer window, point to **Add**, then click **Add Existing Item**. Browse to locate your Chapter07Data directory. Select the file **SingleBind.aspx** from the Chapter07Data directory. Click the **Open** button to import the Web page into your project. Click **Yes** in the dialog box to create a new class file.

7. Double-click **SingleBind.aspx** in the Solution Explorer window to open the page. Double-click on the page to open the code behind the page, which is named **SingleBind.aspx.vb**. Below the last statement that begins with Protected WithEvents, add the code below. This code creates a new property named ImageURL that contains a string. The property is read-only, which means that the property cannot be changed. When the property is called, the string "logo.gif" is returned.

```
ReadOnly Property ImageURL() As String
    Get
        Return "images/logo.gif"
    End Get
End Property
```

8. Below the code you just added, add the code below, which creates a function named GetImageURL. The function returns "logo.gif" when the function is called.

```
Function GetImageURL() As String
    Return "images/logo.gif"
End Function
```

9. In the Page_Load event procedure, after the comment, add the code below. This code binds all of the data controls in the page to the data sources identified in their properties, as shown in Figure 7-1.

```
Page.DataBind()
```

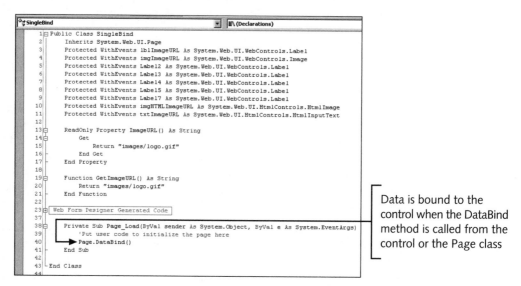

Data is bound to the control when the DataBind method is called from the control or the Page class

Figure 7-1   Return an expression from a property or function

10. Click the **Save All** button and close the SingleBind.aspx.vb page. Click the **SingleBind.aspx** tab to edit the SingleBind.aspx page, if necessary.

11. Click the first control, which is an ASP.NET Label control, to select it. Verify that the ID of the control is lblImageURL. In the Text property, add the code **<%# ImageURL %>**. This code will insert the image name into the label control when the page is rendered.

12. Click the second control, which is the ASP.NET Text Box control, to select it. The control is below the first control. Verify that the ID of the control is txtImageURL. Change the Value property to **<%# ImageURL %>**.

13. Click on the last control, which is below the second, to select it. Verify that the ID of the control is imgImageURL. Change the ImageURL property to **<%# GetImageURL %>**. (*Note*: If you add the image path here, instead of in

the function, the binding expression is returned. Therefore, it is better to have the path included in the function or property, and not in the ASP.NET control.)

14. Click the **Save All** button. Click **Build** on the menu bar, then click **Build Solution**.

15. Right-click on the page, and then click **View in Browser**. Your page should look like the one in Figure 7-2.

16. Close any open pages.

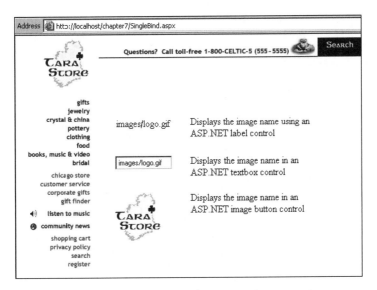

Figure 7-2   Binding Data controls to a single expression

Repeated-expression Binding

Binding a set of data to an ASP.NET control is called repeated-value binding. There are several ASP.NET Data controls that you can use to bind to repeated expressions, as shown in Figure 7-3. The ListControl class and BaseDataList class contain members that can be bound to repeated expressions. Both of these classes inherit from the WebControl class. The DropDownList, ListBox, CheckBoxList, and RadioButtonList controls inherit from a ListControl class. The DataList and DataGrid controls inherit from the BaseDataList class. The Repeater control inherits directly from the System.Web.UI.Control class. Because these controls inherit from different base classes, some properties are not available in all controls. However, all controls use the same technique to bind to data expressions and data sources. All of these controls contain a DataSource property that can be set to a data expression. When the DataBind method of the page is called, the control is bound to the data in the DataSource property.

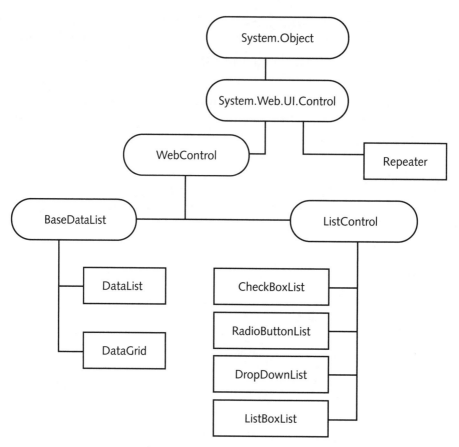

Figure 7-3 ASP.NET Data controls

The repeated expression, which is bound to the data control, can be a collection, such as a hash table, or ArrayList. You can also bind the data to a DataSet, DataView, or DataReader object.

- The **DataSet object** is a cached set of records retrieved from the database. The DataSet works like a virtual data store because it is disconnected from the original database source. The DataSet object can contain one or more DataTables. Because the DataSet can contain one or more DataTables you must identify the table members with DataMember property of the DataSet. The **DataMember property** is used to bind controls to one or more tables within a DataSet.

- A **DataView object** contains a subset of rows of data from a DataTable.

- A **DataReader object** is a read-only, forward-only stream of data from the database. A DataReader object is similar to the DataView because it returns one or more rows of data. However, the DataReader is a not a disconnected source of data. The data connection remains open while the DataReader reads the data. The DataReader object provides better performance than the DataView or DataSet objects. If you use the DataReader object, you can only read the rows once. As a result, you cannot create multiple controls with the data returned from the DataReader.

DATA CONTROLS

ASP.NET supports several types of server controls that can be bound to data sources. These **data-binding controls** are used to bind to the data sources, and then display the data in the Web page. The most commonly used repeated-binding data controls include the DropDownList, the ListBox, the Repeater, the DataList, and the DataGrid controls.

The DropDownList and ListBox controls both display the data using the HTML select tag. However, the DropDownList usually only displays one value at a time, while the ListBox generally displays all the values at the same time.

The Repeater, DataList, and DataGrid controls share a common programming model because they all inherit from the System.Web.UI.Control class. However, the DataList and DataGrid controls both inherit WebControl class functionality, such as the Style and Appearance properties.

- The **Repeater control** is a small, lightweight control. It inherits only the basic Control class functionality, such as the ID property and a child Controls collection. The Repeater control displays the data using HTML controls that you can define. There is no visible interface or formatting available with the Repeater control; it simply repeats the content that you define.

- The **DataList control** is similar to the Repeater control, because it displays the data as a basic list. However, there is a DataList control user interface in the toolbox. You can use the DataList properties to modify the layout of the horizontal or vertical columns.

- The **DataGrid control** allows you to use DataView, DataSource, or DataReader objects as the data source. The DataGrid control repeats content you define once for each data row. When the control is rendered, the page places the data in a table or uses a <br /> tag after each row as a delimiter. An important difference between the DataGrid and DataList controls is that a DataGrid does not contain any template properties.

Binding Data to a DropDownList Control

In the following exercise, you will create a Web page that contains an ArrayList and hash table, binds all the page Data controls, and then displays the bound data DropDownList controls in the Web page. The code to create an ASP.NET DropDownList control is shown below.

```
<asp:dropdownlist id="MyDDL1" runat="server">
</asp:dropdownlist>
```

This example uses the IsPostBack property of the page class to determine if this page has been resubmitted to the server. If the page has not been posted back to the server, then the ArrayList and hash table are populated with values, and are bound to the Data controls. If the page has been posted back to the server, then the values of what was selected from the drop-down lists are displayed in the Web page. This example demonstrates that the DropDownList control can be bound to a variety of data sources. (*Note:* In the next chapter, you will learn to bind the DropDownList control to a DataSet, DataView, and DataReader object.)

In this example, the data source is identified with the **DataSource property** of the DropDownList control. You must specify which item is displayed in the Web page using the **DataTextField property**. You use the **DataValueField property** to specify the value property of the DropDownList items, which is displayed only in the HTML source view of the rendered Web page. The DataValueField corresponds to the value property of the HTML <option> control. The value can be formatted using the **DataTextFormatString property** of the DropDownList control. The expression {0:C} will format the value as currency.

 You can use the DataTextFormat String property of a control to format the output as currency. For example you can use the format: MyDataList.DataTextFormatString = "{0:C}". You can also use the Eval expression to format the value as currency, or another data type. Other regular expression formats, such as percentage, are also available.

1. Open the **Chapter7** project in Visual Studio .NET if it is not already open. Right-click **Chapter7** in the Solution Explorer window, point to **Add**, then click **Add Existing Item**. Browse to locate your Chapter07Data folder, and then select the file **DropDownList.aspx**. Click **Open** to import the Web page into your project. Click **Yes** in the query dialog box to create a new class file.

2. If the page is not open, double-click the **DropDownList.aspx** page icon in the Solution Explorer window to open it. Then double-click on the page to open the code behind the page, which is named DropDownList.aspx.vb. Within the Page_Load event handler, add the code below to create a one-dimensional array named **arr1**. The add method is used to add the items to the array.

```
If Not Page.IsPostBack() Then
  Dim arr1 As New ArrayList(9)
  arr1.Add("Belleek Colleen Vase")
  arr1.Add("Belinda Bradshaw Cat Bowl")
  arr1.Add("Nicholas Mosse Cat Mug")
  arr1.Add("Shamrock Paperweight")
  arr1.Add("Business Card Holder")
```

```
arr1.Add("Large Shamrock Tea Pot")
arr1.Add("Traditional Music of Ireland")
arr1.Add("Bodhran with Trinity Design")
arr1.Add("Belleek Cashill Clock")
```

3. After the array is defined, add the code below to create a hash table. The add method is used to add the elements to the hash table. The first item in the hash table is the called the key, and the second item is called the value.

```
Dim MyHash As New Hashtable(9)
MyHash.Add("Belleek Colleen Vase", 34)
MyHash.Add("Belinda Bradshaw Cat Bowl", 22)
MyHash.Add("Nicholas Mosse Cat Mug", 34)
MyHash.Add("Shamrock Paperweight", 99)
MyHash.Add("Business Card Holder", 59)
MyHash.Add("Large Shamrock Tea Pot", 54)
MyHash.Add("Traditional Music of Ireland", 19.95)
MyHash.Add("Bodhran with Trinity Design", 40)
MyHash.Add("Belleek Cashill Clock", 110)
```

4. Immediately after the code above, add the code to bind the DropDownList control named **MyDD1** to the array named arr1.

```
MyDD1.DataSource = arr1
```

5. Immediately after the code above, add the code to bind the DropDownList control named **DD2** to the hash table. In this instance, the key item in the hash table is assigned to the DataTextField property, and therefore is displayed on the Web page.

```
MyDD2.DataSource = MyHash
MyDD2.DataTextField = "Key"
MyDD2.DataValueField = "Value"
```

6. Immediately after the code above, add the code to bind the DropDownList control to the hash table. In this case, the value items of the hash table are assigned to the DataTextField property of the DropDownList control, and are therefore displayed on the Web page. The value contains the price of the items. The price is formatted as currency, using the DataTextFormatString property.

```
MyDD3.DataSource = MyHash
MyDD3.DataTextField = "Value"
MyDD3.DataValueField = "Key"
MyDD3.DataTextFormatString = "{0:C}"
```

7. Immediately after the code above, bind the data expressions to the DataSource property of the DropDownList controls.

```
    Page.DataBind()
Else
End If
```

7

8. Click the **DropDownList.aspx** tab at the top of the main window. Double-click the **Submit** button. Enter the code below, which runs when the button is clicked. This code changes the Text property of the Label control. It shows the values that the end user selects from each of the DropDownList controls. Use an HTML line break tag to separate the results for each control.

```
lblMyResults.Text = _
"MyDD1 = " & MyDD1.SelectedItem.ToString() & "<br />" & _
"MyDD2 = " & MyDD2.SelectedItem.ToString() & "<br />" & _
"MyDD3 = " & MyDD3.SelectedItem.ToString()
```

9. Click the **Save All** button. Click **Build** on the menu bar, then click **Build Solution**.

10. Click the **DropDownList.aspx** tab at the top of the main window. Right-click on the page, and then click **View in Browser**. Your page should look like the one in shown in Figure 7-4.

11. Click the **Submit** button. The values selected are displayed in the Web page.

12. Close any open pages.

Figure 7-4   Binding data to a DropDownList control

Binding Data to a ListBox Control

The ListBox control can be bound to data. In the following exercise, you will create an ArrayList and hash table, bind all the page Data controls, and then display the bound data ListBox controls in the Web page. The code used to create an ASP.NET ListBox control is shown below.

```
<asp:listbox id="MyLB1" runat="server">
</asp:listbox>
```

The ListBox control generates an HTML <select> tag. The property is set to display more than one value in the list. The ListBox control is often used when the user may select more than one value in the control. The data source in the ListBox control is identified with the **DataSource property**. Each item in the DataSource property will correspond to an <option> in the <select> tag. The text that is displayed for each option is identified with the **DataTextField property**. The **DataValueField property** is used to specify the value property of the ListBox items, which is displayed only in the HTML source view of the rendered Web page. The DataValueField corresponds to the value property of the HTML <option> control. The value can be formatted using the **DataTextFormatString property** of the ListBox control.

1. Open the **Chapter7** project in Visual Studio .NET if it is not already open. Right-click **Chapter7** in the Solution Explorer window, point to **Add**, then click **Add Existing Item**. Browse to locate your Chapter07Data folder, select the file **ListBox.aspx**, and then click **Open** to import the Web page into your project. Click **Yes** in the query dialog box to create a new class file. Open the page from the Solution Explorer window.

2. Double-click on the page to open the code behind the page, which is named ListBox.aspx.vb. Within the Page_Load event handler, add the code to add the code below to create a one-dimensional array named **arr1**. The add method is used to add the items to the array.

```
If Not Page.IsPostBack() Then
   Dim arr1 As New ArrayList(9)
   arr1.Add("Belleek Colleen Vase")
   arr1.Add("Belinda Bradshaw Cat Bowl")
   arr1.Add("Nicholas Mosse Cat Mug")
   arr1.Add("Shamrock Paperweight")
   arr1.Add("Business Card Holder")
   arr1.Add("Large Shamrock Tea Pot")
   arr1.Add("Traditional Music of Ireland")
   arr1.Add("Bodhran with Trinity Design")
   arr1.Add("Belleek Cashill Clock")
```

3. Immediately after the code above, add the code below to create a hash table. The add method is used to add the elements to the hash table. The first item in each hash table element is the called the key, and the second item is called the value.

```
Dim MyHash As New Hashtable(9)
MyHash.Add("Belleek Colleen Vase", 34)
MyHash.Add("Belinda Bradshaw Cat Bowl", 22)
MyHash.Add("Nicholas Mosse Cat Mug", 34)
MyHash.Add("Shamrock Paperweight", 99)
MyHash.Add("Business Card Holder", 59)
MyHash.Add("Large Shamrock Tea Pot", 54)
MyHash.Add("Traditional Music of Ireland", 19.95)
MyHash.Add("Bodhran with Trinity Design", 40)
MyHash.Add("Belleek Cashill Clock", 110)
```

7

4. Immediately after the code above, add the code to bind the ListBox control named **MyLB1** to the array.

```
MyLB1.DataSource = arr1
```

5. Immediately after the code above, add the code to bind the ListBox control named **MyLB2** to the hash table.

```
MyLB2.DataSource = MyHash
MyLB2.DataTextField = "Key"
MyLB2.DataValueField = "Value"
```

6. Immediately after the code above, add the code to bind the ListBox control named **MyLB3** to the hash table.

```
MyLB3.DataSource = MyHash
MyLB3.DataValueField = "Key"
MyLB3.DataTextField = "Value"
MyLB3.DataTextFormatString = "{0:C}"
```

7. Immediately after the code above, bind the data expressions to the DataSource property of the ListBox controls.

```
    Page.DataBind()
Else
End If
```

8. Click the **ListBox.aspx** tab at the top of the main window. Double-click the **Submit** button. Enter the code below, which runs when the button is clicked. This code changes the Text property of the label control. It shows the values that the end user selected from each of the ListBox controls. Use an HTML line break tag to separate the results for each control.

```
lblMyResults.Text = _
"MyLB1 = " & MyLB1.SelectedItem.ToString() & "<br />" & _
"MyLB2 = " & MyLB2.SelectedItem.ToString() & "<br />" & _
"MyLB3 = " & MyLB3.SelectedItem.ToString()
```

9. Click the **Save All** button. Click **Build** on the menu bar, then click **Build Solution**.

10. Close the Output box, then click the **ListBox.aspx** tab. Right-click on the page, and then select **View in Browser**.

11. Select the **Belinda Bradshaw Cat Bowl** from the first ListBox. Select the **Business Card Holder** from the second ListBox. Select the **$54.00** from the third ListBox. Click the **Submit** button. The values selected are displayed in the Web page, as shown in Figure 7-5.

12. Close any open pages.

Figure 7-5   Binding data to a ListBox control

Binding Data to a RadioButtonList and CheckBoxList Control

Both the RadioButtonList and CheckBoxList controls can be bound to data. In the following exercise, you will create an ArrayList and hash table, bind all the page data controls, and then display the bound data using the RadioButtonList and CheckBoxList controls in the Web page. The code to insert an ASP.NET RadioButtonList and CheckBoxList control is shown below.

```
<asp:checkboxlist id="MyCBL1" runat="server">
</asp:checkboxlist>
<asp:radiobuttonlist id="MyRBL1" runat="server">
</asp:radiobuttonlist>
```

Each item in the DataSource property will correspond to an <input> tag where the type is listed as radio or checkbox. The text that is displayed for each Input control is identified with the **DataTextField property**. The **DataValueField property** is used to specify the Value property of the items, which is displayed only in the HTML source view of the rendered Web page. The DataValueField corresponds to the Value property of the HTML <Input> control.

1. Open the **Chapter7** project in Visual Studio .NET if it is not already open. Right-click **Chapter7** in the Solution Explorer window, point to **Add**, then click **Add Existing Item**. Browse to locate your Chapter07Data folder, select the file **CheckBoxRadio.aspx**, and then click **Open** to import the Web page into your project. Click **Yes** in the query dialog box to create a new class file. Open the page from the Solution Explorer window.

2. Double-click on the page to open the code behind the page, which is named CheckBoxRadio.aspx.vb. Within the Page_Load event handler, add the code

below to create an ArrayList named **arr1**. The add method is used to add the items to the ArrayList.

```
If Not Page.IsPostBack() Then
  Dim arr1 As New ArrayList(9)
  arr1.Add("Belleek Colleen Vase")
  arr1.Add("Belinda Bradshaw Cat Bowl")
  arr1.Add("Nicholas Mosse Cat Mug")
  arr1.Add("Shamrock Paperweight")
  arr1.Add("Business Card Holder")
  arr1.Add("Large Shamrock Tea Pot")
  arr1.Add("Traditional Music of Ireland")
  arr1.Add("Bodhran with Trinity Design")
  arr1.Add("Belleek Cashill Clock")
```

3. Immediately after the code above, add the code below to create a hash table. The add method is used to add the elements to the hash table.

```
Dim MyHash As New Hashtable(9)
MyHash.Add("Belleek Colleen Vase", 34)
MyHash.Add("Belinda Bradshaw Cat Bowl", 22)
MyHash.Add("Nicholas Mosse Cat Mug", 34)
MyHash.Add("Shamrock Paperweight", 99)
MyHash.Add("Business Card Holder", 59)
MyHash.Add("Large Shamrock Tea Pot", 54)
MyHash.Add("Traditional Music of Ireland", 19.95)
MyHash.Add("Bodhran with Trinity Design", 40)
MyHash.Add("Belleek Cashill Clock", 110)
```

4. Immediately after the code above, add the code to bind the RadioButtonList and CheckBoxList controls to the ArrayList.

```
CheckBoxList1.DataSource = arr1
RadioButtonList1.DataSource = arr1
```

5. Immediately after the code above, add the code to bind the RadioButtonList and CheckBoxList controls to the hash table.

```
CheckBoxList2.DataSource = MyHash
CheckBoxList2.DataTextField = "Key"
CheckBoxList2.DataValueField = "Value"
RadioButtonList2.DataSource = MyHash
RadioButtonList2.DataValueField = "Key"
RadioButtonList2.DataTextField = "Value"
RadioButtonList2.DataTextFormatString = "{0:C}"
```

6. Immediately after the code above, add the code to bind the data expressions to the data source property of the ListBox controls.

```
  Page.DataBind()
Else
End If
```

7. Click the **CheckBoxRadio.aspx** tab at the top of the main window. Double-click the **Submit** button. Enter the code below, which runs when the button is clicked. Because the user can select more than one check box, variables are used to store the values that the user selected. The code below will store the values from the first CheckBoxList control in the variable named **strResult1**.

```
Dim strResult1 As String
If CheckBoxList1.SelectedIndex > -1 Then
    strResult1 = ""
    Dim i As Integer
    For i = 0 To CheckBoxList1.Items.Count - 1
        If CheckBoxList1.Items(i).Selected Then
            strResult1 += "   " & _
            CheckBoxList1.Items(i).Text + "<br />"
        End If
    Next
Else
    strResult1 = "You did not select a category.<br />"
End If
```

8. Immediately after the code above, enter the code below, which will store the values that the user selected from the second CheckBoxList control in a variable named **strResult2**.

```
Dim strResult2 As String
If CheckBoxList2.SelectedIndex > -1 Then
    strResult2 = ""
    Dim i As Integer
    For i = 0 To CheckBoxList2.Items.Count - 1
        If CheckBoxList2.Items(i).Selected Then
            strResult2 += "   " & _
            CheckBoxList2.Items(i).Text + "<br />"
        End If
    Next
Else
    strResult2 = "You did not select a category.<br />"
End If
```

9. Below the code above, insert the code to change the Text property of the lblCBL control. This will display the values selected in both CheckBoxList controls.

```
lblCBL.Text = _
"<b>CheckBoxList1 = </b><br />" & _
strResult1 & "<br />" & _
"<b>CheckboxList2 = </b><br />" & _
strResult2 & "<br />"
```

10. Below the code above, insert the code to change the Text property of the lblRBL control. This will display the values selected in both RadioButtonList controls.

```
lblRBL.Text = _
"RadioButtonList1 = " & _
RadioButtonList1.SelectedItem.ToString()  & _
"<br /><br />" & _
"RadioButtonList2 = " & _
RadioButtonList2.SelectedItem.ToString()
```

11. Click the **Save All** button. Click **Build** on the menu bar, then click **Build Solution**.

12. Click the **CheckBoxRadio.aspx** tab. Right-click on the page, and then select **View in Browser**.

13. Select the **Belinda Bradshaw Cat Bowl** and **Business Card Holder** from the first CheckBoxList control. Select the **Business Card Holder**, **Belleek Colleen Vase**, and **Belleek Cashill Clock** from the second CheckBoxList control. Select **Shamrock Paperweight** from the first RadioButtonList control. Select the **$22.00** from the second RadioButtonList control. Click the **Submit** button. The values selected are displayed in the Web page, as shown in Figure 7-6.

14. Close any open pages.

Figure 7-6   Binding data to CheckBoxList and RadioButtonList controls

 Access and other file-based database limit the number of concurrent users. You may have to add the user ASP.NET to the Administrators group via the ControlPanel to enable concurrent users and to access the database from a Web page.

Binding Data to a DataGrid Control

The DataGrid control can be bound to various data sources. In this example, you will bind the DataGrid control to a hash table. You will insert columns that will be bound to the key and value items in the hash table, and you will change the heading text property. (*Note*: In the next chapter, you will bind the DataGrid to a DataSet.) The code to insert an ASP.NET DataGrid control is shown below.

```
<asp:DataGrid id="MyDG1" runat="server">
</asp:DataGrid>
```

The DataGrid contains many properties to help format the bound data. The **AutoGenerateColumns property** allows you to specify the columns that you want to bind to your data source. (*Note*: You do not have to bind all of the data columns in your data source to the DataGrid control.) The **HeaderText property** allows you to change the string displayed at the top of the column headings. (*Note*: You can include HTML tags in the heading.) The **DataFormatString property** is used to display currency and is applied to the values displayed within the DataGrid control. The {0:C} will format the value as currency.

1. Open the **Chapter7** project in Visual Studio .NET if it is not already open. Right-click **Chapter7** in the Solution Explorer window, point to **Add**, then click **Add Existing Item**. Browse to locate your Chapter07Data folder, select the file **DataGridSimple.aspx**, and then click **Open** to import the Web page into your project. Click **Yes** in the query dialog box to create a new class file.

2. Double-click **DataGridSimple.aspx** in the Solution Explorer window to open the page. Click the **DataGrid** control to select it. The properties for the DataGrid should appear in the Properties window. Verify that the ID property is **MyDG1**.

3. Change the AutoGenerateColumns property to **False**.

4. Right-click on the page, and then click **View HTML Source**. Locate the code where the DataGrid is inserted. Between the opening and closing tags, insert a blank line.

5. In the blank line you just entered, type the following code, which binds the key and value items to the columns within the DataGrid, and formats the value as currency. Your code should look like the code in Figure 7-7.

```
<Columns>
<ASP:BoundColumn HeaderText="Products" DataField="Key" />
<ASP:BoundColumn HeaderText="Price" DataField="Value"
DataFormatString="{0:C}" />
</Columns>
```

7

The Columns control allows you to create bound and unbound columns in a DataGrid control

Figure 7-7 Adding bound columns to a DataGrid

6. Right-click on the page, and then click **View Design**. Double-click on the page to open the code behind the page, which is named DataGridSimple.aspx.vb. Within the Page_Load event handler, add the code below to create a hash table.

```vb
Dim MyHash As New Hashtable(9)
MyHash.Add("Belleek Colleen Vase", 34)
MyHash.Add("Belinda Bradshaw Cat Bowl", 22)
MyHash.Add("Nicholas Mosse Cat Mug", 34)
MyHash.Add("Shamrock Paperweight", 99)
MyHash.Add("Business Card Holder", 59)
MyHash.Add("Large Shamrock Tea Pot", 54)
MyHash.Add("Traditional Music of Ireland", 19.95)
MyHash.Add("Bodhran with Trinity Design", 40)
MyHash.Add("Belleek Cashill Clock", 110)
```

7. Immediately below the code above add the code to bind the DataGrid control named **MyDG1** to the hash table.

```vb
MyDG1.DataSource = MyHash
```

8. Immediately below the code above, add the code to bind the data expressions to the data source property of the DataGrid control. Notice that here the DataBind method is called specifically for the DataGrid control.

```vb
MyDG1.DataBind()
```

9. Click the **Save All** button. Click **Build** on the menu bar, then click **Build Solution**.

10. Click the **DataGridSimple.aspx** tab at the top of the main window. Right-click on the page, and then click **View in Browser**. Your page should look like the one shown in Figure 7-8.

11. Close any open pages.

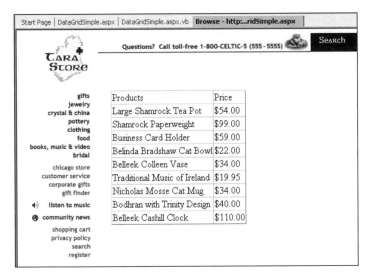

Figure 7-8 Binding data to a DataGrid control

Binding Data to a DataList Control

The DataList control allows you to display values as a simple list. When you add the DataList controls, you need to identify the columns to bind to the data. In the following example, the DataList control is bound to the key and value items of the hash table. DataList and DataGrid support templates to configure the appearance of the control and the values bound to the controls. The code to insert a DataList control is shown below.

```
<asp:DataList id="MyDL1" runat="server">

</asp:DataList>
```

The data-binding instructions are stored within the templates. The DataList control requires you to configure an **ItemTemplate** within the control in order to display the data. Within the ItemTemplate is the **DataItem**. (*Note*: This same DataItem is also applied to the DataGrid control.) The **DataRow** is referenced as a DataItem object within the container control and the field.

1. Right-click **Chapter7** in the Solution Explorer window, point to **Add**, then click **Add Existing Item**. Browse to locate your Chapter07Data folder, select the file **DataList.aspx**, then click **Open** to import the Web page into your project. Click **Yes** in the query dialog box to create a new class file.

2. Double-click the **DataList.aspx** page icon in the Solution Explorer window to open the page. The DataList control appears as a visual gray box in the Design view. Click the **DataList** control to select the control. The properties for the DataList should appear in the Properties window. Verify that the ID property is **MyDL1**.

3. Right-click on the page, and then click **View HTML Source**. Locate the code where the DataList is inserted. Between the opening and closing <asp:DataList></asp:DataList> tags insert the code below to create the ItemTemplate. The <b> tags format the name of the product as bold. The parentheses surround the value that is bound to the items in the hash table. The parameter to format the data as currency can be passed to the DataItem property. Notice that the DataBinder.Eval evaluates the entire expression with the parameters that are passed below.

```
<ItemTemplate>
  <b><%# Container.DataItem.Key %></b>
  (<%# DataBinder.Eval(Container.DataItem, "Value",
  "{0:C}") %>)
</ItemTemplate>
```

4. Switch to Design view. Double-click on the page to open the code behind the page, which is named DataList.aspx.vb. Within the Page_Load event handler, add the code below to create a hash table.

```
If Not Page.IsPostBack() Then
  Dim MyHash As New Hashtable(9)
  MyHash.Add("Belleek Colleen Vase", 34)
  MyHash.Add("Belinda Bradshaw Cat Bowl", 22)
  MyHash.Add("Nicholas Mosse Cat Mug", 34)
  MyHash.Add("Shamrock Paperweight", 99)
  MyHash.Add("Business Card Holder", 59)
  MyHash.Add("Large Shamrock Tea Pot", 54)
  MyHash.Add("Traditional Music of Ireland", 19.95)
  MyHash.Add("Bodhran with Trinity Design", 40)
  MyHash.Add("Belleek Cashill Clock", 110)
```

5. Immediately below the code entered above, add the code to bind the DataList control named **MyDL1** to the hash table.

```
MyDL1.DataSource = MyHash
```

6. Immediately below the code entered above, add the code to bind the data expressions to the Data Source property of the DataList control. Notice that here the DataList method is called specifically for the DataList control.

```
  MyDL1.DataBind()
Else
End If
```

7. Click the **Save All** button. Click **Build** on the menu bar, then click **Build Solution**.

8. Click the **DataList.aspx** tab. Right-click on the page, and then click **View in Browser**. The page should appear as shown in Figure 7-9.

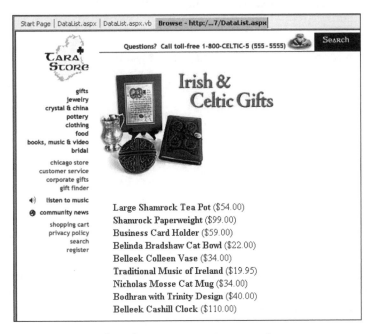

Figure 7-9   Binding data to a DataList control

9. Close any open pages.

Binding Data to a Repeater Control

The Repeater control allows you to bind read-only data to a list. Because the Repeater control has no default appearance, you must use the HTML view of the WebForm to modify the control. You can modify the layout of the list or table using templates. The templates available to the Repeater control include the header, footer, alternating, item, and separator templates. Therefore, the Repeater can be used to create tables, comma-delimited lists, bulleted lists, and numbered lists. The Repeater control is similar to the DataList, but renders additional HTML to allow you more control over the data output.

In order to position the Repeater, you must use additional controls such as the HTML <div> tag or ASP.NET Panel control.

You need to add the code to display the values from the Repeater control. The sample code below inserts a Repeater control into the page. The data is inserted into the Repeater control with an ItemTemplate. The Key property is used to indicate the key from the data source. The Value property is used to pass the value from the data source. The Container.DataItem represents each item within the data source. You can add HTML tags to format the ItemTemplate of the Repeater control.

```
<asp:Repeater id="Repeater1" runat="server">
  <ItemTemplate>
    <b><%# Container.DataItem.Key %></b>
    (<%# Container.DataItem.Value %>)<br />
  </ItemTemplate>
</asp:Repeater>
```

You can format the value of the Repeater control as currency using the same format as the DataList control, as shown in the sample below.

```
<b><%# Container.DataItem.Key %></b>
(<%# DataBinder.Eval(Container.DataItem,
"Value","{0:C}") %>)
<br />
```

The following example shows you how to insert a simple Repeater control into a Web page. The Repeater control is bound to a hash table.

1. Right-click **Chapter7** in the Solution Explorer window, point to **Add**, then click **Add Existing Item**. Browse to locate your Chapter07Data folder, select the file **Repeater.aspx**, and then click **Open** to import the Web page into your project. Click **Yes** in the query dialog box to create a new class file.

2. Double-click the file **Repeater.aspx** in the Solution Explorer window to open the page. Click the **Repeater** control and, in the Properties window, verify that the ID property is **Repeater1**.

3. Right-click on the page, and then click **View HTML Source**. Between the opening and closing Form tags, insert the code below to create the ItemTemplate within the Repeater control tags. The bold tags format the name of the product. (*Note*: In this example, the product price is formatted as currency.)

```
<ItemTemplate>
<b><%# Container.DataItem.Key %></b>
(<%# DataBinder.Eval(Container.DataItem,"Value",
  "{0:C}") %>)
<br />
</ItemTemplate>
```

4. Click the **Design** tab to return to Design view. Double-click on the page to open the code behind the page, which is named Repeater.aspx.vb. Within the Page_Load event handler, add the code below to create a hash table.

```
Dim MyHash As New Hashtable(9)
MyHash.Add("Belleek Colleen Vase", 34)
MyHash.Add("Belinda Bradshaw Cat Bowl", 22)
```

```
MyHash.Add("Nicholas Mosse Cat Mug", 34)
MyHash.Add("Shamrock Paperweight", 99)
MyHash.Add("Business Card Holder", 59)
MyHash.Add("Large Shamrock Tea Pot", 54)
MyHash.Add("Traditional Music of Ireland", 19.95)
MyHash.Add("Bodhran with Trinity Design", 40)
MyHash.Add("Belleek Cashill Clock", 110)
```

5. Add the code below to bind the Repeater control named **Repeater1** to the hash table.

```
Repeater1.DataSource = MyHash
```

6. Bind the data expressions to the data source property of the Repeater control. Notice that here the repeater method is called specifically for the Repeater control.

```
Repeater1.DataBind()
```

7. Click the **Save All** button. Click **Build** on the menu bar, then click **Build Solution**.

8. Click the **Repeater.aspx** tab. Right-click on the page, and then select **View in browser**.

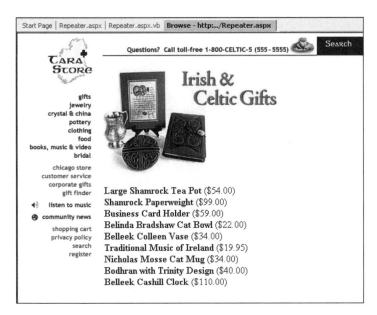

Figure 7-10   Binding data to a Repeater control

9. Close any open pages.

BINDING A DATAVIEW TO A DATAGRID CONTROL

You can use the DataGrid to format the data from a variety of data sources such as a hash table, ArrayList, or database. You can bind a DataGrid to a different data source using the DataSource property. There are two main ways to connect to the database. You can use the DataReader object to create a connection to the database and receive records individually or you can use the DataAdapter to return a DataSet object. The DataSet object is a set of records disconnected from the database.

You can create the connection string and all of the data objects manually within the code, or use the graphical user interface provided within the Server Explorer and Toolbox windows. The sample code below shows how to create a connection string to a database, and a Connection object. You need to pass the connection string to the connection object so that the connection object knows which database to connect to. The ConnectionString (CS) contains data to locate and connect to the database. The ConnectionString includes any authentication requirements such as the UserID and password. The syntax for the ConnectionString varies with the type of database used and the provider chosen, as discussed in Chapter 6. (*Note*: It is important not to break the string across multiple lines of text.) The connection string is stored in a variable CS. The ConnectionString (CS) can also be a global object in the Web configuration or in a User control. (*Note*: If you use the tools in Visual Studio .NET to build your connection, you use a graphical interface to achieve the same results.) Because the Connection object is used to connect to an Access database, the System.OleDb.OleDbConnection class is used to create the Connection object.

```
Dim CS As String =
   "Provider=Microsoft.Jet.OLEDB.4.0;Data " _
& "Source=C:\Inetpub\wwwroot\Chapter7\TaraStore.mdb"
Dim objCS As New System.Data.OleDb.OleDbConnection(CS)
```

The sample code below shows how to create a SQL Select statement that will retrieve all of the records for the first category. The DataAdapter object will be created using the System.Data.OleDb.OleDbDataAdapter class and will create a Connection object using the connection string and SQL statement. The DataAdapter is used to manage the connection and create a DataSet object named objDS. The Connection object and SQL are passed as parameters when the object is created. The DataAdapter is used to get the data from the database and populate the DataSet object. Unless you are using a SQL Server database, use System.Data.OleDb.OleDbDataAdapter as the Provider. (*Note*: You will need to import the `System.Data.OleDb` namespace into your code behind the page using the code `<%@Import Namespace="System.Data.OleDb"%>`. You can also add the namespace reference to your Web References; you don't have to use the fully qualified name.) It is not until the fill method of the DataAdapter is called, when the DataSet is filled with data from the Products table.

```
Dim SQL As String =
   "SELECT * FROM Products where SubSubCategoryID=1"
```

```
Dim objDA As New
   System.Data.OleDb.OleDbDataAdapter(SQL, objCS)
Dim objDS As New DataSet()
objDA.Fill(objDS, "Products")
```

The last part of the code is used to define the DataView. The DataView object is created from the default view of the first table in the DataSource object. The DefaultView will return all of the columns for all of the rows in the table. The table listed is 0, which is the first table in the DataSet. Then, the DataSource property of the DataGrid object is set to the DataView object, and the DataGrid is bound to the DataSource when the Page.DataBind method is called.

```
Dim objDV As DataView
objDV = objDS.Tables(0).DefaultView
MyDG1.DataSource = objDV
Page.DataBind()
```

Although you can enter the code manually, you can use the graphical user interface to create the Data objects and Data controls. In the following exercise, you will use the graphical user interface to bind the DataSource property to a database table named Products, which is stored in the TaraStore.mdb database file. The two tables within the TaraStore.mdb database file are Products and Categories. You will use the DataAdapter to manage the connection with the database and return the DataSet object. The DataSet will contain a single table named Products, with a single DataView. The page uses the default DataView to retrieve the data and displays the default DataGrid. The default DataGrid shows all of the columns—even if they are empty.

1. Right-click **Chapter7** in the Solution Explorer window, point to **Add**, then click **Add Existing Item**. Browse to locate your Chapter07Data folder. Select the files **DataGridDisplay.aspx** and **TaraStore.mdb**. Click **Open** to import the files into your project. Click **Yes** in the query dialog box to create a new class file.

2. Open the Server Explorer window from the View window, if necessary. In the Server Explorer window, create a data connection to the TaraStore database. Right-click **Data Connections**, and then select **Add Connection**. In the Data Link Properties box, click the **Provider** tab. Select **Microsoft Jet 4.0 OLE DB Provider**. This is the OLE-DB provider for the Access database engine. Click the **Next** button, and the Connection tab will open with a different connection form. Click the button labeled with three dots (**...**) and browse to locate your TaraStore database. The default location for the TaraStore database is C:\Inetpub\wwwroot\Chapter7\TaraStore.mdb. By default the username and password is entered. Click the **Test Connection** button. If the Test connection succeeded message is displayed in the alert box, click the **OK** button, then click **OK** to close the Data Link Properties dialog box. If any other message is displayed, verify your database name and user information and create the connection again.

3. Double-click the file **DataGridDisplay.aspx** in the Solution Explorer window to select it, then click the **DataGrid** control. The properties for the DataGrid should appear in the Properties window. Verify that the ID property is **MyDG1**.

4. Close the Server Explorer window, then click the **Data** tab in the Toolbox. Click and drag the **OldDbDataAdapter** control to the Web page. The DataAdapter Configuration Wizard opens. Click the **Next** button. In the Data Connection drop-down list box, select the **Access.C:\Inetpub\wwwroot\Chapter7\ TaraStore.mdb.Admin** data connection, and then click the **Next** button.

5. In the Choose a Query Type pane, only the User SQL statements radio button is selected because Access does not support stored procedures. Click the **Next** button.

6. In the Generate the SQL statements form, click the **Query Builder** button. The Add Table window opens. Select the **Products** table, and then click the **Add** button. Click the **Close** button to close the window. The Query Builder that opens is the same wizard that you used in the previous chapter to create your SQL statements.

7. Click the **Description**, **ModelName**, **SubSubCategoryID**, and **UnitCost** check boxes in the Products column list. In the Criteria box for the SubSubCategoryID column, enter **=1**. Uncheck the **Output** check box for the SubSubCategoryID, as shown in figure 7-11. Then, the SubSubCategoryID will not be shown in the DataGrid. Click **OK**. The SQL code created is displayed in the Generate the SQL statements form. Click **Next** to continue. (*Note:* The Products table does not have a unique identifier, so the wizard will not build an Update or Delete SQL statement.)

8. Click **Finish**. The DataAdapter object named OleDbDataAdapter1 and the Connection object named OleDbConnection1 are added to your Design view. (*Note:* If you click on the OleDbConnection1, the Properties window will display the DataSource, Provider, and ConnectionString information.)

9. Now you need to create a DataSet object. Click **Data** on the menu bar, and then click **Generate Dataset**. In the Generate Dataset window select the radio button labeled **New**. In the text box type **MyDS**. The Products table that is managed by theOleDbDataAdapter1 has already been selected. Leave the Add this dataset to the designer check box checked. Click **OK**.

10. Select the Dataset labeled **MyDS1** in the Design view. Click **Data** on the menu bar, then click **Preview Data.** The DataAdapter Preview window opens. Because the fill method of the DataAdapter has not yet been called, the data is not populated in the DataSet.

11. Click the **Fill Dataset** button, which will call the fill method of the DataAdapter. Your data should be displayed in the window, as shown in figure 7-12. (*Note:* You can change the width of the columns by clicking and dragging the line between the columns. You can also change the size of the window by clicking and dragging the lower-right corner of the window.)

Figure 7-11   Using the Query Builder

7

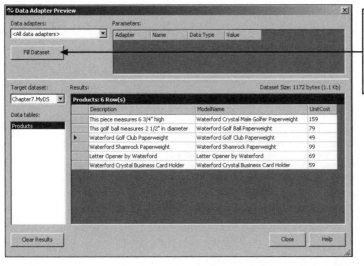

This button calls the fill method of the DataAdapter object, which will fill the DataSet object with data

Figure 7-12   Previewing the DataSet

12. Click the **Close** button.

13. Drag and drop the **DataView** control from the Data tab in the Toolbox to the Web page.

14. You need to assign a table to the DataView. With the **DataView** selected, go to the Properties window, and then click the drop-down list arrow for the **Table** property. Click the **plus sign** next to MyDS1, and then click **Products**. The Table property is listed as MyDS1.Products.

15. Click the **DataGrid** control. You need to set the DataSource property of the DataGrid to the DataView object. Click the drop-down **list arrow** for the DataSource property, and then select **DataView1**.

16. Double-click on the page to open the code behind the page.

17. In the Page_Load handler, add the code below to fill the DataAdapter and to bind the data control to the data source listed in their DataSource property.

```
OleDbDataAdapter1.Fill(MyDS1)

Page.DataBind()
```

18. Click the **Save All** button. Click **Build** on the menu bar, then click **Build Solution**.

19. Click the **DataGridDisplay.aspx** tab. Right-click on the page, and then click **View in Browser**. Your page should look like the one in Figure 7-13. The page displays the product information in a basic table. You can use templates later to format the appearance of the table and the data.

Figure 7-13   Binding a DataGrid to a database

20. Click on the **DataGridDisplay.aspx.vb** page. Click on the **plus sign** next to the Web Form Designer Generated Code. The code displayed is the code that is used by the page to create the connection string, Connection object,

Command object, DataAdapter object, DataSet object, DataTable object, and DataView object.

21. Close any open pages.

By default, all of the columns are displayed. AutoGenerateColumns is used to indicate that all of the columns will be generated by the DataGrid control. You can turn this feature off by setting the **AutoGenerateColumns property** to False. Then, you have to use the Columns template to build your columns manually. The **Columns template** contains all of the bound and unbound columns. A **bound column** is a table column that contains data bound to a field in the database. You specify the data from the database column by using the DataField property. Bound columns are identified with the ASP.NET BoundColumn tag within the Columns template. **Unbound columns** do not automatically contain data from the database.

You can modify the appearance of the individual columns, and display only selected columns. By default, the header text of the column displays the column name in the database. The **HeaderText property** allows you to modify the text message at the top of the column. The DataGrid and DataList controls both support templates. You can build the templates manually or use the tools within Visual Studio .NET.

In the exercise below, you will bind a database to a DataGrid control. Then, you will build and format each of the columns manually.

1. Right-click **Chapter7** in the Solution Explorer window, point to **Add**, then click **Add Existing Item**. Browse to locate your Chapter07Data folder, select the file **DisplayGridColumns.aspx**, then click **Open** to import the Web page into your project. Click **Yes** in the query dialog box to create a new class file.

2. Double-click the file **DisplayGridColumns.aspx** in the Solution Explorer window to open the page.

3. Click the **Data** tab in the Toolbox window. Click and drag the **OleDbDataAdapter** control to the Web page. The DataAdapter Configuration Wizard opens. Click the **Next** button. In the Data Connection drop-down list box, select the **Access.C:\Inetpub\wwwroot\Chapter7\ TaraStore.mdb.Admin** data connection, and then click the **Next** button. Click the **Next** button again.

4. In the Generate the SQL statements form, type **SELECT * FROM Categories**, click the **Next** button, then click **Finish**. The DataAdapter object named OleDbDataAdapter1 and the Connection object named OleDbConnection1 are added to your Design view.

5. To create the DataSet, click **Data** on the menu bar, and then click **Generate Dataset**. In the Generate Dataset window, select the radio button labeled **New**. In the text box, type **MyCatDS**. The Categories table, which is managed by

theOleDbDataAdapter1, has already been selected. Leave the Add this dataset to the designer check box checked. Click **OK**.

6. Drag and drop the **DataView** control from the Data tab in the Toolbox to the Web page.

7. You need to assign a table to the DataView. With the **DataView** selected, go to the Properties window, and then click the drop-down **list arrow** for the Table property. Click the **plus sign** next to MyCatDS1 and then click **Categories**. The Table property is listed as MyCatDS1.Categories.

8. Click the **DataGrid** control. You need to set the DataSource property of the DataGrid to the DataView object. Click the drop-down **list arrow** for the DataSource property, and then select **DataView1**. You can see the headings for the columns that are displayed by default. These columns include CategoryID, CategoryName, description, image, and thumbnail.

9. Double-click on the page to open the code behind the page.

10. In the Page_Load handler, add the code below to fill the DataAdapter and to bind the Data control to the data source listed in the DataSource property.

```
OleDbDataAdapter1.Fill(MyCatDS1)
Page.DataBind()
```

11. Click the **DisplayGridColumns.aspx** tab. Click the **DataGrid** control, and then set the AutoGenerateColumns property to **False**.

12. Click the **HTML** tab to edit the page in HTML view. Locate the <asp:DataGrid> and </asp:DataGrid> tags. Between the DataGrid tags, insert the code below to add a bound column.

```
<Columns>
    <asp:BoundColumn HeaderText="ID"
      DataField="CategoryID">
    </asp:BoundColumn>
    <asp:BoundColumn HeaderText="Name"
      DataField="Categoryname">
    </asp:BoundColumn>
</Columns>
```

Although you are entering the code manually, you could also use the Property Builder to format the HeaderText property, as shown in Figure 7-14.

13. Modify the styles of the columns. Before the closing tag of the closing bracket of the opening <asp:DataGrid> control, insert the code to modify the first column. Add the code below within each of the bound column tags. Notice how the IntelliSense helps display the choices for the property names and values. You can use the Color Picker dialog box to select the color, or

enter it manually, as shown in the sample code below. (*Note:* You can also use the Property Builder to format the properties of the individual columns.)

```
<ItemStyle-Font-Names="Trebuchet MS" ForeColor="#008080">
</ItemStyle>
```

14. Click the **Design** tab to return to Design view.

15. Right-click the **DataGrid** control, and then click **Property Builder**. Notice that the DataSource listed in the Property Builder is DataView1.

16. Click the **Columns** tab. Click **ID** in the Selected columns list. Change the HeaderText property of the ID field from ID to **Category ID**.

17. Click the **Format** tab. Click **Header** in the Objects list box. In the Forecolor drop-down list box, select **Teal**. In the Font name drop-down list box, select **Trebuchet MS**. Check the **Bold** check box. Change the Horizontal alignment drop-down list box to **Center**.

18. Click the **plus sign** next to the Columns item in the Objects list box to expand the selection. Click the **plus sign** next to Columns[1] - Name to expand the selection.

19. Click **Items** to display the properties available, as shown in Figure 7-14. From the Font name drop-down list, select **Trebuchet MS**. From the Forecolor drop-down list, select **Teal**. Click **OK**.

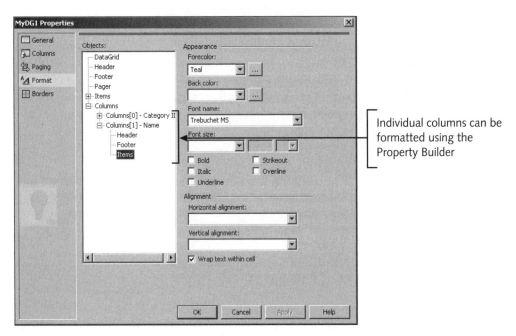

Figure 7-14 The Property Builder

20. Click the **Save All** button. Click **Build** on the menu bar, then click **Build Solution**.

21. Right-click on the page, and then click **View in Browser**. The page displays the category information in a basic table, as shown in Figure 7-15.

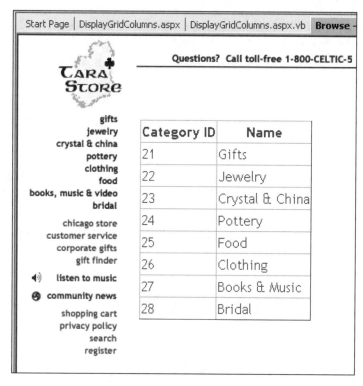

Start Page | DisplayGridColumns.aspx | DisplayGridColumns.aspx.vb **Browse –**

Questions? Call toll-free 1-800-CELTIC-5

gifts
jewelry
crystal & china
pottery
clothing
food
books, music & video
bridal

chicago store
customer service
corporate gifts
gift finder

listen to music

community news

shopping cart
privacy policy
search
register

Category ID	Name
21	Gifts
22	Jewelry
23	Crystal & China
24	Pottery
25	Food
26	Clothing
27	Books & Music
28	Bridal

Figure 7-15   Displaying the DataGrid control

22. Close any open pages.

You can access the wizards and Property Builders for the data objects after the object has been created. Select the object in the Design view and look in the Properties window. A hyperlink will be created to any of the wizards and tools that are used to generate the objects.

WORKING WITH DATA TEMPLATES

In the previous exercise, you created columns in a DataGrid control and used the Property Builder to format the header and the items in the DataGrid. Templates are used to bind data to individual areas within the control and to format the areas within the control. These special areas include the HeaderTemplate, FooterTemplate, and

ItemTemplate. The ItemTemplate is required for both the DataList and the Repeater controls. The template is used to determine what content should appear in the sections of the control. The HeaderTemplate is used to configure the data contained within the header row of the control. The ItemTemplate is used to configure the rows that contain the data from the database. The FooterTemplate is used to configure the data contained within the last row of the control. The appearance of these templates can be modified manually or by using the Property Builder. (*Note:* You can also use templates with the DataGrid control, for example, when you create your own bound and unbound columns. If you create your columns manually in a DataGrid, you should turn the AutoGenerateColumns property to False, or duplicate columns will appear in the DataGrid.)

The DataGrid control contains a Property Builder Wizard that helps you configure the appearance of the header, footer, and item templates. The following is a list of the style objects that can be used to modify the header, footer, and item templates.

- **HeaderStyle** is used to format the HeaderTemplate. You can use the Properties window to modify the styles, or add the style information manually in the Web page.

- **FooterStyle** is used to format the FooterTemplate.

- **ItemStyle** is used to format the rows of data.

- **AlternatingItemStyle** is used to format every other row of data.

- **SelectedItemStyle** is used to format the currently selected row.

- **EditItemStyle** is used to format the row when you are in edit mode and will be making changes to values in the columns.

- **PagerStyle** is used to format the page navigation controls. These controls are used when the number of rows exceeds the number of rows that can be displayed on the Web page. The number of rows that are displayed on the Web page are configured using the PageSize property of the DataGrid control.

Using Templates to Modify the DataGrid Control

You can use the Property Builder or the Properties window to configure the DataGrid control. In the following example, you will use the Property Builder and the Properties window to configure the bound data and the appearance of the DataGrid control.

1. Right-click **Chapter7** in the Solution Explorer window, point to **Add**, then click **Add Existing Item**. Browse to locate your Chapter07Data folder, select the file **DataGridDetails.aspx**, then click **Open** to import the Web page into your project. Click **Yes** in the query dialog box to create a new class file.

2. Double-click the file **DataGridDetails.aspx** in the Solution Explorer window to open the page.

3. Click the **Data** tab in the Toolbox window. Click and drag the **OleDbDataAdapter** control to the Web page. The DataAdapter

Configuration Wizard opens. Click the **Next** button. In the Data Connection drop-down list box, select the **Access.C:\Inetpub\wwwroot\Chapter7\ TaraStore.mdb.Admin** data connection, and then click the **Next** button. Click the **Next** button again.

4. In the Generate the SQL statements form, type **SELECT ProductID, ModelName, Description, UnitCost FROM Products WHERE (SubSubCategoryID = 1)**, click the **Next** button, then click **Finish**. The DataAdapter object named OleDbDataAdapter1 and the Connection object named OleDbConnection1 are added to your Design view.

5. To create the DataSet, click **Data** on the menu bar, and then click **Generate Dataset**. In the Generate Dataset window, select the radio button labeled **New**. In the text box, type **MyProductsDS**. The Products table, which is managed by theOleDbDataAdapter1, has already been selected. Leave the Add this dataset to the designer check box checked. Click **OK**.

6. Drag and drop the **DataView** control from the Data tab in the Toolbox to the Web page.

7. You need to assign a table to the DataView. With the **DataView** selected, go to the Properties window, and then click the drop-down **list arrow** for the Table property. Click the **plus sign** next to MyProductsDS1, and then click **Products**. The Table property is listed as MyProductsDS1.Products.

8. Click the **DataGrid** control. You need to set the DataSource property of the DataGrid to the DataView object. Click the drop-down **list arrow** for the DataSource property, and then select **DataView1**.

9. Double-click on the page to open the code behind the page. In the Page_Load handler, add the code below to fill the DataAdapter and to bind the data control to the data source listed in their DataSource property.

```
OleDbDataAdapter1.Fill(MyProductsDS1)
Page.DataBind()
```

10. Click the **DataGridDetails.aspx** tab. Click the **DataGrid** control to select the control. In the Properties window, click the **plus sign** next to the HeaderStyle item to expand the properties list. Change the BackColor to **#004040** and the ForeColor to **White**. Expand the **Font** property. Change the Font Name to **Trebuchet MS**. Change HorizontalAlign to **Center**, as shown in Figure 7-16.

11. In the Properties window, click the **plus sign** next to the ItemStyle item to expand the properties list. Change the BackColor to **#FFFFCO**. Expand the **Font** property. Change the FontName to **Verdana**. Change the Size to **X-Small**. Change HorizontalAlign to **Center**.

Figure 7-16   The Properties window

12. In the Properties window, click the **plus sign** next to the Alternating Item Style item to expand the properties list. Change the BackColor to **#C0FFFF**.

13. In the Properties Window, click the **plus sign** next to the FooterStyle item to expand the properties list. Change the BackColor to **#C0C0FF**.

14. Right-click the **DataGrid** control, and then click **Property Builder** to open the Property Builder dialog box. On the General tab, click the **Show Footer** check box.

15. Click the **Borders** tab. Change the Border color to **Teal** and the Border width to **2 px**, then click **OK**.

16. Click on the **HTML** tab. Notice the presence of the AlternatingItemStyle, ItemStyle, HeaderStyle, and FooterStyle tags nested within the <asp:DataGrid> control.

17. Click the **Design** tab. Click the **Save All** button. Click **Build** on the menu bar, then click **Build Solution**.

18. Right-click on the page, and then click **View in Browser**. The page should appear as shown in Figure 7-17.

19. Close any open pages.

The tutorials that are installed with Visual Studio .NET are known as walkthroughs. The walkthrough named Adding DataGrid Web Server Controls to a Web Forms Page will walk you through how to format a DataGrid using the Property Builder. The walkthrough is is located at *ms-help://MS.VSCC/ MS.MSDNVS/vbcon/html/vbtskaddingdatagridtowebformspage.htm*.

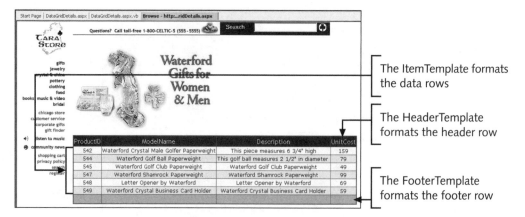

The ItemTemplate formats the data rows

The HeaderTemplate formats the header row

The FooterTemplate formats the footer row

Figure 7-17   Formatting the DataGrid control

Using Templates to Modify the Repeater Control

You can use templates to modify the Repeater control. Remember that the Repeater control repeats only once. In the following example, you will create a header template that contains the heading graphics. You will use a footer template to create an area that contains a company logo and links to the home page. In the body of the Web page, you will use an ItemTemplate, which is bound to the data in the database. You will use the product image names to display the product images, and create hyperlinks. Within the ItemTemplate, you can retrieve the values of the data columns using `<%#  Container.DataItem("ColumnName")  %>`, where ColumnName is the name of the column in the database. You can format the output using any of the standard HTML tags.

1. Right-click **Chapter7** in the Solution Explorer window, point to **Add**, then click **Add Existing Item**. Browse to locate your Chapter07Data folder, select the file **RepeaterTemplate.aspx**, and then click **Open** to import the Web page into your project. Click **Yes** in the query dialog box to create a new class file.

2. Double-click the file **RepeaterTemplate.aspx** in the Solution Explorer window to open the page.

3. Click the **Data** tab in the Toolbox window. Click and drag the **OleDbDataAdapter** control to the Web page. The DataAdapter Configuration Wizard opens. Click the **Next** button. In the Data Connection drop-down list box, select the **Access.C:\Inetpub\wwwroot\Chapter7\ TaraStore.mdb.Admin** data connection, and then click the **Next** button. Click the **Next** button again.

4. In the Generate the SQL statements form, type **SELECT * FROM Products WHERE (SubSubCategoryID = 1)**, click the **Next** button, then click **Finish**. The DataAdapter object named OleDbDataAdapter1 and the Connection object named OleDbConnection1 are added to your Design view.

5. To create the DataSet, click **Data** on the menu bar, and then click **Generate Dataset**. In the Generate Dataset window, select the radio button labeled **New**. In the text box, type **AllProductsDS**. The Products table, which is managed by theOleDbDataAdapter1, has already been selected. Leave the Add this DataSet to the designer check box checked. Click **OK**.

6. Drag and drop the **DataView** control from the Data tab in the Toolbox to the Web page.

7. You need to assign a table to the DataView. With the **DataView** selected, go to the **Properties** window, and click the drop-down list arrow for the **Table** property. Click the **plus sign** next to AllProductsDS1, and then click **Products**. The Table property is listed as AllProductsDS1.Products.

8. Click the **Repeater** control. You need to set the DataSource property of the Repeater to the DataView object. Click the drop-down **list arrow** for the DataSource property, and then select **DataView1**.

9. Double-click on the page to open the code behind the page. In the Page_Load handler, add the code below to fill the DataAdapter and to bind the Data control to the data source listed in the DataSource property.

```
OleDbDataAdapter1.Fill(AllProductsDS1)
Page.DataBind()
```

10. Click the **RepeaterTemplate.aspx** tab to return to the page. Click the **HTML** tab. Within the <asp:Repeater></asp:Repeater> tags, add the code below to create the HeaderTemplate.

```
<HeaderTemplate>
  <div>
      <img src="images/1.jpg"><br />
      <img src="images/560green.gif">
  </div>
</HeaderTemplate>
```

11. Immediately after the code above, add the code below to create the FooterTemplate.

```
<FooterTemplate>
    <img src="images/560green.gif">
    <div align="center">
        <img src="images/logo.gif" align="left">
        <br />
        For more information visit <b>
        <a href="http://www.TaraStore.com">
                http://www.TaraStore.com
        </a></b>
        <br />
        1-800-555-5555
    </div>
</FooterTemplate>
```

12. Immediately after the code above, add the code below to create the SeparatorTemplate. This separates each row visually for the end user. (*Note*: This is not as useful with multiple column displays.)

```
<SeparatorTemplate>
    <img src="images/560green.gif">
</SeparatorTemplate>
```

13. Immediately after the code above, add the code below to create the ItemTemplate. Use a table to make the layout clearer for the viewer. (*Note*: You might want to lay out your table tags first before inserting data, to verify your HTML tags.)

```
<ItemTemplate>
  <table width="500"><tr><td width="170" align="center">
  </td><td width="330">
    </td></tr></table>
</ItemTemplate>
```

14. Within the first table cell tags (`<td width="170"align="center"></td>`), enter the code below to display the product image as a hyperlinked image. Notice that the thumbnail is displayed in the Web page. When the visitor clicks on the thumbnail image, the product image is displayed.

```
<a href="images/<%# Container.DataItem("ProductImage") %>
">
   <img
   src="images/<%# Container.DataItem("thumbnail") %>"
   hspace="2" border="0"/>
</a>
```

15. Within the second table cell tags (`<td width="330"></td>`), enter the code below to display the product image as a text hyperlink. When you click the product name, the product image is displayed. This cell also displays the price formatted as currency and the model number. Notice how the HTML tags are used to format the labels as bold and italic. (*Note*: Do not split strings across two lines of code.)

```
<b><a href=
   "images/<%# Container.DataItem("ProductImage") %>">
<%# Container.DataItem("ModelName")%>
</a></b><br/>
<i>Description: </i>
<%# Container.DataItem("Description") %><br />
<i>Price: </i>
<%# DataBinder.Eval(Container.DataItem, _
"UnitCost", "{0:C}") %><br />
<i>Item #: </i>
<%# Container.DataItem("ModelNumber") %>
```

16. Click the **Save All** button. Click **Build** on the menu bar, then click **Build Solution**. (*Note*: Do not click on the Design View tab. The ItemTemplate is no longer editable within the Design view because of the string that was split within the href property.)

17. Right-click on the page, and then click **View in Browser**. The page should appear as shown in Figure 7-18.

18. Close any open pages.

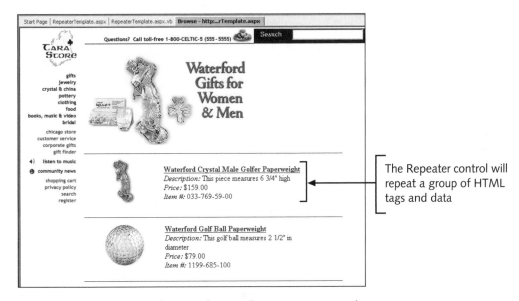

Figure 7-18   Using templates to format the Repeater control

Using Templates to Modify the DataList Control

In the previous exercise, you had to add table tags within the ItemTemplate to format the output of the Repeater control. One of the advantages of using the DataList control rather than the Repeater control is that the DataList can be used to create multiple columns of data without using the table tags in the ItemTemplate. You can alter the number of columns displayed and the direction or layout. The number of columns is the number of columns of data displayed across the Web page. The number of columns repeated is formatted using the **RepeatColumns property**. The RepeatColumns property must be an integer. The **RepeatDirections property** stores the direction of the columns. If the columns repeat horizontally, then the value is RepeatColumns.Horizontal. If they repeat vertically, then the value is RepeatColumns.Vertical. These properties are properties of the DataList control, and not the template.

You can use templates to modify the DataList control. In the following exercise, you will display the data using the DataList control formatted as multiple columns. Within the DataList control, you can use the table tags to format the output more precisely. You need to make sure that the width of the tables is specified in order to ensure that the entire output is visible. In this example, you are going to create the data objects manually in the code behind the page.

 You can reuse the DataSets once they are created within the Web application. When you generated the DataSet, a file with the extension .xsd was created. This file contains the DataSet schema and a reference to a Visual Basic file that contains the code to generate the data. If you show all the files in the Solution Explorer window, you can expand the .xsd file to view the code behind the page.

1. Right-click **Chapter7** in the Solution Explorer window, point to **Add**, then click **Add Existing Item**. Browse to locate your Chapter07Data folder, select the file **DataListTemplate.aspx**, then click **Open** to import the Web page into your project. Click **Yes** in the query dialog box to create a new class file. Open the page.

2. Double-click on the page to open the code behind the page, which is named **DataListTemplate.aspx.vb**. Within the Page_Load event handler, add the code below to create a connection to your database, create the SQL select query, and create the Connection object.

```
If Not Page.IsPostBack() Then
Dim CS As String =
  "Provider=Microsoft.Jet.OLEDB.4.0;Data " & _
"Source=C:\Inetpub\wwwroot\Chapter7\TaraStore.mdb"
Dim SQL As String = _
  "SELECT * FROM Products WHERE SubSubCategoryID=1"
Dim objCS As New System.Data.OleDb.OleDbConnection(CS)
```

3. Immediately after the code above, add the code below to create the DataAdapter object, the DataSet object, and the DataView object.

```
Dim objDA As New
  System.Data.OleDb.OleDbDataAdapter(SQL, objCS)
Dim objDS As New DataSet()
objDA.Fill(objDS, "Products")
Dim objDV As DataView
objDV = objDS.Tables(0).DefaultView
```

4. Add the code below to set the DataSource property of the DataList to the DataView object and bind the Data controls to the data source using the DataBind method of the Page object.

```
MyDL1.DataSource = objDV

Page.DataBind()
```

5. Click the **DataListTemplate.aspx** tab, then click the **DataList** control. Change the RepeatColumns property in the Properties window to **2**.

6. Click the **HTML** tab to edit the DataList control. Locate the
   <asp:DataList></asp:DataList> controls. Between the DataList controls add
   the code below to create the HeaderTemplate and the FooterTemplate.

```
<HeaderTemplate>
  <div>
      <img src="images/1.jpg"><br />
      <img src="images/560green.gif" width="800">
  </div>
</HeaderTemplate>
<FooterTemplate>
    <img src="images/560green.gif" width="800">
    <div align="center">
        <img src="images/logo.gif" align="left">
        <br>
        For more information visit <b>
        <a href="http://www.TaraStore.com">
                http://www.TaraStore.com
        </a></b>
        <br>
        1-800-555-5555
    </div>
</FooterTemplate>
```

7. Add the code below to create the ItemTemplate. Use a table to make the layout
   clearer for the viewer. (*Note:* You might want to lay out your table tags first
   before inserting data, to verify your HTML tags.) The same method used in the
   previous exercise, called DataItem, returns the value for the database column
   specified in the parentheses. You can also use DataBinder.Eval to evaluate the
   results as an expression and apply formatting arguments such as currency.

```
<ItemTemplate>
  <table><tr><td width="200" align="center">
    <a href= "images/<%# ¬
       Container.DataItem("ProductImage") %>">
       <img src=
       "images/<%# Container.DataItem("thumbnail") %>"
       hspace="2" border="0">
    </a>
    </td>
    <td width="200">
    <b>
    <a href= "images/<%# ¬
       Container.DataItem("ProductImage") %>">
       <%# Container.DataItem("ModelName")%>
    </a></b>
  <br />
    <i>Description: </i>
    <%# Container.DataItem("Description") %>
    <br />
```

```
<i>Price: </i>
<%# DataBinder.Eval(Container.DataItem, _
    "UnitCost", "{0:C}") %>
<br>
<i>Item #: </i>
<%# Container.DataItem("ModelNumber") %>
</td></tr></table>
</ItemTemplate>
```

8. Click the **Save All** button. Click **Build** on the menu bar, then click **Build Solution**. (*Note*: Once you have entered the ItemTemplate code, you cannot go back to Design mode because Design mode cannot interpret the quotation marks correctly.)

9. Right-click on the page, and then click **View in Browser**. Click **Build** on the menu bar, then click **Build Solution**. (*Note*: Do not view the page in HTML view.) Figure 7-19 shows how the page appears in the browser.

10. Close any open pages.

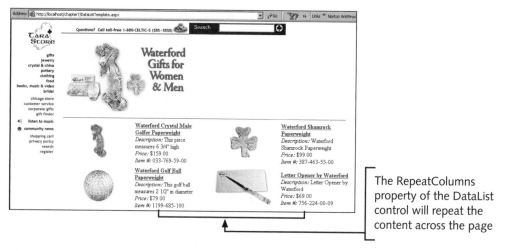

The RepeatColumns property of the DataList control will repeat the content across the page

Figure 7-19   Using templates to format the DataList control

CHAPTER SUMMARY

❑ Data can be displayed using ASP.NET Data controls. The DropDownList, ListBox, CheckBoxList, and RadioButtonList controls inherit from a ListControls class. The DropDownList usually only displays one value at a time, while the ListBox generally displays all the values at the same time.

❑ The DataList and DataGrid controls inherit from the BaseDataList class. The DataList uses an ItemTemplate to display the values. The DataGrid allows you to create bound and unbound columns. Bound columns contain a value that is bound to a value in the database. The DataList and DataGrid controls use templates to create the header, footer, and item sections of the data control. You can format these controls using the graphical Style Builder tool or manually.

❒ The Repeater control inherits directly from the System.Web.UI.Control class. The Repeater control must be edited manually in HTML view. There is no graphical tool to edit the Repeater control.

❒ Data that consists of a repeated expression can be bound to the Data control. Data controls can be bound to many types of data such as a hash table, ArrayList, DataSet, DataView, or DataReader object.

❒ A DataAdapter creates and manages the connection to the database. The Connection uses the connection string to locate the database. The DataAdapter uses the SQL statement and the connection object. The DataAdapter uses the fill method to populate the DataSet with the table specified in the parameter for the Fill command.

❒ The DataSet object can contain one or more DataTables. A DataView object contains a subset of rows of data from a DataTable. A DataReader object is a read-only, forward-only stream of data from the database. The data connection remains open while the DataReader reads the data. The DataReader object provides better performance than the DataView or DataSet.

❒ You can create the Data objects and Data controls manually, or you can use Visual Studio .NET graphical controls to generate the code to create the objects and controls.

REVIEW QUESTIONS

1. Which of the following controls cannot be used to display data in a Web page?
   a. DataList
   b. DataView
   c. DataGrid
   d. Repeater

2. What method can be used to bind the DG1 control to a hash table?
   a. DG1.Bind()
   b. Page.Bind()
   c. DG1.DataBind()
   d. Bind.Page()

3. Which technique can be used to store read-only values that can later be retrieved?
   a. Property
   b. Method
   c. Function
   d. a or b

4. What keyword is used to identify the value returned to a function?
   a. Provider
   b. Return
   c. Function
   d. Else

5. Which Data control is inherited from the BaseDataList class?
   a. CheckBoxList
   b. DropDownList
   c. DataList
   d. RadioButton

6. Which Data control is inherited from the ListControls class?
   a. CheckBoxList
   b. DropDownList
   c. ListBox
   d. All of the above

7. Which object provides a read-only, forward-only stream of data from the database?
   a. DataReader
   b. DataSet
   c. DataView
   d. ArrayList

8. Which data control displays one value at a time?
   a. ListBox
   b. DropDownList
   c. DataList
   d. DataGrid

9. Which control does not have a visual interface in the Visual Studio .NET toolbox?
   a. DataGrid
   b. DataList

c. CheckBoxList

d. Repeater

10. Which method is used to insert a new item into an array?

a. insert

b. add

c. fill

d. InsertCommand

11. Which property of the Data controls identifies where the data is to be located?

a. DataView

b. DataSource

c. DataTable

d. DataTextField

12. What property allows you to format the value as currency?

a. FormatCurrency

b. Format $C

c. DataTextFormatString

d. DataTextField

13. Which property is used to identify the text displayed in a DropDownList control?

a. DataValueField

b. DataTextFormat

c. DataTextFormatString

d. DataTextField

14. What is the fully qualified name of the Connection object for a non–SQL Database?

a. System.Data.OleDb.OleDbConnection

b. System.Data.OleDb.OleDbConnection(CS)

c. System.Data.OleDb

d. System.Data.OleDbConnection

15. What object is used to get the data from the database and populate the DataSet object?

a. DataAdapter

b. DataSet

c. DataConnection

d. DataView

7

16. Which method is used to get the data from the database and populate the DataSet object?

a. fill

b. get

c. select

d. InsertCommand

17. Which property must be set to False before you can change the default DataGrid columns?

a. AutoFormatColumns

b. FormatColumns

c. AutoDataColumns

d. AutoGenerateColumns

18. What ASP.NET tag is used to format a bound column in a DataGrid control?

a. <asp:BoundColumn>

b. <Columns>

c. <ASP:Columns>

d. a and b

19. Which template includes the values from the database?

a. HeaderTemplate

b. FooterTemplate

c. AlternatingTemplate

d. ItemTemplate

20. In the template that contains the value, which expression returns a value from a column named "thumbnail"?

a. <%# Container.DataItem("thumbnail") %>

b. <%# Columns.DataItem("thumbnail") %>

c. <%# Columns ("thumbnail") %>

d. <%# Columns.thumbnail %>

HANDS-ON PROJECTS

Project 7-1

In this project, you will create a Web page that binds an array to a DropDownList control.

1. Start **Visual Studio .NET** and open your **Chapter7** solution if it is not already open.

2. Add a Web page named **Ch7Proj1.aspx** that displays an array using a DropDownList control.

3. Create an array named **arr1**, which has five items.

4. Insert the following values into the array: **Paper**, **Pencils**, **Glue**, **Notepads**, **Pens**.

5. Insert the DropDownList control named **MyDD1**.

6. When the page loads, populate the MyDD1 control with the values in the array, and bind the values to the control.

7. Add an **ASP.NET Label** control to the page. When the user clicks the Submit button, display the value in the Label control.

8. Add headings, graphics, fonts, and colors to enhance the appearance of the page.

9. View your Web page in the browser. Print the Web page, the source code within Visual Studio .NET, and the source code from the browser.

Project 7-2

In this project, you will create a Web page that binds a hash table to a drop-down list control.

1. Start **Visual Studio .NET** and open your **Chapter7** solution if it is not already open.

2. Add a Web page called **Ch7Proj2.aspx** that will display a hash table using a DropDownList control.

3. Create a hash table named **MyHash**, which has five items.

4. Insert the following items into the hash table as the keys: **Yellow Notepads**, **Pencils**, **School Glue**, **Colored Index Cards**, **Ring Index Cards**. The values are yellownotepad1.gif, pencilsfan.gif, gluepinkpaper2.gif, colorednotecards-pink.gif, and ringnotecards.gif, respectively.

5. Insert the DropDownList control named **MyDD1**.

6. When the page loads, populate the MyDD1 control with the values in the hash table, and bind the values to the control.

7. Insert an Image control named **IMG1**. The first image should be the pencilsfan.gif.

8. Add an **ASP.NET Label** control to the page. When the user clicks the Submit button, display the value in the label control.

9. Add headings, graphics, fonts, and colors to enhance the appearance of the page.

10. Save your page and build your solution.

11. View your Web page in the browser. Print the Web page, the source code within Visual Studio .NET, and the source code from the browser.

Project 7-3

In this project, you will create a Web page that binds an array to a DropDownList control.

1. Start **Visual Studio .NET** and open your **Chapter7** solution if necessary.

2. Add a Web page named **Ch7Proj3.aspx** that will display a hash table using a DropDownList control.

3. Create a hash table named **MyHash**, which has five items.

4. Insert the following items into the hash table as the keys: **Yellow Notepads, Pencils, School Glue, Colored Index Cards, Ring Index Cards**. The values are 3.5, 2.75, 3.5, 4.5, and 5.3, respectively.

5. Insert the DataGrid control named **MyDG1**.

6. Change the AutoGenerateColumns property to **False**.

7. Type the code below to add the Columns collection to the DataGrid control to insert the items in the hash table. Format the HeaderText to reflect the contents of the column.

```
<Columns>
<ASP:BoundColumn HeaderText="Product Name"
  DataField="Key" />
<ASP:BoundColumn HeaderText="Product Price"
  DataField="Value"
DataFormatString="{0:C}" />
</Columns>
```

8. When the page loads, populate the MyDG1 control with the values in the hash table, and bind the values to the control.

9. Add headings, graphics, fonts, and colors to enhance the appearance of the page and the templates.

10. Save your page and build your solution.

11. View your Web page in the browser. Print the Web page, the source code within Visual Studio .NET, and the source code from the browser.

Project 7-4

In this project, you will create a Web page that binds a database to a DataGrid control. You will manually add the code to create the data objects. You will modify the DataGrid control using the Property Builder. The page will display all the columns in the products table for all of the products.

1. Start **Visual Studio .NET** and open your **Chapter7** solution if necessary.

2. Add a Web page named **Ch7Proj4.aspx** that displays a table from a database using a DataGrid control.

3. Add the DataGrid control to the page. The ID should be **MyDG1**.

4. In the code behind the page, add the code below to create the data connection to the TaraStore database. Make sure to change the SQL Select statement to choose all the products in the database. Make sure to assign the DataView to the DataSource property of the DataGrid control.

```
Dim CS As String =
   "Provider=Microsoft.Jet.OLEDB.4.0;Data " _
& "Source=C:\Inetpub\wwwroot\Chapter7\TaraStore.mdb"
Dim SQL As String = "SELECT * FROM Products"
Dim objCS As New System.Data.OleDb.OleDbConnection(CS)
Dim objDA As New System.Data.OleDb.OleDbDataAdapter(SQL,
objCS)
Dim objDS As New DataSet()
objDA.Fill(objDS, "Products")
Dim objDV As DataView
objDV = objDS.Tables(0).DefaultView
MyDG1.DataSource = objDV
Page.DataBind()
```

5. Use the Property Builder to modify the DataGrid control. Change the heading color, font name, font size, and background color. Change the background color of the alternating rows to something other than white. Change the heading text properties for all of the columns in the table. Change the font size of the item template to **X-Small** so you can see more of the table on one screen.

6. Add headings, graphics, fonts, and colors to enhance the appearance of the page.

7. Save your page and build your solution.

8. View your Web page in the browser. Print the Web page, the source code within Visual Studio .NET, and the source code from the browser.

Project 7-5

In this project, you will create a Web page that binds a database to a Repeater control. You will modify the Repeater control using Templates.

1. Start **Visual Studio .NET** and open your **Chapter7** solution if necessary.

2. Add a Web page named **Ch7Proj5.aspx** that displays a database using a Repeater control.

3. In the code behind the page, add the code below to create the data connection to the TaraStore database. Make sure to change the SQL Select statement to choose all the products in the database. Make sure to assign the DataView to the DataSource property of the Repeater control.

```
Dim CS As String =
   "Provider=Microsoft.Jet.OLEDB.4.0;Data " _
& "Source=C:\Inetpub\wwwroot\Chapter7\TaraStore.mdb"
Dim SQL As String = _
   "SELECT * FROM Products where SubSubCategoryID=1"
Dim objCS As New System.Data.OleDb.OleDbConnection(CS)
```

7

```
Dim objDA As
    New System.Data.OleDb.OleDbDataAdapter(SQL, objCS)
Dim objDS As New DataSet()
objDA.Fill(objDS, "Products")
Dim objDV As DataView
objDV = objDS.Tables(0).DefaultView
MyRP1.DataSource = objDV
Page.DataBind()
```

4. In the Design view of the Web page, add a Panel control to the page. Delete the text within the Panel control.

5. Add the Repeater control inside the Panel control. The ID should be **MyRP1**.

6. Within the Repeater control tags, add the code below to add a HeaderTemplate to display the category image. (*Hint*: You will have to do this in HTML view.)

```
<HeaderTemplate>
  <div>
      <img src="images/1.jpg"><br />
      <img src="images/560green.gif">
  </div>
</HeaderTemplate>
```

7. Within the Repeater control tags, add the code below to add a FooterTemplate to display the footer.

```
<FooterTemplate>
    <img src="images/560green.gif">
    <div align="center">
        <img src="images/logo.gif" align="left">
        <br />
        For more information visit <b>
        <a href="http://www.TaraStore.com">
                http://www.TaraStore.com
        </a></b>
        <br />
        1-800-555-5555
    </div>
</FooterTemplate>
```

8. Add the code below to add the ItemTemplate.

```
<ItemTemplate>
  <b><%# Container.DataItem("ModelName")%></b>
  <br />
  <i>Description: </i>
  <%# Container.DataItem("Description") %>
  <br />
  <i>Price: </i>
  <%# DataBinder.Eval(Container.DataItem, _
    "UnitCost", "{0:C}") %>
  <br />
  <i>Item #: </i>
```

```
    <%# Container.DataItem("ModelNumber") %>
    <br /><br />
</ItemTemplate>
```

9. Add headings, graphics, fonts, and colors to enhance the appearance of the page.

10. Save your page and build your solution.

11. View your Web page in the browser. Print the Web page, the source code within Visual Studio .NET, and the source code from the browser.

CASE PROJECTS

Tara Store — Data Control Members

Your manager has asked you to provide information about the various data controls that can be bound to data sources. Go to the Help menu within Visual Studio .NET and search for the Data control members listed in this chapter. Create a Web page that describes at least five ASP.NET Data controls. Provide an example of the syntax used to insert each control into the Web page. Add headings, graphics, fonts, and colors to enhance the appearance of the page. Save the page as Ch7Case1.aspx. Print the Web page.

Tara Store — Retrieving the UserID Using a Hash Table

Your boss would like you to create a listing of UserIDs and passwords in a hash table. You are to use the hash table to create a Web page that displays the users in the table. When the user clicks the Submit button, his or her password should be displayed in an ASP.NET Server Label control and display all of the users and passwords should be displayed in a DataList control. Add headings, graphics, fonts, and colors to enhance the appearance of the page. Save the page as Ch7Case2.aspx. Print the Web page.

Tara Store — Displaying a Shopping Cart with the DataGrid Control

Your boss has asked you to create a shopping cart application. In the first phase, you must create a database called Ch7Case345.mdb that contains the product information. You can use SQL Server, Access, or another database application to create the database. Include the name of the product, price, description, product ID, and product image name. Insert some sample data. Create a Web page that displays the data using a DataGrid control. Format the DataGrid using the Property Builder. Change the font color, background color, cell alignment, font name, and font size for the HeaderTemplate and the ItemTemplate for each of the columns. Change the background color of the alternating rows. Add headings, graphics, fonts, and colors to enhance the appearance of the page. Save the page as Ch7Case3.aspx. Print the Web page and the source code.

Tara Store — Displaying a Shopping Cart with the DataList Control

Your boss has asked you to create a shopping cart application. In the first phase, you must create a database called Ch7Case345.mdb that contains the product information. You can use SQL Server, Access, or another database application to create the database. Include the name of the product, price, description, product ID, and product image name. (*Note*: If you created the database in the previous case, you can reuse that database.) Insert some sample data. Create a Web page that displays the data using a DataList control. Format the DataList using the DataList templates. Change the font color, background color, cell alignment, font name, and font size for the HeaderTemplate and the ItemTemplate for each of the columns. Change the background color of the alternating rows. Change the display so that there are always two columns of data displayed on one page. Add headings, graphics, fonts, and colors to enhance the appearance of the page. Save the page as Ch7Case4.aspx. Print the Web page and the source code.

Tara Store — Displaying a Shopping Cart with the Repeater Control

Your boss has asked you to create a shopping cart application. In the first phase, you must create a database called Ch7Case345.mdb that contains the product information. You can use SQL Server, Access, or another database application to create the database. (*Note*: If you created the database in the earlier case, you can reuse that database.) Include the name of the product, price, description, product ID, and product image name. Insert some sample data. Create a Web page that displays the data using a Repeater control. Format the Repeater using the templates. Change the font color, background color, cell alignment, font name, and font size for the HeaderTemplate and the ItemTemplate for each of the columns. Change the background color of the alternating rows. Add headings, graphics, fonts, and colors to enhance the appearance of the page. Save the page as Ch7Case5.aspx. Print the Web page and the source code.

CHAPTER

8

BUILDING DATA-DRIVEN WEB APPLICATIONS

> **In this chapter, you will:**
> ♦ Learn how to use data sources in Visual Studio .NET
> ♦ Build search queries using SQL
> ♦ Page, sort, and filter data using the DataGrid control
> ♦ Insert, modify, and delete records using the DataGrid control
> ♦ Build a reusable Visual Basic .NET component that retrieves a DataSet

Web data management is an ever-evolving component of Web development. Businesses must quickly create Web data-driven applications that display data, allow the user to customize the data displayed, and allow the administrator to manage the data remotely. Visual Studio .NET provides new data objects that you can use to manage your data connections, and new Data controls that you can use to manage your data within the Web page. These new ASP.NET Data controls can also be used to allow the end user to manipulate the data from the Web page.

In this chapter, you will learn how to retrieve data using the DataReader and DataSet controls. Using the DataReader, you will learn how to use SQL statements and stored procedures to retrieve data. Then, you will learn how to modify the appearance of the data using the built-in templates and properties of the DataGrid control. You will also learn how to add, delete, and modify records using the DataGrid control.

USING DATA SOURCES IN VISUAL STUDIO .NET

Web developers must create Web applications that can coexist with evolving data structures. Using Visual Studio .NET, you can create stored procedures to collect data from the database. Then you can create Data controls in the Web page, which are bound to the data source defined within the Data component. When a database administrator decides to change a field name, the administrator can also make the change in the stored procedure. No changes need be made to the application, because the data application tier is separate from the business and presentation tiers. If the Web store owner decides to change the appearance of the Web page, the Web developer can make the change in the Web page, without affecting the data application layer. In previous versions of ASP, you could change the Web page without changing the data application layer. However, the code was intermixed with HTML and was more difficult and costly to maintain.

Visual Studio .NET allows you to create connections to various data sources, such as arrays, hash tables, and databases. The process of binding the data is the same regardless of the data source. To bind the data source to the control, you must assign the data source to the DataSource property of the Data control, and then call either the DataBind method of the control or the DataBind method of the page. It is simpler to access data from a HashTable or ArrayList than from a database because you are only accessing one object, the HashTable or ArrayList.

You can retrieve the data using a DataReader object. The DataReader object provides a read-only, direct connection to the data source. You might choose to use the DataReader when you want to retrieve data that does not change with the client. The DataBind method is used to bind the DataReader to the Data control.

When accessing data from a database, you can access the data from multiple tables. These tables are received as a DataSet object. A **DataSet** contains a DataTables collection. Individual **DataTables** within the DataTables collection can have relationships defined between the DataTable objects. You can use the DataTable to specify the subset of tables and records that you want to access. The DataView object is used to retrieve a subset of one of the tables within the DataSet. In previous versions of ASP and ADO, only one table at a time was accessed with the ADO Recordset object. You could have used the SQL JOIN operations in SQL to access multiple database tables. However, the results were always received by the Recordset object as a single table. With a DataSet object, the data can be received as a group of one or more related tables. The DataBind method is used to bind the DataSet or DataView to the Data control.

The DataReader Object

The **DataReader object** is used to retrieve a read-only, non-buffered stream of data from a database. **Non-buffered** means only one record at any one time is stored in memory. When the new record is read, the old record is first removed from memory. Because the information read is a stream of data, it is retrieved sequentially and is read-only. The DataReader can retrieve the records faster than the DataSet. The DataReader cannot be used to retrieve a disconnected set of data, because the DataReader is directly connected to the database and reads each row individually. The DataReader can retrieve a forward-only set of data, which means that you cannot move backwards through the rows of data. Therefore, the data retrieved by the DataReader can only be bound to a single control.

There are two special types of DataReader objects, which are used for the SqlClient class and the OleDb class. You execute the same steps to implement the DataReader, the SqlDataReader, and the OleDbDataReader, but the objects have different names. There is only a small difference in code between the OleDb and SqlClient DataReader objects. However, there is a substantial difference in performance between them. The **SqlDataReader** is used with SQL Server databases, while the **OleDBDataReader** is used with all other databases, including Access and Oracle. The DataReader can significantly improve the performance of your application. In the current version of Visual Studio .NET, there are no tools in the Toolbox for creating the DataReader object. Therefore, you have to write code to instantiate the DataReader object, and read the data from the code behind the page. The following sample code creates a SQL string and a Connection object. The Command object is created using the active connection and SQL statement. The ExecuteReader method of the Command object returns the OleDbDataReader object. (*Note:* The ¬ symbol is used to show that the code continues on the next line. When you enter the code, type the code on a single line.)

```
Dim CS As String = "Provider=Microsoft.Jet.OLEDB.4.0; ¬
    Data Source=C:\Inetpub\wwwroot\Chapter8\TS.mdb;"
Dim objCN As New OleDb.OleDbConnection(CS)
objCN.Open()
Dim mySQL As String = "SELECT * FROM Categories"
Dim objCM As New OleDb.OleDbCommand(mySQL, objCN)
Dim objDR As OleDb.OleDbDataReader
objDR = objCM.ExecuteReader()
```

You can also use the ConnectionString property of the Connection object, as shown in the sample code below. The first connection string uses a user ID to connect to an Access database.

```
SqlConnection1.ConnectionString = ¬
    "Provider=Microsoft.Jet.OLEDB.4.0; ¬
    Data Source=C:\Inetpub\wwwroot\Chapter8\TS.mdb;"
```

You can also use Visual Studio .NET to create the Data Connection object. You can drag the Data Connection object to the Design view of a Web page. Using the Data Link dialog box you can set up a connection to a specific database. You can also drag the database from an existing data connection listed in the Data Connections in the Server Explorer window. These methods will create the connection string to the database. The second connection string is created by Visual Studio .NET and uses Windows NT trusted security to connect to a SQL Server database.

```
SqlConnection2.ConnectionString = ¬
    "data source=(local)\NetSDK; initial catalogue=Chapter6; ¬
```

```
integrated  security=SSPI;workstation id=COURSE; ¬
packet size=4096";
```

After you have created the DataReader object, you can access the read method to retrieve the data stream. The **read method** of the DataReader reads records in a forward-only direction. Each record is read, and then displayed on the Web page, because only one record is stored in memory at a time. Once you have read the record, you can access the value of a column using the name of the column within quotations, or the index number. The index number is the number of the column in the order in which it is retrieved. The index number for the first column is 0. The following sample code reads the data from the DataReader and returns the value in the CategoryName column for each row. The CategoryName column could have been retrieved using `objDR(0)`.

```
While objDR.Read()
Response.Write(objDR("CategoryName"))
End While
```

Because you have an open connection to the data stream, you must always call the **close method** of the DataReader object when you have finished reading the data. You can also pass the CloseConnection property as a parameter when you call the execute method of the Command object. This causes the Command object to close the connection to the DataReader for you. The code below illustrates how to close the DataReader object using the Command object.

```
objCM.ExecuteReader(CommandBehavior.CloseConnection)
```

You can use stored procedures in combination with the DataReader object. If you run a command that contains any output parameters or return values, these values are not available until you close the DataReader object.

The ASP.NET account must have permission to access each database you create. You will find instructions on assigning database permissions in the ReadMe.doc file, which is located in the Chapter06Data directory.

The steps for implementing a DataReader object with an Access database are as follows:

1. Create a connection string. The connection string contains the database provider name, the data location, and the username and password, which are required to connect to the database. The syntax of the connection string varies with the type of database used. In this example, the name of the provider for the Access database is "Microsoft.Jet.OLEDB.4.0". The code below shows the sample connection string. (*Note:* Because the connection string is a string, it should not be split across multiple lines, unless you concatenate it.)

```
Dim CS As String = "Provider=Microsoft.Jet.OLEDB.4.0; ¬
Data Source=C:\Inetpub\wwwroot\Chapter8\TS.mdb;"
```

2. Create a Connection object. Below is a sample of code that creates a Connection object.

```
Dim objCN As New OleDb.OleDbConnection(CS)
```

3. Open the connection. (*Note*: If you are using Visual Studio .NET, the open method appears on the IntelliSense menu.) Below is a sample of code that opens the connection.

```
objCN.Open()
```

4. Create a variable that contains a SQL command or stored procedure, as shown in the code sample below. (*Note*: Do not split the string across multiple lines of code.) Retrieve the columns from the Categories table.

```
Dim mySQL As String = "SELECT * FROM Categories"
```

5. Create the Command object using the SQL variable and the Connection object, as shown in the code sample below.

```
Dim objCM As New OleDb.OleDbCommand(mySQL, objCN)
```

6. Declare the variable, which contains the DataReader object, as shown in the code sample below.

```
Dim objDR As OleDb.OleDbDataReader
```

7. Use the ExecuteReader method of the Command object to retrieve the data and place the data in the DataReader object, as shown in the code sample below.

```
objDR = objCM.ExecuteReader()
```

8. Read the data from the DataReader object, and write the column values to the Web page, as shown in the code sample below. (*Note*: You are not limited to writing only the values; you can write out other content, HTML code, and expressions.)

```
While objDR.Read()
Response.Write(objDR("CategoryName"))
End While
```

9. Close the DataReader object, as shown in the code sample below.

```
objDR.Close()
```

10. Close the data connection, a shown in the code sample below. (*Note*: You don't have to release the variables because garbage collector will reclaim the variables when they are no longer referenced.)

```
objCN.Close()
```

 You can access the data as a string or in its native data type. For example, you can use the GetDateTime method to retrieve the data as a Date object. You can also retrieve the schema information about the current data returned set by using the GetSchemaTable method. This method returns a DataTable object that contains the schema information as a table. Each column maps to a property of the column returned in the result set, where the ColumnName is the name of the property and the value of the column is the value of the property.

Using the DataReader to Retrieve Data from a Database

In the following exercise, you use the DataReader object to retrieve data and display a listing of categories in the TaraStore database. The Label control at the left of the main image is named lblCat. You will display the values of the categories from the DataReader in the menu Label control.

1. Start **Visual Studio .NET**.

2. Click **File** on the menu bar, point to **New**, and then click **Project**. This opens the New Project window.

3. Click the **Visual Basic Projects** icon, then click the **ASP.NET Web Application** icon under Templates. Type **Chapter8** in the Location text box in place of WebApplication1. Click **OK** to create the solution, project, and default files.

4. In the Solution Explorer window, right-click **Chapter8**, point to **Add**, then click **New Folder**. Type **images** to name the folder, and then press **Enter**.

5. Right-click the **images** folder, point to **Add**, and then click **Add Existing Item**. Change the Files of type drop-down list from VB Code Files to **All Files**. Browse to locate the images folder within the Chapter08Data folder. Select all of the images in the images directory. Click the **Open** button to import the images into the images directory of the Chapter8 project.

6. Right-click **Chapter8** in the Solution Explorer window, point to **Add**, then click **Add Existing Item**. Navigate to your Chapter08Data directory. Select the files **DataReader.aspx** and **TaraStore.mdb** from the Chapter08Data directory. Click the **Open** button to import the Web page into your project. Click **Yes** in the dialog box to create a new class file.

7. Double-click the **DataReader.aspx** page icon in the Solution Explorer window to open the page. Double-click the page to open the code behind the page, which is named **DataReader.aspx.vb**.

8. Within the Page_Load procedure, add the code below. (*Note:* The location of your database may be different, depending on where your Web site is installed on the Web server. Your system administrator can provide you with the physical path to your files.) This code creates the connection string and the Connection object, and opens the connection. The connection string should be on a single line. (*Note:* Do not split the connection string across two lines of code. You cannot split a string across multiple lines of code unless you concatenate the string.)

```
Dim CS As String = "Provider=Microsoft.Jet.OLEDB.4.0; ¬
Data Source=C:\Inetpub\wwwroot\Chapter8\TaraStore.mdb;"
Dim objCN As New OleDb.OleDbConnection(CS)
objCN.Open()
```

9. Below this, add the following code to create the variable to store the SQL command.

```
Dim mySQL As String = ¬
  "SELECT CategoryName FROM Categories"
```

10. Below this, add the following code to create the Command object using the SQL command and the Connection object.

```
Dim objCM As New OleDb.OleDbCommand(mySQL, objCN)
```

11. Below this, add the following code to create the DataReader object. (*Note*: It is more useful to name the DataReader object something like objDR. In most samples installed with Visual Studio .NET the DataReader object is named result.)

```
Dim objDR As OleDb.OleDbDataReader
objDR = objCM.ExecuteReader()
```

12. Below this, add the following code to declare a variable named **MyCat** to store the data from the DataReader object.

```
Dim MyCat As String
```

13. Below this, add the following code to read the record from the DataReader. Concatenate the CategoryName field with the MyCat variable and a line break tag. Store the results from the concatenation in the MyCat variable. This ensures that all records are stored in the MyCat variable.

```
While objDR.Read()
MyCat = MyCat + (objDR("CategoryName") & "<br />")
End While
```

14. Below this, add the code below to close the DataReader and the Connection objects.

```
objDR.Close()
objCN.Close()
```

15. Below this, add the code below to assign the contents of the MyCat variable to the Text property of the label named lblCat. The label displays the results from the DataReader in the Web page.

```
lblCat.Text = MyCat
```

16. Click the **Save All** button. Click **Build** on the menu bar, then click **Build Solution**.

17. Click the **DataReader.aspx** tab to return to the Web page. Right-click on the page, and then click **View in Browser**. Your page should look like the one in Figure 8-1.

18. Close any open pages.

8

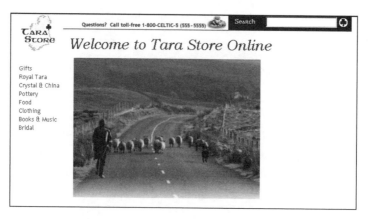

Figure 8-1   Displaying data with the DataReader object

Building Search Queries Using SQL

You can modify the SQL commands to retrieve a select group of records. In the previous exercise, you evaluated a single SQL statement within a single SELECT statement. You can add SQL conditions to retrieve a subset of records from the database. The SQL statement is the **search condition**, which identifies the criterion that is used to filter the records. A search condition evaluates to either true or false. The search condition uses the WHERE keyword to identify the search condition.

The search condition is also referred to as the WHERE condition in SQL. The discussion in this section is focused on building a search condition. You can learn more about how to build SQL statements in *A Guide to SQL, Fifth Edition* by Pratt (© 2000, Course Technology).

The SQL statement `"WHERE username='John'"` would evaluate to true or false. For records in which the username is John, the record is returned in the data set. In Access and SQL, you can create more complex queries using multiple search conditions within the same statement. When the keyword "AND" is used to separate conditions, both search conditions must be resolved to true. If the keyword "OR" is used to separate conditions, only one of the search conditions needs to be resolved to true.

The search condition consists of an expression, followed by a comparison operator, and another expression. An expression can be simple, such as the name of a field, or it can be a string, a number, or a value passed from a form. If the expression is a string, the string must be enclosed within quotation marks. Strings are case sensitive when used as expressions. So, "product" and "PRODUCTS" are not evaluated as equal expressions. An expression that contains a date must append the pound sign (#) before and after the date. The keyword NULL can be used to search for empty fields. An empty string is not the same as a NULL field, because NULL fields do not contain any data. The word NULL is used as the expression. A comparison operator is used to evaluate the expression. Valid comparison operators include +, <, >, <>, IS, and ISNOT. The syntax to create search criteria in a SQL statement is as follows:

```
WHERE [expression1][comparisonoperator][expression2]
```

You can use a static value as the comparative expression or use a variable that contains a value. If the value is a string, single quotes are used around the value. If the value passed is a number, you do not need the single quotes. The following are sample valid expressions that use multiple search criteria and data types. (*Note:* While strings use quotes, the dates use pound signs, and the numbers, variables, and constants do not use quotes.)

```
WHERE user='katie' AND pwd='pass'
WHERE state='IL' OR state='IN' AND people>=10000
WHERE lastVisit>#11/12/2003# OR member='new'
WHERE member='staff' AND salary>35000
WHERE birth=IS NULL OR email=IS NULL
```

By using the keywords "AND" and "OR", you can combine multiple search criteria within the same SQL statement. For example, you can create a query that lists the product names of any product where the number of items is less than five. This information could be provided to the person in charge of ordering new supplies. However, you don't need to order discontinued products. By using combination queries, you can combine all of these search criteria into one SQL statement.

The ORDER BY statement allows you to sort the results based on one or more columns. You can separate multiple sort columns with a comma. When there are multiple sort columns, the rows will be sorted by the first sort column, then the second, and so forth. You can specify the sort order as ascending with ASC or descending with DESC. The following sample SQL statement displays a list of category names, where the CategoryName is Jewelry or the CategoryID is greater than three. The rows returned are sorted by the CategoryName in ascending order.

```
SELECT CategoryName, CategoryID, CatImage, ¬
       Thumbnail, Description
FROM Categories
WHERE (CategoryName='Jewelry') OR (CategoryID>3)
ORDER BY CategoryName ASC;
```

You can use the following SQL statements to insert, update, and delete records.

- INSERT to add a new record
- DELETE to delete one or more rows of data
- UPDATE to modify one or more rows of data

In SQL, you must create an INSERT query in order to create a new record. Insert queries can only be performed on one table at a time, and only one record at a time can be inserted. Furthermore you must specify a value for every field. If no value is available, you can substitute the word "NULL" for the value. You must enter strings using quotation marks. If you enter the fields without specifying the field names, you must enter them in the order that the fields appear in the database structure. If you have used an autonumber field in Access or an identity field in SQL Server, you can't enter a value in that field. The database automatically inserts a value when the record is added. The syntax for inserting a new record into a table that has only five fields using SQL is as follows. The values are entered sequentially in the table. In the example below the string 'chair' is placed in the first column and 153.00 is placed in the second column.

```
INSERT INTO Products
VALUES ('chair',153.00,#12/1/2000#,NULL,'furniture')
```

You can specify the field names in parentheses after the table if you plan to enter values for only a subset of fields. The following sample code demonstrates how to enter only the product name and price. It is better to specify the field names because if the order of the columns is changed, then the SQL query will have to be changed.

```
INSERT INTO Products(name, price, data, number)
VALUES('chair',153.00,#12/1/2000#,NULL)
```

The SQL statement uses the UPDATE command instead of the SELECT or INSERT commands to modify a record. The UPDATE command needs to know which table to update as well as which fields and values. The keyword SET is used to assign the values to the field names. The properties of the Command object are set, and the execute method is called to perform the update. If you do not specify a search condition using the WHERE clause, the value is updated for all records in the database.

```
SQL = "UPDATE Products SET " & _
" ProductName='Claddagh Ring'," & _
" UnitCost='25.45' WHERE ProductID=353"
```

To use the SQL statement with variables, you can replace the static values with variables that contain values, as shown in the sample below. (*Note*: It is important to make sure the single quotation marks are included for strings, and the pound sign for dates. You will have to concatenate the variable between the set of strings such as SQL = "FieldName='" & VariableName & "'," .)

```
SQL = "UPDATE Products SET " & _
" ProductName='" & MyProduct & "'," & _
" UnitCost=" & MyCost & _
" WHERE ProductID=" & MyProductID
```

The SQL DELETE command is used to delete records within the database. When you use the DELETE command, you must specify which records to delete and the name of the table. If you do not specify a specific record or set of records using the WHERE clause, the entire set of records is deleted. The sample below passes a value to the SQL DELETE command so that only a single record is deleted.

```
SQL = "DELETE FROM Products " & _
" WHERE ProductID=" & MyProductID
```

In Chapter 6, you learned how to create SQL queries and stored procedures with Visual Studio .NET. **Stored procedures** are SQL programming statements that can be reused. They can contain SQL commands and can be as simple as a select statement. You can also pass values as parameters to the stored procedures. Stored procedures are queries that reside on the database server, and because they are compiled by database server they are more efficient. Once you create the stored procedure, you can call it from an ASP.NET page and cause it to operate. Popular databases such as Oracle and Microsoft SQL Server support stored procedures. In Microsoft Access, a stored procedure is called a **parameter query**. For example, you can develop a SQL statement that selects all records where the state field contains a value that matches a variable called strState. This SQL statement can be saved as a stored procedure and executed at a later time. When the stored procedure is called, you can then pass the value of the state, such as "IL," to the state variable strState. Not all databases support the concept of stored procedures.

Using the DataReader Object with a SQL Server Database

In the following sample, the connection string Data Source property identifies the name of the SQL Server. The Initial Catalog identifies the name of the database. The names of the Connection, Command, and DataReader objects are SqlConnection, SqlCommand, and SqlDataReader. The steps required to retrieve the data using the DataReader object are the same for both the OleDb and SqlClient databases. Below is the code from the exercise above, rewritten to support a SQL Server database using the SqlDataReader object.

```
Dim CS As String = "Data Source=localhost;Initial ¬
  Catalog=TaraStoreSQL;User Id=sa;password=;"
Dim objCN As New SqlClient.SqlConnection(CS)
objCN.Open()
Dim mySQL As String = ¬
  "SELECT CategoryName FROM Categories"
Dim objCM As New SqlClient.SqlCommand(mySQL, objCN)
Dim objDR As SqlClient.SqlDataReader
objDR = objCM.ExecuteReader()
Dim MyCat As String
While objDR.Read()
MyCat = MyCat + (objDR("CategoryName") & "<br />")
End While
objDR.Close()
objCN.Close()
lblCat.Text = MyCat
```

Localhost is the keyword used to represent the local instance of server. Therefore, the keyword localhost will only work if the SQL Server is on the same physical computer as the Web server. You can also specify the fully qualified name or IP address of the SQL Server.

Upsizing an Access Database to SQL Server

Sometimes you might be hired to work on a Web site that uses an existing database created in Access. Access does not provide the same level of robustness and security as a SQL Server database. You can connect many users simultaneously with SQL Server, but not with Access. Although Access can in theory support up to 20 simultaneous connections to an Access database via the Web, in practice this is not usually the case. You will have more control over security with a SQL Server database. Because Access is file based, the data can be downloaded by merely typing the URL of the database in the browser. The Internet guest account on the Web server needs to have read permission to the database in order to retrieve the data and display the data in the Web page. Because the file has read permission, the end user can download the Access database. (Some users use the password feature within Access to protect the database. Then, when the user downloads the file, they need to enter an additional password to retrieve the data.) With SQL Server, the database is stored by SQL Server and is not downloadable from the browser. Therefore, you can use SQL Server for secure transactions, such as shopping carts.

You can use the Upsizing Wizard to upgrade an Access database to SQL Server. The Upsizing Wizard is available in Access 97, Access 2000, and Access XP. After you have upsized the database, Access provides a report that contains information about the new database. In the exercise below, you will upsize an Access database to SQL Server.

1. Start **Microsoft Access**. (On most computers you click **Start**, point to **Programs**, then click **Microsoft Access**.)

2. Click **File** on the menu bar, then click **Open**. In the Open dialog box, navigate to the **Chapter08Data** folder, select the file **TaraStore.mdb**, and then click **Open**.

3. Click **Tools** on the menu bar, point to **Database Utilities**, then click **Upsizing Wizard**.

4. Verify that the radio button labeled Create new database is selected, and then click **Next**.

5. In the drop-down list box, select **(local)\NetSDK** for the name of the SQL Server database. (*Note:* You can also use the key phrases (local), localhost, or the name of your SQL Server to identify the database server.)

6. Choose the authentication method for your SQL Server that you used in Chapters 5 and 6.

   a. If you use SQL Server authentication, in the Login ID text box type **sa** and leave the Password text box blank. (*Note:* You must use an account with CREATE DATABASE privileges.)

   b. If you use Windows authentication, check the **Use Trusted Connection** check box.

7. In the last text box, type **Ch8TaraStoreSQL** as the name of the new SQL Server database, and then click **Next**.

8. In the Upsizing Wizard dialog box, click the **>>** button to select all the tables in the database to be exported to SQL Server. Click the **Next** button to advance to the next step. The next window allows you to modify how the tables are exported. Do not make any changes to this window. Click the **Next** button to advance to the next step.

9. In the next window, select the radio button labeled **No application changes**. Click the **Next** button to advance to the next step.

10. Click the **Finish** button. The Upsizing Wizard upsizes the database, and then produces a report, which contains information about the tables and objects upsized to SQL Server. (*Note:* You can print or export the report to another application.)

11. Close the Upsizing Wizard Report window by clicking the **Close Window** button.

12. Close the database and Microsoft Access.

Using the DataReader Object to Display Data

Using the upsized database, you will create a page to display the categories list using the SqlClient DataReader object. In the exercise below, you will create a page to display the category list using the DataReader object.

1. Open the **Chapter8** solution in Visual Studio .NET. (*Note:* Your browser must always be online when you are opening a solution. You do not have to be connected to the Internet, but the browser must be configured to be online.)

2. Right-click **Data Connections** in the Server Explorer window, and then click **Add Connection**.

3. In the Connection tab of the Data Link Properties dialog box, type **(local)\NetSDK** in the server name text box. If your application uses SQL Server authentication, select the **Use a specific user name and password** radio button, type **sa** in the User name text box, and then click the **Blank Password** check box to select it. If your SQL Server uses Windows authentication check the **Use Windows NT Integrated security** radio button.

4. In the drop-down list box select the database named **Ch8TaraStoreSQL**, and then click the **OK** button.

5. In the Server Explorer window, expand the Ch8TaraStoreSQL data connection by clicking the **plus sign** (+).

6. Right-click **Chapter8** in the Solution Explorer window, point to **Add**, then click **Add Existing Item**. Navigate to your Chapter08Data folder, select the file **DataReaderSQL.aspx**, and then click **Open** to import the file into your project. Click **Yes** to create the class file for the page.

8

7. Double-click **DataReaderSQL.aspx** in the Solution Explorer window to open the page. Click **(MachineName)\NetSDK.Ch8TaraStoreSQL.dbo** under Data Connections in the Server Explorer window and drag it to the Web page. A SQL Connection object named SqlConnection1 is added to the page.

8. Double-click on the page to open the code behind the page, which is named **DataReaderSQL.aspx.vb**.

9. Within the Page_Load procedure, add the code below to create the objects, and retrieve the data using the DataReader object.

```
SqlConnection1.Open()
Dim mySQL As String = ¬
  "SELECT CategoryName FROM Categories"
Dim objCM As New ¬
  SqlClient.SqlCommand(mySQL, SqlConnection1)
Dim objDR As SqlClient.SqlDataReader
objDR = objCM.ExecuteReader()
Dim MyCat As String
While objDR.Read()
  MyCat = MyCat + (objDR("CategoryName") & "<br />")
End While
objDR.Close()
SqlConnection1.Close()
lblCat.Text = MyCat
```

10. Click the **Save All** button. Click **Build** on the menu bar, then click **Build Solution**. Click the **DataReaderSQL.aspx** tab to select the Web page.

11. Right-click on the page, and then click **View in Browser**. The page should look the same as the page shown in Figure 8-1.

12. Close any open pages.

Using the DataReader Object with Stored Procedures

You can use the DataReader object in combination with the Command object in order to work with stored procedures. Stored procedures are useful for running queries in which input and output parameters are required. When you use a stored procedure, the **CommandType procedure** is set to CommandType.StoredProcedure to indicate that the SQL command is a stored procedure and not a SQL query. When the command is configured, you must specify the stored procedure and the CommandType, as shown in the sample code below.

```
Dim objCM As SqlClient.SqlCommand
objCM = New ¬
SqlClient.SqlCommand("ProductCategoryList", objCN)
objCM.CommandType = CommandType.StoredProcedure
```

In this example, you create a stored procedure to display all of the product categories. The category list is bound to a Hyperlink control. When the user clicks the link, the

DataReaderProducts page opens. The CategoryID field is passed with the hyperlink as a query string to the DataReaderProducts page. Then, you create a stored procedure that displays only the products of the category that was clicked. In this first section, you create the stored procedure to retrieve the categories, retrieve them with the DataReader object, and display them with the DataList object and ASP.NET Hyperlink controls.

1. Open the **Chapter8** project if it is not already open.

2. In the Server Explorer window, under the MACHINENAME\ NetSDK.Ch8TaraStoreSQL.dbo data connection, right-click **Stored Procedures**, and then click **New Stored Procedure**. The stored procedure document opens with the default text for creating the stored procedure.

3. To delete the default text, click **Edit** on the menu bar, then click **Select All**. Click **Edit** on the menu bar again, then click **Delete**.

4. Type the code below, which creates a stored procedure named **ProductCategoryList**. When this stored procedure is run, it returns a list of the product categories.

```
CREATE PROCEDURE dbo.ProductCategoryList
    AS
SELECT CategoryID, CategoryName
    FROM Categories
    ORDER BY CategoryName ASC
RETURN
```

5. Click the **Save All** button. Close the ProductCategoryList stored procedure window.

6. Right-click **Chapter8** in the Solution Explorer window, point to **Add**, then click **Add Existing Item**. Navigate to your **Chapter08**Data folder and select the file **DataReaderStoredProc.aspx**. Click **Open** to import the file into your project. Click **Yes** to create the class file.

7. Double-click **DataReaderStoredProc.aspx** in the Solution Explorer window to open the page.

8. Click **(MachineName)\NetSDK.Ch8TaraStoreSQL.dbo** under Data Connections in the Server Explorer window and drag it to the Web page. A SQL Connection object named SqlConnection1 is added to the page.

9. Double-click on the page to open the code behind the page, which is named **DataReaderStoredProc.aspx.vb**.

10. Within the Page_Load procedure, add the code below to open the connection. (*Note:* You can also create the connection string manually.)

```
SqlConnection1.Open()
```

11. Below this add the following code to create the Command object. When you create the new command, instead of passing a SQL command or the name of the table, pass the name of the stored procedure, ProductCategoryList. Then,

you must specify the CommandType as StoredProcedure. (*Note*: By default the CommandType is Text, which means that you are passing a SQL command. CommandType Table means that you are passing the table name as the command.)

```
Dim objCM As SqlClient.SqlCommand
objCM = New SqlClient.SqlCommand "ProductCategoryList", ¬
SqlConnection1)
objCM.CommandType = CommandType.StoredProcedure
```

12. Below this add the following code to create the DataReader object named **result**. Use the Command object with the DataReader to retrieve the data. Assign the DataReader object to the DataSource DataList control named MyList and bind the data to the control.

```
Dim result As SqlClient.SqlDataReader
result = ¬
objCM.ExecuteReader(CommandBehavior.CloseConnection)
MyList.DataSource = result
MyList.DataBind()
```

13. Click the **Save All** button. Click **Build** on the menu bar, then click **Build Solution**.

14. Click the **DataReaderStoredProc.aspx** tab to view the Web page. Right-click on the page, and then click **View in Browser**. Your page should look like the one in Figure 8-2.

15. Close any open pages.

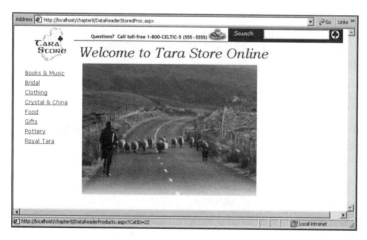

Figure 8-2 Using stored procedures to display data with the DataReader object

Now you must create the second page to retrieve the CategoryID field from the query string of the parameter named CatID. The CategoryID field is the input parameter for the second procedure, named ProductsByCategory. This procedure returns the fields only for the products that belong to that category. In the example below, you create the second procedure, and the page that displays the product list. The page contains a DataList control, similar to the controls that you added in a previous chapter. The control displays a two-column list of product images, product names, and price.

1. Open the **Chapter8** project if it is not already open.

2. In the Server Explorer window, expand the **Ch8TaraStoreSQL** data connection by clicking the **plus sign** (+). Right-click **Stored Procedures**, and then click **New Stored Procedure**.

3. Click **Edit** on the menu bar, and then click **Select All**. Then, click **Edit** on the menu bar again, and click **Delete**.

4. Type the code below to create a stored procedure named **ProductsByCategory**. This returns a list of the products. The @CategoryID input parameter has a datatype of int. (*Note*: In the product table, the column name for the product category is SubSubCategoryID. In real shopping carts, you may have many layers of categories and subcategories or products.)

```
CREATE PROCEDURE dbo.ProductsByCategory
   @CategoryID int
AS
SELECT ProductID, ModelName, UnitCost, Thumbnail
    FROM Products
    WHERE SubSubCategoryID = @CategoryID
    ORDER BY ModelName
RETURN
```

5. Click the **Save All** button. Close the ProductsByCategory stored procedure window.

6. Right-click **Chapter8** in the Solution Explorer window, point to **Add**, then click **Add Existing Item**. Navigate to your **Chapter08Data** folder and select the file **DataReaderProducts.aspx**. Click **Open** to import the file into your project. Click **Yes** to create the class file for the page.

7. Double-click **DataReaderProducts.aspx** in the Solution Explorer window to open the page.

8. Click the **(MachineName)\NetSDK.Ch8TaraStoreSQL.dbo** under Data Connections in the Server Explorer window and drag it to the Web page. A SQL Connection object named SqlConnection1 is added to the page.

9. Double-click on the page to open the code behind the page, which is named DataReaderProducts.aspx.vb.

10. Within the Page_Load procedure, add the code below. This retrieves the category list for the category menu. Notice that the connection is explicitly closed. If you plan to use multiple queries in the same page, you should close the objects explicitly before reopening them.

8

```
SqlConnection1.Open()
Dim objCM As SqlClient.SqlCommand
objCM = New SqlClient.SqlCommand("ProductCategoryList", ¬
  SqlConnection1)
objCM.CommandType = CommandType.StoredProcedure
Dim result As SqlClient.SqlDataReader
result = objCM.ExecuteReader()
MyList.DataSource = result
MyList.DataBind()
result.Close()
SqlConnection1.Close()
```

11. Below this add the following code to retrieve the Category ID from the querystring collection using Request.Params and store it in a variable named CatID. CInt converts the string to an integer.

```
Dim CatID As Integer = CInt(Request.Params("CatID"))
```

12. Below this add the following code to reopen the connection and create a second command object named **objCM2**. A different variable name is provided to differentiate between the two objects.

```
SqlConnection1.Open()
Dim objCM2 As SqlClient.SqlCommand
objCM2 = New SqlClient.SqlCommand("ProductsByCategory", ¬
  SqlConnection1)
objCM2.CommandType = CommandType.StoredProcedure
```

13. Below this add the following code to create a Parameter object named paramCatID. The Parameter object is used to pass the parameter to the stored procedure. The parameter datatype is identified as int, with a length of four bytes. The CatID variable is assigned to the paramCatID parameter, and the parameter is added to the Parameter collection of the Command object. (*Note:* You can add multiple parameters to the Parameters collection of the Command object by calling the add method.)

```
Dim paramCatID As SqlClient.SqlParameter
paramCatID = New ¬
SqlClient.SqlParameter("@CategoryID", SqlDbType.Int, 4)
paramCatID.Value = CatID
objCM2.Parameters.Add(paramCatID)
```

14. Below this add the following code to retrieve the product list for the specific category using the DataReader and Command objects. The data from the DataReader is bound to an ASP.NET DataList control named MyProdList.

```
Dim result2 As SqlClient.SqlDataReader
result2 = ¬
objCM2.ExecuteReader(CommandBehavior.CloseConnection)
MyProdList.DataSource = result2
MyProdList.DataBind()
result2.Close()
SqlConnection1.Close()
```

15. Click the **Save All** button. Click **Build** on the menu bar, then click **Build Solution**.

16. Click the **DataReaderProducts.aspx** tab to view the Web page. Right-click on the page, and then click **View in Browser**. Click the **Pottery** hyperlink. Your page should look like the one in Figure 8-3.

17. Close any open pages.

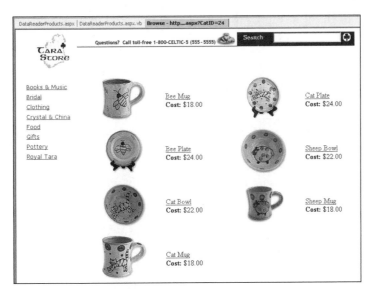

Figure 8-3   Using a stored procedure to retrieve data with the DataReader object

The DataAdapter, DataSet, and DataView Objects

Usually, the DataAdapter, DataSet, and DataView objects are used together to retrieve data from the database. The **fill method** of the DataAdapter object is used to get the data from the database and populate the DataSet object. The DataView object is a collection of data from the DataSet. The default DataView for the DataSet for a specific table is the collection of all the records in the table. There can be many DataViews retrieved from a DataSet. The ASP.NET Data controls, for example the DataGrid control, are bound to the DataView object. Visual Studio .NET contains visual controls to create the DataAdapter, DataSet, and DataView objects. The list below describes one method for inserting a DataAdapter object, creating the DataSet and DataView objects, then displaying the data.

1. Create the WebForm in Visual Studio .NET.

2. Add a DataAdapter from the Data tab in the Toolbox.

3. Select your database connection in the DataAdapter Wizard.

4. Use the Query Builder to build a SQL statement.

5. Add a DataSet object from the Data tab in the Toolbox.

6. Use Generate DataSet Methods from the Data menu. You can preview your data before you insert the data into the Web page.

7. Create a DataView object.

8. Assign a table to the DataView object.

9. Assign the DataSource property of an ASP.NET Data control such as the DataGrid to the DataView object.

10. In the code behind the Web page, call the fill method of the DataAdapter.

11. Bind the controls to the data source.

12. Save and build the solution, and view the Web page in a browser.

The DataAdapter is used to populate the DataSet. The DataSet can consist of multiple related tables. When you create the DataAdapter using the DataAdapter Wizard, you are creating a SQL command and identifying the Connection object. Then, you must manually identify the DataSet object to be filled with data when the fill method is called. After you fill the DataSet, you use a DataView to identify which subset of the DataSet you want to access. If there is only one table involved, then you can simply use the default DataView object, or you can identify the table or SQL statement to use to retrieve a table for the DataView. The following code sample shows how you can fill the DataSet with data using the fill method of the DataAdapter. Then, you can create a DataView from the DataSet, which is a subset of one of the tables within the DataSet. In this example, the default DataView contains all of the rows from the Categories table. Then, the DataGrid control is bound to the DataView object using the DataBind method of the DataGrid control.

```
SQL Data Adapter1.Fill(MyDS)
Dim MyDV As DataView = New DataView(DS, "Categories")
MyDG.DataSource = MyDV
MyDG.DataBind()
```

You can refer to the DataTable in the DataView by the table name or by its index position within the Tables collection. The DataTables collection is a series of tables within the DataSet. When you create the DataView, you are referring to one of the tables within the Tables collection. The DefaultView returns all of the data within the DataTable. But you must identify which table to retrieve. The index position is the number that represents that DataTable within the Tables collection. The sample code below shows how to retrieve all of the data within the first table of the Tables Collection from the DS11 DataSet object. The DataView is then bound to the MyDG DataGrid control.

```
Dim objDV As New DataView()
objDV = DS11.Tables(0).DefaultView
MyDG.DataSource = objDV
MyDG.DataBind()
```

The DataAdapter also has other methods and properties. The **SelectCommand method** allows you to identify the command used to retrieve the records. When the fill method is called, the DataAdapter uses the SQL command identified by the SelectCommand property, to determine which records to retrieve. In the sample below, the DataAdapter is used to fill a dataset using the categories DataTable object.

```
Dim CN As New SqlConnection(CS)
Dim MySQL As String = "Select * From Categories"
MyDS = New DataSet()
MyDA = New SQL Data Adapter(MySQL, CN)
MyDA.Fill(MyDS, "Categories")
```

The DataAdapter contains a Command Builder method to automatically generate commands to insert, modify, and delete data. The database tables must have primary keys defined in order to use the Command Builder. Although you can write the code to access the Command Builder manually, it is much simpler to use the DataAdapter Wizard to activate the Command Builder. The Command Builder creates the SelectCommand, InsertCommand, and DeleteCommand.

Using the DataView to Retrieve Data from a Database

Once you create the DataAdapter object and fill the DataSet object, you define a DataView which will be bound to your Data control. In the following exercise you use Visual Studio .NET to create a DataAdapter, add a DataSet object, generate the DataSet methods, and create a DataView. You will bind the DataView object to an ASP.NET Data control to display the data.

1. Open the **Chapter8** project in Visual Studio .NET.

2. Right-click **Chapter8** in the Solution Explorer window, point to **Add**, then click **Add Existing Item**. Navigate to your Chapter08Data folder and select the file **DataSetProducts.aspx**. Click **Open** to import the files into your project. Click **Yes** to create the class file. Double-click the **DataSetProducts.aspx** page icon in the Server Explorer window.

3. Open the Toolbox if it is not already open, click the **Data** tab, then drag and drop the **SqlDataAdapter** from the Data tab to Web page. The DataAdapter Configuration Wizard opens. Click the **Next** button.

4. In the drop-down list, select the connection to your Ch8TaraStoreSQL database. (*Note*: The connection should be the *MachineName*.Ch8TaraStoreSQL.dbo, where MachineName is the name of your SQL Server.) Click the **Next** button.

5. In the Query Type window, you can design your own query with a SQL Builder, create a new stored procedure, or use an existing stored procedure. Leave the default radio button labeled **Use SQL statements** selected and click the **Next** button.

6. Click the **Query Builder** button to open the Query Builder. Select the **Products** table from the Add Table window, click **Add**, and then click the **Close** button.

8

7. In the Field List box, select the **ProductID**, **SubSubCategoryID**, **ModelNumber**, **ModelName**, **ProductImage**, **UnitCost**, and **Thumbnail** fields. Click the **OK** button. Click the **Next** button. The SQL SELECT, INSERT, UPDATE, and DELETE statements are generated for you, along with table mappings and a command object. The table mappings contain information about the column names within each table. Click the **Finish** button. The DataAdapter and DataConnection objects are added to the page.

8. Now you need to create a DataSet object. Click **Data** on the menu bar, and then click **Generate Dataset**. In the Generate Dataset window, select the radio button labeled **New**. In the text box, type **MyDSAllProducts**. The Products table has already been selected. Click **OK**.

9. Select the DataSet icon in the Design view. Click **Data** on the menu bar, then click **Preview Data**. Click the **Fill Dataset** button. Your data should be displayed in the window. Click the **Close** button.

10. Drag and drop the **DataView** control from the **Data** tab in the Toolbox to the Web page.

11. You need to assign a table to the DataView. With the **DataView** selected, go to the Properties window, and click the drop-down **list arrow** for the Table property. Click the **plus sign** next to MyDSAllProducts1, and then click **Products**.

12. You need to assign a data source to the DataGrid object. Select the **DataGrid** object. In the Properties window, set the DataSource property to **DataView1**. (*Note*: This may already be selected for you.)

13. Click the **DataSetProducts.aspx** tab, then double-click on the page to open the code behind the page, which is named **DataSetProducts.aspx.vb**.

14. Within the Page_Load procedure, add the code below. This code calls the fill method of the DataAdapter to add the data to the DataSet. You must pass the name of the DataSet, MyDSAllProducts1, as a parameter to the DataAdapter. You then have to bind the controls to the Data Source property using the bind method of the Data control or the page. In this example, the bind method of the Page object is used.

```
SQLDataAdapter1.Fill(MyDSAllProducts1)
Page.DataBind()
```

15. Click the **Save All** button. Click **Build** on the menu bar, then click **Build Solution**.

16. Click the **DataSetProducts.aspx** tab to return to the Web page. Right-click on the page, and then click **View in Browser**. Your page should look like the one in Figure 8-4.

17. Close any open pages.

ProductID	SubSubCategoryID	ModelNumber	ModelName	UnitCost	Thumbnail
512	21	503-316-00-32	Abbey Clock by Waterford	99	512.jpg
514	21	537-864-00-62	Westminster Clock by Waterford	198	514.gif
517	21	050-010-55-00	Butterfly by Waterford	50	517.gif
521	21	114-886	Colleen Bell by Waterford	69	521.gif
527	23	tyropne AC-010	Tyrone-Bell-Crystal Makeup Bell - Small	40	527.jpg
528	21	756-224-00-09	Letter Opener by Waterford	69	528.gif
529	21	978-979-53-00	Waterford Crystal Busines Card Holder	59	529.gif
532	21	751-433-95-00	Round Ring Holder by Waterford Crystal	49	532.gif
533	21	WC-333-357 52-00	Heart-shaped Ring Holder by Waterford	49	533.gif
534	23	103543	Waterford Crystal Female Golfer	159	534.gif
535	23	756-224-00-14	Makeup Brush by Waterford	59	535.gif
537	23	387-463-55-00	Waterford Shamrock Paperweight	99	537.gif
542	23	033-769-59-00	Waterford Crystal Male Golfer Paperweight	159	542.gif
544	23	1199-685-100	Waterford Golf Ball Paperweight	79	544.gif

Figure 8-4   Retrieving data with the DataSet and DataView objects

CUSTOMIZING THE DATAGRID CONTROL

The DataGrid control allows you to customize the appearance of the control and the data contained within the columns. In the previous chapter you learned how to modify the appearance of the DataGrid using the Properties window. You learned that you can display bound columns that contain data that is bound to a column in the database. You can display the data or use the data in an expression, such as the source of an image tag. You can also display unbound columns. Unbound columns often contain buttons and other form fields. Some additional features that the DataGrid includes are sorting and filtering. The DataGrid filter allows you to temporarily select a subset of records from the DataGrid. The filter does not remove the data from the database, but only removes the records from the Web page. When the filter is removed, the records are redisplayed within the Web page.

Paging and Sorting Data with the DataGrid Control

Sorting can be performed in the code behind the page, or by using the Visual Studio .NET tools. The default sorting creates a Link Button control for the column name, at the top of the column. When the user clicks the Link Button control, the DataGrid is sorted by that column. The DataGrid does not actually sort the rows. Instead, it raises a **SortCommand event**, which causes the data to be rebound to the DataSource. You must add the code to perform the sorting when the event occurs. The sort expression is passed as an argument, which is represented as e.SortExpression. You have to get the value that is selected as the sort key, and then rebind the DataGrid to the DataView. You can also create your own custom sorting rules, whereby you determine which bound or unbound template columns are sorted. If you create your own custom sorting, you can use an image or an image button for the sort link at the top of the column headings.

Paging is turned off by default. When paging is turned on, you can display a subset of records on a page. A navigation bar at the bottom of the page allows you to page through the data across Web pages. You can format the navigation bar with your own custom text. You can modify the navigation bar to include the number of pages, with links to each page. This allows the visitor to jump to a specific group of records. The default number of records displayed is 10. The paging property of the DataGrid also raises a **PageIndexChanged event** when the user clicks the Link button. Therefore, you also have to add the code to handle the event. The event handler retrieves the NewPageIndex property, which is the page the user wants to browse to. This property is retrieved when the user clicks the link button. Then, you can set the CurrentPageIndex property to the NewPageIndex and rebind the data to the DataGrid control.

In this exercise, you learn how to turn paging on. You will modify the DataGrid control from the previous exercise to support sorting.

1. Open the **Chapter8** project in Visual Studio .NET if necessary.

2. Open the **DataSetProducts.aspx** Web page, if it is not already open.

3. Click the **DataGrid** control and go to the Properties window and make the changes listed below:

   a. Change the Font name to **Verdana**, the size to **X-Small**, and the ForeColor to **#004040**.

   b. Change the AllowSorting property to **True**.

   c. Change the AllowPaging property to **True**.

   d. Click the **plus sign** next to the PagerStyle property. Change the ForeColor to **Red**.

   e. In the NextPageText property replace &gt, with **Next**. Change the PrevPageText property from &lt, to **Previous**. (*Note*: Sometimes the content cannot be displayed on one page. &gt and < display < and > when there are additional pages used to display data.)

   f. Change the Position property to **TopAndBottom**.

4. Double-click on the page to view the code behind the page. Add the code below after the Page_Load event handler, which handles the SortCommand event.

```
Private Sub MyDG_SortCommand(ByVal source As Object, ¬
    ByVal e As ¬
System.Web.UI.WebControls.DataGridSortCommandEventArgs) ¬
    Handles MyDG.SortCommand
```

```
DataView1.Sort = e.SortExpression
MyDG.DataBind()
End Sub
```

5. After the SortCommand event handler, add the code below, which handles the PageIndexChanged event.

```
Private Sub MyDG_PageIndexChanged(ByVal ¬
source As Object, ByVal e As ¬
System.Web.UI.WebControls.DataGridPageChangedEventArgs) ¬
Handles MyDG.PageIndexChanged
MyDG.CurrentPageIndex = e.NewPageIndex
MyDG.DataBind()
End Sub
```

6. Click the **DataSetProducts.aspx** tab top return to the Web page. Right-click the **DataGrid** and select **Property Builder**. Click the **Show footer** check box in the General tab.

7. Select the **Columns** tab and set the following properties.

   a. Deselect the **Create columns automatically at run time** check box.

   b. Select each of the following fields in turn, and click the **>** button to move the fields into the Selected columns text box: **ProductID**, **SubSubCategoryID**, **ModelName**, **UnitCost**, and **Thumbnail**.

   c. Select the **ProductID** field in the Selected columns box. Change the Header text property to **ID**. Change the SubSubCategoryID Header text property to **Category**. Change the ModelName Header text to **Product Name**.

   d. Change the UnitCost Header text to **Price**. In the Data formatting expression text box enter {0:C} to format the field as currency.

   e. Change the thumbnail header text to **Image**. Move the thumbnail up to the top field using the up arrow button.

8. Click the **Format** tab and set the following properties.

   a. Click **Header** inside the Objects text box. Change the ForeColor property of the header to **Navy** and the BackColor to **Silver**.

   b. Click **Footer** inside the Objects text box. Change the BackColor property to **Silver**.

9. In the **Format** tab, center the image column.

   a. Click the **plus sign** next to Columns.

   b. Click the **plus sign** next to the Columns[0]-Image text and select **Header**. Change the Horizontal alignment drop-down list to **Center**.

   c. Select **Items** under Columns[0]-Image in the Object text box, and in the Horizontal alignment drop-down list, select **Center**.

8

10. Click the **Columns** tab. Click **Image** in the Selected Items tab. Click the **Convert this column into a Template Column** hyperlink at the bottom of the dialog box. Click the **OK** button.

11. Click the **HTML** tab to edit the image template column in the HTML code. The code currently displays the image name in the ItemTemplate for the Image column; delete the code between the ItemTemplate tags for the Image column. Add the code below, which displays the image in the column.

```
<a href= ¬
'images/<%# Container.DataItem("ProductImage")%>'>
  <img src= ¬
'images/<%# Container.DataItem("Thumbnail") %>'
  hspace="2" border="0">
</a>
```

12. Click the **Save All** button. Click **Build** on the menu bar, then click **Build Solution**.

13. Click the **Design** tab. Right-click on the page, and then click **View in Browser**. Click the **Product Name** link button. Your page should look like the one in Figure 8-5. (*Note*: If you click on the image, you will link to the image file.)

14. Click the **Abbey Clock** image. The clock image should appear in the browser.

15. Click the **Next** hyperlink to refresh the page with additional products.

16. Close any open pages.

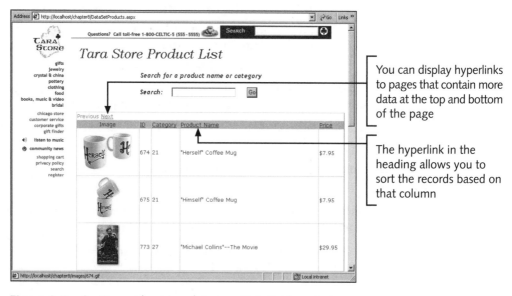

Figure 8-5 Sorting and paging data in a DataGrid control

Filtering Data with the DataGrid Control

Filtering can be performed in the code behind the page or by using the Visual Studio .NET tools. You have to set the **RowFilter property** of the DataView object to the SQL command that queries the DataView to retrieve the records. In this exercise, you modify the code from the previous exercise to support filtering. You retrieve the Category ID from a form field named txtSearch, which is used to filter the data.

1. Open the **Chapter8** project in Visual Studio .NET if necessary.

2. Open the **DataSetProducts.aspx** Web page.

3. Double-click on the page to open the code behind the page. Above the Page_Load event handler, add the below code to create a new variable named **MySearch**, which is used to store the search phrase.

```
Dim MySearch As String
```

4. Add the code below, which searches for any strings that match what the user entered. It compares the string to the ModelName field. If this is the first time the visitor has been at the site, the text box displays Waterford by default. Place this code on the first line below the comment line within the Page_Load event handler.

```
If Page.IsPostBack Then
MySearch = "ModelName LIKE '*" & txtSearch.Text & "*'"
Else
txtSearch.Text = "Waterford"
End If
```

5. Return to the web page. Click the **Design** tab, then double-click the **Go** button to open the btnGo click event handler. Enter the following code within the event handler. This code resets the RowFilter property for the DataView object to the value that was entered in the text box. This value is represented by the MySearch variable. Then, it rebinds the DataView to the DataGrid control.

```
DataView1.RowFilter = MySearch
MyDG.DataBind( )
```

6. Click the **Save All** button. Click **Build** on the menu bar, then click **Build Solution**.

7. Click the **DataSetProducts.aspx** tab to view the Web page. Right-click on the page, and then click **View in Browser**. Waterford is selected by default. Type **Cat** in the search text box, and then click **Go**. Your page should look like the one in Figure 8-6.

8. Close any open pages.

Figure 8-6   Building a search tool using Visual Studio .NET

INSERTING, MODIFYING, AND DELETING RECORDS

To maintain a database you must be able to create new records, modify existing records, and delete records. You can accomplish this by using SQL commands or by using the methods built into the Data controls. You can use the Command Builder method built into the DataGrid, DataList, and Repeater controls to help you build methods and procedures to maintain the database.

Using the DataGrid Control to Maintain a Database

The DataGrid control allows you to bind data to the columns. You can use the DataGrid control to insert, modify, and delete data. In previous exercises you learned that the DataGrid control allows you to create a bound column. You learned that all columns support style properties as listed below.

- *AlternatingItemStyle*—Identifies the style for alternating rows

- *EditItemStyle*—Identifies the style for a row being edited

- *FooterStyle*—Identifies the style for the footer row

- *HeaderStyle*—Identifies the style for the header row

- *ItemStyle*—Identifies the style for individual items within the list or control

- *PagerStyle*—Identifies the style for the page selection controls

- *SelectedItemStyle*—Identifies the style for the currently selected item

All columns within the DataGrid control allow you to configure the appearance of the column, along with the **HeaderText**, **HeaderImageURL**, and **FooterText properties**. You can also set the **Visible property** for a column, which allows you to show or hide the column. The **SortExpression property** can be used to identify the column from the data source that is used when sorting the column.

BoundColumns are used by the DataGrid control to bind data to a column in the DataGrid control. All BoundColumns also allow you to specify the **DataField** property, which identifies the column from the data source bound to the column, and a **DataFormatString property**, which identifies the formatting rules for the contents of the BoundColumn. The **ReadOnly property** is used with BoundColumns to stop the user from editing a column when the DataGrid is in edit mode.

When you pass a request to retrieve the contents of a cell in a bound column, the request is passed as an argument. When you Update a BoundColumn, the columns are sent using **DataGridCommandEventArgs**, which are represented with the variable e. When you want to access a specific cell within a DataGrid object, you must use the **Item property** of the e object. The e.Item property contains an indexed Cells collection that contains one Cell object for each column in the DataGrid control. For a bound control, the data is found in the first control in the Controls collection of the cell. The following sample code retrieves the contents as a string from the TextBox control that is displayed in the second column.

```
Sub UpdateItem(ByVal sender As Object, ¬
     ByVal e As DataGridCommandEventArgs)
  Dim MyData As String
  Dim MyTB As TextBox
  MyTB = CType(e.Item.Cells(1).Controls(0), TextBox)
  MyData = MyTB.Text
End Sub
```

The **TemplateColumn** is used to provide additional content, such as HTML. The column can contain bound data as well as unbound data. You can configure the **EditItemTemplate property** to be used when the DataGrid is in edit mode. The **HeaderTemplate** and **FooterTemplate** appear at the top and bottom of the TemplateColumn, respectively, and may contain HTML elements and controls. The **ItemTemplate column** contains HTML elements and controls within the column.

When you pass a request to retrieve the contents of a cell in a TemplateColumn, the request is passed as an argument. The e.Item property in the TemplateColumn also contains an indexed Cells collection that contains one Cell for each column in the DataGrid. However, the data is contained within the controls you created within the template. You can use the FindControl method and the control's name to retrieve the data within the cell. The sample code below retrieves the data from the TextBox control by using the Name property of the control. The name of the control requested is "ProductName," which is found in the second column of the DataGrid control.

```
Sub UpdateItem(ByVal sender As Object, ¬
    ByVal e As DataGridCommandEventArgs)
Dim MyData As String
Dim box As TextBox
MyTB = CType(e.Item.Cells(1).FindControl("FirstName"), ¬
  TextBox)
MyData = MyTB.text
End Sub
```

A **HyperLinkColumn** is used by the DataGrid control to bind a hyperlink to data. It is often used to select a value, such as the CategoryID from a DataGrid that displays the category list, and open a related set of data such as the list of products for a particular category. The **Text property** identifies the text of the hyperlink, which is formatted with the **DataNavigateURLFormatString property**. The **DataTextField property** is the value of the data source that is displayed as text, and is formatted by the **DataTextFormatString property**. The **NavigateURL property** and the **DataNavigateURL property** both identify a URL the client is redirected to when the hyperlink is clicked. If both properties are set, the NavigateURL takes precedence. The **Target property** identifies which window to open the Web page in. The value of Target can be _Top, _New, _Parent, or _Blank.

A **ButtonColumn** is used by the DataGrid control to insert a user-defined button. You can use the buttons for adding and deleting records, and to execute other commands. By default the buttons created for you in a ButtonColumn or EditCommandColumn are **LinkButtons**. They appear as hyperlink buttons, but have additional functionality similar to a button. You can also specify that the ButtonType property for the ButtonColumn be **PushButton**, which means that the appearance of the button would be similar to a physical button.

Adding and Deleting Records

You can write code to insert or delete records, or you can use the methods built into the data controls. In the following exercise, you build a stored procedure to insert a new record, then create the Web page to call the stored procedure and insert the new record.

1. Open the **Chapter8** project in Visual Studio .NET if necessary.

2. In the Server Explorer window, under the Data Connections, click the **plus sign** next to the Ch8TaraStoreSQL database, click the **plus sign** next to Tables, then click **Categories**. Right-click **Categories**, and then click **Design Table**. In the Properties pane for the CategoryID field, change the Identity to **Yes**. Click the **Save All** button and close the window.

3. In the Server Explorer window, right-click **Stored Procedure** under the Ch8TaraStoreSQL database, and then click **New Stored Procedure**. Select and delete all of the text in the stored procedure. Type the code below, which inserts a new record. The stored procedure takes four parameters, @CatName, @CatImage, @CatThumb, and @CatDesc. The @CatID is also a parameter, but it's an output parameter, so the value is returned when the procedure is called.

```
CREATE Procedure AddCatSQL
  (
    @CatName nvarchar(50),
    @CatImage nvarchar(50),
    @CatThumb nvarchar(50),
    @CatDesc ntext,
    @CatID int OUTPUT
  )
AS
INSERT INTO Categories
  (CategoryName, CatImage, Description, Thumbnail)
  VALUES (@CatName, @CatImage, @CatThumb, @CatDesc)
SELECT
  @CatID = @@Identity
RETURN
```

4. Click the **Save All** button.

5. Right-click **Chapter8** in the Solution Explorer window, point to **Add**, then click **Add Existing Item**. Navigate to your Chapter08Data folder, select the file **InsertCat.aspx**, click **Open**, then click **Yes** to create the new class file. Double-click the page icon in the Solution Explorer window.

6. Click **(MachineName)\NetSDK.Ch8TaraStoreSQL.dbo** under Data Connections in the Server Explorer window and drag it to the Web page. A SQL Connection object named SqlConnection1 is added to the page.

7. Double-click the **Add** category button to open the code behind the page.

8. In the onClick event handler for the btnAdd button, add the code below to retrieve the values from the form.

```
Dim CatName As String = tCatName.Text
Dim CatImage As String = tCatImage.Text
Dim CatThumb As String = tCatThumb.Text
Dim CatDesc As String = tCatDesc.Text
```

9. Below this add the following code to create the connection string variable, the Connection object, and the Command object.

```
Dim oCM As SqlClient.SqlCommand
oCM = New SqlClient.SqlCommand("AddCatSQL", ¬
SqlConnection1)
oCM.CommandType = CommandType.StoredProcedure
```

10. Below this add the following code to create the parameters and assign the values from the text boxes to the parameters. The data type and length of the parameters can be found in the stored procedure.

```
Dim pCatID As SqlClient.SqlParameter
pCatID = New SqlClient.SqlParameter("@CatID", ¬
SqlDbType.Int, 4)
pCatID.Direction = ParameterDirection.Output
```

```
oCM.Parameters.Add(pCatID)
Dim pCatName As SqlClient.SqlParameter
pCatName = New SqlClient.SqlParameter("@CatName", ¬
    SqlDbType.NVarChar, 50)
pCatName.Value = catName
oCM.Parameters.Add(pCatName)
Dim pCatImage As SqlClient.SqlParameter
pCatImage = New SqlClient.SqlParameter("@CatImage", ¬
    SqlDbType.NVarChar, 50)
pCatImage.Value = CatImage
oCM.Parameters.Add(pCatImage)
Dim pCatThumb As SqlClient.SqlParameter
pCatThumb = New SqlClient.SqlParameter("@CatThumb", ¬
    SqlDbType.NVarChar, 50)
pCatThumb.Value = CatDesc
oCM.Parameters.Add(pCatThumb)
Dim pCatDesc As SqlClient.SqlParameter
pCatDesc = New SqlClient.SqlParameter("@CatDesc", ¬
    SqlDbType.NText)
pCatDesc.Value = CatDesc
oCM.Parameters.Add(pCatDesc)
```

11. Below this add the following code to open the connection and execute the command using the **ExecuteNonQuery**. (*Note:* The ExecuteNonQuery does not return the records, only the output parameter.)

```
SqlConnection1.Open()
oCM.ExecuteNonQuery()
SqlConnection1.Close()
```

12. Click the **Save All** button. Click **Build** on the menu bar, then click **Build Solution**.

13. Click on the **InsertCat.aspx** tab. Right-click on the page, and then click **View in Browser**. Your page should look like the one in Figure 8-7.

14. Enter the CategoryName **Waterford**. The description is **Waterford Crystal**. The category image name is **29.jpg**, and the thumbnail image name is **29.gif**. When you are finished, add the new record by clicking the **Add** button. (*Note:* The Web page does not provide any feedback. In a Web application, you will likely want to display some feedback to the user indicating that the record was added successfully. Some developers display the record to the end user, or provide a hyperlink to display the set of records that includes the newly added record.)

15. Double-click the **Categories** table in the Server Explorer window. You should see your new row added to the bottom of the table.

16. Close any open pages.

Figure 8-7   Inserting a new record with the DataGrid control

You can use the DataGrid control to add records to and delete them from the DataSet. You can use a ButtonColumn to trigger the Add and Delete record function, or you can use a TemplateColumn. The table uses the **ItemCommand** to insert add and delete command functions. In the following exercise, you create a Web page that contains a DataGrid control that allows you to delete the record from a table.

1. Open the **Chapter8** project in Visual Studio .NET if necessary.

2. Right-click **Chapter8** in the Solution Explorer window, point to **Add**, then click **Add Existing Item**. Navigate to your Chapter08Data folder, select the file **DeleteCat.aspx**, click **Open**, then click **Yes** to create the new class file. Double-click the **DeleteCat.aspx** page icon in the Solution Explorer window.

3. In the Toolbox, click the **Data** tab and drag and drop the **SqlDataAdapter** control to the Web page. The DataAdapter Configuration Wizard opens. Click the **Next** button.

4. In the drop-down list box, select the connection to your Ch8TaraStoreSQL database. Click the **Next** button. In the Query Type window, leave the default radio button labeled **Use SQL statements** selected and click the **Next** button.

5. Click the **Query Builder** button to open the Query Builder. Select the **Categories** table from the Add Table window, click **Add**, then click the **Close** button.

6. In the Field List box, select the **CategoryID**, **CategoryName**, **CatImage**, **Thumbnail**, and **Description** fields. Click the **OK** button, then click the **Next** button to generate the SQL SELECT, INSERT, UPDATE, and DELETE statements, along with a Command object. Then, click the **Finish** button. The DataAdapter and DataConnection objects are added to the page.

8

7. To create a DataSet object, click **Data** on the menu bar, and then click **Generate Dataset**. In the Generate Dataset window, select the radio button labeled **New**. In the text box type **DSCat**. The Categories table has already been selected. Click the **OK** button.

8. Select the DataSet, click **Data** on the menu bar, then click **Preview Data**. Click the **Fill Dataset** button. Your data should be displayed in the window. Click the **Close** button.

9. Drag and drop the **DataView** control from the **Data** tab in the Toolbox to the Web page.

10. You need to assign a table to the DataView. With the **DataView** selected, go to the Properties window, and click the **Table property** drop-down list. Click the **plus sign** next to the DataSet named DSCat1, and then select the table named **Categories**.

11. To assign a data source to the DataGrid object, select the **DataGrid** object. In the Properties window, set the DataSource property to **DataView1**.

12. Double-click on the page to open the code behind the page, which is named **DeleteCat.aspx.vb**.

13. Within the Page_Load procedure, add the code below to call the fill method of the DataAdapter to add the data to the DataSet. You must pass the name of the dataset, DSCat1, as a parameter to the DataAdapter. Bind the controls to the data sources using the DataBind method.

```
SQL Data Adapter1.Fill(DSCat1)
Page.DataBind( )
```

14. Click the **Save All** button. Click **Build** on the menu bar, then click **Build Solution**.

15. Click the **DeleteCat.aspx** tab to view the page. Right-click on the **DeleteCat.aspx** page, and then click **View in Browser**.

16. Close the browser window and any open pages.

The Web page you just created simply displays the records. Now you need to modify the DataGrid and add the event handlers to the code behind the page. The DataGrid can contain objects such as cells, rows, and other data controls that can initiate events. In order to determine which event sent the command, the events are bubbled up to the DataGrid control. You can also use the onItemCommand property of the DataGrid control to assign a function or event handler to the ItemCommand event. For example, when the user clicks the Delete hyperlink, the **CommandName** is passed to the DataGrid control, which initiates the event. In your code, you can detect which control triggered the event by comparing the CommandName value. In the following exercise, you modify the DataGrid to delete the record. When the user clicks the Delete hyperlink, The CommandName is assigned to "RemoveFromCat". RemoveFromCat is passed to the "Grid_CatCommand" event handler that is triggered when an event is bubbled up to the DataGrid.

1. Open the **Chapter8** project in Visual Studio .NET if necessary. Open the **DeleteCat.aspx** page in Design view.

2. Right-click the DataGrid, then click **Property Builder**. In the General tab, change the Data key field property in the drop-down list to **CategoryID**.

3. In the MyDG Properties window, click the **Columns** tab. Deselect the **Create columns automatically at runtime** check box. You will add the bound and template columns manually.

4. Select the **CategoryID**, **CategoryName**, **CatImage**, **Thumbnail**, and **Description** fields in the Available columns list. Click the **>** sign to move the fields to the Selected columns list. For the CategoryID field, change the header text to **Category ID**. Change the CategoryName header text to **Category Name**. Change the CatImage header text to **Image**.

5. In the Available Columns list, scroll down to Template Column and click the **>** button to copy the entry to the Selected columns list. Move the Template Column to the top of the list by clicking the **up arrow** five times. In the Header text box type **Select a Task**, then click **OK**.

6. Switch to HTML view by clicking the **HTML** tab. In the DataGrid tag, locate the <asp:TemplateColumn> </asp:TemplateColumn> tags. Inside the tags, add the code below which creates an ItemTemplate within the TemplateColumn. The template contains an Add and Delete Link button.

```
<ItemTemplate>
<asp:LinkButton ID="RemoveButton" ¬
CommandName="RemoveFromCat"
     Text="Delete" ForeColor="blue" runat="server" />
</ItemTemplate>
```

7. Click the **Design** tab to return to Design view. Right-click on the page, and then click **View Code** to open the code behind the page.

8. After the Page_Load event handler, add the code below. This code handles the Grid_CatCommand event. If the user clicks the Delete button, then the command name that is passed to the DataGrid is RemoveFromCat.

```
Sub MyDG_ItemCommand(ByVal sender As Object, ¬
     ByVal e As DataGridCommandEventArgs) ¬
     Handles MyDG.ItemCommand
If e.CommandSource.CommandName = "RemoveFromCat" Then
  Else
End If
  Page.DataBind()
End Sub
```

9. Insert a line above the Else statement. Insert the code below to get the value from the second column, which contains the CategoryID, and assign it to the variable CatID.

```
Dim CatIDCell As TableCell = e.Item.Cells(1)
Dim CatID As String = CatIDCell.Text
```

10. Below this add the code below to create the SQL command and the Command object. Notice that the SQL command uses the DELETE SQL command and deletes only the record where the CategoryID matches the value passed in the CatID variable. The CatID variable contains an integer, and therefore you do not need single quotation marks within the SQL command.

```
Dim oCM As SqlClient.SqlCommand
Dim MySQL As String
MySQL = "DELETE FROM Categories WHERE CategoryID =" ¬
  & CatID
oCM = New SqlClient.SqlCommand(MySQL, SqlConnection1)
```

11. Below this add the code below to open the connection and execute the SQL command using the ExecuteNonQuery method of the Command object, so no records will be returned. Rebind the controls to the DataSource to see the changes.

```
SqlConnection1.Open()
oCM.ExecuteNonQuery()
SqlConnection1.Close()
Page.DataBind()
```

12. Click the **Save All** button. Click **Build** on the menu bar, then click **Build Solution**.

13. Right-click on the **DeleteCat.aspx** page, and then click **View in Browser**. The page should look like the one in Figure 8-8. (*Note:* The Web page does not provide any feedback. In a Web application you will likely want to display some feedback to the user indicating that the record was deleted successfully.)

14. Delete the record where the product name was **Waterford**.

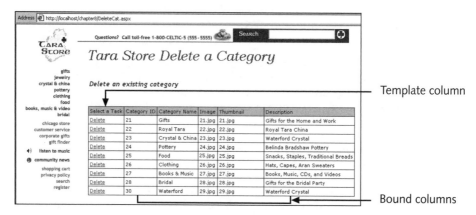

Figure 8-8   Deleting an existing record with the DataGrid control

Updating the Database Using the DataGrid Control

The DataGrid control uses the EditCommandColumn to help add interactivity to your DataGrid. The **EditCommandColumn** helps you edit and update your data in the DataGrid control. You can update a single row of data, or enable all rows to be edited within the DataGrid control by using the **EditCommand** in combination with the TemplateColumn. The **EditCommandColumn** is a button column that contains **LinkButtons** labeled Edit, Update, and Cancel. These LinkButtons are used to edit a single row of data within the DataGrid control. (*Note*: You can also create a Delete LinkButton to delete a record from within the DataGrid control.) The EditCommandColumn also allows you to change the text of the Edit, Update, and Cancel buttons with the **EditText**, **UpdateText**, and **CancelText properties**. You define these properties when you create the EditCommandColumn.

When you click the Edit button the EditCommand event is thrown. You can intercept this event using the **onEditCommand** event handler that is assigned within the DataGrid properties. The **EditItemIndex property** is set by the DataGrid to the selected row, and then the table cells for the single row are displayed as text boxes. After the user enters the new data and clicks the Update LinkButton, the **UpdateCommand event** is triggered. **CancelCommand** is triggered when the user clicks the Cancel LinkButton. You must also include code to handle the **onCancelCommand** and **onUpdateCommand** events.

 Many of the built-in Visual Studio .NET examples demonstrate how to edit data with a DataGrid control by deleting the row, then adding a new row with the data, instead of updating the current row. You should consider the consequences of deleting and recreating rows of data, especially when you are assigning unique IDs.

In the following exercise, you will create a Web page that uses a DataGrid control to display the Categories table. Then, you will modify the DataGrid to edit a record.

1. Open the **Chapter8** project in Visual Studio .NET if necessary.

2. Right-click **Chapter8** in the Solution Explorer window, point to **Add**, then click **Add Existing Item**. Navigate to your Chapter08Data folder. Select the file **EditCat.aspx**, click **Open**, then click **Yes** to create a new class file.

3. Double-click **EditCat.aspx** in the Solution Explorer window. In the Toolbox, click the **Data** tab, then drag and drop the **SqlDataAdapter** to the Web page. The DataAdapter Configuration Wizard opens. Click the **Next** button.

4. In the drop-down list box, select the connection to your Ch8TaraStoreSQL database. Click the **Next** button.

5. In the Query Type window, leave the default radio button selected and click the **Next** button.

6. Click the **Query Builder** button to open the Query Builder. Select the **Categories** table from the Add Table window, and then click **Add**. Click the **Close** button.

7. In the Field list box, select the **CategoryID**, **CategoryName**, **CatImage**, **Thumbnail**, and **Description** fields. Click **OK**, then click **Next** to generate the SQL SELECT, INSERT, UPDATE, and DELETE statements, along with a command object. Then, click the **Finish** button. The DataAdapter and DataConnection objects are added to the page.

8. To create a DataSet object, click **Data** on the menu bar, then click **Generate Dataset**. In the Generate Dataset window, select the radio button labeled **New**. In the text box type **MyDS**. The Categories table has already been selected. Click the **OK** button.

9. Select the Dataset, click **Data** on the menu bar, then click **Preview Data**. Click the **Fill Dataset** button. Your data should be displayed in the window. Click the **Close** button.

10. Drag and drop the **DataView** control from the Data tab in the Toolbox onto the Web page.

11. You need to assign a table to the DataView. With the **DataView** selected, go to the Properties window, and click the **Table** property drop-down list. Click the **plus sign** next to the DataSet named MyDS1, and then select the table named **Categories**.

12. To assign a data source to the DataGrid object, select the **DataGrid** object. In the Properties window, set the DataSource property to **DataView1**.

13. Double-click the page to open the code behind the page, which is named EditCat.aspx.vb.

14. Within the Page_Load procedure, add the code below to call the fill method of the DataAdapter, which adds the data to the DataSet. You must pass the name of the dataset, MyDS1, as a parameter to the DataAdapter. Bind the controls to the data sources using the DataBind method.

```
SQLDataAdapter1.Fill(MyDS1)
Page.DataBind()
```

15. Click the **Save All** button. Click **Build** on the menu bar, then click **Build Solution**.

16. Click the **EditCat.aspx** tab to view the page. Right-click on the page **EditCat.aspx**, and then click **View in Browser**.

17. Close the browser window and any open pages.

You can use Visual Studio .NET to create your code to manage the data within the DataGrid, or build your own code to manage the data. The following sample code would be added to the <asp:DataGrid> tag to indicate which procedures would manage the data.

```
OnCancelCommand="CancelEdit"
OnEditCommand="EditItem"
OnUpdateCommand="UpdateItem"
```

Then, you have to create the code to manage the data for each procedure. In the following sample code, you would cancel the command, or allow the DataGrid to edit the data. You must always bind the data either directly or through a function after the command.

```
Sub CancelEdit(ByVal sender As Object, ¬
    ByVal e As DataGridCommandEventArgs)
    MyDG.EditItemIndex = -1
    BindGrid()
End Sub
Sub EditItem(ByVal sender As Object, ¬
    ByVal e As DataGridCommandEventArgs)
    MyDG.EditItemIndex = e.Item.ItemIndex
    BindGrid()
End Sub
```

Then, for each of the DataGrid text boxes, retrieve the values from the DataGrid text boxes. This code is added within the UpdateItem procedure. (*Note:* You can assign the value to a variable, and then assign the variable to the parameter, or you can assign the value to the parameter directly.)

```
Sub UpdateItem(ByVal sender As Object, ¬
   ByVal e As DataGridCommandEventArgs)
Dim CatNameT As TextBox
CatNameT = e.Item.Cells(2).Controls(0)
Dim CatImageT As TextBox
CatImageT = e.Item.Cells(3).Controls(0)
End Sub
```

You can create the SQL command using parameters instead of variables. Use the UPDATE SQL command to perform an update query, and then add the code to create the Command object using the SQL command.

```
Dim MySQL As String = "UPDATE Categories SET " _
& " CategoryName=@CatName, " _
& " CatImage=@CatImage," _
& " Thumbnail=@CatThumb," _
& " Description=@CatDesc" _
& " WHERE (CategoryID=@CatID); "
Dim oCM As SqlCommand
oCM = New SqlCommand(MySQL, SqlConnection1)
```

You would then need to create the parameters and add them to the Parameters collection of the Command object.

```
oCM.Parameters.Add(New SqlParameter("@CatName", ¬
   SqlDbType.NVarChar, 50))
oCM.Parameters.Add(New SqlParameter("@CatImage", ¬
   SqlDbType.NVarChar, 50))
```

8

You then need to create the parameter for the CatID. Because the CatID is not being edited in the DataGrid form, you need to retrieve the value from the ItemIndex property, and then assign the values from the text box to the Parameter objects.

```
oCM.Parameters.Add(New SqlParameter("@CatID", ¬
  SqlDbType.Int))
oCM.Parameters("@CatID").Value = ¬
  MyDG.DataKeys.Item(e.Item.ItemIndex)
oCM.Parameters("@CatName").Value = ¬
  CType(CatNameT.Text, String)
```

When you edit a record, you should try to determine if the record was added successfully, or if there was an error. If the record is not added successfully, and an exception is triggered, the Web page can catch the exception, which contains information about the error, such as the exception number which helps you determine the type of error that occurred. For example, if you try to add a record and the primary key already exists, the exception number returned is 2627. If you are updating a record and do not correctly form the SQL command, the exception number returned might be 137. In order to determine if an exception occurred, you can enclose the code within a Try-Catch construct. The Try-Catch construct allows you to place code in the Try section that you want to execute. If an exception is thrown within this code, the code within the Catch section runs. The exception can be caught and stored as an object in a variable. You can access the exception number using the Number property of the Exception object. In the following exercise, you will modify the DataGrid to edit a record and use the Try-Catch construct to detect if there was an error when you attempted to update the database.

The sample code below shows how to add the Try-Catch construct. In the Try section, you add the code to open the connection, execute the SQL update command, rebind the data to the DataGrid, close the connection, and reset the EditItemIndect to -1. Also, you change the Text property of the label to indicate the record was successfully updated. If its exception number is 2627, the code displays a message indicating that the record was not added because the primary key cannot have a duplicate value in the table. Otherwise, the code displays a general error message.

```
Try
  SqlConnection1.Open()
  oCM.ExecuteNonQuery()
  SqlConnection1.Close()
  MyDG.EditItemIndex = -1
  BindGrid()
  MyLabel.Text = ¬
  "<b>The record was updated successfully.</b><br>"
End Try
Catch ex As SqlException
  If ex.Number = 2627 Then
    MyLabel.Text = "ERROR: A record already exists" _
    & " with the same primary key"
  Else
    ' Dim Msg As String = ex.Number.GetType.Name
```

```
MyLabel.Text = ex.Number & _
"ERROR: Could not update record," _
& " please review the values you entered." '& Msg
MyLabel.Style("color") = "red"
End If
```

You can write the MySQL variable out in the Catch section. It is useful to write out the SQL command statement and any variables when you are trying to determine why an error occurred.

At the top of the Code View window in Visual Studio .NET, there are two drop-down lists. The drop-down list on the left, called Class Name, lists the class names that exist within the page. These classes are used to instantiate the objects in the page. The drop-down list on the right, called Method Name, lists the events of the objects. You can use these features to help you build your code to edit the DataGrid. In the exercise below, you will use the built-in features of Visual Studio .NET to edit data using a DataGrid control. This exercise will show you how to use significantly less code than if you had created the code manually as shown above.

1. Open the **Chapter8** project in Visual Studio .NET if necessary. Open the **EditCat.aspx** page in Design view.

2. Right-click on the DataGrid, and then click **Property Builder**. In the General tab, change the DataSource to **MyDS1**, change the Data key field property in the drop-down list to **CategoryID**, and change the DataMember to **Categories**. (*Note*: The DataKeyField is used to specify the field that is used to identify the record when changes are requested. The DataMember identifies the table within the DataSet.)

3. In the MyDG Properties window, click the **Columns** tab. In the Available columns list, scroll down to Button Column and click the **plus sign** to expand the list. Click **Edit**, **Update**, and **Cancel**, and then click the **>** button to copy the entry to the Selected columns list. (*Note*: Notice that the HeaderText, FooterText, HeaderImage, SortExpression, EditText, UpdateText, CancelText, ButtonType, and Visible properties can be defined for this column.) Click **OK**.

4. Double-click on the page to open the code behind the page. In the Class Name drop-down list box, select **MyDG**.

5. In the Page_Load event procedure add the code to fill the DataSet and bind the DataGrid control.

```
SqlData Adapter1.Fill(MyDS1)
If Not IsPostBack Then
MyDG.DataBind()
End If
```

6. Reset the Class Name drop-down list to **MyDG**, if necessary. In the Method Name drop-down list box, select **CancelCommand**, which inserts the MyDG_CancelCommand procedure block into the code. Within the MyDG_CancelCommand procedure block, enter the code below, which cancels the edit.

```
MyDG.EditItemIndex = -1
MyDG.DataBind()
```

7. Select **MyDG** from the Class Name drop-down list box. Select **EditCommand** from the Method Name drop-down list box, which inserts the MyDG_EditCommand procedure block into the code. Within the MyDG_EditCommand procedure block enter the code below:

```
MyDG.EditItemIndex = e.Item.ItemIndex
MyDG.DataBind()
```

8. Below this, add the following code, which creates a variable for the values of the Text Box controls for the current row.

```
Dim key As String = ¬
  MyDG.DataKeys(e.Item.ItemIndex).ToString
Dim CatName, CatImage, CatThumb, CatDesc As String
Dim tb As TextBox
tb = CType(e.Item.Cells(2).Controls(0), TextBox)
CatName = tb.Text
tb = CType(e.Item.Cells(3).Controls(0), TextBox)
CatImage = tb.Text
tb = CType(e.Item.Cells(4).Controls(0), TextBox)
CatThumb = tb.Text
tb = CType(e.Item.Cells(5).Controls(0), TextBox)
CatDesc = tb.Text
```

9. Below this add the following code, which uses the FindByCategory method and the key value to locate the row in the DataSet that is being updated. The letter r represents the row. Then, provide the values for each of the columns using the variables from the previous step.

```
Dim r As MyDS.CategoriesRow
r = MyDS1.Categories.FindByCategoryID(key)
r.CategoryName = CatName
r.CatImage = CatImage
r.Thumbnail = CatThumb
r.Description = CatDesc
```

10. Below this add the following code, which calls the update method of the DataAdapter object, which will update the DataSet. Then, reset the command to display mode and rebind the data to the DataGrid.

```
SQL Data Adapter1.Update(MyDS1)
MyDG.EditItemIndex = -1
MyDG.DataBind()
```

11. Click the **Save All** button. Click **Build** on the menu bar, then click **Build Solution**.

12. Click the **EditCat.aspx** tab to select the page. Right-click on the page, and then select **View in Browser**. The page should look like the one in Figure 8-9. Close the browser window and any open pages.

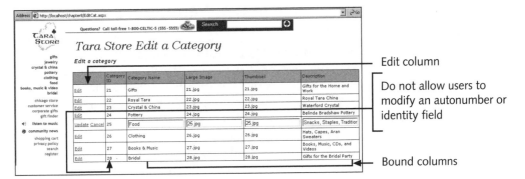

Figure 8-9   Using the DataGrid to update a database

A great way to learn more about data and databinding is by using the walk-throughs within Visual Studio .NET. These walkthroughs are tutorials that help you learn the more complex tasks within the program. A walkthrough on editing the DataGrid control is available at *ms-help://MS.VSCC/MS.MSDNVS/vbcon/html/vbwlkWalkthroughUsingDataGridWebControlTo ReadWriteData.htm.*

BUILDING REUSABLE VISUAL BASIC .NET DATABASE COMPONENTS

In the previous exercises, your code to access the database resides in the code behind the page. If you needed to access the stored procedure again in another page, you must recreate all of the same code. Instead, you can store the code in a central area so that it can be reused in multiple pages. You have already learned how to create a User control to centralize code. However, you can also create a Visual Basic component to store code that is reused across the application. Visual Basic .NET allows you to create components that create objects, access stored procedures, and return data. Because the code is compiled with the application in the namespace, you do not have to register the component in each page as you would a User control.

In this section, you will create a reusable variable and a reusable component. Then you will retrieve the variable and create the component from the Web page. The Web page displays a menu, a home page image, and a list of products. When the user first views the page, the category list is displayed as a menu using a DataList control, along with a home page image. When the user clicks a category, the index number of the selected item and the category ID is passed in the querystring to the same page. When the page is reloaded, the querystring is read, and the values from the selected item and CategoryID are retrieved and stored in variables. These variables are used to retrieve the list of products in the category that was selected. Then, the list of products is bound to a DataList control in the Web page.

Creating a Global Variable in the Web Configuration File

In this section, you will create a global variable, which will contain the connection string. By default, Visual Studio .NET creates a configuration file named Web.config. The Web.config file, which is stored at the root level of the Web site, is a global configuration file. You can create a variable in this file and make it available to the entire application. Web.config is an XML-based text file that is editable using a simple text editor such as Notepad. Because this is an XML-based file, the first line of the file indicates the version of XML that the file is compatible with. The configuration tag is the root node for the configuration file. All tags must be nested within the configuration node. You can include comments within the file using the HTML comment tags. The appSettings tag indicates the global application settings for the Web site.

You use the add tag to create global application variables. The variables are stored as key and value pairs. The key represents the name of the variable, which you use later to retrieve the value. You can add many pairs of keys and values within the appSettings node. In the sample below, the name of the application, Tara Store, is stored as AppName. CS is the name of the key that retrieves the connection string to the database. You can include many connection strings within the Web.config file. You can also include connection strings within Web.config files that are stored in subdirectories. (*Note*: The connection string below is a long string of text and should not be broken across multiple lines in the actual Web.config file.)

```
<?xml version="1.0" encoding="utf-8" ?>
<configuration>
  <!-- application specific settings -->
  <appSettings>
    <add key = "StoreName" value = "Tara Store" />
    <add key = "CS" value = "server=localhost;uid=sa; ¬
      pwd=;database=TaraStoreSQL" />
  </appSettings>
</configuration>
```

To access the key and value pairs, you can assign the values to a variable or access them directly. The following sample code assigns the values from the StoreName and CS keys, and stores them in variables named MyStoreName and MyCS, respectively. Later in the code, you can use the variables to access the values.

```
Dim MyStoreName as String
MyStoreName = ¬
  ConfigurationSettings.AppSettings("StoreName")
Response.write(MyStoreName)
```

```
Dim CS as String
MyCS = ConfigurationSettings.AppSettings("CS")
Response.write(MyCS)
```

In the following exercise, you will modify the configuration file to create a new global variable named CS. The CS variable contains the connection string to your database.

1. Open the **Chapter8** project in Visual Studio .NET if necessary.

2. Double-click the **Web.config** file in the Solution Explorer window. The configuration node and some additional tags are already added for you. Add the following code to create the global connection string. The global connection string is stored in the CS key. (*Note*: Do not reenter the XML declaration and configuration nodes. Make sure to enter the connection string all on one line.) The code should be placed immediately below the opening configuration tag.

```
<appSettings>
<add key="CS" value="server=localhost; ¬
     uid=sa;pwd=;database=TaraStoreSQL" />
</appSettings>
```

3. Click the **Save All** button. Click **Build** on the menu bar, then click **Build Solution**.

Creating a Visual Basic .NET Component

Next, you must create a Visual Basic file. Within the file, you will create a class that contains a function. The function contains the object declarations, and retrieves the data. When you are finished, you can save the file and build the solution. When you build the solution, Visual Studio .Net also compiles the Visual Basic .NET component and stores it in the bin directory along with your other application code. (*Note*: You can store your Visual Basic .NET code within the same application namespace or create additional namespaces.) Each Visual Basic .NET file compiles itself within the applications' namespaces.

In the following exercise you create two functions that are stored within the Chapter8 namespace. The functions create a DataReader object that displays the names of the Categories from the Category table, and retrieve the product list from the Products table for any category. The CategoryID is passed to determine which category of products to retrieve.

1. Open the **Chapter8** project in Visual Studio .NET if necessary.

2. Right-click **Chapter8** in the Solution Explorer window, point to **Add**, then click **Add Component**. In the Name text box type **Ch8Products.vb** to name the component, and then click **Open**. The page opens in Design view.

3. Click the (*MachineName*)**\NetSDK.Ch8TaraStoreSQL.dbo** under Data Connections in the Server Explorer window and drag it to the Web page. A SQL Connection object named SqlConnection1 is added to the page.

4. Right-click on the page, and then click **View Code**. The name of the file Ch8Products is used to create a new class named Ch8Products within the Chapter8 namespace. Later, you will use this class to create an object and access the functions defined within the ProductsDB class.

5. Add the code to import the system, configuration, and data-related namespaces. (*Note*: If you are working with Oracle or Access, you import the System.Data.OleDb instead of System.Data.SqlClient namespace.) In order to add the namespace, you must add the code above the Public Class Ch8Products statement. Click immediately before the first word, **Public**, then press **Enter** to create a new line. Then, add the code to import the SqlClient and Configuration namespaces.

```
Imports System.Data.SqlClient
Imports System.Configuration
```

6. Add the code to create the first function, named **GetCat**. No parameters are passed to this function. This code must be added below the dimmed code that says Component Designer generated code. (*Note*: The dimmed code is used to collapse code that was generated by Visual Studio .NET. This code should not be edited manually.)

```
Public Function GetCat() As SqlDataReader
End Function
```

7. Within the function, add the code below to open the connection to the SqlConnection1 object, create the Connection and Command objects, and specify the CommandType property. In this example, the active connection object and stored procedure parameters of the Command object are passed when the Command object is created.

```
SqlConnection1.Open()
Dim objCM As SqlCommand
objCM = New SqlCommand("ProductCategoryList", ¬
   SqlConnection1)
objCM.CommandType = CommandType.StoredProcedure
```

8. Below this add the following code to create a DataReader named objDR and execute the command in the Command object. The results are passed to the DataReader object, and when the command is completed, it closes the connection. The Return keyword is used to return the DataReader object named objDR to the end user.

```
Dim objDR As SqlDataReader
objDR = ¬
objCM.ExecuteReader(CommandBehavior.CloseConnection)
Return objDR
```

9. Below this add the following code to create the second function, named **GetProducts**. A single parameter is passed to this function. The parameter is an integer, and is referred to as CatID within the function. (Make sure to place this code after the End Function statement.)

```
Public Function GetProducts ¬
  (ByVal CatID As Integer) As SqlDataReader
End Function
```

10. Within the function statements, add the following code to open the connection to the Connection object, create the Command object and specify the CommandType property. In this example, the active Connection object and stored procedure parameters of the Command object are passed when the Command object is created.

```
SqlConnection1.Open()
Dim objCM As SqlCommand
objCM = New SqlCommand("ProductsByCategory", ¬
  SqlConnection1)
objCM.CommandType = CommandType.StoredProcedure
```

11. Below this add the following code to create a Parameter object, passing the parameter the value that is passed to the function, and add the parameter to the Command Object's Parameters collection. (*Note*: In the code below, the name of the parameter object is **pCatID**. The **pCatID** parameter stores the value of the parameter required by the stored procedure. As you learned earlier, you must pass the name of the parameter as it appears in the stored procedure, along with its data type and length properties, when you create the parameter object. The parameter is assigned the value that was passed to the function as CatID. As you learned before, after assigning the Value property to the parameter, you can add the parameter to the Parameter collection of the Command object by calling the add method.)

```
Dim pCatID As SqlParameter
pCatID = New SqlParameter("@CategoryID" ¬
  , SqlDbType.Int, 4)
pCatID.Value = CatID
objCM.Parameters.Add(pCatID)
```

12. Below this add the following code to create a DataReader named objDR, and execute the command in the Command object. The results are passed to the DataReader object, and when the command is completed, it closes the connection. The Return keyword is used to return the DataReader object named objDR to the end user. Your code should look like that shown in Figure 8-10.

```
Dim objDR As SqlDataReader
objDR = ¬
objCM.ExecuteReader(CommandBehavior.CloseConnection)
Return objDR
```

13. Click the **Save All** button. Click **Build** on the menu bar, then click **Build Solution**. Close the component files.

8

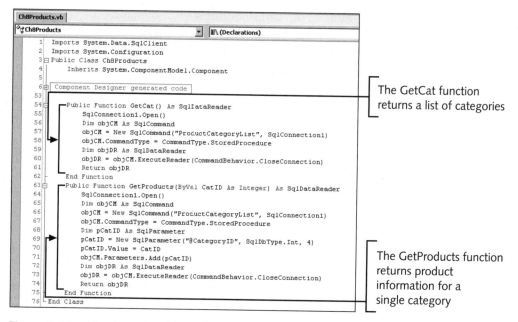

```
Ch8Products.vb
Ch8Products                                      (Declarations)
 1   Imports System.Data.SqlClient
 2   Imports System.Configuration
 3   Public Class Ch8Products
 4       Inherits System.ComponentModel.Component
 5
 6   Component Designer generated code
53
54   Public Function GetCat() As SqlDataReader
55       SqlConnection1.Open()
56       Dim objCM As SqlCommand
57       objCM = New SqlCommand("ProductCategoryList", SqlConnection1)
58       objCM.CommandType = CommandType.StoredProcedure
59       Dim objDR As SqlDataReader
60       objDR = objCM.ExecuteReader(CommandBehavior.CloseConnection)
61       Return objDR
62   End Function
63   Public Function GetProducts(ByVal CatID As Integer) As SqlDataReader
64       SqlConnection1.Open()
65       Dim objCM As SqlCommand
66       objCM = New SqlCommand("ProductCategoryList", SqlConnection1)
67       objCM.CommandType = CommandType.StoredProcedure
68       Dim pCatID As SqlParameter
69       pCatID = New SqlParameter("@CategoryID", SqlDbType.Int, 4)
70       pCatID.Value = CatID
71       objCM.Parameters.Add(pCatID)
72       Dim objDR As SqlDataReader
73       objDR = objCM.ExecuteReader(CommandBehavior.CloseConnection)
74       Return objDR
75   End Function
76   End Class
```

The GetCat function returns a list of categories

The GetProducts function returns product information for a single category

Figure 8-10 Creating reusable Visual Basic .NET components

Calling the Component from the Web Page

After you have created the namespace, your Web page can access the data by simply instantiating the class as a new object from the Ch8ProductsDB class, and then calling the function. In this exercise, you create the Web page that calls the two functions and binds the data to the DataList controls. You also pass a parameter to a function that is used by the stored procedure to retrieve only those products that match the category ID parameter.

1. Open the **Chapter8** project in Visual Studio .NET if necessary.

2. Right-click **Chapter8** in the Solution Explorer menu, point to **Add**, then click **Add Existing Item**. Navigate to your Chapter08Data folder. Select the file **CatMenu.aspx**, click **Open**, then click **Yes** to create the new class file.

3. Double-click the file **Styles.css** in the Solution Explorer window to open the stylesheet.

4. Open Notepad and browse to locate the **MyStyles.txt** file in your Chapter08Data folder. Copy and paste all of the text into the Styles.css page, placing the text so that it starts on the second line. Click the **Save All** icon and close the file.

5. Double-click the **CatMenu.aspx** page icon to open the page. Click and drag the **Styles.css** file icon from the Solution Explorer window to the page to create a link to the stylesheet.

6. Double-click on the page to open the code behind the page. Add the code below to the Page_Load event handler to retrieve the value of the selected item from the querystring. The name of the value from the querystring is selItem. Store selItem in a variable named SelID.

```
Dim SelID As String = Request.Params("selItem")
```

7. Immediately after the code above, enter the code shown below. This code checks if the SelID variable is empty. If there is no SelID, then display the image named HomeImage by setting the Visible property to True. If the SelID property exists, then the user has visited the page before and selected a category from the menu. Therefore, do not show the home page image. Convert the value to an integer using the Cint function, and assign the value to the SeletectIndex property of the MyCatList DataList control.

```
If Not SelID Is Nothing Then
     MyCatList.SelectedIndex = CInt(SelID)
     HomeImage.Visible = False
Else
     HomeImage.Visible = True
End If
```

8. Immediately after the code above, add the code below, which allows you to use the component, and creates a variable named **CatList** to store the object created by the Ch8Products class. (*Note:* You should refer to the class using the namespace in order not to conflict with other classes that might be defined in the application.) Then, assign the DataSource property of the ASP.NET DataList control named MyCatList to the data returned by the DataReader from the GetCat function. Then, you can bind the data using the DataBind method.

```
Dim CatList As Chapter8.Ch8Products
CatList = New Chapter8.Ch8Products()
MyCatList.DataSource = CatList.GetCat()
MyCatList.DataBind()
```

9. Below this add the following code to create another variable named CatID to store the value of the CatID parameter passed by the querystring. Create a variable named **ProdList** to store the object created by the Ch8Products class. Assign the DataSource property of the ASP.NET DataList control named MyProdList to the data returned by the DataReader from the GetProducts function. Then, you can bind the data using the DataBind method.

```
Dim CatID As Integer = CInt(Request.Params("CatID"))
Dim ProdList As Chapter8.Ch8Products
ProdList = New Chapter8.Ch8Products()
MyProdList.DataSource = ProdList.GetProducts(CatID)
MyProdList.DataBind()
```

10. Click the **Save All** button. Click **Build** on the menu bar, then click **Build Solution**.

8

11. Click the **CatMenu.aspx** tab to view the page. Right-click on the page, and then click **View in Browser**. Click the **Gifts** hyperlink. Your page should look like the one in Figure 8-11.

12. Close any open pages.

Figure 8-11   Creating Web pages from reusable Visual Basic .NET components

CHAPTER SUMMARY

❏ ADO.NET provides a variety of data objects that can be accessed from a Web page. By using the .NET Data controls, you can bind the ADO objects dynamically.

❏ The DataSet is used to retrieve the data from the various data sources. The fill method of the DataAdapter object populates the DataSet using a SQL command or stored procedure.

❏ The DataSet consists of a DataTables collection. The DataTables collection consists of one or more DataTable objects.

❏ The DataView is used to retrieve a subset of data from the DataSet. The DataView can combine data from a single table, or a SQL command, but will result in a single DataTable. The default DataView is the first table in the DataTables collection.

❏ You can refer to the DataTable object using the name or the position of the DataTable within the DataTables collection. You can bind your Data controls to a DataView object. You can dynamically display the data by controlling when the BindData method is called, and for which Data controls. You can bind all of the controls at once or do so individually.

❑ The DataGrid control contains several style templates that you can use to format the appearance of the control. The DataGrid control contains different column types such as EditColumn, HyperlinkColumn, ButtonColumn, and TemplateColumn. You can customize the Column properties using the Style properties for each column.

❑ EditColumn is typically used to insert LinkButtons that enable you to update data in a database.

❑ ButtonColumn is typically used to insert Add and Delete buttons, which are used to insert and delete records in the database.

❑ Both BoundColumns and TemplateColumns are used to display data from a data source.

❑ When you use Visual Studio .NET, the DataGrid control creates objects that allow you to insert, modify, and delete data in the database. However, you still need to identify the command to run when the event is triggered. For example, when the user clicks the Delete button, you need to identify the event handler to delete the record.

8

❑ Components allow you to separate business logic from presentation. The Visual Basic .NET component contains classes that are used to create objects within the application. Within the classes, you can define properties and functions. You can create functions that return data from a database. The compiled component is stored in the bin directory in the namespace defined for the application. Therefore, you can access the component from any page within your application.

❑ You can create global variables using the Web.config application configuration file, which is located in the root of the Web site. You can create additional Web.config configuration files within subdirectories within the same site. However, all of the key and value pairs defined in the global Web.config file are available from any Web page in the application.

REVIEW QUESTIONS

1. Which object is not used to retrieve data from a database?
   a. DataView
   b. DataReader
   c. DataSet
   d. DataGrid

2. What method is used to insert the data into a DataSet?
   a. fill
   b. GenerateData
   c. FillAdaptor
   d. FillData

3. Which toolbar is used to generate the DataSet methods?

   a. DataSet

   b. Data

   c. Build

   d. Generate

4. Which object is used to generate a read-only stream of data?

   a. DataAdapter

   b. DataRepeater

   c. DataReader

   d. ADOReader

5. Which features does the DataGrid control support?

   a. Automatic paging

   b. Filtering records

   c. Sorting records

   d. all of the above

6. Which event is raised by the DataGrid control when the use clicks the Page Next button?

   a. PageIndexChanged

   b. NewPageIndex

   c. CurrentPageIndex

   d. GetDataSetPage2

7. Which event handler in the DataGrid control is responsible for intercepting a sort request?

   a. SortCommand

   b. PagePrevText

   c. DataGridPageChangedEventArgs

   d. SortExpression

8. Which property is used to identify the window to open the page when you click the link in a HyperLinkColumn?

   a. DataTextFormatString

   b. Target

   c. DataNavigateURL

   d. DataTextField

9. Which button(s) can be used with the DataGrid EditCommandColumn?

 a. LinkButton

 b. PushButton

 c. ImageButton

 d. all of the above

10. Which window is used to configure the DataGrid control?

 a. Properties window

 b. Property Builder

 c. DataGrid Wizard

 d. a and b

11. Which command(s) appear in the DataGrid EditCommandColumn?

 a. CancelCommand

 b. UpdateCommand

 c. DeleteCommand

 d. a and b

12. Which property allows you to change the LinkButton type in a DataGrid control?

 a. ButtonType

 b. LinkButton

 c. Button

 d. GridButton

13. Which property allows you to specify the column that identifies the unique record in a DataGrid control?

 a. DataKeyField

 b. UpdateCommand

 c. EditItemIndex

 d. ItemIndex

14. Which is not a property of the DataGrid control?

 a. HeaderText

 b. HeaderImage

 c. SortExpression

 d. AcceptButton

8

15. What is the name of the namespace for the OLE-DB .NET managed provider?

    a. `System.Data.SqlClient`

    b. `System.Data`

    c. `System.Data.OleDb`

    d. `System.Data.ODBC`

16. Which SQL command is used to create a new record in the database?

    a. Update

    b. Insert

    c. AddNew

    d. Add

17. What is stored in the field when there is no value?

    a. NULL

    b. Nothing

    c. " "

    d. all of the above

18. Where can you store the connection string so that it is available to all pages within your application?

    a. Global.ASP

    b. Web.config

    c. Config.Web

    d. Default.asp

19. What is the value assigned to the CommandType parameter of the Command object when the page requests a stored procedure?

    a. CommandType.StoredProcedure

    b. StoredProcedure

    c. Command.StoredProcedure

    d. objCM.StoredProc

20. Which of the following statements would retrieve a value from the selItem key in the querystring?

    a. `Dim SelID As String = Request.Params("selItem")`

    b. `SelID = Request ("selItem")`

    c. `Dim SelID As String = Response.Querystring("selItem")`

    d. `Set SelID As String = Request.Params("selItem")`

HANDS-ON PROJECTS

Project 8-1

In this project, you create a connection to the Pubs database and store it in the application configuration file. This project requires you to have the Pubs database installed on your SQL Server.

1. Start **Visual Studio .NET** and open your **Chapter8** solution if it is not already open.

2. If you do not have an existing connection to the Pubs database, you need to create one. (*Note:* If you already have a connection to the Pubs database, proceed to Step 3.) To do this, right-click **Data Connections** in Server Explorer, and then click **Add Connection**. In the Select or enter a server name text box, type **localhost**. In the Username text box, type **sa**. Leave the Password text box blank. Click the **Blank password** check box to select it. In the Select the database on the server drop-down list box, select **Pubs**. Click the **Test Connection** button. Click **OK** in the warning dialog box.

You can use localhost or choose your servername from the drop-down list. You should choose the authentication method provided by your system administrator. If you do not have a username or password, try selecting Windows NT integrated security to establish a connection to the database.

3. Double-click the **Web.config** file in the Solution Explorer window. Add the code below to create the connection string to the Pubs database. (*Note:* You may have to change the user permissions depending upon your SQL Server login configuration. Remember to type the connection string on one line. Do not break strings across lines.)

```
<appSettings>
<add key="CSPubs" value="server=localhost; ¬
  uid=sa;pwd=;database=pubs" />
</appSettings>
```

4. Create a Web page named **Ch8Proj1.aspx**. Add a Label control named **MyLabel**.

5. Double-click on the page to open the code behind the page. In the Page_Load event handler, add the code below to change the Text property of the MyLabel control to the connection string.

```
MyLabel.Text = ConfigurationSettings.AppSettings("CSPubs")
```

6. Click the **Save All** button. Click **Build** on the menu bar, then click **Build Solution**. (*Note:* You can add graphics and text to enhance the appearance of your Web page.)

7. View the **Ch8Proj1.aspx** file in a browser. The connection string is displayed in the Web page. Print the Web page, the source code, and the configuration file, then close all of the files.

8

Project 8-2

In this project, you create a connection to the Northwind database and store it in the application configuration file. This project requires you to have the Northwind database installed on your SQL Server.

1. Start **Visual Studio .NET** and open your **Chapter8** solution if necessary.

2. If you do not have an existing connection to the Northwind database, you must create one. To do this, right-click **Data Connections** in Server Explorer, and then click **Add Connection**. In the Select or enter a server name text box, type **localhost**. In the Username text box, enter **sa**. Leave the Password text box blank. Click the **Blank password** check box to select it. In the Select the database on the server drop-down list box, select **Northwind**. Click the **Test Connection** button. Click **OK** in the confirmation dialog box.

3. Open the **Web.config** file. Under the opening Configuration tag, add the code below to create the connection string to the Northwind database. (*Note:* You may have to change the user permissions depending upon your SQL Server login configuration. Remember to type the connection string on one line. Do not break strings across lines. You can locate the ConnectionString to the Northwind database in the Properties window.)

```
<appSettings>
<add key="CSNW" value="server=localhost; ¬
    uid=sa;pwd=;database=Northwind" />
</appSettings>
```

4. Create a Web page named **Ch8Proj2.aspx**. Add a Label control named **MyLabel**.

5. Double-click on the page to open the code behind the page. In the Page_Load event handler, add the code to change the Text property of the MyLabel control to the connection string.

```
MyLabel.Text = ConfigurationSettings.AppSettings("CSNW")
```

6. Click the **Save All** button. Click **Build** on the menu bar, then click **Build Solution**. (*Note:* You can add graphics and text to enhance the appearance of your Web page.)

7. View the **Ch8Proj2.aspx** file in a browser. The connection string is displayed in the Web page. Print the Web page, the source code, and the configuration file, then close all of the files.

Project 8-3

In this project, you use the DataReader object to display data from the Pubs database using the Label control.

1. Start **Visual Studio .NET** and open your **Chapter8** solution if necessary.

2. Create a new page named **Ch8Proj3.aspx**. Add a Label control named **MyLabel**.

3. Add a Connection object and open the connection. (*Note:* You can drag the database onto the page from the Server Explorer window to create the Connection object.)

4. In the Page_Load procedure, add the code below to open the connection to the Connection object and create the variable to store the SQL SELECT command, which will retrieve the list of authors.

```
SqlConnection1.Open()
Dim mySQL As String = ¬
   "SELECT au_fname, au_lname FROM Authors"
```

5. Below this add the following code to create the Command object using the SQL command.

```
Dim objCM As New SqlClient.SqlCommand(mySQL, ¬
   SqlConnection1)
```

6. Below this add the following code to create the DataReader object by calling the ExecuteMethod of the Command object and storing the object in a variable named objDR.

```
Dim objDR As SqlClient.SqlDataReader
objDR = objCM.ExecuteReader()
```

7. Below this add the following code to declare a variable named **MyAuthor** to store the data from the DataReader object.

```
Dim MyAuthor As String
```

8. Below this add the following code to read the record from the DataReader and store the value with a line break tag in the variable. Make sure to concatenate the data with the MyAuthor variable. This ensures that all records are stored in the MyAuthor variable.

```
While objDR.Read()
MyAuthor = MyAuthor & (objDR("au_fname") & _
(objDR("au_lname") & "<br />"))
End While
```

9. Below this add the following code to close the DataReader and the Connection objects.

```
objDR.Close()
SqlConnection1.Close()
```

10. Below this add the following code to assign the contents of the MyAuthor variable to the text property of the label named **lblAuthor**. The label displays the results from the DataReader in the Web page.

```
MyLabel.Text = MyAuthor
```

11. Click the **Save All** button. Click **Build** on the menu bar, then click **Build Solution**. (*Note:* You can add graphics and text to enhance the appearance of your Web page.)

12. View the **Ch8Proj3.aspx** file in a browser. Print the Web page, the source code, and the configuration file, then close all of the files.

Project 8-4

In this project, you use the DataReader object to display data from a SQL Server database. This project requires you to have the Northwind database installed on your SQL Server.

1. Start **Visual Studio .NET** and open your **Chapter8** solution if necessary. Create a new page named **Ch8Proj4.aspx**. Add a Label control named **MyLabel**.

2. Add a Connection object and open the connection. (*Note:* You can drag the database onto the page from the Server Explorer window to create the Connection object.) Open the code behind the page, and in the Page_Load event procedure, open the connection using the following code.

```
SqlConnection1.Open()
```

3. Below this add the code to create the variable to store the SQL command.

```
Dim mySQL As String = "SELECT * FROM Employees ¬
    WHERE (Country=N'USA') ORDER BY LastName"
```

4. Below this add the code to create the Command object using the SQL command.

```
Dim objCM As New SqlClient.SqlCommand(mySQL,
SqlConnection1)
```

5. Below this add the code to create the DataReader object by calling the ExecuteMethod of the Command object and storing the object in a variable named objDR.

```
Dim objDR As SqlClient.SqlDataReader
objDR = objCM.ExecuteReader()
```

6. Below this add the code to declare a variable named **MyEmployee** to store the data from the DataReader object. Read the record from the DataReader and store the value with a line break tag in the variable. Make sure to concatenate the data with the MyEmployee variable. This ensures that all records are stored in the MyEmployee variable.

```
Dim MyEmployee As String
While objDR.Read()
    MyEmployee += "(" & objDR("EmployeeID") & _
    ")  Ext. "  & _
    objDR("Extension") & "   " & _
    objDR("LastName") & ", " & _
    objDR("FirstName") & "<br /><br />"
End While
```

7. Below this add the code to close the DataReader and the Connection objects. Assign the contents of the MyEmployee variable to the Text property of the label named MyLabel. The label displays the results from the DataReader in the Web page.

```
objDR.Close()
SqlConnection1.Close()
MyLabel.Text = MyEmployee
```

8. Click the **Save All** button. Click **Build** on the menu bar, then click **Build Solution**. (*Note*: You can add graphics and text to enhance the appearance of your Web page.)

9. View the **Ch8Proj4.aspx** file in a browser. Print the Web page, the source code, and the configuration file, then close all of the files.

Project 8-5

In this project, you create a Web page that uses stored procedures from the Pubs database using Visual Studio .NET. You will need to create the DisplayStates stored procedure that displays as hyperlinks the list of states where authors live. Then, you will add the DisplayAuthors stored procedure, which will list the authors in the selected state.

1. Start **Visual Studio .NET** and open your **Chapter8** solution if necessary.

2. In the Server Explorer window, expand the Pubs data connection by clicking the **plus sign** (+). Right-click **Stored Procedures**, and then select **New Stored Procedure**. Click **Edit** on the menu bar, then click **Select All**. Click **Edit** on the menu bar, and then click **Delete**. Type the code below, which creates a stored procedure named **DisplayStates**. This returns an alphabetical list of the states. The DISTINCT command will return only one value for each possible value. In other words, if five authors live in Wisconsin, WI would only be returned once.

```
CREATE PROCEDURE dbo.DisplayStates
    AS
SELECT DISTINCT State FROM Authors
    ORDER BY State ASC
RETURN
```

3. Right-click **Stored Procedures**, and then click **New Stored Procedure**. Click **Edit** on the menu bar, and then click **Select All**. Next, click **Edit** on the menu bar, and then click **Delete**. Type the code below to create a stored procedure named **DisplayAuthors**. This returns a list of the states where the authors live when the state parameter is passed to the stored procedure.

```
CREATE PROCEDURE dbo.DisplayAuthors
    @State nchar(2)
AS
SELECT au_lname, au_fname, phone FROM Authors
    WHERE State = @State
    ORDER BY au_lname ASC
RETURN
```

4. Click the **Save All** button. Close the stored procedure windows.

5. Add a new Web page named **Ch8Proj5.aspx**. Drag a Connection object to the page from the Pubs database, and a Label control named **MyLabel** from the Toolbox. In the Web page, add a Label control named **MyLabel** that displays the list of states from the DataReader.

8

6. Visit *www.lifebeyondyahoo.com/life/graphics.asp*. Visit some of the graphics Web sites. Save a graphic to be used as the home page image. Add the Image to your project files in your images directory. Add a home page image using an Image control. Name the image **HomeImage**. Change the runat property to server to make the image a server-side control.

7. Open the code behind the page. Within the Page_Load procedure, add the code below. This creates the objects and retrieves the data using the DataReader object.

```
SqlConnection1.Open()
Dim objCM As SqlClient.SqlCommand
objCM = New SqlClient.SqlCommand("DisplayStates", ¬
  SqlConnection1)
objCM.CommandType = CommandType.StoredProcedure
Dim objDR As SqlClient.SqlDataReader
objDR = objCM.ExecuteReader()
Dim MyStateList As String
While objDR.Read()
    MyStateList += _
    " <a href='Ch8Proj5.aspx?MyState=" & _
    objDR("State") & "'>" & _
    objDR("State") & "</a><br />"
End While
objDR.Close()
SqlConnection1.Close()
MyLabel.Text = MyStateList
```

8. Immediately below the code above, add the code to retrieve the value from the querystring, assign it to a variable, and store the value in a parameter named **pState**. If there is a value, make the DataGrid visible and open the data connection.

```
Dim State As String = Request.Params("MyState")
If Not State Is Nothing Then
  HomeImage.Visible = False
  MyDG.Visible = True
  SqlConnection1.Open()
```

9. Below this, add the following code, which uses the Command object you created earlier. Pass the name of the stored procedure, DisplayAuthors. Specify the CommandType as **StoredProcedure**. Add a parameter for the State column.

```
objCM = New SqlClient.SqlCommand("DisplayAuthors",¬
  SqlConnection1)
objCM.CommandType = CommandType.StoredProcedure
Dim pState As SqlClient.SqlParameter
pState = New SqlClient.SqlParameter("@State", ¬
  SqlDbType.NChar, 2)
pState.Value = State
objCM.Parameters.Add(pState)
```

10. Below this add the following code, which returns a DataReader object when the Command object executes the stored procedure. Assign the DataReader object to the DataSource property of the DataGrid control named MyDG and bind the data to the control.

```
objDR = ¬
objCM.ExecuteReader(CommandBehavior.CloseConnection)
MyDG.DataSource = objDR
MyDG.DataBind()
```

11. Below this, add the following code so that if there is no value for the state from the querystring, the HomeImage is displayed and the DataGrid control is hidden.

```
Else
    HomeImage.Visible = True
    MyDG.Visible = False
End If
```

12. Save the page and view it in the browser. Click a state, and the list of authors should appear in the window. Print the results displayed in the Output window.

8

CASE PROJECTS

Pubs Database — Displaying the Authors List Using a DataReader Object

Your boss would like to pick the name of the author from a drop-down list box, and then display the author's address information on the Web page. Using the Pubs database, create a stored procedure to retrieve the list of authors by last name (named ListAuthorsByLastNames), and the author's contact information (named AuthorsAddress) for a single author. (*Note:* You can also create a similar database if you do not have access to Pubs.) Create a page named Ch8Case1.aspx. Use a SQL DataAdapter, DataSet, and DataView to bind the results of the ListAuthorsByLastNames stored procedure to the drop-down list named DDAL. When the page loads, display an image named HomeImage and the DDAL drop-down list that contains authors' last names, and a button named btnGo that says Go. The drop-down list will display the last names, but the value will store the author's ID. A Label control named MyLabel will not appear when the page loads. When you click the button, the page will reload, and the MyLabel control will appear, but not the HomeImage. When the user clicks the button, display the author's address information in the MyLabel control using the AuthorsAddress stored procedure. You will have to retrieve the value of the drop-down list. (*Hint:* You can use DDAL.SelectedItem.Value.ToString) Then, you will need to create the Command, Parameter, and DataReader objects. Use the read method of the DataReader to display the data in the label control. Save the page as Ch8Case1.aspx in your data directory. Print the Web page, your source code, and the code behind the page.

Grocer To Go — Displaying the Menu and Products List Using the DataReader Control

Create a stored procedure named DisplayCats to display the category menu. Use the DataReader object to display the list. Bind the DataReader results to a DataList control. The menu should display hyperlinks. When you click a hyperlink, the CategoryID should be passed. Create a stored procedure named DisplayProducts that displays the list of products by category using the CategoryID as the input parameter. You must pass a parameter that contains the category ID to the stored procedure. Then, you need to display the products from the DisplayProducts stored procedure. You should retrieve the results from the DisplayProducts stored procedure using the DataReader object. Then, display the Products using a DataList control. You can display the images by using the ImagePath column value or by importing the images into your images folder from the Chapter8Data\images folder. Save the page as Ch8Case2.aspx in your data directory. Print the Web page, the source code, and the code behind the page.

Grocer To Go — Inserting and Deleting Records with the DataGrid Control

You are to create an administrative area to maintain the GrocerToGo database. You can modify the Categories table so that the CategoryID is an autonumber by changing the Identity property to Yes and making the column a primary key field. Create a page that allows you to add or delete records in the Categories table. Save the page as Ch8Case3_AddCat.aspx in your data directory. Create the stored procedure AddCatSQL that will be used to insert a new record. After the record is inserted, redirect the user to the Ch8Case3_Home.aspx page. Create a second page that allows you to delete a record in the Categories table. Save the page as Ch8Case3_DeleteCat.aspx in your data directory. After the record is deleted, redirect the user to the Ch8Case3_Home.aspx page. Create a third page that allows you to update a record in the Categories table. Save the page as Ch8Case3_EditCat.aspx in your data directory. After the record is updated, redirect the user to the Ch8Case3_Home.aspx page. Add graphics and content to enhance the appearance of your page. Create a Web page that is used as the administrative tool home page with links to the other pages. Save the home page as Ch8Case3_Home.aspx in your data directory. Display the categories on the home page using the DataSet and DataView objects and a DataGrid. Print the Web pages, your source code, and the code behind the page for each of the pages.

CHAPTER

9

CONFIGURING AN ASP.NET APPLICATION

In this chapter, you will:

♦ Learn how to maintain state in an ASP.NET application
♦ Identify the configuration files used in an ASP.NET application
♦ Create a Web page that maintains state using an HTTP cookie
♦ Create a Web page that maintains state without using HTTP cookies
♦ Implement the security methods used in ASP.NET

In previous chapters of this book, you learned how to process forms and share data across Web pages using session variables. In a Web farm, load balancing servers will redistribute the clients based on the workload on the server. If one server crashes, the clients are redirected to a new server. In previous versions of ASP, session data could not be transferred across Web servers, which meant that when a Web server crashed, the session data no longer existed. As a result, a customer could place an order in his or her shopping basket, but if the server crashed, all of the items in the basket could be deleted. In this chapter, you will learn how to maintain session data and implement security using forms authentication. Forms athentication allows you to maintain form information and other data throughout an individual user's session, across the entire application, across multiple sessions, and across multiple servers. You will also learn how to create a Web application that does not rely on HTTP cookies to establish sessions.

WEB APPLICATIONS

A **Web application** is a group of files and folders (including virtual folders) located under the Web application's root directory. A Web application is defined by the Web server software. Internet Information Server (IIS) has the capacity to define multiple Web applications on the same computer. In IIS, the root directory of a Web application may be configured as a virtual Web, or virtual directory.

Configuring your Web sites as Web applications has many benefits. First, you can create application-level and session-level variables that are available to all pages within the Web application. Also, with IIS you can run your Web application in its own memory space, so that an error in one Web application does not bring down the rest of the Web applications on your server. This memory space is referred to as an **isolated process** and is separate from the process that contains the IIS Web server. (*Note*: With ASP.NET, the Web application is run out of the IIS process by default.)

One of the biggest challenges in creating interactive Web pages is maintaining the state of the user. When you visit an interactive Web site, the site maintains information about your session, such as your IP address, what pages you clicked and when, when you visited the site, what browser you are using, and your preferences. User information can be tracked across user sessions and across the entire application. Some of this information is retrieved from the HTTP headers using the ServerVariables collection, which is exposed via the Request object, and some is retrieved from the properties of the Session object, such as the SessionID, a unique identifier that identifies each session. The SessionID is a number whose value is determined by several factors, including the current date, and the IP addresses of the client and server. You cannot change the value of the SessionID property, which uses a special session cookie to maintain the session information. When the session ends, the cookie is discarded. If the user opens a new session, a new SessionID is issued. Therefore, a SessionID can be used to track a user across a single session, but not across multiple sessions. To track a user across multiple sessions, the SessionID can be stored in a client-side cookie or in a database that contains the identity of an individual. Some of the information Web sites track is retrieved from forms submitted by users. Once the user logs on with a user ID, the information collected can be correlated with past visits. The syntax for retrieving the SessionID property of the session object is `Session.SessionID`.

In the database diagram shown in Figure 9-1, you can set up a UsersTable with the UserID and password fields. In a second table, named SessionData, you can store the information gathered from each session. This table would also have a field called UserID, which would be the link between the tables. (*Note*: The UserID is a primary key in the UsersTable, and a foreign key in the SessionData table.) When the user logs in, you can retrieve his or her SessionID, UserID, and write the information directly into the SessionData table. Then, in future visits, you can access the data obtained from past visits.

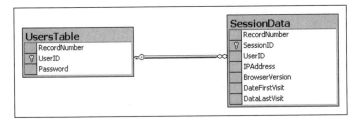

Figure 9-1 Storing session data from a Web application within a database

The Application object allows you to maintain application state. You can maintain information across the entire Web application with the Application object. The Application object stores the application variables in the server's memory, and any user can access them from any page within the Web site. The Session object is used to maintain session state. The session state maintains information across a single user's session. The session variables are also stored in the server's memory. However, session variables can only be accessed within the session that declared and assigned the session variables. When the session ends, the session variables are released from memory. The application variables are only released from memory when the Web application is stopped, when the Web server is stopped, or when the server is stopped.

Privacy Policies

It is important to understand the privacy needs of the user when you are designing your Web site. If you collect information about a user, you should inform the user. A **privacy policy** is often used to inform the user about the type of information that is being collected and about what is being done with that information.

Many users concerned about their privacy do not want Web sites to keep information about them. Below is a list of Web sites that discuss privacy issues and privacy policies.

- TRUSTe—*www.truste.org*
- Electronic Frontier Foundation—*www.eff.org*
- Life Beyond Yahoo!—*www.lifebeyondyahoo.com/life/privacy.asp*
- Privacy.Net—*www.privacy.net*
- CDT - Center for Democracy & Technology—*www.cdt.org*
- ACP - Americans for Computer Privacy—*www.computerprivacy.org*
- Watchdog—*http://watchdog.cdt.org*

APPLICATION CONFIGURATION FILES

In the past version of ASP, the configuration of the Web site was contained primarily within a data structure called the **Metabase**, and some additional data was stored in the registry. The registry is where Windows applications typically store their configuration settings. The Web developer typically accessed the application settings via the **Internet Service Manager** (**ISM**) application, or by using the **Windows Scripting Host** (**WSH**) to create scripts to access the Metabase. The Web site could be configured locally using the Internet Service Manager, as shown in Figure 9-2. In order to remotely access the settings, the Web developer needed access to the Web server console, or used the remote administration Web site known as the **HTMLA**.

Figure 9-2   Configuring the Web server with the Internet Service Manager

Today, you can configure the Web server using the ISM or ASP.NET. It is important to understand the Web server properties that can be configured using the ISM and ASP.NET. In the following exercise you will view the IIS configuration from the ISM, and you will configure the Web site properties using the ISM.

1. Open the **Control Panel**.

2. Double-click the **Administrative Tools** icon. Double-click the **Internet Services Manager** icon. (*Note*: In Windows XP, the ISM is called Internet Information Services.)

3. Double-click the computer name. (*Note*: In Windows XP, the Web and FTP sites are nested within folders labeled Web Sites and FTP Sites.)

4. Right-click **Default Web Site**, and then click **Properties**. The IIS property pages open to the Web Site tab. The **Web Site** tab, as shown in Figure 9-3, contains configurations that identify the Web site, such as the IP address and TCP port. The number of simultaneous connections can be set along with the application timeout. The HTTP Keep-Alives Enabled property allows you to maintain state with newer browsers that support version 1.1 of HTTP.

Figure 9-3   The default Web Site Properties tab

5. The enable logging check box is used to turn logging on. You then must select a log format from the drop-down list. The **W3C Extended Log File Format** contains extended properties that can be logged such as the Client IP Address, the User Name, the Method invoked, the HTTP Protocol Version, the User Agent, the Cookie, and the Referer. (*Note*: In this case Referer is spelled referer.) The default location for the Web server log files are %WinDir%\System32\LogFiles as shown in Figure 9-4. The default directory for the default Web site log files is W3SVC1. Each log filename is named after the data. You can create new log files daily, or set a file size limit. (*Note*: It is recommended that you not allow the log files to increase in size without monitoring them closely. If the log files are on the C: drive and the hard drive disk space fills up, the system will crash.)

6. Click the **Performance** tab. The Performance tab allows you to tune the Web server performance based on the number of expected hits per day. You can also limit the bandwidth available to the Web site, and the amount of CPU time that the Web site can use. (*Note*: The Performance tab is not available in Windows XP.)

7. Click the **Documents** tab. The Documents tab allows you to select a different name for the default document. In ASP.NET, the default name is default.aspx. You can also enable a footer that will appear throughout your entire Web application using the IIS Document Footer property.

9

Figure 9-4   The default Extended Logging Properties

8. Click the **HTTP Headers** tab, which allows you to enable content expiration. You can force the Web application to have the page expire immediately after it is delivered, or configure a relative or absolute date and time for the page content to expire.

9. Click the **Home Directory** tab. You can configure the Web site so it exists in another directory, hard drive, Web server, or, redirect the Web site to another URL, as shown in Figure 9-5. You can configure security properties using the Home Directory tab. The Read property allows visitors to read the Web page. All Web pages must have the Read property enabled. The Directory Browsing property allows you to see the contents of a folder if there is no default Web page in the folder. This is turned off by default. The Log visits property will allow the log file to log visits to the Web site. The Index this resource property will enable Index Server to include this Web resource in the Index Server search engine catalogues. The Write property allows FrontPage and Dreamweaver editors to publish to the Web site using the HTTP Put command that is built into the editor. Script source access allows visitors to access your script source code. Enabling this property is not recommended unless you are debugging your application. The Execute permissions are scripts by default. Scripts permission allows you to read the resource and execute the scripts. Execute permission is reserved for the CGI-BIN directory because it allows the user the ability to run programs on the server.

10. Press the **Configuration** button to get to the Application Configuration Settings. Click the **App Options** (**Options** in Windows XP) tab. The session timeout property, buffering, default language, and script timeout are configured here. Click the **App Debugging** (**Debugging** in Windows XP) tab. You can configure your application to send a detailed ASP error message or a text error message to the client when a script error occurs, and you can also enable script debugging. Click **Cancel**.

11. Click the **Custom Errors** tab. You can configure your own custom error pages within IIS.

Figure 9-5   The default Home Directory tab

12. Click the **Directory Security** tab. You can enable anonymous access, basic authentication, or Windows authentication. You can enable IP address and domain name restrictions if you are running Windows Server. You can also configure client and server certificates within IIS.

13. Click the **Cancel** button to close the property pages.

In addition to the IIS configuration settings, Web applications contain a series of XML-based configuration files that can be edited in a simple text editor such as Notepad. This text-based configuration file system allows Web server and ASP.NET application settings to be easily replicated across Web servers. This allows Web administrators to easily add a new Web server to the Web farm. Furthermore, Web developers can create their own applications to access the Web settings. They can access the Web settings remotely via the configuration files.

Web applications can be configured in the global machine.config file or from within the application configuration files. The application configuration file is named Web.config. The application-level Web.config file is created by default when you create a Web application. Because this file is placed in the root directory of the application, the entire application inherits the settings configured in this file. It is possible to override these settings by placing a Web.config configuration file within a subdirectory, or by configuring the settings within the ASP.NET Web page.

The Web server contains a machine-level configuration file named machine.cfg. This configuration file is located in C:\WINNT\Microsoft.NET\Framework\v1.0. 3705\ CONFIG\machine.config. This file contains configuration settings for the .NET framework, Windows applications, and Web applications. (*Note:* The version of .NET you are running may vary. Also, in Windows XP this file is located in C:\WINDOWS\Microsoft.NET\ Framework\[version]\CONFIG\machine.config.) The version is the .NET Framework build version, such as `v1.0.3705`. The first line of the file is `<?xml version="1.0" encoding="UTF-8" ?>`. This line of code identifies the version of XML used to create the file. The root node of the file is <configuration>. All configuration settings are contained within this root node.

The ConfigSections node is used to identify the configuration sections and section groups. The Web configuration settings are delineated by the system.web section group. The system.web configuration section group is always nested within the system.web section group. There are approximately 30 configuration settings that can be changed within the system.web section group. Each of these settings is nested within the system.web section group. Each Web application configuration setting is configured as a node, and may include child nodes. The default machine.config file contains many preconfigured settings.

Below is the format of the machine.config configuration file. There may be many other nodes in addition to system.web. You can add comments to the file using the HTML comment tags. In this sample, the WebConfigurationNodes represents a Web configuration node with a single child node named WebChildNode. Both types of nodes can contain one or more properties. (*Note:* These properties are also referred to as **attributes**.) Any node that does not contain any content can be written with a single tag. The closing tag is represented by the backslash before the closing angle bracket in the node.

```
<?xml version="1.0" encoding="UTF-8" ?>
<configuration>
  <configSections>
    <sectionGroup name="system.web">
    </sectionGroup>
  </configSections>
  <system.web>
    <!--         Comment goes here
    -->
    <WebConfigurationNodes>
      <WebChildNode/>
    </WebConfigurationNodes>
  </system.web>
</configuration>
```

The Pages Configuration Node

The pages configuration node allows you to configure settings that control how content is delivered to the Web page. Many of these settings are often configured at the page level. Using the pages configuration node, you can modify the buffer, enableSessionState, enableViewState, enableViewStateMac, and autoEventWireup properties.

The **buffer** is an area in memory on the server. As a request is processed, the data generated from the response is stored in the buffer. If the **Buffer property** is set to false, the end user sees content generated by the server faster. As a result, they perceive that the server has a faster response time. There is no increase in the actual performance of the Web server when you change the Buffer property to false. However, once content has been sent to the client, the header content is also sent. You cannot change the header content once content has been sent to the client. When you want to redirect the user to another page, the header content must be modified. Therefore, if you have code in your page that redirects the user to another page, you cannot set the buffer to false. Setting the Buffer property to true allows you to store the response from the request on the server, until the request has completed processing.

As you learned earlier, the **enableSessionState** property allows you to use the Session capabilities of ASP.NET. You must enable sessions to have access to session variables, session IDs, and HTTP cookies. If you do not plan to use sessions, you can disable this property by setting it to false. You can also set the property to read-only so that you can use sessions, but cannot create new session data. The **enableViewStateMac** property is used to validate data. It uses a one-way authentication code based on the MAC address of the server. The enableViewStateMac property is set to false by default because the validation method requires substantial server resources. The **enableViewState** property is used to store data in the _VIEWSTATE hidden form field in the Web page. The property is used to override page-level events such as Load, UnLoad, and Error. Visual Studio .NET automatically allows you to override the Page_OnLoad event, so it sets the default autoEventWireUp property to false.

Below is the default configuration for the pages node in the machine.config file. (*Note*: You can configure the nodes using two tags such as <pages></pages> or use the single tag method <pages/>.)

```
<pages
    buffer="true"
    enableSessionState="true"
    enableViewState="true"
    enableViewStateMac="false"
    autoEventWireup="true"
/>
```

The httpRuntime Configuration Node

The httpRuntime configuration node sets the executionTimeout, maxRequestLength, and UseFullyQualifiesRedirectURL properties. The **executionTimeout** is the time that a resource is allowed to execute before the request times out. The default executionTimeout value is 90 seconds. The **maxRequestLength** is the number of kilobytes that can be accepted from an HTTP request. The default maxRequestLength size is 4096 kilobytes (4 MB). Configuring this property will help you prevent users from uploading large files using HTTP.

Some hackers have been known to send a large number of requests to a Web server to keep the Web server busy. These attacks are called denial of service. By sending many requests, they stop the Web server from responding to legitimate requests. If you set the maxRequestLength to a smaller number, the hackers won't be able to send a large number of requests to the server.

The **UseFullyQualifiedRedirectURL property** is used to fully qualify the URL when the client has been redirected to a new page. For example, the code `response.redirect("/login.aspx")` redirects the user to a login page using a relative address (/login.aspx). However, many clients, such as mobile phones, require fully qualified URLs when they are redirected. Therefore, if the UseFullyQualifiedRedirectURL property is set to true, when the client is redirected, the absolute URL is sent to the client, even if the code in the page identifies a relative address. Below is a sample of the httpRuntime configuration node that would be found in the Web.config file.

```
<httpRuntime
    executionTimeout="90"
    maxRequestLength="4096"
    useFullyQualifiedRedirectUrl="false"
/>
```

The AppSettings Configuration Node

You can use the APPSettings node to configure custom key/value pairs known as **application variables**. This allows you to store data that can be used across the entire application. The key is used to retrieve the value at a later time. In the sample below, a key named SN is created with a value of "Tara Store". A second key named CS is created. The value for the CS is a string that stores the database connection string.

```
<appSettings>
  <add key="SN" value="Tara Store" />
  <add key="CS"
    value="Provider=Microsoft.Jet.OLEDB.4.0; ¬
    Password=''; ¬
    User ID=Admin; ¬
    Data Source= ¬
    C:\Inetpub\wwwroot\Ch9\TS.mdb;" />
</appSettings>
```

Within the Web page, you can easily retrieve the values of the application variables. In the code below, the application variables SN and CS are written to the Web page.

```
dim SN as string
dim CS as String
SN = ConfigurationSettings.AppSettings("SN")
CS = ConfigurationSettings.AppSettings("CS")
Response.Write("Store Name: " & SN)
Response.Write("<BR />")
Response.Write("Connection String: " & CS)
```

Globalization Configuration Node

Users can configure their computers to support a variety of languages. In U.S. English, there are 26 alphabetical characters. But many languages use more than 26 alphabetical characters. The characters on computers using such languages can be displayed in two ways. You can display the text in a language-specific character set or in Unicode. In **Unicode**, each unique character set has its own identity. Therefore, a Unicode-enabled viewer, such as a browser, can view multiple languages at the same time. Internet Explorer versions 4, 5, and 6 support the Unicode character set.

Unicode isn't the only possible method for encoding HTTP requests and responses. The UTF8Encoding class is contained within the **System.Text** namespace. The default value for encoding is UTF-8. **UTF-8** stands for UCS Transformation Format, 8-bit form, which means that all Unicode character values are supported. (*Note:* The Code Page property also represents the encoding values. For UTF-8, the code page value is 65001.)

Using ASP.NET, you can configure the Web site to support the local culture and language. The globalization node is responsible for setting the encoding standard used for incoming requests and outgoing responses. The **requestEncoding property** configures the encoding of incoming requests, while the **responseEncoding property** configures the encoding of outgoing responses. The **fileEncoding property** is used to identify the encoding for ASP.NET resources.

The **Culture** and **uiCulture properties** are used to identify a language and culture string. Possible values for these properties include en-US for United States English, en-GB for British English, en-IE for Irish, and fr-FR for French. This property is used to configure the local settings, such as the language and dates for over 200 cultures. The sample code below shows the settings for the United States English culture.

```
<globalization
    requestEncoding="utf-8"
    responseEncoding="utf-8"
    culture="en-US"
    uiCulture="en-US"
/>
```

These same settings can also be modified in the Web page. In the Web page, you can display the date to see the effects of the Culture properties. In the following exercise you create a new project and modify the culture configuration properties within a Web page.

1. Start **Visual Studio .NET**.

2. Click **File** on the menu bar, point to **New**, then click **Project**. This opens the New Project window.

3. Under Project Types, click **Visual Basic Projects**, and under Templates click **ASP.NET Web Application**. Type **Chapter9** in place of Web Application1 the Location text box, and then click the **OK** button to create the solution, project, and default files.

4. Right-click **Chapter9** in the Solution Explorer window, point to **Add**, then click **New Folder**. Type **images** for the folder name, then press **Enter**.

5. Right-click the **images** folder, point to Add, then click **Add Existing Item**. Browse to locate your Chapter09Data directory. Select all of the images from the images directory within the Chapter09Data directory (you must select **All Files** in the Files of type list box). Click **Open** to import the images into the project images directory.

6. Right-click **Chapter9** in the Solution Explorer window, point to **Add**, then click **Add Existing Item**. Browse to locate your Chapter09Data directory, select the file **france.aspx**, and then click **Open** to import the file into your project. Click **Yes** to create the new class file.

7. Double-click **france.aspx** in the Solution Explorer window. In the Properties window, change the culture from en-US English to **fr-FR-French**. Notice the large number of cultures that can be configured.

8. Double-click on the **france.aspx** page to edit the code behind the page. Add the following code to the Page_Load event procedure.

```
lblDT.Text=DateTime.Now.ToString("D")
```

9. Click the **Save All** button. Click **Build** on the menu bar, then click **Build Solution**.

10. Switch back to the Web page. Right-click on the page, and then click **View in Browser**. Your page should look like the one in Figure 9-6.

11. Close any open pages.

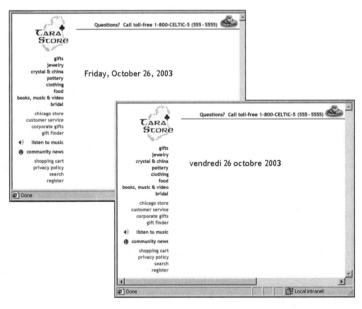

Figure 9-6 Configuring the globalization application settings

Compiler Node Configuration

The compiler node contains configuration settings related to the language compilers use to build the application. By default, the compiler used in a Web application in Visual Studio .NET is Visual Basic .NET. However, you can change the default language for the compiler in the compiler node via the **DefaultLanguage property**. In the code below, the language is set to Visual Basic .NET. The other language compilers that are installed by default with Visual Studio .NET include C#, J#, VBScript .NET and Jscript .NET. (*Note*: Additional compilers such as Perl and Java are available.) The **Debug property** is used to configure the application to show the source code files when you are debugging the application. The Debug property is set to false by default in the machine.config file, but it's set to true by default in the Web.config file. Although the compiler builds the application in a .dll file, you still want to have access to the source code files during the debugging process. The **Explicit property** requires you to declare your variables before they are used. The **Strict property** requires you to declare the data type of a variable before it is used. Both of these properties are set to true by default.

```
<compilation
    debug="false"
    explicit="true"
    strict="true"
    defaultLanguage="vb">
</compilation>
```

You can also change the compiler used in the Web page. In the Web page, you would set the language to the name of the new language.

```
<%@ Page Language="vb">
```

Trace Node Configuration

Tracing is the ability to retrieve data to help identify the data that was communicated during the request or response. The Trace property can be turned on in the page, or in the configuration files. In the page, you can turn tracing on by specifying `Trace="true"` in the @Page command. Figure 9-7 shows an example of trace results generated when tracing is turned on in a Web page.

Within the Web.config file, tracing can be customized. The **Enabled property** allows the application to turn tracing on. In the machine.config file, the enables setting is set to false by default. On a production server, you do not want to display the trace results to the visitor. To avoid this, you can set the **localOnly property** to true, so that tracing results are only displayed to the localhost. To view the trace results, you access the Web site using the URL *http://localhost/*. The **traceMode property** allows you to sort trace results based on time using SortByTime or by category using SortByCategory.

9

Figure 9-7   A Web page with tracing enabled

The **pageOutput property** allows you to display the trace results with the Web page. If the pageOutput property is set to false, then the output is not displayed with the page. Instead, you can access the tracing data using a trace utility program. The trace results are stored in memory and can later be accessed using the trace utility program. The number of trace results stored is configured using the **requestLimit property**. The default number of trace results stored in memory is 10.

```
<trace
    enabled="false"
    localOnly="true"
    pageOutput="false"
    requestLimit="10"
    traceMode="SortByTime"
/>
```

You can configure your application to send additional data to the trace stack. The `trace.write("CategoryName", "Value")` method allows you to send information to the trace utility program. The CategoryName is a string that contains the text label to be displayed in the trace output. The value is a string that contains the value of the CategoryName. You can use an expression to generate the CategoryName or Value. For example, in the following code, the Web page calls a function named GetTotal. The Web page passes two numbers named price and quantity to the GetTotal function. The GetTotal function calculates the product of price and quantity and stores the results in a variable named Total. The function returns the Total variable to the Web page. The variables price, quantity, and total are all sent to the trace stack. The Web page then displays the results using the code `<% Response.write(GetTotal(25, 5))%>` .

```
Public Function GetTotal(Price as Integer, ¬
     Quantity as Integer) As Integer
     Dim Total
     Total = Price * Quantity
     Trace.write("Price: ", Price.ToString())
     Trace.write("Quantity: ", Quantity.ToString())
     Trace.write("Total: ", Total.ToString())
     Return Total
End Function
```

To view the trace data, you can use the Trace property, or use the trace utility program called TraceTool. You can open this program by going to the *http://localhost/ approot/Trace.axd*. (*Note*: It is also available at localhost/Configuration/Tracing/ TraceTool/trace.axd.) The values that you add using Response.write appear in the Category column, and their corresponding values appear in the Message column. The tool provides the trace stack information along with the physical directory of the page being traced. You can enable the Trace feature on any page in any directory even if the enabled property is turned off in the configuration file. It is usually recommended that you disable trace for production applications once the application has been deployed. If you have statements that use Trace.write, you can leave the commands in the page without having an impact on performance. Later, you may want to use those statements again if you have to debug the application.

CustomErrors Node Configuration

When the user requests a page, the Web server provides the page, and an HTTP status message code indicates the status of the request. If the request is successfully met, the HTTP status code 200 is returned. An HTTP status code 404 indicates that the file requested could not be found. (*Note*: HTTP status codes in the 400s usually indicate a client-related error. HTTP status codes in the 500s usually indicate a server-related error.) The Web server and ASP.NET can be configured to send a Web page to the user indicating that an error has occurred.

Both ASP.NET and IIS provide error pages that describe the error, the error codes, and error messages. The IIS Web pages are located in the C:\winnt\Help\iisHelp\common\ directory. You can use the Internet Service Manager tool to configure custom error pages, as shown in Figure 9-8. However, because this tool is often not available to Web developers, custom error pages are seldom used. Furthermore, ASP.NET provides a variety of additional error messages that are not part of IIS. You can create a virtual directory named CustomErrors in which to store your default error pages, and then point the IIS custom error configuration and the ASP.NET configuration to this folder. Then, your application uses a common error message for both ASP.NET and IIS errors.

Figure 9-8 Configuring error pages using the Internet Services Manager

Instead of displaying static error messages, ASP.NET provides a rich error page. When an error occurs, the error page provides detailed information about stack traces and compilation errors. You can use this information to help determine where the error occurred, and how to correct the error. However, you may not want your visitors to see this information. You can configure the CustomErrors node to set the mode to **RemoteOnly**, so that the rich error pages are only displayed locally. The RemoteOnly settings can be set to On or Off. If the RemoteOnly setting is On, then the application contains custom error pages. If the RemoteOnly setting is Off, then the ASP.NET error pages are displayed. The error messages can still be displayed when viewing the Web site using the localhost. But, if the user visits the Web site, and an error occurs, the user is redirected to a default error page or a custom error page. (*Note*: It is recommended that you set the RemoteOnly property to RemoteOnly or On in a production Web server.) You can also set the **defaultRedirect property**, which sets a default error page to be displayed if no applicable custom error page is configured. (*Note*: If an error occurs on the defaultRedirect page, the page does not continually redirect to itself.)

You can configure ASP.NET to use a custom error page for each HTTP status code by using the **error node**. The error node property **statusCode** indicates the status code of the error message. The **Redirect property** indicates the page to redirect the user to when the error is detected. The sample code below shows how to configure the default error page and a custom error page for the HTTP status code 404.

```
<customErrors
  mode="RemoteOnly"
  defaultRedirect="/defaultError.aspx"/>
```

```
<error
    statusCode="404"
    redirect="/error404.aspx"/>
</customErrors>
```

 ASP.NET provides the ability to send messages to the Windows error logs. You can use the Application_OnError event handler to send the message to the Windows Event Log.

MAINTAINING STATE IN AN ASP.NET APPLICATION

There are several techniques that you can use to maintain state information in your ASP.NET Web applications. All three methods use a unique identifier to recognize the client across Web pages. A common method for maintaining state information in early Internet development was client-side cookies. Cookies are small files stored on the client's system. Another method was storing the identification information in a temporary object on the server. ASP.NET uses Application and Session objects to store data. The Session object allows you to store information on the server, but still requires the browser to support a cookie, called the per session cookie. However, this session information is volatile. If the Web server crashes, the session information is unrecoverable. Using ASP.NET you can create cookieless applications. Cookieless applications do not require the user to support client-side or server-side cookies. The identification data is passed with the URL. In this section, you will learn how to create Web applications that use client-side cookies, per session cookies, and cookieless Web applications.

Client-side Cookies

Client-side cookies maintain information about an individual user across sessions. A **client-side cookie** is a small piece of information that is stored on a client's local computer. The **Cookies collection** is a group of cookies that are sent by the server through the header to the client. The browser application on the client receives the cookie and writes the cookie to the client's file system.

All Web servers have the ability to create a client-side cookie. If you are using Netscape Navigator, all cookies are stored in a single text file named cookies.txt, which is usually located in the root directory of the Netscape application. In Internet Explorer, each cookie is stored in a separate text file. In Windows 2000, Internet Explorer stores cookies in C:\Documents and Settings\[UserID]\Cookies.

Because clients can delete their cookies at any time, your Web application should not depend upon the existence of a cookie. Always provide an alternate method for users who elect not to accept cookies, or who delete their cookies. Customers often misunderstand the purpose, value, structure, and security of cookies. You should always create a Web page on your site that informs the user of the privacy and security policies. In this page, you should provide a definition of cookies, inform the user whether the site uses cookies, and if so, indicate what information is stored in the cookie and what the cookie is used for. You should also inform the user that only the server that writes the cookie can read the cookie. TRUSTe (*www.etrust.com*) provides samples of what you might want to include in your privacy and security policy Web page. Below is a list of Web pages that contain more information about cookies, privacy issues, and links to more Web sites that discuss cookies.

- *www.lifebeyondyahoo.com/life/cookies.asp*

- *www.microsoft.com/info/cookies.htm?RLD=291*

- *www.microsoft.com/info/*

- *msdn.microsoft.com/library/default.asp?url=/library/en-us/dninstj/html/cookies.asp*

Most users do not have an accurate understanding of what a cookie is. The cookie file, whether written by Netscape Navigator or Internet Explorer, stores the name of the cookie, the value, and the name of the server that wrote the cookie. Figure 9-9 shows the contents of a client-side cookie. The information stored in a cookie could easily be stored on the server. Storing the cookies with the client provides a means of automating client-side activities, such as the login process form's completion. It's very useful to provide a sample of what a cookie looks like to the user on the security and privacy page. Cookies are limited in size to 4 KB. Most cookies are about 100–200 bytes in size. The maximum number of cookies allowed is currently 300. If the limit is reached, the oldest cookies are deleted. The maximum disk space for cookies is 1.2 MB, which is about the size of a floppy disk. Today, hard disk drives are available that can hold gigabytes of data. Therefore, cookies do not "eat up" a client's hard drive space. (*Note*: It's more likely that large amounts of hard drive space are used by the browser cache file, which contains all of the graphics and Web pages that the client has visited.)

Figure 9-9   A cookie written by the Internet Explorer browser

Reading and Writing Client-side Cookies Using JavaScript

The browser supports a Document object model with its own set of objects, properties, and methods. The Cookie property of the Document object allows you to store and read client-side cookies associated with the document. A cookie consists of the cookie name and a value, separated by an equal sign. For example, you can create a cookie named CookieEmail with the value of kkalata@oakton.edu by writing `document.cookie = "CookieEmail=kkalata@oakton.edu";`. You can assign the cookie an expiration date. The following code from documentCookie.htm sets a cookie named CookieEmail with a value of kkalata@oakton.edu, and an expiration date of January 3, 2003, and reads the cookie into a variable named ReadCookie.

```
<script language="JavaScript">
document.cookie = "CookieEmail=kkalata@oakton.edu;
    expires = Monday, 03-Jan-03 12:00:00 GMT";
readCookie = document.cookie;
</script>
```

 Each cookie name and value pair is separated by a semicolon. You need to separate each pair of cookies, and then separate the name and value.

In the following exercise, you will create a Web page that uses client-side cookies.

1. Open the **Chapter9** application in Visual Studio .NET if necessary.

2. Right-click **Chapter9** in the Solution Explorer window, point to **Add**, then click **Add Existing Item**. Navigate to your Chapter09Data directory. Select the file **clientcookies.aspx**, and then click **OK** to import the file into your project. Click **Yes** to create the new class file.

3. Double-click **clientcookies.aspx** in the Solution Explorer window to open the page. Click the **HTML** tab to view the HTML code.

4. Add the following code above the closing head tag in the heading section.

```
<script language="JavaScript">
function GetCookie(){
  var uid = document.Form1.txtUsr.value
  var pwd = document.Form1.txtUsr.value
  document.cookie = "CookieEmail2=" + uid +
  ";expires=Monday, 01-Jan-03 12:00:00 GMT";
  window.alert("Your cookie is: " + document.cookie);
}
</script>
```

5. Click the **Save All** button. Click **Build** on the menu bar, then click **Build Solution**.

6. Start your Web browser and enter the URL **http://localhost/chapter9/clientcookies.aspx**.

7. Fill in the form with your e-mail address, typing **password** in the password text box, and then click the **Sign In** button. An alert message box appears with the value of your cookie. Your page should look similar to the one in Figure 9-10. (*Note*: Your alert box may also display the per session cookie known as the ASP.NET_SessionId.)

8. Close any open pages.

9

Figure 9-10   Creating a client-side cookie with Visual Studio .NET

HTTP Cookies

HTTP cookies are cookies created by the Web server rather than the browser. They are used to enable the Web server to identify the client. The SessionID is the value of the HTTP cookie that identifies the client's session. This **SessionID** is used to identify a Session object on the server. The Session object can be used to store session variables such as the user's e-mail address, contact information, purchasing habits, browser properties, and personal preferences. HTTP cookies are also known as **per session cookies** because they identify the session. HTTP cookies are only used during the client's session, and are deleted when the session ends.

By default, ASP and ASP.NET applications are configured to use HTTP cookies. The HTTP cookie is sent in the HTTP header, so it can be retrieved as an HTTP server variable called HTTP_COOKIE. You can view the value of the HTTP cookie and the client cookies when the trace property is turned on. Below is the syntax for retrieving a cookie from the HTTP header using the server variable HTTP_COOKIE from a Web page using the server variables.

<% Request.Servervariables("HTTP_COOKIE") %>

In some browsers, such as Internet Explorer 5, users can disable client-side cookies, and still allow HTTP cookies. Figure 9-11 shows how to access the cookie settings in Internet Explorer 5. You should know how to set the cookie settings in older browsers because some of your visitors may be using older browsers. In Internet Explorer 6, the settings have been moved from the Security settings to a new group of settings called **Privacy Settings** as shown in Figure 9-12. You cannot assume that the client supports

HTTP cookies or client-side cookies. Remember that the client can change these settings in the browser, but the programmer can't.

Figure 9-11   Changing the cookie setting in Internet Explorer 5

9

Figure 9-12   Changing the privacy in Internet Explorer 6

Creating Cookies with ASP.NET

The **HttpCookieCollection object** represents the cookie variables. There are two types of HTTP cookie collections within ASP.NET; both can be accessed via the Cookies object. The first type contains cookies that are passed by the client to the Web server from the Cookies header. The second contains cookies that have been generated on the server and transmitted to the client in the **Set-Cookie header**.

Below is the syntax for writing a simple cookie using an absolute date. You can specify the number of days from the current date that you want the cookie to expire. If you expect your visitors to visit daily, then you can set the cookie to expire in "Date.Now.Today.AddDays(1)" days. If your visitors visit monthly, you can set the cookie to expire in "Date.Now.Today.AddDays(30)" days.) If you want the browser to delete the cookie, you can specify a date in the past such as "Date.Now.Today.AddDays(-30)" or "July 4, 1776". The browser then deletes the cookie because the cookie has expired.

```
<% Response.Cookies("myCookie") = "value" %>
<% Response.Cookies(myCookie).Expires = "MM DD,YYYY" %>
```

Notice that the Response object, and not the write method, writes the cookie. The write method is used to write the value of a string to the Web page. The Response.Cookies method actually sends the cookie to the browser, which in turn writes the cookie to the client's file system.

 The named group of cookies is also referred to as a dictionary cookie, and the individual cookies within it are sometimes referred to as cookie keys. Below is the syntax for writing a group of cookies named GroupID, where the cookie expires N days from today.

```
<% Response.Cookies("GroupID")("Cookie_1")="value" %>
<% Response.Cookies("GroupID")("Cookie_2")="value" %>
<% Response.Cookies("GroupID")("Cookie_n")="value" %>
<% Response.Cookies(GroupID).Expires = ¬
    "Date.Now.Today.AddDays(N)" %>
```

You can retrieve a cookie's value—whether from a simple cookie or from a group of cookies—by using the Request object. To retrieve a simple cookie with one value, specify the name of the cookie. One of the benefits of using ASP over client-side scripting is that the Request object parses out the cookie names and values for you. It is easy to retrieve the value of a cookie with one line of code. Below is the syntax for retrieving a simple cookie with one value.

```
<% Request.Cookies("CookieName") %>
```

To retrieve the value of a single cookie from a group of cookies, you must identify the name the cookie group as well as the name of the individual cookie. Below is the syntax for retrieving a single cookie from a group of cookies named GroupID.

```
<% Request.Cookies("GroupID")("CookieName_n") %>
```

You can add additional cookies to the HTTP cookies. You can create an additional cookie with the Response object, read the value of the HTTP cookie using the Request object, and display it in a Web page.

In addition to the Request and Response objects, you can use the HTTPCookie Collection to create and read cookies. The sample code below shows how to write a cookie named CookieEmail with the value from a text box named txtEmail. The MyCookie is then added to the Cookies Collection using the add method of the Response object.

```
Dim MyCookie As New HttpCookie("CookieEmail")
MyCookie.Value = txtEmail.Value
Response.Cookies.Add(MyCookie)
```

In the following example, you will create a Web page that maintains state with HTTP cookies using the Response and Request objects. You will create a cookie named gc that contains the user's name, e-mail address, and SessionID. You will read the value of the cookie and write the value to the Web page.

1. Open the **Chapter9** project in Visual Studio .NET, if necessary.

2. Right-click **Chapter9** in the Solution Explorer window, point to **Add**, then click **Add Existing Item**. Navigate to your Chapter09Data directory, select the file **cookies.aspx**, and then click **OK** to import the file into your project. Click **Yes** to create the new class file.

3. Double-click **cookies.aspx** in the Solution Explorer window to open the page. Double-click the **Sign in** button to open the code behind the page.

4. In the SignIn_ServerClick event procedure, add the code below to retrieve the values from the form. Add a variable to store the SessionID.

```
Dim strName As String = txtName.Value
Dim strEmail As String = txtEmail.Value
Dim SID As String = Session.SessionID
```

5. After the code above, add the code to write the values to a group of cookies named gc. The individual cookie keys are named name, email, and SID. Set the Expires property to specify when the cookie is deleted.

```
Response.Cookies("gc")("name") = strName
Response.Cookies("gc")("email") = strEmail
Response.Cookies("gc")("SID") = SID
Response.Cookies("gc").Expires = ¬
 Date.Now.Today.AddDays(30)
```

6. After the code above, add the code to read the cookies and store the results in a variable named Str Display the value of Str in a text box named Message.

```
Dim Str As String
Str = "Your cookie is: " & _
"<br /><br />Name: " & _
Request.Cookies("gc")("name") & _
"<br />Email: " & _
Request.Cookies("gc")("email") & _
"<br /><br />SessionID: <br>" & _
Request.Cookies("gc")("SID")
Message.Text = Str
```

7. The code should look as shown in Figure 9-13. Click the **Save All** button. Click **Build** on the menu bar, then click **Build Solution**.

8. Open your Web browser and enter the URL **http://localhost/chapter9/cookies.aspx**.

9

```
Private Sub Page_Load(ByVal sender As System.Object, ByVal e As Sys-
    Put user code to initialize the page here
End Sub

Private Sub SignIn_ServerClick(ByVal sender As System.Object, ByVal

    Dim strName As String = txtName.Value
    Dim strEmail As String = txtEmail.Value
    Dim SID As String = Session.SessionID

    Response.Cookies("gc")("name") = strName
    Response.Cookies("gc")("email") = strEmail
    Response.Cookies("gc")("SID") = SID
    Response.Cookies("gc").Expires = Date.Now.Today.AddDays(30)

    Dim Str As String
    Str = "Your Cookie is: " & _
    "<br><br>Name: " & _
    Request.Cookies("gc")("name") & _
    "<br>Email: " & _
    Request.Cookies("gc")("email") & _
    "<br><br>SessionID: <br>" & _
    Request.Cookies("gc")("SID")
    Message.Text = Str
```

Figure 9-13   Final code behind the page for cookies.aspx

9. Fill in the form with your name and e-mail address, and click the **Sign In** button. (*Note:* If a Windows dialog box asks if you want the system to remember the password for this page, click **Cancel**, or **No** in Windows XP.) The text box displays the value of your cookies. Your page should appear similar to the one shown in Figure 9-14.

10. Close any open pages.

Figure 9-14   Creating HTTP cookies in ASP.NET

Maintaining State Without HTTP Cookies

Previous versions of ASP required client support for HTTP cookies. These HTTP cookies were used to link the client's session to the Session object using the SessionID. The SessionID contains several properties. The **Timeout property** specifies when the session ends if no activity occurs. The default value for the session timeout is 20 minutes. The

Session property data is stored as a HashTable of key and value pairs. If the Session ended, the session data contained within the session object was also lost. In ASP.NET, the Session object can be configured to store the data outside of the Web server, without requiring HTTP cookies. In ASP.NET, the session configuration is stored in the **sessionState node**, which is configured in the Web.config file. ASP.NET applications can maintain state without HTTP cookies, and can maintain the session data outside of the Web application. Therefore, more robust and reliable applications can be built with ASP.NET.

ASP.NET applications use the HTTP session cookie by default to maintain session data. The **Cookieless property** in the sessionState node in the Web.config file is used to determine if the session key should require cookies. The Cookieless property is set to false by default, which means that the default application requires cookies to maintain session state. Because users can refuse to accept HTTP cookies, the configuration can be set up to support session key management without requiring HTTP cookies. You can configure the application to use cookies or be cookieless, but you can't use both settings within the same application.

You can modify your application to support sessions without requiring HTTP session cookies. The process of creating a cookieless application is known as **cookie munging**. When the Cookieless property is set to true, the Web Server appends the sessionID to any requested URL, as shown in Figure 9-15. The SessionID does not contain the session data. The session data is still maintained by the Web server, or outside the Web server. When the next page is requested, the Web server can use the SessionID, which is attached to the URL, to identify the client without requiring the client to have a cookie. In the following example, you will modify your application to support visitors who do not accept HTTP cookies.

1. Open the **Chapter9** application in Visual Studio .NET, if necessary.

2. Right-click **Chapter9** in the Solution Explorer window, point to **Add**, then click **Add Existing Item**. Navigate to your Chapter09Data directory, select the file **cookieless.aspx**, and then click **OK** to import the file into your project. Click **Yes** to create the new class file.

3. Double-click **cookieless.aspx** in the Solution Explorer window to open the page. Double-click the **Sign In** button to edit the code behind the page. Add the code below, which creates the same cookies as in the previous exercise.

```
Dim strName As String = txtName.Value
Dim strEmail As String = txtEmail.Value
Dim SID As String = Session.SessionID
Response.Cookies("gc")("name") = strName
Response.Cookies("gc")("email") = strEmail
Response.Cookies("gc")("SID") = SID
Response.Cookies("gc").Expires = ¬
Date.Now.Today.AddDays(30)
Dim Str As String
Str = "Your cookie is: " & _
"<br><br>Name: " & _
Request.Cookies("gc")("name") & _
```

9

```
"<br>Email: " & _
Request.Cookies("gc")("email") & _
"<br><br>SessionID: <br>" & _
Request.Cookies("gc")("SID")
Message.Text = Str
```

4. Double-click **Web.config** in the Solution Explorer window.

5. Under the opening sessionState tag, enter the code below to set the Cookieless property to true. Change the timeout property to two minutes. (*Note*: you may already have some properties, such as Cookieless and Timeout, set with sessionState. If you do, just modify the Cookies and Timeout properties. Do not create a second sessionState node.)

```
<sessionState cookieless="true" timeout="2">
```

6. Click the **Save All** button. Click **Build** on the menu bar, then click **Build Solution**.

7. Open your Web browser and enter the URL **http://localhost/chapter9/ cookieless.aspx**.

8. Fill in the form with your name and e-mail address and click the **Sign In** button. Your page should look like the one in Figure 9-15. Notice that the SessionID appears within parentheses in the URL as the parent directory for the Web page.

9. In the file Web.config, reset the Cookieless property to false, and the Timeout property to 20.

10. Click the **Save All** button. Click **Build** on the menu bar, then click **Build Solution**.

11. Close any open pages.

Figure 9-15   Creating a cookieless Web application

Storing Session Data

You can configure where the Web server stores the session data. In the machine.config and the Web.config files, the **sessionState node** allows you to configure the session management. Storing session data in the Web server memory results in the best performance. But if the Web server crashes, the data is lost. Therefore, you can configure the Web server to store your session data based on your information and performance needs. The **Mode property** is used to identify which storage method to use to store session data. The Mode property can be set to InProc, SQLServer, StateServer, or Off. Turning the mode to Off turns off session management.

The **InProc value** means that the data is stored in process with the Web server. Because the data is not being sent out of process, this method provides the best performance. You should use this method if you are hosting your Web site on a single server, and if your session data is not critical. This method is not appropriate for a Web farm because the user's request can be redirected to another Web server if the Web server load values change, and the session data would not travel with the request.

You can set the mode property to StateServer to store the data with a Windows service called **StateServer**. To use StateServer, the **aspnet_state service** needs to be running. You can start the StateServer by using the DOS commands or the Windows Services applet. Because the service is run out of process from the Web server, the session data is reliably stored. Although the StateServer is reading the data out of process, generally it is located on the same server. Therefore, the performance is better than if the session data is sent to an external server. The StateServer service can be used across multiple Web servers. In the machine.config and Web.config settings, the **stateConnectionString** identifies the TCP/IP connection to the StateServer. The loopback address is used to identify the StateServer. Then, if the IP address of the server is changed, the configuration does not have to be changed. The port number is used to identify the TCP/IP port. The default TCP/IP port for the StateServer is 42424. However, any port can be configured for state management. If you intend to use the same StateServer for multiple Web Servers, you must change the TCP/IP settings for each of the Web servers so that they point to the same StateServer. You must also configure the machine key on each server. The machine key is used to encrypt the data going to the StateServer. In order for the Web servers to be able to encrypt the state session data, they must all have the same machine key. Below is the sample configuration file for a Web server that uses a StateServer.

```
<sessionState
    mode="StateServer"
    stateConnectionString="tcpip=127.0.0.1:42424"
    cookieless="false"
    timeout="20"
/>
```

9

To change the TCP/IP settings you must edit the Windows registry keys. The registry key for the TCP/IP port setting is located in `HKEY_LOCAL_MACHINE` | `System` | `CurrentControlSet` | `Services` | `aspnet_state` | `Parameters`. In the Parameters node, you must click Port in the Name column. In the value data text box, you can enter a new value for the port and click the OK button.

To start the StateServer using the DOS command line:

1. Open the DOS command window by clicking **Start**, then clicking **Run**.

2. Type **CMD** in the text box, and then press **Enter**. The DOS window opens.

3. Type **net start aspnet_state**, and then press **Enter** to start the service.

The StateServer is a Windows service and can therefore be accessed via the Windows Services applet. In the following activity, you will start the StateServer using the Windows Services applet:

1. Click **Start**, point to **Settings**, then click **Control Panel**.

2. Double-click **Administrative Tools**.

3. Double-click **Services**.

4. In the Name column, double-click **ASP.NET State Service**.

5. To start the StateServer service, click the **Start** button. The keyword started in the Status column shows that the service has been started. (*Note:* You can also click the **Start** button on the Services toolbar. You can also open the ASP.NET State dialog box by right-clicking the **ASP.NET State** name and selecting **Properties**.)

6. You can set the service to start manually or automatically by selecting the value in the Startup type drop-down list, as shown in Figure 9-16. Automatic startup means that the service automatically starts whenever the server is restarted.

7. Return to your ASP.NET application in Visual Studio .NET. Edit the **Web.config** file to support the session state parameters. Change the mode to **stateServer**. (*Note:* The connection string may vary with your server. For example, it may include the port number 42424 to identify the service.)

8. Click the **Save All** button. Click **Build** on the menu bar, then click **Build Solution**.

9. Change the mode in the Web.config file session state mode back to **InProc**.

10. Click the **Save All** button. Click **Build** on the menu bar, then click **Build Solution**.

11. Close any open pages.

Figure 9-16 Starting the StateServer to store session data

If you set the mode to SQLServer, you can also use SQL server to store your session data. A scaled-down version of SQL Server is distributed with ASP.NET. SQL Server is run out of process, which means that the SQL Service runs outside of the Web Service, in its own memory space. Although using SQL Server to store session data does not provide the same performance as using StateServer or inProc, it does offer reliable storage of session data. SQL Server can be run on the same Windows server or another Windows server. You must identify the connection string used to connect to the SQL Server database. The connection string identifies the TCP/IP address and the authentication data required to connect to the database. The connection string must be a valid System.Data.SqlClient.SqlConnection string, minus the Initial Catalog.

If you plan to use the SQL Server that is supplied with ASP.NET, you must install it first. You only have to set up the SQL Server once. The name of the executable SQL Server light version is OSQL.exe. When you run the installation script named InstallSqlSate.sql, the TempDB database is created, which stores the session data. Several stored procedures are also created. You need to execute the following steps to install and configure SQL Server to store session data.

A version of SQL Server known as the MSDE was installed when you installed Visual Studio .NET. However, if you are running ASP.NET without Visual Studio .NET, you will have to install SQL Server in order to direct state management to the SQL Server. Your path to the OSQL.exe may be located in a different directory. If you installed the full version of SQL Server, the OSQL.exe file can be located in C:\Program Files\Microsoft SQL Server\80\tools\binn\.

1. Log on to the server as the system administrator. You must have administrative permissions to install the SQL service.

2. Go to the DOS command window by clicking **Start** then clicking **Run**. Type in **cmd** and press **Enter**.

3. Change directory to locate the installation scripts. The installation script is a script written in T-SQL, which installs SQL Server and sets up the session database. To change the directory, type **CD C:\WINNT\Microsoft.net \Framework\[Version]**. (*Note:* Version is the current version of .NET. You can have multiple versions of the .NET framework on the same computer.)

4. Type **OSQL -S localhost -U sa -P <InstallSqlState.sql**. This is the command to start the service and send the output to the SQL Server.

Then, you would have to configure your Web server to use SQL Server to store the session parameters.

1. Edit the **machine.config** file which is located in C:\WINNT\Microsoft.NET\ Framework\V1.0.3705\CONFIG\machine.config to support the session state parameters. (*Note:* Your version of .NET may vary. In Windows XP, this file is located in C:\WINDOWS\Microsoft.NET\Framework\[version]\CONFIG\ machine.config.) Change the mode to **sqlServer** and add the connection string as shown below.

```
<sessionState
    mode="SQLServer"
        sqlConnectionString="data source=127.0.0.1;
        user id=sa;password="
    cookieless="false"
    timeout="20"
/>
```

2. Click the **Save All** button. Go to the **Build** menu and select **Build Solution**.

OVERVIEW OF ASP.NET SECURITY METHODS

There are several ways to protect your ASP.NET Web applications. You can configure the application security settings in the machine.config and Web.config files. The two main principles of security are authentication and authorization. **Authentication** is the process of validating the identity of the request. (*Note:* Although the request is from a user, it is the request, not the user, that is authenticated. There are newer methods, such as biotechnological ones that allow you to validate the user's identity. For example, some computer applications require users to submit their fingerprints or retinal images. However, this requires that additional hardware and software be installed on the client's workstation and the server.) The Authentication mode property can be set to Windows, Passport Forms, or None. If the mode is set to None you can set up your own custom authentication such as validating the username and password with a hashed value.

Windows is the default mode for authentication. When you set the Authentication mode to Windows, you are requiring that the application use Windows authentication. You can specify the authentication method with the Internet Service Manager. The Internet Service Manager identifies how the Web server validates the user. With most Web sites, browsers use the anonymous user account called the **Internet Guest account**. The anonymous user is named by default **IUSR_MachineName**, where MachineName is the name of the Windows server. (*Note:* You can locate the Machine name of the server by going to the Network Identification tab in the System category of the Control Panel. The machine name is the full computer name.) You can configure the server to disable the anonymous user so that all visitors must be authenticated by the server using their own valid Windows user accounts. When you set up the server to use Basic authentication, the username and password are sent as clear text over the Internet, unless you encrypt the login with SSL encryption. If you use Windows authentication, the username and password are not sent over the Internet. Instead, the information is used to generate a hash value that is sent over the Internet. The server knows the username and password and can therefore recreate the hash value. If the values are equal, the user is authenticated. Although Windows authentication is the most secure way to authenticate a user, it is only available in the Internet Explorer browser.

The Authentication mode can also be set to Passport. **Passport** is a single sign-on passport identity system created by Microsoft. In a Web site, the browser collects the user's credentials and sends them to the Passport service. The Passport service authenticates the user and sends a cookie back. The benefit to the user is that he or she only has to login once to access multiple resources and services. The benefit to the administrator it is that he or she does not have to recreate the same account on every computer. The administrator can also use Active Directory to set up an account on a collection of Windows servers called a forest. You can learn more about Passport at *www.passport.com*. The sample code below shows the configuration settings for using the Passport service. When the Authentication mode is set to passport, the passport child node can be used. The redirectURL property of the passport node is used to provide an internal page or URL to redirect the user to when the request is not authenticated, or if the user has not logged in with the Passport service. The value of the redirectURL is typically the Passport login page.

```
<authentication mode="passport">
    <passport redirectURL="gohere"/>
</authentication>
```

Authorization Node Configuration

Authorization is the process of ensuring that you can only access the resources made available to you by the system administrators. The Windows NTFS file system allows you to set permissions on individual files and folders using an **access control list (ACL)**. The ACL determines who has the rights to read, write, modify, and delete resources. Each user who accesses a resource on the server is using a valid Windows account. The configuration files also contain an **identity node** that can be used to impersonate a

9

Windows user account. The **Impersonate property** is used to indicate if impersonation is allowed. The Impersonate property is set to false by default.

The authorization node is used to identify which resources can be accessed after the user is authenticated. The **allow node** is used to configure users that are allowed to access the application. The **deny node** is used to configure users that are not allowed to access the application. The **Users property** is used to identify the user. The wildcard * is used to identify all users. The wildcard ? is used to identify the anonymous user. A name may be provided to explicitly configure a user's access to the applications resources. The **Roles property** is used to identify a group of users. Groups of users are defined as a role in the Windows Active Directory. You can configure several users at the same time by separating the list of users with a comma, as shown below.

```
<authorization>
      <allow users="Joan, John"
      roles="Administrator, Customer"/>
      <deny users="?" roles="BlackList"/>
</authorization>
```

Form-based Authentication

Forms authentication is a cookie-based authentication method. When you log in, using an ASP.NET form, the Web server checks the IP address and domain in the host header of the request.

 The Web server can be configured to deny or allow user access to the Web server based on the client's IP address or domain name. Although this is one way to filter unwanted visitors, it does not prevent hackers from visiting your Web site. Unfortunately, experienced hackers can send a fake IP address in the header of the TCP/IP packet.

Once the Web server has validated the user's IP address, the Web server determines if the anonymous account is enabled. If the anonymous user account is enabled, then IIS passes the request to ASP.NET. ASP.NET determines if an authentication cookie is present in the TCP/IP header packet. If there is no cookie, the client is redirected to the login page. The user must submit credentials and be authenticated. Once the user has been authenticated, a cookie is added to the header packet. After a user has been authenticated, forms authentication uses an HTTP cookie to identify future requests. When ASP.NET has validated that there is a valid authentication cookie in the header, it checks to see if the user is authorized to access the resource. If the user has been authorized, the resource is sent to the client.

The user may be validated using the credential list within the configuration files, or the request may be validated against an XML file, a database, an in-memory structure, an LDAP directory, or even a Web service. A Web service is an application that is sent over HTTP using SOAP. The Web developer needs to know what login information to send to the Web service, and what information is returned, which indicates if the user is a valid account.

Forms Node Configuration

When the Authentication mode is set to Forms, the child node forms may be configured. The **form child node** contains several properties that configure the HTTP cookie. The **Name property** is used to identify the cookie that contains the ID of the user. The default name is .ASPXAUTH. The **Path property** is the path that is valid for the cookie. The cookie is only visible to the path of the server that is identified in this property. The Default Path property is "/" because the server can access the cookie from any directory. The path value in the cookie is case sensitive. Timeout is the valid duration of the cookie. **Timeout** is a sliding value because each time a request is made, the value is reset. The default time-out value is 30 minutes. The **loginUrl** is the page to redirect the user to if he or she has not been authenticated or has been denied authentication. The default is "login.aspx". You have to create the login.aspx page, or change the loginUrl value to your login page.

The **Protection property** is used to protect the data in the HTTP cookie. The possible values for the Protection property are All, None, Encryption, and Validation. The first time the user sends a username and password, the cookie has not been created. Therefore, you must use SSL to encrypt the login information until the HTTP cookie is generated. There is no username or password stored in the HTTP cookie. The HTTP cookie merely identifies the client. If the Protection property is set to **None**, the HTTP cookie is stored as clear text. None is used only when the login is used for personalization purposes. When the Protection property is set to **Encryption**, the cookie is encrypted but the data is not validated. The application will encrypt the HTTP cookie. However, the encrypted cookie is simply an encrypted session ticket. When the Protection property is set to **Validation**, the data is validated but cookie is not encrypted. When the Protection property is set to **All**, both data validation and encryption are used. The default Protection property is all. The encryption of the data is performed using the machine key (*Note:* Triple Data Encryption Standard (TripleDES) is used if it's available and if the machine key is at least 48 bytes long. DES was developed by IBM in about 1974 and was adopted as a national standard in 1977. It is used to encrypt data. However, DES can be broken in less than 3.5 hours. Triple DES is a newer version of DES and is more secure than the original DES.) You must identify the encryption keys used to encrypt the HTTP cookie in the machine.config file.

MachineKey Node Configuration

The **machineKey node** is used to identify a value and method to encrypt data on the server. The machineKey node allows you to set the values for encryption and decryption. The **validationKey** is used as part of the hash algorithm, so only ASP.NET applications that have the validationKey can use the data. Using the validationKey guarantees that the data is valid. The length of the validationKey must be between 40 and 128 hexadecimal characters. The Validation property identifies what type of hash is to be created. Possible values for the validation type include MD5, SHA1, and 3DES. 3DES is the strongest algorithm for creating a hash value. The **decryptionKey** is used to guarantee that nontrusted sources can't read the text.

If you are using a single Web server, do not change the configuration file settings for the machineKey. You can use the AutoGenerate value for the validationKey and decryptionKey. The only time you need to specify the machineKey properties is when your Web server is part of a Web farm. The other Web servers in the Web farm need to access the data that the Web server generates. Therefore, all Web servers in a Web farm must have the same values set for the validationKeys and the decryptionKeys. (*Note:* They do not have to have the same value for both the validationKey and the decryptionKey, as long as the values are consistent across the Web farm.) Below are the default machineKey configuration settings.

```
<machineKey
    validationKey="AutoGenerate"
    decryptionKey="AutoGenerate"
    validation="SHA1"
/>
```

Credentials Node Configuration

The **credentials node** is an optional child node of the forms node. The credentials node is used to provide the credentials for users that may access the application resources. The **passwordFormat property** allows you to specify the encryption method used to encrypt the credentials. The possible values are Clear, SHA1, and MD5. SHA1 and MD5 store the password as a hash value.

The **user node** is a child node of the credentials node used to identify users. The **Name property** identifies the username. The **password** identifies the user's password. The method used to store the password is identified in the passwordFormat property.

```
<authentication>
    <forms
        name=".ASPXAUTH"
        loginurl="login.aspx"
        protection="all"
        timeout="30"
        path="/" >
        <credentials passwordFormat="SHA1">
            <user name="User1" password="password1"/>
            <user name="User2" password="password2"/>
    </forms>
</authentication>
```

Once the user is validated, you can access that user's identity information. The following sample code displays the user's name and the authentication method used in the Web page. (*Note:* This code could be placed in the Page_Load event handler or in a function.)

```
If User.identity.IsAuthenticated then
    Message.Text = "Welcome Member: " & _
    user.identity.name & _
    ". You were authenticated using: " & _
    User.identity.AuthenticationType & "."
```

```
Else
     Message.Text = "Welcome Stranger!"
End if
```

You should provide a method for users to log out, such as a logout button. You can create a click event handler that logs the user out of the application and destroys the temporary HTTP cookie. The following sample code logs out the user when the user clicks a button named DoLogOut. (*Note:* You must import the System.Web.Security namespace into the application.)

```
Public Function DoLogOut(s as Object, e as EventArgs)
     FormsAuthentication.Signout()
     Response.clear
     Response.redirect("login.aspx")
End Function
```

Validating User Credentials

The users credentials file is used to store user authentication data. You can create an XML file to store user information such as e-mail address and password, and later retrieve this information when the user is validated. Below is a sample of a users credentials file named Users.xml.

```
<userlist>
  <users>
    <email>kkalata</email>
    <password>painter</password>
  </users>
  <users>
    <email>jdonnald</email>
    <password>rosewood</password>
  </users>
</userlist>
```

You can validate the user credentials with static data, from the configuration file, from an XML file, or from a database. In the exercise below, you create an XML file that retrieves the user's credentials. The general process is to retrieve the user login information, retrieve the XML data, and locate the user within the XML file. Then, if the user appears, validate the user. If the user is not validated, he or she is redirected by the Web configuration file to the login page. In the first section, you will import the necessary files, and create the default home page. Then, you will change the configuration files to reflect the new user authentication model.

1. Open the **Chapter9** application in Visual Studio .NET, if necessary.

2. Create a new WebForm named **default.aspx**. Double-click the page in the Solution Explorer window to open the page, then double-click on the page to open the code behind the page. In the Page_Load procedure enter **Response.Redirect("home.aspx")**. Save the page and close the window.

3. Right-click **Chapter9** in the Solution Explorer window, point to **Add**, then click **Add Existing Item**. Navigate to your Chapter09Data directory, and select the files **login.aspx, home.aspx** and **XMLUsers.xml** (hold down the Ctrl key to select multiple files). Click **Open** to import the files into your project, and then click **Yes** to create a new class file for each file.

4. Double-click **XMLUsers.xml** in the Solution Explorer window to open the page, then add a username and password to the list of users above the user named kkalata.

5. Click the **Save All** icon and close the file.

6. Double-click the **Web.config** file in the Solution Explorer window. Change the Authentication mode from Windows to **Forms**. Remove the closing forward slash in the Authentication tag. Enter the code below after the Authentication tag to allow the users to log in.

```
<forms name=".ASPXAUTH"
path="/" loginUrl="login.aspx"
protection="All"
timeout="30">
</forms>
```

7. Add the closing authentication tag, **</authentication>**, after the closing forms tag.

8. Click the **Save All** icon and close the file.

In the next step, you will modify the login page to import the relevant namespaces, retrieve the values from the form, and compare the values to the XML file.

1. In the Solution Explorer window, double-click the **login.aspx** page. On the page, double-click the button labeled **Sign In**. The code behind the page opens in the SignIn_ServerClick event procedure. In the first line of code, add the imports statement to import the namespaces required to connect to XML files and DataSets, as shown below.

```
Imports System.Web.Security
Imports System.Data
Imports System.Data.SqlClient
Imports System.Xml
Imports System.IO
```

2. In the SignIn_ServerClick event procedure, enter the code below to retrieve the values from the form and assign it to a variable named cmd.

```
Dim cmd As String = "UserEmail='" & UserEmail.Value & "'"
```

3. Then, create a DataSet object named ds, as follows:

```
Dim ds As DataSet = New DataSet()
```

4. Enter the code below to create a FileStream object named **fs**. The parameters passed include the URL of the XML file named XMLUsers.xml. Open a read-only connection to the file. Create a StreamReader object named **reader**, which will be used to read the file. Use the ReadXML method to insert the data into the DataSet. Close the connection to the file using the close command of the FileStream object.

```
Dim fs As FileStream = New ¬
FileStream(Server.MapPath("users_encrypted.xml"),¬
FileMode.Open,FileAccess.Read)
Dim reader As StreamReader = New StreamReader(fs)
ds.ReadXml(reader)
fs.Close()
```

5. Enter the code below to create a new table named **users** within the DataSet. Create a new row named **matches**. Check to see if there is a row that contains the matching password.

```
Dim users As DataTable = ds.Tables(0)
Dim matches() As DataRow = users.Select(cmd)
If (Not IsDBNull(matches)) And (matches.Length > 0) Then
   Dim row As DataRow = matches(0)
   Dim pass As String = CStr(row("UserPass"))
   If (0 <> String.Compare(pass, UserPass.Value, false))
   Then
   Message.Text = "We couldn't locate your login " & _
      "information.<br />Please try to login again.<br />"
   Else
```

6. Enter the code below. If the password matches, then the user is authenticated against the entire Web site. The finished code behind the page should appear as shown in Figure 9-17.

```
   FormsAuthentication.RedirectFromLoginPage¬
      (UserEmail.Value, false)
End If
End If
```

7. Click the **Save All** icon and close the file.

The last step is to set up the home page. If the user is already authenticated, display a custom message. Otherwise, provide a hyperlink to the login page.

1. Double-click **home.aspx** in the Solution Explorer window to open the page. Double-click the **Log Off** button to open the DoLogOut_ServerClick event procedure.

2. Add the code below to the first line to import the security namespace.

```
Imports System.Web.Security
```

```
Private Sub Page_Load(ByVal sender As System.Object, ByVal e As System.EventArgs) Handles MyBase.Load
    'Put user code to initialize the page here
End Sub

Private Sub SignIn_ServerClick(ByVal sender As System.Object, ByVal e As System.EventArgs) Handles SignIn.
    Dim cmd As String = "UserEmail='" & UserEmail.Value & "'"
    Dim ds As DataSet = New DataSet()
    Dim fs As FileStream = New FileStream(Server.MapPath("XMLUsers.xml"), FileMode.Open, FileAccess.Read)
    Dim reader As StreamReader = New StreamReader(fs)

    ds.ReadXml(reader)
    fs.Close()

    Dim users As DataTable = ds.Tables(0)

    Dim matches() As DataRow = users.Select(cmd)

    If (Not IsDBNull(matches)) And (matches.Length > 0) Then
        Dim row As DataRow = matches(0)
        Dim pass As String = CStr(row("UserPass"))

        If (0 <> String.Compare(pass, UserPass.Value, False)) Then
            Message.Text = "We couldn't locate your login " & _
            "information.<br /> Please try to login again.<br />"
        Else
            FormsAuthentication.RedirectFromLoginPage(UserEmail.Value, false)
        End If
    End If
End Sub
```

Figure 9-17   Validating the user against a database

3. Within the Page_Load procedure, add the code below, which will verify if the user is already authenticated and display a message. If the user is not authenticated, the hyperlink is displayed.

```
If User.Identity.IsAuthenticated Then
        Message.Text = "Welcome <b>" _
        & User.Identity.Name & "</b><br/><br/>" _
        & "Your login was processed using<br/><b>" _
        & User.Identity.AuthenticationType _
        & "</b> Authentication"
Else
        DoLogOut.Visible = False
        Message.Text = "We're sorry," & _
        "<br/>you were not authenticated.<br/><br/>" & _
        "<a href='login.aspx'>Click here to log in</a>"
End If
```

4. Within the DoLogOut_ServerClick procedure, add the code below to destroy the user's authentication cookie and redirect the user to the login page.

```
Response.Clear()
FormsAuthentication.SignOut()
Response.Redirect("login.aspx")
```

5. Click the **Save All** button. Click **Build** on the menu bar, then click **Build Solution**.

6. Open your Web browser and enter the URL **http://localhost/Chapter9/**. Since you are not yet authenticated, the home page provides a link to the login page. (*Note:* You could also redirect the user automatically using response.redirect.) Your pages should look like the ones shown in Figure 9-18. The first page, login.aspx, is redisplayed if the user types in the wrong password. The second page is the welcome page from home.aspx. The third is the logout page from home.aspx.

7. Fill in the login information that you entered in the XMLUsers.xml document, and click **Sign In**. A message welcomes you to the Web site. Click the **Log Off** button. The page displays a hyperlink back to the login page because you are no longer authenticated.

8. Close any open pages.

Figure 9-18   Building a login page using forms authentication with XML

You can also authenticate your resources using a relational database. The process is similar to retrieving the values from the XML file. You must first retrieve the values from the Web page and store them in variables. Then, you must identify the connection string and the connection that is used to access the database. Then, retrieve the values from the database that match the values in the form. Set the Boolean variable to indicate that the user was authenticated. In the steps below, you will import the login database page, create the database and configure the Web.config file.

1. Open the **Chapter9** solution in Visual Studio .NET, if necessary.

2. Right-click **Chapter9** in the Solution Explorer window, point to **Add**, then click **Add Existing Item**. Navigate to your Chapter 09Data directory. Select the file **logindb.aspx**, and then click **Open** to import the file into your project. Click **Yes** to create the new class file.

3. Right-click **Data Connections** in Server Explorer, and then click **Create New SQL Server Database**. The Server text box should read *MachineName***NETSDK** or localhost. In the New Database Name text box, type **Webusers**. Click the **Use SQL Server Authentication** radio button. In the Login Name text box enter **sa**. Leave the Password text box blank and click **OK**. (*Note*: Your system administrator can provide your login information for you. Some systems require Windows NT integrated security.)

4. Expand the **Webusers** database. Right-click **Tables**, and then select **New Table**.

5. In the Column Name column, enter **UserEmail** with the data type **varchar** and length **50**. Deselect the **Allow null** check box.

6. In the Column Name column, enter **UserPass** with the data type **varchar** and length **50**. Deselect the **Allow null** check box.

Your ASP.NET account must have permission to access every database you create. You will find instructions on assigning database permissions in the ReadMe.doc file, which is located in the Chapter9Data directory.

7. Click the **Save All** button. In the Choose Name window, enter **Users** as the name of the table, and then click **OK**. Close the table structure window.

8. In the Solution Explore window, right-click **Stored Procedures**, and then click **New Stored Procedure**. Select all the text and press **Delete**. Then, enter the text below.

```
Create PROCEDURE dbo.InsertData
AS
INSERT INTO users (UserEmail, UserPass )
    VALUES ('kkalata', 'painter')
INSERT INTO users (UserEmail, UserPass)
    VALUES ('jdoherty', 'rosewood')
INSERT INTO users (UserEmail, UserPass)
    VALUES ('lshea', 'barley')
INSERT INTO users (UserEmail, UserPass)
    VALUES ('tgreen', 'grayslake')
INSERT INTO users (UserEmail, UserPass)
    VALUES ('mcavanagh', 'fisherman')
INSERT INTO users (UserEmail, UserPass)
    VALUES ('bmcintosh', 'candlelight')
RETURN
```

9. Click the **Save All** button. With the file open, right-click inside the stored procedure, and then click **Run Stored Procedure**. The data is inserted into the table.

10. Double-click **home.aspx** in the Solution Explorer window to open the file. Double-click the page to edit the code behind the page. Change the href property to **logindb.aspx** and the redirect parameter to **logindb.aspx**.

11. Click the **Save All** icon, and then close all the files.

12. Double-click **Web.config** in the Solution Explorer window to open the file. Change the loginURL from login.aspx to **logindb.aspx**, as follows.

```
<forms name=".ASPXAUTH"
    path="/" loginUrl="logindb.aspx"
    protection="All"
    timeout="30">
</forms>
```

13. Click the **Save All** icon, and then close the file.

In the next set of steps, you will create the code in the login page to retrieve the form values and compare them with the data in the database.

1. In the Solution Explorer window, double-click **logindb.aspx** to open the page. On the page, double-click the button labeled **Sign In**. The code behind the page opens in the SignIn_ServerClick event procedure. In the first line of code in the page, add the imports statement to import the Web.Security and Data namespaces.

```
Imports System.Web.Security
Imports System.Data
Imports System.Data.SqlClient
```

2. In the SignIn_ServerClick event procedure, enter the code below to create a connection string to the database and to retrieve the values from the form. The strUser contains the username, and the strPwd contains the user's password. Create a Boolean variable named blnIsAuth that stores the user's authentication status. The user is not authenticated by default. (*Note:* The connection string for the SqlClient does not have to have the Provider identified. Your connection string will vary with the type of authentication that your SQL Server requires.)

```
Dim CS As String
CS = "data source=localhost;initial catalog=Webusers;user
id=sa;"
Dim strUsr As String = txtUsr.Value
Dim strPwd As String = txtPwd.Value
Dim blnIsAuth As Boolean = False
```

3. Create a SQL string to retrieve the user records as follows.

```
Dim strSQL As String
strSQL = "SELECT * FROM Users WHERE UserEmail='" _
      & strUsr & "' AND UserPass='" & strPwd & "'"
```

4. Enter the code below, which uses the Try-Catch procedure to create the database objects and retrieve the records. Create the Connection object and open the connection. Create the Command object and the DataReader object. Connect to the database with the DataReader object and read in the records. If there is a record, then set the Boolean value to True.

```
Try
      Dim objCN As New SqlClient.SqlConnection(CS)
      objCN.Open()
      Dim objCM As New SqlClient.SqlCommand(strSQL, objCN)
      Dim objDR As SqlClient.SqlDataReader
      objDR = objCM.ExecuteReader()
      If objDR.Read() Then
            blnIsAuth = True
      End If
      objDR.Close()
      objCN.Close()
```

5. Enter the code below, which displays an error message if an error occurs. This is helpful if there is a problem with connection to the database, column names, or other database related errors.

```
Catch objError As Exception
      Message.Text = "<b>* An Error occured</b>.<br/>" _
      & objError.Message & "<br/>" & objError.Source
      Exit Sub
End Try
```

9

6. Enter the code below. If the blnIsAuth variable is true, then redirect the user to the login page that is configured in the Forms child node in the authentication node in the Web configuration file. You must send a Boolean value to indicate if the user's authentication information should persist across browser sessions. If the user is not authenticated, display a custom error message inside the Message label in the Web page.

```
If blnIsAuth Then
    FormsAuthentication.RedirectFromLoginPage ¬
        (txtUsr.Value, False)
Else
    Message.Text = ¬
    "We couldn't locate your login " & _
    "information.<br  /> ¬
    Please try to log in again.<br />"
End If
```

7. Click the **Save All** button. Click **Build** on the menu bar, then click **Build Solution**.

8. Open your Web browser and enter the URL **http://localhost/chapter9/**. The default page normally appears; however, since you are not yet authenticated, the page displays a hyperlink back to the logindb.aspx page.

9. Fill in your login information, and then click the **Sign In** button. A message welcomes you to the Web site. Click the **Log Off** button. The page displays a hyperlink back to the login page because you are no longer authenticated.

10. Close any open pages.

CHAPTER SUMMARY

❐ A Web application is a group of files and folders. The IIS Web server software configures the Web application using the Internet Services Manager, or you can configure it via the Web application configuration files.

❐ The machine.config file maintains information that is used across .NET applications. Within this file, the Web application is configured within the system.web node.

❐ The Web.config file configures the Web application. The Web.config file is an XML-compliant file that can be edited with a text editor. The configurations that are commonly configured in the Web.config file include state management, application timeout, application variables, globalization settings, default compiler language, trace mode, and custom error pages.

❐ The SessionID property is assigned by the server, and provides a way to identify the client during the user session. Sessions require the user to support HTTP cookies.

❐ A cookie can be used to maintain information across multiple sessions for a specific user. The cookie is a text file that is stored on the client's computer.

❑ Your Web sites should educate and inform users about the use of cookies, and about how the cookie affects their computer system. The cookie is passed in the HTTP header with the other HTTP server variables.

❑ Cookies can store single values, and multiple cookies can be stored in a named group of cookies. The cookie is written using the Response object, and retrieved using the Request object. The group of cookies is stored in the HTTPCookieCollection.

❑ You can store session data within the Web server process, within the StateServer, or in a SQL Server database. StateServer is a Windows service that must be turned on before session data can be stored in the StateServer. If the Web server crashes, any session data within the StateServer or SQL Server persists. The StateServer and SQL Server can be used to store session data for a Web farm if the Web servers are configured to use the same server and machine key. The machine encrypts and decrypts data on the server.

❑ Authentication is the process of validating the identity of the request. Authorization is the process of validating the user access privileges to the resources.

❑ You can configure Web applications to support various types of authentication. Anonymous authentication means that the user does not have to log in with a special account. The Internet Guest Account represents the client. Basic authentication sends the login data as clear text. Windows authentication allows the user to log in without sending his or her login over the Internet. Forms authentication is a new technique in ASP.NET to protect the Web application. You can configure forms authentication in the Web.config file.

❑ Authorization within an ASP.NET application is conducted via the Web.config file or via the Windows NTFS permissions.

9

REVIEW QUESTIONS

1. Which method of authentication is new to ASP.NET?

   a. forms authentication

   b. Windows authentication

   c. basic authentication

   d. all of the above

2. Which form of cookies is also known as HTTP cookies?

   a. response cookies

   b. ASP cookies

   c. per session cookies

   d. session cookies

3. A group of files and folders located under the Web applications root directory is called a _____.

  a. Web application

  b. Web directory

  c. Web folder

  d. none of the above

4. A(n) _____ is a unique identifier created by the Web server to maintain the identity of the client.

  a. Session GUID

  b. SessionID

  c. E-mail address

  d. CookieID

5. A(n) _____ is used to inform the user about the type of information that is being collected about the user, and to inform the user what is being done with that information.

  a. privacy policy

  b. security policy

  c. access policy

  d. all of the above

6. Which tool is used to configure IIS?

  a. Windows Scripting Host

  b. Internet Service Manager

  c. HTMLA

  d. all of the above

7. The _____ is used to store most of the IIS configuration data.

  a. Registry

  b. metabase

  c. database

  d. Oracle

8. What log format provides extended properties?

  a. W3C Extended Log File Format

  b. ODBC

  c. Microsoft IIS Format

  d. all of the above

9. The _____ is the default directory for the log files for the IIS Web server.

    a. Window\LogFiles

    b. Documents and Settings\LogFiles

    c. Window\System32\LogFiles

    d. WINNT\System32\LogFiles

10. Which permission is required to run ASP pages?

    a. Write

    b. Script

    c. Execute

    d. a and b

11. The _____ file is the configuration file for the Web server for ASP.NET applications.

    a. machine.config

    b. Web.config

    c. global.asa

    d. none of the above

12. The _____ is the root node in the Web application configuration file.

    a. configuration node

    b. System.Web node

    c. Web node

    d. WebConfigurationNodes node

13. The enableSessionState is configured in the _____ node configuration.

    a. Pages

    b. HTTPRuntime

    c. AppSettings

    d. Globalization

14. The _____ function is used to store data in the _VIEWSTATE hidden form field.

    a. enableViewState

    b. enableViewStateMac

    c. enableSessionState

    d. autoEventWireUp

15. The default value for executionTimeout is _____.
    a. 20
    b. 90
    c. 404
    d. 4096

16. Which of the following would create a new session variable?
    a. <add key="StoreName" value="Tara Store"/>
    b. <add key.value="StoreName" text="Tara Store"/>
    c. <add field="StoreName" value="Tara Store"/>
    d. <add name="StoreName" text="Tara Store"/>

17. Which code sample retrieves a session variable named StoreName?
    a. ConfigurationSettings.AppSettings("StoreName")
    b. AppSettings("StoreName").Value
    c. ConfigurationSettings("StoreName").Text
    d. ConfigurationSettings("StoreName").Value

18. The _____ property is used to restrict trace results to the Web server console.
    a. localhost
    b. localOnly
    c. disabled
    d. pageOutput

19. The HTTP status message code _____ indicates the success of the HTTP request.
    a. 200
    b. 202
    c. 404
    d. 500

20. Your UserID is KALA9876. Client-side cookies are stored in the _____ directory.
    a. C:\Documents and Settings\KALA9876\Cookies
    b. C:\Windows\Cookies\KALA9876\
    c. C:\Program Files\Internet Explorer\KALA9876\Cookies
    d. C:\KALA9876\Cookies

21. The _____ object represents the client's cookie variables.

    a. HttpCollection

    b. ResponseCookieCollection

    c. CookiesCollections

    d. HttpCookieCollection

22. The Windows service used to store session data is called _____.

    a. SQL Server

    b. Oracle

    c. SessionServer

    d. StateServer

23. Your computer's name is DarkStar. The name of the Internet Guest Account is _____.

    a. IUSRDarkStar

    b. localhost

    c. IUSR_Guest

    d. IUSR_DarkStar

24. Which type of authentication sends the username and password as clear text over the Internet?

    a. anonymous authentication

    b. basic authentication

    c. Windows authentication

    d. all of the above

9

HANDS-ON PROJECTS

Project 9-1

In this project, you will create a page that educates the user about cookies.

1. Research the Internet to learn more about cookies. Visit five Web pages that discuss cookies.

2. Open your **Project9** in Visual Studio .NET and create a Web page called **Cookie Research**.

3. Add a heading that says **What You Should Know About Cookies**.

4. Write a paragraph that describes what a cookie is, what a cookie is used for, and what you will do with the information contained in the cookie. Describe the security information that relates to reading and writing cookies.

5. Add a heading that says **Cookie Resources**. Then, create a list of links to five Web pages on the Internet that discuss cookies. Format the list as a bulleted list.

6. Add a heading formatted as heading 2, centered-aligned that says **Your Cookie**.

7. Use the code below to display the cookies that have been written from your domain to the client's computer using the HTTP_COOKIE server variable. The ASP Session cookie is displayed to the user along with any other cookies that have been created by your domain.

```
Here is the cookie that has been written
to your computer from this domain: <br /><br />
<% = Request.Servervariables("HTTP_COOKIE") %>
```

8. Modify the Web page's appearance with your favorite fonts, colors, and images. You can also modify the layout using a table, line breaks, blockquotes, or other HTML or ASP.NET tags.

9. Save the Web page as **Ch9Proj1.aspx**.

10. View the Web page in the browser. Print out the Web page and the HTML code.

Project 9-2

In this project, you will create a privacy policy.

1. Visit the TRUSTe Web site (*www.etrust.com*). Then, go to the Privacy Central Page at *www.truste.org/webpublishers/pub_privacy.html* and read about privacy policies. Read the sample content that they recommend you include in your privacy policy at *www.truste.org/webpublishers/pub_modelprivacystatement.html*. You can also locate Web sites that discuss privacy at Life Beyond Yahoo! at *www.lifebeyondyahoo.com/life/privacy.asp*.

2. Visit at least four Web sites that discuss privacy.

3. Locate at least three Web sites that contain privacy policies.

4. Open your **Project9** in Visual Studio .NET and create a Web page named **Privacy Policy**.

5. Add a heading that says **Privacy Policy Resources**. List the sites you visited.

6. Add a heading that says **Sample Privacy Policy**. Then add a bulleted list of sample policies on the Internet.

7. Add a heading that says **Our Privacy Policy**. Then add at least one paragraph describing your Web site's privacy policy.

8. Modify the Web page's appearance with your favorite fonts, colors, and images. Use blockquote tags, line breaks, tables or other HTML tags to format the layout of the page.

9. Save the Web page as **Ch9Proj2.aspx**.

10. View the Web page in the browser. Print out the Web page and the HTML code.

Project 9-3

In this project, you will create a page with a registration form. The page that processes the form writes the form field values to a cookie. The browser is redirected to a page that retrieves the cookie values, assigns them to session variables, and displays the session variables.

1. Open your **Project9** in Visual Studio .NET and create a Web page called **Registration Form**.

2. Add a heading that says **Registration Form**.

3. Add two text box form fields named **name** and **pass**, with the labels named **username** and **password**.

4. Use the code below to add a hidden field named ID. The value of the field is the SessionID.

```
<input type=hidden id=sid
    value="<% = Session.SessionID%>" runat=server>
```

5. Add a label named **message**.

6. Add a button. In the button, display the text **Register Me!**

7. Double-click the button to edit the code behind the page. Use the code below to retrieve the form values in the code behind the page and write their values to cookies. The cookie group name should be **sc**. Assign the current date to a cookie named **mydate**. Assign the server variables HTTP_REFERER and REMOTE_ADDR to cookies named **referer** and **ip**.

```
<%
Response.Cookies("sc")("name") = Request.Form("name")
Response.Cookies("sc")("pass") = Request.Form("pass")
Response.Cookies("sc")("sid") = Request.Form("sid")
Response.Cookies("sc")("mydate") = ¬
   Now.Date.ToShortDateString
Response.Cookies("sc")("referer") = _
      Request.Servervariables("HTTP_REFERER")
Response.Cookies("sc")("ip") = _
   Request.Servervariables("REMOTE_ADDR")
```

8. Use the code below to display the cookie using the HTTP_COOKIE server variable.

```
message.text = ¬
"Here is the cookie that has been written ¬
to your computer from this domain: <br /><br />" & _
Request.ServerVariables("HTTP_COOKIE")
```

9. Modify the Web page's appearance using your favorite fonts, colors, and images. Use line breaks, blockquotes, tables, or other HTML tags to format the page layout.

10. Save the page as **Ch9Proj3.aspx**.

11. View the **Ch9Proj3.aspx** Web page in the browser. Print the Web page, the HTML source code, and the code behind the page.

Project 9-4

In this project, you will practice reading and writing cookies. You will create a Web page that collects the username and password. The form field values are saved as a cookie. When the user returns to the same Web page, the cookie is used to automatically log the user into the Web page.

1. Open your **Chapter9** project in Visual Studio .NET. Create a new Web page named **Ch9Proj4.aspx**

2. Add a login form with the form fields named **name** and **pass**, with labels that say **username** and **password**. Add a button named **btnLogin** that says **Login**.

3. Add the following code in the code behind the page to determine whether the user filled out the form when the user clicks on the btnLogin button.

   ```
   if name.text<> "") and _
       pass.text <> "") then
   ```

4. Add the code below. If the user filled out the form, then retrieve the values from the form fields and assign them to the cookies. Name the group cookie **lc** and the cookies **name** and **pass**. The cookie should expire in seven days from the current date.

   ```
   Response.Cookies("lc")("name") = ¬
   request.form("name")
   Response.Cookies("lc")("pass") = ¬
   request.form("pass")
   Response.Cookies("lc").expires = ¬
   Date.Now.Today.AddDays(7)
   else
   end if
   ```

5. In the Page_Load event procedure, add a script to detect whether a cookie is present, as shown below. The cookie must have both a name and password stored in the cookie.

   ```
   if (request.cookies("lc")("name") <> "") _
       and (request.cookies("lc")("pass") <> "") then
   ```

6. Add the code below. If there is a cookie, change the message label to **You were logged in with your cookie**. Retrieve the values from the cookie and display them in the browser.

   ```
   message.Text = "You were logged in with your cookie."
   message.Text += "<br />"
   message.Text += Request.Cookies("lc")("name")
   message.Text += "<br />"
   message.Text += Request.Cookies("lc")("pass")
   ```

7. Modify the Web page's appearance using your favorite fonts, colors, and images.

8. Save the Web page as **Ch9Proj4.aspx**.

9. View the Web page. Print your source code. Print out the Web page.

Project 9-5

In this project you will create a Web page that validates the user against a customer database using Visual Studio .NET.

1. Start **Visual Studio .NET** and open your **Chapter9** solution, if it is not already open.

2. In Visual Studio .NET create a database, using the MSDE or SQL Server, named **Ch9Proj5**.

3. Use the table below to determine the column names, datatypes, lengths, and properties.

Column Name	DataType	Length	Allow Nulls
CustomerID	Int	4	No
CustomerName	Nvarchar	50	No
EmailAddress	Nvarchar	50	Yes
Password	char	10	Yes
MembershipLevel	Int	4	Yes

4. In the properties at the bottom half of the window, change the Identity for the CustomerID column from No to **Yes** using the drop-down list arrow. The Identity Seed should be set to **1**, and identity increment should be set to **1**. This creates a new value for each new record entered in the database.

5. Right-click the **CustomerID** column name, and then click **Set Primary Key**. A yellow key appears at the side of the column name to indicate that this column is the primary key column.

6. Click the **Save All** button and save the table as **Customers**.

7. Enter the data listed in the table below in the database.

8. Create a Web page named **Ch9Proj5.aspx**. Add a login form with the CustomerName and Password.

9. Use the CustomerName and Password fields from the database to validate the user.

10. Change the forms authentication in the Web.config file to point to the database.

11. Save the page and view the page in the browser. Print the Web page, the HTML code, the code behind the page, and the Web.config file.

9

Column Name	Row1	Row2	Row3	Row4
CustomerID				
CustomerName	June Mayzer	Ralph Waldon	Joseph Reno	Kevin Marx
EmailAddress	JM@	RW@	JR@	KM@
	tarastore.com	tarastore.com	tarastore.com	tarastore.com
Password	Franklin	Bears	Crypto	Loyola
MembershipLevel	2	1	2	3

Project 9-6

In this project you will create a Web page that validates the user against a customer database using Visual Studio .NET.

1. Start **Visual Studio .NET** and open your **Chapter9** solution if necessary.

2. In Visual Studio .NET create a database named **Ch9Proj6**.

3. Use the table below to create an XML file that contains the username and password. Save the file as **Ch9Proj6.xml**.

Username	JM@ tarastore.com	RW@ tarastore.com	JR@ tarastore.com	KM@ tarastore.com
Password	Franklin	Bears	Crypto	Loyola

4. Create a Web page named **Ch9Proj6.aspx**. Add a login form with Username and Password fields.

5. Use the Username and Password fields from the XML file to validate the user.

6. Change the forms authentication in the Web.config file to point to the XML file.

7. Save the page and view the page in the browser. Print the Web page, the HTML code, the code behind the page, the XML file, and the Web.config file.

CASE PROJECTS

Tara Store — Creating an Individual Membership Login Page

The Tara Store membership has decided that they would like to log in using individual user IDs and passwords. Your task is to create the login page. The members were mailed the default password, TaraOnline, so they can log into the Web site. Create a page where they log in with their e-mail address and the password. When the user logs in, a message is displayed. You are to create the XML file named Ch9Case1.xml. Add graphics and content to enhance the Web page. Print out the Web page, the HTML code, and the code behind the page. Print out the Ch9Case1.xml file.

Tara Store — Testing the Home Page

You are in charge of revising the Tara Store home page. Your manager would like to know how quickly the objects in the page load compared to the current page. Create a new home page named Ch9Case2.aspx. Add content and graphics to enhance the page's layout. Use the trace command to access the trace results. Print the page with the trace results. Circle the value that indicates the total time the page took to load. Circle the control that took the longest time to load.

Tara Store — Configuring Custom Error Pages

You have had number of complaints from customers about the error messages on your Web site. While working with the Web development team to correct the errors, you have been asked to design several custom error pages. Create a new Web page named Ch9Case3.aspx that serves as the default error page. Provide a link to the Web site at *http://help.tarastore.com*. Add graphics and content to enhance the appearance of the page. Create a new Web page named Ch9Case3FNF.aspx, which is used when an HTTP status code 404 is sent. Indicate to the customer that the file he or she has entered has not been found. Provide a link to the Web site at *http://www.tarastore.com*. Add graphics and content to enhance the appearance of the page. Open the Web.config file. In the CustomErrors node, configure the application to use the new default Web page. Configure the application to use the Ch9Case3FNF.aspx page when a file not found error occurs. Print out both pages and the source code. Print out the configuration file source code.

9

10

TROUBLESHOOTING AND DEPLOYING AN ASP.NET APPLICATION

In this chapter, you will:

♦ Identify and handle ASP.NET errors

♦ Use the Visual Studio. NET Debugger tool to identify application errors

♦ Document the Web site using the Code Comment Report Wizard

♦ Use Page Output Caching to increase Web site performance

♦ Learn how to deploy an ASP.NET Web application

Today, customers demand that Web sites run without errors all of the time. Therefore, it is important to build Web applications that are error-free. When an error does occur, the Web developer tools should quickly allow you to detect, locate, and fix the error. One of the most difficult problems ASP programmers faced was debugging their Web applications. With ASP.NET and Visual Studio .NET, the Web programmer has new error-handling and debugging tools. These tools help programmers catch and locate program errors faster, resulting in a more robust application.

ERROR HANDLING

Error handling is a collection of techniques that allow you to identify programming errors in your code, which are called bugs. Many errors are caused by incorrect syntax or spelling errors. These errors are easily identified using the Visual Studio .NET IntelliSense feature. However, some errors, such as programming logic errors, are more difficult to detect. To handle errors that arise during program execution, you can write code that interprets error messages and that executes when an error is detected, and generates custom error messages and global error handlers.

Creating a Custom Error Page Using the Web Configuration File

In the previous chapter, you learned how to use the Page directive to configure a Web page and Web application to display custom error pages when errors occur. The ErrorPage attribute of the Page property identifies the generic error page. When an error occurs, the client is redirected to this error page. The custom error page can also be set in the customErrors node in the Web.config file. When the Mode attribute is set to RemoteOnly, then only remote clients are redirected to the new page. The localhost still displays the default error message. When the application encounters an error, a status code is generated, and the application can be redirected to a new page. The resulting URL will be the URL of the error page, appended with a question mark and a QueryString. The QueryString consists of the name aspxerrorpath and the virtual path to the page that was requested. For example, if you were looking for a page named garden.aspx, and the name of the custom error page was nogarden.aspx, the resulting URL would be *http://localhost/Chapter10/nogarden.aspx?aspxerrorpath=/chapter10/garden.aspx*.

 There is an excellent discussion in the help documentation on configuration of ASP.NET located at *ms-help://MS.VSCC/MS.MSDNVS/cpguide/html/cpcon aspnetconfiguration.htm.*

You can locate the entire list of ASP.NET configuration schema at *ms-help://MS.VSCC/MS.MSDNVS/cpgenref/html/gngrfaspnetconfigurationsectionschema.htm.*

Common Error Status Messages

Below is a listing of the common status codes. These codes are exposed by the **HTTPStatusCode property** of the System.NET namespace.

Table 10-1   Common Status Codes

Status Code	Code Name	Description
200	OK	The request was received successfully.
301	Moved	The URL requested was moved to a new URL.
400	BadRequest	The server did not understand the request.
401	Unauthorized	The request required authentication.
403	Forbidden	Access to the resource was forbidden. This is usually because the ACL refused access to the resource.
404	NotFound	The server cannot locate the resource.
405	MethodNotAllowed	The method Post or Get is not allowed.
500	InternalServerError	A generic error occurred on the server.
503	ServiceUnavailable	The server is unavailable.

There is an excellent discussion of status codes in the help documentation at *ms-help://MS.VSCC/MS.MSDNVS/cpref/html/frlrfSystemWebHttpResponseClass StatusCodeTopic.htm* and at *ms-help://MS.VSCC/MS.MSDNVS/cpref/html/ frlrfSystemNetHttpStatusCodeClassTopic.htm*.

10

In the following exercise, you create a custom error message and enable your Web application configuration file to detect HTTP status errors. You will change the Web.config file to redirect the browser to a custom error page, when the page requested cannot be found.

1. Start **Visual Studio .NET**.

2. Click **File** on the menu bar, point to **New**, then click **Project** to open the New Project window.

3. Under Project Types, click **Visual Basic Projects**, and under Templates, **click ASP.NET Web Application**. Type **Chapter10** in the Location text box in place of WebApplication1. Click **OK** to create the solution, project, and default files.

4. Right-click **Chapter10** in the Solution Explorer window, point to **Add**, then click **New Folder**. Type **images** as the folder name, and then press **Enter**.

5. Right-click the **images** folder, point to **Add**, then click **Add Existing Item**. Switch to All Files in the Files of type text box. Browse to locate your Chapter10Data\images folder and select all the files in the folder. Click **Open** button to import the files into the images folder of your project.

6. Start **Notepad**. Open the file named **styles.txt**, which is located in your Chapter10Data folder. (*Note*: This file contains the style sheet data, which you will use to format your Web pages in this exercise.)

7. Click **Edit** on the menu bar, and then click **Select All**. Click **Edit** on the menu bar, and then click **Copy**. Close the styles.txt file.

8. In the Solution Explorer window, double-click **Styles.css**. Click the second line to place the cursor immediately below the comment. Click **Edit** on the menu bar, and then click **Paste**.

9. Click the **Save All** button, and then close the Styles.css file.

10. Right-click **Chapter10** in the Solution Explorer window, point to **Add**, then click **Add Existing Item**. Browse to locate your Chapter10Data folder. Change the Files of type drop-down list to **All Files**. Select **customError.aspx**, **Error404.aspx**, and **ch10Home.aspx**. Click the **Open** button to import the files into your project. Click **Yes** to create the class file for each of the Web pages.

11. Double-click the **Web.config** in the Solution Explorer window to open the file. Delete the default **customErrors** node. Add the code below to redirect the visitor to a custom error page when a file has not been found. The code should appear as shown in Figure 10-1.

```
<customErrors defaultRedirect="customError.aspx" mode="On">
    <error statusCode="404" redirect="Error404.aspx" />
</customErrors>
```

```
<?xml version="1.0" encoding="utf-8" ?>
<configuration>

 <system.web>

   <!-- DYNAMIC DEBUG COMPILATION
       Set compilation debug="true" to insert debugging symbol
       into the compiled page. Because this creates a larger
       more slowly, you should set this value to true only
       false at all other times. For more information, refer
       debugging ASP.NET files.
   -->
   <compilation defaultLanguage="vb" debug="true" />

   <!-- CUSTOM ERROR MESSAGES
       Set customErrors mode="On" or "RemoteOnly" to enable
       Add <error> tags for each of the errors you want to
   -->
   <customErrors defaultRedirect="customError.aspx" mode="On">
     <error statusCode="404" redirect="Error404.aspx" />
   </customErrors>
```

Figure 10-1 Modifying the Web.config file

12. Click the **Save All** button. Click **Build** on the menu bar, then click **Build Solution**.

13. In the browser, go to **http://localhost/Chapter10/
Chapter10ErrorTest.aspx**. The page should be redirected to the custom
errors page. Your page should look like the one in Figure 10-2.

14. Close any open pages.

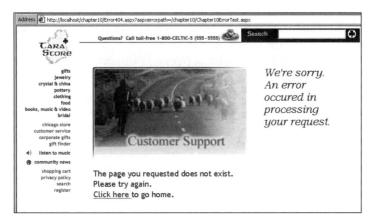

Figure 10-2   Using the Web.config file to configure custom error messages

 Within Internet Service Manager (ISM), the Web site properties contain a tab
called Custom Errors. This lists the common errors and the default messages
that are displayed by the Web server. You can use ASP.NET or IIS to manage
custom errors. However, by using the Web.config file, the programmer does
not need access to the ISM.

Using the Exception Classes to Identify Errors

The .NET System class contains an Exception class that acts as the base class for all
exceptions. An exception is an object that is thrown when a predefined error occurs.
For example, if the page cannot connect to the database, then an exception pointing to
a problem with the database connect is thrown. Catching exceptions can help you
quickly identify errors in your Web application. These predefined errors are categorized
in the SystemException class and ApplicationException class. The **SystemException
class** is the base class for all predefined exceptions. The **ApplicationException class**
provides a base class to create user-defined exception objects. There are several predefined exceptions that are derived from the SystemException class. You can also use a
general exception handler to catch general exceptions.

Common exceptions that are handled with the **Try-Catch-Finally statement** include the SqlException, OleDbException, NullReferenceException, and IndexOutOfRangeException exceptions. The Try-Catch-Finally statement allows you to catch the specific error, and to read information about the exception. The **SqlException** is thrown when an error occurs from the SQL Server DataAdapter. This exception is often thrown when the database server does not exist. The **OleDbException** is thrown when an error occurs from the OleDbDataAdapter. The **NullReferenceException** is thrown when an error occurs when a null object is referenced. The **IndexOutOfRangeException** is thrown when an Array object is improperly indexed. The **ExternalException** class allows other classes to indirectly inherit from the SystemException class. Some objects, such as the OleDbException class, inherit from the ExternalException class, which is derived from the SystemException class.

When the Exception object is created from the SystemException class, several properties and methods are exposed that can help identify the source of the error. The properties are exposed from the objects derived from the SystemException class.

- The **Message property** returns the error message.

- The **TargetSite property** returns the name of the method that threw the exception.

- The **Helplink property** returns the Help file associated with the exception object.

- The **StackTrace property** returns the location where the exception occurred.

- **The InnerException property** returns the first exception within the error stack.

- The **ToString method** returns the fully qualified name of the object, and the other properties.

Application-level Error Handling

An ASP application is a more than a collection of one or more ASP pages. An ASP application includes a Global Application File, called Global.asax, which allows you to tie the pages together so that information can be shared across pages. The **Global Application File** is a text file that contains scripts that are executed when the Web application starts and ends, and scripts that are executed when a browser session starts and ends. A Web application can have only one Global Application File, which must be located in the root directory of the Web application.

The Global Application File contains only server-side scripts. It does not contain any HTML or client-side scripts. The Web application executes the subroutines within the Global Application File before executing server-side includes, or server code. The Global Application File defines four subroutines that run when the application starts and ends and when the sessions starts and ends. The four subroutines that are available in the Global Application File for both ASP and ASP.NET are:

- Application_OnStart
- Application_OnEnd
- Session_OnStart
- Session_OnEnd

 It is useful to keep all four subroutines listed in the Global Application File, even ones that are not used, since you might want to add code later to the subroutines.

By default, in ASP.NET, the global.asax file includes the Application_BeginRequest, Application_AuthenticateRequest, and Application_Error event handlers. The Application_BeginRequest occurs when an HTTP request is made. The Application_AuthenticateRequest occurs when a client attempts to be authenticated.

You can retrieve information about an exception that was thrown from the **HttpContext class**. The **ToString method** provides the details of the exception object. To retrieve the last exception thrown by the application, you can use the **GetLastError method** from the **HttpServerUtility class**. (*Note:* You can also use the Error property of the HttpContext class to retrieve the last exception object thrown by the Web application.) You can clear all errors from the application using the **ClearError method** from the HttpContext class. You can redirect the client to a new URL when a general exception occurs by using the **Error property** of the HttpContext class.

Creating a Global Error Page Using the Global Application File

The following exercise, which consists of several stages, will help demonstrate how you can capture database errors by using the exception object. First, you will create the SQL Server database by upsizing an Access database. Then, you will retrieve the connection string for your database and insert the connection string as an application variable in the configuration file. Next, you will import a page to display the data. Finally, you will enable your Global Application File to detect a general error and redirect the client to a custom error message that displays the error properties of the exception object.

In the first part, you will upsize the Access database to SQL Server; then, you will create the stored procedures.

1. Start **Microsoft Access**. Open the **TaraStore.mdb** file within your Chapter10Data folder. Click **Tools** on the menu bar, point to **Database Utilities**, then select **Upsizing Wizard**. The Create new database radio button is already selected. Click **Next** to continue.

2. In the drop-down list box select the name of your SQL Server, such as [*MachineName*]\NetSDK. Select the authentication scheme for your SQL Server.

10

(*Note*: Some servers may require a trusted connection, and some servers may require you to provide a Login ID and password to connect. You can ask your system administrator for the correct authentication parameters.)

3. In the name text box, enter **Ch10TaraStoreSQL**. Click **Next** to continue. Click the **>>** button to select all available tables, and then click **Next** to continue. Click **Next** to continue twice, then click **Finish**. Close the Upsizing Wizard report window, and then close Access.

4. Open your **Chapter10** project in Visual Studio .NET if it is not already open.

5. In the Server Explorer window, right-click **Data Connections**, and then click **Add Connection**. In the server name drop-down list enter the name of your SQL Server, such as [*MachineName*]\NetSDK. Select the appropriate authentication scheme to access the server. (*Note*: This will depend upon how your SQL Server has been installed.) In the database drop-down list select **Ch10TaraStoreSQL**, and then click **OK**.

6. Click the **plus sign** next to **Ch10TaraStoreSQL** data connection. Then, right-click **Stored Procedures** and select **New Stored Procedure**. Select all text in the procedure. Go to the **Edit** menu, and then select **Delete**.

7. Start **Notepad**. Open the **Ch10StoredProc.txt** file, which is in your Chapter10Data directory. Select all of the code for the ProductCategoryList procedure. (*Note*: The code is found on the first six lines in the file.) Click **Edit** on the menu bar, then click **Copy**.

8. Return to Visual Studio .NET and click inside the empty stored procedure. Click **Edit** on the menu bar, then click **Paste**. The stored procedure code should appear as displayed in Figure 10-3. Again, right-click **Stored Procedures**, and then select **New Stored Procedure**. Select all text in the procedure. Click **Edit** on the menu bar, then click **Delete**.

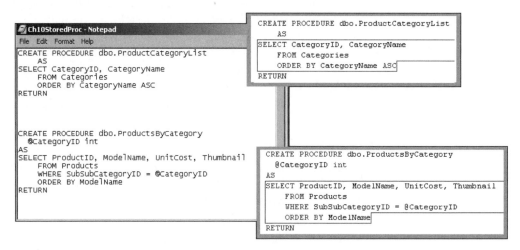

Figure 10-3   Creating the stored procedures

9. Switch to the **Ch10StoredProc.txt** file, which is already open in Notepad, and select all of the code for the ProductsByCategory procedure. Click **Edit** on the menu bar, then click **Copy**.

10. Return to Visual Studio .NET and click inside the empty stored procedure. Click **Edit** on the menu bar, then click **Paste**. The ProductCategoryList and ProductsByCategory stored procedures should appear as displayed in figure 10-3.

11. Click the **Save All** icon. Close both stored procedures.

In this next stage, you will create the application variable that will contain the connection string. Your connection string will vary with the authentication used for your database and SQL Server.

1. In the Solution Explorer window, open **WebForm1.aspx** if it is not already open. Go to the Server Explorer window and drag the **Ch10TaraStoreSQL** database from the Data Connections to the Web page. The SqlConnection object named SqlConnection1 is added to the designer.

2. Click the **SqlConnection1** to select the Connection object. Then, in the Properties window, locate the ConnectionString property. Double-click the value of the connection string to select the entire connection string. Click **Edit** on the menu bar, then click **Copy**.

3. Double-click **Web.config** in the Solution Explorer window to open the file. Add the following code to create the global connection string which is stored in the CS key. The code should be placed immediately below the opening configuration node tag, as shown in Figure 10-4. The value of the variable will be different for your connection, depending upon your database and SQL Server authentication. (*Note*: In the figure below, the SQL Server uses the default authentication with the username sa and no password.)

```
<appSettings>
    <add key="CS" value="[paste your connection here]" />
</appSettings>
```

```
1  <?xml version="1.0" encoding="utf-8" ?>
2  <configuration>
3
4    <appSettings>
5       <add key="CS" value="server=localhost;
6          uid=sa;pwd=;database=TaraStoreSQL" />
7    </appSettings>
8
```

Figure 10-4   Adding an application variable to the Web.config file

4. Click the **Save All** button and close the Web.config file.

In this next stage, you will create the component that will retrieve the data and import an existing page, which will be used to display the data.

1. Right-click **Chapter10** in the Solution Explorer window, point to **Add**, then click **Add Existing Item**. Navigate to your Chapter10Data folder. (*Note:* You may need to change the Files of type drop-down list to **All Files**.) Select **catMenuList.aspx** and **TaraStore.mdb**. Click the **Open** button to import the files into your project. Click **Yes** to create the new class file.

2. Start **Notepad**. Navigate to your Chapter10Data folder and open **Ch10ProductsDB.txt**. Click **Edit** on the menu bar, then click **Select All**. Click **Edit** on the menu bar, then click Copy. Exit Notepad.

3. Right-click **Chapter10** in the Solution Explorer window, point to **Add**, then click **Add Component**. Enter **ch10ProductsDB.vb** as the component name, and click **Open**. The component page will open in Design view.

4. When the file opens, click the hyperlink labeled **Click here to switch to code view**. On the first line add the code to import the data and configuration namespaces, as follows:

```
Imports System.Data.SqlClient
Imports System.Configuration
```

5. Click on the line below the gray text labeled Component Designer generated code. Click **Edit** on the menu bar, then click **Paste**. This code contains the two functions that will retrieve the data, as shown in Figure 10-5.

Figure 10-5 Creating the data access component

6. Click the **Save All** icon and close the window.

7. Double-click **catMenuList.aspx** in the Solution Explorer window to open the file. In the Page_Load event handler add the code below to display the data.

```
Dim SelID As String = Request.Params("selItem")
If Not SelID Is Nothing Then
    MyCatList.SelectedIndex = CInt(SelID)
    homeImage.Visible = False
Else
    homeImage.Visible = True
End If
Dim CatList As Chapter10.Ch10ProductsDB
CatList = New Chapter10.Ch10ProductsDB()
MyCatList.DataSource = CatList.GetCat()
MyCatList.DataBind()
Dim CatID As Integer = CInt(Request.Params("CatID"))
Dim ProdList As Chapter10.Ch10ProductsDB
ProdList = New Chapter10.Ch10ProductsDB()
MyProdList.DataSource = ProdList.GetProducts(CatID)
MyProdList.DataBind()
```

8. Click the **Save All** button and close the catMenuList.aspx page. Click **Build** on the menu bar, then click **Build Solution**.

10

9. Open the browser and go to **http://localhost/Chapter10/catMenuList.aspx** to view the page. The page will appear as shown in Figure 10-6. (*Note:* The link will not display the products because the product DataList control uses a hyperlink catMenu.aspx instead of catMenuList.aspx. This is because later there will be an error that you will catch.)

Figure 10-6   Displaying the category list

Your connection string will vary depending on whether your SQL Server authenticated the user with Windows integrated security or SQL Server security. If your server uses SQL Server security, your system administrator will provide you with the user ID, the password, the name of the database server, and the name of the database. If your server uses Windows authentication, your system administrator will provide you with the properties and values. The code below is an example of a connection string for a database server that uses Windows authentication. (*Note*: Do not split the string across lines.)

```
value = "data source=Course\NetSDK;
initial catalog=Ch10TaraStoreSQL;
integrated security = SSPI;
persist security info= False;
workstation id = COURSE;
packet size=4096"
```

In the next stage, you will add the code to check for general errors using the global configuration file.

1. Double-click the **Global.asax** file in the Solution Explorer window. Click the hyperlink labeled **Click here to switch to code view**. (*Note*: You can see that the event handlers have already added to the file the Application_BeginRequest, Application_AuthenticateRequest, and Application_Error event handlers.)

2. In the Application_Error event add the code below to redirect the use to a custom error page. Pass the error information in the QueryString. The **UrlEncode** method converts the error message to an HTTP compatible message. (*Note*: Special characters such as blank spaces should be converted to HTTP-compatible codes before sending the request or an error may occur in processing the request.) The page should appear as shown in Figure 10-7.

```
Dim EM As String = Server.GetLastError.Message()
Dim EHL As String = Server.GetLastError.HelpLink()
Dim AST As String = Server.GetLastError.StackTrace()
Dim ETS As String = Server.GetLastError.ToString()
Context.ClearError()
Response.Redirect("CustomError.aspx?" & _
"EM=" & Server.UrlEncode(EM) & _
"&EHL=" & Server.UrlEncode(EHL) & _
"&AST=" & Server.UrlEncode(AST) & _
"&ETS=" & Server.UrlEncode(ETS))
```

```
Global.asax.vb [Design]  Global.asax.vb
Global                              ▼  (Declarations)
 37├      End Sub
 38│
 39├⊟     Sub Application_BeginRequest(ByVal sender As Object, ByVal e As
 40│          ' Fires at the beginning of each request
 41├      End Sub
 42│
 43├⊟     Sub Application_AuthenticateRequest(ByVal sender As Object, ByVal
 44│          ' Fires upon attempting to authenticate the use
 45├      End Sub
 46│
 47├⊟     Sub Application_Error(ByVal sender As Object, ByVal e As EventArgs)
 48│          ' Fires when an error occurs
 49│          Dim EM As String = Server.GetLastError.Message()
 50│          Dim EHL As String = Server.GetLastError.HelpLink()
 51│          Dim AST As String = Server.GetLastError.StackTrace()
 52│          Dim ETS As String = Server.GetLastError.ToString()
 53│          Context.ClearError()
 54│          Response.Redirect("CustomError.aspx?" & _
 55│          "EM=" & Server.UrlEncode(EM) & _
 56│          "&EHL=" & Server.UrlEncode(EHL) & _
 57│          "&AST=" & Server.UrlEncode(AST) & _
 58│          "&ETS=" & Server.UrlEncode(ETS))
 59├      End Sub
 60│
 61├⊟     Sub Session_End(ByVal sender As Object, ByVal e As EventArgs)
 62│          ' Fires when the session ends
 63├      End Sub
```

Figure 10-7   Modifying the Global.asax file

3. Click the **Save All** button. Close the Global.asax page.

4. To generate an error, change the reference to the connection in the Ch10ProductsDB.vb page from ConfigurationSettings.AppSettings("CS") to **ConfigurationSettings.AppSettings("CS2")** for both functions.

5. Click the **Save All** button. Click **Build** on the menu bar, then click **Build Solution**.

6. In the Solution Explorer window, double-click on the **customError.aspx** page. Double-click the page to open the code behind the page. Modify the customError.aspx page to display the errors. Enter the code below in the Page_Load event handler as shown in Figure 10-8. (*Note*: There is sometimes no Help link associated with the error, so you need to detect if the error object passed a Help link URL.)

```
lblEM.Text = Request.QueryString("EM")
Dim EHL As String = Request.QueryString("EHL")
If EHL <> "" Then
     lblEHL.Text = Request.QueryString("EHL")
Else
     lblEHL.Text = "There is no help link associated ¬
with this error."
```

```
      End If
      lblAST.Text = Request.QueryString("AST")
      lblETS.Text = Request.QueryString("ETS")
```

```
Global.asax.vb [Design]  catMenuList.aspx  customError.aspx  customError.aspx.vb                    ◁ ▷ ×
⚙ customError                                          ▼  ⚙ Page_Load                                ▼
 1 ⊟ Public Class customError
 2        Inherits System.Web.UI.Page
 3        Protected WithEvents Label2 As System.Web.UI.WebControls.Label
 4        Protected WithEvents lblAST As System.Web.UI.WebControls.Label
 5        Protected WithEvents lblEHL As System.Web.UI.WebControls.Label
 6        Protected WithEvents lblEM As System.Web.UI.WebControls.Label
 7        Protected WithEvents lblMsg As System.Web.UI.WebControls.Label
 8        Protected WithEvents lblETS As System.Web.UI.WebControls.Label
 9        Protected WithEvents Label1 As System.Web.UI.WebControls.Label
10
11 ⊞  Web Form Designer Generated Code
25
26 ⊟     Private Sub Page_Load(ByVal sender As System.Object, ByVal e As System.EventArgs)
27          'Put user code to initialize the page here
28          lblEM.Text = Request.QueryString("EM")
29          Dim EHL As String = Request.QueryString("EHL")
30          If EHL <> "" Then
31              lblEHL.Text = Request.QueryString("EHL")
32          Else
33              lblEHL.Text = "There is no help link associated with this error."
34          End If
35          lblAST.Text = Request.QueryString("AST")
36          lblETS.Text = Request.QueryString("ETS")
37      End Sub
38
39 └ End Class
```

Figure 10-8   Creating the custom error page

7. Click the **Save All** button. Click **Build** on the menu bar, then click **Build Solution**.

Figure 10-9   Viewing the custom error page

8. In the browser, refresh the catMenuList.aspx page by clicking the **Refresh** button. The page should be redirected to the new custom errors page with the errors displayed. Your page should look like the one in Figure 10-9.

9. Double-click the **Global.asax** page in the Solution Explorer window. Comment out the code in the Application_Error event handler. Do not delete the code.

10. Click the **Save All** button. Click **Build** on the menu bar, then click **Build Solution**.

11. Close any open pages.

Using the Try-Catch-Finally to Handle Specific Errors

You can take advantage of ASP.NET's language-independent, structured exception handling within your ASP.NET applications. The exception object forces you to deal with exceptions when they occur. If an exception is raised and you don't explicitly handle the exception, a general ASP.NET exception will occur, forcing the application to terminate without allowing the code to continue executing, resulting in an error page. Using the exception object makes finding errors much easier. To use the exception object, you can use a programming structure called Try-Catch-Finally. The **Try-Catch-Finally statement** allows you to attempt to run a block of code that detects when an error has occurred. The goal of the Try-Catch-Finally statement is to gracefully recover when an exception occurs. Rather than have an error message occur, you can customize the code that is executed. You can even log the error information captured from the error. The **Try statement** attempts to run a block of code. If there is an error, an exception object is created. The **Catch statement** catches the error as an exception object. You can use the Catch statement multiple times to catch multiple types of errors. The **Finally statement** allows you to execute a block of code.

In the following exercise, you will use the Try...Catch...Finally block to capture the SQL Server error and redirect the user to the custom error page, while passing the error object.

1. Open your **Chapter10** project in Visual Studio .NET if necessary.

2. Double-click **catMenuList.aspx** in the Solution Explorer window to open the file, and then double-click the page to open the code behind the page.

3. Add the Try... statement to the code which will retrieve the menu list and the product list. Place the Try statement above the CatList variable declaration, as shown in Figure 10-10.

4. On the line after the MyProdList.DataBind statement, add the code to catch the exception and to redirect the client to the custom errors page. The code should appear as shown in Figure 10-10.

```
Catch Ex As SqlClient.SqlException
    Response.Redirect("/CustomErrors.aspx")
Finally
End Try
```

10

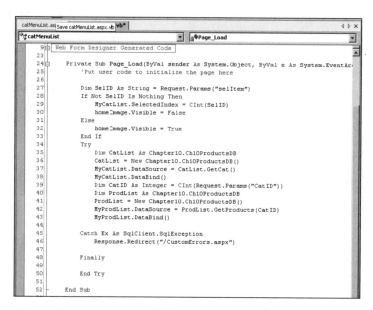

```
catMenuList.as| Save catMenuList.aspx.vb |vb*|                                      ◁ ▷ ×
catMenuList                                  ▼   Page_Load                        ▼
   9|⊞ Web Form Designer Generated Code                                             ▲
  23|
  24|⊟     Private Sub Page_Load(ByVal sender As System.Object, ByVal e As System.EventAr
  25|           'Put user code to initialize the page here
  26|
  27|           Dim SelID As String = Request.Params("selItem")
  28|           If Not SelID Is Nothing Then
  29|               MyCatList.SelectedIndex = CInt(SelID)
  30|               homeImage.Visible = False
  31|           Else
  32|               homeImage.Visible = True
  33|           End If
  34|           Try
  35|               Dim CatList As Chapter10.Ch10ProductsDB
  36|               CatList = New Chapter10.Ch10ProductsDB()
  37|               MyCatList.DataSource = CatList.GetCat()
  38|               MyCatList.DataBind()
  39|               Dim CatID As Integer = CInt(Request.Params("CatID"))
  40|               Dim ProdList As Chapter10.Ch10ProductsDB
  41|               ProdList = New Chapter10.Ch10ProductsDB()
  42|               MyProdList.DataSource = ProdList.GetProducts(CatID)
  43|               MyProdList.DataBind()
  44|
  45|           Catch Ex As SqlClient.SqlException
  46|               Response.Redirect("/CustomErrors.aspx")
  47|
  48|           Finally
  49|
  50|           End Try
  51|
  52|-     End Sub
```

Figure 10-10   Using the Try-Catch-Finally handler to capture errors

5. Click the **Save All** button. Click **Build** on the menu bar, then click **Build Solution**.

6. Open the browser and go to **http://localhost/chapter10/catMenuList.aspx** to view the page. You can see the exception information in the second text box, as shown in Figure 10-11. This error message indicates that there is a problem with the connection string.

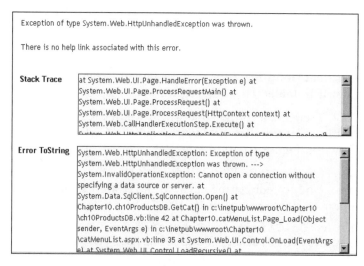

Exception of type System.Web.HttpUnhandledException was thrown.

There is no help link associated with this error.

Stack Trace   at System.Web.UI.Page.HandleError(Exception e) at
System.Web.UI.Page.ProcessRequestMain() at
System.Web.UI.Page.ProcessRequest() at
System.Web.UI.Page.ProcessRequest(HttpContext context) at
System.Web.CallHandlerExecutionStep.Execute() at
System.Web.HttpApplication.ExecuteStep(IExecutionStep step, Boolean

Error ToString   System.Web.HttpUnhandledException: Exception of type
System.Web.HttpUnhandledException was thrown. --->
System.InvalidOperationException: Cannot open a connection without
specifying a data source or server. at
System.Data.SqlClient.SqlConnection.Open() at
Chapter10.ch10ProductsDB.GetCat() in c:\inetpub\wwwroot\Chapter10
\ch10ProductsDB.vb:line 42 at Chapter10.catMenuList.Page_Load(Object
sender, EventArgs e) in c:\inetpub\wwwroot\Chapter10
\catMenuList.aspx.vb:line 35 at System.Web.UI.Control.OnLoad(EventArgs
e) at System.Web.UI.Control.LoadRecursive() at

Figure 10-11   Viewing the stack trace and error ToString property

7. Close the browser window. Return to your Web application within Visual Studio .NET.

8. To eliminate the error, open the **Ch10ProductsDB.vb page**. Change the reference to the connection in the Ch10ProductsDB.vb page from ConfigurationSettings.AppSettings("CS2") to **ConfigurationSettings.AppSettings("CS")** for both functions.

9. Click the **Save All** button. Click **Build** on the menu bar, then click **Build Solution**.

10. In the browser, refresh the catMenuList.aspx page by clicking the **Refresh** button. The page should appear with the menu list and the home page image.

11. Close any open pages, and then close the browser window.

USING THE VISUAL STUDIO .NET DEBUGGER

Visual Studio .NET provides several debugging tools to debug .NET applications. A **debugger** allows you to step through the application at **breakpoints**, which are defined points in the program where processing stops so that you can view the variables, properties, and other application settings. This data can be helpful when trying to locate programming logic errors. (*Note:* You can use the debugger to debug your application across multiple languages.)

To debug your application, you must first enable the page to support debugging. The Page directive includes an attribute named Debug, which allows you to turn on support for debugging. The following sample code shows how to turn on debugging for a single page.

```
<%@Page Debug="True" %>
```

You can also turn on debugging for the entire application by configuring debugging in the Web.config file. The following sample code shows how to turn on debugging for the entire Web application using the Web.config file.

```
<?xml version="1.0" encoding="UTF-8" ?>
<configuration>
    <system.web>
        <compilation
            debug="true" explicit="true"
            strict="true" defaultLanguage="vb">
        </compilation>
    </system.web>
</configuration>
```

10

You can configure the debugger to open whenever an exception is thrown by the application. Then in your Catch block, you can write an exception handler. To enable debugging to handle exceptions, go to the Debug menu in Visual Studio .NET and select Exceptions. In the Exceptions dialog box, check both radio buttons labeled Break into the debugger.

After you have turned on debugging, you need to attach the ASP.NET service process to the debugger. Once the debugger is attached to the ASP.NET service, you do not have to repeat the steps. The debugger remembers the processes that have been attached.

Once the application is in debug mode, you can use the following Debug menu commands to configure how you want to step through the code:

- **Step Over** (F10) allows you to execute the current line of code. Use this command to step through the code line by line.

- **Step Into** (F11) allows you to step into a method that is being called on the current line.

- **Step Out** (Shift + F11) allows you to leave the method and return to the function call.

- **Run to Cursor** (Ctrl + F10) allows you to execute all the code between the current line and the current cursor position.

Once you have stepped into the application, you can view the variables, properties, and application data within Visual Studio .NET using one of the debugger windows. The following are some of the windows used within the Debugger.

- The Locals window and the Auto window display the variables. Local variables are defined within the scope of the current method.

- The Me window displays the properties of the current object.

- The Watch window displays variables that you have specifically requested.

- The Call Stack window displays a hierarchical list of methods that have been called. The **Call Stack window** allows you to identify which statement called the method.

In the following example, you will attach the debugger, set the breakpoints, and step through an application.

1. In Visual Studio .NET, click **Tools** on the menu bar, then click **Debug Processes**.

2. Click the **Show system processes** check box, as shown in Figure 10-12.

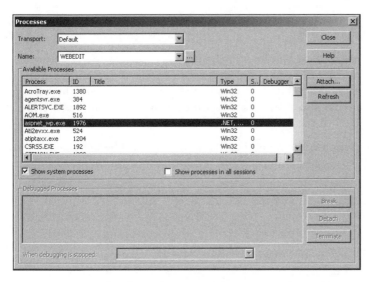

Figure 10-12   Attaching the ASP.NET service to the Debugger

3. In the Process dialog box, select **aspnet_wp.exe**, as shown in Figure 10-12. The aspnet_wp.exe is the executable for the ASP.NET service.

4. Click the **Attach** button.

Figure 10-13   Attach the ASP.NET service to the Common Language Runtime

5. In the Attach to Process dialog box, click the **Common Language Runtime** check box, as shown in Figure 10-13 to select it, and then click **OK**. The **aspnet_wp.exe** process appears in the list of **Debugged Processes**.

6. Click the **Close** button in the Process dialog box.

7. Right-click **catMenuList.aspx** in the Solution Explorer window, and then click **Set as Start Page**.

8. Open the **catMenuList.aspx** page, then double-click on the page to open the code behind the page.

9. Insert a breakpoint by clicking the gray bar next to the code on line 26. (*Note:* This should be the line that contains the Try statement. Your line number may vary.) A red dot appears in the gray bar to mark the breakpoint. (*Note:* You can also insert a breakpoint by right-clicking on the line of code and selecting Insert Breakpoint from the pop-up menu.)

10. Click **Debug** on the menu bar, then click **Start**. The debugger stops the page in the Page_Load method on the breakpoint line, as shown in Figure 10-14.

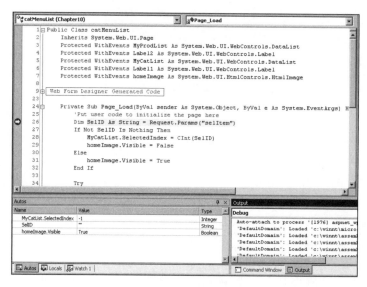

Figure 10-14 The Autos window in the Visual Studio .Net Debugger

11. Click **Debug** on the menu bar, then click **Step Into**, as shown in Figure 10-15. The yellow arrow indicates the current line of code that the debugger is processing. The yellow arrow moves to the next line, as shown in Figure 10-16.

Figure 10-15   The Debug Menu

12. Click **Debug** on the menu bar, and then click **Step Into**. The yellow arrow moves to the next block of code.

Figure 10-16   The Locals window in the Debugger

13. Press **F11** slowly 10 more times. Each time you hit the F11 key, notice how the property names and values in the Auto window changes.

14. Click the **Locals** tab, as shown in Figure 10-16. The Locals window displays the variables that are within the scope of the current method. (*Note:* You can access the debugging commands from the menu, the keyboard, or the toolbars. If the Locals tab is not visible, go to the **Debug** menu, point to **Windows**, then select **Locals**.)

15. To exit the debugger, click **Debug** on the menu bar, then click **Stop Debugging**. The debug windows will close automatically.

16. Click the **red dot** to remove the breakpoint.

17. Close any open windows.

DOCUMENTING THE WEB SITE

It's very important for developers to document their Web applications. If your application is well documented, then other programmers can read the documentation and quickly make the appropriate changes, without spending as much time analyzing the code. One of the features of ASP.NET is the automation of code documentation. You can create an automated Code Comment Report, which contains information about the objects, their inheritance, and their structure. You can view these pages offline using a browser and do not have to include them in the production version of your project.

 The report is stored by default in the Documents and Settings\Visual Studio Projects folder. Each project has a CodeCommentReport folder nested within the project folder. You can learn more about the Code Comment Web Report in the online documentation at *ms-help://MS.VSCC/MS.MSDNVS/vsintro7/html/vxgrfCodeCommentWebReport.htm*.

Creating the Comment Code Report involves creating XML codes that document your application. These XML codes comply with the XML standards, which you learned about in Chapter 4. You can use XML codes to create additional documentation in your project. You can also use these XML codes to add comments that appear in the Web pages to document the code. However, the Comment Code Report feature is only available with C# in the current version of Visual Studio .NET. The C# compiler can be used directly to compile the project with the /doc parameter to process documentation comments to one or more files. Below is a listing of the XML codes that are supported within the Comment Code Report.

- \<c\>
- \<para\>
- \<see\>
- \<code\>
- \<param\>
- \<seealso\>
- \<example\>
- \<paramref\>
- \<summary\>
- \<exception\>
- \<permission\>
- \<value\>
- \<include\>
- \<remarks\>
- \<list\>
- \<returns\>

In the following exercise, you will document the Web page with comments and create the Code Comment Report. The report will list the pages and objects within the application, as well as the controls, and procedures within the page class.

1. In Visual Studio .NET, open your **Chapter10** project if necessary. Double-click **catMenuList.aspx** in the Solution Explorer window, then double-click on the page to open the code behind the page.

2. Modify the code to add comments, as indicated in Figure 10-17.

10

```
Private Sub Page Load(ByVal sender As System.Object,
    ByVal e As System.EventArgs) Handles MyBase.Load
    ' Put user code to initialize the page here.
    ' Declare a variable SelID to contain the
    ' integer passed from the querystring.
    Dim SelID As String = Request.Params("selItem")

    ' If there is a value passed then
    ' the user has not made a menu selection.
    ' So, show the home page image.
    If Not SelID Is Nothing Then
        MyCatList.SelectedIndex = CInt(SelID)
        homeImage.Visible = False
    Else
        ' There is no value passed, then
        ' show the home page image.
        homeImage.Visible = True
    End If
    Try
        ' Get the Menu List
        ' Create a variable to store the new object
        Dim CatList As Chapter10.ch10ProductsDB
        CatList = New Chapter10.ch10ProductsDB()
        ' Call the GetCat method, which returns a DataReader object.
        ' Use the DataReader object returned as the source for the
        ' MyCatList List control.
        MyCatList.DataSource = CatList.GetCat()
        ' Bind the MyCatList List control to the DataReader object.
        MyCatList.DataBind()

        ' Get the Product List.
        ' Create a variable to store the category ID.
        ' The category ID is retrieved from the QueryString.
        ' The CInt converts the string to an Integer data type.
        Dim CatID As Integer = CInt(Request.Params("CatID"))
        Dim ProdList As Chapter10.ch10ProductsDB
        ProdList = New Chapter10.ch10ProductsDB()
        ' Call the GetProducts method, which returns a DataReader object.
        ' You must pass the CatID to the GetProducts method so
        ' that you only return values for the single category.
        ' The method uses a stored procedure that expects an input value.
        ' Use the DataReader object returned as the source for the
        ' MyProdList List control.
        MyProdList.DataSource = ProdList.GetProducts(CatID)
        ' Bind the MyProdList List control to the DataReader object.
        MyProdList.DataBind()

    Catch Ex As SqlClient.SqlException
        ' If there is a problem with the SQL Server database
        ' redirect the user to the error page.
        Response.Redirect("/CustomErrors.aspx")
    Finally
    End Try

End Sub
```

Figure 10-17   Adding comments to document the code

3. Click the **Save All** button. Click **Build** on the menu bar, then click **Build Solution**.

4. Click **Tools** on the menu bar, then click **Build Comment Web Pages**.

5. Click the radio button labeled **Build for selected Projects** to select it. Select **Chapter10**, as shown in Figure 10-18.

Figure 10-18   Saving the Code Comment Report Web page

6. Look at the specified location in the Save Web Pages in the text box. By default, the pages are saved in a folder named **CodeCommentReport**, which is located in the default project folder. It is not automatically saved with the Web pages. Click **OK**.

7. The Code Comment Report opens in Visual Studio .NET. Click the **Chapter10** hyperlink.

8. Click the **plus sign** next to Global in the window on the left side.

9. Click the hyperlink **catMenuList** in the window on the left side.

10. Click the hyperlink in the main window labeled **homeImage**. You can see the homeImage data type in the main window, as shown in Figure 10-19.

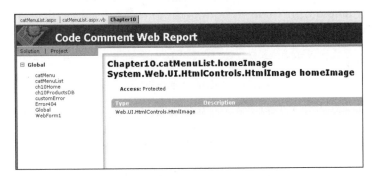

Figure 10-19   Displaying the Code Comment Report

11. Close any open windows.

PAGE OUTPUT CACHING

Page Output Caching is the technique of caching ASP.NET pages on the Web server. When a Web page is compiled, the page is stored on the server in the cache. When another request is made for the same page, the page from the cache is returned to the client. Storing Web pages in the cache increases the performance of your Web application. When a change in the Web page is detected, a newer version of the page is recompiled and replaces the other version in the cache.

You can configure your Web application to use the Page Output Cache via two methods. The OutPutCache directive is used to configure the cache for individual Web pages. The HTTPCachePolicy can be used to programmatically set the page OutPut Cache. In this section, you will learn to enable the OutPutCache directive.

You configure the Page OutPut Cache in the Web page by using the **OutPutCache** directive. Parameters that configure the Page Output Cache include Duration and VaryByParam. The **Duration** identifies how long the document is left in cache. The duration is measured in seconds. After the duration expires, the page is removed from the cache. The next time the page is requested, it is recompiled and stored in cache. The page is rendered from the version stored in the cache.

You use the **VaryByParam property** to cache any parameters passed with the page request. When a page is requested, a QueryString consisting of a series of parameter names and value pairs is attached to the URL. When the VaryByParam is set to the name of the parameter, the page is cached each time the page is requested using a different value. In other words, if the parameter name is LastName and the value is Kalata, the page is cached with the parameter Kalata. The next time the page is requested with the LastName equal to Kalata, the cached page is returned. However, if another user with the LastName equal to Shea requests the page, then the page is cached separately. The next time the page is requested with the LastName equal to Shea, the cached page for Shea is returned. Therefore, multiple versions of the same page can be cached to increase performance. You can separate multiple parameters with a comma as shown below.

```
<%@ Page OutputCache Duration="60"

        VaryByParam="LastName, Department" %>
```

There are different possible settings for VaryByParam. If you set VaryByParam to None, then regardless of the values of the parameters sent with the request, only the default page is cached. If the value is set to an asterisk (*), the page is cached for each possible key and value parameters for both Get and Post methods. You can set the VaryByParam to Mode to a specific parameter key by using the key name. For example, to cache a page sent using the Get method that contains a form field named LastName and EmployeeID, the OutPutCache directive is set to VaryByparam= "LastName;EmployeeID". The VaryByParam setting separates the key names using a semicolon.

There are several additional attributes that you can set with the OutPutCache directive. The **Location** attribute determines where the cached versions are stored. The default value for the Location attribute is Any. If the value is set to Any, then any application caches the document for the duration specified. If the value is set to None, then caching is disabled for the page. If the Location attribute is set to Client, the document is cached on the browser. If the Location attribute is set to Downstream, a new document is generated and is eligible to be cached on the client. If the Location is set to Server, then only the server caches the document.

Web pages that access a data source often use the OutPutCache directive, because parameters that are sent to query the database return different page results. When you use the OutPutCache directive, each version of the page is cached in order to increase performance. The cached versions that are not actively used are removed from cache when the duration expires.

There are additional techniques that allow you to control how the page is cached. The **VaryByCustom** attribute allows you to create custom strings to determine if a page should be cached. The **VaryByHeader** attribute allows you control the cached settings based on the HTTP header that is sent with the request. You can also use fragment caching to cache one or more user controls on the Web page with the **VaryByControl** attribute.

The HTTPCachePolicy uses the Cache Property of the HTTPResponse class. Using the HTTPCachePolicy, you can configure the Web page to expire on a specific date and time. Using the Cache property of the HTTPResponse class, you can also cache pages that have invoked a Web Service. You can find more information on the HTTPResponse class in the Visual Studio .NET SDK.

The following exercise demonstrates how to use the Page OutPut Cache to cache variations of the same Web page that display different data based on different parameters.

1. In Visual Studio .NET, open your **Chapter10** project if necessary. Double-click **catMenuList.aspx** in the Solution Explorer window.

2. Drag a **Label** control to the page and position the control below the yellow label control that says "Visit us online at www.tarastore.com". Change the ID of the new label control to **lblDate**.

3. Drag a **Label** control to the page and position the control below the lblDate control. Change the ID of the new Label control to **lblTime**.

4. Double-click on the page to open the code behind the page.

5. In the code behind the page, add the code in the Page_Load event handler to display the date and time.

```
lblDate.Text = DateTime.Now.ToString("D")
lblTime.Text = DateTime.Now.ToString("T")
```

6. Close the code behind the page.

7. Click the **Save All** button. Click **Build** on the menu bar, then click **Build Solution**.

8. Right-click on the page, and then click **View in Browser**. Click **Refresh** five times. The time continues to advance each time.

9. Return to the **catMenuList.aspx** page. Modify the HTML code to enable page output caching.

```
<%@ OutputCache Duration="60" ¬
VaryByParam="CatID, selItem" %>
```

10. Click the **Save All** button. Click **Build** on the menu bar, then click **Build Solution**.

11. Right-click on the page and select **View in Browser**. Your page should look like the one shown in Figure 10-20. Click the **Reload** button five times. The number of seconds will not change.

12. Close your browser and any open windows within your Visual Studio .NET application.

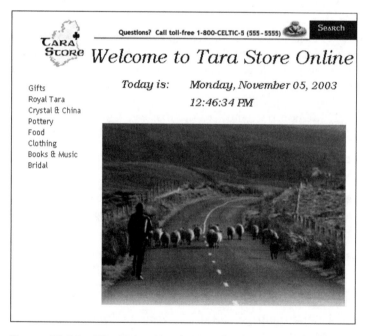

Figure 10-20   Displaying the date and time on a cached Web page

DEPLOYING AN ASP.NET WEB APPLICATION

In previous versions of ASP, before a component would work, you had to stop the Web service, log into the Web server locally, copy the component software to the server, register the component using the **RegServ32.exe application**, then restart the Web Service. Furthermore, once the component was installed, it was available to other installed applications on the server. It was very difficult to install multiple versions of the same application on the same server. In the current version of ASP.NET, deployment of Web applications is simpler and does not require registration of the component or stopping the Web Service.

In ASP.NET, the DLL file contains the application logic, known as the assembly. The two locations for storing assemblies are the local application cache and the global assembly cache. The **local application cache** is the default location for the assemblies for the local application. The local application cache is the bin directory located under the root directory of the application. Only the local application can access the assembly in the local application cache.

To install a compiled DLL, simply copy the DLL file to the bin directory of the application. The **AppDomain class** manages the application process. The AppDomain controls the assemblies and threads, such as loading and unloading assemblies. When a new assembly is copied to the bin directory, the AppDomain class creates an in-memory shadow of the DLL file. The assembly that is loaded is the in-memory shadow. The DLL file is never locked. Therefore, any current connections with the in-memory shadow remain open. Any new connections are started with the new in-memory assembly. When there are no more connections with the current assembly, the assembly is removed. Any time the AppDomain detects a change in the DLL file, the in-memory shadow is replaced with the new version of the assembly.

The **global assembly cache** is the default location for assemblies that are available to the entire server. Therefore, the global assembly cache can be shared by multiple applications. A hosting service provider may install several versions of the same application in the global assembly cache. The DLL is stored on the server, but registered with the global application cache with the GacUtil.exe utility. Because there may be multiple versions of the same assembly, the GacUtil.exe utility registers the assembly and keeps track of the version of the assembly. The GacUtil.exe specifies the default version of the assembly. Applications are allowed to override the default settings.

10

CHAPTER SUMMARY

❐ Error handling is a collection of techniques that allow you to identify programming errors, called bugs, in your code.

❐ Status message codes are exposed by the HTTPStatusCode property.

❑ You can configure custom error pages within the Web page using the Page directive. You can configure customer errors for the application within the Web configuration file. The most common error message is the File NotFound (status 404) error message.

❑ The SystemException class is the base class for all predefined exceptions. The ApplicationException class provides a base class to create user-defined exception objects.

❑ The SqlException is thrown when an error occurs from the SQL Server Data Adapter. This exception is often thrown when the database server does not exist. The OleDbException is thrown when an error occurs from the OleDbDataAdapter.

❑ The Message property of the Exception object returns the error message. The Helplink property returns the Help file associated with the Exception object. The StackTrace property returns the location where the exception occurred. The ToString method returns the fully qualified name of the object, and the other properties.

❑ The Global Application File is a text file that contains scripts that are executed when the Web application starts and ends, and scripts that are executed when a browser session starts and ends. A Web application can have only one Global Application File, which must reside in the root directory of the Web application

❑ The Application_Error event occurs whenever an exception occurs in the Web application.

❑ The UrlEncode method converts the error message to an HTTP-compatible message.

❑ The Try-Catch-Finally statement allows you to attempt to run a block of code that detects when an error has occurred. The Try-Catch-Finally statement can help your applications gracefully recover when exceptions occur.

❑ A debugger allows you to step through the application at defined points, called breakpoints. The Step Into (F11) command allows you to step into a method that is being called on the current line. The Locals window displays the variables that are within the scope of the current method.

❑ The Code Comment Report contains information about the objects, including their inheritance and structure.

❑ You can cache Web pages using several techniques. Page Output Caching is the technique of caching ASP.NET pages on the Web server. The Page OutPut Cache is configured as a directive on the first line of the Web page. When a Web page is rendered, it is stored on the server in the cache. Parameters that are used to configure the Page Output Cache directive include Duration and VaryByParam. Duration identifies how long the document is left in cache. VaryByParam alters any parameters passed with the page request.

❏ The AppDomain class manages the application process, including controlling the assemblies and threads, and loading and unloading assemblies. The local application cache is the default location for the assemblies for the local application. The local application cache is the bin directory located under the root directory of the application. The global assembly cache is the default location for assemblies that are available to the entire server. The GacUtil.exe utility is used to register components in the global assembly cache.

REVIEW QUESTIONS

1. Error handling is a collection of techniques that allow you to identify programming errors in your code; these errors are called _____.

    a. viruses

    b. bugs

    c. worms

    d. parasites

2. Which type of error is not detected by Visual Studio .NET?

    a. spelling

    b. syntax

    c. programming logic

    d. grammatical

3. The Global Application File is located in:

    a. the root directory

    b. the include directory

    c. the cgi-bin directory

    d. the scripts directory

4. The name of the Global Application File in ASP.NET is:

    a. Global.inc

    b. Global.asa

    c. Global.aspx

    d. Global.asax

5. Which of the following subroutines is not contained in the Global Application File?

    a. Session_AuthenticateRequest

    b. Application_OnError

    c. Application_OnStart

    d. Application_OnEnd

10

6. Which attribute of customErrors node in the Web.config file is used to configure error pages to be displayed only on the local server?

   a. RemoteOnly

   b. LocalOnly

   c. Remote

   d. all

7. Which status error code is used to indicate that the method is not allowed?

   a. 301

   b. 403

   c. 405

   d. 501

8. Which status error code is used to indicate that the server is unavailable?

   a. 305

   b. 403

   c. 590

   d. 501

9. The _____ class is not derived directly from the SystemException class.

   a. SqlException

   b. OleDbException

   c. NullReferenceException

   d. IndexOutOfRangeException

10. The _____ property of the current exception object returns the fully qualified name of the object.

   a. TargetSite

   b. StackTrace

   c. InnerException

   d. ToString

11. The _____ method is used to convert the error message to an HTTP-compatible message.

   a. UrlEncode

   b. HTTPEncode

   c. ConvertMsg

   d. none of the above

12. The _____ statement captures the error as an Exception object.

    a. Catch

    b. Try

    c. Finally

    d. Release

13. A _____ is a program used to locate errors.

    a. virus detection program

    b. debugger

    c. dewormer

    d. bug checker

14. You can step through the application at defined points called _____.

    a. breakpoints

    b. stops

    c. hops

    d. endpoints

15. To turn debugging on for the entire application, you must configure the _____ attribute in the compilation node of the Web.config file.

    a. debug

    b. Error

    c. customError

    d. system.web

16. The _____ command is used to execute the current line of code.

    a. Step Over

    b. Step Into

    c. Step Out

    d. Run to Cursor

17. The _____ key allows you to step into a method that is being called on the current line.

    a. F10

    b. F11

    c. F12

    d. Shift+F11

10

18. The _____ window is used to display variables that are within the scope of the current method.

   a. Locals

   b. Watch

   c. Call Stack

   d. a or b

19. When a Web page is compiled, the page is stored on the server in the _____.

   a. buffer

   b. cache

   c. global directory

   d. a and b

20. The Duration = "20" means that the page is recompiled in _____.

   a. 20 milliseconds

   b. 2 minutes

   c. 20 seconds

   d. 20 minutes

HANDS-ON PROJECTS

Project 10-1

In this project, you will create a custom error message, and enable your Web application configuration file to detect HTTP status errors.

1. Start **Visual Studio .NET** and open your **Chapter10** solution.

2. Open the code behind the page for the Web.config file. Locate the customErrors node and modify the code as shown below to redirect the visitor who has been denied access to a Web resource. (*Note*: Do not create a new customErrors node.)

```
<customErrors defaultRedirect=""customError.aspx" mode="On">
    <error statusCode="404" redirect="Ch10Proj1.aspx" />
</customErrors>
```

3. Create a new Web page named **Ch10Proj1.aspx**. Add graphics and content to indicate to the visitor that the resource has not been found. Provide the visitor with a link back to the ch10Home.aspx page. (*Hint*: You can use the NavigateURL property of the Hyperlink control to configure the URL.)

4. Click the **Save All** button. Go to the Build menu and select **Build Solution**.

5. View the Web page in the browser at http://localhost/chapter10/Ch10Proj1a.aspx. Since this page does not exist, you should be redirected to the Ch10Proj1.aspx page.

6. Print the Web page in the browser. Return to Visual Studio .NET and print your source code for the Ch1Proj1.aspx page, and the source code for the Web.config file.

Project 10-2

In this project you will use the Global Application File to detect a general error and redirect the client to a custom error message.

1. Open **Visual Studio .NET** and open your **Chapter10** solution if necessary.

2. Open the **Global.asax** file.

3. Modify the Application_Error event handler to redirect the user to a custom error page named Ch10Proj2a.aspx.

4. Create the custom error page named **Ch10Proj2a.aspx**. Display a message to the user indicating that an error occurred. Display a hyperlink to the Tara Store home page at Ch10Home.aspx. Modify the page with graphics and content to enhance the appearance of the Web page.

5. Import a Web page named **Ch10Proj2b.aspx** from your Chapter10Data folder. This page displays the category list using a data list control named MyCatList.

6. Double-click on the **Ch10Proj2b.aspx** page. In the code behind the page, use the code below to bind the data to the DataReader returned from the GetCat( ) function in the CH10ProductsDB class. Add the code to the Page_Load function.

```
Dim SelID As String = Request.Params("selItem")
homeImage.Visible = True
Dim CatList As Chapter10.ch10ProductsDB
CatList = New Chapter10.ch10ProductsDB()
MyCatList.DataSource = CatList.GetCat()
MyCatList.DataBind()
```

7. Save your Web pages. Build the solution.

8. View the Web page in the browser.

9. Stop the SQL Server: the Taskbar contains an icon representing the SQL Server. Right-click on this icon, and then click **MSSQL Server - Stop**. Click **Yes** in the SQL Server Service Manager.

10. View the Web page in the browser. Print the page that appears.

11. Start the SQL Server: right-click the **SQL Server** icon, and then click **MSSQL Server - Start**.

12. View the Web page in the browser to make sure the database server has started.

13. Print the Web pages, the source code, and the Global.asax file.

14. Double-click the **Global.asax** page in the Solution Explorer window. Comment out the code in the Application_Error event handler. Do not delete the code.

15. Click the **Save All** button. Click **Build** on the menu bar, then click **Build Solution**.

10

Project 10-3

In this project you will use the Try-Catch-Finally statement to attempt to run a block of code that detects when an error has occurred. The Web page shows the code that displays the list of products from the database using the DataSet object and the DataGrid control.

1. Start **Visual Studio .NET** and open your **Chapter10** solution if necessary.
2. In Visual Studio .NET create a new Web page named **Ch10Proj3.aspx**.
3. Add a SQL Server DataAdapter to connect to the Ch10TaraStoreSQL database.
4. Generate a DataSet named **DS1** that retrieves the ProductID, ModelNumber, ModelName, ProductImage, and UnitCost fields from the Products table. (*Note:* Once you create the new DataSet it will be named DS11 by Visual Studio .NET, and then it will be visible within the Design window. Visual Studio .NET suggests the name for the DataSet. However, you can change this when the DataSet is generated.)
5. Add a DataView named **DataView1** to display the Products table in the DS11 dataset. (*Note:* You will need to set the Table property to the Products table in the Properties window.)
6. Add a DataGrid control named **MyDG**. Modify the DataGrid with colors and fonts to enhance the appearance. The first column should be an image of the product thumbnail. The second column should be the product name. The third column should be the product price formatted as currency.
7. In the code behind the page, add the code below to bind the DataView object to the DataGrid control in the Page_Load event handler.

```
SqlDataAdapter1.Fill(DS11)
Page.DataBind()
```

8. Save the page by clicking the **Save All** button. Build the project and view the page in the browser.
9. Go back to the Visual Studio .NET application and apply the Try-Catch-Finally statement to the code to catch SQL Server related errors. If an error occurs, redirect the user to the customError.aspx page. (*Hint:* Since the designer added the data access code behind the page, you can simply add the statement around the fill method as shown below.)

```
Try
    SqlDataAdapter1.Fill(DS11)
Catch
    Response.Redirect("customError.aspx")
Finally
End Try
Page.DataBind()
```

10. Stop the SQL Server: the Taskbar contains an icon representing the SQL Server. Right-click this icon, and then click **MSSQL Server – Stop**.
11. View the Web page in the browser. Print the page that appears.

12. Start the SQL Server: right-click the **SQL Server** icon, and then click **MSSQL Server - Start**.

13. View the Web page in the browser to make sure the database server has started.

14. Print the Web page, your source code for the Web page, and the code behind the page.

Project 10-4

In this project, you will document the Web page with comments and create the Code Comment Report.

1. Start **Visual Studio .NET** and open your Chapter10 solution if necessary.

2. Import **Ch10Proj4.aspx** from your Chapter10Data folder. The page contains a form that includes text boxes for the user's name, e-mail address, and comments.

3. Click the **Save All** button. Build the solution.

4. Click **Tools** on the menu bar, then click **Build Comment Web Pages**.

5. Click the radio button labeled **Build for selected Projects** to select it. Select **Chapter10**. Click **OK** twice to overwrite the existing Code Comment Web Report.

6. Click the **Save All** button. Build the solution. The report will open in Visual Studio .NET.

7. Print the Code Comment Report. Print the report for the Ch10Proj4.aspx page.

Project 10-5

In this project, you will use the Page OutPutCache feature to cache variations of the same Web page that display different data depending upon which parameters are given.

1. Start **Visual Studio .NET** and open your **Chapter10** solution if necessary.

2. Import the **Ch10Proj5.aspx** page from your Chapter10Data folder. This page will display the list of categories from the Category table using a DataList control, and a list of products from the Products table using a DataGrid control.

3. In the code behind the page, add the code in the Page_Load event handler to display the date and time in the lblDate and lblTime Label controls.

4. Add the code below to retrieve the data from the database and bind the data to the controls. This code should be placed in the Page_Load handler so that the data is bound when the page first loads.

```
Dim SelID As String = Request.Params("selItem")
If Not SelID Is Nothing Then
    MyCatList.SelectedIndex = CInt(SelID)
Else
End If
Dim CatList As Chapter10.Ch10ProductsDB
CatList = New Chapter10.Ch10ProductsDB()
```

10

```
MyCatList.DataSource = CatList.GetCat()
MyCatList.DataBind()
Dim CatID As Integer = CInt(Request.Params("CatID"))
Dim ProdList As Chapter10.Ch10ProductsDB
ProdList = New Chapter10.Ch10ProductsDB()
DataGrid1.DataSource = ProdList.GetProducts(CatID)
DataGrid1.DataBind()
```

5. Add the code below in the HTML template to cache the page for 60 seconds based on the CatID.

```
<%@ OutputCache Duration="60" VaryByParam="CatID" %>
```

6. Click the **Save All** button. Build the solution.

7. Open the Web page in your browser. Print the Web page, the source code, and the code behind the page for the Ch10Proj5.aspx page.

CASE PROJECTS

Creating a Custom Error Message

You have been asked to create a custom error message that appears when the user does not find the file he or she requested or when the server is unavailable. When the file not found error occurs, redirect the user to the site map. Create a Web page named Ch10Case1a.aspx that contains a site map of all the pages you created in the chapter. Add graphics and content to enhance the appearance of the page. Add hyperlinks to each page in the Chapter10 Web application. Create a Web page named Ch10Case1b.aspx with a message that the Web server is currently unavailable. Add graphics and content to enhance the appearance of the page. Modify the configuration file to support the new error pages that are displayed when the client visits the Web site. (*Hint*: Status code 404 is means that the file is not found. Status code 500 indicates that there is an Internet server error.) Print the Web pages from the browser, the source code for each page, and the Web configuration file.

Creating a Custom Error Message for Database Server Errors

Your boss has asked you to modify the company's application to support custom errors that detect when a database error occurs. Create a new Web page named Ch10Case2a that explains to the visitor that a database error has occurred. Provide a link to the home page. Create a new page named Ch10Case2b.aspx that displays a listing of products in the Tara Store database only for products where the SubSubCategoryID is equal to 21. Preview the Web page in a browser. Print the Web page from the browser. Modify the Web page to support catching database errors. In the code behind the page, use the Try-Catch-Finally to capture errors related to the SQL Server's Data Adapter. If an error occurs, redirect the user to a page named Ch10Case2a.aspx. Print the Web pages from the browser, and the source code for each page.

Working with the Visual Studio .NET Debugger

Your boss has heard of the new debugger available in Visual Studio .NET. Using the Visual Studio .NET SDK and help documents, read about how to use the debugger tool to identify programming logic errors. Visit five Web pages that describe how to use the debugger tool with ASP.NET and Web applications. You may use any of the Help windows within Visual Studio .NET to locate the help documents. Create a Web page named Ch10Case3.aspx that displays what each resource contains. List the name of the page as a hyperlink to the related Help document. Print out the Web page, the source code, and the code behind the page.

Using Page Output Caching to Increase Performance

The Web page that displays the product list takes a long time to access the database and render the output. Your boss has asked you to increase the download performance. Using the Ch10TaraStore SQL Server database that you created earlier in the chapter, create a page named Ch10Case4.aspx to display a list of all of the products in the database where the SubSubCategoryID is equal to 24. Display the ProductID, SubSubCategoryID, ModelNumber, ModelName, and UnitPrice. View the page in the browser. Modify the page to support page output caching. The duration of time the page should remain cached is 5 minutes. Save the changes in the page and rebuild the solution. View the Web page in the browser. Print out the Web page, the source code, and the code behind the page.

10

11

CREATING XML WEB SERVICES

In this chapter, you will:

♦ Learn how to apply Web Services to business applications

♦ Identify the configuration files used in an ASP.NET application

♦ Identify Web Services standards and protocols

♦ Create a Web Service using Visual Studio .NET

♦ Create a Web page that consumes a Web Service using Visual Studio .NET

♦ Locate Web Services

♦ Explore the security methods used to protect a Web Service

W eb Services are one of the two main applications that are built using ASP.NET technology. While WebForms deliver Web content from a Web server to a Web-enabled client such as a Web browser, Web Services can deliver content to any device, application, or platform that supports XML Web Services.

One example of a Web Service is the business application developed between Dollar Rent-a-Car and Southwest Airlines. Many airlines share a common airline reservation system of which Southwest Airlines is not a part. Dollar Rent-a-Car created an application to provide reservations from within this airline reservation system. Without Web Services, Southwest would have had to join the airline reservation system in order to work with the Dollar Rent-a-Car's system. Instead, Dollar Rent-a-Car and Southwest Airlines developed a Web Service using ASP.NET that allows their two systems to work together. By using Web Services, Southwest saved six months in development time, generated $10 million dollars in incremental revenue, and saved $250,000 dollars in middlemen's fees. They were able to recoup their initial investment. This is one example of how a company can save time and money by using Web Services to connect business systems. Web Services promise to bring information into applications from the Internet in much the same way that browsers have made information available to end users. In this chapter, you will learn to create and consume Web Services using Visual Studio .NET.

OVERVIEW OF WEB SERVICES

Web applications consist of a client, which is the browser application, and a Web server. The Web browser requests a Web page from the Web server. The Web server interacts with other applications, such as a SQL Server database. Then, the Web server delivers the Web page to the browser. But what if the owner of the Web site wants to share the Web site's data with another Web site? In the previous programming model, he or she would use a **Remote Procedure Call (RPC)** to call another application on the Web server. However, this is not useful when you need to create applications that work across platforms. Integrating systems across multiple platforms is time-consuming, costly, and often ineffective. The .NET framework introduces Web Services as an integral part of the architecture, making it easy for you to create and consume these services with minimal amounts of code written.

With Visual Studio .NET and ASP.NET you can quickly build Web Services that expose parts of your Web application to other businesses and applications. The Web Service is part or all of a Web application that is publicly exposed so that other applications can interact with it. The program logic that is exposed via the Web Service is accessible through standard Web protocols such as HTTP, XML, and the Simple Object Access Protocol (SOAP). Therefore, the Web Service is platform independent. This means that any client can access the application using standard protocols.

 The SOAP calls are remote function calls that invoke method executions on Web Service components. The output is rendered as XML and passed back to the user.

Because Web Services are built using open standards, you can use them to develop applications that can be called from a variety of clients on a variety of platforms. As a result, Web Services combine the best aspects of component-based development and Web development. (*Note*: Web Services are like libraries that provide data and services to other applications. That is also why Web Services are sometimes referred to as the Application Programming Interface (API) for the Web application.) Web Services make it easier to build distributed Internet applications.

 Microsoft provides additional information about Web Services at *http://msdn.microsoft.com/webservices*. The .NET platform provides built-in support for invoking standards-based Web Services. Unlike other development platforms, you do not need additional tools or SDKs to build Web Services with .NET. All the necessary support is built into the .NET Framework itself.

Applying Web Services to Business Applications

There are dozens of ways in which Web Services can benefit businesses. One concept is to stream data, such as stock quotes or the weather forecast. The Web Service provides the data, and the client application connects to the Web Service to retrieve it. The client could be a browser or another Web site.

Another example of a Web Service is a real-estate database search application. Several companies list their homes with a multiple listing agent. A real estate company could expose the ability to search for a house in their real estate database. The real estate agents can use the browser to search for homes based on criteria such as the number of bedrooms. The multiple listing service company could allow other Web sites to connect to the real estate database Web Service. Then, they would be able to allow their customers to search for homes via their Web sites. For each sale that originated from the Web Service, the real estate company could pay the Web site a referral fee.

Another recent trend on the Internet is for a Web site, for example an online magazine, to display books from an online bookstore. The Web site receives money, credit, or other bonuses for referring the user to the online bookstore to purchase the book. To create the link between the magazine and the online bookstore, you could hard-code the book-store hyperlinks into your application. If the magazine is a significant business partner to the bookstore, you could create a custom distributed COM application to the bookstore's Web application. A newer and controversial technique that has been used to retrieve product information is scraping. **Scraping** a Web site is the process of using a program to view a Web site and capture the source code. The programmer has to create an appli-cation that parses the HTML from the data. Then, the programmer has to create a pro-gram that integrates the new data into the Web site. This process would have to be repeated as often as the original Web site changed.

A better solution than any of these is for the bookstore to provide a Web Service to its catalogue application. Programmers could then use the Catalogue Web Service within their own Web applications. The bookstore could limit who has access to the Catalogue Web Service. They could expose the entire program as a Web Service, or only certain parts of the catalogue application. By making the catalogue application public, any pro-grammer could use Visual Studio .NET tools to integrate his or her Web site with the bookstore application.

In addition to retrieving data, Web Services can also interact with the Web application. In the online bookstore Web Service, the programmer could expose the ordering func-tions as a Web Service. Then, your Web site could sell the books without the customer having to leave your site. You would provide the user interface for the order form. When the customer submitted the form, you would order the product via the Web Service. Thus, the Web Service allows your Web site to act as a distributor for other goods and services on the Internet.

11

There are many other uses of Web Services. For example, you could use a Web Service to deliver educational materials to schools around the country. Each school could integrate the Web Service into its own curriculum, instead of purchasing a prepackaged curriculum, or building a custom curriculum.

Web Services could also be used to build public service Web sites. For example, volunteer organizations share many common areas of interests and needs. A volunteer organization could build a Web Service that exposed their resources as a community service directory. The resources could be classified by type of service, such as fundraising, or they could be classified by the age of the targeted group. Then, any volunteer organization could use the same directory, or portions of the directory, within their Web site. For example, one organization might want to show only listings for services within its state, for children. Another organization might want to show only services for fundraising in the Midwestern states. By using Web Services, a variety of applications can access the data.

Web Services could be used to retrieve national statistical data such as the census, or government records. You could build the Web Service that contains information about all of the elected government positions. Although all counties in a state have their own governmental bodies, they all share the same state governmental body. Therefore, the counties would be able to access the state-specific data from the Web Service. Individual cities and villages could access the county governmental data and their own local governmental data.

Using Visual Studio .NET to Create and Consume Web Services

Web Services are at the core of the Microsoft .NET vision. Microsoft and IBM worked together to create the XML Web Services standards. However, Web Services can be created using a variety of developer tools and programming languages. The three main parts of building and consuming a Web Service are shown in Figure 11-1. As shown in this example, Tara Store has created a Web Service. They also created a SOAP contract that provides information about how to connect to the Web Service. Tara Store's new partner, MaryKate's Housewares, has contracted to use the Tara Store Web Service. They use the SOAP contract to learn how to connect to the Web Service. They create a proxy client, which connects to the Web Service. MaryKate's Warehouse integrates the data into its own Web site. The end user could be using a variety of applications to access the Internet such as a mobile phone or Web browser. The client sees only the MaryKate's Warehouse Web site. They are not aware of the involvement of Tara Store, or the source of the product listing. Although this is an example of a business-to-business-to-consumer application, some Web Services will be limited to business-to-business transactions.

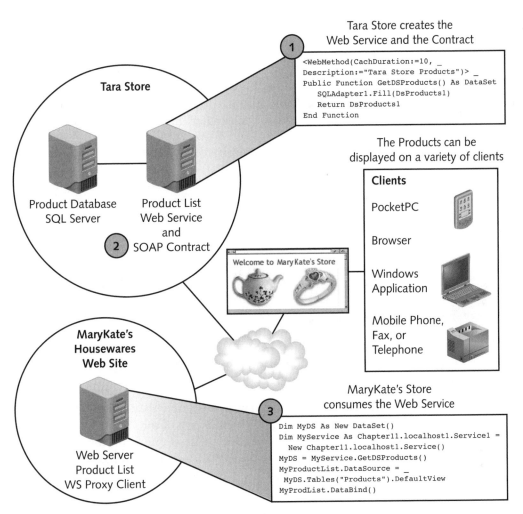

Tara Store creates the
Web Service and the Contract

1

```
<WebMethod(CachDuration:=10, _
Description:="Tara Store Products")> _
Public Function GetDSProducts() As DataSet
    SQLAdapter1.Fill(DsProducts1)
    Return DsProducts1
End Function
```

Tara Store

Product Database
SQL Server

Product List
Web Service
and
2   SOAP Contract

The Products can be
displayed on a variety of clients

Clients

PocketPC

Browser

Windows
Application

Mobile Phone,
Fax, or
Telephone

Welcome to MaryKate's Store

MaryKate's
Housewares
Web Site

Web Server
Product List
WS Proxy Client

MaryKate's Store
consumes the Web Service

3

```
Dim MyDS As New DataSet()
Dim MyService As Chapter11.localhost1.Service1 =
    New Chapter11.localhost1.Service()
MyDS = MyService.GetDSProducts()
MyProductList.DataSource = _
    MyDS.Tables("Products").DefaultView
MyProdList.DataBind()
```

Figure 11-1   Building and Consuming a Web Service

The easiest way to build a Web Service with .NET is to use Visual Studio .NET and create an ASP.NET Web Service project. Visual Studio .NET creates all the necessary files, including the Web Service files. The Web Service is called service1.asmx and service1.asmx.vb by default. The service1.asmx.vb file is the code behind the page for the Web Service.

In order to create a Web Service, you must create a class method with standard input and output parameters and then mark those classes and the specific methods as exposable over the Internet by using the <WebMethod> keyword. There are three major components that make up a Web Service:

- The Web Service on the server side
- The client application that calls the Web Service via a Web reference

- A WSDL Web Service description that describes the functionality of the Web Service

 There are several resources for Web developers on using XML with Web Services. You can learn about using XML with Visual Studio .NET at *ms-help: //MS.VSCC/MS.MSDNVS/vsintro7/html/vxorixmlinvisualstudio.htm*. You can locate sample business applications that contain and consume Web Services on the *www.IBuySpy.com* Web site or at *ms-help://MS.VSCC/ MS.MSDNVS/dwamish7/html/vtgrfWebServices.htm*.

The first part of the Web Service is the server application that is exposed. In ASP.NET, the name of the file for the Web Service must have the file extension .asmx. This Web Service file compiles into a class. So, a Web Service is a class that can be called over a TCP/IP network. As with a traditional Web page, you can create the source file of the Web Service by using a text editor such as Notepad, or a Web development tool such as Visual Studio .NET. You need to import the `System.Web.Services` namespace into the source code for the Web Service. The Web Service is compiled at runtime similarly to ASP.NET pages. Although the Web Service is typically created within a Web application in the same assembly, you can create a separate assembly for the Web Service. Web Services are part of the ASP.NET application model. Therefore, the Web Service must be accessible from a URL that is defined within the Web server. Because the Web Service was built within the ASP.NET framework, it has access to the ASP.NET object model and all the ASP.NET objects such as Request, Session, and Application.

The Web Service page is also divided into the design view and the code behind the page. The code behind the page can be written in any of the .NET languages. You can specify which parts of the Web Service class should be exposed. The keyword <WebMethod> is used to identify the methods that are to be exposed. You can expose properties such as strings, integers, and expressions. Although you can expose objects such as the DataSet object, Web Services do not require you to create or expose programmable objects.

The second step in integrating your application with a Web Service is identifying the method used to locate the Web Service. There are three common ways to locate a Web Service. When a Web Service is created within Visual Studio .NET, a discovery file, known as the **Web Service Description Language (WDSL)** document, is created; this file contains the information on how to interact with the Web Service, and how to format and send data to the Web Service. The Web Service Description Language (WSDL) schema is used to create a WSDL document that describes the functionality of the Web Service. The WSDL is an XML document that describes the methods, namespaces, and URL of the Web Service. You can also use a Web Discovery Service file to locate the Web Service. The **Web Discovery Service** file ends in the file extension .DISCO. This file points to all of the Web Services within your application and the location of the WSDL document. So, when you are using Visual Studio .NET, you can use the Server Explorer window to locate local Web Services on your server and network by reading the discovery files. Another method used to locate a Web Service is to request the URL of the WDSL document from the owner of the Web Service. Another more common way to locate a Web Service is via a **Web Service Discovery Directory**. Microsoft and IBM have teamed up to create the **Universal Description, Discovery, and Integration** (**UDDI**) specification, which can be used to create a third-party Web Service Discovery Directory. You can use these UDDI directories to locate Web Services and the WSDL document. You can learn more about the UDDI standards at *www.uddi.org*.

The third part of a Web Service is the client application that calls the Web Server using a **Web Reference**. Web Services can be consumed programmatically or manually. Web Services can be called from within your Web or Windows application. Adding a Web Reference to your application allows you to treat the Web Service as a local application. Therefore, you can refer to the Web Service class as if it were a local class. Within Visual Studio .NET, the IntelliSense feature provides access to all of the properties and methods of the Web Service class. Even if the Web Service was created on a different platform with a different programming language, you can still call the Web Service class and create programs that interact with the Web Service properties and methods.

The client application does not call the Web Service directly. The application uses the WSDL document to create a **proxy class**. The application calls the proxy class to invoke the Web Service. The proxy class reads the WSDL document and verifies the delivery method. The XML-based request and response messages can be delivered using the HTTPGet method, the HTTPPost method, or SOAP. SOAP calls are remote function calls that invoke method executions on Web Service components. The output is rendered as XML and passed back to the user. SOAP is an important part of creating and consuming Web Services—it's the protocol that's responsible for routing the RPC message from the client to the server and returning the result to the client application. SOAP is based on XML and follows a relatively simple design that's easy to implement. SOAP's simplicity has contributed to its widespread support on just about any platform and development environment. As long as a client application has support for SOAP, it can call the remote Web Service and return data for it, assuming that the user is authorized.

If you are sending the message using SOAP, then, the proxy class creates the **SOAP envelope**, and passes the envelope to the Web Service. The SOAP envelope is used as a wrapper around the messages and provides information about the message format. After the Web server receives the SOAP request, it creates a new instance of the Web Service. After the Web Service has been executed, the return value indicated by the keyword return, passes the output to the SOAP response. The SOAP response is sent over the HTTP connection to the proxy. The client converts the XML document into a format that is understandable by that client application.

If you think that the data within the Web Service will not change frequently, you may want to use the caching techniques you learned in the previous chapter to increase performance. Synchronous calls wait for a response from the Web server. Your application

11

performance degrades if you must wait a long time for the response from a Web Service. Asynchronous calls request the data from the Web server, and then continue processing the application. You can configure your application to send asynchronous calls to the Web Service to increase the performance of your application. In a production environment, you may not be involved in both creating and consuming the Web Service. You may only be creating the Web Service, and providing its description. Another company creates the client application that uses your Web Service Description document to create the interface to your Web server application.

WEB SERVICES STANDARDS AND PROTOCOLS

The HTTP protocol was selected as the primary delivery protocol of Web Services because it can be used to deliver documents through proxy servers and firewalls. The three methods used to route the message over HTTP are HTTPGet, HTTPPost, and SOAP. In addition to calling the Web Service, you can pass parameters to the ASMX page with a QueryString, using the HTTPGet method. The HTTPPost method passes the parameters as a URL-encoded string, which contains the form field variable names and values attached to the body of the message. The SOAP protocol is the default method by which ASP.NET internally calls a Web Service.

Web Services are fully integrated into the Visual Studio .NET development environment. When you use Visual Studio .NET to create your Web Service, the application generates the WSDL document, the DISCO document, and the test Web page. You can use the breakpoints within the debugger tool and the tracing features to debug your Web Service. When you use Visual Studio .NET to consume a Web Service, the application generates a client-side proxy class with both synchronous and asynchronous calls. Then, when you want to access an object, property, or function within the Web Service, the local Web application treats the Web Service as a local object. As a result, all the features of Visual Studio .NET, such as IntelliSense and debugging, are also supported.

The SOAP Contract

The SOAP protocol is an industry standard that is maintained by the WC3. **Simple Object Access Protocol (SOAP)** is an XML-based protocol used for messaging delivery. SOAP is language independent and platform independent. The SOAP message is a remote procedure call over HTTP using XML. Because it's an XML-based message format, it can easily be transmitted over HTTP through firewalls and proxy servers. Because SOAP can represent remote procedure calls and responses from another application, it allows the client application to call the Web Service over HTTP. The SOAP packet contains a SOAP envelope and the response in an XML document. The response may contain the XML data. And, because it serializes the calls and data in XML, SOAP provides a flexible way to express application defined data types. Once the application receives the XML data, the application can deserialize the data into an object such as the DataSet object. So, if you plan to create a Web Service that creates objects, you will likely want to call the Web Service by using SOAP.

SOAP is a simple protocol for publishing available services. The Soap contract is an XML-formatted document called the WSDL. The SOAP contract describes the interface to the Web Service. You can view the SOAP contract by opening a browser and typing the URL of the Web Service followed by "?WSDL". The WSDL file is an XML-formatted file that describes how to call the Web methods using the SOAP protocol. The WSDL document describes the message exchange contract. The WSDL document name has the file extension .sdl. So, the name of a SOAP contract for a Web Service named MyService would be MyService.sdl.

The SOAP contract uses the XML language to describe the location and interfaces that a particular service supports. The WSDL utility looks at the contract and generates the proxy class based on the contract. The WSDL utility is wsdl.exe. The utility requires you to pass the URL of the description. The parameter **?wsdl** is used to generate the proxy. The WSDL utility does not work with the Web Service directly, but through a proxy class. Because the default language used to generate the proxy class default is C#, you may want to use the /language or /l parameter to configure the language as Visual Basic .NET. The /protocol parameter is used for communication with the service. The /namespace parameter is used to configure the global namespace. The default namespace for the proxy class for all Web Services is http://tempuri.org. http://tempuri.org is a generic namespace used in WSDL documents. You can locate more information about the namespaces used in WSDL documents at the *http://tempuri.org* Web site. You should change the reference to the tempuri namespace to your namespace when you are ready to deploy your Web application. (*Note*: If you are using Visual Studio .NET to create and consume Web Services, you can change the Namespace attribute of the <WebMethod> tag.) After you create proxy class, you need to compile it and place it inside the assembly cache. You can compile the application directly with the Visual Basic .NET or Visual C# compiler. Below is a sample of how you can use the WSDL command line utility to look at the contract and generates the proxy class. Wsdl is the command to call the WSDL utility, and /language:VB configures Visual Basic .NET as the language of the class. The URL provides the location of the contract to the Web Service.

```
wsdl /language:VB http://locahost/Service1.asmx?wsdl
```

The DISCO (discovery) document is not the SOAP contract. Rather, it's a pointer to the location of the Web Services within the Web project. The DISCO document is an XML document that examines the SOAP contract to describe the method and data formats within the Web Service. The DISCO document describes how the proxy class should make calls to the Web Service. Although in Visual Studio .NET you can use the tools to create and consume Web Services, you can also use command-line utilities without Visual Studio .NET. The wsdl.exe file is used to create the SOAP contract.

11

You use the disco.exe utility to create the discovery document. You use the VBC.exe compiler to create the proxy class for a Visual Basic .NET class. There are several parameters that can be passed when you use the utility. The /username and /password parameters are provided to authenticate the application to the Web server. The /domain parameter is the domain name that is needed to access the server. By default, the output from the discovery process is saved to a file in the current directory with the file extension .DISCO. You can specify an alternate directory with the /out parameter. You can suppress the output file entirely with the /nosave parameter. The /nologo parameter will suppress the Microsoft logo. The following sample code uses the Discovery tool to send the discovery information to a file in the temp directory.

```
Disco.exe /nologo /out:c:\temp\disco
http://localhost/websx/services.disco
```

The test page uses the HTTPGet method to test the Web Service. Therefore, the names and values are passed with the URL in the QueryString. Because the HTTPGet method was used, the data is returned in an XML format, and not in a SOAP message. However, this gives you the opportunity to verify that you can connect to the Web Service and retrieve data. Because Web Services use standard Web protocols, they follow typical Web rules. For example, Web Services are stateless, which means that, even though Web Services expose classes, they are more of a remote procedure call interface than a remote class interface. None of the major Web Service implementations support properties in any way. You can call methods with parameters rather than storing state in properties between method calls. To maintain state, you will have to use Web-server-specific functionality, such as the ASP.NET Session object, to store the state and retrieve it on subsequent hits. Furthermore, since Web Services use the standard Web architecture, the same tools you have used for HTML-based browser applications can also be used in the Web Services code.

CREATING AND USING A WEB SERVICE

Web Services are fully integrated into the Visual Studio .NET development environment. When you use Visual Studio .NET to create your Web Service, the application generates the WSDL document, the DISCO document, and the test Web page. You can use the breakpoints within the debugger tool and the tracing features to debug your Web Service.

In this exercise, you create a Web Service for Tara Store to allow other stores to display its merchandise. The Web Service returns data from a DataSet object named dsProducts1. You will use the WebMethod in the declaration line to declare the GetDSProducts method as a Web Service method.

1. Start **Visual Studio .NET**.

2. Click **File** on the menu bar, point to **New**, then click **Project**. This opens the New Project window.

3. Click the **Visual Basic Projects** folder icon, then click **ASP.NET Web Service** under Templates. Type **Chapter11WebService** in the Location text box in place of WebService1. Click **OK** to create the solution, project, and default files. The default Web Service page, named Service1.asmx.vb, opens in Design view.

4. In the Solution Explorer window, right-click **Chapter11WebService**, point to **Add**, then click **New Folder**. Type **images** to name the folder, and then press **Enter**.

5. Right-click the **images** folder, point to **Add**, and then click **Add Existing Item**. Change the Files of type drop-down list from VB Code Files to **All Files**. Browse to locate the images folder within the Chapter11Data folder. Select all of the images and then click the **Open** button to import them into the images directory of the Chapter11WebService project.

6. Right-click the **Chapter11WebService** project in the Solution Explorer window, point to **Add**, and then click **Add Existing Item**. Browse to locate the Chapter11Data folder. Select the **TaraStore.mdb** file, and then click the **Open** button to import the file into the Chapter11WebService project.

7. To add a data connection to the TaraStore.mdb database, right-click **Data Connections** in the Server Explorer window, and then click **Add Connection**. Click the **Provider** tab, and select **Microsoft Jet 4.0 OLE DB Provider**. Click the **Next** button to continue. In the database name text box, enter the path to the TaraStore.mdb database that you imported into your project, and then click the **OK** button. (*Note:* The default path would be C:\InetPub\wwwroot\ Chapter11WebService\TaraStore.mdb.) Leave the User name as Admin and the Blank password check box checked. Click **OK** to continue.

8. To add the DataAdapter object, open the **Toolbox** if it is not already open, click the **Data** tab, and drag the **OleDbDataAdapter** tab to the page. The Data Adapter Configuration Wizard opens. Click the **Next** button.

9. Select the **TaraStore** database from the drop-down list if it is not already selected, and then click the **Next** button.

10. Click the **Next** button to create a SQL query.

11. In the SQL text box, enter the code below.

```
SELECT ProductID, ModelName, UnitCost,
   Description, Thumbnail
FROM Products
```

12. Click **Next**, and then click **Finish**. The DataAdapter named OleDbDataAdapter1 and the Connection object named OleDbConnection1 are placed on the designer page.

13. To add a DataSet object, click **Data** on the menu bar, then click **Generate Dataset**.

11

14. In the Generate DataSet dialog box, verify that the New radio button is selected. In the text box, type **dsProducts**.

15. Click the check box labeled **Add this dataset to the designer**, then click **OK**, as shown in Figure 11-2. A DataSet object named DsProducts1 is added to the designer.

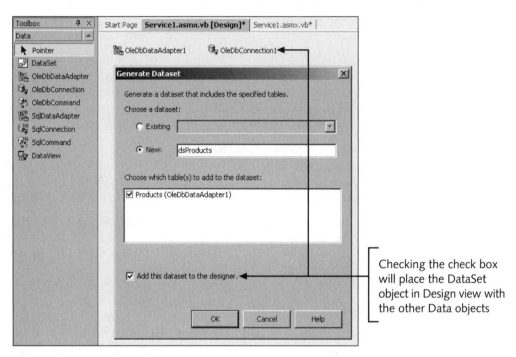

Figure 11-2 Creating the DataSet

16. Double-click the designer to open the Web Service in code view. On the first line, import the **System.Data.OleDb** namespace by typing the following code.

```
Imports System.Data.OleDb
```

17. The green text is a commented-out area that contains a sample Web Service. Below the sample Web Service, create a Web Service by adding the keyword WebMethod, as shown below. Set the CacheDuration attribute to 10 so that ASP.NET caches the results of the Web Service for 10 seconds. Set the Description attribute of the WebMethod to the string shown below. The description appears on the Web Service Help page. (*Note:* To make your code easier to read, you can use the underscore to separate the keyword Method from the function.)

```
<WebMethod(CacheDuration:=10, _
    Description:="Tara Store Products List")> _
```

18. Create the GetDSProducts method by adding the code below. Use the fill method of the DataAdapter to fill the DataSet object named DsProducts1 with the data from the Products table, as shown in Figure 11–3.

```
Public Function GetDSProducts() As DataSet
    OleDbDataAdapter1.Fill(DsProducts1)
    Return DsProducts1
End Function
```

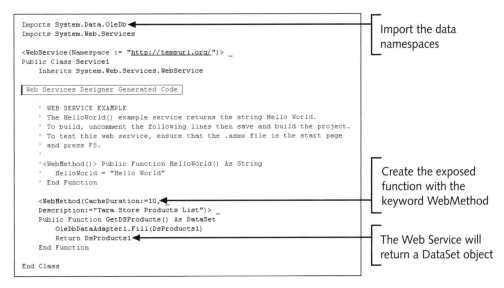

```
Imports System.Data.OleDb                                          Import the data
Imports System.Web.Services                                        namespaces

<WebService(Namespace := "http://tempuri.org/")> _
Public Class Service1
    Inherits System.Web.Services.WebService

Web Services Designer Generated Code

    ' WEB SERVICE EXAMPLE
    ' The HelloWorld() example service returns the string Hello World.
    ' To build, uncomment the following lines then save and build the project.
    ' To test this web service, ensure that the .asmx file is the start page
    ' and press F5.
    '
    '<WebMethod()> Public Function HelloWorld() As String     Create the exposed
    '    HelloWorld = "Hello World"                           function with the
    ' End Function                                            keyword WebMethod

    <WebMethod(CacheDuration:=10,
    Description:="Tara Store Products List")> _
    Public Function GetDSProducts() As DataSet
        OleDbDataAdapter1.Fill(DsProducts1)                   The Web Service will
        Return DsProducts1                                    return a DataSet object
    End Function

End Class
```

Figure 11-3   Filling the DataSet with Data from the DataAdapter

19. Click the **Save All** icon, click **Build** on the menu bar, then click **Build Solution**.

In the next part of the exercise, you will view the Web Service home page in a browser. This will provide you with a list of the functions and properties defined in the Web Service. In this example, there is one function, named GetDSProducts. Clicking on the getDSProducts hyperlink will take you to the HTML test page, where you can test the Web Service. The test page shows sample code that illustrates the sample request and response that is used when communicating with the Web Service using SOAP, HTTPGet, or HTTPPost. From there you can test the Web Service by invoking the function and view the output in an XML-formatted document.

1. Open the browser. Go to the Web Service home page at *http://localhost/Chapter11WebService/Service1.asmx*. Notice that the Web Service Description property is shown in the Web Service Home Page as "Tara Store Products List".

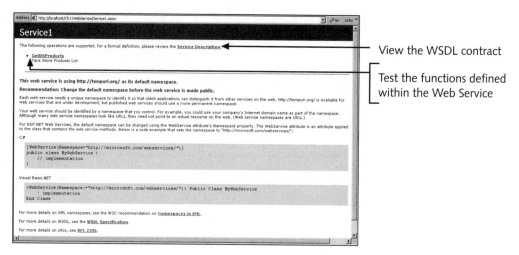

Figure 11-4   Web Service home page

2. Click the hyperlink named **GetDSProducts**. This hyperlink is the method that was defined in the Web Service. (*Note:* The hyperlink takes you to a page with the URL *http://localhost/Chapter11WebService/Service1.asmx?op=GetDSProducts.*)

3. Click the **Invoke** button to test the GetDSProducts method. An XML document is returned that describes the data and contains the data. The URL of the document is *http://localhost/Chapter11WebService/Service1.asmx/GetDSProducts?* as shown in Figure 11-5. The top portion of the document describes the data, and the lower portion contains the product data. There are no additional parameters passed with the QueryString in this example.

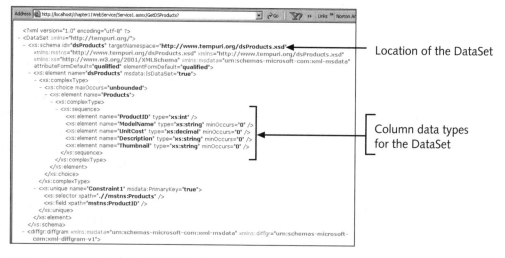

Figure 11-5   Testing the Web Service

4. Close the browser window that contains the XML document.

5. Click the **Back** button in the browser to return to the Web Service home page.

6. Click the hyperlink labeled **Service Description** to view the service contract. The URL of the Service Description page is the same as that of the Web Service home page with ?WSDL appended. The Service Description page in the example is located at *http://localhost/Chapter11WebService/Service1.asmx?WSDL* as shown in Figure 11-6.

The WSDL can be viewed in a browser by entering the URL plus ?WSDL

Figure 11-6   Web Service description page

7. Return to Visual Studio .NET. Click the **Save All** button. Click **Build** on the menu bar, then click **Build Solution**.

8. To close the solution, click **File** on the menu bar, then click **Close Solution**.

11

You can turn the line numbering feature on or off. The line numbering feature is useful when you want to locate specific lines of code. To configure the line numbering feature, go to the Options command on the Tools menu. Click the Text Editor tab, select All Languages, then select General. Click the Line numbers check box to turn line numbering on, then click OK.

Using a Web Service

You can call Web Services via the HTTP Get and Post methods, or via SOAP. Although the HTTP Get and Post methods are limited to sending only primitive data types such as integers, and strings, they can also send arrays of these primitive data types. The SOAP protocol allows you to send any structure, class, or enumerator over the Internet. For example, you can send an ADO object, such as a DataSet object, or an array of Data objects.

When you send the information over the Internet, the information is packaged in a format that can travel over a TCP/IP network. **Serialization** is the process of changing an object into a form that can be readily transported over the network. For example, you can serialize the output of a structure, such as a DataSet object, into a string. With Web Services, you use HTTPGet or HTTPPost to send an object, then the methods, properties, and values of the object can be rendered as elements of an XML document. The process of converting the object to an XML document is known as XML serialization.

Once this has been done, you can use the HTTP Get and Post methods to retrieve the serialized object. You then change the string back into the original structure, which is known as **deserialization**. If the document is in XML format, you can also use LoadXML method of the XML Document Object Model (DOM) to retrieve the XML data. When you use Visual Studio .NET to create and consume Web Services, Visual Studio .NET will create the code necessary to serialize and deserialize your Web Services.

 You can learn more about XML serialization at *ms-help://MS.VSCC/ MS.MSDNVS/cpguide/html/cpconintroducingxmlserialization.htm*.

When you use Visual Studio .NET to consume a Web Service, the application generates a client-side proxy class with both synchronous and asynchronous calls. Then, when you want to access an object, property, or function within the Web Service, the local Web application treats the Web Service as a local object. As a result, all the programming tools of Visual Studio .NET, such as IntelliSense and debugging, are also supported with Web Services.

The application that calls the Web Service is a Web Service client. You create a Web Service client from an ASP.NET page. The Web Service may be called by the HTTP Get and Post methods, or SOAP. The Server Explorer window allows you to see Web Services installed within your local Web Server.

Consuming a Web Service from an ASP.NET Page

In the following exercise, you create a Web page for a partner of Tara Store named MaryKate's Housewares, which wants to distribute Tara Store's products on its Web site. The owners hope to increase their market share by expanding their product line. However, they do not want their customers to know of their relationship with Tara Store. The Web page you create below consumes the Tara Store Web Service and displays Tara Store's products.

1. Start **Visual Studio .NET**.

2. Click **File** on the menu bar, point to **New**, then click **Project**. This opens the New Project window.

3. Click **Visual Basic Projects** in the Project Types pane. Click **ASP.NET Web Application** in the Templates pane. Type **Chapter11** in the Location text box in place of WebApplication1. Click **OK** to create the solution, project, and default files.

4. Right-click **Chapter11** in the Solution Explorer window, point to **Add**, then click **New Folder**. Type **images** to name the folder, and then press **Enter**.

5. Right-click the **images** folder, point to **Add**, and then click **Add Existing Item**. Switch Files of Type to **All Files**. Navigate to your Chapter11Data\images

folder. Select all of the image files, then click **Open** to import the images into the project's images folder.

6. Start **Notepad**. Open the **styles.txt** file in the Chapter11Data folder and select all of the text. Click **Edit** on the menu bar, then click **Copy**. Exit Notepad.

7. In Visual Studio .NET, double-click the **Styles.css** file in the Solution Explorer window. Above the body tag, insert the cursor. Click **Edit** on the menu bar, then click **Paste**. Click the **Save All** icon and close the Styles.css page.

8. Right-click **Chapter11** in the Solution Explorer window, point to **Add**, then click **Add Existing Item**. Select the file **Ch11DisplayProducts.aspx** from the Chapter11Data files directory. Click **Open** to import the files into your project. Click **Yes** to create the new class file for the page.

9. In the Solution Explorer window, right-click the **Chapter11** project, then click **Add Web Reference**. The Add Web Reference dialog box opens. You can search for local or remote Web Services.

10. In the address text box enter the URL of the home page of the Web Service, and then press **Enter**. The URL is *http://localhost/Chapter11WebService/Service1.asmx*. The home page appears in the left window, as shown in Figure 11-7. (*Note*: You can view the contract and definition within the dialog box.)

You can preview the contract and the documentation

Adding a reference allows you to refer to the Web Service as another object within the page

Figure 11-7   Adding a Web reference to a Web Project

11. Click the **Add Reference** button to add the Web reference to the project. (*Note*: A folder named Web References is added to the project. The reference to the localhost is added to the project Web References. There can be more than one Web Service referred to. Therefore, the Web reference contains a map with the URL to the Web Services, and a copy of the service contract for each Web Service.)

12. Double-click **Ch11DisplayProducts.aspx** in the Solution Explorer window to open the page in Design view. Double-click the page to open the code behind the page.

13. On the first line of the page, import the data namespace by typing **Imports System.Data**.

14. In the Page_Load event handler, add the code below, which will create a new instance of the Web Service.

```
Dim MyDS As New DataSet()
Dim MyService As Chapter11.localhost.Service1 = _
    New Chapter11.localhost.Service1()
MyDS = MyService.GetDSProducts()
MyProdList.DataSource = _
    MyDS.Tables("Products").DefaultView
MyProdList.DataBind()
```

15. Click the **Save All** button. Click **Build** on the menu bar, then click **Build Solution**.

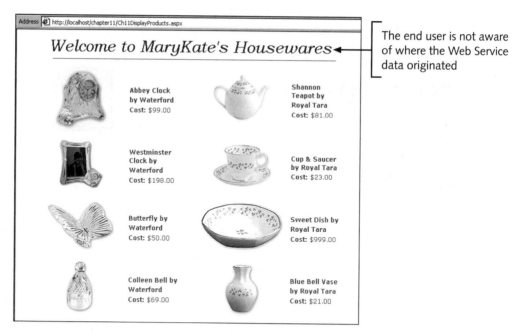

Figure 11-8   Viewing the Web Service from a Web browser

16. Click the **Ch11DisplayProducts.aspx** tab. Right-click the page, and then click **View in Browser**. Your page should look like the one in Figure 11-8.

17. Close any open pages.

Locating Web Services

There are many third-party Web Services available. The UDDI is a directory service that was initially created by Microsoft and IBM to provide businesses a method for registering and searching for Web Services. The UDDI allows you to search for third-party Web Services. The home page for UDDI is located at *www.uddi.org*. Additional information about UDDI can also be located on Microsoft's Web site at *uddi.microsoft.com/*. When you add a Web Reference to your project, instead of typing the URL in the location text box, you can click on the UDDI hyperlink to locate Web Services.

In addition to the UDDI, you can find several third-party Web Services at *www.xmethods.net*, *www.coldrooster.com*, *www.asp.net*, and *www.gotdotnet.com*. In Figure 11-9, you can see that the XMethods Web site provides a listing of SOAP-based Web Services. Not all Web Services are created on Microsoft Windows platforms. However, you can easily integrate non-Windows Web Services into your application in the same way you would integrate Microsoft Windows Web services.

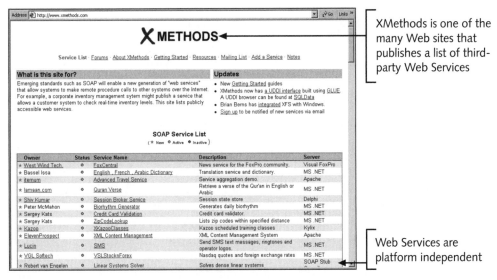

XMethods is one of the many Web sites that publishes a list of third-party Web Services

Web Services are platform independent

Figure 11-9   Sample Web Services available from XMethods

When you add a Web Service, you can locate additional Web Services on your local network or server. To locate local Web Services, add a Web Reference to your project. Instead of typing in the URL of the Web Service in the location text box, click the hyperlink Web References on Local Web Server as shown in Figure 11-10. The discovery document points you to where the Web Services are located. Notice in the image that the Web Service that you created earlier will be listed.

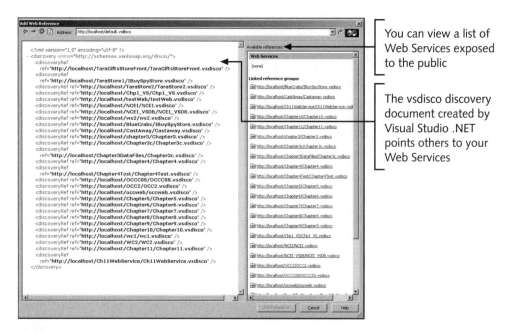

Figure 11-10   Using the discovery documents to Locate Web Services

Securing Web Services

In addition to configuring state management, you will want to make sure your Web Services are secure. You will want to limit access to your Web Services by using an authentication scheme. Although the Web Service architecture doesn't provide security for the developer, you can take advantage of the traditional security methods such as HTTP authentication services and SSL. Creating a secure Web Service is an important factor for business-to-business (B2B) and business-to-consumer (B2C) applications. You can secure a Web Service by using traditional methods such as IIS Web security, Windows authentication and Windows NTFS file permissions, and Passport authentication. Web Services also support the SSL protocol, which is used to encrypt data that is sent using the HTTP protocol. If you need to send the data securely over the Internet, you can also apply HTTPS instead of HTTP. The HTTPS protocol encrypts the message using Secure Sockets Layer (SSL) standards. You can identify when a Web site uses SSL because the HTTPS protocol is used as the protocol within the URL.

Access to the Web Service requires access to the Web Service page. As you recall, this page ends in .asmx. You can protect this file by using the Web Server authentication tools. In IIS, you can configure access to the Web site using the Directory Security tab. The Web server allows you to filter users by IP address or domain name. You can require a specific authentication method such as anonymous access, or a specific Windows user account.

You can require the client to use a secure communications channel such as SSL. (*Note*: You can read more about IIS security at *ms-help://MS.VSCC/MS.MSDNVS/dnasdj01/html/asp0132.htm*. You can also learn more about IIS security at *ms-help://MS.VSCC/MS.MSDNVS/vsent7/html/vxconIISAuthentication.htm*.) In addition, you can protect your Web Service by using ASP.NET security methods. To learn more about these techniques, go to *ms-help://MS.VSCC/MS.MSDNVS/dnbda/html/authaspdotnet.htm*.

You can also apply Windows NTFS file or directory security to protect the Web Service page. Windows NTFS (Windows NT File System) allows you to protect the file by setting permission to the file for specific users and groups. The following code configures the Web.config file to use the Windows security to authenticate the user. Then, within Windows, you need to set the permissions on the file.

```
<authentication mode= "Windows">
</authentication>
```

You can learn more about Windows security at *ms-help: //MS.VSCC/MS.MSDNVS/dnguide/html/msdn_secinst.htm*. You can also learn about the best practices for creating a secure server at *ms-help://MS.VSCC/MS.MSDNVS/vsent7/html/vxconBestPracticesStrategiesForSecurability.htm*.

Although you used Visual Studio .NET to create your Web Service, there are some Web developers who will use other tools, such as the SOAP Toolkit, to create XML Web Services. There are several ways to protect Web Services using SOAP. SOAP can take advantage of HTTP authentication. You can also use SOAP headers with your own encryption algorithms to secure your Web Service. The SOAP header class is a class within the .NET Framework. You can inherit from this class, and then set the properties within the class. You can add data to the header and call methods. The SOAP packet contains a SOAP envelope and the response in an XML document. The response may contain the XML data.

You can learn how to use the SOAP Toolkit at *ms-help://MS.VSCC/MS.MSD-NVS/dnsoap/html/soap_faq.htm*. You can learn more about securing Web Services with the SOAP Toolkit at *ms-help://MS.VSCC/MS.MSDNVS/dnwebsrv/html/websvcs_usingsoap.htm*. You can also learn more about securing Web Services using ASP.NET at *ms-help://MS.VSCC/MS.MSDNVS/cpguide/html/cpconsecuringaspnetwebservices.htm*.

CHAPTER SUMMARY

❑ Web Services are used to expose part or all of an application. In ASP.NET, the name of the file for the Web Service must end in the .asmx extension. The keyword <WebMethod> is used to identify the methods that are to be exposed.

❒ The Web Service Description Language (WSDL) schema is used to create a WSDL document that describes the functionality of the Web Service.

❒ Microsoft and IBM have teamed up to create the Universal Description, Discovery, and Integration (UDDI) specification, which is used to locate Web Services.

❒ Web Services may be called by the HTTP Get and Post methods, or by SOAP.

❒ In Visual Studio .NET, the Web application uses the WSDL document to create a proxy class. The Web application calls the proxy class to invoke the Web Service. The proxy class reads the WSDL document and verifies the delivery method.

❒ The SOAP contract is an XML-formatted document called the WSDL. The test page uses the HTTPGet method to test the Web Service.

❒ You can secure a Web Service by using the traditional methods such as IIS Web security, HTTPS with SSL, Windows authentication, and Passport authentication.

REVIEW QUESTIONS

1. Which method is used to call applications over a TCP/IP network?
   a. RPC
   b. ADO
   c. Web Service
   d. WebForm

2. What file extension is used to identify a Web Service?
   a. .asmx
   b. .aspx
   c. .asp
   d. .ascx

3. What format is used to query the Web Service using the autogenerated test page?
   a. HTTPGet
   b. HTTPPost
   c. SOAP
   d. all of the above

4. The default namespace for all Web Services is _____.
   a. http://tempuri.org
   b. http://www.tempuri.com
   c. http://www.uddi.org
   d. http://www.uddi.net

5. The _____ keyword(s) is/are used to define a function as a Web Service.

   a. <Web Service>

   b. <WebService>

   c. <WebMethod>

   d. <Web Methods>

6. What keyword in the Web Service declaration is used to cache the results from the Web Service?

   a. CacheDuration

   b. Cache

   c. CacheAll

   d. WebCache

7. What keyword in the Web Service declaration is used to describe the Web Service in the default test page?

   a. Description

   b. Name

   c. ID

   d. all of the above

8. Which URL would provide the Service Description Page?

   a. *http://localhost/WebService/Service1?WSDL*

   b. *http://localhost/WebService/WSDL?*

   c. *http://localhost/WebService/?WSDL*

   d. *http://localhost/WebService/Service1.asmx?WSDL*

9. Which method of the XML Document Object Model (DOM) is used to retrieve the XML data?

   a. GetXML

   b. LoadXML

   c. LoadXMLData

   d. ReadXMLData

10. Which object is used to call the Web Service?

    a. a Web Service Alias

    b. a Proxy Service

    c. a Proxy Class

    d. a Web Service Public Class

11

11. What does the SOAP stand for?

    a. Simple Object Access Protocol

    b. Simple Object ASP Protocol

    c. Simple Object Access Pages

    d. Serialized Object Access Protocol

12. What method should be used to call a Web Service that accesses a Data object?

    a. HTTPGet

    b. HTTPPost

    c. SOAP

    d. all of the above

13. What companies initiated the UDDI standards?

    a. Microsoft

    b. IBM

    c. Sun

    d. a and b

14. The _____ is a directory service that provides businesses with a method to register and search for Web Services.

    a. UDDI

    b. ASP

    c. WebServices

    d. ASMX

15. What method(s) can be used to secure Web Services?

    a. IIS Web security

    b. Windows authentication

    c. SOAP headers

    d. all of the above

16. What third-party tool(s) from Microsoft provide(s) authentication services?

    a. NTFS

    b. Passport

    c. SSL

    d. all of the above

17. Which tool within Visual Studio is used to add a Web Service to a Web project?

   a. Web reference

   b. Web Service

   c. XML Web Service

   d. all of the above

18. What is the file extension of the discovery document that is created when you create a Web Service in Visual Studio .NET?

   a. .DCO

   b. .ASMX

   c. .DISCO

   d. .DISC

19. If your company uses a firewall, when should you use Web Services?

   a. Never. You can't use Web Services with firewalls.

   b. Use them only if the company uses a proxy server.

   c. Anytime. Web Services can send files through a firewall.

   d. Use them only when the firewall supports the SOAP protocol.

20. What type of applications can call a Web Service?

   a. Web applications

   b. Window applications

   c. Java applications

   d. all of the above

HANDS-ON PROJECTS

Project 11-1

In this project, you create a banner ad database that can be used with a banner ad Web Service.

1. Start **Visual Studio .NET** and open your **Chapter11** solution.

2. Right-click **Data Connections** in Server Explorer, and then click **Create New SQL Server Database**. Name the database banners as shown in Figure 11-11. (*Note:* Your server name and authentication permissions may vary with your SQL server.)

3. Create a new table.

4. Add the fields to the table as shown in Figure 11-12. Make the AdID an identity field and the primary key.

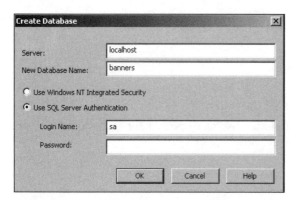

Figure 11-11   Creating the Banners database

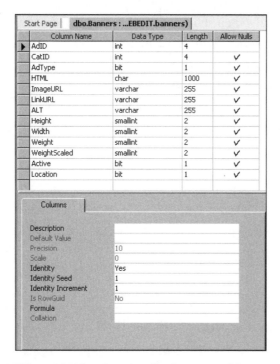

Figure 11-12   Creating the Banners table

5. Save the table as **Banners**, then add the data to the Banners table as shown in Figure 11-13.

AdID	CatID	AdType	HTML	ImageURL	LinkURL	ALT	Height	Width	Weight	WeightScaled	Active	Location
1	1	1	<NULL>	home.jpg	www.tarastore.com	Tara Store Home Page	50	500	10	10	1	0
2	2	1	<NULL>	waterford.jpg	www.tarastore.com	Waterford Products	50	500	10	20	1	0
3	3	1	<NULL>	china.jpg	www.tarastore.com	China Products	50	500	10	30	1	0
4	4	1	<NULL>	pottery.jpg	www.tarastore.com	Pottery Products	50	500	10	40	1	0
5	5	1	<NULL>	movies.jpg	www.tarastore.com	Movies About Ireland	50	500	10	50	1	0
6	6	1	<NULL>	books.jpg	www.tarastore.com	Books About Ireland	50	500	10	60	1	0
7	7	1	<NULL>	music.jpg	www.tarastore.com	Irish Music	50	500	10	70	1	0

Figure 11-13   Inserting the data for the Banners table

6. Create a new table named **Categories**.

7. Add the fields to the Categories table as shown in Figure 11-14. Make the CatID an identity field and the primary key.

Column Name	Data Type	Length	Allow Nulls
CatID	int	4	
Name	varchar	255	✓
Keywords	varchar	1000	✓

Columns

Description	
Default Value	
Precision	10
Scale	0
Identity	Yes
Identity Seed	1
Identity Increment	1
Is RowGuid	No
Formula	
Collation	

Figure 11-14   Creating the Categories table

8. Add the data to the Categories table as shown in Figure 11-15.

CatID	Name	Keywords
1	TaraStore	Tara Home
2	Waterford	Waterford Crystal Glassware
3	China	China Royal Tara Plates
4	Pottery	Pottery Belinda Bradshaw Nicholas Mosse
5	Movies	Movies About Ireland
6	Books	Books About Ireland
7	Music	Irish Music

Figure 11-15   Inserting the data for the Categories table

9. Create a new table named **BannerHits**.

11

10. Add the fields to the BannerHits table as shown in Figure 11-16. Make the HitID an identity field and the primary key.

Figure 11-16   Creating the BannerHits table

11. Print the records in the Banners table in your database.

Project 11-2

In this project, you create a banner ad Web Service using a random number generator. You must have completed Project 11-1 in order to complete this project.

1. Start **Visual Studio .NET** and create a new Web Service project named **Chapter11Project2**.

2. Double-click the **Service1.asmx.vb[Design]** page, to edit the code behind the page. In the Code view, add the code below to create two properties, ImageURL and NavigateURL, which are both strings, as shown in Figure 11-17.

```
Public Class BannerAd
    Public ImageURL As String
    Public NavigateURL As String
End Class
```

Figure 11-17   Creating the Banner Ad Web Services

3. Add the code below to create the **WebMethod**, which displays the banner randomly. Then, add the GetAd function to generate a banner ad object with two properties, ImageURL and NavigateURL, which are both strings, as shown in Figure 11-17.

```
<WebMethod()> _
Public Function GetAd() As BannerAd
Dim Ad As BannerAd = New BannerAD()
Dim AdID As String = CInt(Int((7 * Rnd()) + 1)).ToString()
Ad.ImageURL = "http://localhost/chapter11/images" & ¬
AdID & ".jpg"
Ad.NavigateURL = "http://www.tarastore.com"
Return Ad
```

4. Click the **Save All** icon. Go to the **Build** menu and select **Build Solution**. Close the solution.

5. Open the **Chaper11** solution. Add a **Web Reference** to the new Banner Ad Web Service at *http://localhost/chapter11Project2/Service1.asmx*.

6. Create a new page named **Ch11Proj2DisplayBanner.aspx** that will retrieve one of the banner ads. Add a hyperlink object from the WebForms tab. The hyperlink object's name is Hyperlink1 by default.

11

7. In the Code view, add the code below to call the Web Service and retrieve the image name and URL from the Web Service, as shown in Figure 11-18.

```
Dim MyService As Chapter11.localhost2.Service1 = _
New Chapter11.localhost2.Service1()
Hyperlink1.ImageUrl = MyService.GetAd().ImageURL
Hyperlink1.NavigateUrl = MyService.GetAd().NavigateURL
```

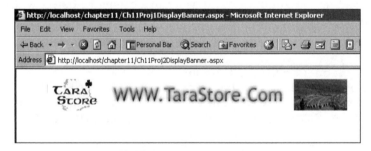

Create an instance of the Web Service, which returns the ad

Assign the properties to the Hyperlink1 object

Figure 11-18   Retrieving the banner ad from the Web Services

8. Save the page and build the solution. View the page at *http://localhost/chapter11/Ch11Proj2DisplayBanner.aspx* in the browser, as shown in Figure 11-19. Click the **Refresh** button several times to see the banner ad rotate images randomly. Print the Web page, your source code, and the source code for the Web Service.

Figure 11-19   Viewing the banner ad

Project 11-3

In this project, you create a banner ad Web Service using the values from the database. You must have completed Project 11-1 in order to complete this project.

1. Start **Visual Studio .NET**.

2. Create a new Web Service Solution named **Chapter11Project3**.

3. On the Service1.asmx page, use the SqlDataAdapter to connect to the **Banners** SQL Server database. Select all of the records within the Banners table. Then, generate a DataSet named **dsBanners** based on the Banners table, and add the DataSet to the designer. Add a **DataView** and set the Table property to the **Banners** tab.

4. Double-click the **Service1.asmx** page to edit the code behind the page. In the Code view, add the code below to create a function to generate a Banner Ad object with properties for each of the properties in an image hyperlink such as **ImageURL**, **NavigateURL**, **ImageWidth**, **ImageHeight**, **AltText**. All of the properties are strings, as shown below.

```
Public Class BannerAd
        Public ImageURL As String
        Public NavigateURL As String
        Public ImageWidth As String
        Public ImageHeight As String
        Public AltText As String
End Class
```

5. Add the code below to create the **WebMethod**, which displays the banner ads randomly. There are only seven banner ads in this example. So, in this instance, simply use the random function to generate a random number between 1 and 7, as shown below.

```
<WebMethod()> _
Public Function GetAd() As BannerAd
Dim Ad As BannerAd = New BannerAd()
Dim AdID As String = CInt(Int((7 * Rnd()) + 1)).ToString()
Dim RecordPos As Integer = CInt(AdID)
```

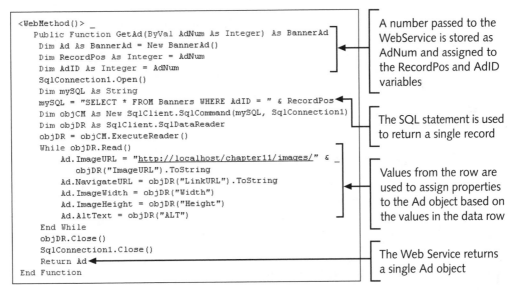

```
<WebMethod()> _
    Public Function GetAd(ByVal AdNum As Integer) As BannerAd
    Dim Ad As BannerAd = New BannerAd()
    Dim RecordPos As Integer = AdNum
    Dim AdID As Integer = AdNum
    SqlConnection1.Open()
    Dim mySQL As String
    mySQL = "SELECT * FROM Banners WHERE AdID = " & RecordPos
    Dim objCM As New SqlClient.SqlCommand(mySQL, SqlConnection1)
    Dim objDR As SqlClient.SqlDataReader
    objDR = objCM.ExecuteReader()
    While objDR.Read()
        Ad.ImageURL = "http://localhost/chapter11/images/" & _
            objDR("ImageURL").ToString
        Ad.NavigateURL = objDR("LinkURL").ToString
        Ad.ImageWidth = objDR("Width")
        Ad.ImageHeight = objDR("Height")
        Ad.AltText = objDR("ALT")
    End While
    objDR.Close()
    SqlConnection1.Close()
    Return Ad
End Function
```

A number passed to the WebService is stored as AdNum and assigned to the RecordPos and AdID variables

The SQL statement is used to return a single record

Values from the row are used to assign properties to the Ad object based on the values in the data row

The Web Service returns a single Ad object

Figure 11-20   Retrieving a single row of data from a DataView

6. Add the code to retrieve the values from the database. Use the DataReader to retrieve only a single row based on the AdID property, as shown in Figure 11-20.

7. Click the **Save All** icon. Click **Build** on the menu bar, then click **Build Solution**. Close the solution.

8. Open the **Chapter11** solution and add a **Web Reference** to the new Banner Ad Web Service at *http://localhost/Chapter11Project3/Service1.asmx*.

9. Create a new page named **Ch11Proj3DisplayBanner.aspx** that will retrieve one of the banner ads. Add a hyperlink object from the WebForms tab. The hyperlink object's name is Hyperlink1 by default.

10. In the Code view, add the code to call the Web Service and retrieve the image name and URL from the Web Service, as well as the ImageWidth, ImageHeight, and AltText properties, as shown in Figure 11-21.

```
Private Sub Page_Load(ByVal sender As System.Object, ByVal e As System.EventArgs)
    'Put user code to initialize the page here
    Dim MyService As Chapter11.localhost2.Service1 = _
    New Chapter11.localhost2.Service1()
    HyperLink1.ImageUrl = MyService.GetAd.ImageURL
    HyperLink1.NavigateUrl = MyService.GetAd.NavigateURL
    HyperLink1.Width = Parse(MyService.GetAd.ImageWidth)
    HyperLink1.Height = Parse(MyService.GetAd.ImageHeight)
    HyperLink1.ToolTip = MyService.GetAd.AltText
End Sub

Public Overloads Shared Function Parse(ByVal s As String) As Unit
End Function
```

Figure 11-21   Creating a banner ad from a Web Service

11. Save the page. Build the solution. View the page at *http://localhost/chapter11/Ch11Proj3DisplayBanner.aspx* in the browser. Click the **Refresh** button several times to see the banner ad rotate images randomly. Print the Web page, your source code, and the source code for the Web Service.

CASE PROJECTS

Creating a Banner Ad Distribution Web Service

Your store manager would like to provide a banner ad Web Service that other companies can use to display your banner ad on their Web sites. Create a Web Service that allows another company to view your Web banner. Create a single banner ad. Create the Web Service named Ch11Case1. Create a page to demonstrate how to implement your Web Service. Print your Web page, the source code, and the Web Service source code.

Consuming Web Services

Your boss would like to use a third-party Web Service already established on the Internet. Your task is to implement a third-party Web Service. Visit a Web site such as *www.uddi.org, www.xmethods.net, www.asp.net,* or *www.gotdotnet.com.* Locate one Web Service that you would like to implement within your Web site. Create a Web page named

Ch11Case2.aspx that consumes the Web Service. In your Web page, document the information about the Web Service such as:

- Name of the Web Service
- URL where you found the Web Service
- Description of the Web Service
- Who owns the Web Service
- The costs required to use the Web Service
- The requirements to consume the Web Service
- The procedure for consuming the Web Service
- View the Web page in the browser, print out the Web page and the source code.

Creating and Consuming a Membership Web Service

Your boss would like you to create a membership database that can be accessed by other companies. You decide to implement a membership Web Service named Chapter11Case3WS. Create a database named Ch11Members that contains member information. You can use Access or SQL Server to create your database. Then, create a Web Service named Ch11Case3WS that exposes the membership data. Create a new page named Ch11Case3.aspx that consumes the Web Service and displays the membership data. Print out your Web pages and the source code.

11

Creating a Banner Ad Web Service from a Database

Your store manager wants to provide a Web banner ad service that other companies can use to display one of your ten banner ads on their Web sites. Create a Web Service that allows another company to view your Web banner ads on their Web pages. Create at least 10 banner graphics. Create the Case4Banners database and the Banners table. Add the 10 graphics' data into the Banners table. Create the Web Service named Ch11Case4. Create a page to demonstrate how to implement your Web Service, as shown in Figure 11-22. Create a login page. If the company is validated, allow them to view all 10 banners ads. If they are not, only allow them to view one default banner ad. Show them the code to implement each of the banner ads using the Web Service. Print your Web page, the source code, and the Web Service source code.

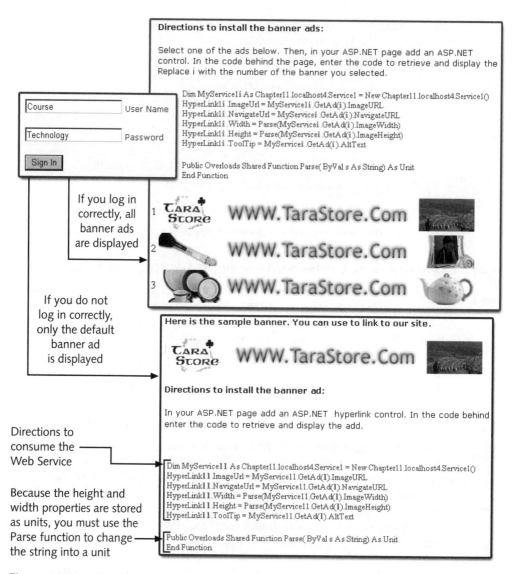

Figure 11-22   Sample Banner Ad Web Service

CHAPTER 12

EXTENDING ASP.NET
APPLICATIONS

In this chapter, you will:

♦ Send e-mail from the Web application

♦ Store and retrieve data from the Web server's file system

♦ Create and read files from an ASP.NET page

♦ Use Mobile controls to deliver content from a Web application

Businesses have learned through experience that they must provide additional services via their Web sites, rather than just delivering HTML content. In this chapter, you will learn how ASP.NET can work with other applications to increase the utility of the Web site. You will learn how to send e-mail from a Web page, so that when users complete a form, you can send them a customized e-mail message with their user information. You can also send the information to the administrator with a different custom message. You will also learn to save data to a file. Web sites often use databases and files to store user data, product information, or company data. In addition, you will learn to create Web applications that generate HTML Web pages on the fly, so that the Web content displayed can reflect user preferences. For example, you can create Web pages that store the users' favorite stock quotes, or display a list of newly published books by their favorite authors. Also, since a growing percentage of Internet customers use mobile devices to connect to the Internet, you will learn how to use Mobile controls to display your Web page content on a mobile device.

SENDING E-MAIL FROM THE WEB APPLICATION

In earlier chapters of this book, you learned how to process and validate form data. Often you will want to generate a customized automated e-mail reply that uses this form data, for example, to send an order confirmation to a customer. To send outbound e-mail from a Web page, you must use an e-mail server, along with an e-mail object or application to communicate with the e-mail server.

The E-mail Server

The e-mail server, known as the SMTP server, is included when you install the IIS Web Server. The SMTP server provides an easy way to transmit Internet mail. Simple Mail Transfer Protocol (SMTP) is a protocol, or set of rules, used to transfer mail between servers. The SMTP server contains several default folders, including Pickup, Queue, Badmail, Drop, and SortTemp. These folders are located by default in C:\Inetpub\MailRoot\. The Pickup folder is used to store outgoing mail messages. These messages are sent from the SMTP server to other servers. The default port for the SMTP Server is 25. Mail messages can be placed in this directory by hand or by other software applications.

In the following exercise, you will verify that the e-mail server is installed and running. The property pages and configuration settings for the SMTP server will vary between Windows 2000 and Windows XP.

1. To verify that the SMTP services are running, click **Start**, point to **Settings**, then click **Control Panel**. Double-click the **Administrative Tools** icon. Double-click the **Services** icon. The Services window opens with the list of running and stopped services.

2. Scroll down the window until you locate the Simple Mail Transport Protocol (SMTP) service in the Name column, as shown in Figure 12-1. The Status column should say that the Simple Mail Transport Protocol (SMTP) has been Started. (*Note*: If it is stopped, you can right-click the Simple Mail Transport Protocol (SMTP) name and click Start.)

3. Close the Services window by clicking the **Close** button and then close the Administrative Tools folder.

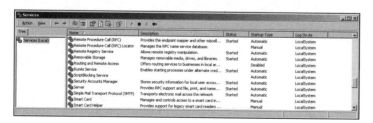

Figure 12-1 Verifying that the SMTP service is running

You can right-click the Simple Mail Transport Protocol (SMTP) service to access the SMTP server properties. You can configure the service to automatically start when the server is booted by setting the startup type to Automatic. You can also identify what action you want to take if the service has failed. For example, you can run a file, restart the service, or reboot the computer. Your Webmaster or system administrator is usually the one responsible for configuring your e-mail server.

The Microsoft Management Console (MMC) is the main interface to the administrative programs such as IIS and SMTP. The Internet Services Manager is a snap-in for the MMC. You can access the SMTP server and IIS server through the Internet Services Manager. In the following exercise, you view the SMTP settings through the Internet Services Manager.

1. To open the ISM, click **Start**, point to **Settings**, then click **Control Panel**. Double-click the **Administrative Tools** folder, and then double-click **Internet Information Services.** (*Note:* The shortcut to your Internet Services Manager console may vary depending on how you installed IIS. Also, the ISM is called Internet Information Services in Windows XP.) The Internet Information Services window opens.

2. Click the **plus sign** next to the computer icon to expand the list of FTP sites, Web sites, and SMTP servers available. (*Note:* You can also double-click the name of the computer or the computer icon to expand the menu.)

3. Click the name of the server. In Figure 12-2, the name of the server is course. On the right, you should see that the SMTP server named Default SMTP Virtual Server is running on Port 25, as shown in Figure 12-2. (*Note:* The window in Figure 12-2 varies between the ISM in Windows 2000 and IIS in Windows XP. The IIS places the Web sites and FTP sites in folders.)

12

Figure 12-2   Verifying that the Default SMTP Virtual Server is running

4. Right-click the **Default SMTP Virtual Server** icon, and then click **Properties** to open the Default SMTP Virtual Server Properties window. You can configure the server properties on these property pages. Notice that on the General tab, you can enable logging. By default, if logging is enabled, the SMTP log files are stored in the C:\WINNT\System32\LogFiles\SmtpSvc1 directory.

5. Click the **Connection** button on the General tab. You can configure the number of connections and number of minutes per connection. Verify that the TCP port selected is 25, as shown in Figure 12-3. Click **Cancel**. (*Note:* In Windows XP you do not have a Connection button. This information is located on the General tab.)

Figure 12-3   Verifying the TCP settings for the Default SMTP Virtual Server

6. Click the **Access** tab. The Access property sheet allows you to configure which accounts will be allowed to send e-mail through the Default SMTP Virtual Server.

7. Click the **Authentication button** to view the Authentication property page. You can allow the Internet anonymous user account to send e-mail, or restrict access using Basic or Windows authentication, as shown in Figure 12-4.

Figure 12-4   Verifying the authentication settings for the Default SMTP Virtual Server

8. Click **Cancel** to return to the Access tab.

9. Click the **Connection** button to access the Connection property page as shown in Figure 12-5. The Computer and Relay property pages, also shown in Figure 12-5, allow you to configure which servers can access the Default SMTP Virtual Server to send or relay e-mail messages. You can configure access to the Default SMTP Virtual Server based on the IP address of the computer, the network ID, or the domain name.

Figure 12-5   Verifying the connection and relay settings for the Default SMTP Virtual Server

10. Click **Cancel** to close the Connection property page.

11. Click the **Messages** tab, as shown in Figure 12-6. The Messages tab allows you to configure the size of the message, the session size, the number of messages per connection, and the number of recipients per connection. When an e-mail message is not sent, the message is deposited in the Badmail directory, which is located by default at C:\Inetpub\mailroot\Badmail. You can specify that a Non-Delivery report be e-mailed to you.

12. Click the **Delivery** tab, as shown in Figure 12-6. The Delivery tab allows you to configure how the message is delivered. For example, if the e-mail cannot be sent, you can specify the number of minutes to wait before attempting to e-mail the message again.

13. Click **Cancel** to close the Default SMTP Virtual Server properties window.

14. In the Internet Services Manager, click the **plus sign** next to the envelope icon that represents the Default SMTP Virtual Server.

12

15. Click **Domains**. In the right window, your Web server is listed under the Domain Name column.

16. Right-click the domain name in the Domain Name column, and then click **Properties**.

Figure 12-6 Configuring the Messages and Delivery properties for the Default SMTP Virtual Server

17. Click **Cancel** to close the window.

18. Click the **Close** button to close the Internet Information Services window.

 The configuration of the e-mail server and network affects how you can send outbound e-mail from your ASP pages. If you have a firewall, or special routing, you must modify your code. For example, in some networks, if your e-mail address is john@yourschool.edu, you might have to explicitly state the domain of the e-mail server. If the e-mail server's name is darkstar, the e-mail address is john@darkstar.yourschool.edu.

E-mail Objects

An e-mail software application or component is used in order for the Web page to communicate with the e-mail server. A component known as CDONTS is provided with the SMTP server to allow third-party applications such as ASP.NET to communicate with the SMTP server. CDONTS is located in a server component called cdonts.dll, which is located in C:\winnt\system32\ and is made available when you install the Microsoft SMTP Server. The CDONTS component places your message in the Pickup folder. The CDONTS component is a scaled-down version of a collection of objects known as **Collaborative Data Objects (CDO)**. CDO is typically used to integrate your applications with active messaging systems such Microsoft Outlook and Microsoft Exchange Services. CDONTS is a collection of objects, properties, and methods that connect the SMTP service with the Web application. CDONTS is only available with the XP or 2000 versions of the Windows

Professional or Windows Server operating systems. It is not available with Windows Millennium or Windows XP personal home systems.

 You can find additional information on how to use CDONTS at *http://msdn.microsoft.com/library/periodic/period99/email.htm* and *http://msdn.microsoft.com/library/periodic/period99/asp9951.htm*.

You can access CDONTS by using three built-in classes within the .NET Framework. The `System.Web.Mail` **namespace** provides access to the MailMessage, MailAttachment, and SmtpMail classes. The **MailMessage class** provides access to the properties and methods used to construct an e-mail message. The **MailAttachment class** is used to identify a file that is to be sent with the e-mail message. These attached files are often called **attachments**. The **SmtpMail class** is used to send the e-mail message that is specified in the MailMessage class.

The MailMessage class allows you to send the body of your message using different formats, such as basic text and HTML. The format of the e-mail message in the MailMessage class can be specified with the **MailFormat** enumeration. The possible enumerated values for e-mail format are MailFormat.HTML and MailFormat.Text. The **MailFormat.Text** enumeration means that the format of the MailMessage is plain text. You should use Text when it is important that all e-mail applications be able to read the message. Some e-mail programs do not interpret HTML codes, and so these codes would be visible to the recipient. The **MailFormat.HTML** sends the output as HTML. E-mail programs that support the HTML format interpret the HTML commands in the same way that a browser interprets the HTML commands.

The priority of the e-mail message in the MailMessage class is configured with the **MailPriority** enumeration. You can use the MailPriority enumeration to indicate to the e-mail application the importance of the message. Some e-mail applications provide indicators, such as an exclamation point, to indicate that a message has been given a certain priority level. The MailPriority property does affect how quickly a message is sent. The three MailPriority property levels that you can set with the MailMessage class are **MailMessage.Normal**, **MailMessage.High**, and **MailMessage.Low**. The MailPriority is set to Normal by default.

The MailAttachment class provides properties and methods to construct an e-mail attachment. You need to specify the location of the attachment and the encoding format of the attachment. The location of the attachment is specified with the Filename property of the MailAttachment class. The **filename** is assigned a string value, which specifies the drive, path, and filename of the attachment. (*Note:* You can use the FileField text box to locate the filename of a local file within an ASP.NET page.) The encoding of the attachment is specified with the **MailEncoding** enumerator. **MailEncoding.UUEncode** is the default encoding format. Some files, such as graphics, must be encoded as binary before they are sent. You can specify binary encoding with the **MailEncoding.Base64** enumeration.

12

The MailMessage class consists of several properties that must be set before the message can be sent. These properties include the recipient, the sender, the subject, and the message body. The **MailMessage.To** property gets or sets the e-mail address of the recipient of the e-mail message. So, you can specify multiple recipients using the To property by separating each e-mail address with a semicolon.

The **MailMessage.From property** gets or sets the e-mail address of the sender of the message. The From property is used to identify the sender. Although it is possible to send anonymous e-mail by omitting the From property entirely, it is not recommended. You should specify a complete e-mail address for the sender. Some e-mail programs do not accept e-mail when the sender's address is not valid. It is useful to change the From property according to the message. For example, if the e-mail is being sent to customers, you might set the From property to "help@mydomain.com". That way, your customer can identify who is sending the e-mail. You cannot specify more than one address using the From property.

You must take precautions when sending e-mail from a Web application. A network administrator is usually the person who is responsible for the network security and for setting up the network servers. Because you can configure the To, From, Subject, Message, and attachments programmatically, it is important to configure your Web server so that it does not support e-mailing visitors without their permission. For example, you can configure the To property within the ASP.NET code so that the end user cannot change the e-mail address of the recipient. It's also important to configure your Web server and SMTP server to disable hackers from sending e-mail from your server. For example, you can configure the mail server to not relay messages from other servers.

The **MailMessage.Subject property** gets or sets the subject line of the e-mail message. You should not leave the subject blank. It is important to pick a meaningful phrase for the Subject property. Because many viruses are sent via e-mail, recipients often delete e-mail from unknown e-mail addresses, or with suspicious subject phrases like "Click here to win a car."

The **MailMessage.Body property** gets or sets the body of the e-mail message. You can create a variable to hold the entire message, or retrieve the value from a form field. Then, you can assign the contents of the variable or form field to the Body property.

The default encoding, format, and priority level are chosen from the default values of the MailEncoding, MailPriority, and MailFormat enumerations, unless you configure them using the MailMessage class. The MailMessage class also contains properties that you can use to configure the individual e-mail message with the **MailMessage.BodyEncoding**, **MailMessage.Bodyformat**, and **MailMessage.Priority properties**. (*Note*: Each of these properties uses the same values as their counterpart enumerations.)

There are several optional e-mail properties. The **MailMessage.Attachments property** is a list of attachments that is transmitted with the message that is identified with the MailAttachment class. The **Carbon Copy (MailMessage.CC) property** gets or sets a semicolon-delimited list of e-mail addresses that receive a carbon copy (CC) of the e-mail message. You can separate multiple recipient addressees with semicolons (;).

The **Blind Carbon Copy (MailMessage.BCC) property** sets a semicolon-delimited list of e-mail addresses that receive a blind carbon copy (BCC) of the e-mail message. Blind carbon copies are used when you do not want the recipients to know that other individuals have been sent the same message. For example, you could send your customer an e-mail message, and send a blind carbon copy to your manager. The customer would not know that you sent a copy to your manager, and your manager's e-mail address would not be visible to the customer.

You can use the UrlContentBase and UrlContentLocation properties to insert content from another URL into the e-mail message. The **MailMessage.UrlContentBase property** gets or sets the URL base of all relative URLs used within the HTML-encoded body. The **MailMessage.UrlContentLocation property** is used to identify the location of content within the e-mail message. You can use the **MailMessage.Headers property**, of the MailMessage class to specify custom headers that are sent with the e-mail message. Using the **MailMessage.Headers property**, you can add additional headers, such as a Reply-To header.

The SmtpMail class provides properties and methods to send an e-mail and attachments using the SMTP e-mail service built into Microsoft Windows operating systems. After the MailMessage class has been configured, you can call the Send method of the SmtpMail class to actually send the message. The Send method of the MailMessage object creates the message in the required format and writes it to the Queue folder; eventually the message is moved to the Pickup folder. Therefore, all e-mail is, by default, queued, ensuring that the calling program does not block network traffic. The SMTP server then delivers the message. (*Note*: After the message has been sent you should set the object to the keyword Nothing to release the object from memory.)

By default, the e-mail is sent using the default local SMTP server. However, you can change the SMTP server used to send the message with the **SmtpServer property** of the SmtpMail class. You can locate the name of the SmtpServer in the property pages of the Default SMTP Virtual Server within the Internet Services Manager console.

You can call also configure the MailMessage properties directly when you send the message with the SmtpMail class. You can pass the properties as parameters of the send method instead of defining each property individually. Each of these properties is passed as a string to the send method. The From property is placed first, followed by the To property, the Subject, and the MessageText. The following code illustrates how an e-mail message can be sent in one line of code.

```
SmtpMail.Send("sender@sender.com",
        "recipient@recipient.com", "Subject", "Message")
```

Sending an E-Mail Message from an ASP.NET Web Page

In the following exercise, you will create a Web page that sends a static message to a single recipient. You must have access to a directory on a computer with a SMTP server running and with CDONTS installed in order to complete this activity.

You should discuss with your system administrator how to connect your pages with your mail server. Some SMTP servers use the same Configuration object to define the configuration settings. Fields in the configuration object, such as sendusing, can be configured to specify where to place the message. You may be required to specify a username and password to authenticate the send message request.

1. Start **Visual Studio .NET**, then click **File** on the menu bar, point to **New**, and click **Project**. This opens the New Project window.

2. Click the **Visual Basic Projects** folder icon, then click **ASP.NET Web Application** under Templates. Type **Chapter12** in the Location text box in place of WebApplication1. Click the **OK** button to create the solution, project, and default files.

3. Right-click **Chapter12** in the Solution Explorer window, point to **Add**, then click **New Folder**. Type **images** to name the folder, and then press **Enter**.

4. Right-click the **images** folder, point to **Add** and then click **Add Existing Item**. Navigate to your Chapter 12Data\images folder. Select all of the image files, then click the **Open** button to import the images into the project's images folder.

5. Right-click **Chapter12** in the Solution Window, point to **Add**, then click **Add Web Form**. To name the page, type **SendMessageSingle.aspx** in the Name text box, and then click **Open**.

6. Double-click on the page to view the code behind the page. On the first line of code enter the following text to import the Mail classes from the `System.Web.Mail` namespace.

```
Imports System.Web.Mail
```

7. Enter the following code in the Page_Load handler to declare a variable MM to store the MailMessage objects.

```
Dim MM As New MailMessage()
```

8. Add the code below to configure the properties of the MailMessage object. Assign your e-mail address to the From and To properties.

```
MM.From = "[your_email@your_address.edu]"
MM.To = "[your_email@your_address.edu]"
MM.Subject = "CDONTS Exercise"
MM.Body = "I have completed the CDONTS exercise"
MM.BodyFormat = MailFormat.Text
MM.Priority = MailPriority.Normal
```

9. Add the code below to use the send method of the SmtpMail object to send the message. Then, release the variables that are storing the Mail object.

```
SmtpMail.Send(MM)
MM = Nothing
```

10. Click the **Save All** button. Click **Build** on the menu bar, then click **Build Solution**.

11. Right-click on the aspx page, and then click **View in Browser**. Your page should look like a blank page. The e-mail message has been created and placed in your Queue folder.

12. Close the window.

13. On your desktop, double-click the **My Computer** icon, and then double-click the drive on which your Web server is installed. (By default the Web server is installed on drive C.) Double-click **Inetpub**, then **mailroot**, and then **Pickup**.

14. Right-click the **envelope** icon, and then click **Open with**. In the window, scroll down until you see Notepad. Click **Notepad**, and then click **OK**. Your e-mail message should look similar to the one shown in Figure 12-7. (*Note*: If you select Open, the e-mail message opens in your default e-mail application.)

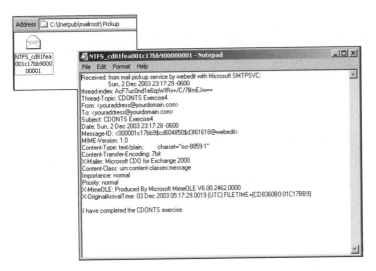

Figure 12-7   Viewing the e-mail message in Notepad

15. Close the file and close the Pickup folder. (*Note*: When your e-mail server is ready, it places the e-mail message into the Pickup folder and sends it. Your e-mail server may not be configured to send the message. Some network settings prevent servers from sending mail via their networks. You should check with your system administrator for the e-mail server settings to send outbound mail through your network.)

Not all hosting service providers use the SMTP mail server as their e-mail server. You need to contact your HSP to determine what components interface with their e-mail server. Some hosting service providers may use the SMTP server, but require you to use a different e-mail component. For example, ServerObject.com (*www.serverobjects.com*) provides two mail components, named ASPMail and ASPQMail (*www.serverobjects.com/products.htm*), that are commonly used to enable an ASP page to send e-mail. Although the syntax is slightly different, the programming methods of CDONTS and ASPMail are very similar. You can view the documentation on ASPMail 3.0 at *www.serverobjects.com/comp/Aspmail3.htm* and on ASPQMail 2.x at *www.serverobjects.com/comp/AspQmail.htm*.

STORING AND RETRIEVING DATA IN THE WEB SERVER'S FILE SYSTEM

Another challenging task for Web developers is storing Web information in a file. There are several classes and objects within the `System.IO` namespace that allow you to interact with the Web servers' file system. The `Sytem.IO` namespace allows synchronous and asynchronous reading and writing of data streams and files. In the following section, you will learn to access the directory structure, create and remove directories, and create, read, and delete files. There are several ways to create, read, and delete files and directories on the Web server. The `System.IO` namespace contains several classes, such as File, FileStream, and Directory, that allow you to create, read, and delete files. However, the newer classes, DirectoryInfo and FileInfo, allow more flexibility and easier access to the file system. In this section, you will learn to work with the DirectoryInfo and FileInfo class. The DirectoryInfo class allows you to obtain the properties of a directory and its subdirectories. The FileInfo class allows you access to the properties of a file, using the FileAttributes.

Working with Directories

The **DirectoryInfo** class provides several pieces of information about a directory. When you create a DirectoryInfo class, you must pass the complete path to a directory. The Directory property of the DirectoryInfo class identifies whether the object is a directory. The Attribute for the Directory object is 16, which means that it is a directory. The **GetDirectories** method of the DirectoryInfo class is used to retrieve the collection of subdirectories. You can use a For-Each loop to iterate through the collection to retrieve information about the subdirectories. In the following example, you will retrieve the directory properties for C:\Inetpub\wwwroot\Chapter12, and the list of subdirectories within the Chapter12 directory.

1. Open your **Chapter12** solution. Right-click **Chapter12** in the Solution Window, point to **Add**, and then click **Add Web Form**. Enter **DisplayChapter12Dir.aspx** to name the page.

2. Add an ASP.NET Label control. The control is named Label1 by default.

3. Double-click on the page to view the code behind the page. On the first line of code, enter the following text to import the DirectoryInfo classes from the `System.IO` namespace.

```
Imports System.IO
```

4. Enter the following code in the Page_Load handler. First, create the DirecroryInfo object. Use the default Web Server directory C:\Inetpub\wwwroot\Chapter12.

```
Dim DD As DirectoryInfo = _
    New DirectoryInfo("C:\Inetpub\wwwroot\Chapter12\")
```

5. Add the following code to display data about the directory. Notice that the Date and Time properties must be formatted using the ToShortDateString or another date-to-string conversion method. The Name property is used to retrieve the values of the parent directory.

```
Dim br As String = "<br />"
Label1.Text = _
"<b>Directory Properties for " &
"C:\InetPub\wwwroot\Chapter12\</b>" _
& br & br & _
"Full Name = " & DD.FullName & br & _
"Name = " & DD.Name & br & _
"Attributes = " & DD.Attributes & br & _
"Creation Date = " _
& DD.CreationTime.ToShortDateString & br & _
"LastAccessTime = " _
& DD.LastAccessTime.ToShortDateString & br & _
"LastWriteTime = " _
& DD.LastWriteTime.ToShortDateString & br & _
"Root Drive Letter = " & DD.Root.Name & br & _
"Parent Directory Name = " & DD.Parent.Name & br & _
"Extension = " & DD.Extension & br & _
"Exists = " & DD.Exists & br
```

6. Add the following code to display information about the subdirectories of the wwwroot directory. You must create a variable named SD, which represents each subdirectory, and use a For-Next loop to rotate through the subdirectories in the Chapter12 directory.

```
Dim SD As DirectoryInfo
Label1.Text = Label1.Text & br & "<hr /><b>" & _
"Subdirectories of C:\InetPub\wwwroot\Chapter12\" & _
"</b>" & br & br
For Each SD In DD.GetDirectories()
    Label1.Text &= SD.Name & br
Next
```

7. Click the **Save All** button. Click **Build** on the menu bar, then click **Build Solution**.

8. Click the **DisplayChapter12Dir.aspx** tab. Then, right-click on the page and select **View in Browser**. A listing of the subdirectories will appear, as shown in Figure 12-8. (*Note*: Because your Chapter12 folder may contain different directories your listing may appear different from the listing in Figure 12-8).

12

```
Directory Properties for C:\InetPub\wwwroot\Chapter12\

Full Name = C:\Inetpub\wwwroot\Chapter12\
Name = C:\Inetpub\wwwroot\Chapter12\
Attributes = 16
Creation Date = 5/8/2002
LastAccessTime = 5/8/2002
LastWriteTime = 5/8/2002
Root Drive Letter = C:\
Parent Directory Name = Chapter12
Extension =
Exists = True
_____

Subdirectories of C:\InetPub\wwwroot\Chapter12\

bin
images
```

Figure 12-8   Displaying the properties of a directory

9. Close the file.

Creating and Deleting Directories

You can use the DirectoryInfo class to create and delete directories. You can use the **CreateSubdirectory** method to create a new directory. You must pass the name of the directory to the DirectoryInfo object. If the path to the directory is too long, or if the directory already exists, an exception may be thrown. You can catch these exceptions using the Try-Catch-End Try structure. The **ArgumentException** is used when you try to create a directory with invalid characters such as <>*?" or \\. If the directory already exists, the **IOException** is thrown. If the name of the path to the directory exceeds 248 characters, the **PathTooLongException** is thrown. If you don't have permission to create the folder, the **SecurityException** is thrown. When you delete the directory, you use the delete method of the DirectoryInfo object. If you attempt to delete a directory that does not exist, an IOException named **DirectoryNotFoundException** is thrown.

The delete method is used to delete a directory with the DirectoryInfo class. You just have to call the delete method. You can also use the Directory class directly to delete files. You must specify a file, and an optional Boolean value. With the Directory class you specify True or False as a parameter when you call the delete method. If you specify True, then all files and subdirectories are deleted. If you specify False, then if there are any files within the subdirectory, an exception is thrown. (*Note*: You can also use the Directory class of the FileSystemObject to create and delete directories.) In the following example, you will create and remove directories with the DirectoryInfo class. You will use a form to retrieve the name of the directory to create and delete.

Before completing the following exercise, you may need to modify the permissions in your Security tab. To do this, double-click My Computer, double-click the C: drive, double-click Inetpub, and then double-click the wwwroot directory. (In Windows XP, Inetpub is located on the C: drive.) Right-click the Chapter 12 folder, and then click Properties. Click the Security tab, click the Add button, select ASPNET from the Name column, and then click Add. Click OK. With the aspnet_wp account selected in the Name column, click the Modify and Write check boxes to select them. Click Apply, and then click OK. To select the ASPNET account in Windows XP, you can type in [*MachineName*]\ASPNET in the text box and click the OK button.

The Security tab is only visible on drives formatted with NTFS. The Security tab may not be visible on a Windows XP computer if simple file sharing is enabled. To disable simple file sharing, click Start, and then click My Computer. On the Tools menu, click Folder Options, and then click the View tab. In the Advanced settings section, clear the Use simple file sharing (Recommended) check box. Then click the OK button to close the window.

1. Open your **Chapter12** solution. Right-click **Chapter12** in the Solution Explorer window, point to **Add**, and then click **Add Web Form**. Enter **CreateDir.aspx** to name the page.

2. Add a text box in the upper left-hand corner. The name of the text box is TextBox1 by default. To the right of the text box, add a button that says **Create Directory**, a button that says **Delete Directory**, and a button that says **Display Directory**. By default, the buttons are named button1, button2, and button3, respectively.

3. Below the text box, add an ASP.NET Label control. The Label control is named Label1 by default.

4. Double-click on the page to view the code behind the page. On the first line of code, enter the following code to import the DirectoryInfo classes from the `System.IO` namespace.

```
Imports System.IO
```

5. Enter the following code in the Page_Load handler to display the default message.

```
If Not Page.IsPostBack Then
Label1.Text = _
"Enter the name of the subdirectory to create or delete."
End If
```

6. Click the **CreateDir.aspx** tab. Then, double-click the first button, which says **Create Directory**. In the Button1_Click event procedure, add the following code to create the subdirectory using the value entered into the text box. First, create the DirecroryInfo object named DD. Use the default Web server

directory C:\Inetpub\wwwroot\Chapter12. Write out the name of the directory using the FullName property. Write out a message indicating that the subdirectory was created.

```
Dim DD As DirectoryInfo = New
DirectoryInfo("c:\inetpub\wwwroot\Chapter12\")
Label1.Text = _
"<b>The Parent Directory " & "</b><br /><br />" & _
"The full name of the parent directory was: " _
& DD.FullName & "<br />"
DD.CreateSubdirectory(TextBox1.Text)
Dim SD As DirectoryInfo
Label1.Text = Label1.Text & _
"<br /><hr /><b>Create a Subdirectory named: " & _
TextBox1.Text & "</b><br /><br />"
For Each SD In DD.GetDirectories()
    If SD.Name = TextBox1.Text Then
        Label1.Text &= TextBox1.Text & _
        " was created successfully.<br />"
    Else
    End If
Next
```

7. Click the **CreateDir.aspx** tab. Then, double-click the second button, which says **Delete Directory**. In the Button2_Click event procedure, add the following code to delete the directory, and display a message indicating that the directory was deleted.

```
Dim DD2 As DirectoryInfo = New
DirectoryInfo("c:\inetpub\wwwroot\Chapter12" & ¬
TextBox1.Text)
Label1.Text = _
"<b>The Parent Directory " & "</b><br /><br />" & _
"The full name of the parent directory was: " & _
DD2.FullName & "<br /><br /><hr /><br />"
DD2.Delete()
Label1.Text &= TextBox1.Text & " was deleted."
```

8. Click the **CreateDir.aspx** tab. Then, double-click the third button, which says **Display Directory**. In the Button3_Click event procedure, add the code to redirect the browser to the page that displays the Chapter12 directory information.

```
Response.Redirect("DisplayChapter12Dir.aspx")
```

9. Click the **Save All** button. Click **Build** on the menu bar, then click **Build Solution**.

10. Click the **CreateDir.aspx** tab. Right-click on the page, and then click **View in Browser**.

11. Type **MyTest12** in the text box, and then click the **Create Directory** button, as shown in Figure 12-9. The message stating that the directory was created is displayed. Then, click the **Display Directory** button, and the entire subdirectory list is displayed. Close the browser window.

12. Click the **CreateDir.aspx** tab. Right-click on the page, and then click **View in Browser**. Type **MyTest12** in the text box, and then click the **Delete Directory** button. The message that the directory was deleted is displayed. Then, click the **Display Directory** button, and the entire subdirectory list is displayed. MyTest12 is not listed in the subdirectory list. Close the browser window.

13. Close any open files.

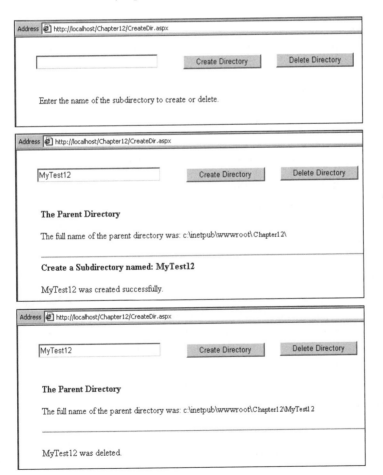

Figure 12-9   Managing directories from a Web page

Creating and Reading Files from an ASP.NET Page

You use the **FileInfo** class to create a file, read the contents of a file, and delete a file. The GetFiles method of the FileInfo object returns the files collection. You can retrieve the properties of a file with the FileInfo class. Some of the commonly used properties of the FileInfo class include **Attributes**, **CreationTime**, **lastAccessedTime**, **LastWriteTime**, **Name**, **FullName**, and **Exists**. The following is a list of additional properties that can be retrieved using the FileInfo class.

- The *Encrypted property* identifies that the object is encrypted.

- The *Hidden property* hides the file in the directory view.

- The *Compressed property* indicates whether or not a file is compressed.

- The *Archive property* indicates whether the file has been archived.

- The *NotContentIndexed property* identifies whether the Index Server will index the page.

- The *Offline property* identifies whether the file is to be available while the computer is offline.

- The *ReadOnly property* identifies whether the file is not to be modified by the user.

- The *System property* identifies whether the file is a system file. You can limit the directory view to avoid displaying system files. Then, the user can't accidentally modify or remove the system file.

- The *Temporary property* identifies whether the file is a temp file.

You can use the FileInfo class to create a basic text file or HTML file, copy a file to a new location, move a file to a new location, or delete a file. The **CopyTo** method copies a file from one path to another. The **MoveTo** method copies a file from one path to another, and then deletes the original file. The delete method removes a file from the hard drive.

There are several objects that you can use to create, modify, read, and delete files. The File object contains methods for working with files. The File, Directory, and Path classes are derived from the System.Object. However, the DirectoryInfo and FileInfo classes are derived from the System.IO.FileSystemInfo class. Both groups of classes allow you to interact with FileStream, BinaryReader, BinaryWriter, StreamReader, and StreamWriter classes, which allow you to read and write to files.

In the following exercise, you will create a new file, add material to the file from a form, display its properties using the FileInfo class, and delete the file. When you load the page, the default directions appear in the label. When you enter a filename and click the Create File button, the file is created using the name of the file and the CreateText method. The **CreateText** method returns a **StreamWriter** object. The create and CreateText methods are used to create files. You can create a plain text file or an HTML file. You must pass the path of the new file to the CreateText method. The CreateText method returns the StreamWriter object and opens the file for editing. The write method can be used to write HTML contents to the file. If you plan to create an HTML file, and want to display the contents at a later time, you should use the <XMP> tag to ignore the HTML tags in the file. Then, the HTML tags are displayed with the text and not interpreted by the browser. When you create the file, you can specify a relative path or a Universal Naming Convention (UNC) path for a server and share name. For example, the path to the file can be specified as "C:\\ MyDirectory\\MyFileName.txt", "C:\\ MyDirectory", "MyDirectory\\MySubdirectory", or "\\MyServerName\MyShareName".

The **write** method of the StreamWriter object is used to write to the file. When you are finished, you need to use the close method of the StreamWriter object to close the file. You can read the contents of the newly created file with the OpenText method of the FileInfo class. The **OpenText method** returns a **StreamReader object**, which can read through each line from the file. When you are finished, you need to use the close method of the StreamReader object to close the file.

1. Open your **Chapter12** solution. Right-click **Chapter12** in the Solution Window, point to **Add**, and then click **Add Web Form**. Name the form **CreateFile.aspx**.

2. Add a text box to the form, which will hold the name of the file. The text box is named TextBox1 by default.

3. Add a button that says **Create File**, and a button that says **Delete File**. By default, the buttons are named Button1 and Button2. Add a third button that says **Display File Contents**, which is named Button3 by default.

4. Add an ASP.NET Label control, which is named Label1 by default.

5. Double-click on the page to view the code behind the page. On the first line of code, enter the following code to import the FileInfo classes from the System.IO namespace.

```
Imports System.IO
```

6. Enter the following code in the Page_Load handler to display the default message.

```
If Not Page.IsPostBack Then
    Label1.Text = _
        "Enter the name of the file to create or delete."
End If
```

7. Click the **CreateFile.aspx** tab. Then, double-click the button that says **Create File**. In the Button1_Click event procedure, add the following code to create the file using the value entered into the text box. Store the path to the new file in the FN variable. Create the FileInfo object named **NF**. Use the default Web Server directory C:\Inetpub\wwwroot\Chapter12. Write out a message

stating that the file was created. Create the **StreamWriter** object using the CreateText method in order to create the file, and open the file for writing.

```
Dim FN As String = "c:\inetpub\wwwroot\Chapter12\" & ¬
TextBox1.Text
Dim NF As FileInfo = New FileInfo(FN)
Label1.Text = _
"<b>The File was created! " & "</b>"
Dim SW As StreamWriter = File.CreateText(FN)
```

8. Use the Write and WriteLine methods to send content to the file. The WriteLine method places a return character at the end of the line. You can also use the Visual Basic .NET constant vbCrLf to represent a return character. You can assign the values using strings or content from the text box in the form. Replace [Your Name] with your own name.

```
SW.Write("This file was ")
SW.WriteLine("created by: ")
SW.Write("[Your Name] ")
SW.Write(vbCrLf)
SW.WriteLine("on " & Now.Date.ToShortDateString)
SW.WriteLine()
SW.WriteLine()
SW.Write(TextBox1.Text)
```

9. Add the following code, which closes the TextStream object when you are finished. Then, release the object by setting the variable to nothing.

```
SW.Close()
NF = Nothing
```

10. Click the **CreateFile.aspx** tab. Then, double-click the button that says **Delete File**. In the Button2_Click event procedure, add the following code to delete the file using the value entered into the text box. Use the delete method of the FileInfo object to delete the file. (*Note*: If the file is in use by another process, it cannot be deleted.)

```
Dim FN As String = "c:\inetpub\wwwroot\Chapter12\" & ¬
TextBox1.Text
Dim DF As FileInfo = New FileInfo(FN)
Label1.Text = _
"<b>The File was deleted! " & "</b>"
DF.Delete()
DF = Nothing
```

11. Click the **CreateFile.aspx** tab. Then, double-click the button that says **Display File Contents**.

12. In the Button3_Click event procedure, add the following code to read the file using the value entered into the text box.

```
Dim FN As String = "c:\inetpub\wwwroot\Chapter12\" & ¬
TextBox1.Text
```

13. Add the following code, which uses the StreamReader object to retrieve the file from the File object and open the file with the OpenText method. The ReadToEnd method reads the entire file line by line until it reaches the end of the file.

```
Dim RF As FileInfo = New FileInfo(FN)
Dim SR As StreamReader = RF.OpenText()
Dim strContents As String = SR.ReadToEnd
```

14. Add the following code, which places the contents inside a string variable named strContents. The strContents variable is assigned to the Text property of the Label control in the Web page.

```
Label1.Text = strContents
SR.Close()
SR = Nothing
```

15. Click the **Save All** button. Click **Build** on the menu bar, then click **Build Solution**.

16. Click the **CreateFile.aspx** tab. Right-click on the page, and then click **View in Browser**.

17. Type **MyChapter12.txt** in the text box, and then click the **Create File** button.

18. Click the **Display File Contents** button. The contents of the file are displayed in the browser.

19. Click the **Delete File** button. Your file is deleted.

20. Close the file. To close the solution, go to the **File** menu and select **Close Solution**.

Notice that the carriage returns are not recognized in the browser. HTML ignores carriage returns and white space such as tabs. You must use HTML tags to ensure that the contents are placed on the correct line. In the following exercise, you will create a file named CreateHTMLFile.aspx, which includes HTML commands.

1. Open your **Chapter12** solution. Right-click **Chapter12** in the Solution Window, point to **Add**, and then click **Add Web Form**. Enter **CreateHTMLFile.aspx** to name the form.

2. Add a text box, which is named TextBox1 by default. Add a second text box, which is named TextBox2 by default. TextBox2 will hold the new contents of the file.

3. Add one button that says **Create File,** and another button that says **Delete File**. The buttons are named Button1 and Button2 by default.

4. Change the TextMode property of TextBox2 from SingleLine to **MultiLine**. Then, change the Rows property to **10**.

5. Add a Hyperlink control that will store the URL to the new HTML page. The Hyperlink control is named HyperLink1 by default.

12

6. Add an ASP.NET Label control, which is named Label1 by default.

7. Double-click on the page to view the code behind the page. On the first line of code enter the following text to import the FileInfo classes from the System.IO namespace.

```
Imports System.IO
```

8. Enter the following code in the Page_Load handler to display the default message.

```
If Not Page.IsPostBack Then
   HyperLink1.Text = ""
   Label1.Text = _
      "Enter the name of the HTML file to create or ¬
      delete."
End If
```

9. Click the **CreateHTMLFile.aspx** tab. Then, double-click the button that says **Create File**. In the Button1_Click event procedure, add the following code to create the file using the value entered into the text box. Set the hyperlink to an empty string so that it is not displayed.

```
Dim FN As String = _
"c:\inetpub\wwwroot\Chapter12\" & TextBox1.Text
Dim NF As FileInfo = New FileInfo(FN)
HyperLink1.Text = ""
Label1.Text = _
"<b>The File was created! " & "</b>"
Dim SW As StreamWriter = File.CreateText(FN)
```

10. Add the following code, which enters the basic HTML tags. The body of the page content comes from the TextBox2 control.

```
SW.WriteLine("<html><head>")
SW.WriteLine("<title>Creating an HTML File: ")
SW.WriteLine(TextBox1.Text)
SW.WriteLine("</title>")
SW.WriteLine("<body>")
SW.WriteLine(TextBox2.Text)
SW.WriteLine("<hr /><br /><br />Created on ")
SW.WriteLine(Now.Date.ToShortDateString)
SW.WriteLine("</body></html>")
SW.Close()
NF = Nothing
```

11. Add the following code to set the properties of the hyperlink and display the hyperlink.

```
HyperLink1.Text = "Click here to read the HTML file!"
HyperLink1.NavigateUrl = _
"http://localhost/Chapter12/" & TextBox1.Text
Label1.Text = ""
```

12. Click the **CreateHTMLFile.aspx** tab. Then, double-click the button that says **Delete File**. In the Button2_Click event procedure, add the following code to delete the file.

```
Dim FN As String = _
"c:\inetpub\wwwroot\Chapter12\" & TextBox1.Text
Dim DF As FileInfo = New FileInfo(FN)
HyperLink1.Text = ""
Label1.Text = _
"<b>The File was deleted! " & "</b>"
DF.Delete()
DF = Nothing
```

13. Click the **Save All** button. Click **Build** on the menu bar, then click **Build Solution**.

14. Click the **CreateHTMLFile.aspx** tab. Then, right-click on the page and click **View in Browser**.

15. Type **MyChapter12.htm** in the first text box. In the second text box, type **Welcome to my Web site**.

16. Click the **Create File** button. The file is created and the new hyperlink is displayed. Click the hyperlink to open the page in the browser. The contents of the file are displayed in the browser.

17. Click the **Back** button in the browser.

18. Click the **Delete File** button. Your file is deleted. (*Note*: If you were to refresh the page, the File Not Found error message would appear.)

19. Return to Visual Studio .NET and close the file. To close the solution, go to the **File** menu and select **Close Solution**.

12

WORKING WITH ALTERNATIVE PLATFORMS: PDAS AND MOBILE DEVICES

Today, a Web application is thought of as a series of Web pages viewed with a browser. However, each year more consumers are viewing Web content via alternative devices such as mobile phones. There are several major issues that affect the development of a Web application for mobile devices. First, because there is a wide range of hardware and software for these devices, not all of them have the same screen size, resolution, color, graphics, and multimedia capabilities. Some devices support a scaled-down version of a browser, and others only support text. Although some users connect directly via a network or wireless LAN, other users connect via modems or cellular phones. Therefore, Web developers have less control over the end-user interface than ever before. Therefore, you should focus on what you can control, which is the content you are providing to the end user.

The main platforms for portable devices are Palm, Windows Pocket PC, and Windows CE. Some platforms, such as the Pocket PC, use a browser to display Web pages, and some platforms use other HTML and XML interpreters. There are a wide range of mobile devices and platforms. Displaying Web pages is very difficult on a mobile device because of the limited screen size. However, new technologies, such as the Mobile Internet Toolkit, have made it easier for developers to create a single mobile application that can be displayed on a variety of mobile devices and platforms. As the telecommunications and network infrastructures are upgraded to newer technologies, more mobile and Internet capabilities will be built into mobile and portable devices. As a result, you will see a greater demand for Web applications to expand to these new markets.

 The current home Web site for Microsoft mobile solutions is at *www.microsoft.com/mobile*. The Mobile Internet Information Server Toolkit and Microsoft Mobile Explorer are available from Microsoft at *www.microsoft.com/mobile/phones/mme/mmemulator.asp*. You can download the Mobile Internet Information Server, toolkits, and Mobile Explorer and other related items from *msdn.microsoft.com/vstudio/nextgen/device/mitdefault.asp*.

Creating a WML Document

The standard used to program on a mobile device is the **Wireless Application Protocol (WAP)**. WAP is an open standard that is available at *www.wapforum.com*. Within the WAP is the **Wireless S Protocol (WSP)**, which is a transport protocol that performs the same functions as HTTP for mobile devices. To work with Web content, the WAP standards use an application standard known as **Wireless Markup Language (WML)**. Files that use the WML end with the file extension .wml. These files can contain small programs written in a scripting language such as VBScript. If the file contains programming scripts, the file extension ends in .wmls. Wireless bitmap images end in .wbmp.

When you develop applications for wireless devices, you need to view the results on the device, or use a device simulator. Most mobile devices supply a simulator for developers. Device emulators simulate several devices and allow you to apply different templates, called skins, to the emulator. Each device has its own skin, which you can view on the device emulator. The simulator is installed on your desktop computer to test your applications. The Nokia 7110 phone device simulators are available at *http://forum.nokia.com*. You can also use the OpenWave device simulator to test several types of phones. The **OpenWave Simulator** allows you to simulate phones from Ericsson, Mitsubishi, and Samsung. Openwave can be found at *http://developer.openwave.com*. A list of tested devices and emulators that are supported within Visual Studio .NET can be found at *http://msdn.microsoft.com/vstudio/nextgen/device/mitdevices.asp*.

You can configure your Web Server to support WML files by adding a Mime Map for the file extension .wml with content type text/vnd.wap.wml as shown in Figure 12-10.

Figure 12-10   Configuring the IIS Web Server MIME types to support the WML files

WML is compliant with the XML protocols, and therefore is case sensitive. You must also close each tag, with a closing tag or by adding a forward slash to the end of the opening tag. All WML files contain the MIME type declared in the document type declaration:

```
<?xml version="1.0"?>
<!DOCTYPE wml PUBLIC =-//WAPFORUM??DTD WML 1.1//EN
"http:///www.wapforum.org/DTD/wml_1.1.xml">
```

The rest of the document is enclosed in a single pair of WML tags, which serve as the root element of the WML document. The WML card metaphor is used to organize content delivered to a mobile device. So, a WML file consists of a deck of cards. Each card is a screen of content. Although the entire file is sent to the device, only one screen is displayed at a time. Each card is identified with the card tag: <card>. The title attribute of the card is used to provide a description of the content within the card. You can link WML documents using a hyperlink created with an anchor tag <a>. The href property of the anchor tag is used to identify the target in the WML document. You can set the target to an internal target or to another URL. Additional tags, such as the line break, paragraph, and bold tags, are commonly used in mobile devices.

Installing the Mobile Internet Toolkit in Visual Studio .NET

The Mobile Internet Designer is free and available in the Microsoft Internet Toolkit. You can download the Mobile Internet Toolkit from Microsoft, which enables you to use mobile controls within ASP.NET applications. The current version requires 4.0 MB and an additional 10 MB of free space. The toolkit is a set of ASP.NET server controls that generate WML 1.1, cHTML 1.0, and HTML 3.2 content for different devices.

Once you install the Mobile Internet Toolkit, you will be able to create ASP.NET pages that can be displayed on mobile devices. The ASP.NET Web pages that contain mobile controls are known as **mobile forms**. The tool within Visual Studio .NET that allows you to create mobile forms using a GUI is called the **Mobile Internet Designer**. You do not have to create the WML code. ASP.NET will generate the code that is appropriate for the mobile device. So, if you use ASP.NET, the ASP.NET Mobile controls will generate the

WML output for your Web application. Just as with WebForms, you can also create mobile forms by using Visual Studio .NET or in a simple editor such as Notepad.

> Additional information about the Microsoft Mobile Internet Toolkit is available at *http://msdn.microsoft.com/vstudio/device/mitdefault.asp*. An overview of the Mobile Web Forms technology is available at *http://msdn.microsoft.com/vstudio/techinfo/articles/clients/mobilewebforms.asp*.

In the following exercise, you will install the Mobile Internet Toolkit. The installation will include the mobile Internet controls and the Internet Designer for Visual Studio .NET, which is available for both Visual Basic .NET and C#. The installation will also include the Mobile QuickStart site, which is installed at *http://localhost/mobilequickstart/*. This site contains information on how to use the Mobile Internet Toolkit and create Mobile WebForms.

The Mobile controls inherit from the `System.Web.Mobile` namespace, as shown in Figure 12-11. You can configure the Toolbox in order to add these controls to a Toolbox tab. You can add mobile forms to an ASP.NET Web application, or create a mobile Web project and create the mobile forms within it.

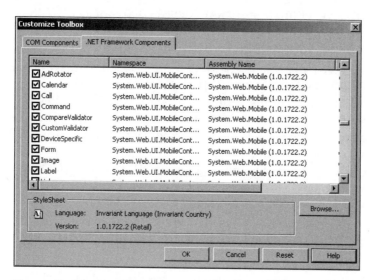

Figure 12-11   Configuring the mobile form controls in Visual Studio .NET

1. Close your Chapter12 solution and exit Visual Studio .NET. Start your Web browser and go to *http://msdn.microsoft.com/downloads/default.asp?url=/msdn-files/027/001/817/msdncompositedoc.xml*. or go to *www.microsoft.com* and search for the Microsoft Mobile Internet Toolkit.

2. Click the **Download** hyperlink.

3. Read the license agreement, and then click the **Yes** button. The File Download message is displayed.

4. Click **Save** to begin the download process.

5. In the Save As dialog box, select your **Chapter12** Data directory to download the Mobileit.exe file to, and then click the **Save** button.

6. When your download is finished, click the **Open Folder** button.

7. Double-click the **Mobile Internet Toolkit executable** file to launch the installer program. The Install Wizard opens. Click the **Next** button to continue.

8. Click the **I accept the terms in the license agreement** radio button, and then click the **Next** button.

9. Select the **Complete** application. (*Note*: The custom application allows you to select the items to install. You can also view the location where the toolkit is installed. By default, the toolkit is installed in C:\Program Files\ Microsoft.Net\Mobile Internet Toolkit\.) Click the **Next** button to continue. Click **Next** to begin the install, then click Finish.

10. Start **Visual Studio .NET**. Click **File** on the menu bar, point to **New**, and then click **Project**.

11. Under the Templates section click **Mobile Web Application**. In the Location text box, replace http://localhost/MobileWebApplication1 with http://localhost/Chapter12Mobile. This creates a mobile application.

12. Click **OK**. Click the **Mobile Web Forms** tab in the Toolbox. The Mobile controls will appear on the Mobile Forms tab, as shown in Figure 12-12.

Figure 12-12   The Mobile Form controls

Using Mobile Controls in an ASP.NET Application

Mobile controls inherit a code behind the page named System.Web.UI. MobileControls.MobilePage. Each Web page contains a register directive that is used to register the mobile tag controls with the Mobile control namespace. So, on the first line of code in the Web page, you will see the following code. This code is automatically placed on the mobile form by Visual Studio .NET when you create the mobile form.

```
<%@ Page Language="vb" AutoEventWireup="false"
Codebehind="MobileWebForm1.aspx.vb"
Inherits="Chapter12Mobile.MobileWebForm1" %>
<%@ Register TagPrefix="mobile"
Namespace="System.Web.UI.MobileControls"
Assembly="System.Web.Mobile" %>
```

In the following exercise, you will create a basic mobile form using the Mobile Internet Designer. Because the WML is XML compliant, you can view the document in an XML reader such as Internet Explorer if you do not have a mobile device simulator installed.

1. Open your **Chapter12Mobile** solution if it is not already open. Right-click **Chapter12Mobile** in the Solution Explorer window, point to **Add**, then click **Add New Item**. In the Templates pane, click **Mobile Web Form**. In the Name text box type **MFDisplayList.aspx**. Click the **Open** button. The mobile form appears smaller on the Web page. This is the default width of the form.

2. Add a Label control from the Mobile Forms tab.

3. With the Label control selected, view the properties in the Properties window. Change the (ID) of the label to **lblStoreName**.

4. Change the font to **Trebuchet MS,** the ForeColor to **#004040**, the Alignment property to **Center**, and the Bold property to **True**.

5. Change the Text property to **Tara Store Home Page**.

6. Add a List control to the mobile form. For each item within the List control, the Text attribute assigns the value and the displayed text. The Decoration property identifies the type of list. By default, the List control Decoration property is set to none. The Decoration property may also be assigned to Numbered or Bulleted.

7. Change the List control properties for the font to **Trebuchet MS** and for the ForeColor to **#004040**.

8. Double-click on the page to view the code behind the page.

9. In the Page_Load event procedure, add the following code to create an array named AR1 and populate the array with values. Then, bind the List control named List1 to the AR1 Array control.

```
Dim AR1 As New ArrayList(9)
AR1.Add("Current Events in Ireland")
AR1.Add("Fishing in Ireland")
```

```
AR1.Add("An Ghaeilge (The Irish Language)")
AR1.Add("Hiking in Ireland")
AR1.Add("Irish History")
AR1.Add("Irish Music")
AR1.Add("Irish Step and Set Dancing")
AR1.Add("Travel in Ireland")
AR1.Add("Sports in Ireland")
List1.DataSource = AR1
List1.DataBind()
```

10. Click the **Save All** button. Click **Build** on the menu bar, then click **Build Solution**.

11. View the page in the browser at *http://localhost/Chapter12Mobile/MFDisplayList.aspx*. The page is displayed as shown in the Internet Explorer window in Figure 12-13. The figure depicts how the page looks both in a browser and on a Pocket PC emulator. The same code generated both displays. (*Note*: If you have a device emulator installed, you can also view the page in the device emulator.)

12

Figure 12-13   Viewing a mobile form

12. View the source code for the Web page in the browser. Notice that there is no sign of mobile forms or WML. The ASP.NET Web Application sent the code that was supported by the device.

13. In Visual Studio .Net, view the HTML source code for the mobile form by clicking the **HTML** tab. Notice that the form is tagged with the mobile prefix, and each of the form fields, Label and List, are tagged with the mobile prefix. Although these controls look similar to ASP WebForm controls, they have additional properties to support mobile forms.

14. Close all the files and the solution.

In the example above, not all of the content is displayed on the screen. You must scroll down to view additional content. You can set the **Wrapping property** of the form to NoWrap to stop the control from wrapping. Wrapping allows content that extends over a long line to wrap to the next line. If wrapping is turned off, the user must scroll horizontally to view long lines. You can also set the **TextView property** to enable pagination for large amounts of text. You can set the **Paginate property** for the mobile form to true. Using pagination allows you to divide the list into multiple pages. When you create the list, you can display the default pagination properties, or set the values of the displayed text with the **PagerStyle properties**. In the sample code below, the **PageLabel** property of the PagerStyle properties identifies the number of pages that are available. You can also add the **NextPageText** and **PreviousPageText** PagerStyle elements to your page and assign them a text value to display in the window, as shown in the sample code below.

```
PagerStyle —PageLabel="Page {0} of {1}"
PagerStyle —NextPageText="Continue"
PagerStyle —PreviousPageText="Back"
```

Each card can be represented by a separate mobile form within the WML document. You can then create a Link control to link to other cards within the same file, or to another WML file. The **NavigateURL** is used to identify links. The pound sign (#) is used to indicate an internal link.

With the WML file, you can easily insert scripts within the mobile form document. You can interact with page events, such as Page_Load. You can detect if the form has any mobile capabilities in the Page_Load event handler or in the Machine.config file. Within the Machine.config file, the <browserCaps> section identifies the support for mobile devices, which are exposed through the MobileCapabilities class. You can also use form templates to provide reusable content, such as the HeaderTemplate and FooterTemplate. Several Mobile Form controls can contain other controls such as the paragraph, line break, bold, italic, and anchor HTML tags.

In the following activity, you will create additional mobile forms in the same document.

1. Open the **Chapter12Mobile** solution. Right-click **Chapter12Mobile** in the Solution Explorer window, point to **Add**, then click **Add New Item**.

In the Templates pane, select **Mobile WebForm**. In the Name text box type **MFHomePage.aspx**. Click the **Open** button. The Mobile Form appears smaller on the Web page. This is the default width of the form.

2. Add a label control from the Mobile Forms tab. With the Label control selected, view the properties in the Properties window. Change the (ID) of the label to **lblStoreName**. Change the font to **Trebuchet MS**, the ForeColor to **#004040**, the Alignment property to **Center**, and the Bold property to **True**. Change the Text property to **Tara Store Home Page**.

3. Add a List control to the mobile form. For each item within the List control, the Text attribute assigns the value and the displayed text. Change the Decoration property to **Numbered**. The Decoration property identifies the type of list such as bulleted or numbered lists. Change the List control properties for the font to **Trebuchet MS** and for the ForeColor to **#004040**. Change the ItemsAsLinks property for the list to **True**. The ItemsAsLinks property displays the items in the list as hyperlinks.

4. Drag a second form tag to the page from the Mobile Forms tab. Form2 is created. Change the (ID) property of Form2 to **Products**. Change the Title property to **Product Categories**. Add an **ObjectList** control to the form.

5. Drag a third form tag to the page from the Mobile Forms tab. Form2 is created. Change the (ID) property of Form2 to **ChicagoStore**. Change the Title property to **Chicago Store**.

6. Drag the **Image** tag to the ChicagoStore Mobile Form. You can specify the ImageURL property as **images/ChicagoStore.jpg**. The ImageURL property is the location of the graphic file. Specify the AlternateText property as **Chicago Store Image** so that if no images are supported, an alternate text message is displayed. (*Note*: On some devices, bitmapped graphics (BMP) are preferred over GIF files. You can use the **DeviceSpecific** filter property within the page or within the Web configuration file to identify the preferred format for the entire application. In general, browsers prefer the GIF format, whereas cellular devices prefer the BMP format.)

7. Drag a new Form to the page from the Mobile Form tab. Change the ID property to **CustomerService**. Change the Title property to **Customer Service**.

8. Drag the **PhoneCall** control to the form. (*Note*: In Internet Explorer 5.5 or earlier, a label with a link is displayed instead of placing the call.) Change the PhoneNumber property to **800-555-1212**. If the user's device is enabled, the control places the phone call. Change the AlternateURL to **#ChicagoStore** for devices that are not able to place calls. Change the Text property to **Call Tara Store at 800-555-1212**. Change the font to **Trebuchet MS** and the ForeColor to **#004040**.

12

9. View the HTML source code by clicking the **HTML** tab, as shown in Figure 12-14.

10. Click the **Design** tab to return to Design view. Double-click the page to view the code behind the page.

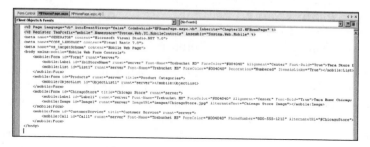

Figure 12-14 HTML code with Mobile Form controls

11. In the Page_Load event procedure, add the following code to create a HashTable named AR1 and populate the array with values. Then, bind the List control named List1 to the AR1 structure. Notice that the Hash table was used to display a different value than what is sent when the user clicks on the link.

```
Dim AR1 As New Hashtable(8)
AR1.Add("#Products", "Products")
AR1.Add("#ChicagoStore", "Chicago Store")
AR1.Add("#CustomerService", "Customer Service")
List1.DataSource = AR1
List1.DataTextField = "Value"
List1.DataValueField = "Key"
List1.DataBind()
```

12. Add the following code to create the second array and bind the second array to the objects list.

```
Dim AR2 As New ArrayList(9)
AR2.Add("Gifts")
AR2.Add("China & Crystal")
AR2.Add("Pottery")
AR2.Add("Music, Books, Video")
AR2.Add("Bridal")
AR2.Add("Clothing")
AR2.Add("Food")
AR2.Add("Jewelry")
ObjectList1.DataSource = AR2
ObjectList1.DataBind()
```

13. Click the **Save All** button. Click **Build** on the menu bar, then click **Build Solution**.

14. View the page in the browser at *http://localhost/Chapter12Mobile/ MFHomePage.aspx*. The page is displayed as shown in Figure 12-15. (*Note*: If you have a device emulator installed, you can also view the page in the device emulator.)

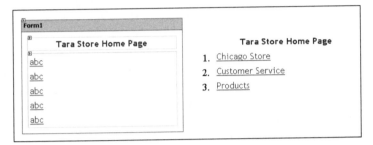

Figure 12-15   Viewing a mobile form in a browser and in the Pocket PC Emulator

15. Click the **Products** link. Click the **Back** button in the browser.

16. Click the **Chicago Store** link. Click the **Back** button in the browser.

17. Click the **Customer Service** link.

18. Click the **Call** hyperlink. The browser is redirected to the Chicago Store page.

19. Close the browser.

20. Close all the files and the solution.

There are many other mobile form controls that you can insert into a mobile form. You can add AdRotator controls and Calendar controls to the mobile forms. You can also create a form with text boxes. However, the text fields can only exist on one line. Multiple-line text boxes are not supported. You can also use TextView control to insert long text blocks. The TextView can support some formatting such as bold, italic, and hyperlinks. You can use the Numeric Text controls with WML devices only. The Password Text control displays an asterisk instead of the number in the screen window, but it does not hide the value from the code behind the page. You can use Validation controls to validate the form fields, similarly to how they are used with Web Forms. You cannot use client-side JavaScript to display error messages with the Validation controls. If you use a ValidationSummary control, you must keep the control on a separate form and use the formToValidate property to assign the control to a mobile form. The error messages are not displayed interactively as you move from control to control. Because the List object is created with a control, you can change the list items programmatically. You can insert command buttons that can be used to send a command with the OnItemCommand property for the ItemCommand Event.

12

CHAPTER SUMMARY

❏ The SMTP server is the default mail service that is installed with the Internet Information Service Web Server. The mail server's default root directory is C:\Inetpub\MailRoot\. The Pickup folder is used to store outgoing mail messages. Mail that cannot be delivered is sent to the BadMail directory. You can configure the SMTP server via the property sheets in the Internet Services Manager application. The default port for the SMTP server is 25.

❏ The CDONTS object, from cdonts.dll, is installed with the SMTP server and enables you to send outbound e-mail from a Web page. The CDONTS component is only available if the SMTP mail server is installed. You can access the properties of the CDONTS object via the `System.Web.Mail` namespace. The MailMessage class provides the sender and recipient data, as well as the message content. The MailAttachment class is used to identify a file that is to be sent with the e-mail message. The SMTPMail class is used to send the e-mail message. E-mail can be sent as plain text or formatted with HTML. The send method of the SmtpMail class creates the message in the required format and writes it to the Pickup folder, from where the SMTP server sends it.

❏ The `System.IO` namespace provides you with classes that interact with the Web server's file system. It contains several classes such as File, FileStream, and Directory, which allow you to create, read, and delete files. However, the newer classes, named DirectoryInfo and FileInfo, are more flexible and provide easier access to the file system.

❏ The DirectoryInfo class allows you to obtain the properties of a directory and its subdirectories.

❏ The GetDirectories method of the DirectoryInfo class is used to retrieve the collection of subdirectories. The CreateSubdirectory method is used to create a new directory. You can capture exceptions when creating directories and files with the Try-Catch-End Try structure.

❏ You can use the FileInfo class to copy a file to a new location, move a file to a new location, or delete a file. The FileInfo class allows you access to the properties of a file, using the FileAttributes. You can use the FileInfo class to create a basic text file or HTML file.

❏ The CreateText and create methods of the FileInfo class return a StreamWriter object, which is used to create files. The open, OpenRead, OpenText, and OpenWrite methods allow you to open and read the file. The write method of the StreamWriter object is used to write to the file. The OpenText method returns a StreamReader object, which can read through each line from the file.

❏ The Wireless Application Protocol (WAP) is an open standard used to create programs on a mobile device. Wireless Markup Language (WML) is the programming language used to create the code for the mobile applications. WML is compliant with the XML protocols. The WML files use cards to organize and divide the structure of the WML document. You can use additional HTML tags within the WML language, such as the anchor tag.

❑ Device simulators, such as the OpenWave Simulator, allow you to simulate phones from a variety of vendors. The Web server must be configured to recognize the mobile application file extensions, and to run the mobile applications. By using .NET developer applications, such as Visual Studio .NET and the Mobile Internet Toolkit, developers can create mobile applications, using ASP.NET mobile server controls. A Web page that contains Mobile controls is called a mobile form. Mobile controls inherit a code behind the page named System.Web.UI.MobileControls.MobilePage. You can view the output of the WML file within a browser.

REVIEW QUESTIONS

1. Which service is used to deliver e-mail to another server?
   a. PopMail Server
   b. Web Publishing
   c. FTP Server
   d. SMTP Server

2. The CDONTS component creates the e-mail message and places the message in which folder?
   a. Pickup
   b. Queue
   c. Drop
   d. Badmail

3. Where is the e-mail message placed after all attempts to deliver the message have failed?
   a. Pickup
   b. Queue
   c. Drop
   d. Badmail

4. Where is the default main e-mail folder located?
   a. c:\Inetpub\Mail
   b. c:\Inetpub\MailRoot
   c. d:\Inetpub\Mail
   d. d:\Inetpub\mailroot

12

5. Which administrative tool is used to determine if the Simple Mail Transport Protocol (SMTP) has been started?

   a. SMTP Server

   b. Internet Services Manager

   c. Services

   d. SMTP Mail Manager

6. Which class provides access to the properties and methods to construct an e-mail message?

   a. MailMessage

   b. MailAttatchment

   c. SmtpMail

   d. System.Web.Mail

7. Which class is used to identify a file that is to be sent with the e-mail message?

   a. MailMessage

   b. MailAttatchment

   c. SmtpMail

   d. System.Web.Mail

8. Which property is used to indicate that the output of the message is HTML?

   a. MailFormat.Text

   b. MailFormat.HTML

   c. MailMessage.Normal

   d. MailEncoding.UUEncode

9. Which property is required when creating a MailMessage?

   a. MailMessage.UrlContentBase

   b. MailMessage.From

   c. MailMessage.CC

   d. MailMessage.BCC

10. Which character does not throw an ArgumentException when you create a directory?

    a. <

    b. z

    c. *

    d. ?

11. If you attempt to delete a directory that does not exist, an IOException named
    _____ is thrown.

    a. DirectoryNotFoundException

    b. SecurityException

    c. IOException

    d. PathTooLongException

12. Which of the following is not a property of the FileInfo class?

    a. CreationTime

    b. lastAccessedTime

    c. LastWriteTime

    d. DirectoryKey

13. What property is used to identify if the file is not to be modified by the user?

    a. ReadOnly

    b. Compressed

    c. NotContentIndexed

    d. Archive

14. If you want to copy a file to a new location, and delete the original file, which
    method of the FileInfo class should you use?

    a. CopyTo

    b. MoveTo

    c. Delete

    d. MakeFile

15. Which method returns a StreamWriter object?

    a. CreateText

    b. Create

    c. CreateFile

    d. a and b

16. Which tag causes the browser to ignore the HTML tags in the file?

    a. <XMP>

    b. <!-- -->

    c. <// >

    d. <Comment>

12

17. If you open a file using the OpenText method, you need to close the file with what method?

   a. Close

   b. EndFile

   c. CloseAll

   d. FreeObjects

18. Which pane in the SQL Editor shows the criteria as visual icons?

   a. Table Pane

   b. Grid Pane

   c. SQL Pane

   d. Results Pane

19. What organization maintains the WAP standards?

   a. Internic

   b. Network Solutions

   c. World Wide Web Consortium

   d. WapForum.com

20. Which markup language is used to build WAP applications?

   a. WML

   b. ASP

   c. VB.BET

   d. ASP.NET

HANDS-ON PROJECTS

Project 12-1

In this project, you create a Web page that sends an e-mail message to a single recipient.

1. Start **Visual Studio .NET** and open your **Chapter12** solution.

2. Add a Web Form named **Ch12Proj1.aspx** to the project.

3. Double-click on the page to view the code behind the page. On the first line, enter the following code to import the Mail classes from the `System.Web.Mail` namespace.

   ```
   Imports System.Web.Mail
   ```

4. Enter the following code in the Page_Load handler. First, declare the variable MM to store the MailMessage object.

   ```
   Dim MM As New MailMessage()
   ```

5. Add the following code to configure the properties of the MailMessage object.

```
MM.From = "yourname@yourdomain.com"
MM.To = "yourname@yourdomain.com"
MM.Subject = "Chapter 12 Project 1"
MM.Body = "I have completed Chapter 12 Project 1"
MM.BodyFormat = MailFormat.Text
MM.Priority = MailPriority.High
```

6. Add the following code, which uses the send method of the SmtpMail object to send the message. Then, release the variable that stores the Mail object.

```
SmtpMail.Send(MM)
MM = Nothing
```

7. Print your source code for the Ch12Proj1.aspx page.

8. Save the files and build the solution.

9. Right-click on the design page, and then click **View in Browser**. Your page should be blank. The e-mail message has been created and placed in your Pickup folder.

10. On the desktop, double-click the **My Computer** icon, and then double-click the letter of the drive on which your Web server is installed. By default the Web server is installed on drive C. Double click on **Inetpub**, then **mailroot**, and then **Pickup**.

11. Right-click the envelope icon, and then click **Open with**. In the window, scroll down until you see Notepad. Click **Notepad**, and then click the **Yes** button.

12. Print the page in Notepad.

13. Close the file, close the Pickup folder, and close the solution.

Project 12-2

In this project, you will create a Web page that sends an e-mail message to a single recipient. You will retrieve the values for the e-mail message properties from a form.

1. Start **Visual Studio .NET** and open your **Chapter12** solution.

2. Add a Web form named **Ch12Proj2.aspx** to the project.

3. Add four TextBox controls to the page. The text boxes should be named **txtFrom, txtTo, txtSubject,** and **txtMsg**. Add a Label for each control. Change the Text property of the labels to **From, To, Subject,** and **Message**.

4. Change the TextMode property of the txtMessage control to **MultiLine** and the Rows property to **10**.

5. Add a button to the page named **btnSend**. The label of the button should say **Send My E-mail Message**.

6. Double-click the **btnSend** button to view the code behind the page. On the first line of code on the entire page, enter the following text to import the Mail classes from the System.Web.Mail namespace.

```
Imports System.Web.Mail
```

7. Enter the following code in the **btnSend_Click event** handler. First, declare the variable MM to store the MailMessage x object.

```
Dim MM As New MailMessage()
```

8. Add the following code to retrieve the values from the variables and assign them to the MailMessage object properties.

```
MM.From = txtFrom.Text
MM.To = txtTo.Text
MM.Subject = txtSubject.Text
MM.Body = txtMsg.Text
```

9. Add the following code to configure the additional properties of the MailMessage object.

```
MM.BodyFormat = MailFormat.Text
MM.Priority = MailPriority.High
```

10. Add the following code, which uses the send method of the SmtpMail object to send the message. Then, release the variable that is storing the mail object.

```
SmtpMail.Send(MM)
MM = Nothing
```

11. Print your source code for the Ch12Proj2.aspx page.

12. Save the files and build the solution.

13. Right-click on the page, and then click **View in Browser**. Fill out the Web form with your email in the To and From textboxes. In the Subject text box, enter **Chapter 12 Project 2** and in the Message text box enter **I have completed project 2**.

14. Locate your Pickup file, right-click on the **envelope** icon, and then select **Open with**. In the window, scroll down until you see Notepad. Click on **Notepad**, and then click the **OK** button.

15. Print the Pickup page in Notepad. Close the file, close the Pickup folder, and close the solution.

Project 12-3

In this project, you display the directory properties. The visitor provides the directory URL in a form.

1. Open **Visual Studio .NET** and open your **Chapter12** solution.

2. Add a Web form named **Ch12Proj3.aspx** to the project.

3. Add a text box named **txtDirectoryName** and a button named **btnGetDirInfo**.

4. Add an ASP.NET Label control named **lblDirInfo**.

5. Double-click on the page to view the code behind the page. On the first line of code, enter the following text to import the Mail classes from the **System.IO** namespace.

```
Imports System.IO
```

6. Enter the following code in the Page_Load handler. If the page has been loaded before, then you can retrieve a value from the text box, and create the DirectoryInfo object.

```
If Page.IsPostBack Then
```

7. Add the following code to display data about the directory in the Label control.

```
Dim myPath As String = txtDirectoryName.Text
Dim DD As DirectoryInfo = _
New DirectoryInfo("c:\inetpub\wwwroot\Chapter12\")
lblDirInfo.Text = _
"<b>Directory Properties for " & myPath _
& "</b><br /><br/>" & _
"<b>The Parent Directory " & _
"</b><br /><br/>" & _
"The full name of the parent directory was " _
& DD.FullName & "<br />"
DD.CreateSubdirectory(txtDirectoryName.Text)
```

8. Add the following code to display information about the subdirectories of the directory. You must create a variable named SD, which represents each subdirectory, and use a For-Next loop to rotate through the subdirectories in the directory.

```
Dim SD As DirectoryInfo
lblDirInfo.Text = lblDirInfo.Text & _
"<br /><hr /><b>Subdirectories of " & _
myPath & "</b><br /><br />"
For Each SD In DD.GetDirectories()
        If SD.Name = txtDirectoryName.Text Then
                lblDirInfo.Text &= myPath & _
                " was created successfully. <br />"
        Else
        End If
Next
```

9. Add the following code to display a default message if the user has not visited the page before. (*Note:* The code for assigning the Text property of the Label control should be entered on one line.)

```
Else
    lblDirInfo.Text = _
        "Enter the complete path to a directory on the Web
        server."
End If
```

10. Save the files and build the solution.

11. View the page in the browser at *http://localhost/Chapter12/Ch12Proj3.aspx.* Insert **Ch12Proj3** in the text box and click the button to submit the form.

12. Add graphics, color, fonts, and content to enhance the appearance of the form.

13. Print the Web page, the source code, and the code behind the page.

14. Close the File.

Project 12-4

In this project, you create a Web page from the contents of a form.

1. Open your **Chapter12** solution.

2. Add a Web Form named **Ch12Proj4.aspx** to the project.

3. Add a text box named **txtFileName**, which stores the name of the HTML file. Add a label that says **Filename** next to the text box.

4. Add a text box named **txtContents**, which will hold the new contents of the file. Add a label that says **Body** next to the text box.

5. Add a text box named **txtTitle**, which will hold the title of the new page. Add a label that says **Title** next to the text box.

6. Add a text box named **txtBGColor**, which will hold the background color of the new page. Add a label that says **Background Color** next to the text box.

7. Add a text box named **txtFGColor**, which will hold the foreground color of the new page. Add a label that says **Text Color** next to the text box.

8. Add a button named **btnCreateFile** that says **Create File**.

9. Add a hyperlink control named **HLReadFile**, which will be used to store the URL to the new HTML page.

10. Add an ASP.NET label control named **lblFileInfo**.

11. Double-click on the page to view the code behind the page. On the first line of code, enter the following text to import the FileInfo classes from the System.IO namespace.

    ```
    Imports System.IO
    ```

12. Enter the following code in the Page_Load event handler to display the default message.

    ```
    If Not Page.IsPostBack Then
      HLReadFile.Text = ""
      lblFileInfo.Text = _
        "Enter your data in each text box to create your Web ¬
         page."
    End If
    ```

13. In Design view, double-click **Create File** button. In the btnCreateFile_Click event procedure, add the following code to create the file using the value entered into the text box. Set the hyperlink to an empty string so that it is not displayed.

    ```
    Dim FN As String = _
    "c:\inetpub\wwwroot\Chapter12\" & txtFileName.Text
    Dim NF As FileInfo = New FileInfo(FN)
    lblFileInfo.Text = _
    "<b>The File was created! " & "</b><br /><br />"
    HLReadFile.Text = "Click here to read the HTML file!"
    HLReadFile.NavigateUrl = "http://localhost/Chapter12/" _
    & txtFileName.Text
    ```

14. Add the following code to create variables for the txtTitle, txtBGColor, and txtFGColor fields. Add the code to detect if the user has entered values for the txtTitle, txtBGColor, and txtFGColor fields. If no value was detected, insert a default value.

```
Dim BGC, FGC, MyTitle As String
If txtTitle.Text = "" Then
        MyTitle = "Creating a Web Page"
Else
        MyTitle = txtTitle.Text
End If
If txtBGColor.Text = "" Then
        BGC = "#ffffcc"
Else
        BGC = txtBGColor.Text
End If
If txtFGColor.Text = "" Then
        FGC = "#336600"
Else
        FGC = txtFGColor.Text
End If
```

15. Add the following code to create the page and enter the basic HTML tags. The body of the page content comes from the text boxes.

```
Dim SW As StreamWriter = File.CreateText(FN)
SW.WriteLine("<html><head><title>")
SW.WriteLine(myTitle)
SW.WriteLine("</title></head><body BGColor=")
SW.Write(BGC)
SW.WriteLine(" Text=")
SW.Write(FGC)
SW.WriteLine(">")
SW.WriteLine(txtContents.Text)
SW.WriteLine("<hr /><br /><br />Created on ")
SW.WriteLine(Now.Date.ToShortDateString)
SW.WriteLine("</body></html>")
SW.Close()
NF = Nothing
```

16. Save the files and build the solution.

17. View the page in the browser at *http://localhost/Chapter12/Ch12Proj4.aspx*.

18. Enter **Ch12Proj4.htm** in the File Name text box. In the Title text box, enter **Community News**.

19. In the BackgroundColor text box, enter **#99CCCC**. In the Color text box, enter text **#330099**.

20. In the Body text box, enter **Welcome to my Web site.**

21. Click the **Create File** button.

12

22. Click the hyperlink to open the page in the browser. The contents of the file are displayed in the browser.

23. Click the **Back** button in the browser.

24. Go back to Visual Studio. NET and close the file.

Project 12-5

In this project, you create a Microsoft Word document from the contents of a form on a Web page.

1. Open your **Chapter12** solution.

2. Add a Web Form named **Ch12Proj5.aspx** to the project.

3. Add a text box named **txtFileName**, which stores the name of the HTML file. Add a label that says **Filename** next to the text box.

4. Add a text box named **txtContents**, which will hold the new contents of the file. Add a label that says **Body** next to the text box.

5. Add a button named **btnCreateFile** that says **Create File**.

6. Add a hyperlink control named **HLReadFile**, which will be used to store the URL to the new HTML page.

7. Add an ASP.NET Label control named **lblFileInfo**.

8. Double-click on the page to view the code behind the page. On the first line of code, enter the following text to import the FileInfo classes from the `System.IO` namespace.

```
Imports System.IO
```

9. Enter the following code in the Page_Load handler to display the default message.

```
If Not Page.IsPostBack Then
  HLReadFile.Text = ""
  lblFileInfo.Text = _
  "Create your own Word document."
End If
```

10. In Design view, double-click on the **Create File** button. In the btnCreateFile_Click event procedure, add the following code to create the file using the value entered into the text box. Set the hyperlink to an empty string so that it is not displayed.

```
Dim FN As String = _
"c:\inetpub\wwwroot\Chapter12\" & txtFileName.Text
Dim NF As FileInfo = New FileInfo(FN)
lblFileInfo.Text = _
"<b>The File was created! " & "</b><br /><br />"
HLReadFile.Text = "Click here to read the doc file!"
HLReadFile.NavigateUrl = "http://localhost/Chapter12/" _
& txtFileName.Text
```

11. Add the code to create the page.

```
Dim SW As StreamWriter = File.CreateText(FN)
SW.WriteLine(txtContents.Text)
SW.Close()
NF = Nothing
```

12. Save the files and build the solution.

13. View the page in the browser at **http://localhost/Chapter12/Ch12Proj5.aspx**.

14. Enter **Ch12Proj5.doc** in the File Name text box.

15. In the Body text box, enter **This is a test**.

16. Click the **Create File** button.

17. Click the hyperlink to open the page in the browser. The contents of the file are displayed in the browser. If the File Download dialog box appears, click **Open**. If you do not have Microsoft Word, the file opens in Microsoft Word Pad. (*Note*: If your browser does not open the file, open Microsoft Word directly, then browse to your Chapter12 directory, and open the file from Microsoft Word.)

18. Click the **Back** button in the browser.

19. Return to Visual Studio .NET and close the file.

CASE PROJECTS

12

E-mailing a Feedback Form

Your manager at Tara Store has asked you to create a feedback form page. He wants the form to go to the support team. Create a Web page named Ch12Case1.aspx. Add a form with that collects the To, From, Subject, and Message data. The subject should be Customer Feedback. Make the To field have a value of your e-mail address and make the subject read-only so that the visitor cannot change the value of the field. Add a submit button that says Send My E-Mail Message. When the user clicks the button, configure the e-mail objects and send the e-mail message. Set the priority of the e-mail message to high. Enhance the appearance of the form with color, fonts, content, and graphics. Print the form, the source code, and the results from the e-mail message.

Configuring an E-mail Message from a Database

Your manager would like to be able to send bulk e-mail messages to the store's customers. Create a database named Ch12Case2. (*Note*: You may use SQL Server or Microsoft Access to create your database.) Create a table named Members. Within the table, create a field named MemberID that is an identity field and a primary key field. Create an additional field named MemberEmail that contains the member e-mails. The MemberEmail field should be type varchar and 50 bytes long. Enter three new members with your e-mail address. Create a Web page named Ch12Case2.aspx. Add a form that will collect the From, Subject, and Message data. Make the From field have a value of your e-mail address and make it read only so that the visitor cannot change the value of the field. Add a submit button that says Send My E-Mail Message; the subject should be Announcement. Create a multiline ASP.NET List Box Server control named dlTo that will contain the list of member e-mail addresses. The dlTo field should be populated by the Ch12Case2 database. Then, the list should be sorted by MemberEmail address. (*Hint:* You can use the DataAdapter to create the Data Connection object. Then, create a dataset using the data from the DataAdapter. After this, create a DataView from the DataSet Members table. Then, if the page has not been posted back, fill the DataAdapter and bind the DataView to the list box control. When the page loads, retrieve the values of the member e-mails and place them in the txtTo drop-down list box.) Display the e-mail address in the list box, but the value of each option should be the MemberID field. When the user clicks the button, configure the e-mail objects and send the e-mail message to each member in the drop-down list box. (*Hint:* Because there are multiple items selected, you need to handle this in your code. You can use a For-Each-Next statement to loop through each of the items within the list box items collection. You can then retrieve the specific text value for the list box item that was selected.) Set the priority of the e-mail message to high. When the message has been sent, display a message to the user indicating that the e-mails have been sent. Enhance the appearance of the form with color, fonts, content, and graphics. Print the form, the source code, and the results from the e-mail messages. (*Note:* You can print the e-mail messages from the Pickup folder if your e-mail server will not allow you to send mail out of your network.)

Creating a File Management System

Your manager has heard that it's more effective to manage files on the Web than to use a file transfer program (FTP) to create and upload files to the Web server. Create a simple Web-based file management system. Create the initial page as Ch12MobileCase3.aspx. Allow the end user to enter the name of the file or directory. The path should be hard-coded as your Chapter12 directory. Add buttons that allow you to create and delete directories as well as files. The buttons should be named Create Directory, Delete Directory, Display Directory, Create File, Delete File, and Read File. Add a hyperlink to view the Web page in a browser. The directory information should be displayed in a label control in the same page. When the Read File button is clicked, the file contents should be displayed in the label control. Save your Web pages in your Chapter12 directory. Enhance the Web pages with graphics, color, and text. Print the page and the source code.

Creating a Mobile Web Application

Your customers are starting to use wireless and PDA devices to connect to the Web site. Create a series of five cards that display information about the online store. Save your Web application to your Chapter12 directory. The cards should be named Ch12Case4_1, Ch12Case4_2, Ch12Case4_3, Ch12Case4_4, and Ch12Case4_5. Enhance the Web pages with graphics, color, and text. Print the page and the source code.

Index